TAKE IT OFF!

2,872
Tax Deductions
Most People
Overlook

TAKE
IT OFF!

2,872
TAX DEDUCTIONS
MOST PEOPLE OVERLOOK

Completely revised and enlarged 1984 edition

Robert S. Holzman, Ph.D.

1817

HARPER & ROW, PUBLISHERS, New York
Cambridge, Philadelphia, San Francisco, London
Mexico City, São Paulo, Sydney

ISBN 0-06-015186-2   83 84 85 86 87 10 9 8 7 6 5 4 3 2 1

ISBN 0-06-464065-5 (pbk.)   83 84 85 86 87 10 9 8 7 6 5 4 3 2 1

THIS TENTH annual edition of *Take It Off!* contains 2,872 deductions, a net increase of 509 over the number included in last year's version. This represents an increase of 21.5 percent (well over the current inflation rate) in the number of deductions reported. In order to make the new edition even more useful, 161 cross-references have been added.

This edition has been designed for use in preparing Federal tax returns for 1983 early in the year of 1984. For that reason, changes made by legislation that goes into effect after 1983 are not considered here.

Changes in deductions made by the 1982 Tax Equity and Fiscal Responsibility Act (TEFRA) that will affect most persons who itemize are in the areas of *medical expenses* and *casualty losses*. Medical expenses now are deductible only to the extent that in aggregate they exceed 5 percent of an individual's adjusted gross income, instead of the previous 3 percent. There is a new limitation on deductible nonbusiness casualty losses, which now must in aggregate exceed 10 percent of adjusted gross income; the rule that the first $100 of nonbusiness casualty losses is nondeductible remains. This may mean that medical expenses and casualty loss deductions will become unavailable to some people; it may mean that others will have to recognize all properly deductible items in these categories in order to take advantage of the tax laws. You should know *what* is deductible: for example, the cost of elastic stockings or of whiskey is a deductible medical expense in certain circumstances. And you must know *how* to prove a deduction: a casualty loss deduction may depend upon your remembering to take some prompt photographs or consulting with an appraiser with the proper credentials. These steps can't be taken retroactively.

This edition has greatly expanded coverage on subjects in which there have been new developments or in which readers of prior editions have expressed special interest—such as hobby losses, transactions entered into for profit, maintenance of an office in the home, and shareholders' expenses. New emphasis has been placed on steps to take in order to furnish *proof* of entitlement to a particular deduction—for instance, through the use of photographs or the keeping of contemporary documentation.

It can't be overemphasized that taxpayer ingenuity is an important ingredient in proving entitlement to deductions. For example, one individual convinced a court that he indeed had gambling losses, despite absence of paper records, by testimony as to the frequent heated arguments he had with his wife about his continuous losses. In a recent case, one businessperson was shown to have convinced the court that he was entitled to deduct payments to truck loaders and assistants, despite his failure to identify any of the payees; because of the prevailing underground economy, no one would have done this type of work for him if names and Social Security numbers had been recorded.

Using this book, you may save money not only by discovering forms of deduction that had not occurred to you but also by discovering how to prove what the Internal Revenue Service or the courts require. Penalty is imposed upon a person who is not able to point out his authority for taking a certain deduction. That puts a heavy premium on knowledge of sources. Every one of the deductions shown here is accompanied by a citation of the authority for it: the law, a court decision, an IRS ruling or illustration. Logic and reason are not authorities for claiming a deduction. In the words of the court in a recent decision, "Unfortunately, common sense and the tax law are rarely even waving acquaintances." (*Skoglund v. United States,* . . . F.2d . . . [Ct. Cl., 1982].)

ROBERT S. HOLZMAN

Preface

TAX DEDUCTIONS, the courts have frequently stated, are a matter of legislative grace. You are not entitled to any deduction unless Congress specifically has provided for it. The courts, in interpreting the laws, have approved the deductibility of many other items and subitems. In addition, the Internal Revenue Service, in practical implementation of the tax laws, has authorized the taking of deductions in various forms. So in order to keep one's taxes at their legitimate minimum, it is necessary to know what deductions are *allowed;* none can be presumed. As the United States Supreme Court has said, the legal right of a taxpayer to reduce his taxes or to eliminate them altogether *by means which the law permits* cannot be doubted.

By means which the law permits . . . Your barber, bartender, taxi driver, and other helpful acquaintances are brimful of bright ideas for tax deductions. But when you have that encounter session with a steely-eyed Internal Revenue Agent and he questions your deductions with a suspicious "Who says so?" the moment of truth has arrived. A disallowed deduction means more than payment of what you would have paid in the first place had you not been so venturesome. There is interest (deductible). There are penalties (nondeductible). If you are so distinguished a businessperson or are presumptively so well versed in taxation that you are deemed to have known better, there can be fraud penalties. The entire climate of a tax audit can change. Should a Revenue Agent find improper deductions so readily, not illogically he will believe that there's more gold to be found in your return, and now he will really get to work on it.

This book, as it must be, is thoroughly documented. Each deduction named bears an identifying footnote number, which leads to the answer to that infuriating question of the Revenue Agent, "Who says so?" The so-sayer may be the Internal Revenue Code itself. It may be the Treasury Regulations. It may be an official government release. It may be a court decision. But it won't be your spouse's second cousin. Or, for that matter, your spouse.

Who needs tax deductions? If the zero bracket amount wipes out your entire Federal income tax liability, that's fine (in one limited sense, anyway). But if you still have taxable income, there are almost certain to be some valid deductions awaiting discovery. One cannot accept a defeatist attitude that he really has nothing to deduct. For a modest start, there is the modest cost of this book. Do you have medical expenses (such as a wig), revolving credit accounts with department stores, or sessions with a tutor of some sort to patch up chinks in your executive armor before Higher Authority discovers them? When you take your best customer to that appropriately expensive restaurant after getting a particularly lucrative order, do you know what proportion of the tab you may properly deduct? Were you ever "taken" by a glib-tongued dealer or salesman? If you are summoned to appear as a witness before a Congressional committee (and 1973 showed that this can happen even to the most respectable and unsuspecting of gentlefolk), under what circumstances can you deduct the fees of the lawyer who counsels you there? Do you regularly take work home from your place of business at night? Are you involved in litigation? Are you an investor? Have you any expenditures which involve estate planning, insurance, or taking heavy paraphernalia to your place of work?

An allowable deduction requires more than merely *taking* it. If you find a Supreme Court authority here for a certain deduction, there is still the matter of proving *your* right to it. Can you demonstrate *your* entitlement to that deduction for business entertainment or charitable contributions or child-care expense? One clever lawyer proved that his client, an entertainer, was entitled to deduct the cost of expensive dresses as *business expense* rather than personal apparel which could be worn for everyday use; he had her demonstrate in the courtroom the sheer impossibility of sitting down in her exquisite form-fitting finery. But, generally, your right to a deduction is substantiated by such unspectacular routines as keeping pieces of paper. Do you keep letters from your customers on business letterheads which thank you for that lovely evening at the fights where you discussed the new winter line? (A good place to file such correspondence is right next to a purchase order dated a few days later.) Do you remember to take photographs immediately after casualty losses? In order to get a deduction, you may have to plan a transaction in advance to have the proper dates on receipts or in employee manuals. Should your transaction be with stipulated related parties, the Internal Revenue Service can refuse to recognize losses or certain other consequences for tax purposes; so it might be better to make your sales or deals with more distant relatives or with outsiders. Some of the deductions, such as the net operating loss carry-over, may be of sufficient complexity in operation to require the assistance of tax counsel.

If you are entitled to a tax deduction, take it. As Judge Learned Hand once wrote, a person does not owe a patriotic duty to pay one cent more in taxes than he is required to do. But if a deduction is not proper in your situation, don't take it. It has been held that when a taxpayer persistently claimed deductions such as had been disallowed in prior years, he was guilty of fraud; that is, willfully seeking to evade taxes which by now he had learned were due.

Even though courts have stated that taxation is not based upon logic or equity, the rule of reason must not be overlooked in claiming deductions.

Ordinary food cannot be deducted as medical expense, even though your health would be affected should you terminate your input. The cost of a business suit is not deductible, although without such garb you would be unable to retain your job in most walks of life. But tax deductions may be allowed even where an expenditure seems to stretch beyond the reasonable concept of a word or phrase, as where clarinet lessons as well as the cost of the clarinet were properly deducted as medical expense. Whether unrepaid advances to your business can be deducted may depend upon your own personality; the nastier it is, the greater your chance of getting the deduction.

It is strongly advisable to think about your tax deductions before the filing date of your tax return. In order to become legitimately a minimum taxpayer on a nonminimum income, you must become accustomed to deductive thinking.

A

Abandonment loss. If business assets are rendered economically useless to a taxpayer, the remaining undepreciated cost may be written off when the property cannot be used or disposed of.[1]* Such was the case where a place of business became useless because the state had condemned its parking lot for use as a highway. Without a parking lot for customers, there would be no customers, and the business would have to move to a new location.[2]

An individual sold his land to a utility company, reserving the right to remove all buildings within a year. Certain structures proved too costly to take away. The value of these could be deducted as an abandonment loss at the end of that year.[3]

Deduction was allowed for the cost of a compressor for a business air-conditioning unit that became unusable and was replaced during the same year.[4]

Taxpayers owned land and an ancient hotel that stood on it. The city enacted a building code calling for strict safety standards, which, however, did not extend to existing structures until the nature of their use changed. A Federal agency leased the building for a job corps training center but after a year relinquished the building to its owners. They could not resume hotel operations after this lapse of time without spending more money than was available to them to comply with the building code. They decided to abandon the hotel. The building doors and windows were barricaded; insurance was cancelled. This qualified for a deductible abandonment loss for the structure even though, because of high demolition costs, the building physically remained in existence.[5]

A deduction is permitted only where there is a complete elimination of all value, coupled with recognition by the owner that the item no longer has any utility or worth to him.[6]

An individual installed service recorders on his trucks to note the time during which the vehicles were running. The drivers disliked them and broke a number of the devices. The individual decided to discontinue their use, removed them from the trucks, and abandoned them before the end of the year of installation. The cost of the recorders was deductible.[7]

If a taxpayer has elected to amortize research and development expenses, abandonment of the research projects results in an allowable deduction for any amounts not yet deducted.[8]

Ordinarily, an architect's fees are not currently deductible but must be considered a cost of the building he designed to be depreciated over the period of its useful life. But if a proposed building never leaves the drawing-board stage and the plans are abandoned, the architect's fees are deductible at that time.[9]

Architects' fees may be deducted where the plans for a building are scrapped.[10] Deduction was allowed for an architect's fees where the building as designed was too expensive and consequently was rejected. This was so even though the same architect designed a second, dissimilar, structure which eventually was built.[11]

A taxpayer could deduct costs in connection with the construction of two gas compressor engines. Ordinarily costs of business assets lasting more than one year are not deductible, the expenditures being deductible as depreciation over a period of years. But these engines proved to be defective and were scrapped. None of the materials or plans in connection with the equipment could be used for subsequent construction. As the taxpayer had nothing to show for these outlays, the costs were deductible.[12]

Ordinarily, rezoning expenses are not deductible when incurred, inasmuch as they represent a capital outlay: engineering, architectural, legal, and similar expenses which are considered to be part of the cost of the property involved, recoverable over the remaining life through depreciation. Even an unsuccessful attempt to obtain a zoning modification ordinarily does not make the expenditure deductible when incurred, because whatever engineering or other work was done in connection with this request may serve on some future occasion. But when rezoning expenses were incurred in order to consummate a lease with a major department store which was contingent upon obtaining approval for commercial occupancy, the costs were fully deductible at the time the zoning variance was disapproved. The intention of leasing this property was abandoned completely at that point, so the expenditures could provide no future benefit.[13]

When a water well used by a farmer for irrigation and other agricultural purposes dried up, no casualty-loss deduction was allowed on the ground that the loss was the result of long-term deterioration rather than something sudden and hence did not meet the statutory definition of a casualty.[14] But a well can be abandoned by some overt act, such as by filling or sealing the well excavation or casing, which terminates the existence of the well and all economic benefits therefrom. So the abandonment is deductible as a business loss.[15] *See also* **Demolition; Farmers; Inventory write-downs; Investors; Termination of a business; Transactions entered into for profit.**

Abnormal retirement. *See* **Obsolescence.**

Abortion. A woman who, at her own request, undergoes an abortion operation to terminate her pregnancy can claim the expense as a medical deduction if the operation is performed in a general hospital and the operation is not illegal under state law. This is true because the operation is for the purpose of affecting a structure or function of the body and therefore is a deductible expense.[16] *See also* **Medical expenses.**

Absconding, losses from. *See* **Casualties; Reliance upon misrepresentation.**

Absenteeism, reduction of. *See* **Day-care center, financing of; Training expenses.**

Accident and health insurance premiums. *See* **Medical expenses.**

Accidents. Although the types and variations of deductible casualty loss are virtually beyond count, the triggering event must fall within the general framework of a fire, storm, or the like. Thus, payments for the support of a minor child could not be claimed as a casualty loss resulting from an accident.[17] But a deductible casualty loss can result from an everyday accident, as in a case where a diamond disappeared after an automobile door had slammed against an individual's ring.[18] Here the court observed that "the casualty need not be of great or near-tragic proportions in order to qualify."

Sonic-boom damage to a residence caused by jet aircraft qualified in one instance for the casualty-loss deduction.[19] Similarly, vandalism qualified.[20] Loss from damage to the exterior paint of a house, which was caused by sudden and severe smog containing an unusual concentration of chemical fumes, constituted a casualty loss for tax purposes. The painted surface of the house was eaten through in one night by smog, which caused the paint to blister and to peel from the wood. The home had recently been painted, and the damage was the result of an identifiable event, sudden in nature, fixing a point at which loss to the damaged property could be measured; it also was unexpected in the context in which the damage occurred.[21] *See also* **Casualties; Settlement payments.**

Accountant. *See* **Conventions; Education.**

Accounting, businessperson's guidance in. Amounts paid by a businessperson to an accountant to instruct an employee in keeping the business books were deductible.[22] Similarly, the cost of instruction from an accountant in how to figure costs to bid on government contracts was allowable.[23] *See also* **Education.**

Accounting expenses. The costs of accounting work performed in applying for a Federal income tax ruling are deductible.[24]

Accounting fees are deductible if they represent an ordinary and necessary business expense, as opposed to expenses of purchasing capital assets.[25]

Deduction was allowed for fees paid to an accountant to look into the advisability of a change in the taxpayer's accounting system.[26]

Attorneys' fees paid in connection with the purchase of an apartment building were nondeductible, as they represented an expenditure for an asset having a useful life of more than one year. (*See also* **Legal fees.**) But payments to a certified public accountant for advice on the tax aspects of such an acquisition were deductible. Here the taxpayer already owned the asset, so these payments were deemed to be for advice on taxes and not property acquisition.[27]

An individual could deduct fees paid to a CPA for tax advice in connection with the purchase of investments.[28]

An individual, even without documentation, was permitted to deduct a moderate accounting fee where the income tax returns on which he had claimed the deduction had been signed by an accounting firm.[29]

A holder of properties that produce rentals and oil royalties could deduct the fees he paid to the accountant who kept the books for the recording of these transactions.[30]

A corporate director was allowed to deduct accounting fees for services in connection with his defense against a stockholder suit for violation of fiduciary duties.[31]

An investor may deduct fees paid to a certified public accountant and to a bookkeeper in connection with his investment activities.[32]

If a person incurs accounting expenses to produce both taxable and tax-exempt income, but he cannot identify specifically the expenses which produce each type of income, then he must prorate them in order to determine the amount deductible.[33]

Account juggling, losses from. *See* **Check kiting.**

Acquisition charges. The amounts paid by a customer to a retail store under a retail installment contract for the privilege of prepaying accounts were deductible as interest.[34]

Acquisition fees. Fees paid for the acquisition of a capital asset such as stock or a building in most instances are not deductible but are added to the other costs of the property. But fees paid for a broker's recommendations that certain property be acquired were deductible as investment counsel.[35] *See also* **Mineral leases, cost of acquiring.**

Actors. The cost of clothing destroyed while performing stunts as an actor was held to be deductible.[36] An actor who lost some teeth during the screening of a fight sequence was allowed a deduction for replacement parts.[37] A prominent actor was allowed to deduct the cost of clothing which was suitable for personal wear and which was in current fashion. This clothing was purchased specifically for television use and was kept at the studio. At the end of the shooting season, this garb was placed in mothballs and was never taken home.[38]

The cost of costumes purchased at an actor's own expense was deductible.[39] One actor was permitted to deduct the cost of "period" clothing which he purchased for a play set in the 1930s.[40]

Amounts paid for hairpieces suitable only for professional use were deductible by an actor whose income would have been affected adversely by a mature appearance.[41]

A motion-picture actor was allowed to deduct expenses incurred in keeping himself in first-class condition to meet the requirements of his calling, including massage treatments, a physical trainer, rent for handball courts and gymnasium facilities, plus sundries.[42]

Deduction was allowed for fees paid to the Screen Actors Guild.[43]

A motion-picture actor had business reasons for giving tips to studio employees in an effort to obtain good cooperation.[44]

Costs of sending photographs and résumés to studios, casting directors, and agents were deductible by a professional actor.[45] *See also* **Chauffeur; Legal fees; Tips.**

Acupuncture. Payments for acupuncture treatments are deductible even though the person performing them may be acting in a manner not approved by the appropriate medical association. The determination of what medical care is depends on the nature of the services rendered, not on the experience, qualifications, or title of the person rendering them.[46] *See also* **Medical expenses.**

Admission to the bar. An attorney can deduct his costs for gaining admission to the bar only if he can demonstrate that he had intended to have this status for not more than one year. Otherwise it is a nondeductible capital expenditure.[47]

Adoption expenses. Deduction of up to $1,500 is allowed for the expenses that are paid or incurred in connection with the adoption of a qualifying child, which generally means a child who is difficult to place. These expenses are allowable in the case of children who have been found by a state to be eligible for adoption assistance on the basis that they have special needs: that is, that there is a specific factor which leads the state to conclude that they cannot be placed without adoption assistance.[48]

Ad valorem tax. An *ad valorem* automobile license fee was deductible as a property tax.[49]

Advance commissions, repayment of. If a salesperson is permitted to draw commissions against sales which have not been made yet, he can deduct amounts which he must repay.[50] Example: where a sale which he had made was cancelled by the customer.

Advanced degree, study for. An individual held a temporary appointment as a tutor at a university. It was made clear to him that it was necessary for him to make substantial progress toward attaining his doctorate to keep his position as a tutor. The expenses of tuition, etc., in working for his doctorate were deductible because that doctorate was necessary to earn the income that the Internal Revenue Service would tax.[51]

A full-time university instructor took courses to improve his skills and to accumulate credits that would lead to a university degree. In addition to tuition costs, he could deduct expenses for research and typing.[52]

An assistant professor at a university had no assurance of continued employment unless he was granted tenure; that is, a status of permanency after he had served for a certain length of time. It was university policy to require a doctor's degree before tenure was granted. To influence the university to grant him tenure, he gave written assurance that he would start work on his doctorate at once. He was granted tenure, and the Internal Revenue Service sought to disallow education expenses after the date that tenure was granted. But the deduction was allowed because the assistant professor had made his commitment to get the advanced degree primarily to hold his present status, even though he knew that possession of the degree would also bring promotion and more money. Had he terminated his studies once tenure had been granted, his conduct obviously would have been that of deceit, and the university could have found effective ways of showing its disapproval. Therefore the expense of earning his doctorate was still deductible inasmuch as it was a necessary requirement of maintaining his present status.[53]

A dentist engaged in general practice could deduct costs incurred in taking postgraduate studies in orthodontics, the correction of irregularities or abnormalities of the teeth. Thereafter he limited his practice to orthodontic patients. He was allowed to deduct the expenses for postgraduate studies, since they had not been incurred to qualify him for a new trade or business but were to improve his skills as a dentist, although now he was known as an orthodontist.[54]

A practicing attorney, although he already had a bachelor of law or doctor of jurisprudence degree, was permitted to deduct the cost of tuition for a master of law degree. The courses improved his skills in his present employment and did not qualify him for a new trade or business.[55] *See also* **Doctoral dissertation; Education; Research; Teachers, expenses of.**

Advances. *See* **Bad debts; Loans and advances.**

Advertising. Advertising is deductible as an ordinary and necessary business expense.[56]

In the main, the cost of advertising is deductible because it is regarded as a stimulus for getting business.[57] As one court observed, "In the tremendous competition of today [a businessman who did not advertise] would be more like a bashful boy who threw his sweetheart a kiss in the dark. He knew what he was doing, but nobody else did."[58]

To be deductible, an advertisement need not directly praise the payor's product.[59]

Deductible advertising can be in as original and unorthodox a form as a businessperson's imagination and ingenuity can conceive. The advertising expense is not confined to any stereotyped pattern that might have been set by unimaginative competitors.[60] Some discretion must be left to a taxpayer in deciding what kinds of advertising and promotion are necessary to obtain and to hold business.[61] For example, the principals of a retail dairy company took an African safari, the expenses of which were deductible by the business. The firm maintained a museum, and tickets distributed by milk-truck drivers invited customers to visit it. The business had maintained a museum even before this safari, and the obtaining of more exotic specimens involved such "roughing it" by the principals who made the trip that it scarcely seemed describable as a pleasure jaunt. The court was convinced that it was extremely good advertising at a relatively low cost and that conventional advertising of equal value could not have been obtained for the same amount of money.[62]

A restaurant was allowed to deduct the cost of wolfhounds that never left the premises except to attend dog shows where they were entered in the name of the restaurant. Furthermore, the cost of show horses was deductible when it could be established that they were entered in horse shows in the name of the restaurant and wore the colors which adorned the front of the restaurant.[63]

Samples are deductible as advertising, unless there is a state law which prohibits the distribution of samples. But deduction is allowed even under this circumstance if the state law is not being enforced.[64]

The owner of an automobile service station could deduct the cost of beer that was freely available to his customers as a promotional item. Previously he had given trading stamps to customers, but he felt that beer would be more attractive to them. The court was favorably impressed with his explanation: "Sir, I really don't feel in my heart how a small businessman can be put down because he had an idea and made it work."[65]

A taxpayer in a numbers racket was allowed to deduct 25 percent of the total advertising expenses he claimed.[66] (*See also* **Illegal business activity.**)

A manufacturer, who sold his products over a wide district, sponsored a baseball team that participated in games with teams from other organizations. The manufacturer received considerable publicity because of the team's appearances in various parts of the district where it did business and because the games were reported in local newspapers. Amounts spent in outfitting and supporting the team were deductible by the manufacturer as advertising.[67]

Advertising expense sometimes takes the form of an expense that is not for advertising. This verbal paradox simply means that in order to advertise, an expenditure is made with advertising as the objective but not the medium. To be deductible for tax purposes, payments in lieu of advertising have to be something that is designed to achieve the same function as advertising, with the same limitations. Thus, expenses of selling associate memberships in a recreation club were deductible by a real-estate company. The company had no advertising program; instead, property was sold to persons who became interested when, from the club premises, they could see other picturesque land which was for sale. This was deemed to be a substitute for ordinary advertising.[68]

In the case of a breeder of horses, one court held that "Horse shows are the best form of advertising." Costs of entering and showing the animals, therefore, were deductible.[69]

Payments to a state in order to provide for highway safety advertising were deductible.[70]

A physician who wished to become known in a new community in which he was now living decided to join the county sheriff's mounted posse, using his own horse. He was permitted to deduct out-of-pocket expenses, such as shoeing and stabling, as unreimbursed expenditures made incidental to service to a tax-exempt organization.[71]

Deduction is allowed for advertising which emphasizes and promotes government objectives, such as conservation.[72] Expenditures for institutional or goodwill advertising which keeps the taxpayer's name before the public are generally deductible provided the expenditures are related to patronage the taxpayer might reasonably expect in the future. Deduction is allowed for the cost of advertising which keeps the taxpayer's name before the public in connection with encouraging contributions to such organizations as the Red Cross, purchase of United States Savings Bonds, or participation in similar causes. In like fashion, expenditures for advertising which present views on economic, financial, social, or other subjects of a general nature, but which do not involve lobbying or attempts to influence legislation, are deductible.[73]

The cost of newspaper space used to encourage people to go out and vote for candidates of their own choice was deductible. The advertisements identified the taxpayer as their sponsor.[74]

The advertising need not be of the taxpayer's product or service. A landlord could advertise on behalf of a tenant whose prosperity would help the landlord to collect the rent. Had the tenant failed, the landlord might have had trouble in leasing the aged building and other properties in the neighborhood.[75]

An insurance agent could deduct matured claims against an insurance company that he represented, and which he paid to clients out of his own pocket, to "promote the taxpayer's business," as the court stated.[76] (That, after all, is what advertising is all about.)

Advertising deductions are permitted for companies whose production facilities are devoted entirely to governmental work, so that their names and the qualities of their products will be known to the public when they return to nongovernmental production. But in evaluating the amount of the deduction, cognizance must be taken of the taxpayer's prior advertising budgets, public patronage reasonably to be expected in the future, and the unavailability of components used in the advertised products.[77]

Ordinarily, an expenditure is not currently deductible if the benefits to be obtained are expected to last for more than one year. But advertising and promotion for a campaign covering the next five years were deductible at the time of the expenditure.[78]

A business could deduct the cost of advertising placed in magazines published by labor unions.[79]

The general rule is that a deduction is not permitted for advertising in a political convention program. Deduction is permitted for such advertising in connection with a convention for nominating candidates for the offices of President and Vice-President of the United States, providing the cost of the advertising is reasonable in light of the business expected to be received (1) directly as the result of the advertising, or (2) as a result of the convention's being held in an area where the taxpayer has a principal place of business.[80]

A taxpayer was allowed a business expense deduction for an advertisement placed in the official program of such a national convention, without having to show an expectation of increased business to justify the deduction.[81]

Advertising expenses of a gambling establishment were deductible although state law banned gambling.[82]

The cost of tickets for benefit performances, purchased to maintain goodwill in the community, was deductible as a form of advertising.[83] A tavern owner was permitted to deduct as advertising the cost of a Christmas party given for the children of the neighborhood to promote goodwill with their parents.[84] A restaurant could deduct the cost of an automobile given to the patron who drew a winning ticket.[85]

A market research consultant could deduct the cost of parties given to promote the services of a client.[86]

To promote sales and net profits, a business agreed to pay to an approved charitable organization a certain amount for each label from one of its products that the charitable organization mailed to the business enterprise. In return, the charitable organization agreed to permit the use of its name in the business's advertising and to obtain testimonial letters for use in a sales campaign. The amounts turned over to the charity by the business were deductible as ordinary and necessary expense, without the percentage limitations imposed upon charitable contributions.[87]

If expenses for advertising items such as signs have a life of more than one year, the deductible cost must be spread over the estimated number of years of use.[88]

Advertising expenses do not require the detailed documentary substantiation of travel and entertainment, such as the amount, time, place, and business purpose of every expenditure. Thus credible estimates may be acceptable.[89] A New Orleans businessperson could deduct part of the maintenance costs (as determined by the court) of horses he entered in a Mardi Gras parade, although his records were sketchy as to the clientele that was developed at the parade.[90] *See also* **Business gifts; Contributions; Employees; Expenses of another person; Ordinary and necessary business expenses.**

Aftershocks. *See* **Casualties.**

Agreement not to compete, payments for. *See* **Expenditures for benefits lasting more than one year.**

Agricultural allotment cancellation. When the Secretary of Agriculture cancelled a cotton acreage allotment, a farm operator could deduct the amount he had paid for this allotment.[91]

Air-conditioning equipment. Ordinarily, the cost of property with a life of more than one year cannot be deducted for tax purposes; if the property is used for business purposes, the cost can be written off as depreciation over the period of its life. If equipment with a life of more than one year is purchased for medical reasons, the cost is deductible only to the extent that it does not add value to the property of a house in which it may be permanently installed. If air-conditioning equipment is acquired to relieve an allergy or to facilitate breathing for patients with a heart condition, deduction is allowed under the following conditions: The initial cost of the air-conditioning equipment plus the operating expense minus the resale or salvage value is allowed, *provided* that the medical need for the equipment is substantiated by evidence and that the equipment is used primarily for the alleviation of a person's illness, and provided further that the equipment does not become a permanent part of a dwelling. If you can't take it with you, then you can't take it off your taxes.[92] *See also* **Medical expenses.**

Airline pilot, expenses of. A commercial pilot could deduct the cost of uniforms worn only on duty, as well as costs for the maintenance and replacement of navigation instruments, computers, and plotters.[93]

The cost of shoeshines was deductible where a pilot was required by his employer to present a well-groomed appearance to the public and where other pilots actually had been discharged for not doing so.[94]

"Incidentals of his profession" justify deduction of commuting expenses where items such as heavy tools must be carried from home to place of work. But this rule does not apply to airline pilots who carry flight bags and overnight bags.[95]

Airspace. *See* **Depreciation.**

Alcoholics Anonymous. An individual who joined an Alcoholics Anonymous club in his community pursuant to competent medical advice could deduct as medical expenses the transportation costs of attending the meetings of the club. This was true because the medical adviser stated that membership in AA was necessary for the treatment of a disease involving the excessive use of alcohol.[96]

Alcoholism, treatment for. An individual entered a therapeutic center for alcoholism, where he remained as an inpatient for several months. The center was maintained for alcoholics by a private, nonprofit organization, and inpatients were required to pay for their care, which included room, board, and treatment at the center. Amounts thus paid were deductible as medical expense.[97] *See also* **Medical expenses.**

Aliens. *See* **Nonresident alien, deductions of.**

Alimony (periodic payments). Periodic payments (alimony) made by a husband to a wife (or vice versa) are deductible by the spouse making the payments, if such payments are made after a legal divorce or separation. Such periodic payments (whether or not they are made at regular intervals) must be made to satisfy a court order or decree divorcing or legally separating the husband and wife, *or* to satisfy a written form relating to such divorce or legal-separation action.[98] A letter satisfies the written-instrument requirement if it embodies the terms of a prior oral agreement or understanding.[99]

Support payments may be amended after the divorce decree to take account of changed support requirements. An amended agreement produces an alimony deduction if the new arrangement satisfies the requirements mentioned previously.[100]

Under a divorce decree, the husband was required to pay the wife

$600 a month as alimony and $500 as part of a "full, complete and final division of the estate." He could not deduct the $500 if it was part of a property settlement. But as the parties did not live in a community property state, she had no basis for receiving the $500 in addition to the agreed $600 alimony other than her claim for support, nor did she relinquish rights of significant value, other than her claim for support in order to receive the $500. So the $500 monthly payments were deductible by him, as they were made because of the marital relationship and thus were support.[101]

In cases where a husband and wife are separated, and they have executed a written separation agreement, periodic payments made under it are deductible, whether or not the agreement is legally enforceable.[102] But if a husband wrote his wife a letter saying that he would give her $800 a month for support, he could deduct nothing. She had never agreed to this amount, accepting his checks only because she needed money. The court did not believe that this had been intended to be a legal agreement, because parties would not have entered into such an important agreement in such a casual manner.[103]

When, for reasons of economy or otherwise, a couple continues to live in the same house, deduction of alimony depends upon whether they actually are living separately. This is a fact and not a definition, and deduction was allowed in a case where the court was persuaded that they were indeed living separately.[104]

An individual paid a certain amount each month to his former wife under a settlement agreement. She suffered severe head injuries in an automobile accident and was placed in a convalescent home, the expenses of which were considerable. A court named a conservator for her, and he requested the ex-husband to assume the new heavy medical and support costs. The onetime husband could deduct the amounts he thus paid out, even though he never had agreed in writing to do so. By accepting the conservator's letter of understanding and by making the payments specified in the letter, he was deemed to have consented to his new obligations.[105]

Periodic payments are defined as payments of a fixed amount for an indefinite period (*e.g.*, $10,000 per year until death or until remarriage) or as payments of an indefinite amount for either a fixed period (*e.g.*, 10 percent of a husband's income for ten years) or an indefinite period (*e.g.*, 10 percent until death). The payments need not be made at regular intervals, such as on the fifteenth of each month, to be defined as periodic payments.[106]

Even if a principal sum is specified in the decree and the sum is payable over a period of less than ten years, the payment still may be deducted as alimony, if it is in the nature of a support allowance, and if it is subject to modification on the death, remarriage, or change of economic status of the spouses.[107]

If the period for the payments is fixed and it is for more than ten years, the payor may deduct each installment payment, but only to the extent that the sum of the installments does not exceed 10 percent of the total specified in one taxable year. This 10 percent limitation applies to installment payments made in advance of their due date, but not to delinquent installment payments received by the payee during one taxable year. For instance, suppose that under a court order John Smith owes Mary Smith, his ex-wife, $100,000 to be paid over a period of twelve years. If in the first year of his obligation he gives Mary $20,000 he can claim only $10,000 of that money during that taxable year.

In addition to the alimony payments themselves, the husband or wife may deduct any other amounts which are a part of the alimony settlement. For instance, a husband under a separation agreement was obligated to pay his ex-wife $20,000 a year as long as she lived and was unmarried and also to pay $5,000 a year to his mother-in-law "for and in behalf of" his ex-wife. He could deduct the payments made to the mother-in-law.[108]

A divorce decree provided that the husband should furnish his wife with a residence without charge. He could deduct his payments for the house's rent and heat, even though the building was owned by a corporation in which he owned stock.[109]

Where a separation agreement gave the wife the right to occupy free of charge a cooperative apartment owned by the husband, he could deduct the "rent" fixed in the proprietary lease affecting this apartment, as well as his payments for expenses for painting and repairs.[110]

If a court order requires the husband to pay medical expenses of the wife, these are deductible as alimony. That includes medical insurance premiums for the wife which the court order has mandated.[111] The husband also may deduct medical insurance premiums where the court has merely provided the payment by him of actual medical expenses. Here the payment serves as his method of providing the wife's medical support required by the court order.[112]

Annual vacation payments to one's former wife, as provided in the divorce decree, were deductible.[113]

A separation agreement between two spouses provided among other things that the husband would pay a specified amount each year to the wife for the payment of her "contemplated life insurance." This agreement was incorporated into the divorce decree. The wife purchased the insurance, the husband having no ownership or any rights under the policy. He could deduct the payments for the insurance as alimony, even though they were not labeled as such in the divorce decree.[114]

Deductible alimony does not include payments under a property settlement agreement. But in one case, a husband could deduct payments made to the wife which the separation agreement said were "by way of property settlement." Actually she had no property rights which she could have exchanged for the property, as the couple had owned nothing jointly. The lawyers representing each party had never discussed a division of the husband's property but only the payment to the wife of an amount related to her current needs.[115]

Whether mortgage payments made by one spouse on property awarded to the other spouse under a divorce decree are deductible depends upon whether these payments were part of a property settlement or were support payments. The payments were deductible as alimony when they were made in discharge of a general obligation of support.[116]

If, under a divorce decree or alimony settlement, an individual pays his ex-spouse's medical and/or dental expenses, these may be deducted as alimony provided that they qualify as periodic payments and that separate returns (other than a joint return for the two parties involved) are filed.[117]

The spouse receiving the payments must include these payments in his or her gross income, but they may be deducted by that spouse as medical expenses if deductions are itemized.[118]

A deduction is also allowed for periodic payments made in lieu of alimony (but which amount to the same thing), or an allowance for support is correct if the payments provided for that support are made during the year in which the payor's income tax is filed. The amount of payment has to be included in the income of the payee, however, for the deduction to be legal.[119]

The above could cover payments made by a husband (or a wife) periodically under a divorce decree granting legal separation from bed and board.[120]

A separation agreement between two spouses provided that the wife would waive alimony rights. There was a property settlement which, among other things, required the wife to convey her interest in the family house to the husband, who was obliged to sell it and to give her a specified amount out of the proceeds. Until money was received from the sale of the house, he was bound to pay her $170 a month rent for an apartment, unless the actual rent came to a lesser figure. He was permitted to deduct the rental payments he gave to her, even though he gave her the required rents rather belatedly in the form of a lump-sum payment.[121]

Payments made under a divorce decree of questionable validity are deductible because a divorce decree is presumed to be valid for tax purposes until a court having proper jurisdiction either declares the divorce invalid or formally invalidates it by a subsequent divorce decree.[122]

A wife brought suit against her husband for divorce and was awarded

$200 a week as alimony. Subsequently he won an annulment on the ground that she had been married to a prior husband at the time of the marriage. Although the court held his marriage to her had been void from the beginning, he gave her $150 a week for support. Inasmuch as his payments were made in recognition of a general legal obligation arising from the marital relationship, which was made specific by the annulment decree, he was allowed to deduct these amounts as alimony, even though under state law that is not what they were.[123]

Where arrears (overdue alimony payments) are paid by one spouse in a lump sum, this sum is treated for tax purposes in the same manner as periodic payments would have been treated if paid when due. See previous discussions.[124]

Payments for child support are not deductible by the payor, nor are they included in the income of the payee, such as alimony must be, even if provided for under the same decree or order as the deductible alimony payments.[125]

Regardless of what the parties may have intended, if the decree, and the agreement prepared in accordance with the decree, makes no reference to how much of the payment is for child support, the entire amount is treated for tax purposes as alimony and is therefore deductible by the payor and must be included in the income of the payee.[126]

The payor gets a tax deduction for any portion of the payment he makes which is not specifically earmarked in the agreement for support of the children.[127]

A divorce settlement provided that the husband would pay a specified monthly sum to the wife for the care, support, and maintenance of their five minor children, and for the support, maintenance, and alimony of the wife. This sum was to be reduced by one-sixth as each child would reach age eighteen, die, or become financially independent. Although this one-sixth provision may have implied that equal payments had been allocated to each child and to the wife, the agreement itself nowhere stated that five-sixths of the payments were for child support and one-sixth was for alimony. The amount paid as child support under the reduction clause could be determined only by inference or conjecture. So the entire amount paid by the onetime husband was deductible as alimony.[128]

The payor is entitled to an alimony deduction even where the amount actually paid is of a lesser sum than called for by the divorce decree, if the payment took into account other amounts owed by the payee to the payor.[129]

Deductible alimony payments include credits to which the payor was entitled by reason of valid counterclaims against the payee.[130]

Expenses which are incurred by the alimony-receiving spouse in getting an increase in that alimony are deductible.[131]

Legal fees to collect previously awarded (and delinquent) alimony are deductible.[132]

Under the terms of a property-settlement agreement approved in the divorce decree, a husband had to pay, in addition to alimony and child support, the premiums on two life insurance policies on his own life. Policy A was assigned absolutely to the ex-wife, she being designated, in legal terms, as the irrevocable beneficiary and the children as irrevocable contingent beneficiaries. Policy B designated the children as beneficiaries, and the ex-wife as contingent beneficiary. Policy B was not assigned to the ex-wife and remained in the husband's custody. The premiums paid on Policy A were deductible by the husband, but those on Policy B were not.[133]

An individual was ordered by a divorce decree to pay stipulated annual sums to his former wife. He made some payments in cash, he paid bills from her creditors which she forwarded to him, and he rounded out the required payment in the taxable year by having his broker send her the balance in a margin account he had opened in her name some years previously. Although the divorce decree had provided that his alimony payments to her were to be in cash, the payments to her creditors were deemed equivalent to his having paid these amounts to her, followed by her payments to the creditors. The margin account had been created by his funds, he alone gave the broker instructions to execute transactions, and he paid all the margin calls with his own funds. There was no evidence that he had ever given her the brokerage account as a gift or otherwise, and hence it still was his when he had the account converted into cash for her. Inasmuch as he had paid to or for her the amount mentioned in the divorce decree with his own funds, he was entitled to the alimony deduction even though the payments had not been in the form of cash flowing directly from him to her.[134]

For taxable years beginning after December 31, 1976, alimony is deductible by persons using the zero bracket amount as well as by taxpayers who itemize their deductions.[135] *See also* **Interest; Legal fees; Medical expenses; Taxes.**

Ambulance hire. *See* **Medical expenses.**

Amortization. *See* **Depreciation; Election to deduct or to capitalize; Expenditures for benefits lasting more than one year; Investors.**

Amortization of bond premium. If a person buys a taxable bond (as opposed to a tax-free state or municipal bond) at a price above its face value, this excess is referred to as bond *premium.* For example, he pays $1,040 for a $1,000 face value bond which will reach its maturity date in ten years. He may elect to deduct one-tenth of the $40 premium, or $4, each year for the next ten years.[136]

If the corporation which issued the bond is entitled to redeem ("call") the bond before its stated maturity date, any unamortized portion is deductible as an ordinary loss in the year of the call. For example, four years after the investor purchases his bond, the corporation calls it for retirement. At that time he may deduct $24 (six years of unamortized premium times $4 a year).[137]

Annuities from charitable organizations. The purchaser of an annuity may recover tax-free each year the cost of his annuity divided by the number of years in his life expectancy; that is, he excludes from income each year the *cost* divided by the number of years in his life expectancy.[138] For example, Amos Turner is fifty years old when he purchases an annuity for $3,000. His life expectancy is twenty more years, so he divides the $3,000 by twenty, which is $150. The $150 is excluded from his income that year.

In response to one of the many advertisements which appear in newspapers and magazines, an individual may buy an annuity from a charitable organization. If he pays more than the going rate for comparable annuities from a commercial company, the annuity cost which may be recovered over the years tax-free is limited to the fair market value of the annuity. The balance of his cost is deductible as a charitable contribution.[139]

Annuity contract, refund. The original purchaser of a single premium *refund* annuity contract who surrendered it for a cash consideration was permitted to deduct the difference between the basis of the contract (the cost less amounts previously recovered under the contract) and the amount received upon surrender.[140]

Answering service. An attorney who had given up his professional office when he became a state employee, but who continued to handle some of his former clients on a "moonlighting basis," could deduct the charges of a telephone answering service which received calls on what had been his business phone.[141]

Antitrust suits. *See* **Legal fees.**

Apartment used for business purposes. When a businessperson regularly travels to another city to take care of his commercial affairs, his hotel expenses there are deductible. But if he maintains an apartment in the city to which he travels from his home, a portion of the rent is deductible, the amount depending upon the business as opposed to the personal use made of it. One individual lived in Cleveland and maintained a three-room apartment in New York which was used by himself and by several employees when in the latter city on business. He was permitted to deduct 75 percent of the full rental.[142]

Apportionment of realty taxes. *See* **Taxes.**

Appraisal fees. *See* **Casualties; Condemnation awards, expenses related to; Contributions; Farmers; Investors; Taxes.**

Appreciated-value property, contributions of. *See* **Contributions.**

Arbitration. Fees paid to an arbitrator are deductible where the dispute was business-oriented.[143]

Architect's fees. *See* **Abandonment loss.**

Armed forces. In general, the cost of uniforms, including laundry, cleaning, repair, and alterations, is not deductible because the uniform takes the place of civilian clothing. Where local military regulations require that the fatigue uniform be worn, and then only while on duty or while traveling to and from duty, provided the individual does not leave his car or other means of transportation, the cost of such uniforms and their maintenance is deductible to the extent that it exceeds any uniform gratuity or allowance received.

Here are examples of uniforms which may qualify if these tests are met: Navy dungaree working uniforms and chief petty officer and officer khaki working uniforms (wash khakis); Marine fatigues; Army fatigue (field or utility) uniforms and wash khakis; and Air Force fatigue (utility) uniforms for men and three-piece field suits for women.[144]

In order to get a deduction for a particular uniform, one must show that military regulations prohibit one from wearing it while off duty.[145]

In the case of a member of a Reserve component of the Armed Forces who is required to wear his uniform for temporary periods when on active duty for training, when attending Reserve school courses, or when attending training assemblies, and who is prohibited by military regulations from wearing his uniform except on such occasions, the uniform does not merely take the place of articles required in civilian life.[146] Then the cost of uniforms and their maintenance is deductible.

Students of Armed Forces service academies cannot deduct the cost of uniforms to the extent that they replace regular clothing, but deductions may be taken for the cost of their status insignia which are purchased.[147]

All members of the Armed Forces are permitted to deduct the cost of items or equipment specially required of them which do not take the place of civilian clothing. Examples include the cost of all items of insignia of rank and corps, including gold lace and devices on the uniform coat, black braid on the aviation winter working uniform, collar devices, shoulder marks, chin straps, cap devices, and the excess cost of a cap for officers which is attributed to the gold lace on the visor; the cost of campaign bars, wings, full-dress belts, epaulets, and aiguillettes. Deduction likewise is allowed for the expense of altering uniforms and equipment upon change of rank by promotion or demotion.[148] The cost of company bars is deductible.[149] The cost of a sword is an allowable deduction,[150] presumably because it is not something which can be expected to be used in civilian life.

As previously noted, the cost of cleaning fatigues is deductible, but the cost of haircuts is not.[151]

A person in the Armed Forces may deduct the cost of professional magazines which are appropriate to his work.[152]

The cost of a correspondence course is deductible if it meets the regular educational-expense requirements. (*See* **Education.**) The deductible educational expenses of a veteran of the Armed Forces do not have to be reduced by tax-exempt educational benefits received from the Veterans Administration.[153]

If a member of the Armed Forces is on temporary or temporary additional duty, travel and other expenses (such as those incurred for meals, lodging, taxicabs, laundry, and cleaning) in excess of reimbursements are deductible while he is away overnight from home, be it on a ship or at a base or station.[154]

Reserve personnel required to work and to drill on the same day at each of two different locations within the same city or general area may deduct one-way transportation expenses in going from one place of business to another. When they return home before drills, one-way expenses, not to exceed those from place of work to place of work, may be deducted. But round-trip transportation expenses are deductible only when such duty area is situated beyond the city or general area which constitutes the principal place of business, provided free transportation between such locations is not furnished by the Armed Forces. This applies to all personnel who are employed at two locations on the same day.[155] This rule applies regardless of whether the individual attends such drills in the evening after his regular working hours or on an otherwise non-working day.[156]

Travel expenses, including meals and lodging, of Reserve personnel who under competent orders, with or without compensation, are required to remain away from their principal place of business overnight in the performance of authorized drills and training duty are deductible.[157]

A member of the Armed Forces who is serving on temporary active duty in the Ready Reserve and who has a principal or regular place of business or employment which he has not given up and to which he will return after his period of service, is considered in a travel status; that is, provided he is stationed away from the general area where his civilian place of employment or other business is located. In such cases, a member who pays for his meals and lodging at his official post of duty is entitled to a deduction for expenses necessarily incurred for that purpose to the extent that such expenses exceed any nontaxable basic subsistence and quarters allowances received for these expenses. In determining the amount deductible, the expenses are limited to those which are directly attributable to the member's own presence at his military post and do not include expenses for members of his family.[158]

An executive of a manufacturing company was commissioned as an Army officer and was assigned to work on wartime procurement activities. He could deduct the expenses of using his own car in fulfilling his duties, where the need for prompt action made it impossible for him to obtain regular government transportation.[159]

A naval officer may deduct as a traveling expense the cost of his meals aboard ship while the ship is away from its home port.[160]

Losses incurred by military and naval disbursing officers in replacing shortages which were not due to negligence are deductible.[161]

Losses sustained as a result of destruction or seizure of personal property in the course of military or naval operations, to the extent not reimbursed by insurance or otherwise, are deductible.[162]

A United States Army retiree could deduct legal fees in connection with a suit instituted by him to contest the rank and rate of retirement pay at which he had been retired. Here the court found that he should have been retired at a higher rank and awarded him back pay which he included in his income.[163] A noncommissioned Army officer could deduct the expenses connected with his successful litigation to obtain an increase in his retirement pay.[164]

An individual who was in the Army Reserve was charged with falsifying his educational accomplishments on two Statements of Personal History and on an Army Reserve Qualification Questionnaire, as well as falsifying time and attendance vouchers while employed as a budget and finance officer. After employing counsel, he defended a court-martial arising out of the charges, was acquitted, and was retained as an officer in the Army Reserve. Inasmuch as conviction could have resulted in loss of his position, his expenses were deductible.[165]

A captain in the Army Reserve could deduct the legal expenses of defending himself in a court-martial which had been appointed to try him on the charge of conduct unbecoming an officer in that he had dishonorably refused to pay his wife the alimony provided for her. It was held that he was engaged in the trade or business of being an officer. This was a business expense, for if he had been convicted, he would have been discharged from the trade or business.[166]

A member of the Armed Forces was allowed to deduct expenses incurred in moving his dependents to his new duty station in a foreign country. They were not eligible for moving at government expense because he was in pay-grade E-4 with less than four years of active military service and hence did not qualify. It did not matter that his dependents had to renew their visas every ninety days, for they were members of his household and he met the requirement of being a full-time employee in the general area of his new principal place of work for twelve months. Nor did it matter that the new duty station had a rule which denied housing to family members who had not been moved at government expense.[167]

The cost of moving to report for active duty by a member of the Armed Forces on permanent change of duty may be deductible even though he used a tax table or the zero bracket amount in computing his Federal income tax. Moving expenses may qualify for deduction even if the new place of employment is at least thirty-five miles from the old residence and if the employment meets the thirty-nine- or seventy-eight-week tests.[168] Such also is the case where he had no old place of employment when he entered the service. (*See* **Moving expenses.**)

If an individual received a reenlistment bonus which he previously included in gross income on a Federal income tax return, and, because his enlistment is terminated, he must refund a portion of the bonus, he is entitled to a deduction for that amount.[169]

Personal money allowances received by certain high-ranking military officers for their discretionary use are includable in gross income but are deductible in determining adjusted gross income, whether or not the officer itemizes his deductions. But if the expenses exceed the personal money allowance, he may claim an itemized deduction for such excess as a business expense provided he itemizes deductions.[170]

Amounts reimbursed to military attachés for entertaining in connection with their official duties are similarly treated, subject to proper substantiation.[171]

The unreimbursed expenses incurred by a veteran as a member of the American Legion in attending a Legion convention as a delegate, as well as unreimbursed expenses directly connected with and solely attributable to the rendition of such voluntary services by him to the Legion, constitute deductible charitable contributions. This applies equally to other organizations which have tax-exempt status.[172]

Expenses in connection with one's trade or business ordinarily are deductible. That applies to expenses related to military service by a retired army officer who is subject to recall to active duty.[173] *See also* **Education; Employees; Travel.**

Artificial teeth and limbs. *See* **Medical expenses.**

Artist, contributions of. A professional artist who contributed three of his own paintings to an approved charitable organization could not deduct the value of the pictures or of his own artistic services, but only his cost of the canvas and other materials used.[174]

Artist, expenses of. In general, a professional sculptor was allowed to deduct the cost of materials and labor.[175]

An artist who prepared television commercials could deduct the cost of art supplies and books.[176]

A full-time painter was permitted to deduct the cost of maintaining his art studio.[177] *See also* **Office at home.**

Assessment of tax, interest on. *See* **Interest.**

Asset Depreciation Range (A.D.R.) system. *See* **Depreciation; Repairs.**

Assets. *See* **Depreciation; Obsolescence; Purchase of stock to get assets.**

Assistant, lunches for. *See* **Entertainment.**

Athletic-club dues. Dues or fees paid to an athletic club or organization after December 31, 1978, in taxable years ending after that date are deductible if the taxpayer establishes that the facility was used primarily for the furtherance of his trade or business and that the expense was related directly to the conduct of his trade or business.[178] *See also* **Entertainment.**

Attorney's fees. *See* **Legal fees.**

Audit, expenses of representation. A taxpayer could deduct the fees of a certified public accountant who represented him at the Internal Revenue Service audit of a prior year's tax return.[179]

Audit fees. *See* **Accounting expenses.**

Author. *See* **Research; Travel.**

Author's expenses. A professional writer was able to deduct his expenses in researching, writing, and arranging material for a book. The court stressed the fact that he had demonstrated that he was in the trade or business of writing.[180] *See also* **Writers, expenses of.**

Automatic dividend reinvestment plan. A bank offered its checking account customers an automatic investment service, under which a customer could elect to invest a portion of his checking account each month in the common stock of one or more of twenty-five specified corporations. For each corporation in which a participant invested, there was a monthly service charge equal to 5 percent of the amount deducted from his checking account, the figure not to exceed a specified amount in any one month. This monthly service charge was ruled to be deductible.[181]

Automobile financing interest. Even where a person uses the standard mileage rate instead of itemizing expenses of using his car for business purposes, he can deduct interest paid to finance the purchase of a car.[182]

Automobile, use of. Expenses paid or accrued in the operation and repair of an automobile used in making business or professional calls are deductible.[183]

Where a person uses his automobile for business purposes and chooses to itemize his deductions instead of using the standard mileage rate, he may elect to exclude from the Accelerated Cost Recovery System a car placed in service after December 31, 1980.[184] *See also* **Casualties; Commuting; Contributions; Employees; Expenditures for benefits lasting more than one year; Medical expenses; Mileage allowance; Ordinary and necessary business expenses; Settlement payments; Travel; Wrongful death claim.**

Awards. *See* **Employee awards; Long-service award; Productivity award; Rewards; Safety award.**

"Away from home." *See* **Travel.**

"Who Says So?"

Except in a few areas which most persons never encounter, the burden of proof in a tax matter is on the taxpayer. Unless an individual uses the zero bracket amount with its minimal opportunity for tax savings, he must be prepared to demonstrate an authority for every deduction claimed.

These sections of the book list the authorization or citation for each deduction which has been mentioned alphabetically. The authorities may be the Internal Revenue Code, Treasury Regulations, or various administrative rulings by the Internal Revenue Service. A substantial number of the citations represent court decisions. The monographs, booklets, and brochures listed are all publications of the Internal Revenue Service, except for *Armed Forces Federal Income Tax,* which was issued by the office of the Judge Advocate General of the United States Navy, and *Protecting Older Americans Against Overpayment of Income Taxes,* published by the Special Committee on Aging of the United States Senate.

IRS letter rulings are Internal Revenue Service letters sent in response to specific questions asked by taxpayers. These rulings may not be cited as precedents but they are useful in forming an opinion as to how the Service will apply its thinking to situations of a like kind.

A

1. Regulations Section 1.167(a)-9.

2. *Tanforan Co., Inc., v. United States,* 313 F. Supp. 796 (DC, ND Cal., 1970).

3. *Reeder et al. v. Commissioner,* T.C. Memo. 1980-165, filed May 7, 1980.

4. *San Marco Shop, Inc.,* T.C. Memo., Docket No. 39738, entered July 22, 1953.

5. *Hanover et al. v. Commissioner,* T.C. Memo. 1979-332, filed August 23, 1979.

6. *Commissioner v. McCarthy,* 129 F.2d 84 (7th Cir., 1942).

7. *Mark C. Nottingham et al.,* T.C. Memo., Docket Nos. 31414-5, entered May 8, 1953.

8. *A.J. Industries, Inc., v. United States,* 503 F.2d 660 (9th Cir., 1974).

9. *Continental Trust Company et al.,* 7 BTA 539 (1927).

10. *Tom (Fayette T.) Moore,* 19 BTA 140 (1930).

11. *Robert Buedingen,* 6 BTA 335 (1927).

12. *Dresser Manufacturing Company,* 40 BTA 341 (1939).

13. *Chevy Chase Land Company of Montgomery County, Maryland v. Commissioner,* 72 T.C. 481 (1979).

14. Revenue Ruling 55-367, 1955-1 CB 25.

15. Revenue Ruling 56-599, 1956-2 CB 122.

16. Revenue Ruling 73-201, 1973-1 CB 141.

17. *William Morse, Jr., et al.,* T.C. Memo. 1968-222, filed September 30, 1968.

18. *John P. White et al.,* 48 T.C. 430 (1967).

19. *Your Federal Income Tax,* 1976 edition, page 149.

20. *Burrell E. Davis,* 34 T.C. 586 (1960).

21. Revenue Ruling 73-201, 1973-1 CB 140.

22. *Clanton Motors, Inc.,* BTA Memo., Docket No. 89957, entered June 29, 1939.

23. *Kamen Soap Products, Inc.,* T.C. Memo. 1956-157, filed June 29, 1956.

24. Revenue Ruling 67-401, 1967-2 CB 123.

25. *Malone & Hyde. Inc. v. United States,* 568 F.2d 474 (6th Cir., 1978).

26. *Meldrum & Fewsmith, Inc.,* 20 T.C. 780 (1953).

27. *James A. Collins et al.,* 54 T.C. 1656 (1970).

28. *Michael J. Ippolito et al.,* T.C. Memo. 1965-167, filed June 14, 1965, *aff'd on another issue,* 364 F.2d 744 (2d Cir., 1966).

29. *Abe Brenner et al.,* T.C. Memo. 1967-239, filed November 28, 1967.

30. *Myrhl Frost,* T.C. Memo., Docket No. 112333, entered March 31, 1943.

31. *Lomas & Nettleton Company v. United States,* 79 F. Supp. 886 (DC, Ct., 1948).

32. *Albina Bodell,* T.C. Memo., Docket No. 109651, entered January 9, 1943.

33. *Tax Deduction on Investment Income and Expenses,* IRS Publication 550, 1976 edition, page 23.

34. Revenue Ruling 73-137, 1973-1 CB 68.

35. *Picker et al. v. United States,* 371 F.2d 486 (Ct. Cl., 1967).

36. *Charles Hutchison,* 13 BTA 1187 (1928).

37. *Reginald Denny,* 33 BTA 738 (1935).

38. *Oswald "Ozzie" Nelson et al.,* T.C. Memo. 1966-224, filed October 11, 1966.

39. *Charles Hutchison,* 13 BTA 1187 (1928).

40. *Regan v. Commissioner,* T.C. Memo. 1979-340, filed August 28, 1979.

41. *Reginald Denny,* 33 BTA 738 (1935).

42. *Charles Hutchison,* 13 BTA 1187 (1928).

43. *Regan v. Commissioner,* T.C. Memo. 1979-340, filed August 28, 1979.

44. *William L. Tracy,* 39 BTA 578 (1939).

45. *Regan v. Commissioner,* T.C. Memo. 1979-340, filed August 28, 1979.

46. Revenue Ruling 72-593, 1972-2 CB 180.

47. *Arthur E. Ryman, Jr., et al.,* 51 T.C. 799 (1969).

48. Economic Recovery Tax Act of 1981, Section 125.

49. *Geraldine R. Mann et al.,* T.C. Memo. 1975-74, filed March 24, 1975.

50. Revenue Ruling 72-28, 1972-1 CB 45.

51. *Marlor v. Commissioner,* 251, F.2d 615 (2d Cir., 1958).

52. Revenue Ruling 67-421, 1967-2 CB 84.

53. *Devereaux et al. v. Commissioner,* 292 F.2d 637 (3d Cir., 1961).

54. Revenue Ruling 74-78, 1974-1 CB 44.

55. *Albert C. Ruehmann III,* T.C. Memo. 1971-157, filed June 30, 1971.

56. *Shroyer et al. v. Commissioner,* T.C. Memo. 1981-327, filed June 24, 1981.

57. Regulations Section 1.162-14.

58. *Southwestern Electric Power Company v. United States,* 312 F.2d 437 (Ct. Cl., 1963).

59. *Denise Coal Company et al.,* 29 TC 528 (1957), *rev'd in part and aff'd in part on other issues,* 271 F.2d 930 (3d Cir., 1959).

60. *Poletti et al. v. Commissioner,* 330 F.2d 818 (8th Cir., 1969).

61. *Duffey v. Lethert,* DC, Minn. 1963.

62. *Sanitary Farms Dairy, Inc.,* 25 T.C. 463 (1955).

63. *Rodgers Dairy Company et al.,* 14 T.C. 66 (1950).

64. *Sterling Distributors, Inc. v. Patterson,* 236 F. Supp. 479 (DC, ND Ala., 1964).

65. *Sullivan et al. v. Commissioner,* T.C. Memo. 1982-150, filed March 24, 1982.

66. *Nowland v. Commissioner,* 244 F.2d 450 (4th Cir., 1957).

67. Revenue Ruling 70-393, 1970-2 CB 34.

68. *Aptos Land and Water Company, Inc.,* 46 BTA 1232 (1942).

69. *Engdahl et al. v. Commissioner,* 72 T.C. 659 (1979).

70. Revenue Ruling 54-532, 1954-2 CB 93.

71. *Hahn et al. v. Commissioner,* T.C. Memo. 1979-429, filed October 15, 1979.

72. IT 3581, 1942-2 CB 88.

73. Regulations Section 1.162-15.

74. Revenue Ruling 62-156, 1962-2 CB 47.

75. *Hennepin Holding Co.,* 23 BTA 119 (1931).

76. *Edward J. Miller,* 37 BTA 830 (1938).

77. IT 3581, 1942-2 CB 88.

78. *Consolidated Apparel Co.,* 17 T.C. 1570 (1952).

79. *Alexander Sprunt & Son, Inc.,* 24 BTA 599 (1931).

80. IRC Section 276(c).

81. *Denise Coal Company et al.,* 29 T.C. 528 (1957), *rev'd in part and aff'd in part on other issues,* 271 F.2d 930 (3d Cir., 1959).

82. *George G. Ebner et al.,* T.C. Memo. 1958-108, filed June 9, 1958.

83. *Victor J. McQuade,* 4 BTA 837 (1926).

84. *A. D. Miller,* T.C. Memo., Docket No. 23754, entered January 18, 1951.

85. IT 1667, II-I CB 83.

86. *Miller v. Commissioner,* T.C. Memo. 1980-136, filed April 23, 1980.

87. Revenue Ruling 63-73, 1963-1 CB 35.

88. *Alabama Coca-Cola Bottling Company, Inc.,* T.C. Memo. 1969-123, filed June 18, 1969.

89. *Sealy et al. v. Commissioner*, T.C. Memo. 1980-7, filed January 14, 1980.

90. *Pollard et al. v. Commissioner*, 285 F.2d 760 (5th Cir., 1961).

91. *Condit et al. v. Commissioner*, T.C. Memo. 1980-536, filed December 4, 1980.

92. Revenue Ruling 55-261, 1955-1 CB 307.

93. *Dean L. Phillips*, T.C. Memo., Docket Nos. 18410-18, entered June 9, 1950.

94. *C. Fryer et al.*, T.C. Memo. 1974-26, filed January 30, 1974.

95. *Fausner et al. v. Commissioner*, 413 U.S. 838 (1973).

96. Revenue Ruling 63-273, 1963-2 CB 112.

97. Revenue Ruling 73-325, 1973-2 CB 75.

98. Regulations Section 1.71-1(b).

99. *Randal W. Clark, Jr.*, 58 T.C. 519 (1972).

100. *Alice L. Heath*, 30 T.C. 339 (1958), *aff'd*, 265 F.2d 662 (2d Cir., 1959).

101. *Graham et al. v. Commissioner*, T.C. Memo. 1981-692, filed December 3, 1981.

102. Regulations Section 1.71-1(b)(2).

103. *Saniewski v. Commissioner*, T.C. Memo. 1979-337, filed August 27, 1979.

104. *Sydnes v. Commissioner*, 577 F.2d 60 (8th Cir., 1978).

105. *Osterbauer et al. v. Commissioner*, T.C. Memo. 1982-266, filed May 17, 1982.

106. Regulations Section 1.71-1(d).

107. *Martin et al. v. Commissioner*, 73 T.C. 255 (1979).

108. *Robert Lehman*, 17 T.C. 652 (1951).

109. *Doris B. Marinecco*, 54 T.C. 877 (1970).

110. *Rothschild et al. v. Commissioner*, 78 T.C., No. 10 (1982).

111. *Illene Isaacson et al.*, 58 T.C. 659 (1972).

112. *Lebeau et al. v. Commissioner*, T.C. Memo. 1980-201, filed June 12, 1980.

113. *Illene Isaacson et al.*, 58 T.C. 659 (1972).

114. *Phillips et al. v. Commissioner*, T.C. Memo. 1977-296, filed August 31, 1977.

115. *Schottenstein et al. v. Commissioner*, 75 T.C. 451 (1980).

116. *Mace v. United States*, DC, SD Cal., 1964.

117. Revenue Ruling 62-166, 1962-2 CB 21.

118. *Income Tax Deductions for Alimony Payments*, IRS Publication 504, 1976 edition, page 1.

119. IRC Section 215(a).

120. *Income Tax Deductions for Alimony Payments*, IRS Publication 504, 1976 edition, page 2.

121. *Hinish et al. v. Commissioner*, T.C. Memo. 1978-207, filed June 6, 1978.

122. *Income Tax Deductions for Alimony Payments*, IRS Publication 504, 1976 edition, page 2.

123. *Andrew M. Newburger et al.*, 61 T.C. 437 (1974).

124. Revenue Ruling 55-457, 1955-2 CB 527.

125. IRC Section 71(b).

126. *United States v. Paurowski*, 457 F.2d 1401 (4th Cir., 1973).

127. *Commissioner v. Lester*, 366 U.S. 299 (1961).

128. *Blakey et al. v. Commissioner*, 78 T.C., No. 68 (1982).

129. *Martha P. Pierce et al.*, 66 T.C. 840 (1976).

130. *Clarence W. Smith et al.*, 54 T.C. 1 (1968).

131. *Elsie B. Gale*, 13 T.C. 661 (1949), *aff'd on another issue*, 191 F.2d 79 (2d Cir., 1951).

132. *Jane V. Elliott*, 40 T.C. 304 (1963).

133. Revenue Ruling 70-218, 1970-1 CB 19.

134. *Robert W. Drummond et al.*, T.C. Memo. 1976-55, filed February 26, 1976.

135. Tax Reform Act of 1976, Section 502.

136. IRC Section 171(a)(1).

137. IRC Section 171(b)(2).

138. IRC Section 72.

139. Revenue Ruling 70-15, 1970-1 CB 20.

140. Revenue Ruling 61-201, 1961-2 CB 46.

141. *Leisner et al. v. Commissioner*, T.C. Memo. 1977-205, filed July 5, 1977.

142. *Wallace L. Chesshire*, T.C. Memo., Docket No. 30969, entered February 19, 1952.

143. *James A. Mount*, T.C. Memo., Docket No. 9401, entered November 29, 1946.

144. *Armed Forces Federal Income Tax*, 1976 edition, page 40.

145. IRS Letter Ruling 8120036, February 18, 1981.

146. Revenue Ruling 55-109, 1955-1 CB 261.

147. *Your Federal Income Tax*, 1976 edition, page 107.

148. *Armed Forces Federal Income Tax*, 1976 edition, page 40.

149. IT 1965, III-I CB 201.

150. Regulations Section 1.262-1(b)(8).

151. *Richard W. Drake*, 52 T.C. 842 (1969).

152. *Charles A. Harris et al.*, T.C. Memo., Docket No. 34256, entered January 28, 1953.

153. *Tax Information on Educational Expenses*, IRS Publication 508, 1976 edition, page 1.

154. *Armed Forces Federal Income Tax*, 1976 edition, page 27.

155. Ibid.

156. Revenue Ruling 55-109, 1955-1 CB 261.

157. *Armed Forces Federal Income Tax*, 1976 edition, page 27.

158. Revenue Ruling 63-64, 1963-1 CB 30.

159. *Howard Veit et al.*, T.C. Memo. Docket Nos. 15552-3, entered October 11, 1949.

160. Revenue Ruling 55-571, 1955-2 CB 44.

161. *Armed Forces Federal Income Tax*, 1976 edition, page 39.

162. Ibid.

163. Revenue Ruling 72-169, 1972-1 CB 43.

164. IT 3325, 1939-2 CB 151.

165. Revenue Ruling 64-277, 1964-2 CB 55.

166. *Howard v. Commissioner,* 202 F.2d 28 (9th Cir., 1953).

167. Revenue Ruling 70-520, 1970-2 CB 66.

168. *Armed Forces Federal Income Tax,* 1976 edition, page 26.

169. Ibid., page 40.

170. Revenue Ruling 77-350, 1977-2 CB 21.

171. Revenue Ruling 77-351, 1977-2 CB 23.

172. Revenue Ruling 58-240, 1958-1 CB 141.

173. *Imhoff et al. v. Commissioner,* T.C. Memo. 1980-30, filed January 31, 1980.

174. *Maniscalco v. Commissioner,* 632 F.2d 6 (6th Cir., 1980).

175. *Rood et al. v. United States,* 184 F. Supp. 791 (D.C., Minn., 1960).

176. *Herman E. Bischoff et al.,* T.C. Memo. 1966-102, filed May 19, 1966.

177. *Benjamin E. Adams et al.,* T.C. Memo. 1966-242, filed October 28, 1960.

178. Technical Corrections Act of 1979, Section 103(a)(1)(A), (B).

179. *Blair et al. v. Commissioner,* T.C. Memo. 1981-634, filed October 27, 1981.

180. *Stern et al. v. United States,* DC, CD Calif., 1971.

181. Revenue Ruling 75-548, 1975-2 CB 331.

182. Internal Revenue News Release IR-81-121, October 6, 1981.

183. Regulations Section 1.162-6.

184. Revenue Procedure 81-54, I.R.B. 1981-44, 21.

B

Bad debts. Business bad debts are deductible in full. Nonbusiness bad debts are deductible as short-term capital losses.[1] A business bad debt must be connected with the taxpayer's trade or business. A business bad debt can arise even out of an isolated transaction if it is related to a person's trade or business.[2]

In determining whether a bad debt is related to a person's trade or business, the test is his dominant motive in incurring a debt.[3]

An attorney could deduct unrecoverable advances that he made to a client to meet operating expenses so that the borrower could continue to be a client.[4]

Even if a person makes a loan to a corporation which might have become a good source of business income at a time which was *before* the lender had the necessary permit to engage in this business, loss on noncollectibility of a business bad debt is deductible if the lender already had the properties and was actively soliciting customers.[5]

Ordinarily, where an officer or other employee lends money to the business which employs him, any resulting loss is a nonbusiness bad debt, for an employee is not likely to be in the business of lending money and therefore the loss is not the result of a business transaction. Similarly, loss on his purchase of his employer's stock is a capital loss. But where the loan or purchase was for the purpose of obtaining or retaining one's position, a resultant loss is business-related. An individual as a result of major surgery was virtually unable to use his voice and one arm. He was offered employment only if he lent money to a certain corporation, in the stock of which he was also obligated to make an investment; the justification was that the corporation could not expand sufficiently to offer him employment unless the funds were made available. His subsequent losses were fully deductible as expenses in connection with his business of being an employee. He could not have been employed here or, presumably, anywhere else without his making the advance and the investment.[6]

An individual was informed when he was hired as vice-president and business manager of a corporation that he would be expected to make loans to the company until its cash position improved. He made such loans from time to time. There came a time when he was told that if he did not make further advances, the company would not be able to pay his salary and he would be fired. He declined and was fired. His prior unpaid advances were fully deductible business bad debts. The advances had been made in connection with his trade or business of rendering services for pay.[7]

A father and son created their own corporation in the used-metal business. They could deduct their losses when their advances to the corporation were not repaid. The father had made loans because, being over seventy, he had reason to feel he never would be able to get another job, and such proved to be the case after the corporation failed. The son was of employable age but was characterized by the court as unemployable for all practical purposes because of his personality, which did not lend itself to serving as an employee for a company other than his own. Both father and son were motivated by the desire to protect their trade or business as employees, and the advances were business bad debts.[8]

The president and sole stockholder of a textile corporation could deduct his advances to a corporation when they became uncollectible. The loans had been made to protect his job. His psychiatrist testified that his patient had very serious personality problems and was unable to work with persons in superior or equal positions. He had to retain his position as executive by owning his company; he could protect his employment only by helping the corporation to survive. The psychiatrist had advised him to form his own company so that he could carry on his trade or business of being a stylist.[9]

A corporate executive had difficulty living on his salary in view of the objectives he entertained for his family. He formed a corporation that performed the same type of work he previously had done for his employer, believing that he could generate a larger income for himself in this manner. When the corporation went bankrupt, he could deduct the amounts he had put into it. His stock had been acquired with the expectancy of increasing his salary, not as an investment (a capital asset). No dividends ever had been paid by the corporation and there had never been a prospect that there would be. There was no market for the stock, and there had been no expectation that it would increase in value.[10]

A well-regarded executive was hired by a new bank as its president in the belief that his reputation as a successful businessperson would bring in other commercial accounts. Actually his own business was in financial trouble, and it was for this reason that he accepted the generously salaried job at the bank. He advanced funds of his own to his company, which was unable to repay him. The Internal Revenue Service could not treat the advance as an effort to protect his investment, which would have been a short-term capital loss of limited usefulness. It was, however, fully deductible as an expenditure to protect his job with the bank. He was justified in believing that the bank would not have continued to employ as its president a person who could not even keep his own company solvent.[11]

Two individuals formed a corporation to create television shows and promotion. They personally guaranteed corporate notes to banks for the purchase of equipment. When the corporation failed, they could deduct the amounts paid out as guarantors as business bad debts. The court believed that the guarantees were not to protect their investments (which totaled only $3,000) but their salaries (aggregating $93,000). The arithmetic indicated that the individuals' primary purpose was to preserve their status as employees.[12]

In deciding whether protection of one's investment or of one's salary was the more important motivation, the figures at the date of the advances and not at the date of the original investment is determinative. Protection of salary was held to be the primary purpose of a stockholder's advance to his corporation. Even though his annual salary was only about one-twentieth the size of his investment in the stock, the relevant figure was the value of the investment at the time of the advance, which was zero.[13]

The sales manager of a shoe-manufacturing company was concerned that if the company failed, as seemed likely, customers would not get the footwear which they had purchased from him personally. Nondelivery would hurt his reputation. He guaranteed loans by a financial institution to the company, which he had to make good when the company could not pay. He was permitted to deduct his losses as business bad debts. His loan guarantees had been made for the purpose of maintaining his reputation and employability as a sales executive.[14]

The rules for determining whether a direct loan gives rise to a non-business bad debt also apply to debts which an individual has guaranteed.[15] So a person must prove that when the guarantees were made, they were in connection with what his trade or business was at the time.[16]

After its insolvency, an individual could deduct as a business bad debt the amounts he had advanced to a corporation he owned that bore his name. The loan had been made in an effort to protect his credit rating for bonding purposes in his construction business.[17]

One individual was employed to be president and general manager of a corporation for a stipulated salary and profit-sharing percentage. He also became a stockholder at that time. He cosigned a corporate note for bank financing when the company could not get funds on its own. He was obliged to honor the note from his own pocket when the corporation failed. He could deduct this payment in full as a business bad debt incurred primarily to protect his employment and not to protect his stock investment. Even though he was not yet receiving a salary, the obligation was related to his business of being an employee.[18]

A manufacturer's representative lent money to several small corporations whose products he sold. Purpose: to maintain his status as representative with its potential for commissions. He felt that without this financial assistance to them, the corporations would be disinclined to continue the relationship once he had introduced customers to the manufacturers. Amounts that could not be repaid to him could be deducted as business bad debts.[19]

The manager of a division of an insurance company received compensation based upon a percentage of the premium income produced by the unit under his control. To develop and to maintain loyalty and dedication which paid off in employee productivity, he made thirty-two loans to his staff members in an eight-year period. When one borrower went into bankruptcy, the loan to him could be deducted fully as a business bad debt. The manager's action in making loans to his employees was appropriate and useful in furtherance of his business as an insurance producer.[20]

The president of a financially distressed corporation lent money to two key employees so that they could buy stock in the company. He figured that if they owned a piece of the action, they would have an incentive to stay with the corporation and work harder for its success. When they were unable to repay the loans, he was able to deduct the amounts as business bad debts incurred for the purpose of protecting his job, which he would lose should the corporation fail.[21]

The cancellation of a debt which is in fact uncollectible amounts to a bad debt loss, in the absence of any relationship between debtor and creditor that would deny tax recognition of a loss between related parties.[22]

A business bad debt deduction was allowed where loans were made by an advertising agent to a corporate client in order to retain the corporation's business. These loans were related to the taxpayer's business of being an advertising agent.[23]

A cardiologist and several other doctors formed a group practice. He and the others transferred equipment used in their individual practices to a corporation at appraisal values, paid in notes. Subsequently the arrangement was terminated. That part of the notes which had not been paid off represented a business bad debt to the cardiologist. Although he was not regularly engaged in the business of selling medical equipment, this transaction was directly related to his business of a practicing physician and was for the purpose of enabling him to carry on his business in a form which seemed to better serve his professional interests.[24]

The president of a corporation made misrepresentations of the company's financial status to prospective investors, who then purchased stock. He could deduct the amount he paid to satisfy a court judgment against him in favor of the investors after the corporation went out of business.[25]

If a lien is placed against a taxpayer's property because of another person's unpaid debt, the taxpayer is considered to be this other person's creditor when he (the taxpayer) pays the debt in order to protect his own property. He is entitled to a bad debt deduction if the other person's debt is worthless.[26]

In the words of the United States Supreme Court, "The taxing act does not require the taxpayer to be an incorrigible optimist."[27]

The deduction of a debt as bad is established by some *identifiable event* which puts an end to the hope and expectation of repayment.[28]

Deduction was justified where an investigation of the business and of endorsements gave no hope of recovery.[29] Worthlessness was established in a year when a national accounting firm and the telephone company were unable to collect their bills. When such seasoned professionals cannot collect their money, what chance does an ordinary businessperson have?[30]

The unlikelihood of collection can be indicated by the illness of the proprietor of a business that makes termination of the business a certainty.[31] Uncollectibility can be established by disappearance of the debtor, with an apparent lack of leviable assets.[32] Worthlessness was evident where a customer corporation had sold all of its operating assets and had notified the Internal Revenue Service that liquidation was contemplated.[33]

A receivership, bankruptcy, liquidation, or cessation of a business may give evidence of the worthlessness of its debts.[34]

Noncollectibility may be established by an authoritative balance sheet showing that liabilities exceed assets.[35]

Accounting evidence may show that value is extinct without demonstration of an identifiable event.[36]

It is necessary to show what efforts have been made to collect the debt, that there is no property out of which the debt can be satisfied.[37]

If a taxpayer can establish that a debt appears to be recoverable only in part, he has the election of waiting until the debt is fully bad or of charging off that part of the debt which seems to be worthless at the time of this charge-off. In order to get a deduction for a partially bad debt, it must be a business bad debt and it must actually be charged off on the books to the extent claimed on the tax return.[38] The write-off must be of specific debts; it is not proper to take a flat percentage of total receivables or any other generalized figure.[39]

In the past, worthless debts of political parties could not be written off by frustrated creditors, except in the case of banks. For taxable years beginning after December 31, 1975, deduction is allowed for worthless debts owed by political parties or campaign committees if the debts arose from good-faith sales of goods or services and if substantial efforts were made to collect the debts.[40] Thus, suppliers of campaign office furniture, printers, landlords, and the like, who were stuck with unpaid bills can now regard campaigns with less bitterness, regardless of which horse comes in.

Spending money in an effort to collect a debt that a person previously deducted as bad can endanger this deduction, for it suggests that the creditor wasn't fully convinced that the debt *was* uncollectible. Deduction was permitted, however, where suit had been brought against a company, the unpaid account of which had been written off as worthless, when it could be established that the taxpayer still believed the company was unable to pay its debt but there was some possibility of personally involving an officer of the delinquent company.[41]

Bad debts are deductible when they are charged off. Alternatively, amounts added to a reserve for bad debts to bring this reserve up to what experience has shown to be a proper percentage of receivables or sales are deductible.[42]

An alternative method of accounting for bad debts is the *reserve method*. Based upon past experience, a taxpayer can deduct whatever amount is necessary to bring the year-end balance in the reserve up to an acceptable measuring rod, such as 2 percent of closing receivables. This assumes that in the past, 2 percent of receivables became worthless. But inflation can ruin the validity of this approach. With soaring prices for goods, a single default can exceed the amount in the seller's previous reserve, which was based upon the *previous* year's receivables balances. Changed circumstances must be taken into account in determining the reasonableness of a taxpayer's addition to reserve.[43] *See also* **Guarantors, payments by; Reliance upon misrepresentation.**

Bail-bond fee. An individual could deduct the fee he had paid for a bail-bond when he was accused of taking kickbacks while serving as a purchasing agent for a major city. The expenditure was deductible because it arose in connection with his trade or business.[44]

Bankruptcy. A trustee in bankruptcy can deduct costs in connection with a corporate liquidation, except costs connected with the sale of assets, which must be charged against the proceeds of the sale.[45] *See also* **Creditors, payments to; Fiduciaries; Legal fees.**

Bar association dues. An attorney may deduct dues paid to bar associations.[46]

Bargain sales. *See* **Contributions.**

Barter-club commissions. In an effort to escape tax on sales of goods and services, an "underground economy" has sprung up. One technique is to form a "barter club," which makes available to members pertinent information concerning property and services that other members are offering for exchange. The club debits or credits members' accounts for goods or services received from or rendered to other members. Exchanges are made on the basis that one credit unit equals $1 of value. The club charges the member purchaser a 10 percent commission payable in cash on barter purchases. If the commission was paid to the barter club to acquire an item for use in connection with the member purchaser's trade or business, the amount of the commission is deductible as a business expense just as though a cash purchase was made.[47]

Baseball player, expenses of. A professional player is permitted to deduct the cost of his own uniforms if he has to supply them.[48] *See also* **Family transactions; Travel.**

Baseball team, support of. *See* **Advertising.**

Bathroom, cost of installing. *See* **Medical expenses.**

Beach cottage. *See* **Entertainment.**

Beneficiaries. If, on the termination of an estate or a trust, there is a net operating loss carry-over or a capital loss carry-over, or for the last taxable year of the estate or trust there is an excess of deductions over gross income for that year, the carry-over may be used by the beneficiary succeeding to the property of the estate or trust.[49]

In determining whether there is an excess of deductions over gross income, deductions exclusive of the personal exemption and the charitable deduction are to be totaled and matched against the gross income of the terminating estate or trust. If the deductions so computed in fact exceed that gross income, there will be excess deductions available for use by the beneficiary.[50]

A remainder beneficiary's payment of property taxes accrued and chargeable to a trust were deductible, where under state law the beneficiaries had at least a secondary obligation to pay these taxes.[51] A remainder beneficiary will receive what remains in a trust fund after other persons, such as someone who gets income for life, no longer have to be provided for. *See also* **Capital losses; Depreciation; Interest; Legal fees.**

Benefit performances, tickets for. Here are the ground rules if one purchases tickets for a benefit performance by an approved charitable organization:
1. If the charity sells one ticket for about the established price of a concert, etc., no part of the "contribution" is deductible.
2. If the charity charges an amount in excess of the established price of the ticket, only this excess is deductible as a contribution.
3. If the buyer of a ticket sold by the charity at the established price has no intention of using the ticket and in fact does not use it, he still gets no deduction. However, he would get the deduction if he refused to accept the ticket and merely made his contribution of the same amount to the charity.

4. If a charity solicits contributions on a form where the "contributor" designates his check mark as either being for a ticket to an event produced by the tax-exempt organization or as being a straight contribution, the person checking the first option gets no tax deduction.

5. If friends of the charity pay the entire cost of staging an event for which tickets are sent to contributors to the charity, no part of the cost of the tickets is deductible.[52]

If there is no established charge for an event for which tickets are "distributed" by a charitable organization to "contributors," an individual claiming a tax deduction must establish that the amount paid is not the purchase price of the privileges or benefits and that part of the payment, in fact, does qualify as a gift.

The amount indicated on a ticket (or other evidence of payment) to be a "contribution" does not necessarily have a bearing on the amount deductible. Such a statement, however, may be meaningful if it shows not only the value of the admission or other privilege but also the amount of the gift. If an individual pays $10 to see a special showing of a movie, the net proceeds of which go to a qualified organization, he cannot take too seriously the words "Contribution—$10." If the regular price for the movie is $2, he has made a contribution of $8.[53]

Betting losses. *See* **Gambling losses.**

Birth-control measures. The purchase of birth-control pills by a woman for her personal use was a deductible medical expense because she obtained the pills under a prescription provided by her physician.[54]

A woman who, at her own request, undergoes an abortion operation to terminate her pregnancy can claim the expense as a medical deduction if the operation is performed in a general hospital and if the operation is not illegal under state law. This is true because the operation is for the purpose of affecting a structure or function of the body and therefore is a deductible expense.[55]

A vasectomy performed in a doctor's office under local anesthetic and for the purpose of preventing conception is a deductible medical expense, even if the operation is performed at the man's own request.[56] *See also* **Medical expenses.**

Blackout losses. Losses from casualties or thefts sustained during an electricity blackout are deductible. The loss is fully deductible if business property is involved. In the case of nonbusiness property, the deduction is limited to the amount which exceeds $100.[57]

Blind persons, expenses of. The expenses paid by a blind person or for him in connection with maintaining a Seeing Eye dog are deductible as medical expenses.[58]

Amounts expended to have someone accompany the payor's blind child solely for the purpose of guiding the youngster in walking throughout the school day constituted medical care.[59]

Corporate executives or professional persons who are blind may have to engage readers in order to perform their business duties satisfactorily. The cost generally is paid by the handicapped persons themselves and not by their employers. The payments are deductible as ordinary and necessary expenses for labor directly connected with or pertaining to the taxpayer's trade or business. But being medical expenses, they are limited in deductibility to the extent that total medical expenses exceed 5 percent of the taxpayer's adjusted gross income. In a case where it is questionable whether an expense is deductible as a business or medical expense, business expense deductibility applies if all three of the following elements are present: (1) the nature of the taxpayer's work clearly requires that he incur a particular expense to perform his work satisfactorily, (2) the goods or services purchased by the expense are clearly not required or used, other than incidentally, in the conduct of the individual's personal activities, and (3) the tax law and its explanatory regulations are otherwise silent as to the treatment of such expenses.[60]

Where an item is purchased in a special form primarily for the alleviation of a physical defect (such as a braille edition of a book or magazine purchased for the blind) and where it is one that ordinarily is used for personal, living, and family purposes, the excess of the cost of the special form over the normal cost of the item is an expense for medical care. Therefore, where a parent has a child attending a school for the blind, amounts paid to purchase braille books and magazines in excess of the cost of their regular printed editions are expenses for medical care.[61]

An individual's child was afflicted with an eye condition that was diagnosed as a disease which eventually would cause the child to become totally blind. At the time the child was enrolled in a state university, and competent physicians recommended that certain special aids be obtained to facilitate the child's further education. The costs of a tape recorder, special typewriter, projection lamp for enlarging written material, and special lenses were considered to mitigate the condition of losing the sense of sight and were deductible as medical expenses.[62]

The cost of hand railings installed in a home to accommodate a blind dependent was deductible as medical expense.[63] *See also* **Medical expenses.**

Board of trade fees. Dues paid to a board of trade or chamber of commerce by individuals are deductible as business expenses where this membership is used as a means of advancing the business interests of the individual.[64]

Bodyguard. Hiring a bodyguard was a deductible expense in the case of a professional person who was the recipient of a kidnap threat.[65] *See also* **Protection.**

Boll weevils. Expenses for the elimination of boll weevils were deductible.[66]

Bond, furnishing of. An employee who is required to furnish bond to his employers at his own expense can deduct the cost.[67]

Bondholders' protective committee, payments to. *See* **Investors.**

Bond premiums. *See* **Investors.**

Bonds, tax-exempt. *See* **Tax-exempt bonds.**

Books. Amounts paid by a business or professional person for books used in connection with his work are deductible, if the useful life of such a book is short (for example, an almanac would be useful for one year).[68]

An Internal Revenue Agent was able to deduct the cost of tax books he used in connection with audits when he was away from his IRS office and its library. New editions of these books were published annually, so that the lives were not more than one year.[69]

Depreciation is allowed on books with a life of more than one year which are used for business or professional purposes.[70]

The cost of books purchased for the purpose of passing a professional engineering examination was deductible.[71]

An individual purchased an instructional text from a publisher of materials for forming family trusts. Inasmuch as these trusts proved to have no effect in reducing his Federal income taxes, the cost of the book was not deductible as an expense in connection with the determination of taxable income. But he could deduct the cost of books brought out by a major publishing house which were designed for use in connection with the preparation of tax returns and the determination of tax.[72]

A managerial consultant could deduct the cost of technical books.[73]

A college teacher was allowed to deduct the cost of books which he used for research to prepare for classroom instruction.[74]

A doctor could deduct the cost of a medical library.[75]

Education expenses include amounts spent for books.[76]

An executrix was permitted to deduct the cost of law texts purchased for use in discharging her responsibilities.[77]

Bowling alleys. *See* **Entertainment.**

Brace. A brace for a bad back was deductible as a medical expense.[78]

Breach of contract, payments for. Damages paid for breach of contract entered into in the ordinary course of a taxpayer's business and directly related thereto normally are considered to represent deductible business expense.[79]

An individual signed a contract for his employment as a salesperson. He ignored a contractual provision that he was not to sell the products of a competing firm, and his employer sued him for breach of contract. He could deduct the value of what he gave his employer to settle the suit.[80] *See also* **Settlement payments.**

Breach of fiduciary duty. *See* **Compensable injuries.**

Breach of trust. Payments made by an attorney to a client for failing to protect his interests were deductible.[81]

Payments by a corporate director to attorneys for defense of stockholder suits were deductible.[82]

Breakage by employee. A research scientist could deduct expenses for breakage he incurred and paid for.[83]

Bribes and kickbacks. Bribes and kickbacks, whether direct or indirect, are not deductible if made to an official of any government (United States, state, or foreign) or to any agency or instrumentality in violation of Federal or state law. They are allowed in the case of other payees unless the taxpayer-payor is convicted of an illegal bribe or kickback in a criminal proceeding or if he enters a plea of guilty or *nolo contendere.* (*Nolo contendere* means that the defendant does not contest the accusation against him.)[84]

Payments to an official or employee of a foreign government are deductible as business expenses if made in connection with the operation of a business, unless prohibited by the Foreign Corrupt Practices Act of 1977.[85]

If a bribe or kickback, other than to a governmental employee, does not constitute a criminal act in the jurisdiction where it took place, or if the taxpayer is not successfully prosecuted, the deduction is not disallowed.[86]

Some states, such as New York, make it a misdemeanor to give any gratuity to another party's employees without the knowledge and consent of the employer, "with intent to influence such employee's . . . action in relation to his . . . employer's . . . business." The tax deduction is available if the payor gets the consent of the employer of the buyer, inspector, etc.[87] Actually this may not be impossible. The employer may have complete confidence in the integrity of his employees, who have been told that they would be fired if they overpaid for merchandise or approved shoddy performance. And he may believe that if the customer gives the employee a sizable bonus, he will not have to do so.

A corporation allowed cash discounts to certain customers, contrary to state law. The Internal Revenue Service sought to disallow the payments as bribes and kickbacks. But inasmuch as these discounts took the form of lower net prices to customers, this constituted reductions in gross income as opposed to deductions for illegal purposes, which automatically would be disallowed. So the discounts were recognized for tax purposes as reductions in gross income.[88]

Kickbacks made to induce purchasing agents or other employees to promote purchases by their employers or principals from a taxpayer are not deductible when made by taxpayers subject to the Federal Trade Commission Act, if they constitute unfair methods of competition or deceptive practices in commerce. But the payments are deductible if (1) they are normal, usual, and customary in the industry and in the community; (2) they are appropriate and helpful in obtaining business; and (3) they are made with the knowledge and consent of the customer or prospective customer.[89]

Even if a type of payment is barred by state law, deduction is permitted when the payment is business-oriented if this law is not enforced by the state. An unenforced law is scarcely a law for this purpose. In one example of this, a wholesale beer distributor gave away free samples in violation of state law and the regulations of the state alcoholic beverage control board. Deduction was permitted in this case because the state officials consciously chose not to enforce these rules and had advised the appropriate enforcement personnel to that effect.[90]

A state act declared as unlawful the giving by an insurance agent of any premium rebate to a person as an inducement to buy a policy. One insurance agent, unaware of this law, made such rebates to buyers. He could deduct them, for there was no record that in the past twelve years the state had taken any disciplinary action in such a situation; there was only one state investigator for conducting all investigations involving insurance agents and he concentrated on consumer swindles; and by the time of the tax case, no investigation of the taxpayer's activities had been made by the state, although it had knowledge of his having given rebates inasmuch as the Internal Revenue Service had supplied this information twelve months previously.[91]

A state law is not "generally enforced" if the only persons normally charged with violations are infamous or their violations are extraordinarily flagrant: that is, if violations of the statute brought to the attention of the authorities do not result in enforcement action in the absence of unusual circumstances.[92]

The cost of liquor used to entertain customers was deductible where the state knew of the custom and did nothing about it, although state law banned the practice. The state's nonaction negated the idea of a sharply defined public policy against the practice.[93]

A manufacturer entered into an agreement with other companies to fix prices at a high level. On occasion, the manufacturer granted price rebates on merchandise purchased by certain customers who otherwise would have bought their requirements from companies which were not part of the arrangement. In time, the manufacturer was convicted under a Federal law against deals to maintain higher prices. But the price rebates were not illegal payments; they were paid so the manufacturer could remain competitive with companies not part of the price-rigging scheme. So the rebates were deductible.[94]

Where state law sets minimum prices for certain items, such as liquor, a seller may in effect make the prices lower to pet customers by supplying some free merchandise. For tax purposes this is regarded as a price adjustment and not a prohibited deduction. The seller's closing inventory valuation is reduced, and that increases the cost of goods sold, which in turn reduces gross profit. So the merchandise kickback has the effect of a deduction, in the words of one decision, "regardless of the parties' bookkeeping hypocrisies."[95]

Tips to employees of other employers are deductible if such employers are not governmental and there is no local law prohibiting the practice. Tips to employees of a railroad company to expedite the movement of the payor's shipments were deductible where this was essential to the success of the business and where the practice was common.[96] Tips to truck drivers to assure prompt deliveries were allowable.[97] *See also* **Tips.**

However, tips to railroad ticket offices to obtain extra services such as were not offered to "ordinary" customers of these offices were disallowed on the ground that they merely gratified the desire of the payor for unusual and extraordinary personal comfort or convenience and therefore were not business expenses but personal expenditures.[98] *See also* **Rebates.**

Brokers' fees. *See* **Investors.**

Budget charge account. A department store required customers signing up under a budget charge account to pay 1 percent of the balance in the account after a twenty-day payment period. Such payments were deductible as interest.[99]

Burglary, losses from. *See* **Casualties.**

Bus drivers, uniforms of. Costs of acquisition and maintenance of uniforms of bus drivers are deductible if the drivers must wear distinctive types of clothing while at work and this garb is not suitable for ordinary wear.[100] *See also* **Uniforms.**

Business associates, lunches for. *See* **Entertainment.**

Business bad debts. *See* **Bad debts.**

Business expenses. *See* **Ordinary and necessary business expenses.**

Business gifts. Ordinarily, a business gift is subject to the same strict rules of contemporary documentation as entertainment; that is, who, what, when, where, and business purpose.[101]

But where it could be shown that the items (tie tacks in this particular case) were used to call his business to the attention of customers, a salesperson could deduct the cost as a promotional expense without the detailed substantiation requirements.[102]

Although ordinarily no deduction is allowed for the cost of gifts made directly or indirectly to an individual to the extent that the total expense of all or any gifts made in the same taxable year exceeds $25, deduction is allowed in the following situations:

1. An item having a cost to the taxpayer of not more than $4, on which the taxpayer's name is clearly and permanently imprinted and which is one of a number of similar items generally distributed.

2. A sign, a display rack, or other promotional material to be used on the recipient's business premises.

3. An item of tangible property having a cost to the taxpayer not in excess of $400, which is awarded to an employee by reason of length of service, for safety achievement, or for productivity.[103]

Payments to the New York Stock Exchange gratuity fund, maintained for the benefit of families of deceased members of the Exchange, by a member who actually is engaged in business there are deductible as ordinary and necessary expenses in carrying on a trade or business.[104]

Gifts to entertainers made by an agent for vocalists were held to be deductible.[105]

Deductibility of the cost of a business gift depends upon evidence of each of the following: (1) the cost; (2) evidence that the cost, when added to the cost of other gifts to the same donee during the taxable year, does not exceed $25; (3) the date of the gift; (4) a description of the gift; (5) the business purpose of the gift; and (6) information establishing the business relationship of the donee to the donor.[106]

Where the cost of business gifts to an individual exceeds $25 in a single year, deduction is allowed for the first $25, as where fruit baskets costing $35 each were sent to certain customers. Only $10 of each gift was nondeductible.[107]

Wedding and baby presents represent deductible expenses if it can be shown, in the words of one court, "that they were made solely for a business purpose and not to gratify [the taxpayer's] social inclinations."[108]

Voluntary payments to persons who have assisted a taxpayer in his or her business career are deductible.[109] *See* **Tips.**

A physician-anesthesiologist could deduct, up to a ceiling of $25 each, the cost of gifts made to referral physicians, employees, and business associates that were related to the trade or business.[110]

A businessperson could deduct the cost of liquor purchased in reasonable amounts for people who regularly supplied merchandise.[111]

A business could take deductions for liquor given to customers under the supervision and direction of its controller, who had the only key to the room where the liquor was kept.[112]

A builder could deduct the cost of a gift (subject to the $25 limitation) made to the construction foreman of a project because of the latter's excellent work in getting the job completed very quickly.[113]

Gifts to subordinates by a sales supervisor were deductible because greater cooperation from these persons was likely to increase his own performance.[114]

When witnesses of accidents or pilferage were taken to lunch so that details of the happening could be developed, the restaurant bills were regarded as payments for assistance and not gifts that would require very detailed contemporary documentation.[115] *See also* **Ordinary and necessary business expenses.**

Business losses. *See* **Abandonment loss; Bad debts; Business-related losses; Cancellation and forfeiture; Carry-overs; Family transactions; Partnerships; Property used in the trade or business and involuntary conversions; Sale and leaseback.**

Business overhead insurance. Insurance premiums for specified business overhead expenses during extended disability are deductible.[116] *See also* **Insurance.**

Business-related clothing. *See* **Costumes; Uniforms; Work clothes.**

Business-related losses. Amounts paid in satisfaction of a claim arising from an individual's trade or business are deductible.[117] Amounts paid in settlement of such a claim, in the exercise of good-faith business judgment, are likewise deductible.[118]

A teller, cashier, or similar party may be required by the conditions of his employment to pay his employer the amount of any shortages before he is permitted to continue on the payroll. This is deductible as an expense in earning his compensation if he itemizes his deductions. But if he uses the zero bracket amount instead of itemizing deductions, this is not a deduction in determining adjusted gross income.[119]

The cost of rectification of errors made in advising customers of the cost of policies was deductible.[120] A salesman sold securities to a customer with the agreement that he would be entitled to 50 percent of the customer's profits but would absorb 50 percent of his losses. When the transaction ended with a loss, the salesman could deduct the amount he paid in discharge of his obligation under the guaranty agreement, for the guaranty was given in the course of his business activities.[121]

An individual, while driving in connection with his business activities, injured a child. He lost a negligence suit. The judgment was deductible as a business expense; the expenditure was proximately connected with a business activity, not a personal one.[122]

The Internal Revenue Service seized property owned by an antiques dealer for alleged unpaid tax liabilities. This property was sold for less than its tax cost to the dealer. Loss from the seizure, which had been improper, could be deducted as arising from loss of inventory in a transaction entered upon for profit.[123]

A taxpayer's warehouse was totally destroyed by fire, and properties belonging to its customers were lost. Although some customers were insured under personal policies, and others were covered by the taxpayer's general insurance policy, still other customers had no insurance protection at all. They were unhappy about their losses and complained that they had been insufficiently informed about their insurance options. To preserve customer goodwill and to protect its business reputation, the taxpayer made at least partial monetary restitution to uninsured customers. Although in most instances payments for goodwill are regarded as nondeductible capital expenditures, these payments were allowed to be deducted as ordinary and necessary business expenses to protect the taxpayer's business reputation.[124]

An employee who sells on commission is dependent for his income upon the amount of wares the employer is willing to make available to him for marketing. When a brokerage firm "suggested" to an employee that he buy stock in the company to provide it with survival funds, he bought shares. True, his arm wasn't actually twisted nor were there threats of discharge if he refused to buy company stock. But it was obvious to him that his employer could control his level of income by restricting new stock which in the past had been a good source of income to him. When the brokerage firm failed, his stock loss was fully deductible as a business transaction—protecting his job and earning power—rather than as a capital loss, such as customarily would accompany a sour investment.[125]

The publisher and editor of a newspaper stated in an interview with a magazine writer that one of his (the publisher's) executive committee members evidently was selling or telling secrets of the publication to competitors. A recently discharged executive sued the publisher for libel and won. Deduction was allowed for the court's award. The libelous statement was made during the course of his trade or business, and allowance of the deduction was not contrary to public policy because it was a private wrongdoing rather than a public one.[126] *See also* **Executives; Farmers; Guarantor, payments by; Judgment payment.**

Business reputation, defense of. *See* **Business-related losses; Executives; Legal fees.**

Buy-out, expenses to prevent. An executive bought shares in his employer corporation when it appeared that outside interests intended to buy enough shares to acquire control. When he later sold his stock at a loss, this was deductible as an expenditure for the purpose of maintaining his existing employment.[127]

Legal fees incurred in an effort to prevent a takeover of a corporation were deductible by the controlling shareholder.[128]

B

1. IRC Section 166.

2. *Robert Cluett 3d et al.*, 8 T.C. 1178 (1947).

3. *United States v. Generes*, 405 U.S. 93 (1972).

4. *Garlove et al. v. Commissioner*, T.C. Memo. 1965-201, filed July 23, 1965.

5. *Syracuse et al. v. Commissioner*, T.C. Memo. 1981-340, filed June 30, 1981.

6. *Wallace L. Hirsch et al.*, T.C. Memo. 1971-235, filed September 14, 1971.

7. *Trent et al. v. Commissioner*, 291 F.2d 679 (2d Cir., 1961).

8. *Isidor Jaffee et al.*, T.C. Memo. 1967-215, filed October 30, 1967.

9. *Kent Average Estate*, T.C. Memo. 1969-64, filed April 3, 1969.

10. *Kuhnen et al. v. Commissioner*, T.C. Memo. 1981-600, filed October 19, 1981.

11. *LaStaiti et al. v. Commissioner*, T.C. Memo. 1980-547, filed December 8, 1980.

12. *Halpern et al. v. Commissioner*, T.C. Memo. 1982-31, filed January 25, 1982.

13. *Hutchinson et al. v. Commissioner*, T.C. Memo. 1982-45, filed February 1, 1982.

14. *Maurice Arnstein et al.*, T.C. Memo, 1970-220, filed July 29, 1970.

15. *Putnam v. Commissioner*, 352 U.S. 82 (1956).

16. *Tolzman et al. v. Commissioner*, T.C. Memo. 1981-689, filed December 2, 1981.

17. *Oddee Smith et al.*, 60 T.C. 316 (1973).

18. *Goodenough et al. v. Commissioner*, T.C. Memo 1980-28, filed January 28, 1980.

19. *Gilboy et al. v. Commissioner*, T.C. Memo. 1978-114, filed March 22, 1978.

20. *Harlan v. United States*, DC, ND Texas, 1974.

21. *Carter et al. v. Commissioner*, T.C. Memo. 1979-447, filed November 8, 1979.

22. *Giblin v. Commissioner*, 227 F.2d 692 (5th Cir., 1955).

23. *Stuart Bart*, 21 T.C. 880 (1954).

24. *Arthur Bernstein et al.*, T.C. Memo. 1960-213, filed October 7, 1960.

25. *Ostrom et al. v. Commissioner*, 77 T.C. 608 (1981).

26. *Deduction for Bad Debts*, IRS Publication 508 (Rev. Nov. 1980), page 1.

27. *United States v. S.S. White Dental Manufacturing Company of Pennsylvania*, 274 U.S. 398.

28. *Sterling Morton*, 38 BTA 1270 (1938), aff'd, 112 F.2d 320 (7th Cir., 1940).

29. *Clark v. Commissioner*, 85 F.2d 622 (3d Cir., 1936).

30. *Paul J. Byrum et al.*, 58 T.C. 731 (1972).

31. *Providence Coal Mining Company v. Glenn*, 88 F. Supp. 975 (DC, WD Ky., 1950).

32. *Roth et al. v. Commissioner*, T.C. Memo. 1981-699, filed December 9, 1981.

33. *Genecov et al. v. United States*, DC, ED Tenn., 1968, aff'd, 412 F.2d 556 (5th Cir., 1965).

34. *Hans Christiansen*, T.C. Memo. 1969-112, filed May 29, 1969.

35. *Mahler v. Commissioner*, 119 F.2d 869 (2d Cir., 1941).

36. *Sterling Morton*, 38 BTA 1270 (1938), aff'd, 112 F.2d 320 (7th Cir., 1940).

37. *Straub Distributing Co., Inc.*, T.C. Memo. 1971-46, filed March 15, 1971.

38. IRC Section 166(a)(2).

39. Regulations Section 1.166-3(a).

40. Tax Reform Act of 1976, Section 2104.

41. *Bruce V. Green et al.*, T.C. Memo. 1976-127, filed April 22, 1976.

42. IRC Section 166(c).

43. *Gurentz et al. v. Commissioner*, T.C. Memo. 1978-238, filed June 26, 1978.

44. Revenue Ruling 80-52, 1980-1 CB 100.

45. Revenue Ruling 77-204, 1977-1 CB 40.

46. *Henry P. Keith*, T.C. Memo., Docket No. 108883, entered December 9, 1942.

47. *Murphy et al. v. Commissioner*, T.C. Memo. 1980-25, filed January 28, 1980.

48. Revenue Ruling 70-476, 1970-2 CB 25.

49. IRC Section 642(h).

50. *O'Bryan v. Commissioner*, 75 T.C. 304 (1980).

51. *Hord v. Commissioner*, 95 F.2d 179 (6th Cir., 1938).

52. Revenue Ruling 67-246, 1967-2 CB 104.

53. *The Tax Deduction for Contributions*, IRS Publication 526, 1976 edition, page 3.

54. Revenue Ruling 73-200, 1973-1 CB 140.

55. Revenue Ruling 73-201, 1973-1 CB 140.

56. Ibid.

57. Revenue Ruling 55-261, 1955-1 CB 307.

58. Revenue Ruling 68-295, 1968-1 CB 92.

59. Revenue Ruling 64-173, 1964-1 CB (Part 1) 12.

60. Revenue Ruling 75-316, 1975-2 CB 54.

61. Revenue Ruling 75-318, 1975-2 CB 424.

62. Revenue Ruling 58-223, 1958-1 CB 156.

63. *Beyers et al. v. Commissioner*, T.C. Memo. 1979-353, filed September 5, 1979.

64. OD 421, 2 CB 105 (1920).

65. *Frederick Cecil Bartholomew Estate*, 4 T.C. 349 (1944).

66. *Alexander Sprunt & Son, Inc.*, 24 BTA 599 (1931).

67. TD 2090, CB December 14, 1914.

68. Regulations Section 1.162-6.

69. IRS Letter Ruling 8124101, March 19, 1981.

70. *Beaudry v. Commissioner*, 150 F.2d 20 (2d Cir., 1945).

71. *Kincheloe v. Commissioner*, T.C. Memo. 1980-527, filed November 25, 1980.

72. *Contini et al. v. Commissioner*, 76 T.C. 447 (1981).

73. *Thomas M. B. Hicks, Jr., et al.*, T.C. Memo. 1960-48, filed March 24, 1960.

74. *Ginkel et al. v. Commissioner*, T.C. Memo. 1980-424, filed September 23, 1980.

75. *William Q. Wolfson et al.*, T.C. Memo. 1978-445, filed November 7, 1978.

76. *Educational Expenses*, IRS Publication 508 (Rev. Nov. 1980), page 2.

77. *A. M. Barnhart Estate*, T.C. Memo. 1959-42, filed February 27, 1959.

78. *Rendell Owens et al.*, T.C. Memo. 1977-319, filed September 19, 1977.

79. *Great Island Holding Corporation*, 5 T.C. 150 (1945).

80. *DeVito et al. v. Commissioner*, T.C. Memo. 1979-377, filed September 17, 1979.

81. *Henry F. Cochrane*, 23 BTA 202 (1931).

82. *Lomas & Nettleton Company v. United States*, 79 F. Supp. 886 (DC, Ct., 1948).

83. *Mathilda M. Brooks*, 30 T.C. 1087 (1958), *rev'd on other grounds*, 274 F.2d 96 (9th cir., 1960).

84. IRC Section 162(c)(3).

85. Tax Equity and Fiscal Responsibility Act of 1982, Section 288.

86. Senate Finance Committee Report on the Revenue Bill of 1971, Section 162(c)(3).

87. New York Penal Laws, Section 439.

88. *Haas Brothers, Inc., et al. v. Commissioner*, 73 T.C. 1217 (1980).

89. Revenue Ruling 54-27, 1954-1 CB 44.

90. *Sterling Distributors, Inc., v. Patterson*, 236 F. Supp. 479 (DC, ND Ala., 1964).

91. *Custis et al. v. Commissioner*, T.C. Memo. 1982-296, filed May 26, 1982.

92. Regulations Section 1.162 18(b)(3).

93. *Stacy et al. v. United States*, 231 F. Supp. 304 (DC, SD Miss., 1963).

94. Revenue Ruling 77-243, 1977-2 CB 57.

95. *Max Sobel Wholesale Liquors v. Commissioner*, 630 F.2d 670 (9th Cir., 1980).

96. *F. L. Bateman*, 34 BTA 351 (1936).

97. *August F. Nielsen Co., Inc., et al.*, T.C. Memo. 1968-11, filed January 18, 1968.

98. *Julius (Jay) C. Henricks*, T.C. Memo., Docket No. 16192, entered November 8, 1949.

99. Revenue Ruling 67-62, 1967-1 CB 1 CB 44.

100. Revenue Ruling 70-474, 1970-2 CB 34.

101. IRC Section 274.

102. *Hobson, Jr., et. al. v. Commissioner*, T.C. Memo. 1980-132, filed April 21, 1980.

103. IRC Section 274(b), as amended by the Economic Recovery Tax Act of 1981, Section 265.

104. Revenue Ruling 70-342, 1970-2 CB 32.

105. *Lou Levy et al.*, 30 T.C. 1315 (1958).

106. Regulations Section 1.274-5(b)(5).

107. *Jetty et al. v. Commissioner*, T.C. Memo. 1982-378, filed July 7, 1982.

108. *Julius (Jay) C. Henricks*, T.C. Memo., Docket No. 16192, entered November 8, 1949.

109. *Olivia de Havilland*, 20 T.C. 323 (1953).

110. *Beltran et al. v. Commissioner*, T.C. Memo. 1982-153, filed March 25, 1982.

111. *Rodgers Dairy Co.*, 14 T.C. 66 (1950).

112. *Lynch-Davidson Motors, Inc. v. Tomlinson*, 172 F. Supp. 101 (DC, SD Fla., 1958), *rev'd and rem'd'd on another issue*, 5th Cir., 1961.

113. *Gilman II et al. v. Commissioner*, 72 T.C. 730 (1979).

114. *Harold A. Christensen*, 17 T.C. 1456 (1952).

115. *Heller et al. v. Commissioner*, T.C. Memo. 1980-417, filed September 22, 1980.

116. Revenue Ruling 55-264, 1958-1 CB 11.

117. *Helvering v. Hampton*, 79 F.2d 358 (9th Cir., 1935).

118. *Levitt & Sons v. Nunan*, 142 F.2d 795 (2d Cir., 1944).

119. *Butchko et al. v. Commissioner*, T.C. Memo. 1978-209, filed June 7, 1978.

120. *Boyle, Flagg & Seaman, Inc.*, 25 T.C. 43 (1955).

121. *Irving L. Schein*, T.C. Memo., Docket No. 32717, entered February 29, 1952.

122. *Plante et al. v. United States*, 226 F. Supp. 314 (DC, N.H., 1963).

123. *E. Gerald Lackey et al.*, T.C. Memo. 1977-213, filed July 12, 1977.

124. Revenue Ruling 76-23, 1976-1 CB 45.

125. *Elmer Carsello et al.*, T.C. Memo. 1976-193, filed June 15, 1976.

126. *Cornelius Vanderbilt, Jr.*, T.C. Memo. 1957-235, filed December 23, 1957.

127. *Steadman et al. v. Commissioner*, 424 F.2d 1 (6th Cir., 1970).

128. *Powell, Jr., v. United States*, 294 F. Supp. 977 (DC, SD S.D., 1969).

C

Cadets, expenses of. A cadet at the United States Coast Guard Academy was allowed to deduct expenditures for insignia, shoulder boards, and similar items.[1]

Cancellation and forfeiture. A payment by a lessee for cancellation of a business lease was held to be deductible.[2]

As a general rule, amounts paid by a lessor to a lessee for cancellation of a lease prior to its expiration date are capital expenditures, amortizable over the unexpired portion of the cancelled lease. But where the unexpired term was less than one year, although extending into the following year, payment for the cancellation was deductible in full.[3]

A tenant failed to go through with its commitment on a business lease and its deposits thereupon were forfeited. The amounts were deductible in the year of the forfeiture.[4]

Where a portion of the purchase price of a plantation was forfeited upon failure of the would-be buyer to make the additional payments called for, the forfeited down payments were deductible.[5]

Deduction was allowed when a deposit to guarantee observation of the rules of a service bureau was forfeited.[6] *See also* **Farmers.**

Capital improvements. Capital expenditures are not currently deductible, but in the case of business assets with a measurable life, annual write-offs are permitted in the form of depreciation and amortization.

In general, all construction costs of a business must be capitalized and written off over the estimated useful life of the facility. But when the purpose of temporary partitions, heating, and the like was to allow existing buildings to operate during major construction operations, the cost was deductible.[7] Deduction was also allowed for the cost of enlarging and improving an office where the work was not in the nature of permanent improvements but was to facilitate the transaction of increasing business.[8]

Expenses related to the installation of capital equipment with a useful life of more than one year customarily must be capitalized. But labor and transportation costs in connection with moving certain of a taxpayer's capitalized assets to another location were deductible, for the relocation did not add to the value nor appreciably prolong the useful lives of these assets.[9]

For capital improvements to one's home for medical reasons, *see* **Expenditures for benefits lasting more than one year; Medical expenses.**

Capital losses. In the case of sales of capital assets after October 31, 1978, an individual may deduct from income 60 percent of the net long-term capital losses which are in excess of the net short-term capital gains.[10]

It is immaterial whether the motive prompting the sale was to secure a tax deduction, so long as the sale was *bona fide* and fair value was paid, provided the buyer was not closely related to the seller.[11]

Losses resulting from the sale of stocks and bearer bonds on the last day of the taxable year are deductible for the year the contract was entered into, even though delivery was made in the following year.[12]

Long-term capital losses are deductible from long-term capital gains, but $2 of the former are needed to offset $1 of the latter.[13]

If capital losses exceed capital gains, a deduction against taxable income is allowed up to $3,000.[14] The deduction of capital losses against ordinary income for married persons filing separate returns is limited to $1,500 for each spouse.[15]

To the extent that an individual cannot use a capital loss in the year sustained, he may carry it forward for an unlimited period of time. The unused capital-loss carry-over, after being used to reduce net capital gains of the year to which it is carried, is available to offset ordinary income in the manner just mentioned.[16]

An unused capital-loss carry-over at the time that an estate or trust terminates is allowed as a deduction to the beneficiaries succeeding to the property.[17]

A capital loss is of limited tax usefulness, not being fully deductible in the manner of an ordinary business loss. But whether a particular property is a capital asset for this purpose can depend upon *why* it was held. If someone has purchased a stock exchange seat as an investment, it is a capital asset. But when a broker purchased a New York Stock Exchange seat so that he could conduct transactions for customers on the floor of that exchange, this was not a capital asset. So loss on sale of this seat was fully deductible.[18]

As to capital loss transactions involving certain related parties, *see* **Family transactions.**

Career counseling. Expenses for career counseling are deductible where they assist a person to obtain other employment in the same trade or business. This includes (1) a job evaluation which is an appraisal of a party's capabilities and personal characteristics, (2) establishment of attainable goals consistent with a person's abilities, (3) interview preparations, and (4) evaluation of salary and fringe benefits, including job acceptance protection procedure.[19]

Carpenter, expenses of. A carpenter could deduct the cost of his overalls.[20] *See also* **Work clothes.**

Carrying charges on installment purchases. *See* **Interest.**

Carrying charges on loans. Carrying charges on a loan were deductible when they were equivalent to interest.[21] *See also* **Interest.**

Carrying charges on unproductive realty. *See* **Election to deduct or to capitalize.**

Carry-overs. If an individual has sustained a loss in the operation of his trade or business during a taxable year, or a casualty or theft loss in excess of the year's income, there is a net operating loss. A net operating loss is the excess of allowable deductions over gross income after prescribed adjustments have been made. An individual with a net operating loss may carry the loss as a deduction to certain other taxable years in a stipulated time sequence to reduce tax liability for such years or to obtain a refund of taxes previously paid.[22]

An individual's net operating loss is computed in the same way as his taxable income, with these adjustments:

1. Taxable income is determined without regard to the particular net operating loss being carried back or over, or to any later net operating loss. But account is taken of any earlier net operating losses being carried back or over from the previous years.
2. Capital losses may not exceed capital gains. Nonbusiness capital losses may not exceed nonbusiness capital gains, even though there may be an excess of business capital gains over business capital losses.
3. Deduction of 50 percent of the excess of a net long-term capital gain over a net short-term capital loss cannot be taken.
4. Personal exemptions and exemptions for dependents cannot be taken into account.
5. Nonbusiness deductions cannot exceed nonbusiness income.[23]

If a husband and wife file separate returns for a taxable year but file a joint Federal income tax return for any or all of the years involved in computing the carry-over or carry-back to the taxable year, the separate carry-overs or carry-backs to the taxable year are to be computed as if on separate returns with certain modifications. A husband was engaged in the coal business. His wife served as billing clerk and bookkeeper and she handled sales, all without compensation. In addition, she cosigned company notes, pledged her own property as security for business loans, and paid off some of the business notes with her own funds. The business lost money for the three years ending with her husband's death. Then she took a salaried position in another business. A net operating loss that is incurred in a joint-return year and carried forward to a separate tax return must be allocated to ensure that it is used to offset only the income of the spouse who incurred the loss. But in this case it was held that the losses of the coal business had been incurred equally by each spouse. So when she filed a separate income tax return for the year after the death of her husband, she could carry forward one-half of the losses of the coal business for the preceding three years to offset her business income, which consisted of her salary.[24]

Except for charitable contributions, any deductions claimed by an individual which are based on or limited to a percentage of adjusted gross income (such as medical expenses) must be recomputed on the basis of the adjusted gross or taxable income after the application of these adjustments. The deduction of charitable contributions is determined using the same adjustments except that account is not taken of any net operating losses being carried back.[25]

Except in the case of any foreign expropriation losses (which are discussed under **Foreign expropriation losses**), a net operating loss must first be carried back to the third year preceding the year in which it was sustained. Any amount of the loss that is not used to offset taxable income (adjusted, as mentioned previously) for the third preceding year is carried back to the second preceding year.[26] Any amount of the loss that is not used to offset taxable income for the third and second preceding years must be carried to the first preceding year. If the loss is not entirely used to offset taxable income as adjusted in the three preceding years, the balance may be carried over to specified future years in the order of their occurrence. For net operating losses incurred in taxable years after December 31, 1975, losses may be carried forward for fifteen years. In addition, taxpayers entitled to carry-back periods for their net operating losses may elect to forgo the entire carry-back period for a net operating loss in any taxable year.[27]

Loss resulting from the worthlessness of any security which is a capital asset in the taxpayer's hands is treated as a loss from the sale or exchange of a capital asset on the last day of the taxable year.[28]

If, in the year of a casualty or theft, the amount of loss sustained exceeded taxable income computed without allowance of the loss, the excess is treated as a net operating loss.[29] This means that the net operating loss carry-back and carry-forward rules applicable to excess business losses apply, rather than the carry-forward rules applicable to excess capital losses.[30]

Married persons may carry back or forward a loss sustained by one spouse and reported on a separate tax return to offset joint income.[31] If the parties consistently file joint returns, they may carry a net operating loss jointly to the other years irrespective of which one incurred the loss.[32] An individual may deduct a net operating loss from the income of his or her spouse reported on a joint return only where a joint return can also be filed at the time the loss is sustained.[33] So a net operating loss sustained by a wife after her husband's death cannot be carried back and applied against income reported on joint returns in past years where all the income was earned by the husband.[34]

Where, in a community property state such as California, there is a change in the marital status by divorce, and subsequently one of the parties to the marriage sustains a net operating loss, the loss may be carried back only to that portion of the taxable income reported on a previously filed joint return of the community income which is vested in the party who sustained the loss.[35] (John and Mary, for example, had until the time of their divorce in 1984 filed joint income tax returns. All the community income had been produced by John's businesses. The terms of the divorce gave John title to those businesses. In 1985 John sustained a net operating loss. He could carry the loss back in a manner which is ordinarily applicable in computing business losses, whereas if Mary had sustained the loss, she could not have done so.)

Such also is the case in a noncommunity property state where one of the parties dies and the survivor sustains a net operating loss in a subsequent year.[36]

A husband and wife filed a joint return for one year and separate returns for the following year. The husband had a business loss for the earlier year, while the wife had nontaxable income. The husband's loss for the first year which could be carried forward and claimed as a deduction in the second year had to be reduced by the nontaxable income of the wife for the same year.[37]

A partnership agreement will determine the proportionate loss deductions of the several partners, but if any provision has as its principal purpose tax avoidance, the Internal Revenue Service can disregard it.[38] A partner may deduct his proportionate share of partnership losses for each year, but only to the extent of his adjusted basis in the partnership at the close of each year.[39] He can increase the amount of his loss which is deductible, by increasing his basis in any of the following ways: (1) by contributing additional capital to the partnership, (2) by lending money to the partnership, or (3) by any increases in the liabilities of the partnership. A partner's basis for his interest is increased by his share of the partnership liabilities.[40]

A limited partner's share of partnership liabilities does not exceed the difference between his actual contribution credited to him by the partnership and the total contribution which he is obligated to make under the limited-partnership agreement. But where none of the partners has any personal liability with respect to a partnership liability (as in the case of a mortgage on real estate acquired by the partnership without the assumption by the partnership or by any of the partners of any liability on the mortgage), then all partners, including limited partners, are considered as sharing such liability in the same proportion as they share profits.[41]

A limited partner cannot deduct losses in excess of his investment. But unused losses can be carried forward to offset future income of the partnership.[42]

If an estate or trust, when it is terminated, has a net operating loss carry-over, the carry-over is allowed as a deduction to the beneficiaries succeeding to the property. The same rule applies if the estate or trust, in its last taxable year, has deductions in excess of gross income, not taking the personal exemption into consideration.[43]

The total of the unused loss carry-overs or the excess deductions on termination which may be deducted by the successor beneficiaries is allocated proportionately according to the share of each in the burden of the loss or deduction.[44]

Carry-overs, unused charitable contributions. *See* **Contributions.**

Car telephone. *See* **Medical expenses.**

Cash discounts on purchases. Cash discounts on purchases may be deductible by businesspersons as discounts, or the amounts may be reflected in inventory. The taxpayer has this election on the first tax return where there are such purchases. Once made, this election is irrevocable and permanent.[45]

Cash shortages. A salesman properly deducted the amounts of cash shortages he was obligated to make up to his employer because of mistakes in making change, loss of inventory in his custody, and reimbursements to his customers for which he in turn was not reimbursed.[46] Collections from customers which were lost by a salesman were deductible by him as a business expense.[47] *See also* **Armed Forces.**

Casualties. A deduction is allowed for any loss sustained during the taxable year which has not been compensated for by insurance or in any other manner.[48] The loss need not be in any way connected with a taxpayer's trade or business.[49]

"In any way" includes payments received under the Uniform Relocation Assistance and Real Property Acquisition Policies Act of 1970, commonly referred to as the Relocation Act.[50] Likewise included are payments received from the Client's Security Trust Fund, an organization established under Maryland law to reimburse losses caused by lawyers taking client funds.[51]

The loss deduction is not necessarily in the year of the casualty. Typically, a fire occurred in one year, but deduction was proper two years later, when the taxpayer settled with the insurers.[52] In another case, trees were damaged by a freeze in December. The owner tried to revive them during the next two years but was unsuccessful. It was held that for tax purposes the loss occurred in the third year after the freeze, when it became apparent that the trees could not be saved.[53] A farmer erected evergreens as a windbreak for his buildings and livestock. An extraordinary blizzard injured the trees, but it was not until the following year that so many trees withered and died that the windscreen no longer could perform its intended function. Deduction was allowed in the year after the blizzard occurred.[54]

Pending litigation against an insurance company or other party does not postpone the deduction of loss where there is no reasonable prospect for recovery.[55]

Ordinarily, a casualty loss is deductible only by the person who owns or has an economic interest in the damaged property. But deduction was allowed in the case of an individual who rented a residence, subject to the condition that at the end of the lease he would return the premises in a condition as good as they were at the start of the lease. He could deduct his expenses in having the property restored to its original condition after a fire during the period of the lease. There had been no insurance coverage.[56]

The amount of the loss to be taken into account for tax purposes is the lesser of (1) the fair market value of the property immediately before the casualty or (2) the amount of the adjusted basis for determining loss.

In the case of business property, if the fair market value of the property immediately before the casualty is less than the adjusted basis, the amount of the adjusted basis is deemed to be the amount of the loss.[57]

In the case of nonbusiness (or personal) property, the deduction is the amount by which the casualty loss exceeds $100. Or the deduction may be the cost of repairing the damage.[58] For taxable years beginning after December 31, 1982, the deduction is limited to the amount by which the losses (after this reduction of $100 for each casualty loss) exceed 10 percent of a person's adjusted gross income.[59]

In the case of depreciable nonbusiness property, the deduction may not exceed the amount of the loss actually sustained, measured by the then depreciated value of the property.[60]

In other words, to determine your deductible loss on personal property, take the following three steps:

1. Determine the difference between the market value of the property immediately before the loss and the market value of the property immediately after the loss. The result is the loss in fair market value.

2. Then determine the adjustment basis for the property. This is, in most cases, the original cost of the property plus the cost of improvement minus previously taken deductions for casualty loss.

3. Take the lower amount of step 1 or step 2 and subtract the salvage value, insurance proceeds (or other compensation for the loss), and $100. The resulting amount is your deductible casualty loss for personal property.

If the property is business property, these steps should be taken:

1. Same as step 1 above.

2. Determine the adjusted basis for the business property. This is usually the original cost of the property plus the cost of improvements minus previously taken deductions and depreciation.

3. Take the amount of step 1 or step 2, whichever is lower—with the following exception: If the business property was totally destroyed and the market value of the property before the casualty was less than the adjusted basis for the property, then the deduction taken is the adjusted basis less the compensation received for the loss. Note the 10 percent limitation in the paragraph with footnote reference [59].

To determine the amount of loss deduction, the fair market value of the property immediately before and immediately after the casualty "shall generally be ascertained by competent appraisal."[61] This means that the deduction can depend upon the quality of the appraiser you use.

When assets are damaged in part, the owner can have a real problem in proving how fair market value has been reduced by events which have not yet occurred. In one case, a taxpayer owned tracts of trees for use in the manufacture of a product. Storms seriously damaged some of the trees. Fair market value after the casualty could be reduced by damage to the property's income potential as well as to its physical state. It was up to the taxpayer to offer believable evidence as to how the storm had affected the trees' rate of future growth and the amount of wood which could thereafter be utilized. The impact of the storm on access roads to the trees also had to be taken into consideration.[62]

Deduction was allowed for the value of trees which were so damaged by an ice storm that their beauty and distinction were lost.[63]

An individual's deductible losses are limited to (1) losses incurred in a trade or business, (2) losses incurred in any transaction entered into for profit, although not connected with a trade or business, and (3) losses of property not connected with a trade or business, where the losses arise from a fire, storm, shipwreck, or other casualty, or from theft.[64] Examples are: subterranean disturbances,[65] ice storm,[66] flood.[67]

The intervention of a human agency in the sequence of events other than theft does not deprive the incident of its character as a casualty.[68]

To be deductible, the happening need not be cataclysmic in character. For example, deduction was allowed when a diamond was dislodged from a finger ring by the impact of a slamming automobile door. The gem was never found.[69]

"Other casualty" means an event or happening which was destructive of the property and was sudden in its occurrence.[70] An "other casualty" must also be unexpected, violent, and not due to the deliberate or willful actions of the taxpayer.[71]

The question is not whether *damage* was sudden but whether the *cause* of the casualty was sudden.[72]

Deduction was allowed for an uninsured diamond which disappeared from the ring on which it had been mounted. The wearer's husband had cleaned the ring within the past month, as he did several times a year. A jeweler had examined it within eighteen months of the loss. An expert testified that in his thirty-five years of experience, he never had seen a diamond drop from such a setting except as the result of an identifiable cause, such as a sharp blow or other accident. The court was willing to assume that that was what had happened.[73]

Suddenness is measured by the lapse of time between the precipitating event and the loss directly resulting from that event.[74]

Loss because of termites rarely qualifies as a casualty-loss deduction because of the absence of suddenness. The rotting away of building foundations, trees, and the like has been some time in coming. Loss was allowed for destruction of trees by southern pine beetles, for this particular form of infestation killed the trees in a matter of days, which was fast enough to constitute the required suddenness.[75] Destruction of trees by a mass attack of such beetles in epidemic proportions qualified as a casualty, having occurred within a period of five days to two weeks.[76]

An exception to this rule exists in the case of the "fast termite," where it has been held that termite damage may qualify as a casualty loss if it can be shown to have occurred within a relatively short period of time. So it was in one case where an experienced builder and architect had tested a building twelve months before the infestation and had found no termites present.[77] In another case, the purchaser of a building and the real-estate agent representing the seller made an inspection for termites and found no evidence of them. Infestation fourteen months later resulted in a casualty-loss deduction.[78]

Loss of a diamond from its ring mounting was regarded as having the necessary degree of suddenness, when its owner had seen the gem while manicuring her nails within an hour before the disappearance. After the loss, it was noted that two prongs were broken and the claws on the opposite side of the ring were also broken, indicating that a fairly strong blow had been struck on one side of the ring.[79]

In 1971, a severe earthquake did no visible damage to a business building. A year later, there was another quake, which caused stresses less than one one-hundredth of those of the first earthquake. But this time there were cracks over the full length of the concrete walls, which would have permitted the entry of water that might have caused rust or deterioration of the reinforcing steel over a period of time. A casualty-loss deduction was allowed in the amount of the repair bill at the time of the second, less severe quake. The abrupt manifestation of cracks indicated that the damage had resulted from a *sudden* if slight event. A deductible casualty loss does not have to be one of catastrophic proportions.[80]

A casualty loss was deemed to be sudden where a residence was flooded after a heavy rainfall. The Internal Revenue Service had argued that inasmuch as there had been an even heavier rainfall four years previously, the later flooding resulted from continued and gradual deterioration after that time. But the court allowed the deduction, pointing out that the more recent rainfall had caused a sudden casualty inasmuch as the house had remained unscathed by rains in the intervening four years.[81]

A casualty-loss deduction was allowed when a floor buckled two years after a hurricane had damaged a taxpayer's house. The sand in which posts had been set became loose as a result of the hurricane's action; the subsequent collapse of the posts and the flooring they supported was a delayed reaction to the hurricane.[82]

A casualty may be deemed to exist when honeybees are destroyed by pesticide.[83] The death of cattle by accidental poisoning qualifies as a casualty loss.[84]

An individual's *ordinary* negligence is not a bar to a casualty loss, although *gross* negligence is.[85]

Under the safety codes of some places (for example, Pennsylvania) a person is guilty of a felony if he is found to have caused a fire or explosion by using volatile materials in a reckless manner, which exposes the general public to a catastrophe. After one manufacturer of illegal drugs sustained a fire which wrecked his plant, the Internal Revenue Service claimed that a casualty loss was not deductible because state policy against reckless endangerment would be frustrated by permitting this deduction resulting from an illegal act. Deduction was, however, allowed. Although the taxpayer had been engaged in an illegal activity, the fire had resulted from carelessness, not conscious disregard of the public welfare such as state law would have penalized. He had not been found guilty of consciously violating the safety code.[86]

Deduction was allowed for the complete destruction of a diamond ring which a woman had placed in a waterglass of ammonia for the purpose of cleaning the gem. Her husband, not knowing of the presence of the ring, emptied the glass into the garbage-disposal unit, which he then activated. Negligence on the part of either spouse, or both of them, may have brought about the loss of value, but it nonetheless amounted to a casualty deduction.[87]

Casualty-loss deduction is allowed where it results from the faulty driving of the taxpayer or other person operating his car if the damage is not the result of the willful act or willful negligence of the taxpayer or of anyone acting in his behalf.[88]

The cost of repairing damage to a person's car was deductible where he carried no insurance and the accident had not been occasioned by his willful act of negligence.[89] The value of a personal car was deductible when the vehicle unexpectedly fell through the ice on a frozen lake on which it was parked.[90] Deduction was allowed when a car was destroyed by overturning on an icy road while it was in the unauthorized possession of a chauffeur. The driver may have been negligent, but "casualty" for income tax purposes expresses rather the result than the cause of the damage.[91]

An individual owned some *Asparagus plumosus* ferns which he had intended to sell. He was allowed to deduct their cost when they were destroyed by a severe freeze, even though a commercial fern grower might have made proper provisions for heating the plants on cold nights.[92]

Deliberate destruction of his own property by a taxpayer can produce a deductible casualty loss. So it was when a farmer destroyed some of his own vineyards and orchards in order to check further destruction by disease.[93]

Damage to property by the explosion of a time bomb constituted a casualty loss.[94]

While a casualty loss must ordinarily have the element of suddenness, a loss sustained in the case of residential property as a result of subsoil shrinkage during a period of drought was deemed to be a casualty loss.[95] Damage to a house because of an "earth movement" following a heavy rain was deductible as a casualty loss. Actually, a clogged drain was the immediate precipitating event. Though the taxpayer might have prevented the damage by the exercise of due care, the characterization of the loss as a casualty deduction was not denied.[96]

Inasmuch as a casualty for tax purposes must be from a sudden or unexpected cause, loss resulting from gradual deterioration of property does not qualify. Cracks in walls and foundations of a house, attributable to settling, ordinarily do not constitute casualties. But casualty loss was recognized where cracks in a house suddenly appeared one day as the result of an extraordinary tremor.[97]

Similarly, loss was deductible where the damage was attributable to an "underground disturbance" which resulted in the sudden subsidence of the surface portion of the land on which the taxpayer's house was built.[98]

The use of statistics can show that a happening such as the collapse of a building was not due to progressive deterioration. Deduction was allowed where problems with a residence's foundations were not the result of gradual deterioration. During an eighteen-day period, precipitation was 35 percent in excess of the ten-year average and the number of days of freezing and thawing were 127 percent above the average for that December. These conditions contributed to prevent the ground from drying out as rapidly as usual and created a wet and soggy condition which caused the earth to assert abnormal pressures under the taxpayer's home.[99]

Similarly, collapse of a living-room ceiling was ruled a casualty for tax purposes where U.S. Department of Commerce Weather Bureau records showed that in the first six months of the year of the collapse, precipitation in the taxpayer's city had a substantial deficiency (10.90 inches against a normal 18.14), followed by 9.90 inches in July, the wettest July since 1880. The collapse was attributed not to a gradual deterioration of the structure but to unusual action of the elements.[100]

Where a taxpayer's concrete driveway broke up during a four-month period and statistics indicated that rainfall during this period was 36 percent above normal, this was sufficiently "unexpected." The unusually severe weather and rain conditions *during the period* constituted a casualty loss, this not being progressive damage "through a steadily operating cause."[101]

Damage to property through a prolonged drought ordinarily is not regarded for tax purposes as a casualty loss, since damage is not due to sudden invasion by a hostile agency. A couple had substantially landscaped their property with trees, shrubs, plants, and lawns. Elaborate irrigation systems were installed. But because of a severe drought, county officials imposed rigid water restrictions. The irrigation systems could not be used, and the vegetation was dead within four months. A casualty deduction was allowed, because the death of the plantings was relatively rapid; that is, sudden, "It resulted," said the court, "from extraordinarily calamitous drought."[102]

Deduction was allowed for complete loss of value in the case of a diamond ring which a woman placed in a waterglass of ammonia for cleaning. Her husband, who was washing dishes, inadvertently emptied the contents of the glass into the kitchen-sink drain and then activated the garbage-disposal device in the sink; appraisal value of the ring: zero.[103] Deduction was allowed when a diamond was dislodged from a finger ring by the impact of a slamming automobile door. The gem never was found.[104]

Losses arising from highway mishaps may be deducted even though caused by the ordinary negligence of the taxpayer.[105] Thus, it is necessary in such cases to establish that even though the person was careless, he was not *grossly* negligent. When a physician asked a salesman in a seed store for something which would kill "quack grass" and was given a bottle which allegedly bore a label warning that the product should not be used on desirable vegetation, the resulting loss of the lawn was a casualty. While the taxpayer may not have exercised due care by omitting to read the label, he did rely upon the salesman's recommendation. This was not a case of gross negligence on the part of the taxpayer, which would bar a casualty-loss deduction.[106]

Loss sustained in a fire in a taxpayer's home was deductible, although the fire-department report had listed the cause as "cooking carelessness."[107]

Deduction was allowed for damage to a car's starter when a child pushed the starter button while the vehicle was in motion.[108]

When a water heater in a private home burst, no deduction was allowed for the loss of the boiler, for there was no evidence that the casualty was sudden; quite likely the boiler had been deteriorating gradually for a long period of time. But damage to the taxpayer's rugs and draperies could be deducted, for the injury to them was sudden.[109]

A casualty loss may be indirect. A taxpayer's home was destroyed by fire. After the fire, underground water pipes, now uncovered, froze and burst. The pipes would not have been uncovered so that freezing occurred, save for the fire, and the damage therefore was part of the casualty-loss deduction.[110]

Flood damage was caused to an individual's house when a plumber carelessly stepped on a pipe. Even though there may have been faulty construction, which would not be considered a casualty loss, the flood damage had been caused directly by the careless plumber, and casualty-loss deduction was allowed.[111]

Subsoil shrinkage from unusually severe drought can weaken either vertical or lateral support for building foundations. Cracking of walls and other serious damage to buildings amounts to a deductible casualty loss where this shrinkage is relatively rapid.[112]

The fact that a damaged structure was between seventeen and twenty-six years old does not necessarily mean that the damage was the result of deterioration through age rather than a casualty created by storm. The taxpayer has the opportunity of producing evidence.[113]

Deduction was allowed for the loss from the freezing of water pipes in a residence during the absence of the occupant.[114]

When ornamental pine trees were destroyed by a mass attack of beetles, the event was deemed to be unexpected because no known massive assault of beetles had occurred in the area of this property.[115]

Deduction similarly was allowed where a 100-year-old oak was destroyed in a matter of weeks by chestnut borers. Attack by such borers, according to expert testimony, was not a common problem of oaks and thus could be characterized as "unexpected or unusual in nature." So it was necessary to find out *precisely* what had caused the destruction.[116] Proof of a deductible casualty loss may require expert testimony concerning its suddenness and unexpectedness.

Where there was evidence that the loss of trees was attributable to "an unusual and unprecedented drought," a casualty-loss deduction was permitted.[117]

Loss of trees because of chestnut blight was deductible.[118]

A taxpayer's truck was damaged severely in an accident, and there was no possibility of recovery. He carried no collision insurance, and the driver of the vehicle which caused the accident could not be found. The amount of the deductible loss was the difference between the trade-in allowed him on a new truck and the amount which would have been allowed had damage not been sustained in the collision.[119]

When there is no proof of the value of an asset damaged, both before and after the event, the cost of restoration to prior condition is deductible.[120]

The cost of repairs to the damaged property is acceptable as evidence of the loss of value if (1) the repairs are necessary to restore the property to its condition immediately before the casualty, (2) the amount spent for such repairs is not excessive, (3) the repairs do not account for more than the damage suffered, and (4) the value of the property after the repairs does not as a result of the repairs exceed its value immediately before the casualty.[121] This rule applies only where the repairs actually have been made.[122]

A taxpayer must be able to prove that the work done was limited solely to repairing damage caused by the casualty.[123]

Where furniture and furnishings were damaged in a fire, deduction was limited to the repair costs.[124]

Where the amount of a casualty loss is determined by subtracting the fair market value of property immediately after the casualty from the fair market value immediately preceding it, an appraiser may take into account in estimating the postcasualty fair market value the probable cost of repairing the damaged property. Under this method, it doesn't matter that the repairs actually have not yet been made.[125]

But a receipt for the cost of repairs which was dated more than a year after the damage had been sustained was accepted as proof that the repairs actually had been made, where the taxpayer explained that he repeatedly had requested the receipt only after he realized that it was needed for income tax purposes.[126]

The amount of casualty loss to a building which was fully depreciated could not be deducted, but the cost of replacing the damage was ordinary and necessary expense and was deductible as such.[127]

Deduction was allowed for the cost of restoring sand that had been washed away from a taxpayer's beach by abnormal storms.[128]

One of the measures of a deductible casualty loss is fair market value of the property immediately before the casualty reduced by fair market value immediately afterward.[129] Often fair market value of realty immediately after the casualty drops sharply because of buyer resistance. For example, if there is a landslide, hurricane, or the like, potential buyers do not want to purchase property in that area. Ordinarily, the courts do not allow a casualty-loss deduction based upon such psychological or economic losses, because the property has not been sold and hence there is no closed transaction by which to measure the amount of loss sustained. But in one case, when Internal Revenue Service appraisers said that loss in value was only temporary, inasmuch as buyers would forget all about a hurricane in nine months, the court came up with a brand-new approach. Fair market value of the property immediately after the casualty could be reduced by a buyer resistance factor: a fair interest rate for a nine-month period on the proceeds likely to be realized on the sale of the property at the end of this nine-month period.[130]

The deduction for property destroyed in a fire at one's residence includes property belonging to the owner's minor child.[131]

In determining this value immediately after the casualty, a lessening of the property's value other than by the casualty itself can be taken into account. Beach-front property in an expensive residential area was damaged by a severe storm, which destroyed a natural barrier between the house and the lake that protected the house against wave action. As a result of the destruction of this attractive, highly vegetated natural barrier, the householder had to erect an unsightly artificial barrier in the form of a seawall. This detracted from the appearance of the property and permanently reduced its attractiveness to potential buyers. So the value of the property after the casualty could be reduced further in accordance with what a knowledgeable realtor said had been done to the saleability of the property.[132]

When a casualty has been sustained with respect to trees on residential property, generally the trees are treated as a part of the overall property.[133] But in placing a value for deduction purposes on trees which had been destroyed by a tornado, it was held to be appropriate to give a higher "location" value to those trees which were closest to the taxpayer's residence, that is, which provided the most shading, noise abatement, or wind screening.[134]

When a portion of a taxpayer's road is destroyed by flood, more than the destroyed portion may be affected. The entire road may decline in value.[135]

Where there is a casualty loss to a home owned by a husband and wife as tenants by the entirety, if the husband pays for the cost of restoring the house to its original condition, each spouse may claim one-half of the cost on his or her Federal income tax return, assuming the parties itemize their deductions. Neither spouse is permitted to deduct the entire cost if separate returns are filed.[136] Similarly, the casualty-loss deduction in the case of a residence owned by husband and wife as tenants by the entirety may be reported to the extent of one-half on each of their separate income tax returns, but neither may report the full amount.[137]

A theft, for tax purposes, occurs when there is an appropriation of property which constitutes the crime of larceny by false pretenses, kidnapping for ransom, or embezzlement.[138] A taking of property in the course of extortion also constitutes theft.[139] The exact nature of the crime is of little importance so long as it amounts to theft.[140]

Theft losses are deductible as casualties. The problem here, frequently, is that of establishing the loss as having been caused by a theft rather than by carelessness or by causes unknown. That the victim promptly reports the loss to the police is a factor which tends to corroborate that a theft indeed has taken place. But loss on the theft of a diamond ring was allowed for tax purposes in a case where a new cleaning person failed to come back to work directly after the ring disappeared. And the victim did not accuse this cleaning person of the theft and did not report the incident to the police, lest she be charged with false arrest as had happened in the case of a personal friend.[141]

A theft-loss deduction was allowed in one case although no report had been filed with the police. The taxpayer believed that reporting the incident would have been useless, as he lived thirty miles from the sheriff's office. A pushed-in window indicated that his house had been broken into, and there were juveniles in the neighborhood who were suspected of having broken into other houses. But as the taxpayer was a high-school teacher, there was justification for his belief that he should make no accusations against suspected youths without any proof.[142]

It is almost mandatory in the case of loss by theft or vandalism to prove that the casualty was reported immediately to the police. But deduction may still be allowed if an individual can show why the police were not notified. A teacher discovered that persons unknown had broken into his house and that various items of property were missing. The Internal Revenue Service sought to disallow the loss deduction because the incident had not been reported to the law-enforcement authorities. But a pushed-in window indicated unlawful entry. And there were special reasons why he had not reported his loss. Juveniles were known to be stealing from unoccupied homes in the vicinity, and the youths he suspected were his own students, whom he could scarcely accuse of the crime without some proof. In addition, the nearest policeman was a sheriff some thirty miles away.[143]

Prompt reporting of a car burglary to the police enabled the authorities to investigate at once and to establish that a door had been forced open by unknown persons.[144]

A theft-loss deduction was allowed where part of the collateral for a bank loan disappeared while in the bank's possession. The deduction was that amount not reimbursed by the bank.[145] The taxpayer's schedule of collateral that had been deposited with the bank was lost when the Internal Revenue Service, which was examining some of his records, admittedly sent them back to the wrong person.

An individual was permitted to deduct the cost of a stereo, a television set, and a diamond ring stolen from his apartment. He had not reported the happening to the police because, as a result of an unsuccessful search by the constabulary for property he had reported after a prior break-in, he believed that this would have been useless.[146]

Deduction was allowed for a diamond ring which was kept in the taxpayer's room in a locked apartment, the key to which was kept in a dressing table that was accessible to her maid. When the taxpayer returned from a trip, the jewelry was missing, as was some clothing, and the maid had departed. The court was willing to infer that the ring had been removed from its place of safekeeping by some unauthorized person who had gained access to the key in the taxpayer's dressing table. Whether or not this person was the maid was deemed irrelevant.[147]

If a theft loss is not reported promptly to the police, the victim must offer as a substitute the testimony of anyone who witnessed the event or its aftermath. If records were burglarized, steps must be taken to reconstruct the records by gathering substitutes, such as copies of checks for travel.[148]

An individual claimed a theft-loss deduction for jewelry, furs, and a postage-stamp collection which allegedly had been removed from his home. Only the value of the stamps was deductible in the absence of proof of the value or even of the existence of the other items. His stamp collection consisted solely of full sheets and plate blocks of new issues of unused United States stamps. The postmaster of the local post office where most of the stamps had been purchased in the last ten years, himself a collector, testified that he had visited the taxpayer's home several times to view the collection. Said the court: "If anyone would be competent to estimate the worth of sheets of stamps it would be the postmaster."[149]

Proof of the amount of a theft loss is difficult in the case of cash, where there is little likelihood that there is any documentation of how much a taxpayer had on his person or in his home. Deduction was allowed in full, however, where the victim had evidence of why he had such a large amount of money with him. Here, the record showed that he was on his way to complete the closing on the acquisition of a house.[150]

In one case, a large amount of cash was claimed to have been taken by thieves at gunpoint from a retail liquor store owner one evening. Presence of the cash was justified by the explanation that it was to be used to pay for liquor that was to be delivered by a wholesaler the next day.[151]

Deduction was allowed for unauthorized withdrawals by an employee to the extent not recoverable by insurance or otherwise.[152]

A theft loss is deductible regardless of whether the alleged thief is prosecuted, so long as there was an illegal taking of property under the laws of the state where it occurred.[153]

Property taken without the owner's consent by a friend qualified as a casualty-loss deduction. Such is the case even where no legal proceedings, civil or criminal, were taken to recover the stolen property, in reliance upon the advice of the taxpayer's lawyer that recovery costs would exceed the value of the property.[154]

In allowing a deduction for theft losses, Congress did not distinguish between losses sustained by the naive or greedy from those suffered by others. "Indeed," commented one court, "gullibility or cupidity of the victim is often the crucial factor that enables the swindler to succeed in his fraud."[155]

An individual paid a contractor who was building a swimming pool for her on the strength of false representations made by the contractor that he had already paid subcontractors and material suppliers. The individual was allowed a deduction, as a theft loss had taken place.[156]

A taxpayer engaged a lawyer to recover property which had been stolen from her. When without authorization the lawyer kept as his fee part of the property which he had recovered, the taxpayer could deduct as a theft loss that portion which the attorney kept.[157]

Deduction was allowed where money was entrusted to a faithless trustee and subsequently appropriated by him for his own use.[158]

Losses which are sustained by reason of criminally false pretenses are deductible as casualty losses. Such was the finding in the case where an individual was induced to buy certain annuity contracts by a pension consultant in order to obtain reputed tax savings. Later the consultant told him that a pending change in the law would prevent the alleged tax advantages and offered to buy back the contracts for $500. The offer was accepted. When the trusting client discovered that the contracts were actually worth $104,000, the difference was deductible as a theft loss, having been taken from the taxpayer by the consultant with the intent to defraud. It was no less a theft by reason of the fact that had the victim read the printed words of his contracts he would have been aware of the substantial value they had. He had relied upon the statement of a person in a position to know the circumstances.[159]

An individual loaned money to a corporation in exchange for a short-term note. His decision to make the loan was based on financial statements issued by the corporation. The corporation failed, after which the president was convicted by a court of violating the state securities law through the issuance of false and misleading financial statements. The unfortunate lender could deduct a theft loss, inasmuch as the corporation president knowingly had obtained money by false representation, with intent to defraud.[160]

An individual bought 100 shares of stock in G Corporation. Six years later, the company's directors approved a merger into X Corporation, subject to the approval of two-thirds of the stockholders of each corporation. X Corporation provided G with detailed information about its financial condition, which was included in proxy statements sent to the G stockholders when they voted on the merger plan, which was passed. Each G shareholder got X shares for his stock. Within two years X went into bankruptcy, and an unfortunate investor claimed a theft loss. Deductibility depended upon whether he had lost his money as the result of what the law characterized as theft in the state where all of this took place. It did. Theft was defined by the state's law as the obtaining of money by the false representation of a material fact with intent to defraud and with knowledge of the falsity of the statement, as a result of which the perpetrator obtains money or something else of value from someone who has relied upon the false representation to his own detriment.[161]

A taxpayer paid out sums of money, by reason of misrepresentations, to enter into certain tax-avoidance schemes. He would not otherwise have paid out these sums. It was determined that he was swindled and had sustained a theft loss. It mattered not that the person sponsoring the scheme thought his machinations would succeed and therefore lacked any intent to commit a fraud.[162]

Whether money paid out as a result of fraud, trickery, and deceit is deductible may depend upon whether the *modus operandi* was treated as theft under the laws of the state where the incident took place. A loss such as that incurred on the sale of forged notes is treated differently in different states.[163]

A hat-check girl in a nightclub became friendly with a wealthy older man, who provided her with a nice home and valuable gifts, including a block of Xerox stock. The nightclub owner learned of her considerable net worth and began dating her, sometimes taking along his brother and their attorney. Collectively, they convinced the well-endowed but financially unsophisticated woman that she should turn over $300,000 to them for investment purposes. That was the last she saw of the money. But at least it qualified for a casualty-loss deduction, for under the law of that state, "theft" includes obtaining money by false pretenses.[164]

While a criminal conviction in a state court may establish conclusively that a theft has occurred, the deduction does not depend upon whether the thief has been convicted, prosecuted, or even whether the taxpayer has chosen to move against the malefactor.[165] Rather, the taxpayer merely must prove by a preponderance of evidence that, under the state law, a theft occurred.[166]

Money lost in a confidence game known in the profession as a "Spanish swindle" was deductible, for the transaction had occurred in Mexico, where local law defined the activity as theft.[167]

Loss resulting from embezzlement of funds by a business associate is deductible as a theft loss.[168]

Sums withdrawn by a husband from a joint checking account with his wife may be deductible as theft losses if this action takes place in a state where intraspousal thefts are recognized as "legitimate" thefts.[169]

When a wife, co-owner of a joint bank account with her husband, withdrew money from the account in circumstances constituting embezzlement, a theft loss was allowed.[170]

An individual could deduct amounts he gave to another person for the purpose of making investments for the former. The latter lost the money in gambling and had no remaining assets. The moneys could be deducted as theft losses by embezzlement, that is, the fraudulent appropriation of property by one to whom it had been entrusted.[171]

A partner takes into account as an ordinary loss deduction his distributive share of a partnership loss occasioned by another partner's embezzlement of cash.[172]

Deduction was allowed where a taxpayer was forced to pay a sum of money for the return of securities withdrawn by his son for Junior's own use.[173]

A child was kidnapped. Under threats of injury to the child, the kidnappers extorted ransom payments from the taxpayer. Theft loss is defined by state law. But to be permitted a theft loss in this circumstance, the Internal Revenue Service has ruled that a taxpayer needs only to prove that his loss resulted from a taking of property which is illegal under the law of the state where it occurred and that the taking was done with criminal intent. So even though the ransom demand and payment did not amount to the statutory crime of "theft" under local law, the taking of the taxpayer's money had been illegal under the laws of the state where the incident took place, and the taking could be presumed to have been done with criminal intent. Hence, the theft-loss deduction was allowed.[174] But inasmuch as the first $100 of a nonbusiness casualty loss is nondeductible, a $500,000 payment to a kidnapper would be deductible only to the extent of $499,900.

An employer was permitted to deduct various payments made to a kidnapper to obtain the release of an employee, despite the fact that the kidnapper's demands had not been addressed to the employer but to the victim's family. The employer derived a business benefit by getting back the employee.[175]

Ordinarily, expenses to prevent a casualty are not deductible, for the expenditures are likely to involve acquisition of property with an estimated useful life of more than one year. But deduction is allowed where the preventive measures do not add to the value of property. In one example, a plant had sustained cave-ins under flooring, and further trouble of the same sort was anticipated. Drilling and grouting to forestall this was a deductible expense.[176]

A farmer could deduct the cost of fuel to heat the superintendent's house, even though it was unoccupied at the time. The expenses had been incurred to prevent freezing of the water pipes in the structure.[177]

An individual used temporary dikes to protect his personal residence (property that was not held for investment or used in his trade or business) as well as his business property from flooding. The dikes were constructed of earth and sandbags and were removed immediately after the floodwater receded. The cost of constructing and removing the temporary dikes was not allowed as a casualty loss with respect either to the business or the nonbusiness properties. But the cost of constructing and removing the temporary dikes to protect business property was deductible as an ordinary and necessary business expense.[178]

Deduction was allowed for fees paid to private detectives for protection of business premises and equipment where police protection was not available during a labor dispute.[179]

One type of expense which was incurred for the purpose of preventing an accident and which was held to be deductible was the cost of a vasectomy.[180]

Ordinarily, a casualty loss, as by storm, is deductible in the year the event took place. But if the casualty is sustained in what the President of the United States subsequently proclaims to be a disaster area, the loss may be deducted in the taxable year immediately preceding the year in which the casualty occurred.[181] This is optional.

Appraisal fees paid in order to establish the amount of a casualty loss sustained to residential property by reason of a prolonged drought are deductible.[182]

A fee was paid to an insurance adjuster to develop data to be used in connection with proving the amount of a tax-loss deduction to be claimed. This was deductible. Because settlement with the insurance company had already been made, this was not an expenditure dealing with the appraisal of property but was an expense in connection with the determination of income tax.[183] The cost of hiring adjusters to collect insurance claimed on business property was deductible. The claim was for money damages, not to protect title or to improve or to increase the value of any capital asset.[184]

While the owners of property are competent to testify as to its value, the weight given to their testimony will depend upon their knowledge, experience, method of valuation, and other relevant considerations.[185]

A major problem in the claiming of a casualty-loss deduction is *proof.*

Unless one thinks to take action immediately after a casualty has occurred, it may not be possible to prove the amount and extent of the loss. The day after her home was wrecked by a storm, an individual went through the house and wrote down a list of the articles she saw, adding items she remembered having been there, though many had been blown or washed away. She inserted her recollection of where each item had been purchased and what it had cost. There were almost 1,900 items on the list. The Internal Revenue Service allowed $1,500.19 for loss of household and personal effects; the Tax Court allowed $12,000, or the difference between the lower amount of fair market value or adjusted basis immediately before the casualty and the value immediately afterward.[186]

When major storms buffeted an individual's shorefront property, an immediate inspection by an experienced realtor disclosed that the land had been washed away by sudden waves and not by erosion. Erosion, as a progressive deterioration through a steadily operating cause, would not qualify as a deductible casualty. This damage did, thanks to a prompt examination of how the property had been destroyed.[187]

Credence was lent to a damage report prepared by an appraiser employed by the taxpayer where made *shortly* after the casualty.[188]

Loss deduction could be established by photographs which were taken immediately after a storm and which depicted valuable trees destroyed by a hurricane.[189] Diminution in the value of a person's home after a storm was demonstrated to the court's satisfaction by photographs that revealed in some detail the fact that the storm had destroyed several beautiful trees which provided privacy, a sense of spaciousness, and beauty to the backyard.[190]

In another case, photographs showed the complete destruction of a road section on the taxpayer's property which was washed out by a flood.[191]

Another individual documented the tornado damage sustained by his residential property by exhibiting contemporary photographs of destroyed trees, damage to the supporting piers of the foundation of his house, and the like.[192] Along the same line, at the time of Hurricane Agnes in 1969, the Internal Revenue Service announced that photographs of damage done by the storm would be helpful in establishing the amount of loss.[193]

After Hurricane Camille, a taxpayer's photographs were accepted as establishing the amount of the damage sustained.[194]

In one case, an individual wrote on his income tax return, "Casualty Damage to Fence and Swimming Pool by Sudden Wind, June 1959, per Pictures Attached."[195]

The extent of damage to a retaining wall by a storm was established by photographs.[196] The amount of casualty loss in one case was determined in part from photographs taken shortly after a windstorm.[197]

A businessperson claimed a casualty-loss deduction when a car crashed into his building, causing a fire which severely damaged the property and records contained there. The IRS sought to disallow part of the deduction because the records which could have substantiated it were not presented, having been destroyed by the fire. Negligence penalty also was imposed for failure to maintain proper records. But photographs saved the day for the taxpayer on two fronts. The pictures showed the extent of the damage sustained. And they showed that the failure to maintain adequate records was not due to the taxpayer's negligence.[198]

You must be sure that (1) the photographer understands what his picture must show and (2) that he is competent to depict this. In one case, a flood-loss deduction was denied where photographs of the damage did not indicate that it was either serious or widespread.[199]

One taxpayer was unable to establish the amount of casualty loss when his house was gutted by fire, because his complete inventory of belongings and their suppliers' names was simultaneously destroyed by the flames.[200] Copies of household inventories should be kept both at home and in a place of safety, such as a bank vault. If, however, the only copy is in the bank, a person is unlikely to review the inventory regularly either for revaluation purposes or for making changes.

Vandalism qualifies as a casualty loss, as where a house was broken into and a stove, washing machine, dryer, and deep freeze were taken.[201] Looting also qualifies as a casualty.[202]

A wife was entitled to a theft-loss deduction where, during her absence from the family home, her husband gave her personal belongings to his girl friend.[203]

Mine cave-in damage to one's property is regarded as a casualty for tax purposes.[204]

Damage to a taxpayer's boat when it ran aground was a casualty loss.[205]

Ordinarily, an otherwise qualifying casualty loss is not deductible if the taxpayer could have been reimbursed by filing a claim with his insurance company. Reason: Here the loss was really the insurance company's and not the taxpayer's. But where one taxpayer sustained a fourth burglary in eight years, he did not file a claim for reimbursement because he feared his insurance policy would be cancelled if he did so. Here the court felt that insurance-company reimbursement, if claimed, would be costly to the taxpayer. So a casualty-loss deduction for the unclaimed loss was allowed.[206]

A transporter of petroleum products had to have insurance on his boats and barges, both for protection and for indemnification of other parties who might have been injured by the taxpayer's vessels. Insurance coverage was insisted upon by shippers, and there were mortgage requirements mandating such coverage. Previously the taxpayer had had coverage cancelled because of unfavorable loss experience, other standard carriers had refused to insure the taxpayer, and the existing insurance had been obtained with great difficulty from a substandard carrier through the assistance of a specialized broker in this field. When the taxpayer suffered damage within two months of obtaining coverage, the broker advised against filing a claim with the insurance company. The loss was deductible because choosing not to seek reimbursement from the insurer was a real business necessity in order that the taxpayer could continue his business.[207]

An individual's boat was damaged. He did not file a claim with his insurance company because, two years earlier, that company had notified him that it would not renew his policies because of excessive prior damage claims. His broker was able to reinstate coverage at that time but advised the taxpayer not to make further claims unless there was a catastrophic loss. He could deduct the loss although he had not sought reimbursement from the insurance company, which also had issued policies covering his automobile and his apartment.[208]

When one individual's fishing boat was seized by Bahamian authorities for allegedly fishing in that nation's territorial waters, he could deduct the uninsured cost of his boat as a casualty loss. It was not unrealistic for him to decide to abandon the vessel rather than to incur legal costs necessary to obtain repossession and to pay towing costs to bring the boat home if he was successful, for it was in a state of disrepair.[209]

An American with a business in South Vietnam was outside of the country when the business was invaded. The Internal Revenue Service claimed that he could not deduct a casualty loss for his property, because he was unable to say that what had happened to it was the result of a casualty. The court allowed the deduction because it had occurred as a result of an unexpected accidental force which the taxpayer had been unable to prevent either because of its suddenness or some disability on his part.[210]

Another court allowed a casualty deduction where it could not be established just what had caused a diamond to disappear from the ring in which it had been mounted. According to expert testimony, the gem simply could not have come loose except as the result of a sudden blow, which ruled out loss by reason of gradual deterioration of the mounting.[211]

When money disappeared from a business's premises and was claimed as a theft loss, the Internal Revenue Service claimed that there was no proof of theft and suggested that the funds might have been taken by the chief executive. The court allowed the missing funds to be deducted. The chief executive had reported the cash shortage to the police, tightened up bookkeeping procedures, and placed strict cash controls on the business. Had he been appropriating company funds for himself, it was unlikely that he would have plugged this alleged source of money so effectively.[212]

A loss for tax purposes due to the nationalization of property by a foreign government is deducted at that time when the taxpayer no longer has a reasonable prospect of recovery.[213]

Losses due to flooding of buildings and basements as a result of a storm are deductible casualty losses.[214]

An individual purchased real estate for long-term investment. Oil was discovered under the ground, so the fair market value of the property shot up. Then salt water filtered into the oil deposit and ruined it. Down went the value of the property, and a casualty-loss deduction was claimed. The Internal Revenue Service sought to disallow this on the theory that there was no loss affecting cash flow. The Service insisted that there was a loss of only unexpected and unrealized appreciation of the original investment in land. The court disagreed. There is no tax distinction between casualty losses to property which has appreciated in value and to property which has not. The only thing that counts is that as a result of a casualty involving the taxpayer's property, there was a permanent loss of value in the marketplace.[215]

Casualty or theft losses and casualty gains with respect to (1) depreciable property and real estate used in a trade or business and (2) capital assets held for more than twelve months are consolidated. If the casualty losses exceed the casualty gains, the net loss is treated as an ordinary loss, fully deductible, without regard to whether there may be noncasualty gains of business depreciable and real property. If, however, the casualty gains exceed the casualty losses, the net gain on business depreciable and real property must be consolidated for tax purposes with other gains and losses on such properties.[216]

Attorneys' fees paid in recovering stolen property are deductible.[217]

Included in a loss, such as a fire, are cleanup expenses after the fire.[218]

Cleanup expenses for removing debris after a hurricane were deductible.[219] Cleanup expenses after a hurricane include such items as labor and stump removal.[220]

The cost of moving dead and blown-down trees could be deducted by a farmer.[221]

Cleanup and repair expenditures incurred as a result of a southern pine beetle attack on the taxpayer's trees were deductible.[222]

The cost of felling trees which had been damaged by a casualty was deductible.[223]

In determining the measure of a deductible casualty loss, sales tax is included in the value of property.[224]

As noted, a casualty loss is deductible in the taxable year only when there is no reasonable possibility of reimbursement by insurance or otherwise. Business property was damaged in a flood, but the insurance company still was disputing the amount of settlement by year's end. The cost of recovering and repairing the equipment, however, could be deducted that year as an ordinary and necessary expense to keep the business operating. Should any insurance be recovered in a later year, the amount of the business-loss deduction in the year of the casualty would not be affected, only the income of the year of recovery.[225] The possibility of a future settlement or favorable court decision on the claim does not affect the deduction if it can be shown by the taxpayer that at the close of the taxable year, no reasonable prospect of recovery existed.[226]

A casualty-loss deduction is not allowed in a year when there is a reasonable prospect of recovery, and the bringing of suit against the party responsible for the loss is ordinarily regarded as evidence that recovery still appeared to be possible. But an embezzlement loss was allowed in the year of discovery even though suit against the perpetrator was started more than a year later. Here the suit had been brought, not with any real hope of recovery from a person without funds, but because of anger at being bilked by a trusted employee. The suit later was dropped.[227]

A casualty loss, to the extent not reimbursable by insurance or otherwise, is deductible even if the property owner actually benefits. Such was the situation where a business lost a valuable merchandising right. Subsequently, an even more valuable merchandising right was obtained from a different source, a right which could not have been obtained had the original one still been held. Declared the court: "A deduction cannot be denied simply because the loss may not be wholly disadvantageous to the taxpayer."[228] *See also* **Carry-overs; Check kiting; Drought losses; Farmers; Foreign expropriation losses; Government seizure; Investors; Reliance upon misrepresentation; Replacement of damaged property.**

Cats. *See* **Deaf persons, expenses of.**

Cattle feed, deductibility of. Certain persons engaged in a cattle-feeding program reported on a cash basis. Shortly before the end of their taxable year, they purchased large quantities of feed, most of which was to be used in the following taxable year. Deduction of the full amount was allowed at the time of purchase. Although tax benefits may have been gained by purchase at that time, there were business reasons for purchasing the feed before it was to be used. On the basis of professional experience, it appeared that feed prices were more favorable at that time than they would be later in the winter. Feed producers were anxious to sell before storage charges were incurred.[229] *See* **Farmers.**

Ceilings to charitable contributions. *See* **Contributions.**

Cemetery company, contributions to. *See* **Contributions.**

Certified public accountant. *See* **Education.**

Certified public accountant, payments to. *See* **Accounting expenses; Stockholders' suit, defense of; Tax rulings, expenses in obtaining.**

Chamber of Commerce dues. A realtor properly deducted dues that he paid to the chamber of commerce in the community where he operated.[230]

Charge accounts, interest on. *See* **Interest.**

Charitable contributions. *See* **Contributions.**

Chauffeur. That portion of payments to a driver which was for business purposes was deductible.[231]

A professional actor who was too young to obtain a driver's license could deduct the salary paid to a chauffeur who drove the trailer used by the juvenile actor as a dressing room on location.[232]

A securities adviser could deduct the expenses of a chauffeur-driven luxury car used to take clients, many of whom were wealthy Europeans, to see brokers. The court noted "the generally obnoxious traffic situation" and the fact that the Europeans were accustomed to this luxurious treatment in their homeland.[233]

Check kiting. Two persons worked out a scheme for kiting checks: that is, checks drawn on one bank were deposited in a second bank, from which moneys were taken out before the original check cleared. A time came when one of the banks discovered it had paid out dollars from an account which was bare. The money was not recovered. The overdraft was not regarded as a claim against the bank's reserve for bad debts but was a fully deductible loss, as state law characterized check kiting or account juggling as theft.[234]

Child-care and disabled-dependent care. This book is concerned solely with tax *deductions*. But an exception is made in the case of this item, for prior to 1976 it was a deduction. Now it is a *credit*; that is, it can be used to reduce the tax you have computed on Form 1040 itself.

In the case of taxable years beginning after December 31, 1981, there is a credit equal to 30 percent of such employment-related expenses of persons with incomes of $10,000 or less. The credit is reduced by 1 percent for each $2,000, or fraction thereof, of income above $10,000. For taxpayers with adjusted gross incomes above $28,000, the credit rate is 20 percent. The maximum amount of employment-related expenses taken into account is increased to $2,400 (one dependent) and $4,800 (two or more dependents).[235]

To qualify, you (together with your spouse, if married) must furnish more than half the cost of maintaining a home that is your principal residence as well as that of a qualified individual, which means: (1) your dependent under age fifteen for whom you are entitled to a personal exemption, (2) your dependent (or a person you could claim as a dependent if it were not for the gross-income test used in determining dependent status) who is physically or mentally incapable of self-care, or (3) your spouse who is physically or mentally incapable of self-care.

Child-care expenses are not confined to services performed within your household. Disabled-dependent or disabled-spouse-care expenses are includable only if they are for services performed in your home to enable you to be gainfully employed.[236]

The requirements were met where a mother took her child out of a junior high school in a major city because she and the child were terrified by the frequent violence and gang warfare going on there. She could not have paid for his expenses at a nonurban private school without getting a job, and, if she kept a constant eye on her child at the strife-torn school, she could not have held a job. School expenses included tuition, room, and board, and the court made its own estimate as to how much of the total qualified as child care for purposes of the tax computation.[237]

Payments for child-care services by a taxpayer to certain relatives formerly qualified for the child-care credit only if the services constituted "employment" as defined for Social Security purposes. Under the Social Security definition, child-care services rendered by a grandparent generally do not constitute employment. But for taxable years beginning after December 31, 1978, payments to grandparents for the care of their grandchildren may qualify for the child-care credit.[238]

Expenditures for out-of-home noninstitutional care of a disabled spouse or dependent are eligible for the credit. Expenditures for services provided by a dependent-care center not in compliance with state or local regulations are not eligible for the credit.[239]

Child-care center for employees' children. *See* **Ordinary and necessary business expenses.**

Child support. *See* **Alimony.**

Chiropodists, payments to. *See* **Medical expenses.**

Chiropractors, payments to. *See* **Medical expenses.**

Christian Science practitioners, payments to. *See* **Medical expenses.**

Christmas cards. *See* **Ordinary and necessary business expenses.**

Christmas gifts. Getting a tax deduction for out-of-pocket business expenses is troublesome because of lack of substantiation. But an alert businessperson can prove his entitlement to a deduction by saving notes of appreciation, which he himself may have solicited. The professional pilot of a manufacturing company's airplane could deduct as a business expense his contributions to the cost of a Christmas party given by an airport for its personnel, for it was necessary for pilots to establish good working relations with the airport staff. Proof of the expenditures, usually lacking in Christmas-gift cases, was provided in a thank-you note from the airport's president.[240] *See also* **Business gifts; Postcards.**

Christmas gifts to employees. *See* **Compensation.**

Christmas parties, cost of. A businessperson could deduct the cost of Christmas parties which were attended by employees, customers, and suppliers. The parties contributed to employee morale and promoted good feelings between the businessperson and people of value.[241]

A physician could deduct expenses associated with a Christmas party given for his nurses.[242] *See also* **Ordinary and necessary business expenses.**

Cigars. Ordinarily, it is impossible to justify the cost of cigars as a tax deduction. But the full cost was deductible by a businessperson who could establish that he (or she) was a nonsmoker of the items.[243]

Civil damages. Civil damages arising from the ordinary and necessary operation of a business are deductible, even though expenses in connection with criminal actions are not.[244]

Civil-defense volunteer, expenses of. A civil-defense volunteer is permitted to deduct out-of-pocket expenses incurred in the performance of his duties, such as travel to observe atomic-bomb tests.[245]

Claim of right. If income is received in any taxable year under circumstances where it appears from all the facts available at the time that an individual has an unrestricted right to this income (known as a "claim of right"), but subsequent to that year it is established that he really was not entitled to the income in the first place, his repayment in a later year ordinarily does not affect his tax in the year of the original receipt; his deduction for the repayment is in the year when it is made. But if the deduction is more than $3,000, he may elect to take the deduction either in the year of original receipt or in the year of repayment.[246]

This election as to the year of deduction is not available in the case of the return of embezzled funds of more than $3,000, inasmuch as they were not received under a claim of right. Repayment of amounts embezzled in prior years is deductible in the year in which the repayment is made. The election does not apply to the repayment by corporate officers or employees of compensation they must repay to their corporation, as where they had agreed to reimburse the corporation for any portion of their compensation which has been disallowed to the corporation as a deduction as a result of a tax audit by the Internal Revenue Service.[247]

Claim settlements. *See* **Settlement payments.**

Claims, satisfaction of. *See* **Business-related losses.**

Class action, cost of. Where an individual took legal action for recovery of property on behalf of himself and the other stockholders of a corporation, he was permitted to deduct the amount of legal fees he had paid.[248]

Cleanup expenses. *See* **Casualties.**

Client reimbursement. *See* **Ordinary and necessary business expenses.**

Clothing. *See* **Actors; Armed forces; Uniforms; Work clothes.**

Clothing, cleaning of. Where uniforms or work clothes not adaptable to general use must be worn on the job, cleaning expenses are deductible as well as the cost of the garb.[249] *See also* **Armed Forces; Uniforms; Work clothes.**

Club dues. *See* **Entertainment.**

Coaching. *See* **Education.**

Coexecutor's fees. An executor who is not acquainted with the task of administering a decedent's estate is permitted to deduct fees which he pays to a more experienced coexecutor to assume the full burden.[250]

"Cohan rule." *See* **Entertainment.**

Collection of income, expenses for. *See* **Legal fees.**

Commercial bribes. *See* **Bribes and kickbacks.**

Commercial fishermen. *See* **Compensation; Ordinary and necessary business expenses; Travel; Work clothes.**

Commissions. *See* **Referral fees.**

Commitment fees. A commitment fee paid as a prerequisite to an agreement that funds would be available as required was deductible.[251]

A merchant negotiated a commitment agreement with several banks, under which they agreed to purchase, at the end of each monthly period for a specified time, its installment accounts receivable arising out of current sales, up to a stipulated ceiling. The banks' "purchase price" was the amount of the receivables less discount at a certain percent per year. If, each quarter, the merchant did not offer for sale to the banks an agreed amount of receivables, a commitment fee on the unused amount had to be paid by the merchant. This was not interest but was deductible business expense.[252]

Where a loan is for an extended period, commitment fees must be amortized over the period of loan or mortgage.[253] Where the amortization of the fees paid for a construction loan falls within the construction period, the amount amortized must be capitalized as a part of the cost of construction.[254] *See also* **Construction costs; Interest.**

Commodity futures contract, purchase of. *See* **Farmers.**

Commuting. The expenses of getting from one's home to one's place of business, and vice versa, are deemed to be personal and not tax-deductible. If an individual has several regular places of business, he may drive to one or more places of work on any given day. On days when he drives to any one place of work and then returns home, there is no deductible transportation expense. On days that involve stops at more than one place of work, no deduction is allowed for the cost of his transportation from his home to the first work location and from the last work location back home. But transportation costs incurred between work locations are deductible business expenses.[255]

Travel costs were deductible commuting expenses where a person drove from his house to perform repair and maintenance services at the residences of customers. The Internal Revenue Service had claimed that his costs "resembled" commuting costs. The court allowed the deduction because there was business justification for his traveling from his home office to the places where he performed services; that is, his customers' residences.[256]

A physician who used his car to visit patients all over the county could deduct his automobile expenses. Where a person operates his own trade or business which necessitates the use of automobile transportation, the costs of his trade or business are deductible, although he returns home at the close of each day.[257]

A physician who performed services at his office, a hospital, nursing homes, and patients' residences was permitted to deduct automobile expenses incurred in traveling 150,000 miles in one year, except for 920 miles which the court deemed to represent actual commuting expenses. Declared the court: "The nature of a medical doctor's business, when he is engaged in the private general practice of medicine, making house calls and visiting the various medical institutions, precludes an arbitrary application of the commuter expense rule holding that every time a physician leaves his home on business he is 'commuting.' . . ."[258]

Once or twice a week, a manufacturing company's controller used his own car to go to other facilities of the corporation in the same city. His unreimbursable expenses for local transportation, incurred in carrying out the duties of his employment, were deductible on the basis of the standard mileage deduction. This was not regarded as commuting, for it did not involve travel to or from his home.[259]

When a person's principal place of business with respect to one of his two businesses happens to be his home, he may deduct his expenses of getting to his other place of business.[260]

A university professor went on a year's leave to work as a scientist at a government agency in a distant city. He rented out his home at the university during his temporary assignment period. He could deduct the cost of commuting between his temporary residence and the government agency.[261]

Where a person has several offices, the cost of travel between them is deductible. Where he has an office at home, this must be his principal office if the cost of travel to and from his home office is to be deductible.[262]

A person may deduct transportation expenses in going from his home to see clients or customers when this home is his only place of business.[263]

Expenses of driving between jobs were held to be deductible, as well as the cost of extra trips to pick up tools and the like which had been left at a prior place of employment because the equipment was not needed at the next assignment.[264]

Hauling tools or instruments in your car in commuting to and from work does not make your commuting costs deductible. But you may deduct additional costs, such as renting a trailer that is towed by your car, for carrying equipment to and from your job.[265]

An individual can deduct expenses in excess of ordinary commuting expenses which can be shown to have been incurred in transporting job-related tools and materials to and from a work site.[266]

An individual has the opportunity of showing (if he can) that he would not have used his automobile to drive to and from his work except for the necessity of transporting his tools. One court found that a taxpayer would have used his car to get to and from work even if he hadn't lugged his equipment, and 50 percent of the total costs could be deducted as pertaining to business rather than to personal considerations.[267]

Where a person can establish that additional expenses were incurred for transporting work implements to and from work, a reasonable and feasible method of allocation is to allow a deduction only for the portion of the cost of transporting the work implements by the mode of transportation used that is in excess of the cost of commuting by the same mode of transportation without the work implements. Internal Revenue Service example: An individual commuted to and from work by public transportation before he had to carry necessary work implements. It cost $2 per day to commute to and from work. When it became necessary to carry the implements back and forth, it cost $3 per day to drive a car and an additional $5 a day to rent a trailer in which the implements were carried. The allowable deduction was the $5 per day additional expense that he incurred in renting the trailer to carry the work implements.[268]

An individual worked about forty miles from his home. He showed that there was a public bus within one hundred yards of his home, with scheduled trips every thirty minutes. The court believed that that was the way he would have traveled were it not for the tools he had to carry. Inasmuch as the car was deemed to be for carrying the tools and not for his personal commuting, deduction was proper in this instance.[269]

A musician may deduct the expenses of using his car to carry instruments between his residence and his place of work if such transportation is necessary because the instruments are too bulky to be carried otherwise and he would not use his automobile except for that reason.[270]

But "incidentals of [one's] occupation" are not given the same favorable treatment as tools. A commercial airline pilot transported his flight bag and his overnight bag in his car which he regularly drove from his home to his place of employment. Inasmuch as he would have used his car even if he went to the airport empty-handed (a nondeductible commuting cost) the United States Supreme Court refused to allow any deduction or allocation, in the justices' language, "because by happenstances the taxpayer must carry incidentals of his occupation with him."[271]

Ordinarily, daily travel expenses to one's place of employment are nondeductible personal commuting expenses. But unreimbursable business travel expenses are deductible when a person travels to and from a temporary site. Such was the situation where an individual had reason to believe his employment would be for a short time only, and hence he would not be justified in moving his home to be closer to the work site. The court held that whether work was to be regarded as "temporary" depended upon the prospects of the length of employment and not upon the subsequent actual length.[272]

The Internal Revenue Service has stated that one year should be the cut-off point after which a job should no longer be considered temporary.[273]

"[A]n exception to the commuter rule has developed a deduction for travel expenses where the commute is longer than usual and is to a temporary place of work—temporary as contrasted with indefinite or indeterminate."[274] (See "Away-from home" expenses under **Travel**.)[274]

An individual was advised by her physician to seek remunerative employment as and for occupational therapy. She could deduct taxi fares in implementing this advice.[275]

For other examples of deductions where physicians advised incapacitated persons to go to work as a therapy measure, see **Medical expenses; Office at home**.

Companion. *See* **Blind persons, expenses of; Medical expenses.**

Compensable injuries. Compensable injuries are those sustained as a result of a patent infringement, a breach of fiduciary duty, or antitrust injury for which there is a recovery under Section 4 of the Clayton Act. In these cases, a special deduction is allowed which has the effect of reducing the amounts required to be included in income to the extent that the losses to which they relate do not give rise to a tax benefit. This is accomplished by a provision stating that when a "compensable amount" is received or accrued during a taxable year for a "compensable injury," a deduction is allowed for the compensable amount or, if smaller, the unrecovered losses sustained as a result of the compensable injury.[276]

Compensating use tax. *See* **Taxes.**

Compensation. Compensation paid for business services is deductible. But even if no services are performed, compensation may be deductible, as in the case of payments to employees who are on vacation. Similarly, payments of a guaranteed annual wage and of dismissal pay are deductible although they are not paid for services.[277] Payments to onetime employees who are now in the Armed Services are deductible when they are made as an inducement to return after separation from military duty.[278] Payments to an employee absent from work as a result of being summoned to serve the Federal government in any capacity at nominal consideration are deductible if he plans to return to the employer at the end of his service.[279]

Persons who work in civilian businesses sometimes are invited to accept governmental positions for a period which is not intended to be permanent. For example, a successful corporation executive may be called to Washington to serve as a member of the Cabinet at a salary which is far less than he had been earning in civilian life. Where such a person intends to return to his private employer at the conclusion of his government service, continuance of salary payments (or portions of them) by his civilian employer are deductible as ordinary and necessary expenses.[280]

Compensation is deductible only to the extent that it is reasonable. Evidence of one employee's indispensability to the payor was established by the fact that the employee had rushed back from his honeymoon to deal with a business problem of the employer.[281]

A corporation executive could deduct the compensation he had paid out of his own funds to a person assisting him in his duties.[282] Such also was the situation where a partner hired an individual to relieve him of some of his partnership duties.[283]

Compensation paid to one's brother was deductible as reasonable where the payee's ability, the nature of his work, the degree of his responsibility, and his past earnings record showed that he had earned his salary.[284]

Wealthy persons could deduct the amount of compensation paid to employees who provided clerical assistance in the making of contributions to approved charitable organizations.[285]

Deductible compensation need not be in the form of cash. For example, compensation to members of the crew of a fishing vessel may be in the form of lodging, meals, or a portion of the catch.[286]

An employer may deduct the cost of turkeys, hams, or other items of merchandise of nominal value given to employees at Christmastime. There is an annual limitation of $25 for such a gift.[287]

A businessperson who absorbs the employee portion of Social Security taxes can deduct them as compensation, providing the rule of reasonableness is followed.[288] The cost of flowers sent to an employee in a hospital is deductible.[289] Improvements to a recreation lodge conveyed to a foremen's association for use by its employees for recreation purposes were deductible.[290]

Loans and advances to an employee which the employer does not expect him to repay are deductible as compensation if they are for personal services actually rendered and the total is reasonable when added to other compensations.[291]

Payment by the employer of an employee's ordinary life insurance premiums are deductible by the employer, where the policy specifies that proceeds upon death are payable to the employee's nominee.[292]

Group-term life-insurance premiums paid or incurred by the employer on policies covering the lives of employees who designated their own beneficiaries are deductible by the employer if he does not retain any incidents of ownership and he is not directly or indirectly the beneficiary under the contract. This is true for both permanent group life and nonpermanent group life insurance.[293] Group hospitalization and medical-care premiums which the employer pays for the benefit of his employees are deductible.[294] Medicare premiums for both active and retired employees are deductible.[295]

Amounts paid by an employer to employees because of injuries, including lump-sum amounts paid or acrued as compensation for injuries, are allowable deductions, which, however, are limited to amounts not compensated for by insurance or otherwise.[296] *See also* **Family transactions.**

Compensation, repayment where excessive. *See* **Executives.**

Competition, payments to eliminate. *See* **Expenditures for benefits lasting more than one year.**

Compromise of taxes, fees in connection with. *See* **Legal fees.**

Compromise payments. *See* **Legal fees; Settlement payments.**

Condemnation awards, expenses related to. Where awards upon the condemnation of property by governmental authority were held to be taxable to the person whose property was seized, deduction was allowed for legal, engineering, and appraisal fees he incurred in getting this award.[297]

Condominiums and cooperative housing corporations. An individual who qualifies as a tenant-stockholder of a cooperative housing corporation may deduct from his gross income amounts paid or accrued within his taxable year to the cooperative housing corporation which represents his proportionate share of (1) the land and building and (2) the interest allowable to the corporation on its indebtedness contracted in the acquisition, construction, alteration, rehabilitation, or maintenance of the building. The deduction cannot exceed the amount of the tenant-shareholder's proportionate share of the taxes and interest. His proportionate share of the stock of the corporation is that portion owned by him of the total outstanding stock of the corporation. For taxable years beginning after December 31, 1969, if the corporation has issued stock to a governmental unit, then in determining the total outstanding stock, the governmental unit is deemed to hold the number of shares it would have held if it had been a tenant-stockholder.[298]

A tenant-stockholder in a cooperative housing corporation may deduct as interest an amount which he paid to the corporation toward the permanent financing of the corporation.[299]

When a tenant-stockholder uses the proprietary lease or right of tenancy, which he has solely by reason of stock ownership in a trade or business or for the production of income, rather than for personal use, the stock is subject to depreciation or (in the case of a lease) amortization.[300]

An individual qualifies as a tenant-stockholder even though he is entitled to occupy more than one dwelling unit in the cooperative housing corporation. He need not actually live in any of the units himself and may rent them to other parties.[301]

In a condominium arrangement, a purchaser owns outright a dwelling unit in a multidwelling structure, and he also owns a proportionate undivided interest in the common elements of the structure, such as land, lobbies, elevators, and service areas. Real-estate taxes on the individual owner's interest in the land and on the common parts of the structure are deductible on a proportionate basis.[302] If he is liable to the local taxing authority for the tax assessment on his interest in the condominium, he may deduct taxes which he pays with respect to the apartment.[303] He may deduct interest on an overall mortgage if the amount he pays is specified in his purchase deed. He also may deduct interest on an individual mortgage on his particular property. He may deduct for his share of casualty losses, such as an uninsured boiler explosion, in the same manner as other homeowners.[304]

Ordinarily, a condominium is purchased for its tax advantages, notably the deduction by the purchaser of interest and property taxes not available to a person who rents his home or apartment, despite the fact that a major portion of his rent actually represents interest and taxes on the property. But a condominium also can represent a transaction entered upon for profit, all the expenses of which are deductible. Upon the advice of an investment counselor, an individual bought a condominium. The purchaser's facilities were made available for rental by outsiders, and use by the owner was negligible. Accordingly, depreciation and other costs incurred in owning and operating the property were deductible by the owner as business expenses.[305] (*See also* **Interest; Taxes.**)

With the prospects of their daughters going to college in the not too distant future, a married couple sought an investment which might generate income to defray these bills. They purchased a condominium unit with the purpose of renting it out, but efforts by brokers and the building's management were only partially successful, and the upkeep of the condominium exceeded income from it. The couple could deduct this excess as an expense related to the production of income. They never had used the unit for personal purposes, and it was not intended as the place for their ultimate retirement.[306]

Similarly, such expenses were deductible where an owner-stockholder notified the manager that he wanted to rent his unit, hired a real-estate agency to manage rentals for a year, and placed advertisements in the *Wall Street Journal* and elsewhere. Although he was not too successful in finding tenants at first, over a period of four years he was able to convert from a totally unrented apartment to a continuously rented one. He almost never went to the apartment, spending less than four weeks there in his five years of ownership.[307]

Confiscation. Losses arising from the seizure (or confiscation) of business property generally are deductible in the absence of a showing by the Internal Revenue Service that the deduction will frustrate a sharply defined national or state policy.[308] *See also* **Casualties; Foreign expropriation losses; Government seizure; Property used in the trade or business and involuntary conversions.**

Con games. *See* **Casualties.**

Congressman, expenses of. For taxable years beginning after 1981, the place of residence of a member of Congress (including any delegate and resident commissioner) is considered to be within the state which he represents.[309]

A United States congressman can deduct the expenses of taking a constituent to luncheon where there is no other time to discuss the latter's problem with a governmental agency.[310] *See also* **Moving expenses.**

Conservation expenditures. *See* **Farmers.**

Construction costs. Commitment fees to have moneys available in specified amounts for construction purposes were deductible.[311] *See also* **Capital improvements; Expenditures for benefits lasting more than one year.**

Construction-period interest and taxes. Individuals are not permitted to deduct real property construction period interest or taxes that were paid on account in the taxable year on property that is expected to be used in a trade or business or in an activity conducted for profit. These amounts may be capitalized as a construction cost, but they may be deducted as a percentage amount for each amortization year. For nonresidential real property, the rate is 10 percent. For residential real property, the rate is 11 ⅑ percent in 1983 and 10 percent thereafter.[312]

Consultation fees. Deduction was allowed for payments for advice on the solving of day-to-day business problems.[313] *See also* **Accounting expenses; Expenditures for benefits lasting more than one year; Family transactions; Financial counseling fees; Investors; Legal fees; Tax preparation, fees related to.**

Contact lens insurance. *See* **Medical expenses.**

Contested inheritance, expenses of. Expenses paid or incurred for the production or collection of income are deductible. Legal fees incurred in settling a claim for an inheritance are not deductible insofar as what is received is characterized as inherited property, for such property is excludable from gross income and hence the legal fees allocated to obtaining the property are not related to the production or collection of income. But legal fees for any part of what is received which represents improperly withheld income is deductible, legal fees being prorated according to the type of payment involved for this purpose.[314] *See also* **Legal expenses.**

Continuing professional education. *See* **Advanced degree, study for; Education; License maintenance.**

Contraceptives. *See* **Medical expenses.**

Contract, breach of. *See* **Settlement payments.**

Contracts, expenses. A business was obligated to deposit United States Government bonds as security for the performance of a contract. Such bonds were purchased, and after the completion of the contract, the bonds were promptly sold. The resultant loss was deductible as an ordinary and necessary business expense, not as a capital loss of limited availability. The cost of procuring security for the performance of the contract was not distinguishable from the ordinary premium expense of a surety company, a usual part of a contractor's cost.[315] Penalties for nonperformance of a contract are deductible. If a taxpayer makes a contract to construct a building by a certain date and is obligated to pay a certain amount for each day the building is not finished after the date set for completion, the amounts paid or incurred by him are deductible.[316] *See also* **Family transactions.**

Contributions. Within certain limits (to be defined later in this section), an individual may deduct contributions for exclusively public purposes to:

1.   The United States or any of its political subdivisions.

2.   A domestic corporation, trust, or community chest, fund, or foundation organized and operated exclusively for religious, charitable, scientific, literary, or educational purposes or for the prevention of cruelty to children or animals, or to foster national or international amateur sports competition if the organization does not use any of its funds to provide athletic facilities or equipment.

This applies provided that no part of the earnings goes for the benefit of any individual and no substantial part of the activity is lobbying. Under certain circumstances, the recipient of the contribution may be a veterans' organization or cemetery company.[317]

An organization which had a membership comprising churches of various denominations qualified as an association of churches, an organization to which contributions are deductible for tax purposes. Here its activities consisted of provision of clergymen at hospitals and college campuses and the coordination of efforts to aid the poor.[318]

A contribution was deemed to be exclusively for public purposes when made to a committee of court officials and attorneys in order to commission a portrait of a recently appointed judge for permanent display in a courthouse in accordance with local custom.[319]

An individual may deduct contributions which he voluntarily makes to a nonprofit cemetery corporation for its perpetual maintenance, if the contribution was not made for the perpetual care of a particular lot.[320]

The Internal Revenue Service publishes a list of organizations, contributions to which are deductible within specific limits. If an organization's name is deleted from this list by the IRS because it is no longer entitled to recognition as charitable, etc., deduction ordinarily is allowed where the contribution was made *before* removal of the name. But deduction is not allowed if the contributor knew the exempt status was going to be revoked or if he was himself in any way responsible for activities leading to the revocation of charitable status.[321] Deduction was permitted where exempt status subsequently was revoked, for here the donor, although he enjoyed a close personal relationship with the charitable organization's president, had no reason to know about any questionable activities.[322]

Often a contribution to a private school is disallowed because the institution is practicing discrimination. A potential donor should ask to see a copy of the form that the school has to file with the Internal Revenue Service entitled "Annual Certification of Racial Nondiscrimination for a Private School Free from Federal Income Tax."[323] Failure by a school to allow this form to be examined should be considered thoughtfully by the potential donor.

A charitable organization has been defined as one with "any benevolent or philanthropic objective not prohibited by law or public policy which tends to advance the well-doing and well-being of man." The furtherance of recreational and amateur sports falls within this broad definition and should be so classified. A deduction was accordingly allowed for contributions to a nonprofit organization that sponsored Little League and other amateur athletics.[324]

A charitable contribution is allowable even if it is made without the slightest charitable impulse. In the words of one court:

Community good will, the desire to avoid community bad will, public pressures of other kinds, tax avoidance, prestige, conscience-salving, a vindictive desire to prevent relatives from inheriting family wealth—these are a few of the motives which may lie close to the heart, or so-called heart, of one who gives to charity. If the policy of the income tax laws favoring charitable contributions is to be effectively carried out, there is good reason to avoid unnecessary intrusions of subjective judgments as to what prompts the financial support of the organized but non-governmental good works of society.[325]

To be deductible, a charitable contribution must be made voluntarily, without expectation of getting anything in return. But deduction was upheld where a tornado-displaced person, who was provided with food and shelter by the American Red Cross, made a contribution to a local chapter in gratitude for what he had received.[326]

An attorney owned a number of low-income houses which had no indoor plumbing and provided little more than shelter. A storm of criticism about substandard housing in the city arose, as a result of which he donated the use of these houses to a tax-exempt organization, for the use of the existing tenants without rent for a three-year period, after which they were scheduled for demolition under an urban renewal program. He could deduct the value of this gift, measured by the income flow he was giving up, even though the purpose of the contribution was to avoid further controversy attaching to his name and destroying his effectiveness as a lawyer.[327]

For Federal income tax deduction purposes, the mere delivery of a check to an approved charitable organization is considered a payment and is sufficient to permit a deduction.[328]

Pew seats, building fund assessments, and periodic dues paid to an approved church are regarded as methods of making contributions to the church and are deductible contributions.[329]

If an individual makes a charitable contribution of an item of property other than money and claims a deduction in excess of $200 for that item, he must attach to his Federal income tax return information as to the name and address of the donee, the date of the contribution, a description of the property including its physical condition, how the property had been acquired, fair market value at the time of the contribution, the method used in determining the value, and its cost or other basis.[330] But where contributions of property do not include any *single* item of property claimed as a deduction in excess of $200, these detailed requirements need not be met.[331]

In general, contributions in the form of appreciated-value property are deductible only to the extent of the donor's costs, and the appreciation element is not included in the amount of the deduction. But there are some important exceptions to this general rule:

1. In the case of gifts of appreciated-value property which, if sold, would have produced ordinary income or short-term capital gain, the appreciation is not part of the tax deduction. Let's say that Fred Jones gives to charity some stock held for less than one year. The stock cost Fred $500 initially but now is worth $700. He can use as a basis for his charitable deduction only the $500 which he originally paid for the stock and must forget the appreciated $200 value of the stock as far as his tax deduction goes. In other words, the amount of the appreciation in value results in a reduction of the contribution deduction to the extent of the appreciation. Inventory is an example of this type of appreciated-value property.

The charitable deduction for gifts of property which would to some extent, at least, produce ordinary income if sold, as a result of various depreciation recapture rules, is also reduced by the amount subject to recapture as ordinary income.[332]

2. Gifts of property which would produce long-term capital gain if sold are deductible at fair market value when they are made to organizations which can use the property for the purpose for which the donee's tax-exempt status has been granted (*e.g.,* sculpture donated to an art museum).

In the case where tangible property is given to an exempt organization whose use of the property is unrelated to the purpose constituting the donee's basis for tax exemption (*e.g.,* that same piece of sculpture donated to a haven for dogs and cats), the amount of the deduction is reduced by 40 percent of the appreciation which would have been a long-term capital gain if the property had been sold at fair market value.

Consider a piece of sculpture originally purchased by Erma Black for $400. Its market value is now judged to be $4,000. If Erma donates the sculpture to her favorite art museum, her deduction for charity is $4,000. If she decides to donate the same sculpture to a dog and cat haven, she can now deduct only $1,840, or the original purchase price ($400) plus half of the appreciated value (40 percent of $3,600, or $1,440).[333]

One individual could deduct the fair market value of porcelain art objects that he gave to a tax-exempt nonprofit retirement center. Although ordinarily decorative objects might not be related to the retirement home's exempt purpose, here they were functionally related to the home's principal activity of creating a living environment for the residents because the display of the porcelains directly enhanced that environment.[334]

3. Similarly, appreciation is taken into account in determining the amount of deduction in the case of gifts of appreciated-value property to certain private foundations.[335]

4. In the case of so-called "bargain sales" to charitable organizations, where the taxpayer sells property to such an organization for less than its fair market value (often at his cost), the cost or other basis of the property must be allocated between the portion of the property "given" to the charity and the portion "sold" on the basis of the fair market value of each portion.[336]

Thus, if an individual sold land with a fair market value of $20,000 to a charitable organization (not a private foundation) at his cost of $12,000, he would be required to go through the following steps: He must find the percentage that the actual sale price of the property is to the property fair market value. In this case it is 60 percent. He must then apply this percentage to the adjusted basis of the land (in this case $12,000) and he finds that he has a recognized taxable gain of $4,800 on which he must pay taxes. (Sixty percent of $12,000 is $7,200, which when subtracted from $12,000 equals the gain of $4,800.) This is his allocation for that part of the property "sold" to charity.

His deduction of that part "given" to charity is allocated as 40 percent of the potential $20,000 realization, or $8,000. He would be required to include the $4,800 as gain from the sale of a capital asset in his tax return and would be allowed a charitable deduction of $8,000.

A simple gift of property to charity can have complex tax consequences. One person transferred real estate with a fair market value of $25,000, subject to a $10,000 mortgage, to an approved charitable organization. He had held the property, which was a capital asset, in his hands for more than one year. Because he had been relieved of an indebtedness by getting rid of encumbered property, his disposition was partially a deductible contribution and partially a realization of income to the extent of the indebtedness discharged. Here are the tax consequences of this deceptively simple transaction:

1.	Fair market value of the property	$25,000
2.	Less mortgage indebtedness	10,000
3.	Adjusted basis of the property	15,000 (Amount of the charitable deduction).

But he also had taxable gain (relief from indebtedness).

4.	Adjusted basis of the property (Item 3)	15,000

5. Times income realized by relief of
indebtedness (Item 2)   10,000
6. Equals   150,000,000

7. Divided by fair market value of the
property (Item 1)   25,000
8. Equals adjusted basis for determining
bargain sale (sale of property for
less than its fair market value)
(Item 6 divided by Item 7)   6,000
9. Amount realized (Item 5)   10,000
10. Gain on bargain sale to charity
(Item 9 minus Item 8)   4,000

So his charitable deduction is $15,000 (Item 3) and he has a long-term capital gain of $4,000 (Item 10).[337]

As previously mentioned, contributions to valid charitable organizations are deductible at fair market value in most situations. Fair market value, in turn, is defined as what a willing buyer pays a willing seller where each has knowledge of all of the facts. So if a charitable organization promptly sells the gifted property to a third party, the price customarily measures the amount of the donor's deduction. But he has the opportunity to show that the actual sales price was not realistic under the circumstances. In one case, it was shown that the charitable organization had no need for this property, a yacht (it might just as well have been a work of art or a home), and the property was sold as rapidly as possible to avoid maintenance and insurance charges. This haste to sell may very well have resulted in a lower price than more leisurely and careful selling efforts would have brought. If the donor can show that such indeed was the case, his deduction is not limited to the price at which the actual sale was made.[338]

Nor is the donor's deduction limited to the amount realized by the recipient charitable organization at an unrestricted auction, which in this case was attended primarily by wholesalers or dealers who were buying for resale.[339]

A donor's deductible amount is not restricted to the proceeds of a forced sale, such as a bankruptcy sale.[340] Such also was the finding in the case of a sheriff's sale.[341]

United States Government publications (including the *Congressional Record*) that a person gets from the government without charge, or below the price at which they are sold to the general public, are considered ordinary income property. If later he gives these publications to an approved organization, his deduction is the fair market value minus the amount that would be ordinary income if he had sold them at fair market value.[342]

Where an individual purchases an annuity contract from an approved tax-exempt organization, that part of his cost which is in excess of the fair market value of the annuity as established by Internal Revenue Service tables is deductible as a charitable contribution.[343]

The contribution may be in the form of any kind of property which the donor possesses. He may deduct the value of a form of assignment he makes to a charitable organization. For example, a man signs a dance-lesson contract and pays for a specified number of hours at a stated price per lesson. He may contribute to a charitable organization his right to receive dancing lessons which he purchased from the dancing school.[344]

An individual irrevocably named an approved charitable organization as beneficiary of a policy of insurance on his life. He was permitted to deduct annual premiums he paid to keep the policy in force.[345]

If a person has any interest in property, the value of his interest can be the basis of a deductible contribution when he gives or assigns it to an approved charity. For example, where an individual owns a policy of insurance upon his own life and he gives this policy to a charity, he is entitled to a deduction on his tax return. The amount of the deductible contribution is what insurance people call the interpolated terminal reserve, which is similar to the cash surrender value.[346]

Deduction is allowed for charitable contributions in easements and other partial interests in real estate for conservation purposes. These are defined as (1) the preservation of land areas for outdoor recreation of the general public; (2) the protection of a relatively natural habitat of fish, wildlife, or plants, or a similar ecosystem; (3) the preservation of open space (including farmland and forest land) where such preservation is for the scenic enjoyment of the general public or pursuant to a clearly delineated Federal, state, or local governmental policy and will yield a significant public benefit; or (4) the preservation of a historically important land area or a certified historic structure.[347]

A "restrictive easement" in favor of the Federal government to enable the government to preserve a scenic view which at the time was open to certain public properties was found to be deductible for a taxpayer complying with this restrictive easement. In one case, a taxpayer generously donated the "restriction" of his parcel of land, which presented a scenic view to a nearby Federal highway. The restrictions he imposed pertained to the type and height of buildings, types of activities for which they could be used, size of parcels to be sold, etc. His "restrictive easement" enabled him to claim a charitable deduction.[348]

Other restrictive easements which a taxpayer may grant provide that the donor agrees to restrictions on the use of his property, such as limitations on the type and height of buildings that may be erected, the removal of trees, the erection of utility lines, the dumping of trash, and the use of signs.[349] Although contribution deductions are no longer permitted for interests in property which consist of less than a taxpayer's entire interest in the property, deduction is allowed in the case of an undivided portion of his entire interest. So deduction is permitted for a charitable contribution of an open-space easement in gross forever. An easement in gross is a mere personal interest in, or right to use, the land of another party. In order to value the easement, the difference between the fair market value of the total property after the grant is the fair market value of the easement given up.[350] Here is an illustration. A governmental body, in order to preserve open space in a particular location and to prevent its development with a structure of any kind, secured from the owner of farm land a contribution of an easement for all time to prohibit development, but to permit continued use as farm land.

A taxpayer transmitted an open-space easement in gross for all time to an approved operating foundation, which qualified as a tax-exempt organization. The deed of easement provided for a thirty-foot-wide right-of-way along the edge of the taxpayer's property to be used by the foundation for the creation and maintenance of a recreation trail that was to be used year-round by the general public for hiking and skiing purposes. The donor agreed not to interfere with use of this property by the public. The fair market value of the easement, as determined by a realtor or other expert in values, was allowable as a charitable deduction.[351]

In the event that a taxpayer who is the recipient of a reversionary interest from the principal of a trust declines the interest in favor of a charitable organization, he is allowed the deduction of that amount as a charitable deduction.[352]

Ordinarily, no charitable deduction is allowed for a donation of less than the donor's entire interest in property to a charitable organization. Deduction is allowed, however, if the interest is a *remainder* interest in a personal residence or farm. Similarly, a partial interest can be deductible if transferred to a trust. A donor may take a charitable contribution deduction for an outright transfer of property to a qualified organization even though he transfers less than his entire interest in the property. In such a case, he is entitled to a contribution deduction in the amount which would have been allowed had he transferred the same property in trust for the charitable organization.[353]

In the case of contributions for conservation purposes, the types of partial interests which qualify include the entire interest of the donor in real property other than the rights to subsurface minerals.[354]

A donor may deduct the value of an undivided portion of his entire interest which he contributes. If he owns 100 acres of land and donates an undivided 50 acres to a qualified charity, a deduction is allowed for that portion which he gives away.[355]

Deduction is allowed for a partial interest in one's property which is a "qualified conservation contribution." This refers to a transfer of what is defined as qualified real property to a qualified organization exclusively for conservation purposes.[356]

For a contribution to a charitable organization to produce a tax deduction, the donor must rid himself of all dominion and control over the property given. The owners of manuscripts and similar materials related to the theater, radio, and television donated this property to the New York Public Library for use by the public at large. The contributors stipulated, however, that none of the materials could be copied without the donors' permission. The Internal Revenue Service claimed that full control of the property had not been relinquished by the donors because of this restriction. The court concluded, however, that the donation had a genuine charitable intent and amounted to a completed gift despite certain very minor restrictions imposed upon its use.[357]

An individual is entitled to a charitable deduction if he transfers property to an approved organization, including the United States Government, and retains only an unsubstantial right. This was the case when a person donated his entire interest in 800 acres of land to the government, reserving only the right to train his dogs there during the remainder of his life.[358]

Undocumented contributions also were deductible, in an amount estimated by the court rather than the larger amount claimed on the tax return, where a minister wrote in a letter that the taxpayer had been a regular contributor to the church.[359]

Charitable contributions of individuals generally are limited to 50 percent of adjusted gross income. The limitation is 30 percent for gifts of appreciated-value property unless in computing the amount of the contribution the appreciation element is reduced by one-half.

The limitation of 20 percent of adjusted gross income is imposed on contributions to private foundations which are not operating foundations unless within two and one-half months after the year of receipt they distribute the contributions to an operating foundation or to a public charity, college, etc., in which event the higher contribution limitation is available.[360]

Contributions were found to be deductible in a larger amount than could be documented where evidence showed that an individual had been going through the trauma of a second divorce. Observed the court, "As so often happens during time of stress (he) . . . looked for solace in the church.[361]

An individual's charitable contributions, although undocumented, were allowed where his estranged wife rather surprisingly testified on his behalf.[362]

If it chooses, a court may allow deduction of contributions even in the absence of documentation. In one case where deduction was allowed, the court stated that "Our observations of [the taxpayers] at trial were that they were forthright, open, and honest and that they tried to recall the facts to the best of their ability . . . [W]e believe that [the taxpayers] did maintain records and that they were lost and the witness who could verify their existence is dead." The establishment of *credibility* is highly important.[363]

One of the major problems in the case of contributions to charities is whether the donor receives anything in return. In the words of one court, "If a payment proceeds primarily from the incentive of anticipated benefit to the payor beyond a satisfaction which flows from a generous act, it is not a gift."[364]

But it is not always true that there is automatically something wrong with a contribution which also benefits the donor. Two businessmen gave some modest acreage in their real-estate enterprise to the local school board. The Internal Revenue Service claimed this was not a charitable contribution because at the time the enterprise was trying to get the planning board to approve its subdivision plan. Also, the presence of a school right in the middle of the subdivision would attract family buyers to the area, and the properties would be enhanced in value. But the court saw nothing objectionable about that. It was a transfer without consideration to an organization which qualified under the tax law as a charity. The fact that the donors may have derived financial benefits was quite irrelevant.[365]

A manufacturer of sewing machines made sales of his products at substantial discounts to schools and to approved charitable organizations other than schools. Discounts on the sales to schools did not qualify for the charitable deduction, as the purpose of discount sales here was to encourage the schools to interest and to train the students to learn to sew and thus to become potential buyers of such machines. Discounts on sales to other charitable organizations, however, qualified for the charitable deduction.[366]

Membership fees or subscriptions paid to an approved charitable, educational, scientific, or literary organization are deductible if any rights and privileges of membership (advance exhibitions, reduced rates of admission, and the like) are incidental to making the organization function according to its charitable purpose. Privileges such as being associated with or being known as a benefactor of the organization are not regarded as significant return benefits that have a monetary value which would cause disallowance of the deduction.[367]

A business firm contributed land to a state highway department. This land ran through the firm's property. The highway department improved and beautified the lands given by the taxpayer and by other parties at the same time. A contributions deduction was permitted. The contributions section of the law, observed the court, is not to be construed as applicable only in the event the donor receives no benefit. Nor are the motives of the donor in making his contributions relevant if compliance with the tax law is otherwise realized.[368]

Voluntary payments by merchants and property owners to a municipality to provide public parking facilities in the general area of the businesses and properties of the contributors were deductible as contributions *only* in cases where the parking was not limited to use by contributors and their customers and where the amount of the contributions was not based on the proximity or probable use of the facilities by contributors, their tenants, or customers.[369]

Contributions to a city to enable it to furnish new facilities outside the city to two railroads in return for the removal of their inner city facilities and relinquishment of their rights-of-way through the city were deductible.[370]

The contributions deduction is allowed where the donor receives merely an incidental benefit from the tax-exempt organization by way of a trade-off. The owners of a trailer park donated its sewer system to a municipality. Nothing of value, such as a zoning change, was received in exchange. True, the donors were relieved of maintenance responsibility for the sewer system after the transfer, and that was a benefit. But as nonowners, they would be paying a use charge, which should amply cover any repair costs that henceforth would be borne by the city.[371]

Amounts paid to a state-established commission to study the problems of industrial life in a particular geographical area were deductible. The commission sought to benefit the residents of the region by attracting and maintaining industry by subsidies or by arranging to have new funds pumped into the area.[372]

Payments to a state highway department for posters and advertising signs promoting highway safety were deductible.[373]

A payment made to an approved welfare organization as reimbursement for services in the adoption of a child was deductible. State law prevented the organization from charging a fee for the service which it rendered.[374]

A hopelessly ill individual paid a substantial sum of money into the building fund of a nursing home one day prior to her acceptance as a patient in the home's infirmary. This was allowed as a contributions deduction, as there was no showing that such payment was required to procure her admission there or that the home thereafter charged and collected less for her regular care than it otherwise would have charged her.[375]

Contributions to nonprofit volunteer fire companies are deductible as contributions.[376] It does not matter that the contributor may be getting something very substantial in return, such as his life.

The deductibility of a contribution is not forfeited by the fact that the donor obtained benefits from making the contribution. In the words of one court, "a taxpayer is entitled to decrease the amount of his tax liability by means which the law permits."[377]

Contributions to charitable organizations are limited to a specified percentage of the taxpayer's adjusted gross income, as mentioned previously. Ordinary and necessary business expenses, however, are fully deductible, subject only to the requirement that they be reasonable (*see* **Ordinary and necessary business expenses**), but no deduction is permitted as ordinary and necessary if it would be allowable as a charitable contribution except for the fact that it exceeds that portion of the donor's income which qualifies as a charitable contribution. In other words, you can't sneak extra money into the charitable deduction disguised as a business expense if the only reason for doing so is that you have already used up your allowable 50 percent of adjusted gross income deduction.[378] The problem is to show that the payment, even to a charitable or similar organization, was really for business rather than charitable purposes.

A business firm was engaged in retailing in a resort city and derived a significant part of its income from the tourist industry. An oil-well blowout caused crude oil to pollute the beaches, and tourists stayed away in droves. The local city council solicited voluntary funds to protect local business through an oil-pollution control fund, which was to be used to seek ways of preventing pollution problems other than through lobbying. The firm made a contribution to this fund. It was deductible as ordinary and necessary expense; it was not a contribution inasmuch as the donor expected a financial return commensurate with the amount of money he had given. The payment was calculated to improve the donor's future business.[379]

A taxpayer who depended upon the general public for patronage made payments to various charitable and religious organizations. The benefit to the donor was an acknowledgment of the donation in a printed bulletin or leaflet distributed to the membership of the organizations. Customers of the donor were mostly local citizens. Advertising was the principal motive of the expenditures, which were deductible as advertising.[380]

A cement manufacturer's contribution to a YMCA building fund was deductible as a business expense. The "Y" had to buy cement for its building. The manufacturer's contribution was made for the purpose of directly acquiring more business; thus it was a business expense.[381]

A businessperson made contributions to an approved hospital because the chairman of the fund drive was the owner of a company which was a potential customer of his. The payment could be deducted as a business expense rather than as a charitable contribution.[382]

A woman who operated her own travel agency dealt primarily with charitable organizations. She made sizable contributions to some of them, which she regarded as sales promotion, for she did not advertise or use promotion techniques as her competitors did. She considered the value of each account when making the contributions and reflected them in a business account. The Internal Revenue Service claimed they were not deductible to the extent they exceeded the contributions limitation. She won. These were payments in the expectation of getting business.[383]

A business firm agreed to pay a certain charitable organization a specified amount for each label of the payor's product which was mailed back to the payor by its customers. In return, the charity agreed to permit its name to be used in connection with the firm's advertising and to secure testimonial letters from prominent individuals extolling the firm's product. It was held that the amounts paid by the firm to the charitable organization were not charitable deductions, subject to limitation as such, but were ordinary and necessary business expenses for the purpose of stepping up the sales of its product.[384]

In order to promote business in the neighborhood of his office, a stockbroker, as an inducement to customers, paid an amount equal to 6 percent of all brokerage commissions to an authorized charitable organization. The purpose of this tax-exempt organization was to reduce neighborhood tensions and to combat community deterioration in the neighborhood in which the broker's office was located. The broker advised the charitable organization of the procedure used in soliciting business, and the latter was agreeable to the technique. Inasmuch as the broker's payment of 6 percent of his commissions to the charity was related to the payor's business and could reasonably be expected to further his business commensurately, the payments were deductible as ordinary and necessary business expenses.[385]

An employer made payments to a nonprofit organization organized and operated for the purpose of eliminating prejudice and discrimination in the securing of housing by minority groups. As part of its activities the exempt organization entered into agreements with various business concerns in the community in which it acted as general adviser and consultant to employees. These payments were deductible without limitation as business expenses.[386]

If a donor to a charitable organization receives (or reasonably expects to receive) a financial benefit that is commensurate with the "gift" he makes, no deduction is allowed. If he receives a financial benefit that is substantial but is less than the value he gives, then the transaction may involve both (1) a gift and (2) a contribution. Then deduction is allowed only for the excess of the value of what he gives over (1). A tax-exempt organization conducted weekend seminars for the purpose of bringing harmony into marriages. A husband and wife attended one such seminar. Participants were not obligated to pay any fee but were invited to make a donation to the actual *pro rata* participant costs of the seminar. The couple was permitted to deduct any part of its contribution to the extent it could be shown that the contribution exceeded the monetary value of all benefits and privileges received.[387]

An employer could deduct as ordinary and necessary expenses its payments to an association for the purpose of setting up a school for company employees and their families. The payments were a direct business benefit to the employer because they encouraged family persons not to move away to locations where schools were available.[388]

A manufacturer could deduct payments made to a local hospital as business expenses. Two-thirds of the population of this community were employees or their dependents.[389]

A contribution to charitable organizations in the form of property is deductible, even though the donor buys it back in a later year, if the contribution was valid when it was made and if there was no requirement or condition that it be sold back, the charitable organization having all rights to keep the property or to sell it elsewhere.[390]

When a contribution is made to an approved organization in the form of property which the donee can use in connection with its tax-exempt function, the donor is allowed a deduction for the fair market value of the property for its highest and best use. In the case of property on which stands a structure which the donee cannot use, removal costs must be subtracted from the value of the property, unless the donee can make some interim use of it until plans can be put into effect utilizing the land for its highest and best use.[391]

Where a state legislature established an official committee to receive unsolicited contributions to defray the expense of providing state units for a parade attendant on a Presidential inauguration (with any unexpended balance in the fund to go the state), contributors were allowed to deduct the full amount of their gifts.[392]

Amounts paid for stock of the Ohio Valley Industrial Corporation, a nonprofit organization, were deductible by a clothier as ordinary and necessary business expenses. The nonprofit organization had been organized to promote business in the area where the clothier operated.[393]

Sometimes an individual is interested in making a contribution to a charitable organization, but he has nothing of value to give, all his wealth being tied up in the family business corporation. A tax-free reorganization may be the solution to this problem. If the corporation were capitalized solely with one-class voting stock, a recapitalization would allow the replacement of such shares by common (voting) stock and preferred stock on a tax-free basis.[394] The individual could then contribute each year to charitable organizations as few or as many of the preferred shares as he might choose, thereby obtaining charitable deductions without in any way diluting his control of the voting stock of the corporation and without using his cash or other forms of wealth.

A nonprofit hospital admitted patients who came without the recommendation of a doctor, and these patients were treated by interns and residents under the supervision of a hospital staff physician. Some of the patients had health insurance coverage that entitled the staff physicians to receive fees for their services. Doctors who voluntarily assigned these fees to the educational training program of their own departments could deduct the amounts as charitable contributions.[395]

Medicare fees earned by staff physicians of a private hospital were voluntarily assigned to a fund used for the education of resident physicians and graduate nurses. Charitable deductions were allowed for these fees.[396]

If a member of a religious order who has taken an oath of poverty is assigned to teach at a public school by this order, to which she remits her salary, this remuneration is includable in her gross income. But she is entitled to a deduction of the excess of her salary over the value of the living expenses which the religious order furnishes to her.[397]

No deduction is allowed for services rendered to a charitable organization. But an individual who gratuitously gives his services to a charity may deduct his unreimbursed travel expenses (including meals and lodging) while away from home in connection with the affairs of the charity.[398] Also deductible are unreimbursed expenses of salaried assistants directly attributed to services rendered by a person to an approved charitable organization.[399] Also the cost and upkeep of uniforms which have no general utility and are required to be worn while performing donated services are deductible.[400] This includes the cost and upkeep of uniforms used in charitable or educational activities, as by a scoutmaster.[401]

A ski buff who volunteered to assist a tax-exempt organization in safeguarding ski areas could deduct the cost of the distinctive parka and trousers the patrol wore as uniforms.[402]

An individual who owned a collection of tape recordings of classical music made copies of this material which he contributed to charitable organizations. The value was deductible, for it did not represent, as had been alleged by the Internal Revenue Service, a contribution of nondeductible services, materials being involved as well as his copying time.[403]

A professional artist contributed three of his paintings to an approved charitable organization. His efforts in producing the paintings were not deductible services, but he could deduct the cost of his materials and canvas.[404]

A contributions deduction is not allowed for the contribution of one's own services. But an individual's car, however deeply he is attached to it, is not a part of him for tax purposes. When Hurricane Agnes struck the area in which an individual lived, he worked as a volunteer and used his automobile to distribute food to evacuated flood victims. His car expenses, on a mileage basis, were deductible.[405]

A volunteer Red Cross worker could deduct the cost of her uniforms.[406]

Out-of-pocket expenses directly attributed to the use of personally owned aircraft and automobiles were deductible.[407]

Frequently mayors, councilmen, and other elected or appointed governmental officials serve without compensation in the performance of their official functions. If such a person can show that he had expenses directly connected with these duties and solely connected with these duties (that is, they were not personal expenses), then he can deduct as contributions the amount of such expenses to the extent that he has not been reimbursed for his out-of-pocket expenditures.[408]

Out-of-pocket expenses incurred by an individual for transportation to and from a local hospital or church for the purposes of rendering voluntary services to the Red Cross or a church are deductible, but not meals unless the taxpayer is away from home overnight.[409]

A physician who recently had moved into the county sought to become well known by joining the sheriff's mounted posse. He used his own horse. He could deduct costs such as horseshoeing and stabling as unreimbursed expenses in connection with services rendered to an exempt organization.[410]

One individual was a member of a church that had as its basic function evangelism, the spreading of faith through preaching, teaching, and personal suasion. In carrying on the evangelistic work, he was deemed to be rendering services "to or for the use" of his church, so he could deduct out-of-pocket travel expenses to areas where he sought to carry out his mission.[411]

Unreimbursed out-of-pocket expenses of a retired businessman performing volunteer services as a consultant were allowed on the ground that his services furthered the purpose of the Small Business Administration to provide management services to small firms.[412]

Individuals invited by the Department of Justice to attend a conference to contribute their advice regarding methods of meeting legal problems of the poor could deduct their out-of-pocket expenses.[413]

The Volunteer Income Tax Assistance (VITA) program is an ongoing project established under the auspices of the Internal Revenue Service to assist taxpayers in complying with the tax laws and to help individuals to meet their obligations in this respect. Free assistance is provided to low-income, elderly, and non-English-speaking people in the preparation of their returns. The volunteers are permitted to deduct transportation expenses to and from the tax assistance sites, the cost of writing materials used in the work, and any costs of publicizing their availability.[414]

Similarly deductible are out-of-pocket expenses incurred by a civil-defense volunteer in the performance of his duties, such as travel expenses to watch simulated emergencies and to attend state meetings of civil-defense volunteers.[415]

An approved charitable organization conducted a program of assisting needy unmarried pregnant women. As part of this program these women were placed during the middle of their pregnancies in the homes of families which volunteered their help to the organization. Participating families took these women into their homes, paid for their food and clothing, and gave them a small weekly allowance, for which they were not reimbursed. Inasmuch as the out-of-pocket expenses incurred by the participating families were directly connected with and solely attributable to the rendition of uncompensated services to the charitable organization, they were deductible as contributions.[416]

Foster parents may deduct unreimbursed out-of-pocket expenses they pay out to provide gratuitous foster-home care for children placed in their home by a charitable organization.[417]

If an individual uses his car in connection with rendering gratuitous services, the standard mileage deduction is nine cents a mile. The taxpayer does not have to take the deduction in this manner. If the actual cost of operating his car exceeds the nine-cent-per-mile allowance, the taxpayer may deduct his actual expense.[418] Parking fees and tolls may be deducted in addition to the standard mileage rate deduction.[419]

Unreimbursed, reasonable, out-of-pocket expenses incurred by a volunteer who treats selected groups of children to such activities as swimming, going out to dinner, and fishing, are deductible in the same manner and to the same extent as other contributions. But the portion of the expense attributable to the admission tickets or similar expenses of the volunteer is not deductible because he is receiving a benefit or privilege for this portion of the expenditure.[420]

Unreimbursed out-of-pocket expenses incurred in sponsoring cocktail and dinner parties to promote a ball held by a charitable organization are deductible.[421]

An individual donated land to a community for a park and properly claimed a charitable deduction. Many years later, a highway project sought to open a roadway through this park. The original donor of the land was permitted to deduct as a contribution the legal fees spent in resisting efforts to encroach upon property now owned by a tax-exempt organization.[422]

An individual permitted two charitable organizations to use office space in his premises. Deduction was allowed for the value of the space used by one of the organizations; the other organization was not on the official list of organizations contributions to which are deductible for tax purposes.[423]

Should an individual pay more than fair market value to a qualified charitable organization for merchandise or goods, the amount paid in excess of the value of the item may be a charitable contribution. Assume he pays $20 for a box lunch at a church picnic. If the lunch, plus any entertainment or other services provided, has a fair market value of $1.50, the excess of $18.50 is a contribution to the church, assuming that the net proceeds of the picnic go exclusively to the church.[424]

Where an individual purchases an annuity for himself from an approved charitable organization, he may deduct as a contribution any part of his cost which is in excess of the fair market value as established in standard annuity tables.[425]

An appraisal fee paid by a contributor of property to a tax-exempt organization for the purpose of ascertaining the proper amount to claim as a deduction on his income tax return is deductible. It is an expense in connection with the determination of income tax liability.[426]

An individual may deduct the amount he paid to maintain in his home a full-time student in the twelfth or any lower grade at an educational institution located in the United States. The student cannot be a dependent or relative. He can be a foreign student or an American student, but he must be a member of the taxpayer's household under a written agreement between the taxpayer and a qualified organization. The purpose of the agreement must be to provide educational opportunities for the student. If the taxpayer receives any compensation or reimbursement for the student's maintenance, no deduction is allowed. Only money actually spent by the taxpayer is taken into account (the fair market value of the student's lodging or any other similar item is not considered money spent by the taxpayer). The amount which may be deducted cannot exceed $50 times the number of full calendar months in the taxable year during which the student was a member of the taxpayer's household. Any month in which the student resides there for fifteen or more days is considered a full calendar month for this purpose.[427]

To be deductible, a contribution in the taxable year must convey under the law applicable where it takes place an ascertainable legal interest in the property, unencumbered by conditions in the transfer document or in the law relating to the transfer which might deny the interest.[428]

Ordinarily, contributions made directly to individuals, however deserving the recipients may be, are not deductible. Occasionally they are. The officials of a state which had suffered a hurricane disaster appealed to householders to open their homes to the thousands of persons made homeless by the storm. The persons displaced by this disaster were advised to check at centers set up by the Red Cross, Salvation Army, Civil Defense, and the United States Office of Emergency Planning, which tried to find temporary shelters for the displaced people. The charitable organizations assumed the responsibility of caring for the hurricane evacuees. So actual unreimbursed expenses incurred by an assisting individual, which were directly connected with and solely attributable to providing necessities, such as lodging, food, and clothing to the storm victims, were regarded as contributions for the use of the charitable organizations. Deduction was permitted as contributions.[429]

Reasonable unreimbursed out-of-pocket expenses of a person for meals and recreation of a child who has been referred to this person's temporary care by an approved charitable organization are deductible.[430]

An organization whose purpose is to foster national or international amateur sports competition can be qualified as an exempt charitable organization if no part of its funds is used to provide athletic facilities or equipment. One such organization induced various "host families" to provide lodgings in their homes, transportation between lodgings and places of competition, and meals for visiting competitors. None of the host families' expenses was reimbursed. Such families could deduct their out-of-pocket expenses in this connection as contributions.[431]

Contributions are deductible when made "to or for the use of" an approved organization. One individual set up a fund to provide scholarships for high-school students, recipients to be selected by school principals on the basis of need and scholastic merit. The donor actually wrote out all of the checks, each one payable jointly to a selected student and to the college he would attend. The Internal Revenue Service vainly sought to disallow a contributions deduction on the ground that the donees' names were known to the donor and he was making payments to them as individuals. But the court concluded that deduction was proper, for neither the contributor nor anyone acting under his direction had any control over which deserving student would receive a scholarship.[432]

A charitable contribution is a gift "to or for the use of" a corporation, fund, or foundation organized and operated exclusively for charitable, religious, educational, etc., purposes. A donor tends to believe that this means the contribution must be directly to the fund or corporation. But the recipient may be more broadly construed. An individual directed his bank to send a check to a missionary who was serving in South America under the auspices of a church. As instructed, the bank notified the missionary that the money was to be used "for the Presbyterian mission work" in Brazil. So the funds were not for the missionary's personal use but were to be employed in carrying out the church's activities. In substance, the donor contributed the funds to the church, and the missionary received the money as its agent or representative. Result: deductibility.[433]

Although contributions made directly to a foreign organization are not deductible, an individual may deduct contributions to a United States organization that transfers funds to a foreign charitable organization, provided the United States organization controls the foreign organization's use of the funds or if the foreign operation is merely an administrative arm of the United States organization.[434]

If an individual's charitable contributions are of the type that qualify for the 50 percent ceiling discussed earlier, any contributions which he makes in excess of 50 percent of his adjusted gross income may be carried over for use in the next five years to the extent that contributions in those years do not exceed the 50 percent figure at such time. No carry-over is provided in the case of contributions geared to 20 percent of adjusted gross income where such contributions exceed 20 percent in any year.[435]

Even where a taxpayer could not substantiate the amount of cash contributions made to his church, the court accepted the amount claimed because of the proven regularity of his church attendance and the generosity demonstrated by his substantial contributions to other charities.[436] Many churches have instituted their own envelope systems that provide documentary evidence of an individual's contributions.[437]

If husband and wife file a joint Federal income tax return in a taxable year in which they made valid charitable contributions in excess of the percentage of their adjusted gross income allowed by the tax law, this *excess charitable contribution* can be carried forward to each of the next five taxable years, starting with the earliest. But if separate tax returns are filed in a succeeding year, the carry-over must be allocated according to the amount of any excess contribution that each spouse would have computed had separate returns rather than a joint return been filed for the year in which the excess contribution was made. Any agreement made by the spouses as to how they will divide the excess contribution should they subsequently file separate returns will be disregarded by the Internal Revenue Service.[438]

For taxable years beginning after December 31, 1978, the former deduction for political or newsletter fund contributions has been discontinued. There is now a *credit* against the contributor's Federal income tax for political contributions of $50 ($100 on a joint return). Contributions eligible for this credit may be made to (1) candidates for nomination or election to a Federal, state, or local office in general, primary, or special elections; (2) committees sponsoring such candidates; (3) national, state, or local committees of a national political party; and (4) newsletter funds of an official or candidate.[439]

A so-called check-off system took effect on January 1, 1973. An individual can designate that $1 of his tax liability be set aside in a special fund in the Presidential Election Campaign Fund for the candidates of a political party he specifies. Alternatively, he can direct that the $1 be set aside in a nonpartisan general account in the fund. In the case of a joint return having a tax liability of $2 or more, each spouse may designate that $1 be paid into an account.[440]

In the past, persons who used the zero bracket amount (formerly called the standard optional deduction) instead of itemizing deductions were not allowed to deduct contributions to approved charitable organizations. For taxable years beginning after December 31, 1981, deduction is allowed for a percentage of contributions up to a fixed dollar amount of contributions in this manner:

Year	Percentage	Deduction Limit
1982 and 1983	25	$25
1984	25	$75
1985	50	None
1986	100	None
1987	Provision expires	

The maximum contribution is the same for married persons filing joint returns and single taxpayers. For married persons filing separately the maximum is one-half of the applicable amount.[441] *See also* **Annuities from charitable organizations; Credit card, charges to; Lobbying; Ordinary and necessary business expenses; Retirement homes.**

Convalescent homes. *See* **Medical expenses; Retirement homes.**

Conventions. Expenses related to one's trade or business are deductible. Thus deduction was allowed for the cost of attending a professional seminar[442] and a professional convention.[443]

An accountant could deduct expenses of going to the National Association of Cost Accountants convention, where he derived business from his attendance and his activities.[444] A clergyman could deduct his costs of going to church conventions.[445] An executive of a lumber company was able to deduct his costs of going to lumbermen's conventions.[446]

A lawyer was allowed to deduct expenses of attending a meeting of the American Bar Association.[447] A legal secretary's expenses in attending a convention of the National Secretaries Association were deductible.[448] A university teacher was allowed to deduct expenses of attending conventions and scientific meetings.[449] A professional cartoonist could deduct his expenses of attending a political convention.[450] An insurance agent who specialized in truck insurance could deduct his expenses while attending a truck association convention.[451]

Expenses incurred in attending conventions are deductible if an individual by attending is benefiting or advancing the interests of his trade or business. This test is met if the agenda of the convention or other meetings is so related to the individual's position as to show that attendance was for business purposes. The agenda need not deal specifically with the official duties and responsibilities of the person's position in order for his expenses of attendance to be business-oriented and deductible for tax purposes as business expenses.[452]

A bank required its employees who went to annual conventions of the industry to take their wives as registered participants. At these conventions, executives fraternized with key personnel of other banks with whom they regularly discussed such mutual problems as loans, investments, and leverage lease transactions. Wives entertained and socialized with other bankers and their spouses. The Internal Revenue Service sought to disallow wives' expenses as business deductions on the ground that what the wives did was not *necessary* to the employer's business activities. But it was ruled that the conventions were working sessions and not vacations for the executives or their spouses. The employer found the presence of spouses was so useful in fostering good working relations with other companies that executives *had* to bring their wives. An expenditure qualifies for a necessary expense when it is appropriate and helpful to the taxpayer's business.[453]

In the case of meetings abroad beginning after December 31, 1980, no deduction is allowed for expenses related to a convention, seminar, or similar meeting held outside of the United States, its possessions, the Trust Territory of the Pacific, and Canada and Mexico, unless it is as "reasonable" for the meeting to be held outside of this area as within it. Expenditures for amounts which are lavish and extravagant are not allowed. Deduction is no longer allowed for expenses incurred in attending conventions held on cruise ships.[454]

The factors to be taken into account in determining "reasonableness" are (1) the purpose of the meeting and the activities taking place there; (2) the purposes and activities of the sponsoring organizations or groups; and (3) the places at which other meetings of the sponsoring organizations or groups have been or will be held. If the convention lasts for more than one week, and at least one-quarter of the taxpayer's time is spent on nonbusiness activities, special allocation rules are applicable. Transportation expenses are deductible only if incurred principally for business purposes.[455]

Conveyance taxes. State and local transfer taxes on the conveyance of real estate or securities in a transaction entered upon for profit are deductible.[456]

Cooperative health association membership. The cost of membership in an association furnishing cooperative or "free-choice" medical service, or group hospitalization and clinical care, is deductible.[457]

Cooperative housing, deductions of tenant-shareholder in. *See* **Condominiums and cooperative housing corporations.**

Co-owners, transfer of property between. *See* **Family transactions.**

Corporate officers. *See* **Executives.**

Corporate officers' expenses. *See* **Entertainment; Executives; Legal fees; Travel.**

Corporations. *See* **Contributions; Legal fees; Small-business corporation stock; Tax-option corporations.**

Correspondence course. The cost of a correspondence course is deductible if the course meets all of the requirements for a deductible educational expense.[458]

Cosmetic surgery. *See* **Face-lifting; Medical expenses.**

Cost depletion. *See* **Depletion.**

Cost of eliminating competition. *See* **Expenditures for benefits lasting more than one year.**

Cost recovery provisions. *See* **Depreciation.**

Costumes. A professional actor could deduct the cost of costumes purchased at his own expense.[459]

A concert harpist was allowed to deduct the cost of her playing costumes.[460]

Where such costumes have a useful life of more than one year, the Internal Revenue Service position is that there is no immediate deduction but there is an annual depreciation deduction spread over the assumed remaining life of the costumes.[461]

In one case, the court drew this distinction: items such as stage footwear and similar items of a very short useful life are currently deductible, while costumes, concert gowns, and stage equipment are subject to depreciation write-offs.[462]

Cotton allotment allocation, loss of. *See* **Agricultural allotment cancellation.**

Country-club dues. Dues or fees paid to a country club are deductible only if the taxpayer establishes that the facility was used primarily for the furtherance of his trade or business and that the expense was directly related to the conduct of his trade or business.[463] *But see* **Entertainment.**

Covenant not to compete, payments for. *See* **Expenditures for benefits lasting more than one year.**

Credential renewal fees. *See* **Teachers, expenses of.**

Credit card, charges to. Contributions to approved charitable organizations by use of a credit card are validly made and deductible in the year made; deduction does not await the formal billing day, and payment to the bank or other issuer of the credit card.[464] A similar rule exists in the case of use of a credit card for the payment of medical expenses, such as to a hospital.[465]

Credit cards, interest on. *See* **Interest.**

Credit insurance. *See* **Insurance.**

Creditor insurance policy, premiums on. A seller of real property on the installment plan can deduct premiums covering the lives of purchasers.[466] Premiums on life-insurance policies held as security for debts were deductible.[467]

Creditors, payments to. Payments to creditors after a discharge of debts in bankruptcy proceedings were held to be deductible, being expenses to reestablish the bankrupt's credit in the commercial world. An insurance broker wrote insurance in several companies. When one of these failed he paid off claims which had matured against that company and reinsured his customers in another company at additional cost to himself. His payments for such purposes were deductible. Although he was under no obligation to make these payments, he did so in order to retain customers and to promote his business.[468]

Crutches, deduction of cost of. *See* **Medical expenses.**

Cuban expropriation losses. *See* **Foreign expropriation losses.**

Custodian services. *See* **Investors.**

Custody fee. A subscriber to a sponsored investment plan may deduct annual custody fees which he pays.[469]

Customer, medical expenses of. The owner of a bakery could deduct the cost of a physician's treatment of a thumb injury sustained by a customer (Tom Thumb?) in the shop.[470]

C

1. Revenue Ruling 62-122, 1962-2 CB 12.
2. Revenue Ruling 69-511, 1969-2 CB 23.
3. *Boucher et al. v. Commissioner*, T.C. Memo. 1981-258, filed May 27, 1981.
4. *R. E. L. Holding Corporation*, BTA Memo., Docket No. 34961, entered March 23, 1931.
5. *Mrs. E. B. Lawler*, 17 BTA 1083 (1929).
6. *Chicago Lumber Company of Omaha et al.*, 18 BTA 916 (1930).
7. *Robert Buedingen*, 6 BTA 335 (1927).
8. *Connecticut Mutual Insurance Company v. Eaton*, 218 F. 206 (DC, Conn., 1914).
9. Revenue Ruling 70-392, 1970-2 CB 33.
10. Revenue Act of 1978, Section 402(a).
11. *Maurice Bower Saul et al.*, T.C. Memo., Docket No. 7679, entered June 26, 1947.
12. Revenue Ruling 70-344, 1970-2 CB 4.
13. IRC Section 1211(b)(1).

14. Tax Reform Act of 1976, Section 1401.
15. IRC Section 1211(b)(2).
16. IRC Section 1202.
17. IRC Section 642(h).
18. *Becker Warburg Paribas Group Incorporated v. United States*, 514 F. Supp. 1273. (DC, ND Ill., 1981).
19. Revenue Ruling 78-93, 1978-1 CB 38.
20. *Busking et al.*, T.C. Memo. 1978-415, filed October 16, 1978.
21. *Oliver W. Bryant et al.*, T.C. Memo., Docket No. 27114, entered May 2, 1952.
22. IRC Section 172(c).
23. Regulations Section 1.172-3(a).
24. *Vivian W. Rose*, T.C. Memo. 1973-207, filed September 17, 1973.
25. *Losses from Operating a Business*, IRS Publication 536, 1976 edition, page 2.

26. IRC Section 172(b)(1).

27. Tax Reform Act of 1976, Section 806(a), as amended by Economic Recovery Tax Act of 1981, Section 207.

28. IRC Section 165(g).

29. IRC Section 172(d)(4)(c).

30. Regulations Section 1.172-3(a)(3)(iii).

31. Regulations Section 1.172-7(b).

32. Regulations Section 1.172-7(c).

33. Revenue Ruling 65-140, 1965-1 CB 127.

34. *Security First National Bank v. United States*, DC, SD Cal., 1966.

35. Revenue Ruling 60-216, 1960-1 CB 126.

36. Revenue Ruling 65-140, 1965-1 CB 127.

37. *Samuel G. Adams et al.*, 14 BTA 781 (1930).

38. Regulations Section 1.704-1(b)(2).

39. IRC Section 704(d).

40. IRC Section 752.

41. Regulations Section 1.752-1(e).

42. IRC Section 704(d).

43. IRC Section 642(h).

44. *Federal Tax Guide for Survivors, Executors, and Administrators*, IRS Publication 559, 1978 edition, page 15.

45. *Warfell-Pratt-Howell Company*, 13 BTA 506 (1928).

46. *Marshall J. Hammons et al.*, T.C. Memo., Docket No. 31518, entered November 24, 1953.

47. *Marion S. Perkins et al.*, T.C. Memo., Docket No. 31053, entered May 29, 1952.

48. IRC Section 165(a).

49. *Shearer v. Anderson*, 16 F.2d 995 (2d Cir., 1927).

50. *Smith et al. v. Commissioner*, 76 T.C. 459 (1981).

51. *Louise D. Bryan Estate v. Commissioner*, 74 T.C. 725 (1980).

52. *Rose Licht*, 37 BTA 1096 (1938).

53. *United States v. Barret*, 202 F.2d 804 (5th Cir., 1953).

54. *Nourse v. Birmingham*, 73 F. Supp. 70 (DC, Iowa, 1947).

55. *Rainbow Inn, Inc. v. Commissioner*, 433 F.2d 640 (3d Cir., 1970).

56. Revenue Ruling 73-41, 1971-1 CB 74.

57. Regulations Section 1.164-7(b).

58. Regulations Section 1.165-7(a)(2).

59. Tax Equity and Fiscal Responsibility Act of 1982, Section 203.

60. *Helvering v. Owens et al.*, 305 U.S. 468 (1939).

61. Regulations Section 1.165-7(a)(2)(i).

62. *Westvaco Corporation v. United States*, 639 F.2d 700 (Ct. Cl., 1980).

63. *Whipple v. United States*, 25 F.2d 520 (DC, Mass., 1928).

64. IRC Section 165(c)(3).

65. *Harry Johnson Grant*, 30 BTA 1028 (1934).

66. *Frederick H. Nash*, 22 BTA 482 (1931).

67. *Ferguson v. Commissioner*, 59 F.2d 893 (10th Cir., 1932).

68. Revenue Ruling 54-395, 1954-2 CB 143.

69. *John P. White et al.*, 48 T.C. 430 (1967).

70. *Louis Broido*, 35 T.C. 786 (1961).

71. *John P. White et al.*, 48 T.C. 430 (1967).

72. *Pebley v. Commissioner*, T.C. Memo. 1981-701, filed December 10, 1981.

73. *Kielts et al. v. Commissioner*, T.C. Memo. 1981-329, filed June 24, 1981.

74. *Maher et al. v. Commissioner*, 76 T.C. 593 (1981).

75. *Black et al. v. Commissioner*, T.C. Memo. 1977-337, filed September 27, 1977.

76. *Smithgall et al. v. United States*, DC, MD Ga., 1980.

77. *Rosenberg v. Commissioner*, 198 F.2d 46 (8th Cir., 1952).

78. *Shopmaker et al. v. United States*, 119 F. Supp. 705 (DC, ED Mo., 1953).

79. *Kielts et al. v. Commissioner*, T.C. Memo. 1981-329, filed June 24, 1981.

80. *Abrams et al. v. Commissioner*, T.C. Memo. 1981-231, filed May 7, 1981.

81. *Butschky et al. v. United States*, . . . F. Supp. . . . (DC, Md., 1981).

82. *Willard T. Burkett*, T.C. Memo., Docket No. 37344, entered September 28, 1951.

83. Revenue Ruling 75-381, 1975-2 CB 25.

84. Revenue Ruling 59-102, 1959-1 CB 200.

85. *Jack R. Farber et al.*, 57 T.C. 714 (1972).

86. *Hossbach v. Commissioner*, T.C. Memo. 1981-291, filed June 15, 1981.

87. *William H. Carpenter et al.*, T.C. Memo. 1966-228, filed October 18, 1966.

88. Regulations Section 1.165-7(a)(3).

89. *Elwood J. Clark et al.*, T.C. Memo., Docket Nos. 9059, 9135, and 9167, entered April 1, 1956, *aff'd*, 158 F.2d 851 (6th Cir., 1947).

90. Revenue Ruling 69-88, 1969-1 CB 58.

91. *Shearer v. Anderson*, 16 F.2d 995 (2d Cir., 1927).

92. *Stanley Kupiszewski et al.*, T.C. Memo. 1964-258, filed September 30, 1964.

93. *F. H. Wilson*, 12 BTA 403 (1928).

94. *George G. Ebner et al.*, T.C. Memo. 1958-108, filed June 9, 1958.

95. Revenue Ruling 54-85, 1954-1 CB 58.

96. *Sid J. Klawitter et al.*, T.C. Memo. 1971-289, filed November 9, 1971.

97. *Tank et al. v. Commissioner*, 270 F.2d 477 (6th Cir., 1959).

98. *Harry Johnston Grant*, 30 BTA 1028 (1934).

99. *Ferris, Jr., et al. v. United States*, DC, Vt., 1962.

100. *Delbert P. Hesler et al.*, T.C. Memo. 1954-176, filed October 18, 1954.

101. *O'Connell et al. v. United States*, DC, ND Cal., 1972.

102. *Ruecker et al. v. Commissioner*, T.C. Memo. 1981-257, filed May 27, 1981.

103. *William H. Carpenter et al.*, T.C. Memo. 1966-228, filed October 18, 1966.

104. *John P. White et al.*, 48 T.C. 430 (1967).

105. *Anderson v. Commissioner*, 81 F.2d 457 (10th Cir., 1936).

106. *Jack R. Farber et al.*, 57 T.C. 714 (1972).

107. *Ion Z. Josan*, T.C. Memo. 1974-144, filed June 6, 1974.

108. *Harry M. Leet et al.*, T.C. Memo. 1955-13, filed January 24, 1955.

109. Revenue Ruling 70-91, 1970-1 CB 37.

110. *Betty L. Young*, T.C. Memo. 1977-38, filed February 16, 1977.

111. *Irving J. Hayutin et al.*, T.C. Memo. 1972-127, filed June 12, 1972.

112. Revenue Ruling 54-85, 1954-1 CB 58.

113. *Dady et al. v. Commissioner*, T.C. Memo. 1981-440, filed August 19, 1981.

114. *Seward City Mills*, 44 BTA 173 (1941).

115. Revenue Ruling 79-174, 1979-1 CB 99.

116. *McKean et al. v. Commissioner*, T.C. Memo. 1981-670, filed November 19, 1981.

117. *Buttram v. Jones*, 87 F. Supp. 322 (DC, WD Okla., 1943).

118. *Cinelli et al. v. Commissioner*, 502 F.2d 695 (6th Cir., 1974).

119. *Luther Wickline*, T.C. Memo, 1971-205, filed August 18, 1971.

120. *Dominick Calderazzo et al.*, T.C. Memo. 1967-25, filed February 13, 1967.

121. *Lamphere et al. v. Commissioner*, 70 T.C. 391 (1978).

122. Ibid.

123. *Butschky et al. v. United States*, . . . F. Supp. . . . (DC, Md., 1981).

124. *Johnson, Jr., et al. v. Commissioner*, T.C. Memo. 1981-55, filed February 11, 1981.

125. *Abrams et al. v. Commissioner*, T.C. Memo. 1981-231, filed May 7, 1981.

126. *Dady et al. v. Commissioner*, T.C. Memo. 1981-440, filed August 19, 1981.

127. *Ralph S. Clark et al.*, T.C. Memo. 1966-22, filed January 27, 1966.

128. *Clapp et al. v. Commissioner*, 321 F.2d 12 (9th Cir., 1963).

129. Regulations Section 1.165-7(b)(1)(i).

130. *Cantrell et al. v. Commissioner*, T.C. Memo. 1978-237, filed June 26, 1978.

131. *Scharf et al. v. Commissioner*, 4th Cir., 1976.

132. *Strutz et al. v. Commissioner*, T.C. Memo. 1980-274, filed July 28, 1980.

133. *Western Products Company*, 28 T.C. 1196 (1957).

134. *Bowers et al. v. Commissioner*, T.C. Memo. 1981-658, filed November 12, 1981.

135. *Johnston et al. v. Commissioner*, T.C. Memo. 1980-477, filed October 23, 1980.

136. Revenue Ruling 75-36, 1975-1 CB 143.

137. Revenue Ruling 75-347, 1975-2 CB 70.

138. *Evelyn Nell Norton*, 40 T.C. 500 (1963), aff'd, 333 F.2d 1005 (9th Cir., 1964).

139. *Sidney Dembner et al.*, T.C. Memo. 1974-180, filed July 9, 1974.

140. Revenue Ruling 72-112, 1972-1 CB 60.

141. *Frederick C. Moser et al.*, T.C. Memo. 1959-25, filed February 11, 1959.

142. *Robert W. Jorg*, 52 T.C. 288 (1969).

143. *Robert W. Jorg*, 52 T.C. 288 (1969).

144. *Blair et al. v. Commissioner*, T.C. Memo. 1981-634, filed October 27, 1981.

145. *Doud et al. v. Commissioner*, T.C. Memo. 1982-158, filed March 29, 1982.

146. *Novick v. Commissioner*, T.C. Memo. 1981-446, filed August 24, 1981.

147. *Warner L. Jones et al.*, 24 T.C. 525 (1955).

148. *Blackshear v. Commissioner*, T.C. Memo. 1977-231, filed July 25, 1977.

149. *Sol Whiteman*, T.C. Memo. 1973-124, filed June 11, 1973.

150. *Harris v. Commissioner*, T.C. Memo. 1978-332, filed August 23, 1978.

151. *Anthony Marcella et al.*, T.C. Memo. 1955-205, filed July 22, 1955.

152. *Pfeiffer Brewing Company*, T.C. Memo., Docket No. 28825, entered June 12, 1952.

153. *David K. Carlisle et al.*, T.C. Memo. 1976-314, filed October 6, 1976.

154. *Wilson v. Commissioner*, T.C. Memo. 1982-107, filed March 4, 1982.

155. *Perry A. Nichols et al.*, 43 T.C. 842 (1965).

156. *Evelyn Nell Norton*, 40 T.C. 500 (1963), aff'd, 333 F.2d 1005 (9th Cir., 1964).

157. *Vesta Peak Maxwell*, BTA Memo., Docket Nos. 86186-7, entered February 7, 1940.

158. *Vincent v. Commissioner*, 218 F.2d 228 (9th Cir., 1955).

159. *Robert S. Gerstell et al.*, 46 T.C. 161 (1966).

160. Revenue Ruling 71-381, 1971-2 CB 126.

161. Revenue Ruling 77-18, 1977-1 CB 46.

162. *Perry A. Nichols et al.*, 43 T.C. 842 (1965).

163. *The Morris Plan Company of St. Joseph*, 42 BTA 1190 (1940).

164. *Russell v. United States*, DC, Ore., 1976.

165. *Paul C. F. Vietzke*, 37 T.C. 504 (1961).

166. *Warner L. Jones et al.*, 24 T.C. 525 (1955).

167. *Curtis H. Muncie*, 18 T.C. 849 (1952).

168. *Frank DeGoff et al.*, T.C. Memo. 1966-89, filed April 28, 1966.

169. *Vesta Peak Maxwell*, BTA Memo., Docket Nos. 86186-7 entered February 7, 1940.

170. *Saul M. Weingarten*, 38 T.C. 75 (1962).

171. *Frank DeGoff et al.*, T.C. Memo. 1966-89, filed April 28, 1966.

172. *Mann et al. v. Commissioner*, T.C. Memo. 1981-684, filed November 25, 1981.

173. *Earle v. Commissioner*, 72 F.2d 366 (2d Cir., 1934).

174. Revenue Ruling 72-112, 1972-1 CB 60.

175. IRS Letter Ruling 7946010, no date given.

176. *American Bemberg Corporation*, 10

T.C. 361 (1948), aff'd, 177 F.2d 200 (6th Cir., 1949).

177. *Otis Beall Kent*, T.C. Memo., Docket No. 37332, entered December 31, 1953.

178. Revenue Ruling 70-90, 1970-1 CB 37.

179. *Carlos W. Munson*, 18 BTA 232 (1929).

180. Revenue Ruling 73-201, 1973-1 CB 140.

181. IRC Section 165(h).

182. Revenue Ruling 58-180, 1958-1 CB 153.

183. *Ben R. Stein et al.*, T.C. Memo. 1972-140, filed June 29, 1972.

184. *Ticket Office Equipment Co., Inc.*, 20 T.C. 272 (1953), aff'd on another issue, 213 F.2d 318 (2d Cir., 1954).

185. *Bailey v. Commissioner*, T.C. Memo. 1980-70, filed May 12, 1980.

186. *Gilbert J. Kraus*, T.C. Memo., Docket No. 22594, entered October 31, 1951.

187. *Tatham et al. v. Commissioner*, T.C. Memo. 1979-205, filed May 22, 1979.

188. *Bowers et al. v. Commissioner*, T.C. Memo. 1981-658, filed November 12, 1981.

189. *Carl A. Hasslacher*, T.C. Memo., Docket No. 21662, entered April 7, 1950.

190. *Zardo et al. v. Commissioner*, T.C. Memo. 1982-94, filed February 23, 1982.

191. *Johnston et al. v. Commissioner*, T.C. Memo. 1980-477, filed October 23, 1980.

192. *C. E. R. Howard et al.*, T.C. Memo. 1969-277, filed December 18, 1969.

193. IRS News Release 1237, July 16, 1972.

194. *Cantrell et al. v. Commissioner*, T.C. Memo. 1978-237, filed June 26, 1978.

195. *Donald H. Kunsman et al.*, 49 T.C. 62 (1967).

196. *Dady et al. v. Commissioner*, T.C. Memo. 1981-440, filed August 19, 1981.

197. *Chichester et al. v. United States*, 185 Ct. Cl. 591 (Ct. Cl., 1968).

198. *Cavell v. Commissioner*, T.C. Memo. 1980-516, filed November 20, 1980.

199. *Taylor et al. v. Commissioner*, T.C. Memo. 1979-261, filed July 11, 1979.

200. *Incopero v. Commissioner*, T.C. Memo. 1979-22, filed January 15, 1979.

201. *Burrell E. Davis et al.*, 34 T.C. 586 (1960).

202. *Charles Gutwirth et al.*, 40 T.C. 666 (1963).

203. *Jacobson et al. v. Commissioner*, 73 T.C. 610 (1979).

204. *Tax Guide for Small Business*, 1978 edition. IRS Publication 334, page 111.

205. *Miller v. Commissioner*, T.C. Memo. 1980-550, filed December 11, 1980.

206. *Hills et al. v. Commissioner*, 76 T.C. 484 (1981).

207. *Waxler Towing Company, Inc. v. United States*, 510 F. Supp. 297 (DC, WD Tenn., 1980).

208. *Miller v. Commissioner*, T.C. Memo. 1981-431, filed August 13, 1981.

209. *Ramos et al. v. Commissioner*, T.C. Memo. 1981-473, filed August 31, 1981.

210. *Popa v. Commissioner*, 73 T.C. 130 (1979).

211. *Kielts et al. v. Commissioner*, T.C. Memo. 1981-329, filed June 24, 1981.

212. *Reno Turf Club, Inc. v. Commissioner*, T.C. Memo. 1979-381, filed September 17, 1979.

213. *Frank Fuchs Estate et al. v. Commissioner*, 413 F.2d 503 (2d Cir., 1969).

214. Revenue Ruling 76-134, 1976-1 CB 54.

215. *Cox et al. v. United States*, 537 F.2d 1066 (9th Cir., 1976).

216. IRC Section 1231.

217. *Katherine Ander*, 47 T.C. 592 (1967).

218. *Louis V. Coughlin et al.*, T.C. Memo. 1973-243, filed October 29, 1973.

219. Revenue Ruling 71-161, 1971-1 CB 76.

220. *Cantrell et al. v. Commissioner*, T.C. Memo. 1978-237, filed June 26, 1978.

221. *Smithgall et al. v. United States*, DC, ND Ga., 1980.

222. *Thomas O. Campbell et al.*, T.C. Memo. 1973-101, filed April 25, 1973.

223. *Black et al. v. Commissioner*, T.C. Memo. 1977-337, filed September 27, 1977.

224. *Daniel B. Kenerly et al.*, T.C. Memo. 1975-139, filed May 12, 1975.

225. *R. R. Hensler, Inc. v. Commissioner*, 73 T.C. 317 (1979).

226. *Ramsay Scarlett & Co., Inc.*, 61 T.C. 795 (1974).

227. *Mann et al. v. Commissioner*, T.C. Memo. 1981-684, filed November 25, 1981.

228. *George Freitas Dairy, Inc. et al. v. United States*, 582 F.2d 500 (9th Cir. 1978).

229. *Berglund et al. v. United States*, DC, Minn., 1981.

230. *Gilman II et al. v. Commissioner*, 72 T.C. 730 (1979).

231. *A. L. Miller*, 29 BTA 1061 (1933).

232. *Frederick Cecil Bartholomew Estate*, 4 T.C. 349 (1944).

233. *Denison et al. v. Commissioner*, T.C. Memo. 1977-430, filed December 22, 1977.

234. Revenue Ruling 77-215, 1977-1 CB 51.

235. IRC Section 44A, as amended by the Economic Recovery Tax Act of 1981, Section 124.

236. *Child Care and Disabled Dependent Care*, IRS Publication 503, 1977 edition.

237. *Brown v. Commissioner*, 73 T.C. 156 (1979).

238. Revenue Act of 1978, Section 121.

239. Economic Recovery Tax Act of 1981, Section 124.

240. *Klutz v. Commissioner*. T.C. Memo. 1979-169, filed April 30, 1979.

241. *LeSage et al.*, T.C. Memo., Docket Nos. 11239 and 11246, entered December 3, 1947, aff'd and rev'd on other issues, 173 F.2d 826 (5th Cir., 1949).

242. *Beltran et al. v. Commissioner*, T.C. Memo. 1982-153, filed March 25, 1982.

243. *Abe Brenner et al.*, T.C. Memo. 1967-239, filed November 28, 1967.

244.   *Helvering v. Hampton,* 79 F.2d 358 (9th Cir., 1935).

245.   Revenue Ruling 56-509, 1956-2 CB 129.

246.   IRC Section 1341.

247.   Revenue Ruling 65-254, 1965-2 CB 50.

248.   *Powell, Jr., et al. v. United States,* 294 F. Supp. 977 (DC, SD, 1969).

249.   *Jerome Mortrud et al.,* 44 T.C. 208 (1965).

250.   Revenue Ruling 55-447, 1955-2 CB 533.

251.   Revenue Ruling 74-395, 1974-2 CB 45.

252.   Revenue Ruling 54-43, 1954-1 CB 119.

253.   *Andover Realty Corporation,* 36 T.C. 671 (1960).

254.   *H. K. Francis et al. v. Commissioner,* T.C. Memo. 1977-170, filed June 2, 1977.

255.   Revenue Ruling 76-453, 1976-2 CB 86.

256.   *Adams et al. v. Commissioner,* T.C. Memo. 1982-223, filed April 26, 1982.

257.   *Lang v. United States,* 134 F. Supp. 214 (DC, ND Ga., 1955).

258.   *Bovington et al. v. United States,* DC, Mont., 1977.

259.   *Kahl et al. v. Commissioner,* T.C. Memo. 1981-222, filed May 4, 1981.

260.   *Curphey v. Commissioner,* 73 T.C. 766 (1980).

261.   IRS Letter Ruling 8121050, February 26, 1981.

262.   *Wisconsin Psychiatric Services, Ltd. et al. v. Commissioner,* 76 T.C., No. 72 (1981).

263.   *Worden et al. v. Commissioner,* T.C. Memo. 1981-366, filed July 15, 1981.

264.   *Howard A. Pool,* T.C. Memo. 1977-20, filed January 31, 1977.

265.   *Your Federal Income Tax,* 1980 edition, page 69.

266.   Revenue Ruling 63-100, 1963-1 CB 34.

267.   *Tyne v. Commissioner,* 385 F.2d 50 (7th Cir., 1972).

268.   Revenue Ruling 75-380, 1975-2 CB 59.

269.   *Grayson et al. v. Commissioner,* T.C. Memo. 1977-304, filed September 7, 1977.

270.   Revenue Ruling 63-100, 1963-1 CB 34.

271.   *Fausner et al. v. Commissioner,* 413 U.S. 838 (1973).

272.   *Frederick et al. v. United States,* 457 F. Supp. 1274 (DC, ND, 1978), aff'd, 8th Cir., 1979.

273.   Revenue Ruling 60-189, 1960-1 CB 60.

274.   *Kasun et al. v. United States,* 510 F. Supp. 228 (DC, ED Wis., 1981).

275.   *Misfeldt v. Kelm,* DC, Minn., 1952.

276.   IRC Section 186.

277.   Regulations Section 1.162-10(a).

278.   *Berkshire Oil Co.,* 9 T.C. 903 (1947).

279.   Revenue Ruling 71-260, 1971-1 CB 57.

280.   Ibid.

281.   *Foos et al. v. Commissioner,* T.C. Memo. 1981-61, filed February 18, 1981.

282.   *Lillian M. Goldsmith,* 7 BTA 151 (1927).

283.   Revenue Ruling 70-253, 1970-1 CB 31.

284.   *J. D. O'Connor et al.,* T.C. Memo. 1954-90, filed June 30, 1954.

285.   *Rockefeller et al. v. Commissioner,* 676 F.2d 35 (2d Cir., 1982).

286.   *Tax Guide for Commercial Fishermen,* IRS Publication 595, 1979 edition, page 14.

287.   *Tax Information on Business Expenses,* IRS Publication 535, 1976 edition, page 5.

288.   *R. J. Nicholl Co.,* 59 T.C. 37 (1972).

289.   *Marvin T. Blackwell et al.,* T.C. Memo. 1956-184, filed August 9, 1956.

290.   *Slaymaker Lock Company,* 18 T.C. 1001 (1952).

291.   *Tax Information on Business Expenses,* IRS Publication 353, 1976 edition, page 5.

292.   *N. Loring Danforth,* 18 BTA 1221 (1930).

293.   *Tax Guide for Small Business,* 1976 edition, page 85.

294.   Ibid., page 79.

295.   Ibid.

296.   *Tax Information on Business Expenses,* IRS Publication 535, 1976 edition, page 7.

297.   Revenue Ruling 71-476, 1971-2 CB 308.

298.   IRC Section 216.

299.   Revenue Ruling 73-15, 1973-1 CB 141.

300.   Regulations Section 1.216-2(a).

301.   Revenue Ruling 66-341, 1966-2 CB 101.

302.   *Tax Information for Homeowners,* IRS Publication 530, 1976 edition, page 8.

303.   Revenue Ruling 64-31, 1964-1 CB (part 1) 300.

304.   *Tax Information for Homeowners,* IRS Publication 530, 1976 edition, page 8.

305.   *Wachter et al. v. United States,* DC, WD Wash., 1974.

306.   *Ong et al. v. Commissioner,* T.C. Memo. 1979-406, filed September 25, 1979.

307.   *Nelson et al. v. Commissioner,* T.C. Memo. 1978-287, filed July 26, 1978.

308.   *Ramos et al. v. Commissioner,* T.C. Memo. 1981-473, filed August 31, 1981.

309.   IRC Section 162(a).

310.   Revenue Ruling 78-373, 1978-2 CB 108.

311.   Revenue Ruling 56-136, 1956-1 CB 92.

312.   IRC Section 189.

313.   *United States Freight Company et al. v. United States,* 422 F.2d 887 (Ct. Cl., 1970).

314.   *Parker et al. v. United States,* 573 F.2d 42 (Ct. Cl., 1978).

315.   *Commissioner v. Bagley & Sewell Co.,* 221 F.2d 944 (2d Cir., 1955).

316.   *Tax Information on Business Expenses,* IRS Publication 535, 1976 edition, page 3.

317.   IRC Section 170(c).

318.   Revenue Ruling 74-224, 1974-1 CB 61.

319.   Revenue Ruling 81-219, IRB 1981-39, 5.

320.   Revenue Ruling 58-190, 1958-1 CB 15.

321.   Revenue Procedure 64-25, 1961-1 CB (Part 1) 694.

322.   *Cooper et al. v. Commissioner,* T.C. Memo. 1978-178, filed May 15, 1978.

323.   IRS Form 5578.

324.   *Hutchinson Baseball Enterprises, Inc. v. Commissioner,* 73 T.C. 144 (1979).

325. *Crosby Valve & Gauge Company v. Commissioner,* 380 F.2d 146 (1st Cir., 1967).

326. Revenue Ruling 80-77, 1980-1 CB 56.

327. *Pearsall et al. v. Commissioner,* T.C. Memo. 1977-230, filed July 25, 1977.

328. IRS Letter Ruling 7816001, August 19, 1977.

329. Revenue Ruling 70-47, 1970-1 CB 49.

330. Regulations Section 1.170A-1(a)(2)(ii) (a)-(f).

331. *Reis et al. v. Commissioner,* T.C. Memo. 1982-213, filed April 21, 1982.

332. IRC Section 170(e)(1)(A).

333. IRC Section 170(e)(1)(B).

334. IRS Letter Ruling 8143029, July 29, 1981.

335. IRC Section 170(e)(1)(B).

336. IRC Section 1011(b).

337. Revenue Ruling 81-163, IRB 1981-24, 5.

338. *United States v. Wolfson,* 573 F.2d 216 (5th Cir., 1978).

339. *Daniel S. McGuire et al.,* 44 T.C. 801 (1965).

340. *Cassidy Company, Inc.,* 11 BTA 190 (1928).

341. *Park Amusement Co.,* 15 BTA 106 (1929).

342. *Determining the Value of Donated Property,* IRS Publication 561 (Rev. Nov. 1980), page 4.

343. Revenue Ruling 70-15, 1970-1 CB 20.

344. Revenue Ruling 68-113, 1968-1 CB 80.

345. *M. C. Adler,* 5 BTA 1063 (1926).

346. Revenue Ruling 69-79, 1969-1 CB 63.

347. *Summary of Miscellaneous Tax Bills Passed by the Congress in the Post-Election Session.* Prepared by the Staff of the Joint Committee on Taxation, December 23, 1980, page 16.

348. Revenue Ruling 64-205, 1964-2 CB 62.

349. IRC Section 170.

350. Revenue Ruling 73-339, 1973-2 CB 68.

351. Revenue Ruling 74-583, 1974-2 CB 80.

352. Revenue Ruling 67-363, 1967-2 CB 118.

353. IRC Section 170(f)(3).

354. *Summary of Miscellaneous Tax Bills Passed by the Congress in the Post-Election Session.* Prepared by the Staff of the Joint Committee on Taxation, December 23, 1980, page 16.

355. *Income Tax Deduction for Contributions,* IRS Publication 526, 1976 edition, page 7.

356. Public Law 96-541, Section 6, approved December 17, 1980.

357. *Lawrence et al. v. United States,* DC, CD Cal., 1974.

358. Revenue Ruling 75-66, 1975-1 CB 85.

359. *Chipman, Jr., et al. v. Commissioner,* T.C. Memo. 1981-794, filed April 22, 1981.

360. IRC Section 170(b).

361. *Church, Jr., v. Commissioner,* T.C. Memo. 1978-252, filed July 10, 1978.

362. *Bodine v. Commissioner,* T.C. Memo. 1978-340, filed August 29, 1978.

363. *Carpenter et al. v. Commissioner,* T.C. Memo. 1981-551, filed September 28, 1981.

364. *Harold DeJong,* 36 T.C. 896 (1961), *aff'd,* 309 F.2d 373 (9th Cir., 1962).

365. *Ben I. Seldin et al.,* T.C. Memo. 1969-233, filed November 3, 1969.

366. *The Singer Company v. United States,* 449 F.2d 413 (Ct. Cl., 1971).

367. Revenue Ruling 68-432, 1968-2 CB 104.

368. *The Citizens & Southern National Bank of South Carolina v. United States,* 243 F. Supp. 900 (DC, WD SC, 1965).

369. Revenue Ruling 69-90, 1969-1 CB 63.

370. Revenue Ruling 67-446, 1967-2 CB 119.

371. *Myers et al. v. United States,* DC, ND Ala., 1980.

372. Revenue Ruling 79-323, 1979-2 CB 106.

373. Revenue Ruling 54-532, 1954-2 CB 93.

374. *Wegner et al. v. Lethert,* 375 F.2d 351 (DC, Minn., 1967).

375. *O. J. Wardwell Estate v. Commissioner,* 301 F.2d 632 (8th Cir., 1962).

376. *Income Tax Deduction for Contributions,* IRS Publication 526, 1976 edition, page 1.

377. *DeWitt et al. v. United States,* 503 F.2d 1406 (Ct. Cl., 1974).

378. IRC Section 162(b).

379. Revenue Ruling 73-113, 1973-1 CB 65.

380. *Smith et al. v. Commissioner,* T.C. Memo. 1980-523, filed November 25, 1980.

381. *Old Mission Portland Cement Company v. Commissioner,* 69 F.2d 676 (9th Cir., 1934).

382. *Marcell v. United States,* DC, Vt., 1961.

383. *Sarah Marquis,* 49 T.C. 695 (1968).

384. Revenue Ruling 63-73, 1963-1 CB 35.

385. Revenue Ruling 72-314, 1972-1 CB 44.

386. Revenue Ruling 68-2, 1968-1 CB 61.

387. Revenue Ruling 76-232, 1976-1 CB 62.

388. *Sugarland Industries,* 15 BTA 1265 (1929).

389. *Corning Glass Works v. Commissioner,* 37 F.2d 798 (CA, DC, 1929).

390. *DeWitt et al. v. United States,* 503 F.2d 1406 (1974).

391. *Rainier Companies, Inc., et al. v. Commissioner,* T.C. Memo. 1977-351, filed October 3, 1977.

392. Revenue Ruling 58-265, 1958-1 CB 127.

393. *Commissioner v. The Hub, Incorporated,* 68 F.2d 349 (4th Cir., 1934).

394. IRC Section 368(a)(1)(E).

395. Revenue Ruling 69-275, 1969-1 CB 36.

396. Revenue Ruling 70-161, 1970-1 CB 15.

397. IRS Letter Ruling 8105008, September 29, 1980.

398. Revenue Ruling 55-4, 1955-1 CB 291.

399. *Rockefeller et al. v. Commissioner,* 76 T.C. 178 (1981), *aff'd,* 676 F.2d 35 (2d Cir., 1982).

400. *Income Tax Deduction for Contributions,* IRS Publication 526, 1976 edition, page 2.

401. *Protecting Older Americans Against Overpayment of Income Taxes,* Special Committee on Aging, United States Senate, 1976, page 3.

402. *McCollum et al. v. Commissioner,* T.C. Memo. 1978-435, filed November 1, 1978.

403. *Robert H. Orchard et al.*, T.C. Memo. 1975-31, filed February 24, 1975.

404. *Maniscalco v. Commissioner*, 632 F.2d 6 (6th Cir., 1980).

405. *Wilhelm et al. v. Commissioner*, T.C. Memo. 1978-327, filed August 17, 1978.

406. Revenue Ruling 56-508, 1956-2 CB 126.

407. Revenue Ruling 58-279, 1958-1 CB 145.

408. Revenue Ruling 59-160, 1959-1 CB 59.

409. Revenue Ruling 56-508, 1956-2 CB 126.

410. *Hahn et al. v. Commissioner*, T.C. Memo. 1979-429, filed October 15, 1979.

411. *Travis Smith et al.*, 60 T.C. 988 (1973).

412. Revenue Ruling 67-362, 1967-2 CB 117.

413. Revenue Ruling 65-285, 1965-2 CB 56.

414. Revenue Ruling 80-45, 1980-1 CB 54.

415. Revenue Ruling 56-509, 1956-2 CB 129.

416. Revenue Ruling 69-473, 1969-2 CB 37.

417. Revenue Ruling 77-280, 1977-2 CB 14.

418. Revenue Procedure 70-26, 1970-2 CB, 507, as amended by Revenue Procedure 80-32, IRB 1980-29, 27.

419. *Determining the Value of Donated Property*, IRS Publication 561 (Rev. Nov. 1980), page 11.

420. Revenue Ruling 70-519, 1970-2 CB 62.

421. IRS Letter Ruling 7726018, May 29, 1977.

422. *Archbold v. United States*, 449 F.2d 1120 (Ct. Cl., 1971).

423. *Hubert Rutland et al.*, T.C. Memo. 1977-8, filed January 17, 1977.

424. *Income Tax Deduction for Contributions*, IRS Publication 526, 1976 edition, page 4.

425. Revenue Ruling 70-15, 1970-1 CB 20.

426. Revenue Ruling 67-461, 1967-2 CB 125.

427. IRC Section 170(h).

428. *Smith et al. v. Commissioner*, T.C. Memo. 1981-371, filed July 20, 1981.

429. Revenue Ruling 66-10, 1966-1 CB 47.

430. Revenue Ruling 70-519, 1970-2 CB 62.

431. IRS Letter Ruling 8121070, February 27, 1981.

432. *Bauer et al. v. United States*, 449 F. Supp. 755 (DC, WD La., 1978).

433. *Thomas E. Lesslie et al.*, T.C. Memo. 1977-111, filed April 14, 1977.

434. *Miscellaneous Deductions and Credits*, IRS Publication 529, 1976 edition, page 4.

435. IRC Section 170(d).

436. *William V. Moylan et al.*, T.C. Memo. 1968-15, filed January 22, 1968.

437. *Proctor et al. v. Commissioner*, T.C. Memo. 1981-436, filed August 17, 1981.

438. Revenue Ruling 76-267, 1976-2 CB 71.

439. Revenue Act of 1978, Section 113.

440. IRC Section 6096.

441. Economic Recovery Tax Act of 1981, Section 126.

442. *Musser v. United States*, DC, ND Cal., 1957.

443. *Robert C. Coffey*, 21 BTA 1242 (1930).

444. *Charles O. Gunther, Jr., et al.*, T.C. Memo. 1954-181, filed October 21, 1954.

445. *Marion D. Shutter*, 2 BTA 23 (1925).

446. *L. F. Ratterman et al.*, T.C. Memo., Docket Nos. 11319, 11913, and 12080, entered July 6, 1948, *aff'd*, 177 F.2d 204 (6th Cir., 1949).

447. *Ellis v. Burnet*, 50 F.2d 343 (CA, DC, 1931).

448. *Rita M. Callinan*, T.C. Memo., Docket No. 38626, entered February 19, 1953.

449. *Alexander Silverman*, 6 BTA 1328 (1927).

450. *Jay N. Darling*, 4 BTA 499 (1926).

451. *J. Gordon Gaines, Inc.*, T.C. Memo., Docket Nos. 24662 and 29056, entered March 2, 1951.

452. Revenue Ruling 63-266, 1963-2 CB 88.

453. *Bank of Stockton*, T.C. Memo. 1977-24, filed January 31, 1977.

454. IRC Section 274(h).

455. IRS News Release IR-81-10, January 22, 1981.

456. Revenue Ruling 65-313, 1965-2 CB 47.

457. *Medical and Dental Expense*, IRS Publication 502 (Rev. Nov. 1979), page 2.

458. *Miscellaneous Deductions*, IRS Publication 529 (Rev. Nov. 1979), page 3.

459. *Chas. Hutchison*, 13 BTA 1187 (1928).

460. *Elliott v. United States*, 250 F. Supp. 322 (DC, WD N.Y., 1965).

461. Regulations Section 1.167(a)-2.

462. *George Loinaz et al.*, T.C. Memo. 1975-17, filed January 28, 1975.

463. IRC Section 274(a)(2), as amended by Revenue Act of 1978, Section 361.

464. Revenue Ruling 78-38, 1978-1 CB 67.

465. Revenue Ruling 78-39, 1978-1 CB 73.

466. Revenue Ruling 70-254, 1970-1 CB 31.

467. *Charleston National Bank*, 20 T.C. 253 (1953), *aff'd*, 213 F.2d 45 (4th Cir., 1954).

468. Revenue Ruling 56-359, 1956-2 CB 115.

469. Revenue Ruling 55-23, 1955-1 CB 275.

470. *Fred W. Staudt*, T.C. Memo., Docket No. 32244, entered December 17, 1953.

D

Day-care center, financing of. A manufacturer entered into an agreement with an established day-care center to provide child care for the preschool children of employees. The stated purposes of the taxpayer in providing for the availability of the day-care center were (1) to provide employees with a place to send their children during working hours, knowing that the children would receive proper care, (2) to reduce absenteeism and to increase productivity, and (3) to reduce employee turnover. The amounts paid by the manufacturer to the day-care center were directly related to his business and hence were deductible business expenses.[1]

Deaf persons, expenses of. Less well known than the Seeing Eye dog is the Hearing Ear dog. Amounts paid for the acquisition, training, and maintenance of a Hearing Ear dog for the purpose of assisting a taxpayer or his dependent who is deaf are deductible. A taxpayer's daughter had a severe congenital hearing loss. In order to alleviate, in part, the effect of his daughter's defect in hearing, he purchased a dog and paid to have it trained by a professional trainer to alert her to dangerous conditions.[2]

A medical expense deduction also was allowed for the cost of maintaining a cat in one's home. An individual with a severe hearing impairment obtained peace of mind by being alerted by a cat which had been trained to respond to unusual sounds in an instantaneous and directional manner. The tabby had been registered with the county animal-control division as a hearing-aid animal.[3] There may be wide applications of this ruling on helpful animals. In about 390 B.C., Rome would have been overcome by Gauls in a sneak attack during the night had not the sacred geese of the Temple of Juno cackled an alarm.

Medical care for a deaf student can include such expenses as payments to a notetaker. The taxpayer for whom the deaf student is a dependent is allowed the deduction.[4]

When such specialized equipment[5] is used primarily to help a taxpayer's condition or that of his spouse or dependents, any amounts spent by him to repair the equipment may also be deducted as medical expenses.[6]

Special equipment is available which displays the audio portion of television programs as subtitles on the screen of a TV set, so that programs can be understood by the deaf. Both the cost of a self-contained unit that can be attached to any conventional television set and the excess cost of a specially equipped color TV set over the price of the same model conventional color television set are expenses for medical care.[7]

The cost of instruction in lip reading is deductible.[8] Deduction was allowed for expenses of a school for the teaching of lip reading.[9] Deduction also is allowed for expenses to qualify an individual for future normal education or for normal living.[10]

Medical insurance includes health and accident insurance. A father had a deaf child who had learned lip reading. But if anything was now to happen to his sight . . . The father took out an insurance policy covering the total permanent loss of sight in the child's right eye. Premiums were deductible as medical expense.[11] *See also* **Medical expenses.** (For a study of this problem, see Alan Ander, "Tax Law Benefits and Problems for the Deaf," a thesis presented to the Graduate School of Business Administration, New York University, 1977.

Dealers in securities, stock transfer taxes of. *See* **Taxes.**

Debtor insurance. A creditor was permitted to deduct premiums on insurance on the life of a defaulting debtor where a policy on the latter's life had been assigned to the creditor as collateral.[12] *See also* **Creditor insurance policy, premiums on; Insurance.**

Debts. *See* **Bad debts.**

Decedent, medical care of. *See* **Medical expenses.**

Deceit, loss because of. *See* **Casualties.**

Defense of title. *See* **Legal fees.**

Deferred payment plan charges. Such charges on the purchase of a refrigerator were held to be deductible.[13] *See also* **Interest.**

Delinquent insurance premiums. When a cash-basis taxpayer was obliged to pay premiums on a fidelity bond in order to maintain his employment, the fact that one particular payment actually was for an earlier taxable year did not disqualify the deduction.[14]

Delinquent payments. *See* **Interest.**

Demolition. If land and buildings are acquired for business purposes, and subsequently the building is torn down, tax treatment depends upon the buyer's intention when he acquired the property. If he intended to use the building, and the decision to demolish is made *subsequent* to the acquisition, the cost of the building as well as the demolition expense may be deducted.[15] Such was the case in which the buyer had every intention of using the building he had acquired, but at a later date it was determined that necessary reconstruction work to allow the building to be used was economically unfeasible.[16] Demolition deduction was permitted where it was decided after the acquisition that the building could not be used because of the hidden defects which had been discovered, specifically, rotten beams.[17]

Deduction was allowed for the cost of razing what remained of a building acquired for rental purposes, after a fire had substantially wrecked the structure. The edifice had not been purchased with the intent of tearing it down and replacing it with a new building, though that was what actually happened as the result of severe fire damage.[18]

In another case, a demolition loss was deductible when a year after land and building had been purchased, the building had to be torn down as a result of unexpected action by the city in widening a street.[19]

The fact that demolition occurred pursuant to a plan formed subsequent to the acquisition of property, thus permitting deduction, may be suggested by: (1) substantial improvement of the buildings immediately after the acquisition, (2) prolonged use of the buildings for business purposes after their acquisition, (3) suitability of the buildings for investment purposes at the time of acquisition, (4) substantial change in economic or business conditions after the date of acquisition, (5) loss of useful value occurring after the date of acquisition, (6) substantial damage to the buildings occurring after their acquisition, (7) discovery of latent structural defects in the buildings after their acquisition, (8) decline in the taxpayer's business after the date of acquisition, (9) condemnation of the property by municipal authorities after the date of acquisition, or (10) inability after acquisition to obtain building material necessary for the improvement of the property.[20]

The operator of a service business believed that there were growth possibilities in a nearby community, and he purchased land and a building there in order to rent the property to tenants. A month later, he learned that one of his competitors was going to establish a branch in the new community. So the property owner concluded that to retain his business in that area, he would have to open a branch there. Inasmuch as realtors he engaged were unable to find property available for this use, he decided to tear down the building he had acquired for rental purposes, and he bought back the tenants' leases. He could deduct his demolition loss, as changed conditions and circumstances had led him to abandon his recently formed intention of using the structure for rental purposes.[21]

Where at the time of purchase the buyer had intended to abandon some of the properties at a later date, part of the purchase price could be allocated to the assets which would be abandoned at a later date. These assets certainly had some value to the purchaser when acquired. At the subsequent time when the assets were in fact abandoned, deduction was allowable for the allocated part of the original purchase price.[22]

If a lessee has the right to tear down buildings which are on the property in order to erect his own, the landlord is entitled to a demolition-loss deduction.[23]

The owner of an old business building in a deteriorating neighborhood has a tax dilemma. If a potential tenant does not want a structure in run-down condition on the land he is going to use, and the owner is required by the terms of the lease to tear the edifice down, no demolition loss is deductible. But if the owner has the structure razed for his own business reasons before he even has a tenant, the tax cost of the building is deductible. Such deduction was allowed in the case of a structure in a badly deteriorated neighborhood where continuance of insurance coverage was doubtful because of vandalism, arson, and accidents to passersby by reason of the dilapidated nature of the building. No agreement to lease the structure had been made before fear of accidents led to the decision to demolish.[24]

An automobile distributor erected a building to the specifications of Ford Motor Company. About fifteen years later, Ford insisted that the distributor would have to move to a new location with greatly enlarged facilities in order to retain the franchise. This was done. As the old building was of such a specialized nature that no one wanted it, it was torn down by the distributor at his own expense, for a new tenant required that the land be made available free of any structures. Demolition loss was deductible, as the old building had been constructed for a specific purpose that had to be abandoned by the owner because of an economic event not of his own making. The building became as worthless as if it had been destroyed by fire or other casualty.[25]

The demolition deduction is available even where only part of a building is torn down.[26]

The same principle applies where land is purchased with the intention of destroying what is on it. For example, there are fruit trees on land to be used for real-estate investment. Deduction of the value of the trees is permitted if there was no intent to destroy the trees prior to purchase.[27]

Demotion. Expenditures to protect one's position are deductible.[28]

Dental expenses. *See* **Medical expenses.**

Dentists, professional expenses of. A dentist engaged in general practice returned to dental school for postgraduate study in orthodontics, which deals with treatment of abnormalities or irregularities of the teeth. He attended the school on a full-time basis, continuing his dental practice on a part-time basis. Upon completion of his postgraduate training he became an orthodontist and limited his practice to orthodontic patients. He could deduct his expenses for postgraduate study, as they had not been incurred in connection with qualifying him for a new trade or business but were in connection with improving his skills as a dentist.[29] *See also* **Advanced degree, study for; Education; License maintenance; Professional instruments and equipment; Professional negligence.**

Department-store service charge. A customer may deduct as interest a service charge of a specified percentage of his unpaid balance after a twenty-day payment period.[30] *See also* **Interest.**

Dependent care expenses. *See* **Child-care and disabled-dependent care.**

Dependents. *See* **Family transactions; Medical expenses.**

Depletion. The owner of an economic interest in mines, oil and gas wells, other natural deposits, and timber is allowed a deduction for a reasonable amount of depletion.[31]

The annual depletion allowance is permitted where (1) the taxpayer has an investment in mineral in place or standing timber and (2) he may look only to income derived from the extraction of the mineral or severance of the timber for a return of his capital.[32]

Cost depletion is computed by dividing the total number of recoverable units (tons, barrels, etc., determined in accordance with prevailing industry methods) in the deposit into the adjusted basis of the mineral deposit and multiplying the resulting rate per unit (1) by the number of units for which payment is received during the taxable year of the taxpayer if the cash method is used or (2) by the number of units sold if he uses the accrual method.[33] (The adjusted basis of the mineral deposit is the original cost less depletion allowed. The adjusted basis cannot be less than zero.)

A taxpayer may deduct under the percentage-depletion method a stipulated percentage of his gross income from the property during the taxable year. But the deduction for depletion under this method cannot exceed 50 percent of his taxable income from the property, computed without the deduction for depletion.[34] The stipulated percentage for oil and gas wells, for example, was set at 22 percent by the Tax Reform Act of 1960.[35]

Even if a person has recovered his cost or other basis of property, he may take a deduction for percentage depletion.[36] This is because the percentage depletion allowance is up to 50 percent of a taxpayer's taxable income from the property, computed without allowance for depletion.[37]

Effective January 1, 1975, the 22 percent depletion allowance for oil and gas wells was terminated, except in the case of (1) regulated natural gas, (2) natural gas sold under a fixed contract, (3) certain geothermal deposits, and (4) independent producers and royalty owners. In the case of (4), the rate has dropped each year, reaching 15 percent in 1984, and depends upon a production schedule contained in the Tax Reduction Act of 1975.[38]

Deposit, forfeiture of. *See* **Cancellation and forfeiture.**

Depreciation. The cost of business assets with an estimated useful life of more than one year cannot be deducted as an expense. But if the useful life can be estimated with reasonable accuracy, these costs in many instances can be amortized with a tax deduction in each year of estimated useful life. That is, gradual using up of the asset used for business purposes is written off. The most common form of this is depreciation.

Depreciation is deductible only in the case of property used in the trade or business or held for the production of income.[39]

Where a person has an office in his home or otherwise uses his residence partially for business purposes, depreciation is taken only on the portion he uses for business purposes. Apportionment may be on a space basis, such as the number of rooms used for business purposes and for personal purposes.[40]

Where property had been held for the production of income during a taxable year, depreciation was allowed even though, in fact, the property produced no income.[41] Depreciation can be taken on the Federal income tax return for such items as a radio, a cocktail table, a grandfather clock, and a painting if the items are used in the taxpayer's trade or business.[42]

A lawyer who was working on a photographic book that he intended to publish and sell could deduct depreciation on his photographic equipment even though the book was not yet ready for publication.[43]

Works of art are not subject to depreciation. But paintings which are placed in a business office as decoration and not as works of art may be eligible for depreciation deductions.[44]

Depreciation is allowed for business equipment which was placed on a customer's premises, although placing the equipment there was contrary to state law.[45]

A concert harpist could deduct depreciation on her musical instrument.[46]

Costumes used exclusively in a business, such as theatrical clothing, may be depreciable.[47]

A teacher was allowed to take depreciation on the cost of books used in his trade or business of being a teacher.[48]

Depreciation may be taken on a professional library, as by a physician.[49]

A veterinarian was allowed to take depreciation on names and addresses of pet owners and medical histories of the animals.[50]

A retiring obstetrician sold the personal property used in his practice to another gynecologist. The former's patient charts and medical histories also were sold. The charts were of no value in inducing patients to come to the purchaser but saved him much time in compiling data for use in his practice. The purchaser could take depreciation on the cost of the charts over a six-year period. Women usually had babies in a relatively short time period, and if they did not return within five years, it was unlikely they would do so. In addition, former patients might move away or change doctors.[51]

Depreciation is allowed on animals such as horses and dogs that are used for advertising purposes.[52]

Land is not depreciable but airspace is. Builders, excavators, and truckers are often faced with disposal dirt, debris, and other materials which they remove. One solution is to purchase property for use as a landfill. In time, the usefulness of this land for further dumping will come to an end, as there will be no room for additional waste materials. Consequently, the airspace exhausted in the operation of the site is subject to annual depreciation deductions. Cost of the property may be divided by the total number of cubic yards of capacity. This unit cost, multiplied by the number of units dumped each year, is the depreciation deduction.[53]

The depreciation deduction is allowed as medical expense in the case of equipment used primarily for the alleviation of sickness or disability, such as a car fitted with handicap controls for a war-disabled veteran. Here there was no possibility of salvage value.[54]

Depreciation is allowed on assets used in a taxpayer's trade or business, even for that portion of the year when the property cannot be used because of slack business conditions.[55]

Only a taxpayer who has a depreciable interest in property may take the deduction.[56] But the depreciable property may be upon another party's land. A manufacturer of military aircraft erected barricades on each end of a runway on land owned by a municipality. This was done in view of safety requirements in landing aircraft, in order to catch aircraft using the maximum roll-out afforded by the runway. The manufacturer was permitted to take depreciation on the barricades.[57]

Where property was acquired and held for business purposes, depreciation could be taken even during periods when the property was leased to charitable organizations for nominal amounts. The owner continued to hold the property for business purposes and hoped to be able to sell it to one of these charitable organizations.[58]

Where depreciable business property is held by an estate or a trust, a life tenant is entitled to a depreciation deduction. Income beneficiaries of property held in trust, or heirs, legatees, or devisees of an estate, may deduct allowable depreciation not deductible by the estate or trust.[59]

A deduction for a portion of the depreciation is allowable where property is used partially for business and partially for personal purposes.[60] The amount of the allocation is to be proved by the taxpayer.

For property placed in service in taxable years before 1981, depreciation could be taken in any one of a variety of ways. These choices are still in effect until the cost of business assets placed in service prior to 1981 is recovered through depreciation deductions.[61]

The annual depreciation deduction must be in accordance with a reasonably consistent plan, but it is not necessarily at a uniform rate.[62] Even straight-line depreciation, which customarily is thought of as being a consistent figure year after year regardless of actual usage of the asset, may vary markedly. Depreciation of this type may be taken at a faster rate than previously if it can be proved that during a taxable year the assets were subjected to faster wear and tear than had been contemplated when the rates were set. In the case of road-building equipment, for example, accelerated straight-line depreciation was recognized where the contractor worked the equipment for an excessive number of hours a day, where the equipment was subjected to abnormal weather conditions such as salt water or flooding, and where untrained operators worked with the equipment and subjected it to grueling stresses.[63] Abuse of equipment justified more rapid depreciation even under the straight-line method.[64]

The depreciation deduction is taken in the taxable year in which the property is placed in a condition or state of readiness and availability for a specifically assigned function.[65]

Depreciation on a barge commenced when it was ready for use, even though the barge could not be put into operation at that time because it was frozen into a canal.[66]

The period of deduction begins when the asset is ready for use, despite the fact that weather conditions prevent the start of operations for several months.[67]

Depreciation on a crane commenced in the taxable year when it would have been put into operation except that a utility company was unable to supply energy at that time because of litigation about whether power lines could be erected across a certain highway.[68]

Any reasonable and consistently applied method of computing depreciation may be used, but deductions cannot exceed the amounts necessary to recover the cost or other basis during the remaining useful life of the property.[69] But so-called accelerated depreciation, such as the double-declining-balance method or the sum-of-the-years'-digits method, may be used only in the case of (1) tangible property having a useful life of three years or more where (2) the original use of the property commenced with the taxpayer.[70] (If either of these methods of depreciation is unfamiliar to you, ask your accountant for an explanation.)

In addition to the depreciation methods mentioned previously, any other method may be used, provided depreciation allowances computed in accordance with such method do not result in accumulated allowances at the end of any taxable year greater than the total of the accumulated allowances which would have resulted from the use of the double-declining method. This limitation applies only during the first two-thirds of the useful life of the property.[71]

For example, there is the operating-day method. Life of an asset, such as a rotary oil-drilling rig, is estimated in terms of the total number of days it can be operated, and the depreciable basis is prorated according to the actual number of days the asset is used.[72]

One of the major depreciation deduction problems is estimating the useful life of an asset, so that annual deductions can be computed. One recent technique for coping with this was the Asset Depreciation Range (ADR) system.[73] For taxable years beginning after December 31, 1970, taxpayers were allowed to elect to use ADR to compute the reasonable depreciation allowance for all eligible property placed in service during a taxable year. Eligible property was tangible personal and real property placed in service by the taxpayer after 1970 for which there was in effect an asset guideline class and an asset guideline period. An election could be made for each year on Form 4832 for assets acquired during that year which, at the taxpayer's choice, might be anywhere in the range of 20 percent above or below the guidelines figures. If a taxpayer adopted the *modified half-year convention,* all property placed in service during the first half of a taxable year was considered as placed in service on the first day of that year; all property placed in service during the second half of the taxable year was considered as placed in service on the first day of the second half of the taxable year. If he adopted the *half-year convention,* all property placed in service during the taxable year was treated as if it had been placed in service on the first day of the second half of the taxable year. Special provisions were made for allowances for salvage and for repairs.[74]

Depreciation deductions could be taken without reference to the physical life of the property. Deductions could be taken over the remaining economic life of the property if shorter than the physical life.[75]

Deduction is allowed for expenditures necessary to maintain a mine's normal output made necessary by the recession of the working face, so long as these expenditures (1) do not increase the value of the mine, (2) decrease the cost of production of mineral units, or (3) represent an amount expended in restoring property or in making good the exhaustion thereof for which an allowance is or has been made.[76] Where coal was mined, the mine's face obviously must have been receding. So additional conveyor equipment was needed simply to maintain production and its cost was deductible.[77]

Under ADR, the Treasury Department specified average rates for equipment used in most industries. *The ADR system of apportioning depreciation over the useful life of property was terminated for recovery property placed in service after December 31, 1980.*[78]

Recovery property is tangible depreciable property used in a trade or business or held for the production of income.

The Accelerated Cost Recovery System (ACRS) has taken the place of ADR. Here the cost of an asset is written off ("recovered") over a predetermined period which is shorter than under ADR. It is used for both new and used equipment and takes no account of estimated salvage values. The depreciation deduction is determined by applying the appropriate percentage for each class of property to its cost (unadjusted basis).

Most tangible depreciable business property (real and personal) is covered by ACRS. Exceptions: (1) property which is not depreciable in terms of years, such as under the unit of production method; (2) property amortized over a specified period, such as leasehold improvements which are written off over the life of the lease; (3) property acquired after December 31, 1980, in a transaction with stipulated related parties or in certain tax-free reorganizations or exchanges.

Under ACRS, eligible personal property and certain real property is depreciated over three, five, ten, or fifteen years.

> Three-year recovery property: automobiles, light-duty trucks, research and development equipment, and personal property with a midpoint life of four years or less.
> Five-year recovery property: most other equipment except long-lived public utility property and certain single-purpose agricultural structures and petroleum storage facilities.
> Ten-year recovery property: residential and manufactured homes and certain public utility property which under ADR had a life of more than eighteen but less than twenty-five years.
> Fifteen-year recovery property: public utility property with ADR life exceeding twenty-five years.

A taxpayer may elect to use a longer recovery period under certain circumstances.

A taxpayer electing to use an optional recovery method must elect the same recovery for all property placed in service for the year the election is made. This election applies to all property in that class and other classes and is irrevocable.[79]

Although the use of the Accelerated Cost Recovery System is mandatory, a taxpayer may elect to exclude an automobile used for business, charitable, medical, or moving purposes if he uses the standard mileage allowance.[80]

Note: this is merely a summarized overview of the newer depreciation provisions. It is suggested that if they apply to your tax return, you discuss them with your accountant.

Election may be made to deduct rather than to capitalize the cost of personal property for use in a trade or business but not property held merely for the production of income. Property does not qualify for this deduction if acquired from a related party or in an exchange. The amount of the deduction is limited.

If the taxable year begins in:	The deductible amount is:
1982	$5,000
1983	5,000
1984	7,500
1985	7,500
1986 and thereafter	10,000[81]

Special depreciation rules have been provided for expenditures to rehabilitate low-income rental housing under specified conditions. Here, the expenditures may be computed under a straight-line method over a period of sixty months, if the additions or improvements have a useful life of five years or more. The Revenue Act of 1978 provided a three-year extension of this rule in the case of expenditures paid or incurred with respect to low- and moderate-income rental housing after December 31, 1978, and before January 1, 1984 (including expenditures made pursuant to a binding contract entered into before January 1, 1984.)[82]

Depreciation may be taken on intangible property with a limited useful life.[83] Patents and sales franchises for a specified number of years are examples.

Depreciation on intangible assets, commonly referred to as amortization, is deductible over the remaining life of the asset. But the annual write-off for tax purposes of a franchise could be based upon the actuarial life expectancy of the owner of a business rather than upon the franchise itself as stated in the contract where the franchise could be cancelled by the franchisor if the holder of the franchise died. Such was the case where General Motors Corporation was permitted to cancel a Pontiac agency franchise in the event of the owner's death.[84]

Normal obsolescence is included in the depreciation allowance; that is, there is a general assumption that in time depreciable property is likely to be supplanted by something better even though there is a remaining useful life. *Abnormal* obsolescence, a write-off necessitated by some specific fact or action, can be a separate deduction. *See also* **Obsolescence; Office at home.**

Detectives. *See* **Bodyguard; Casualties; Private investigators; Protection.**

Development. *See* **Research and experimental expenses.**

Development expenses of farmers. *See* **Farmers.**

Diet, expense of. *See* **Medical expenses; Weight-loss program.**

Directors. A director is an individual, in the words of one decision, who "when acting as a director and officer of The . . . Company was engaged in carrying on a trade or business. . . ."[85] Therefore any business related to his acts as a director is a business expense.

Bankruptcy trustees of a corporation brought suit against the directors for having declared dividends at a time they knew the corporation was bankrupt. A director who made a compromise settlement payment to the trustees, with approval of the bankruptcy court, could deduct this payment as one arising from his business activity.[86]

To effect a compromise settlement of a threatened suit against him for mismanagement of a corporation of which he was president and a director, an individual paid to a holder of that company's preferred stock a certain sum. The payor could deduct this as a business expense.[87]

A building and loan association became insolvent as the result of embezzlement by an employee. Believing the directors to be negligent in not discovering the embezzlement sooner, management requested the directors to assign certain amounts to the corporation and threatened to sue directors who failed to do so. A director who was not repaid the amount he had advanced could deduct this as an expense in connection with being a paid director.[88] *See also* **Accounting expenses; Breach of trust; Executives; Fiduciary responsibility, defense of; Legal fees; Reputation, maintenance of; Stockholders' suit, defense of.**

Disability insurance payments. *See* **State disability insurance.**

Disabled-dependent care. *See* **Child-care and disabled-dependent care.**

Disallowance of deductions in transaction with related parties. *See* **Family transactions.**

Disaster area. *See* **Casualties.**

Disaster losses. If a casualty is sustained in what the President of the United States subsequently proclaims to be a disaster area, the loss may be deducted in the taxable year immediately preceding the year in which the casualty is sustained rather than in the year of the happening. This choice is optional. The election is available whenever a deductible disaster loss is incurred, whether or not that loss technically is a "casualty loss" as narrowly defined in the tax law. This choice as to year of tax deduction now is available for *any* kind of loss, even if not casualty-related. Now included are such items as obsolescence, worthless stock or securities, losses from sale or exchange of capital assets, loss on stock of affiliated companies, provided the property is used in a trade or business or in a profit-seeking transaction. Individuals, however, may deduct losses to personal property only if the loss arises from a fire, storm, shipwreck, or other such casualty, or from theft.[89] The election to deduct for the preceding year must be made on or before whichever is later: (1) the original due date of the taxpayer's income tax return for the year in which the disaster occurred or (2) the due date of the preceding year's tax return (taking into account any extensions of time for filing which had been granted).[90]

Disbarment, expenses to resist. An attorney could deduct his legal fees for defending himself in disbarment proceedings.[91]

Disbarment proceedings, defense in. *See* **Legal fees.**

Discount. Where a business note was discounted at a bank, the amount received which was less than face value was deductible as interest.[92]

The excess between the amount of a loan and what the borrower receives is deductible as interest.[93]

Dismissal pay. A businessperson can deduct severance pay which he gives, whether in the form of cash or property.[94] *See also* **Compensation.**

Disposable diapers. *See* **Medical expenses.**

Dissenting stockholder, expenses of. *See* **Legal fees.**

Divorce settlements. *See* **Alimony.**

Doctoral dissertation. A teacher was permitted to deduct the cost of obtaining his Doctor of Philosophy degree as a business expense. In consequence, he also was able to deduct the cost of having his dissertation typed.[95]

Doctors' fees. *See* **Medical expenses.**

Doctors' fees assigned to hospital. Where a staff physician at a hospital is entitled to health insurance payments made on behalf of patients who have such coverage, he is taxed upon the fees. But he is entitled to a charitable deduction if he assigns the fees to the hospital.[96] The same treatment is applied to Medicare reimbursements.[97]

Doctors, professional expenses of. *See* **Advertising; Automobile, use of; Commuting; Conventions; Depreciation; Dues, professional societies; Education; Entertainment; Expenditures for benefits lasting more than one year; Hobby losses; Hospital staff fees; House calls; Insurance; Legal fees; Malpractice insurance; Office at home; Ordinary and necessary business expenses; Professional instruments and equipment; Professional negligence; Settlement payments; Subscriptions to periodicals; Telephone; Travel; Work clothes.**

Dogs. *See* **Advertising; Blind persons, expenses of; Deaf persons, expenses of; Entertainment; Medical expenses; Transactions entered into for profit.**

Donations. *See* **Contributions.**

Donee, expenses of. *See* **Legal fees.**

Down payments, forfeiture of. *See* **Cancellation and forfeiture.**

Dredging expenses. *See* **Repairs.**

Dress clothes. *See* **Uniforms.**

Driver. *See* **Chauffeur.**

Drought losses. In most instances drought-related losses, to be deductible, must be incurred in a trade or business or in a transaction entered upon for profit. But in 1977, the Internal Revenue Service announced it had changed its mind and now will not go so far as to say that a drought loss may never qualify as a casualty loss.[98] *See also* **Farmers.**

Drug abusers. Maintenance of such persons at a center providing treatment is deductible.[99] For treatment of drug addicts, *see* **Medical expenses.**

Drunkenness. *See* **Alcoholism, treatment for.**

Dry rot. Damage to property through dry rot usually is not recognized as a casualty loss, which requires that there must have been a *sudden* activity or action. But it is *possible* to show that such indeed was the case.[100]

Dues, association. A businessperson could deduct dues paid to an association that disseminates trade information for the general welfare of the industry. The association was not engaged in lobbying activities.[101]

A realtor was allowed to deduct dues paid to the local chamber of commerce.[102]

Dues, club. *See* **Entertainment.**

Dues, professional societies. A physician could deduct the dues that he paid to medical societies.[103] An attorney was allowed to deduct bar association dues.[104]

D

1. Revenue Ruling 73-348, 1973-2 CB 31.
2. Revenue Ruling 68-295, 1968-1 CB 92.
3. IRS Letter Ruling 8033038, May 20, 1980.
4. *Reuben A. Baer Estate*, T.C. Memo. 1967-34, filed February 27, 1967.
5. Revenue Ruling 71-48, 1971-1 CB 156.
6. Revenue Ruling 73-53, 1973-1 CB 139.
7. Revenue Ruling 80-340, 1980-2 CB 81.
8. *Donovan et al. v. Campbell, Jr.*, DC, ND Texas, 1961.
9. *Lawrence D. Greisdorf et al.*, 54 T.C. 1684 (1970).
10. Regulations Section 1.213-1(e)(1)(v)(*a*).
11. *Donovan et al. v. Campbell, Jr.*, DC, ND Texas, 1961.
12. Revenue Ruling 75-46, 1951-1 CB 55.
13. *Carl E. Noe*, T.C. Memo., Docket No. 27682, entered May 2, 1952.
14. *Raymond Warren Jackson*, T.C. Memo. 1975-301, filed September 30, 1975.

15. Regulations Section 1.165-3(b)(1).

16. *Panhandle State Bank*, 39 T.C. 813 (1963).

D

126

17. *Parma Company*, 18 BTA 429 (1929).

18. *Savage et al. v. Commissioner*, T.C. Memo. 1981-278, filed June 2, 1981.

19. *Hartford Courant Company v. Smith*, DC, Conn., 1942.

20. Regulations Section 1.165-3(c)(1).

21. *Lawver et al. v. Commissioner*, T.C. Memo. 1981-192, filed April 22, 1981.

22. *J.B.N. Telephone Company, Inc. v. United States*, 638 F.2d 227 (10th Cir., 1981).

23. *Feldman v. Wood*, 335 F.2d 264 (9th Cir., 1964).

24. *Grossman et al. v. Commissioner*, 74 T.C. 1147 (1980).

25. *Yates Motor Company, Inc. v. Commissioner*, 561 F.2d 490 (6th Cir., 1977).

26. *Gilman II et al. v. Commissioner*, 72 T.C. 130 (1979).

27. *Wilson et al. v. Commissioner*, T.C. Memo. 1980-514, filed November 20, 1980.

28. IRS Letter Ruling 8032084, no date given.

29. Revenue Ruling 74-78, 1974-1 CB 44.

30. Revenue Ruling 67-62, 1967-1 CB 44.

31. IRC Section 611.

32. Regulations Section 1.611-1(b)(1).

33. Regulations Section 1.611-2.

34. Regulations Section 1.613-2.

35. IRC Section 613(b)(1).

36. *Tax Guide for Small Business*, IRS Publication 334 (Rev. Nov. 1981), page 70.

37. IRC Section 613(a).

38. Tax Reduction Act of 1975, Section 501.

39. IRC Section 167(a)(1),(2).

40. *Allen et al. v. Commissioner*, T.C. Memo. 1982-93, filed February 23, 1982.

41. *Riis & Company, Inc., et al.*, T.C. Memo. 1964-190, filed July 14, 1964.

42. *Beaudry v. Commissioner*, 150 F.2d 20 (2d Cir., 1945).

43. *Snyder et al. v. United States*, 549 F.2d 171 (10th Cir., 1982).

44. *D. Joseph Judge et al.*, T.C. Memo. 1976-283, filed September 7, 1976.

45. *Marigold Foods, Inc. v. United States*, DC, Minn., 1965.

46. *Elliott v. United States*, 250 F. Supp. 322 (DC, WD NY, 1965).

47. Regulations Section 1.167(a)-2.

48. *Ginkel v. Commissioner*, T.C. Memo. 1980-424, filed September 25, 1980.

49. *Wolfson et al. v. Commissioner*, T.C. Memo. 1978-445, filed November 7, 1978.

50. *Central Animal Hospital, Inc.*, 68 T.C. 269 (1977).

51. *Johnson, Jr., et al. v. United States*, DC, WD Texas, 1961.

52. *Rodgers Dairy Company et al.*, 14 T.C. 66 (1950).

53. *Sanders et al. v. Commissioner*, 75 T.C. 157 (1980).

54. *Sanford H. Weinzimer et al.*, T.C. Memo. 1958-137, filed July 16, 1958.

55. *Gallagher v. Commissioner*, T.C. Memo. 1979-412, filed September 12, 1979.

56. *Reisinger v. Commissioner*, 144 F.2d 475 (2d Cir., 1944).

57. Revenue Ruling 54-579, 1954-2 CB 91.

58. *Lorraine Corporation*, T.C. Memo. 1958-141, filed July 21, 1958.

59. IRC Section 167(b).

60. *Glynn N. C. Jones*, T.C. Memo. 1959-98, filed May 19, 1959.

61. Economic Recovery Tax Act of 1981, Section 201(a).

62. Regulations Section 1.167 (a)-1(a).

63. *United States v. Livengood et al.*, DC, ED Pa., 1969.

64. *Pilot Freight Carriers, Inc.*, T.C. Memo. 1956-195, filed August 27, 1956.

65. Regulations Section 1.46-3(d).

66. *Sears Oil Company v. Commissioner*, 359 F.2d 191 (2d Cir., 1966).

67. *Schrader v. Commissioner*, 582 F.2d 1374 (6th Cir., 1978).

68. *SMC Corporation v. United States*, DC, ED Tenn., 1980.

69. Regulations Section 1.167(b)-o.

70. IRC Section 167(c).

71. Regulations Section 1.167(b)-4(a).

72. Revenue Ruling 65-652, 1956-2 CB 125.

73. IRC Section 167(m).

74. Regulations Section 1.167(a)-11.

75. *Adda, Inc.*, 9 T.C. 199 (1947), *rev'd on another issue*, 171 F.2d 367 (2d Cir., 1948).

76. Regulations Section 1.612-2(a).

77. *Leland Adkins et al.*, 51 T.C. 957 (1969).

78. Economic Recovery Tax Act of 1981, Section 209.

79. Ibid., Section 201.

80. Revenue Procedure 81-54, I.R.B. 1981-44, 21.

81. Ibid., Section 202(a).

82. Revenue Act of 1978, Section 367, as amended by PL 96-541, approved December 17, 1980.

83. Regulations Section 1.167(a)-3.

84. *Hampton Pontiac, Inc. v. United States*, 294 F. Supp. 1073 (DC, SC, 1969).

85. *Hochschild v. Commissioner*, 158 F.2d 764 (2d Cir., 1947).

86. *Donald V. Smith et al.*, T.C. Memo., Docket Nos. 5836-9, entered May 21, 1947.

87. *William Ziegler, Jr., et al.*, 5 T.C. 150 (1945).

88. Revenue Ruling 68-131, 1968-1 CB 73.

89. Treasury Decision 7522, December 15, 1977.

90. Regulations Section 1.165-11.

91. *Morgan S. Kaufman*, 12 T.C. 1114 (1949).

92. *United States v. Collier et al.,* 104 F.2d 420 (5th Cir., 1939).

93. *John R. Hopkins,* 15 T.C. 160 (1950).

94. *Albin J. Strandquist et al.,* T.C. Memo. 1970-84, filed April 3, 1970.

95. *Donald C. Hester,* T.C. Memo. 1963-107, filed April 15, 1963.

96. Revenue Ruling 69-275, 1969-1 CB 36.

97. Revenue Ruling 70-161, 1970-1 CB 15.

98. Revenue Ruling 77-490, 1977-2 CB 64.

99. Revenue Ruling 72-226, 1972-1 CB 96.

100. *Rosenberg v. Commissioner,* 198 F.2d 46 (8th Cir., 1952).

101. *Robert S. LeSage et al.,* T.C. Memo., Docket Nos. 11239 and 11240, entered December 3, 1947, *aff'd and rev'd on other issues,* 173 F.2d 826 (5th Cir., 1949).

102. *Gilman II et al. v. Commissioner,* 72 T.C. 730 (1979).

103. *Kenneth Blanchard,* T.C. Memo., Docket No. 24010, entered May 21, 1953.

104. *Henry P. Keith,* T.C. Memo., Docket No. 108883, entered December 9, 1942.

D

E

Earthquake damage. *See* **Casualties.**

Easement, contribution in form of. *See* **Contributions.**

Economic analysis. Expenditures which will produce benefits expected to last for more than one year must be capitalized and not deducted at the time. Economic analysis of projects which never were undertaken, however, could be written off when the projects were abandoned.[1]

Economic value, loss of. *See* **Casualties.**

Education. Ordinarily, an individual cannot deduct expenses for his education. This is because such expense is regarded as a personal expense or as the expenditure for the acquisition of capital asset (learning), the advantages of which last for more than one year. But certain educational expenses which occur in connection with one's trade or business are deductible. An individual may deduct educational expenses which were necessary
1. To meet the express requirements of his current employer.
2. To keep his current salary, status, or employment.
3. To maintain or to improve skills required in performing his current duties.[2]
 Educational expenses are also deductible when:
1. The courses which an individual takes are *not* required to meet the minimum educational requirements for his employment. In other words, if the minimum educational requirement of the individual's employer is a high-school education, and the employee (already possessing a high-school education) takes a course at a college or business school, then the expenses of the courses he takes to improve his skills are deductible.
2. The education was *not* undertaken to qualify him for a new trade or profession.

 Once a person has met the minimum educational requirements for qualification in his employment, he is thought of as continuing to meet those requirements even though they are changed.[3] A woman who was already certified to teach in Toronto, Canada, thus could deduct the cost of taking courses required to obtain her certification in New Jersey. Having acquired certification to teach in Toronto, she had met the minimum educational requirements for qualification in her employment, and the cost of additional courses required by New Jersey was deductible because they maintained and improved her skills as a teacher.[4]

Deduction was allowed for the cost of courses taken to improve a teacher's skills and to satisfy a state's recertification requirements.[5]

A teacher at an elementary parochial school, who did not have a bachelor's degree, signed an agreement at the start of her employment that she would take a minimum of six college credits a year until she obtained such a degree. She could deduct the costs of study for her degree.[6]

A low-echelon manager on his own initiative took courses at a university which dealt specifically with marketing management in the industry in which he was engaged. Eventually he was promoted to higher managerial positions in his company. Tuition was deductible because what he studied had honed his knowledge of the business and improved his managerial capabilities. A change in duties is not considered a new trade or business if the new duties involve the same general type of work. The court cited as an example an individual who progressed from personnel assistant to assistant personnel director and finally to personnel director in the same company; he did not change his trade or business in any technical or practical sense.[7]

An individual served as a personnel representative for a large corporation, where she made recommendations and suggested personnel policy improvements. Although not required to do so, she undertook night courses which led to her obtaining a Master of Business Administration degree. While she still was working for her degree, she was promoted to personnel manager. Her duties remained the same, although she now made decisions and not merely recommendations. Her employer's tuition reimbursements she reported as income, offsetting these by showing tuition costs as business expenses. These were allowed because the program did not equip her for a new trade or business but merely sharpened her skills in her existing line of work. One of her courses had been in accounting, but that scarcely qualified her for a new career as an accountant.[8]

A business administrator could deduct the expenses of working for a Master of Business Administration degree when he was not currently employed and used his sharpened skills to get a different job. He wished to participate in a university's MBA program on a full-time basis but could not get a leave of absence from his employer. He resigned and worked full-time for two years to get his degree. Then he went to work as an administrator for another business. He was allowed to deduct his expenses in getting this advanced degree because (1) he had worked long enough in the past to show that he was in the business of being a salaried employee; (2) a period of absence does not affect one's status of carrying on a trade or business while attending graduate school; (3)

the MBA training would not equip him for a different type of career; (4) the education was expected to equip him to be a better administrator than he was before; and (5) he continued in the same business of being an administrator, although it happened to be for another company.[9]

The test is: Do the courses studied bear a proximate and direct relationship to a person's duties?[10]

A person may have a dual objective in incurring education expense. Deductibility then depends upon the more immediate objective of the expenditure.[11]

A section foreman in a manufacturing company's quality control department was not permitted to deduct that portion of his tuition costs unreimbursed by his employer for university courses in business law, advanced finance, corporate strategy, economics, and marketing, as they were not related to his *present* employment. But he could deduct his unreimbursed tuition costs for production and operations management, bookkeeping and cost accounting, and business finance, as they sharpened his skills for his existing work in quality control.[12]

An attorney could deduct tuition for courses leading to an advanced law degree. His skills were being sharpened, and he was not being trained for a new trade or business.[13]

If one is not diligently seeking a job, one cannot deduct the cost of studying for it. An elementary-school principal resigned to work full-time for his doctorate. But then he could not find another administrative position. Deduction for his costs was disallowed by the Internal Revenue Service on the ground that he was not actually in the trade or business of teacher or educational administrator while his expenses were incurred. The court allowed the deduction. A person still can be engaged in a trade or business, although currently unemployed, if he was previously engaged in it and intends to return to the same trade or business. The court stressed the fact that he "was more than an inactive member of his profession."[14] In an earlier case, deduction was disallowed where a teacher lacked diligence in seeking employment after the completion of her graduate courses.[15] Here the evidence may be that it is not unusual for a teacher to do such graduate study.

The Internal Revenue Service has stated that where an individual, in order to undertake education or training to maintain or to improve skills required in his employment or other trade or business, temporarily ceases to engage actively in this employment, he is still regarded as being engaged in his employment or business if his suspension of the work is for a period of one year or less. But courts have been more liberal as to the time of cessation of work where a teacher has resigned in order to take the courses when leave of absence has been denied.[16]

It does not matter that an individual chooses to acquire the additional education to improve his skills by attending a university in a foreign country rather than one in the United States.[17]

Educational costs are deductible, even though the education may lead to a degree and possibly a new trade or profession, if the expense is incurred to meet the express requirements of the individual's employer.[18]

Where a parochial school required one teacher to sign a statement that he would obtain a college degree, and there was no greater educational requirement for a parochial-school teacher, whether by state law or otherwise, than a high-school diploma, the cost of obtaining the bachelor's degree was deductible.[19]

An individual was hired by International Business Machines as a patent trainee with a stipulation that he acquire a law degree in a prescribed four-year course of study. He could deduct the cost of his educational expense, for this was a condition of the retention of his present employment.[20]

When a commercial airline switched from propeller to jet planes, flight engineers on the old type of aircraft could retain their status only if they held commercial pilot's licenses. The cost of the education necessary to acquire such licenses was deductible because the purpose was to meet a specific requirement of the employer for the retention of their status as flight crew members. That the training might also qualify a person for a higher position as copilot was irrelevant if the primary purpose was to retain the existing status.[21]

A high-school teacher had tenure; that is, he had taught long enough so that under the school's employment policy he could not be discharged. However, to be eligible to participate in any salary increase made available by the school, he had to obtain additional training. One acceptable method was to take a summer course at a foreign university. The cost of this training was deductible as a business expense. True, because of the tenure he didn't *have* to study further in order to keep his job, but this additional training was undertaken to preserve rights to annual advancements that would be lost if he did not comply with the additional training requirements.[22]

If a person has met the minimum educational requirements for qualification in his employment, but his employer requires him to obtain further education in order to retain his present salary status or employment, that person may deduct the expenses for the education he must get to meet the employer's minimum requirements. If one college course is all that is needed to meet those minimum requirements and the person takes two courses, he may deduct only the cost of the one course.[23]

Educational expenses incurred for the purpose of improving one's skills in his existing position or field of specialization are deductible. An Internal Revenue Service reviewer in the Estate and Gift Tax Division was entitled to deduct law-school tuition. It was custom, if not the rule, that all examiners in this division be attorneys, and the custom, observed the court, "should be even more true of a reviewer who is their superior." Inasmuch as in his position a law degree was the custom, the expenditure was primarily for the purpose of maintaining or improving the skills required by his business. The "summit of knowledge," the court concluded, "like the fruit of Tantalus, is never reached."[24]

A practicing physician specializing in internal medicine voluntarily undertook training in the techniques of psychiatry primarily for the purpose of maintaining or improving his skills in the practice of internal medicine. He continued to practice as an internist following the completion of his psychiatric training. The claimed deductions were allowed as education expenses incurred for the purpose of enabling him better to carry on his own practice, notwithstanding the fact that incidental to such education he acquired a new specialty.[25]

A physician was engaged in the practice of psychiatry. He pursued a lengthy institute-sponsored training program in psychoanalysis. Even though psychoanalysis is a specialty which is practiced exclusively by some physicians, this doctor intended to utilize his new skills simply to improve his existing work as a psychiatrist. In consequence, deduction was allowed.[26]

A physician, while engaged in the private practice of psychiatry, undertook a program of study and training at an accredited psychoanalytic institute which would lead to his qualification to practice psychoanalysis. His expenditures for such study and training were deductible because the study and training maintained or improved skills required by him in his trade or business and did not qualify him for a new trade or business.[27] A general practitioner of medicine took a two-week course reviewing new developments in several specialized fields of medicine. His expenses for the course were deductible because the course maintained or improved skills required by him in his trade or business and did not qualify him for a new trade or business.[28]

A licensed physician was a resident in psychiatry at a hospital. He could deduct his expenses for undergoing psychoanalysis. What he learned improved his skills as a physician treating psychiatric patients by enhancing self-awareness and enabling him to recognize psychological "blocks" on certain material. The psychoanalysis maintained and improved his skills in his *present* employment. Deductibility was not lost because the psychoanalysis also might improve his skills in the future as a certified psychiatrist, which the Internal Revenue Service alleged was a different trade or business.[29]

A dentist took postgraduate courses in orthodontics, that division of dentistry dealing with irregularities of the teeth. He had engaged in a general dental practice, but he now attended dental school on a full-time basis, continuing his professional practice on a part-time basis. Upon completion of his postgraduate training he became an orthodontist and limited his practice to patients in need of this field of specialization. He was permitted to deduct the cost of his postgraduate studies, for these expenses were not incurred in connection with qualifying him for a new trade or business but were for the purpose of improving his skills as a dentist.[30]

An individual with a bachelor's degree in business administration was employed by a municipality as a social services case worker. He enrolled in a university graduate school of social work as a nondegree candidate. In the taxable year, he took courses directly related to social services work. The Internal Revenue Service sought to disallow deduction of the tuition, as possession of the Master of Social Work degree would have qualified him for a new trade or business as a social worker. Deduction was allowed because he could not qualify for the higher position without possession of the advanced degree for which he was not even a candidate at that time. It was irrelevant that the course did qualify him for promotion in a *later* year when possession of a higher degree could qualify him for a new trade or business.[31]

Deductible expenses which are voluntarily incurred for education to maintain or to improve skills needed for one's occupation include refresher courses or courses dealing with current developments, as well as academic or vocational courses.[32]

A dentist could deduct the cost of continuing professional education courses approved by the state dental association to satisfy the requirements for license maintenance.[33]

An engineer employed by a corporation as an electronics technician could deduct his nonreimbursable tuition for courses in high-frequency transistor circuitry and design.[34]

An attorney was permitted to deduct his expenses in attending a tax institute. The institute had as an objective the presentation of current developments in the field of taxation. The court noted that the attorney was morally bound to keep currently informed as to the law of Federal taxation. Attendance at the institute, declared the court, "was a way well adopted to keep sharp the tools he actually used in his going trade or business."[35]

Education may include improving the managerial skills needed in one's employment, and therefore the expenses incurred in obtaining such improvement are deductible.[36]

A United States Navy captain whose assignments involved primarily command and administration of personnel could deduct the cost of graduate courses which he took on his own initiative as part of a program that led to the degree of Master of Arts in Personnel Administration. The education he undertook was not pursuant to a specific requirement of his employer imposed as a condition to the retention of his salary, status, or employment. But the courses undertaken by him were so closely related to his employment duties that they served to maintain or to improve the skills required of him in his employment. Inasmuch as the courses taken by him were not part of a program of study which would qualify him for a new trade or business and were not required of him in order to meet the minimum educational requirements for qualification in his employment, the expenditures he incurred in taking the courses were deductible.[37]

A deputy district attorney in Los Angeles frequently worked with persons who spoke Spanish. He took instruction in that language to enable him to interview witnesses and victims involved in criminal cases. Deduction was allowed, for the tuition expense enabled him to perform his job better.[38]

An individual who was born and educated in Korea was employed by a major corporation as a workmen's compensation supervisor. He was allowed to deduct the cost of courses he took to study methods of comprehension, logic, accounting, and government. These courses helped him to think, to express himself, and to write in the English language, to analyze the reports received, and to comprehend the methods by which laws are enacted and interpreted in the United States. The education improved his skills in his employment in a direct way.[39]

An engineering aide employed by a major corporation was permitted to deduct the cost of attending night school in order to maintain and to improve the skills required by his employer.[40]

A housing assistant in the New York City Housing Authority could deduct the cost of taking graduate courses in housing and public administration. Although his employer did not require him to take these courses in order to maintain his employment, the taxpayer was helped by showing the court a pamphlet issued by his employer, *Guide for the Housing Assistant,* which stated in part, "The Authority believes that greater knowledge of the housing field will lead to greater interest, job satisfaction and competence in carrying out your job."[41]

An ordained minister could deduct educational expenses incurred while taking certain undergraduate courses at a college. He chose his courses according to their helpfulness to his ministry: psychology, public speaking, teaching methods, business-related subjects, and drama. Such courses enhanced skills which were appropriate and helpful to him in solving the problems of his congregation. His degree did not qualify him for a new trade or business; he neither sought nor obtained the teaching certificate customarily awarded to those being graduated from his college.[42]

An industrial psychologist employed by a national life-insurance firm as an assistant research analyst in industrial psychology could deduct the cost of courses which he undertook in that field in order to improve his skills. The courses were leading to a Doctor of Philosophy degree, but his employer did not insist upon the higher degree as a basis for promotion.[43]

An engineer at a major corporation was in charge of a project to develop technical systems. Frequently he was called upon to resolve conflicts among persons who worked for him and outside parties. To acquire the skills needed for technical management, he became a candidate for the degree of Master of Science in Administration at a university. Inasmuch as he already was engaged in work which combined the essential ingredients of administration and management, the courses did not equip him for a new trade or business. Tuition was deductible.[44]

A teacher who already had her state teaching credentials was permitted to deduct the cost of working for a Ph.D. degree. The additional education was not undertaken to obtain a new position or a substantial advancement in position, or primarily for the purpose of fulfilling general educational aspirations; nor was it undertaken for the purpose of qualifying her for her intended profession, as she already had her credentials. It was, however, held that the expenditure was for the primary purpose of maintaining or improving the skills required in her present employment.[45]

An instructor at a university was able to deduct his expenses in studying for his Ph.D. degree. He was reemployed each year on the basis that he maintain his qualifications, and he took courses related to his field of teaching. His status, rank, and salary remained the same after he received his doctorate.[46]

A university lecturer had a temporary teaching appointment. To obtain a permanent appointment, he was required to obtain his Ph.D. degree. His tuition costs were deductible, because they were necessary to obtain an established employment relationship and did not equip him for a different trade or business.[47]

A certified public accountant was accepted as an assistant professor at a university, his certificate being considered to be the equivalent of the master's degree required in the case of other faculty members. He could deduct the costs of working for a master's degree when his superiors suggested, but did not require, that he undertake the study of other business courses, the better to demonstrate to his students the functions of accounting as a tool of, and aid to, business management. That his study led to a master's degree was of secondary importance to the improving of his skills.[48]

An individual employed as an engineering aide by a major corporation was informed by his superior that he should take a leave of absence and take courses to complete his work for a college degree so that he would have a more secure future with the company, especially during slack periods when lesser-trained employees would be laid off. He did so. Deduction of the cost of taking these courses was permitted, for although he was not required to take the courses, he did so to maintain or improve skills required by his employer.[49]

Voluntarily strengthening one's business weaknesses can be equated with sharpening one's skills. An individual was an executive with a construction company. When the president was killed in an automobile accident, this individual was promoted to the position of vice-president and general superintendent. He felt that although he was generally knowledgeable about the construction business, he was deficient in certain key aspects of corporation management, such as financing, bonding, accounting, and personnel problems. So he went to an experienced management consultant who was then training and advising a number of corporate executives on an individual basis in his own home. The new vice-president deducted his payments as "Business Management Training Consultant Fees." Deduction was allowed despite the Internal Revenue Service claim that a self-educated private tutor, who had never attended an institution of higher learning, cannot qualify as a management consultant. The tax deduction is not limited to formal or institutional education. What the vice-president learned from his tutor served to improve the managerial skills needed in his present employment. In order to *maintain* his employment, which he probably could not have done had his superiors discovered the chinks in his executive armor, he had to learn to cope with problems with which he was unfamiliar.[50]

A professional singer could deduct payments which she made to a voice coach. The payments were to maintain her present employment by profiting from the voice coach's instructions.[51]

A professional harpist was allowed to deduct the cost of music lessons taken from someone the court called "one of the few persons in that world capable of giving valuable instruction to [her] to maintain or improve her proficiency as a harpist."[52]

After he left high school, a young man engaged a former semiprofessional baseball player, in order to have the veteran teach him the skills necessary to be a professional player. The Internal Revenue Service was not permitted to disallow the payments as personal education expenses. The payments related to services in connection with the young man's business: playing ball.[53]

If a person takes courses simply in order to carry out his present job more competently, his costs are deductible. A Special Agent of the Federal Bureau of Investigation had a private pilot's license, which did not permit him to fly in poor weather. Frequently his work assignments had to be cancelled because of adverse flying conditions. He could deduct the cost of lessons in instrument flying and other courses which could have qualified him to become an airline pilot. His real intent in taking advanced flight training was to improve his flying skills and to enhance his job performance for his existing employer.[54]

A flight engineer of a major airline was required to have a commercial pilot's license with instrument rating. In the belief that his ability to maintain basic instrumental flying skills would deteriorate unless he operated a plane himself with some regularity, he purchased a small, single-engine propellor-driven aircraft. His instructional expenses were job-related in part because they improved his skills and did not fit him for a better position; promotions from his rank were based entirely upon seniority. But inasmuch as he also used his plane for personal purposes as well as maintaining his skills, the court made an estimate of how much of his education expense was deductible.[55]

A staff photographer for a major New York newspaper also served as a free-lancer. He learned to fly solely to get to the locale of news events quickly and to take aerial views of spot news. This enabled him to improve his skills as to timeliness, range, and graphic portrayal. The time gained might well make the difference between a valuable and a worthless picture, and many events which would have been mundane or even unphotographable from ground level became spectacular from the air. The photographer exhibited to the court "enlightening examples" of how he was maintaining his status as a photographer. His deduction for the flying lessons was allowed.[56]

A physician employed by the Federal Aviation Agency could deduct the cost of flying lessons. His duties included passing upon the qualification of applicants for flying licenses; and what he learned from flying helped him to evaluate the performances of other persons.[57]

Where an expenditure is for both business and personal purposes, customarily it must be allocated between business and nonbusiness usage, only the former being deductible. Example: costs of operating an automobile. But necessary educational expenses which are not for the purpose of qualifying the taxpayer for a new job require no allocation between the relative business and personal benefits. Example: an individual utilized his own plane for business purposes for most but not all of the time it was used. He could deduct the entire cost of instrument flying instruction, which broadened the business use of the plane in all types of weather, even though he also could use the vehicle more frequently for personal purposes now.[58]

An unlicensed accountant, head of his own accounting firm, was not permitted to deduct his tuition for the accounting courses preparing him to take the state examination for certified public accountants, for such courses would have qualified him for a new trade or business. But inasmuch as his accounting firm gave business and financial advice to its clients, he could deduct the tuition for courses which improved his skills in giving business and financial advice.[59]

An officer assigned to the Naval Safety Center could deduct a portion of the expense of operating a privately owned airplane as a business-related education expense. He needed to maintain his flying skills, although because of budgetary limitations the Navy could not provide him with flying facilities. As an aviator, he was regarded by the Navy fliers as a full "member of the club" and provided with help essential in his work of accident investigator.[60]

Expenses for education are not deductible when that education is part of a program of study being pursued by the taxpayer that will lead him to qualifying for a new trade or business. In the case of an employee, however, *a mere change of duties is not the same as a new trade or business* if the change of duties involves the same general type of work as is involved in his present employment.[61]

The most frequent example of nondeductible educational expenses involves law-school tuition and related expenses. Or at least, it is the one most often brought to court. To a very large proportion of all persons engaged in a trade or business, the advantages of an education in the law would be helpful. But that is not enough to justify a tax deduction, for by getting the law degree a person has at least *qualified* himself for a new trade or business. In the words of one decision, "Law is a field so pervasive as to be 'helpful' to some extent in virtually every type of employment. But that does not mean that everyone who is gainfully employed is entitled to deduct the expenses of acquiring a legal education."[62]

To be entitled to deduct law-school expenses, an individual must show that his primary purpose in attending the school is to enable him to do his *present* job better. An insurance claims adjuster could deduct his expenses in attending night law school, for the knowledge he acquired improved the skills required of him as an adjuster. His duties, said the court, involved "frequent contact with legally oriented problems."[63]

Law-school expenses were properly deductible by a civilian employee with the Air Force because his employment required him to write technical regulations in the area of procurement and he constantly worked with contracts. His skill as a lawyer would certainly enhance his ability in his present occupation.[64]

A physician served the coroner's office in a major city. His expenses in attending law school were deductible, for his employment dealt with investigations of sudden, violent, and suspicious deaths. His work brought him into constant contact with law-enforcement agencies, lawyers, and the law itself. Certainly an improved knowledge of the law would be an asset to the physician in his present position.[65]

A certified public accountant served as a partner in his father's accounting firm. At the suggestion of his father, the son attended law school. His legal education enabled him to do his accounting work better. He could analyze legal documents to determine their effect upon financial statements and he was better able to understand the laws affecting tax returns which he prepared. But his work for his firm did not change after he obtained his law degree; he never presented himself to the public as a lawyer; and he was satisfied with his earnings as a certified public accountant. There was no indication that he intended to use his law-school education or degree to obtain changed or better employment. Therefore the expenses for attending law school were an allowable deduction.[66]

An individual could deduct the costs of attending law school while he was an Internal Revenue Service Special Agent; that is, while he was engaged in the investigation of suspected criminal violations of the tax law. Although he accepted a position with a law firm shortly after obtaining his degree, he had taken the courses to improve and to maintain his skills as a Special Agent. He was an Armed Services veteran on whom the war had left an unerasable mark and for whom government service offered the security his doctor had prescribed. The court felt that he wouldn't have chosen to burden himself with evening law school so that he might leave the security of government service in order to enter the legal profession. Whatever else the legal profession offers, concluded the judge, is difficult to catalog, but its principal attraction has never been security. This indicated to the court that the taxpayer really had gone to law school to improve his skills as a Special Agent, which made the tuition deductible despite his later change of intention.[67]

Very frequently an individual will lose his deduction for law-school expenses for either or both of two reasons. First, law school application forms customarily ask why the applicant wishes to attend the school, and applicants are afraid to say anything except the desire to practice law, lest the admissions committee reject a person whose objective really is something other than being an attorney. But the Internal Revenue Service frequently uses the application form to prove that the individual really was seeking to qualify for a new profession.

Second, even if the individual has not left his old business, he frequently tries his own tax case involving disallowance of the education deduction. That pretty well establishes that he is qualified for a new profession. Persons who do not try their own cases in this situation fare better.[68]

A chemical engineer who was switching to a career on the professional stage could deduct his costs in attending drama school.[69]

A child was afflicted with dyslexia, a neurological condition which results in great difficulty in learning to read. Education rather than medicine or therapy is the means to offset the effect of dyslexia. The parents were permitted to deduct as medical expenses the fees paid to a teacher for training and study skills which enabled the child to overcome the results of his handicap.[70]

Education need not be restricted to formal instruction. A corporate executive could deduct the cost of being tutored, in areas where his skills were weak, by a retired executive who himself had no formal educational background.[71]

A social worker was allowed to deduct amounts paid to a certified psychoanalyst for aid in equipping the social worker to deal with her patients' problems.[72]

Education expenses include amounts spent for books, supplies, laboratory fees, and similar items. Also covered is the cost of correspondence courses.[73]

The deduction is for the amount not reimbursed as education by one's employer or other party.[74]

Expenditures for travel are deductible under appropriate circumstances as a form of education.[75] Such expenditures are deductible only to the extent that the period of travel covered is directly related to the duties of the individual in his employment or other trade or business. There is such a direct relationship only if the major portion of the activities during the period is of a nature which directly maintains or improves skills required by the individual in his employment, trade, or business.[76]

The following examples should give a better idea of how expenditures for travel as a form of education can be deductible:

A physician who specialized in the problems of alcoholism could deduct the expenses of a trip to Europe. While he was there, he visited hospitals and clinics to study their methods and procedures. The expenses contributed substantially to his knowledge and technique of treating the disease of alcoholism.[77]

A high-school teacher of world history, emphasizing the development of Western civilization, could deduct summer travel expenses to France. She visited abbeys, châteaux, cathedrals, palaces, museums, and other places of historical interest which enabled her to present her course material to students with added meaningfulness.[78]

A high-school teacher of Latin and French could deduct as an expense of maintaining and improving her skills in her employment the money she paid in traveling to various places in the Mediterranean area that had a relationship to the courses she taught.[79] Travel expenses were allowed as educational expenses even where the teacher's activities consisted largely of visiting French schools and families, attending motion pictures, plays, and lectures in the French language, and similar activities.[80]

A school librarian could deduct the costs of a trip abroad. Her principal duty was to lend various forms of assistance to other teachers in their classroom teaching. She acted as "educational resource person," utilizing or making available to teachers and students various relevant audio-visual and other educational media, such as slides, film strips, recordings, and books. Her trip abroad, which took several hundred hours to plan, was centered around subjects the faculty wished to teach. She purchased or took hundreds of slides which were maintained in the school; she collected other materials such as posters and pamphlets for use in the school. Her travel itinerary and travel goals bore close relationship to the emphasis placed on foreign cultures by the social studies department. The trip, in the court's words, "directly maintained and improved important job skills. She is therefore entitled to her deduction."[81]

Travel expenses on sabbatical leave are deductible by a teacher when the places and activities encompassed by the trip are related directly to his teaching position.[82]

An individual may deduct transportation expenses for qualified educational activities which he incurs in going between (1) his place of employment and a school within the same general area or (2) his place of employment and a school located beyond the general area. But if he returns home before going to school, he may deduct the expense in going from home to school only to the extent that it does not exceed the transportation expense which he would have incurred had he gone from work to school.

One individual lives and works in Jersey City and goes to New York City three times a week to attend night classes at a university there. If his educational expenses are deductible under the allowable deduction guidelines, he may also deduct his round-trip transportation expenses, including toll and parking fees.[83]

Where education expenses are otherwise deductible, it does not matter that courses are taken at a foreign university.[84]

If an individual travels away from home primarily to obtain education, the expenses of which are deductible, his expenditures for travel, meals, and lodging while away from home are also deductible. But if he, as an incident of the trip, engages in some personal activity such as sightseeing, social visiting, or entertaining or other recreation, that portion of the expenses attributable to the personal activity constitutes nondeductible personal or living expenses. If his travel away from home is primarily personal, his expenditures for travel, meals, and lodging (other than meals and lodging during the time spent in participating in the deductible educational pursuits) are not deductible.

Whether a particular trip is primarily personal or primarily to obtain education depends upon all the facts and circumstances of each case. An important factor to be taken into account is the relative amount of time devoted to personal activity as compared to the time devoted to educational pursuits.[85]

Expenses of a trip involving both educational and personal pursuits may be allocated into deductible and nondeductible expenses. A physician took a cruise on a ship where lectures on developments in medicine were given. He could deduct that portion of the cost which he could establish was appropriate to the time he spent on educational endeavors.[86]

An otherwise valid education expense is not deductible to the extent that it is reimbursable. But expenses paid by veterans, which properly are deductible for Federal income tax purposes, do not have to be reduced by the nontaxable benefits received during the taxable year from the Veterans Administration. These are not reimbursement payments but are in the nature of a living stipend, determined without reference to amounts received.[87] *See also* **Advanced degree, study for; Armed forces; Deaf persons, expenses of; License maintenance; Ordinary and necessary business expenses; Training expenses; Tuition-postponement plan payments.**

Educational materials. A teacher was allowed to deduct the cost of games and other items he bought to use in his classes for trainable mentally retarded students, or as a student in courses for the handicapped in which he was enrolled.[88]

Efficiency awards. Amounts paid by an employer for increased efficiency by an employee are treated as additional compensation and thus are deductible.[89]

Efficiency engineer, payment to. *See* **Expenditures for benefits lasting more than one year.**

Election to deduct or to capitalize. Certain expenditures may be treated as deductible expenses or as capital expenditures at the taxpayer's election.
1. In the case of unimproved and unproductive real property: annual taxes, interest on a mortgage, and other carrying charges.
2. In the case of real property, whether improved or unimproved and whether productive or unproductive:
    a. Interest on a loan (but not theoretical interest of a taxpayer using his own funds).
    b. Taxes of the owner of such real property measured by compensation paid to his employees.
    c. Taxes of such an owner which are imposed on the purchase of materials or on the storage, use, or other consumption of materials.
    d. Other necessary expenditures paid or incurred for the development of the real property or for the construction of an improvement to the property up to the time the development or construction work has been completed.
3. In the case of personal property:
    a. Taxes of an employer measured by compensation for services rendered in transporting machinery or other fixed assets to the plant or installing them there.

b.   Interest on a loan to purchase such property or to pay for transporting or installing it.

c.   Taxes of the owner thereof imposed on the purchase of such property or on the storage, use, or other consumption of such property, paid or incurred up to the date when such property is first put to use by the taxpayer, whichever date is later.

4.   Any otherwise deductible taxes and carrying charges with respect to property which in the opinion of the Commissioner of Internal Revenue are under sound accounting principles chargeable to capital accounts.[90]

Intangible drilling and development costs are deductible expenses or are chargeable to capital, as the taxpayer elects.[91] Development expenses are subject to a similar election.[92] A like election is available in the case of certain mining exploration expenditures.[93]

The owner of a certified historic structure who rehabilitates it may elect to amortize over sixty months certain expenditures attributable to certified rehabilitation. The rehabilitation must be certified by the Secretary of the Interior to the Internal Revenue Service as consistent with the historic character of the structure.[94]

Research and experimental expenses may be deducted in the year paid or incurred, or the amount may be deferred and amortized ratably over a period of not less than sixty months, as selected by the taxpayer, beginning with the month in which the taxpayer first realizes benefits from these expenditures.[95] Thus, if it takes some time before the research expenses produce income, he is not wasting a deduction by claiming it in a year when there is no income. But if the research pays off more rapidly, the expenses may be deducted should that method be the taxpayer's election. Research and experimental expenditures for new products or processes which are not related to the current product lines or manufacturing processes of his trade or business are still regarded as research and experimental expenditures which, at the taxpayer's election, may be deducted if paid or incurred in connection with his trade or business.[96]

A drug manufacturer was not allowed to sell new products until final approval of the Food and Drug Administration. Costs of listing and developing a potential drug constituted research and developmental expenses until final approval for the *marketing* of the drug was obtained from the FDA.[97]

This election provision covers costs incurred in developing the concept of a product as opposed to the product itself.[98] Research and experimental expenditures include, in general, all costs incident to the development of an experimental or pilot model, a plant process, a product, a formula, an invention or similar property, and the improvement of an already existing property of the types mentioned.[99]

Ordinarily, a taxpayer likes to take a deduction as soon as possible. But research and development expenditures sometimes require several years to produce financial success. Thus, a taxpayer might prefer to amortize research and development over a period of years, so that expenditures are not claimed until there is income to offset them. An election either to deduct or to amortize is permissible. Previously, a taxpayer merely made this election by taking the deduction at once or on a prorated basis. For taxable years ending after August 29, 1976, the election can be made only by attaching a written statement to this effect to the Federal income tax return for the first taxable year in which the election is applicable. For details of what is to be stated in this election, consult Treasury Regulations Section 1.174-4(b)(1).[100] *See also* **Farmers; Removal of impediments to the physically handicapped.**

Electrolysis. *See* **Hair removal.**

Elevator in home. *See* **Medical expenses.**

Eligible charitable contributions. *See* **Contributions.**

Embezzled funds, return of. Embezzled funds are taxed to the embezzler in the year of their acquisition and are deductible in the year of their return.[101]

Embezzlement. If an embezzler returns money he has embezzled from someone else, he has a deduction for this repayment in the year that it is made.[102] Deduction is in the taxable year when the funds are actually returned to the victim, not in a prior year when the embezzler's assets may have been "frozen" by a sheriff to assure that repayment would be made.[103] *See also* **Casualties; Claim of right.**

Embezzlement loss. *See* **Casualties.**

Emotional disorders. *See* **Medical expenses.**

Employee awards. Business gifts are not deductible to the extent that the cost exceeds $25. But an item of tangible personal property having a cost to the taxpayer not in excess of $400 is deductible, where it is awarded to an employee by reason of length of service or for safety achievement.[104]

Employee benefit-plan losses. Somehow the computations of the advantages of qualified employee benefit plans always assume that an employee will get back more than he puts into the plan. It doesn't always work that way. An employer's pension plan called for employees to contribute part of the cost of the plan. When one employee retired some years later, his retirement contribution from the fund, as a result of investment losses sustained by the fund, amounted to less money than he had contributed over the years. This differential was deductible by him as an ordinary loss in the year of the lump-sum distribution to him.[105]

Another employee was a participant in his employer's contributory stock-bonus plan. The employer went bankrupt, and the employee, his services being ended, received his portion of the stock, which was worthless. In the year he received the stock he was entitled to an ordinary loss deduction in the amount of the contributions he had made over the years.[106]

Employee benefits. *See* **Compensation; Employee benefit-plan losses.**

Employee loans, unrepaid. *See* **Bad debts.**

Employee morale, expenses to improve. *See* **Improvement of employee morale.**

Employees. Expenses related to one's trade or business are deductible. But these expenses are not confined to that of a business enterprise. The performance of services as an employee constitutes the carrying on of a trade or business. Therefore, the ordinary and necessary business expenses of an employee in connection with his employment are deductible.[107] This includes expenses of being an elected public officeholder.[108]

The president of a corporation is in the business of being an executive and can deduct unreimbursable expenditures in that capacity.[109]

An Army officer is in the business of being an Army officer (that is, an employee of the Army) and can deduct his expenses in that connection.[110]

A retired Army colonel still was in the business of being a military officer, inasmuch as he was subject to recall to active duty.[111]

A professional jockey is in the business of being a jockey and can deduct his expenses in conducting his duties.[112]

Expenses incurred in order to retain an established employment relationship are deductible.[113]

Where a congressman paid the cost of newsletters sent to his constituents, this was deductible as an expense in connection with his being employed as a congressman.[114] (*See also* **Congressman, expenses of.**) A member of the state legislature is in the business of being a legislator.[115]

Expenses to prevent discharge are deductible because related to the continuance of one's present employment.[116]

An individual who had lost his position as the result of a highly publicized controversy could deduct his expenses in negotiating a settlement with the employer.[117]

Expenses to resist attempted demotion in one's job are deductible.[118]

An elected public official could deduct his expenses in resisting efforts to have him voted out of office in a special election.[119]

The general counsel of a corporation could deduct the cost of buying stock in the company which another person was intending to buy, so that he would be able to keep the job he feared would be given to someone else by the would-be purchaser.[120]

A municipal fireman who was required to familiarize himself with the entire territory served by his company and who had to be able to pass a test on the location of fire hydrants in this territory could deduct his automobile expenses in connection with gaining this information.[121]

To combat discrimination, a major city required all the firemen of each company to have their meals together while on duty. Each person was assessed his share of the cost of meal preparation. As a fireman was required as a condition of his employment to pay this amount, the payment was deductible as an expense in connection with his business of being a fireman.[122]

An individual could deduct the costs a court ordered him to pay after his car had injured a child, for, inasmuch as the car was being used for business purposes at the time, the expenditure was related to his trade or business.[123]

Legal expenses paid by an employee who needs help in matters relating to his employment, whether in performing his duties or keeping his job, are deductible.[124]

An employee can deduct the cost of a personal physical examination when the employer requires it.[125]

An employee could deduct club membership costs when he could show that his membership was designed to make his services more valuable to his employer in expectation of an increased salary.[126]

A sales manager was allowed to deduct payments for business journals and magazines.[127]

A securities salesman properly deducted expenses for a marketing-service publication used by him in pursuance of his selling activities.[128]

Deduction is allowed for living expenses while an individual is away from home on business. This is to lessen the burden of a person who, because of the requirements of his trade or business, must maintain two places of abode and thus incur additional and duplicate living expenses.[129] In furtherance of this purpose, when a person with a principal place of employment goes *elsewhere* to take work which is merely temporary, he may deduct the living expenses incurred at the temporary post of duty, because it would not be reasonable to expect him to move his residence under such circumstances.[130] For this purpose, temporary employment is the type which can be expected to last for only a short period of time.[131]

An employee whose permanent residence is in this country but who is given a foreign assignment by his employer sometimes is required to spend his leave in the United States on the ground that the nature of his duties abroad calls for him to be fully familiar with present living patterns in America. Then his expenses of living and traveling in the

United States are deductible expenses in connection with his employment if he is not reimbursed for them.[132]

Outside salesmen, who do their selling away from their employer's place of business, are permitted to deduct all ordinary and necessary expenses paid or incurred in connection with their sales activities. Except for meals, an outside salesman can deduct all such expenses even if he is not away from home overnight. He may deduct the cost of his meals only if he is traveling away from home overnight or if his meals qualify as entertainment expenses.[133] In determining adjusted gross income, an employee can deduct these types of traveling expenses incurred while he is away from home on business if he is not reimbursed by his employer: travel, lodging, baggage, samples, display materials, cost of sample rooms, telephone and telegraph, stenographic services, and expenses (including depreciation) of maintaining and operating an automobile for business purposes. Loss on the sale of a car used for business purposes is deductible by an employee in computing adjusted gross income.[134] Automobile expenses for this purpose specifically include the cost of lubrication, repairs, tires, supplies, parking fees, and tolls. Also included are interest on a car loan, taxes in connection with maintaining the car, and insurance.[135]

An employee who is required to travel in connection with his job is entitled to deduct the unreimbursed costs of local transportation[136] and traveling expenses.[137]

A person's tax home is deemed to be where he works, and if he chooses for such reasons as convenience to reside elsewhere, the costs of meals, lodging, and transportation are not deductible as away-from-home business expenses. A salesman who lived in Virginia was assigned a territory centering on Philadelphia; 80 percent of his trips were to places within eighty-eight miles of that city. The Internal Revenue Service claimed that Philadelphia was his tax home, so that his expenses while visiting customers in that area were not deductible away-from-home expenses. But the court allowed deduction. He continued to live in Virginia after he got the Philadelphia territory because his wife worked close to his Virginia home and he wished to avoid loss of her job and the inconvenience of moving. His employer did not require him to live or to have an office in his sales territory. The concentration of his income-producing activity in the Philadelphia area was insufficient, by itself, to create a principal place of business or tax home there. So his costs while away from Virginia were deductible commuting expenses. His costs while staying overnight in the Philadelphia area were deductible away-from-home expenses.[138]

An outside salesman who kept valuable samples in his room could deduct as a business expense the cost of a security lock to protect these samples. He could also deduct the cost of a post-office box for business use, and a home telephone used for business purposes before and after his day's visits.[139]

A life-insurance company opened a new building, where appropriately new furniture was supplied by the company for all individual offices except that of a district sales manager, who thereupon purchased his own desk, sofa, draperies, etc. The company had not supplied him with new equipment because of a personality conflict between him and the employee designated to furnish the new building. The district sales manager felt that he could not maintain his status with clients, agents, and other persons that he saw in his dilapidated surroundings, but he wanted to avoid interoffice conflicts and hence did not complain. He sought no reimbursement from the company, and none was offered even when the matter became public knowledge. He could deduct depreciation on this equipment, which had been acquired for business reasons, to maintain status in connection with doing his job as an employee.[140]

A legal stenographer was permitted to deduct the cost of advertisements for employment which she inserted in the *New York Law Journal*.[141]

A nurse could deduct amounts she paid to a nurses' registry.[142]

A hospital attendant was permitted to deduct the cost of repairs to a watch which he was *required* to wear by his employer.[143] In other cases, where possession of a watch was not required, deduction of repairs was not permitted.

An insurance broker could deduct premium differences absorbed by him when he improperly advised his clients of the costs of policies.[144]

A physician who worked for an employer could deduct premiums he paid for malpractice insurance.[145]

A salesperson could deduct premiums on a fidelity policy which his employer required him to carry.[146]

A university research associate was expected by his employer to publish articles on his scientific pursuits. One article of particular value was not accepted by any scholarly publication, possibly because of professional dissension about the research technique used. He finally decided to finance the printing of this piece himself. The cost was deductible on the ground that his employer expected (although did not require) his research staff to publish the results of the research.[147]

The cost to an employee of a routine physical examination to establish his physical fitness in order to retain his position was deductible as a business expense, but any additional expense for medical or physical correction would only have been deductible if it met the medical-expense requirements.[148]

Defense of one's professional acts is also deductible.[149]

When a city's purchasing agent was charged with taking bribes in return for the awarding of contracts, he could deduct the cost of his legal fees as an expense related to his employment.[150]

Liquidated damages paid to one's former employer because of breach of an employment contract are deductible as a business loss if they are attributable to compensation received for services rendered.[151] For example, Jesse Hunt, a mason, worked for the Miller Industrial Corporation under the terms of a contract which called for Hunt to construct a brick wall around the entire perimeter of the Miller complex in one year's time. The entire cost of the project was $20,000, one-half of which was to be paid in advance. The amount of liquidation damages established by the contract was $7,000. After working for three months, Hunt found that he could not complete the project under the terms of the contract for less than twice the original cost agreed upon. In order to save himself from such a big loss, Hunt defaulted on the employment contract, thereby having to pay the $7,000 liquidation damages out of his $10,000 advance. He could properly deduct the $7,000 as a business loss.

An airlines flight officer was allowed to deduct the cost of his navigation kits and maps.[152]

A college professor may deduct his research, lecturing, and writing expenses.[153]

A sales representative for a graphics company was obliged to install, maintain, and service equipment sold to his customers. In order to perform this work, it was necessary for him to have a full complement of hand tools. These were not supplied by his employer, and the cost was not reimbursable. He could deduct the cost.[154]

The initiation fee required to be paid by an individual to a labor union in order to obtain employment is deductible.[155]

Monthly dues and assessments paid by members of a labor union are deductible business expenses except for any portion of the assessments used to provide death benefits.[156]

An unemployed electrician was allowed to deduct the costs of going to his union's hall twice daily for extended periods so that he could learn of any jobs that were posted. Although unemployed, he was still engaged in the electrical construction trade, even though not working for any particular employer at these times.[157]

Assessments for benefit payments to unemployed union members are deductible to the extent that they are applied to out-of-work benefit payments to unemployed members capable of working.[158]

Payments for union assessments which members are required to make for the support of an old-age pension fund are deductible where a member must pay his assessment in order to remain in the union and to retain his job.[159]

An employee who was obligated to pay a fine imposed against him by his union could deduct the amount of the payment when the fine had to be paid in order to remain in the union.[160]

Persons who are not members of a union may deduct check-off fees payable to the union which must be withheld from the compensation of *all* employees under a union contract.[161]

Employee contributions to the New Jersey Nonoccupational Disability Benefit and its New York equivalent are deductible by employees as state income taxes.[162]

An employee may deduct business transportation expenses in computing adjusted gross income even though they are neither reimbursable by his employer nor incurred while traveling away from home.[163] Among the expenses included in traveling expenses are charges for transportation of persons or baggage, expenditures for meals and lodging, and payments for the use of sample rooms for the display of goods.[164] But an employee must be away from home overnight in order to deduct the cost of his meals on business trips.[165]

An employee away from home on business could deduct the cost of his meals and nonalcoholic beverages in excess of the amount of reimbursement he received from his employer.[166]

Despite the rule that an individual cannot deduct the cost of his own meals unless he is away from home overnight on business, employer requirements can create employee deductions. An employee was permitted to take a deduction for the cost of his meals when he was required by his employer to have his meals on the work premises at his own expense. Here, to prevent racial discrimination, all employees were ordered to eat at the same time and place which, because of the requirements of the job, had to be on the employer's premises. Each employee was billed, and could deduct, the proportionate share of actual expenses.[167]

A salaried person ordinarily may not deduct entertainment expenses. But if he can show that his employer required or expected him to incur entertainment expenses in connection with his work, he may deduct the expenses, assuming that he can satisfy the record-keeping requirements.[168]

A field manager of a pharmaceutical manufacturer supervised fifteen salesmen. He spent some of his own money on salesmen or their families for bowling, theater, candy, toys, and the like in order to bring about good relations so that the business of his employer could prosper and his own earnings would increase. Deduction was allowed.[169]

A plant production manager could deduct the cost of entertaining the entire production supervisory staff and their spouses at a catered dinner given each year. He was also allowed to deduct expenses of entertaining associates and company customers at his home. There was no provision for reimbursement.[170] *See also* **Entertainment.**

An employer's business expenses are deductible by the employer. If an employee pays for company expenses, he is entitled to receive reimbursement, and hence the expenses are not his to deduct, even if, for some reason, he fails to seek reimbursement. But if he is not entitled to reimbursement, the expenses of the employer which he pays are deductible by him provided the expenditures also are in furtherance of his own business career.

An individual was an advertising solicitor for *Time* magazine. He was able to deduct entertainment expense because of evidence that he was expected to entertain company clients and would not be reimbursed. A memorandum from his business manager stated:

Mr. Luce and other Management officers have often emphasized that TIME salesmen are paid high salaries because selling is not a routine job and makes demands on a man's time and money that cannot be accounted for minute-by-minute or penny-by-penny. There are many expenses incidental to selling which a salesman is not expected to recover from the Company on top of his salary. In a very true sense, a salesman's job never ceases. And almost without exception his business life is closely interwoven with his personal social life. I make this point again because there are new men on the TIME staff who may never have heard of it. And because it explains why the Management does not expect an expense account to contain every phone call, every taxi ride, every luncheon and every drink bought by a salesman in the course of his business and social existence.[171]

The presentations manager of a magazine won his claimed entertainment deduction by attaching to his income tax return a letter from the assistant treasurer of the publication, stating that the nature of the magazine business was such that it was necessary for him (the manager) to incur entertainment expenses beyond those for which he was specifically reimbursed.[172]

An employee could deduct his travel expenses incurred while on his employer's business, where emergencies had to be dealt with without waiting for authorization or approval of his superiors.[173]

A corporation executive was entitled to reimbursement from his employer for most types of expenditure relating to client entertainment. He could deduct amounts paid for gifts to clients and for home entertainment of a business nature, as reimbursement specifically was not available for these types of outlay.[174]

An Air Force officer lived at an air base, although some of his duties were at other locations. The Air Force had military transportation facilities, assigned on the basis of rank, which meant that this major frequently had a jolly long wait. He was permitted to deduct the cost of using his own car to carry on his assignments. Inasmuch as his base was considered a place that had government transportation available, he was not entitled to claim reimbursement.[175]

An executive, who was directed by his home office to reduce expenses at the branch office he headed, notified his staff that reimbursement would not be given by the company to employees who used their cars for business purposes. He could deduct his expenses for using his car for a business purpose because he had to bear the cost himself. Had he claimed reimbursement from the company despite this rule, he might have gotten it. But he would have undermined the effectiveness of the rule and failed to meet the conditions of his employment, one of which was reducing company costs.[176]

Deduction by the employee requires that he show that he was expected to pay company entertainment expenses or specified company expenses from his own pocket according to an agreement with his superior.[177]

The general manager of a corporation could deduct his expenses of entertaining company customers when a jury was satisfied that he could not have obtained reimbursement from his employer.[178]

A bakery-route salesman working on a strictly commission basis could deduct his expenses in occasionally taking grocers to lunch and in buying soft drinks and coffee for certain customers in order to promote goodwill and to increase his sales and commissions. The court agreed with his labeling of these transactions on his income tax return: "Entertainment expense (to secure and/or retain patronage)."[179]

An employee of a management-consulting firm spent much of his time on the road, where he was allowed reasonable traveling expenses. He could deduct payments for public stenographers, typewriter rentals, calculator rentals, blueprints, drafting materials, and technical books for which he could not get reimbursement from his employer.[180] *See also* **Bad debts; Child-care and disabled-dependent care; Commuting; Education; Employee benefit-plan losses; Employment-agency fees; Employment, expenses in seeking; Government employees; Individual retirement account; Interviews; Legal fees; Mileage allowances; Moving expenses; Office at home; Overtime meals; Research; Self-employed plans; Speeding charges, expenses to go to court hearing; Telephone; Transactions entered into for profit; Uniforms; Union dues.**

Employees of other persons, payments to. *See* **Bribes and kickbacks.**

Employee turnover, reduction of. *See* **Day-care center, financing of; Improvement of employee morale; Ordinary and necessary business expenses.**

Employer, expenses of. Amounts paid on account of injuries received by employees and lump-sum payments as compensation for injuries are proper deductions.[181]

An employer may deduct payments made to an unrelated party for assisting transferred employees in selling their homes.[182] *See also* **Business gifts; Compensation; Contributions; Conventions; Day-care center, financing of; Efficiency awards; Group legal services plan; Improvement of employee morale; Ordinary and necessary business expenses; Sick-leave payments; Training expense; Violation of rights, payments to settle.**

Employment-agency fees. Fees paid to an employment agency for *securing* employment are deductible.[183] For executives seeking top positions and the compensation packages which go with them, much individualized effort may be necessary to find the ideal place, which no employment agency will undertake without an assured fee (usually substantial, in view of the work necessary), regardless of whether suitable employment is ultimately found. Payments made to an executive-search agency (not an employment agency) were deductible at the time when paid where employment was not found until long after the close of the taxable year when the payment was made.[184] Payments to an executive-search agency were deductible even though the executive never accepted a new position that was offered, his old employer having agreed to match the offered terms.[185]

Such payments were held to be deductible even though, because of economic conditions or otherwise, the payor did not succeed in obtaining a better position.[186] And fees of this nature were deemed to be deductible even though the payor had become disenchanted with the executive-search agency and terminated the relationship before anything was done for him.[187]

The executive vice-president of a corporation was fired by his long-time employer. The ex-officer paid a substantial fee to an executive-search agency, but he was not able to deduct the payment. Expenses incurred in connection with one's trade or business are deductible. But an employee who is out of work cannot be said to be in the trade or business of being an executive. One is not considered to be performing one's trade or business when out of a job. "It stretches the imagination to say that one is carrying on his trade or business as a corporate executive when he has no corporation for which to be an executive," observed the court.[188] To get the deduction an individual should be sure to make the payment to an executive-search agency before he loses his position.

Where an employee received reimbursement from his employer for placement agency fees after the former had completed a specified period of service, the amount received was taxed as additional compensation. But the employee could deduct the fee.[189]

Employment, expenses in seeking. In 1975, the Internal Revenue Service reconsidered the position which it had previously taken. The Service now takes the position that expenses incurred in seeking new employment *in the same trade or business* are deductible if the expenses are directly connected with that trade or business as determined by all the facts and circumstances. But such expenses are not deductible if an individual is seeking employment *in a new trade or business* even if employment is secured. If the individual is unemployed at the time of the expenditure, his trade or business would consist of the services previously performed for his past employer where no substantial lack of continuity occurred between the time of the past employment and the seeking of the new employment. Such expenses are not deductible by an individual where there is a substantial lack of continuity between the time of the past employment and the seeking of the new employment, or by an individual who is seeking employment for the first time.[190]

An individual became disenchanted with his employer's future prospects and decided to seek a comparable position elsewhere. Expenses in attending scheduled interviews with interested would-be employers were allowable as deductions from gross income in computing his adjusted gross income. Expenses for typing, printing, and postage related to sending out of résumés could be deducted by a person who itemized his deductions.[191]

An attorney worked for a state agency. He was worried lest this agency's activities be curtailed. His transportation expenses in going to another city to take an examination for a position as court administrator were deductible, being expenses in seeking new employment in the same trade or business; that is, being a lawyer.[192]

An actor was allowed to deduct the expenses of mailing out photographs and résumés to studios, agents, and casting personnel.[193]

Endorsers. *See* **Guarantor, payments to.**

Entertainers. *See* **Commuting; Education; Uniforms.**

Entertainment. No deduction is allowed for entertainment unless an individual establishes (1) that the expenditure was directly related to the active conduct of his trade or business or (2) in the case of an expenditure directly preceding or following a substantial and *bona fide* business discussion (including business meetings at conventions or otherwise), that the expenditure was associated with the active conduct of the individual's trade or business.[194]

An expenditure is deemed to be directly related to an individual's trade or business if it meets all four of the following tests:
1. At the time of the expenditure, the individual must have more than a general expectation of deriving income or a business benefit other than goodwill at some indefinite future time.
2. During the entertainment period, the individual is actually engaged in a business meeting, negotiation, discussion, or other *bona fide* transaction, other than entertainment, for the purpose of obtaining a business benefit.
3. The principal character of the expenditure must be the active conduct of the individual's trade or business. It is not necessary that more time

be devoted to business than to entertainment to meet this requirement.

4. The expenditure is allocable to the individual and a person or persons with whom he engages in the active conduct of trade or business during the entertainment or with whom he would be so engaged if it were not for circumstances beyond the individual's control.

In all the above instances, the expenditure must be in a "clear business setting."

The following expenditures are generally considered not directly related to an individual's business and would not be allowed as deductions:

1. Where the individual is not present.

2. Where the distractions are substantial; *e.g.,* meetings or discussions are held at nightclubs, theaters, sporting events, or cocktail parties.

Expenditures for food and drink will be allowed without reference to the above limitations where the circumstances are conducive to business discussions, even if business is not actually discussed. But the surroundings must provide an atmosphere where there are no substantial distractions.[195]

There are nine exceptions to these rules. They are business meals, food and beverages for employees, expenses treated as compensation, reimbursed expenses of employees and independent contractors, recreational expenses for employees, employee or stockholder business meetings, meetings of business leagues, items available to the public, and entertainment sold to customers. Expenses covered by these exceptions are not subject to the regular restrictions for entertainment expenses; they are deductible if they qualify as ordinary and necessary business expenses.[196]

It is not necessary that income or business benefits actually result from every entertainment expenditure for which a deduction is claimed.[197]

"Goodwill" entertainment involves entertainment where business is not discussed. The cost or expense is deductible if the entertainment takes the form of a "quiet" business setting, which directly precedes or follows a substantial business discussion. "The surroundings should be such," declared the Internal Revenue Service, "that there are no substantial distractions to dinner."[198] For example, the parties may completely avoid any business discussions at dinner if these discussions take place right before or after the meal.

If an individual entertains a business customer under circumstances where the cost of entertaining a customer is deductible, and the customer's wife joins the individual and the customer because it is impracticable to entertain the customer without her (*e.g.,* the customer is from out of town and has his wife traveling with him), the cost of entertaining the customer's wife is also deductible as an ordinary and necessary business expense. And if the taxpayer's wife joins them during the entertainment because the customer's wife is present, the cost of entertainment allocable to the taxpayer's wife also is deductible.[199]

If a person takes a customer to lunch for business goodwill purposes, and the customer's wife comes along, the expense will be allowed, even if they do not discuss business, where the surroundings are of the type generally considered conducive to discussing business. Should the host's wife accompany him in entertaining a customer in such surroundings, her part of the bill is also deductible whether or not the customer's wife is present. The fact that the business-meal entertaining takes place at the taxpayer's home does not disqualify the deduction, as long as the food or beverages are served under circumstances conducive to business discussion. But in the case of business-meal entertaining, the taxpayer must clearly show that the expenditure is commercially rather than socially motivated.[200]

Entertainment in one's home can be justified by showing that the home is more conducive to a confidential discussion than a public place would be; for example, when, as in one case, many of the guests are well-known people. It is also helpful if, as here, it can be shown that some of the persons for whom home entertainment deduction is claimed have been entertained at home on occasions when no business entertainment expense has been claimed.[201]

An individual, then, may deduct the cost of entertaining a customer, the customer's wife, and even his own wife under appropriate circumstances. But the deductibility of his own meal when he is not away from home overnight is a big question mark. Widely unnoticed is the fact that a number of decisions have held that unless the taxpayer demonstrates that the cost of a business meal exceeded that amount which he would have been required to spend in any event for his sustenance, no deduction will be allowed, for one's own meals represent a personal, nondeductible cost, and the individual would have had to feed himself even if a customer had not been present. The fact that the taxpayer would not have spent nearly so much on his own meal had he not been entertaining a *bona fide* customer is something for him to prove, if he can.[202] Bar bills where a customer was present were not the basis for *any* deduction where there was no indication of purchases for the taxpayer's own consumption.[203]

The manager of a bowling alley took to lunch various social or personnel directors of companies that sponsored bowling activities for their employees. He could deduct the expenses of the persons he thus entertained but not the cost of his own meals except to the extent that he could show they exceeded his normal costs for lunch.[204]

One court has noted that "if taxpayer can show . . . the maximum cost of his own lunches, a deduction for the remaining amount should be allowed."[205] It is an unusual situation when a taxpayer can do this. In one case, however, the taxpayer was a diabetic who was on a strict diet and did not use intoxicating liquors. He ate most of his meals, except lunches, at home. His lunches cost between seventy-five cents and $1, except when he entertained customers at lunch or dinner. Then he ordered mostly vegetables and coffee. Sometimes he ate nothing when he was with customers. Here the Internal Revenue Service was not able to assume that the portion of each lunch or dinner check chargeable to the host's food was equal to that chargeable to each guest, for the host had evidence to the contrary.[206]

In another case where there was evidence that an executive was interested only in his business and had no time for vacations and hobbies, the full cost of taking clients to lunch in his home city was deductible. There was reason to believe that he did not enjoy business lunches, and there was evidence that on those rare occasions when he did eat alone, he spent only about thirty-five cents or forty-five cents on his own meals.[207]

The IRS has announced that this rule as to nondeductibility of an individual's own portion of entertainment expenses will be applied only in "abuse" cases.[208] Where this approach is taken, it is up to the taxpayer to demonstrate that there was no abuse in his particular situation.

Deduction of entertainment facility items has been curtailed sharply in the case of items paid or incurred after December 31, 1978, in taxable years ending after that date. Deduction no longer is allowed for expenses of an entertainment, amusement, or recreation facility. "Facility" for this purpose means any real or personal property which is owned, rented, or used by a taxpayer in connection with an entertainment activity, including yachts, hunting lodges, fishing camps, swimming pools, tennis courts, and bowling alleys. Facilities also include airplanes, cars, hotel suites, apartments, and houses (such as beach cottages and ski lodges) located in recreational areas. But business expense deduction is proper provided that a facility is not used in connection with *entertainment*. Thus, expenses of a car used primarily for business purposes other than entertainment still are deductible if properly substantiated. "Facility" includes dues or fees paid to any social, athletic, or sporting club or organization. But otherwise deductible business meals are not disallowable merely because the expense was incurred in the dining room of a club or organization where dues or fees are not deductible under this rule. Dues or fees paid to a country club are deductible only if the taxpayer establishes that the facility was used primarily for the furtherance of his trade or business and that the expenses were directly related to the conduct of his trade or business.[209] Deduction similarly is allowed in the case of fees paid to social, athletic, or sporting clubs or organizations which satisfy this same test.[210]

This illustration was furnished by the Congressional committee which wrote the legislation:

> For example, if a salesman took a customer hunting for a day at a commercial-shooting preserve, the expenses of the hunt (such as hunting rights, dogs, a guide, etc.) would be deductible provided that the current law requirements of substantiation, adequate records, ordinary and necessary, directly related, etc., are met. However, if the hunters stayed overnight at a hunting lodge on the shooting preserve, the cost attributable to the lodging would be nondeductible but expenses for any meals would be deductible if they satisfied the requirements of current law. The shooting preserve should provide the taxpayer with an allocation of charges attributable to the overnight lodging for the taxpayer and guests.[210]

That a facility actually was used for the obtaining of business and not for entertainment, amusement, or recreation can be shown by credible contemporary documentation. In one case, a broker of foodstuffs owned a yacht. The log contained entries such as the presence of guests from a named canning company, followed by the informative and helpful statement, "sold 7,500 cases to them."[211]

Proof that an entertainment expense was business-related can come from showing why a particular person was entertained. An individual who was seeking investment advice could deduct the cost of meals furnished to persons in a position to give him such advice.[212]

An anesthesiologist was allowed to deduct entertainment costs for physicians who referred patients to him.[213]

Deduction was approved for the purchase of tickets from customers to promote goodwill.[214]

A businessperson could deduct the cost of season tickets to baseball and hockey games because they brought customers to his hotel.[215]

A business was unsuccessful in attracting customers during the normal daytime working hours. Dinners were therefore given for important clients. Expenses for these were allowed after the taxpayer produced charts which showed that business growth had paralleled increased promotional activities.[216]

Deduction was allowed even where entertainment of potential customers did not result in purchase orders, for the inability to obtain business was solely because of the failure of the intending buyers to secure bank financing.[217]

Where entertainment of customers unquestionably was for business purposes, full deduction of the expenses was allowed even though some of the nonbusiness guests used the entertainment facilities (in this case, a yacht) on the same days that customers were aboard. No allocation was necessary.[218]

A business could deduct its entertainment expenses where customers of its made-to-order machine parts were invited to partake of the host company's hospitality. Here the customers were urged to bring their personal manufacturing problems for discussion with the host's staff and with other guests who had had to cope with the same or similar situations. The personal pleasure of persons invited may have been a factor in their attendance, but undeniably they hoped to derive business benefits from being there, and so did the host, who therefore could deduct business entertainment expenses.[219]

Entertainment expenses may be accepted as business-related rather than personal where an individual is able to show that he *would not* have made an expenditure for himself. The cost of cigars was deductible by a person who established that he was a nonsmoker. It was only his customers who smoked.[220]

An executive who entertained customers at his club could deduct the cost of handball games there when he testified convincingly that he never had held a handball.[221]

Deduction was allowed for the cost of taking partners and business associates to lunch where there was evidence that business was discussed.[222]

A person could deduct the cost of lunches for assistants with whom he discussed business.[223]

Proof is the essential ingredient in the allowance of travel and entertainment expenses. Unlike most deductions, reasonable estimates cannot be used; the so-called "*Cohan* rule," which permits a court to make its own estimate of undocumented expenses where it can be established that there were such expenditures, does not apply to travel and entertainment expenses.[224] In addition to the regular rules which control tax deductions with reference to being ordinary, necessary, reasonable, and the like, a special section of the Internal Revenue Code disallows travel and entertainment expenses which do not meet stringent additional requirements as to documentation.[225] There must be contemporary records for each such expenditure, showing cost, date, place, business purpose, nature of the business benefit expected, and business relationship to the taxpayer of the person or persons entertained.[226]

Where the documentation offered by an insurance agent showed all of the required information except business purpose of the entertainment, deduction was allowed in instances where he could identify the names of persons who shortly afterward had purchased insurance from him.[227]

In one case, where all of the requirements were documented in the record except for business purpose, the court was willing to assume there had indeed been such a purpose, for there was evidence that an executive devoted practically every waking moment of every weekday (and frequently weekends) to his employer, a bank. The bank was his sole avocation and, noted the court, "he is more than a banker; he is a flesh and blood extension of [the] . . . Bank."[228]

If any information relating to an expenditure, such as place, business purpose, or business relationship, is of a confidential nature, this information need not be set forth in the account book, diary, statement of expense, or similar record, provided the information is recorded at or near the time of expenditure and is available elsewhere to the Internal Revenue Service to justify this element of the expenditure.[229]

Where a person's travel is purely local in nature, he does not have to meet stringent substantiation requirements. A court, if it chooses, can allow a deduction in an amount of the court's own determination upon the basis of credible estimates.[230]

The strict rules for business entertainment deduction require a contemporary listing of who was entertained, where, etc., as detailed earlier in this section. A liquor salesman bought drinks at bars where he solicited orders, picking up the tab for owners, managers, bartenders, and their friends who happened to be on the spot. He recorded each day where he had spent the money, naming each bar and the proprietor, plus other persons unspecified. The Internal Revenue Service sought to disallow expenses where names were not named. But the court allowed full deduction. The requirement is that persons entertained be identified by name, title, or *other designation.* "Friends" or "customers" was sufficient identification of the business relationship of the expenditures to the salesman's business. The purpose of the substantiation requirement is only to encourage the taxpayer to maintain proper records; not to penalize him unduly for compliance peculiar to his trade or business.[231]

Proof of the business nature of an expenditure can be *circumstantial,* as when the relationship between the expense and the taxpayer's business is obvious.[232]

Likewise, the strict rules for business entertainment deduction do not apply where a manufacturer of consumer products authorized his salespersons, in the course of regular calls on customers, to purchase company products for free distribution to the customer's patrons. (A brief presentation on the quality of the taxpayer's products also was delivered.)[233]

To ride herd on business appointments, a person probably keeps an office diary showing the dates, times, places, and names of persons whom he wines and dines. The diary would substantiate the deductions in case of an audit. Deduction of otherwise proper business expenses is not authorized where this diary or other contemporary record does not disclose the "occupation or other information relating to the person or persons entertained, including name, title, or other designation, sufficient to establish relationship to the taxpayer."[234] A businessperson must not omit this information, because by law the Internal Revenue Service is not allowed to recognize the deduction without it.[235]

You do not have to record each name if there is a readily identifiable class of individuals involved. For example, if you entertain all the stockholders of a small corporation, a designation such as "all the stockholders of the Amy Corporation" is enough. If, however, the identity of a class is not enough to identify the persons entertained, then an individual designation of each person is required.[236]

The proprietor of a gambling establishment could deduct his expenses for providing sandwiches and liquor to his customers. Substantiation that he had provided "free lunches" was furnished to the court's satisfaction by several former patrons.[237]

The operator of an automobile service station could deduct the cost of beer which was available to customers of his establishment. Recipients of the beer reasonably knew that his motive in incurring the expenditure was directly furthering his business.[238]

One court has repudiated the Internal Revenue Service regulation that such data be in writing. Even without meeting the Service requirements, declared this decision, a taxpayer can deduct travel and entertainment expenses if he backs up the expenses with adequate records or with sufficient evidence corroborating his own statement. There may be alternative methods of substantiation other than written records. "Thus," ruled this court, "oral testimony of the taxpayer, together with circumstantial evidence available, may be considered 'sufficient evidence' for the purpose of establishing the business purpose required under the new provision."[239] This means that properly substantiated oral testimony may be sufficient to back up travel and entertainment expenses.

Even without contemporary written evidence of the business purpose of taking persons to lunch, where the written record showed only the places, dates, and amounts charged, a court accepted as proper documentation the testimony of several businesspersons that there had been business purpose for the meetings at which the taxpayer as host was "gracefully allowed . . . to pick up the check."[240]

If a taxpayer maintains a diary showing each person entertained, no receipts or other corroborating documentary evidence are required in the case of expenditures up to $25, except for lodging, and where receipts are readily available, for transportation.[241]

The tough substantiation requirements can be bypassed if entertainment expenses can be properly categorized under another classification. A business awarded trips to deserving dealer-customers; such trips covered an individual and his spouse. The wives of two of the business's principals acted as hostesses, performing personal services on week-long trips in the interest of building customer goodwill. The court accepted the denomination of the $1,000 payments to each of the wives as compensation rather than entertainment expense; and hence the lack of detailed substantiation data was not fatal to the deduction.[242]

In applying the test of whether the detailed requirements for entertainment must be met, a person's trade or business must be considered.

Thus, although attending a theatrical performance generally would be considered entertainment, it would not be so regarded in the case of a professional theater critic, attending in his professional capacity.[243]

The manager of a cocktail lounge could deduct the cost of drinks he purchased for himself when he went to other lounges to evaluate the competition and to try to recruit entertainers. He was not obliged to maintain the detailed contemporary records required to substantiate entertainment expenses, because his expenditures were not for entertainment but were in effect, to quote the court's decision, "tickets of admission."[244]

Entertainment expenses are not deductible to the extent that they are lavish or extravagant. But deductions by a broker of the costs of transporting certain customers to and from his office in a chauffeur-driven Cadillac were allowed when it was shown that they were wealthy foreigners who were accustomed to this sort of treatment in their homeland.[245]

Deduction is allowed for entertainment of public officials where it is of a type prevalent in the industry and there is no administrative action in the state prohibiting the providing of such entertainment.[246]

Out-of-pocket expenditures spent on entertainment to promote a charitable ball by means of giving cocktail parties and dinners were deductible. It was noted in this ruling that the sponsor of these affairs had no control over the invitation list.[247]

The general rule (given at the beginning of this section) for the disallowance of deductions for entertainment, amusement, or recreation expenses does not apply to expenses which are includable in the gross income of a recipient of the entertainment, etc., who is not an employee, as compensation for services or as a taxable prize or award. But in order to avoid disallowance of expenses which do not have elaborate entertainment expense substantiation, the payor must file an information return (Form 1099) with the Internal Revenue Service, showing the amount of the payment and the name of the individual benefited.[248] If a taxpayer's substantiation data for entertainment expenses cannot be produced because of loss of such records through circumstances beyond his control, he has the right to substantiate a deduction by reasonable reconstruction of his expenditures.[249]

For example, a salesperson was evicted from his apartment for nonpayment of a month's rent. When he came home that night, there in the street were his possessions—except for what had been stolen, which included his business records. He was permitted a deduction of entertainment expenses which he was able to reconstruct.[250]

A persistent question in the case of a closely held corporation is whether the IRS will recognize as a corporate deduction entertainment expenses incurred by an officer-shareholder. This is especially a problem where, as so often is the case with a closely held corporation, substantiation of the *business* nature of the entertainment is sketchy. To safeguard the corporation's interest, some companies in their bylaws provide that if the firm's entertainment expense deduction is disallowed by the Service because the expenditure appeared to be for the officer's personal benefit, he must repay the corporation for its lost deduction. He can then deduct the amount of this reimbursement as an expense in carrying on his trade or business.[251] *See also* **Advertising; Congressman, expenses of; Executives; Ordinary and necessary business expenses.**

Entrance fee. *See* **Retirement homes.**

Erosion. *See* **Water erosion, correction of.**

Errors, rectification of. *See* **Business-related losses; Executives; Shortages, repayment of.**

Errors and omissions, policy premiums. A fiduciary was allowed to deduct premiums on errors and omissions insurance where he was paid a fee for his services. This made the expenditures a payment incurred for the production or collection of income.[252] *See* **Fiduciaries.**

Escrow, deduction of taxes paid in. *See* **Taxes.**

Estate planning. Estate planning involves many items in connection with the disposition of a person's property, including in most instances Federal income, estate, and gift taxes. A fee related to the preparation of a tax return or the establishment of the tax is one of the relatively few personal expenditures which an individual can deduct for tax purposes. So payments for estate planning are deductible to the extent that it can be shown that the fees paid for the estate planning relate to taxes. An individual therefore should make certain that bills for estate-planning services clearly identify the portion of the charge which relates to taxes rather than the drawing up of a will, setting up of a trust, transfer of insurance policies, and the like.[253]

Excess charitable deductions. *See* **Contributions.**

Excessive compensation, repayment of. *See* **Executives; Repayment of excessive compensation.**

Executives. The president of a gigantic, prestigious, publicly held corporation is after all an employee, and he has the type of deduction available to employees in general. But because of the nature and scope of his duties, an executive may be entitled to various other additional deductions.

Serving as president of a corporation constitutes the carrying on of a trade or business.[254] Thus, expenses in connection with an officer's trade or business are deductible by him.

An executive could deduct the cost of entertaining salesmen under his supervision, for this tended to build up business, which in turn affected his compensation.[255] A corporation president was allowed to deduct his membership fees in a chamber of commerce whether or not the corporation required him to take out the membership. He used this affiliation as a means of carrying out the essential duties of his employment; it enabled him to keep more readily abreast of business plans and of business and economic conditions in the community.[256]

In order to encourage directors and officers to make the "right" decision regardless of possible personal consequences, some corporations take out liability insurance to indemnify these persons if they are sued or otherwise held financially accountable for business acts. Lower-level executives customarily are not covered by such insurance, perhaps because they are less likely to be sued, perhaps because top management is not willing to have the corporation absorb costs involving the second team. When a corporation took out such liability insurance to indemnify nonofficer executives for the financial consequences of their business acts, and the executives were back-charged their proportionate shares of the premiums, the executives individually could deduct the costs as ordinary and necessary business expenses.[257]

Two individuals who were major but not the sole stockholders of a corporation transferred some of their stock back to the company in order to improve its financial condition. They could deduct their cost of this stock as an expense in connection with being employees, as their solution to the company's financial problem was intended to help the company pay their salaries.[258]

A corporate officer could deduct attorneys' fees when defending himself against an effort to remove him from control and management.[259]

Legal expenses in resisting attempts to dislodge an executive as an officer were deductible by him.[260]

A corporation president properly deducted his expenses in connection with a lawsuit against the corporation for his ouster.[261]

Legal fees in connection with one's business or the production of income generally are deductible. Fees for personal, nonbusiness services are not. But the president of a corporation was permitted to deduct attorneys' fees in connection with changing the trustees of trusts she had created for her children. Some of the stockholders wanted to oust her from her high-salaried position, and the company shares which she had transferred to these trusts (5 percent of the total stock outstanding) might have been voted by the trustees against her. So replacement of these trustees with persons willing to vote the stock in her favor constituted a deductible business expense: to continue on the payroll.[262]

An individual was a corporation executive and also a trustee and life-income beneficiary of a trust which owned all of the corporation's stock. Charges against him for mismanagement were filed by the trust's remaindermen. In settlement of this dispute he relinquished his life income in the trust. The value of the transferred interest was an ordinary and necessary business expense as an officer and director of the corporation. His malfeasance in the conduct of his paid corporate duties was a major part of the action against him.[263]

A corporate officer was permitted to deduct amounts he paid to settle a claim that he had violated a position of trust in permitting his wife to profit from transactions in the corporation's securities.[264]

The board chairman of a major steel-manufacturing company swore to all of the company's tax returns as chief executive officer. He was charged with conspiracy to defraud the government of taxes but was acquitted. The necessity of paying legal fees was occasioned by acts done in connection with his trade or business, and deduction was allowed.[265]

Similarly, a corporate officer whose responsibilities included the filing of his company's Federal income tax returns was indicted for having caused the filing of a false corporate return where company funds were diverted to his own use. His legal fees in defending himself were deductible because they arose in connection with acts committed by him in his trade or business as an executive.[266]

Amounts expended in defending a suit against charges of breach of duty as a corporate officer are deductible.[267]

Expenditures by an officer and director of a corporation in the successful defense of a stockholder's derivative suit were held to be deductible business expenses. While acting as an officer and director, he was engaged in carrying on a trade or business.[268]

A retired officer of a corporation could deduct legal fees arising out of transactions in which he participated while he still was an officer.[269]

A director of a corporation could deduct amounts paid to settle a stockholders' suit alleging incompetency in his duties.[270]

Stockholders sued the directors of a corporation for recovery of damages based upon alleged wrongful acts and omissions, and a court awarded judgment for a certain sum against one of the directors. He was not permitted to deduct the costs as being incurred in a trade or business, or in a transaction entered for profit. He did not, and did not expect to, receive any compensation or other monetary benefit for his services, having become a director solely out of friendship for the chief stockholder. He rarely attended a board meeting and was totally uninformed about the corporation's financial affairs. He could not be regarded as in the business of being a director. This decision illustrates what *should* be established in order to be allowed the deduction.[271]

An individual was president and a stockholder of a corporation which became insolvent. An employee threatened to sue him personally because the corporation had violated state law by not protecting its employees with Workmen's Compensation Insurance. The president's lawyer advised him that he might be personally liable to the claimant because the corporation could not provide any funds for employee demands. So the official compromised the claim for $2,000, which he paid. Even though his lawyer's advice might have been erroneous, he was justified in relying upon it, and he properly deducted the payment as an expense in connection with being an officer of the corporation.[272]

Stockholders of a corporation brought suit against the officers and directors of a corporation for alleged improper conduct. A settlement was reached under which each defendant would transfer a certain number of his shares or the cash equivalent to an agent for the stockholders. A director who transferred stock to this agent in order to satisfy his obligation was deemed to have made a disposition of his stock. So the difference between what he had paid for the shares and the value at the time of disposition was gain or loss. But inasmuch as his settlement obligation arose from his trade or business of being a director, loss was not capital but was a fully deductible business expense.[273]

A director of a corporation undergoing a reorganization was permitted to deduct his share of a settlement payment (including his attorney's fees) which arose from suits against him and the other directors in their respective capacities as directors.[274]

An officer of a corporation could deduct legal fees involving a question of how an option given to him to buy company stock at a favorable price should be taxed. This related to his *business* income.[275]

An executive could deduct the amount of judgment obtained against him by his corporation for losses resulting from his unauthorized use of corporate funds for speculating in commodities, which he carried on solely for the benefit of the corporation.[276]

A financial consultant acted as an officer and consultant of public utility companies. He served as an officer and director of a corporation undergoing Section 77B Bankruptcy Act reorganization. He paid a sum in settlement of a claim which arose from an alleged breach of fiduciary duty because of certain profits made by his wife with respect to sales and purchases of the corporation's bonds. His payment was deductible, having been made in connection with his trade or business.[277]

Section 16(b) of the Securities Exchange Act of 1934 provides, in part, that for the purpose of preventing the unfair use of information which may have been obtained by an officer, director, or beneficial owner of more than 10 percent of the stock of a corporation, any profit realized by him from any purchase or sale, or any sale and purchase, of any equity security of the corporation within any period of less than six months shall inure to and be recoverable by the corporation. A deduction by reason of an insider's payment to a corporation pursuant to or as a result of this provision in the amount of profits derived in dealings with stock will not be denied on the ground that it frustrates sharply defined public policy.[278]

A corporate executive held various directorships, including a major listed motion-picture producing company. He had purchased enough of that stock to ensure his becoming a director. His purpose was to make a profit by improving the company's performance. When the Securities and Exchange Commission brought the matter to the company's attention, reminding the company that insider profits belong to the corporation, he was so advised. He believed that he was not covered because the violation, if such it was, resulted from inadvertence. But to avoid any adverse impact on his business reputation which a disclosure would occasion, he turned his profits over to the company. That amount was deductible by him as a business expense, to protect his reputation, which he considered to be his most important asset.[279] Although several other decisions have held that such payments are not deductible, those cases involved payment which the insider legally was obligated to make. Here the individual never consulted a lawyer but immediately repaid the amount, not because he felt it was a legal obligation but to safeguard his reputation for integrity. The payment was not made purely because he was required by law to make it; he had a business reason for making the payment.

The president and chief stockholder of a corporation was approached by a potential acquirer of the company, and all financial data were requested. The president became an officer of the acquirer after negotiations were completed. Subsequently the acquirer filed suit against him, alleging that he had fraudulently misrepresented his old company's liabilities, as a result of which substantial losses were incurred by the acquirer. Deeming this suit to be an attack upon his integrity and business reputation, he vigorously defended the suit, incurring substantial legal and accounting fees which he deducted as ordinary and necessary expenses. The court permitted these as expenses in connection with his trade or business of being a corporate officer. Counsel for his new employer had advised him that if the charges were substantiated, he would have to resign as an officer and director because the new employer was a listed company which might be harmed by the publicity.[280]

Expenses to protect one's business reputation are deductible, such as in the case of the president of a personal service corporation which bore his name. The company was unable to pay trade creditors. He feared that if the company with his name went bankrupt, that would damage his own reputation. He could deduct the amount of the company bills which he paid with his own funds.[281]

The chief executive officer of a manufacturing company was responsible for operations. When the shareholders sold their stock to another company, the latter subsequently demanded a reduction in price because of shortages and errors, which was granted. The equivalent of this amount was deducted from moneys payable to the chief executive on account of his alleged poor performance. He in turn could deduct this amount as an expense in connection with his business of being an executive.[282]

Ordinarily, a shareholder may not take a tax deduction for a payment made on behalf of the corporation. But the payment may be deducted as an ordinary and necessary expense of a trade or business of the shareholder. An individual was an officer and purchasing agent of an industrial-plumbing corporation, *I*. He also owned all the stock of a corporation, *G*, which was engaged in residential heating. *G* was in severe financial trouble, and the directors of his employer company, *I*, were worried about the impact of the insolvency of a firm with which he was known in the trade to be closely identified. In fact, the *I* directors felt it would be impossible for him to continue as purchasing agent, where he would have to make terms with creditors who were familiar with the impending bankruptcy of his own company, *G*. It was remembered that some years before he had also been associated with a bankrupt firm, and suppliers might be reluctant to sell on credit to a company, *I*, whose purchasing agent had consistently been associated with losers. Feeling that his job was in danger, he attempted to protect his position by personally making settlement with *G*'s creditors. The payments were made by him, not to put new life into *G* nor to protect his investment in it, but to protect his job with *I*. Accordingly, he could deduct the payments he made to *G*'s creditors as expenses related to his business of being an employee of Corporation *I*.[283]

In states and cities where sellers are obliged to charge sales tax to customers, officers of corporations which fail to transmit such taxes are *personally* liable for the untransmitted funds. But the individuals who must pay these amounts personally can deduct them on their own Federal income tax returns.[284]

When an executive bought stock in his corporation to prevent a buy-out that would have cost him his job, subsequent loss upon disposition of the stock was fully deductible as a business expense, for the business was transacted in order to maintain his employment.[285]

An executive may deduct as education expenses his costs for improving the managerial skills needed in his employment.[286]

An executive could deduct expenses of a telephone in his home during a period when he was confined there by illness.[287]

The executive head of a corporation worked on a commission basis. He employed other persons, whom he personally paid, to help him increase his sales and commissions. The salaries he paid were deductible as expenses in connection with his business of being the head of the company.[288]

A corporate officer claiming a deduction for travel and entertainment expenses will get the deduction if he can show that such expenses relate directly to his own business activities.[289]

In general, expenses of corporate entertaining are deductible only by the corporation; the expenses are corporate and not those of the officers, however much they may identify themselves with the company. But if payment of entertainment expenses helps an officer to do his job better, the fact that the corporation also benefits does not bar the officer's deduction. The vice-president of a New York City bank could deduct his substantiated expenses for entertaining persons whose favor the bank wanted, for the entertainment enabled the officer to discharge his implied duty. As the bank had given him to understand that he was to extend hospitality to certain clients, and nothing was said about reimbursement, the expenses were necessary for his office.[290]

One executive was allowed to deduct nonreimbursable expenses of entertaining customers of his bank where the court found that the directors "not only approved of [his] conduct, but expected and required it. They knew that little if any business would come [his] way if he spent eight hours a day in his office waiting for customers to seek him out."[291]

A bank officer received "suggestions" from his superiors that he join certain clubs for the better performance of his duties, and after his salary was increased, they made it clear to him that he was personally expected to bear the expense of his club dues. "To be sure," observed the court, "they did not threaten to discharge him if he failed to comply with their suggestions; but the purport of such suggestions was obvious."[292]

A vice-president in charge of production for a major listed tobacco company had responsibilities which included extensive entertaining. It was held that his bills were properly deductible by him because they were incurred in connection with earning his income.[293]

The president of a corporation was not on a guaranteed salary. A significant part of his compensation represented commissions on sales he made for the corporation. He was on an incentive basis, and in order to earn these commissions, it was necessary to entertain prospective customers to get their business. He was entitled to the deduction for this entertainment cost, not being able to get reimbursement from the corporation for his expenses.[294]

In another case, a vice-president and regional manager of a leading paper company had as his principal responsibility the maintenance of "first-name" contacts and relationships with top-echelon officers of major business enterprises throughout his region. To keep such high-level contacts, he joined a number of clubs. His arrangement with the company president was that entertainment expenses for large parties were subject to reimbursement, while usual and ordinary expenses were to be paid from his own funds. To maintain his status position and appropriate image with the company's board of directors and president, he believed that it was necessary that he pay for ordinary expenses. These expenditures were deductible.[295]

A corporate officer who claims deductions for travel and entertainment expenses incurred on behalf of a corporation must bear the burden of proof that *he* is entitled to the deduction. A directors' resolution requiring the assumption of such expenses by him tends to indicate that they are a necessary expense of his office.[296]

An executive may be required by corporate bylaw or otherwise to reimburse the corporation to the extent of any entertainment expense the company paid on his behalf, if the Internal Revenue Service disallows it as unsubstantiated from the point of view of the corporation's business. Then he is permitted to deduct the amount which he pays the corporation to make good its lost deduction.[297]

In an interoffice memorandum a company advised its executives that although entertainment expenses for existing customers would be reimbursed, expenses for potential new business would not be reimbursed by the company and would have to be borne by the individual incurring them unless the president and the treasurer specifically authorized them. An executive's entertainment expenses for potential customers were deemed to be deductible to a considerable extent and perhaps would have been allowed in full had his records been better kept.[298]

Where the officers of a corporation were required to incur travel and other expenses of the corporation without expectation of reimbursement, these expenses were deductible as ordinary and necessary expenses of being an executive of the corporation.[299]

If an executive personally pays the salary of someone to handle his duties when he is not available, the cost of the substitute is a deduction for the executive.[300]

A partner who paid with his own funds the salary of a partnership employee engaged to take over some of the partner's duties was permitted to deduct these payments.[301]

An individual paid a fee to a psychological-study organization for a basic psychological examination and for counseling services to the degree of success he might obtain as a business executive. Through these efforts he actually obtained a position. He could deduct the fees as expenses in securing employment.[302]

Some corporations pay consulting firms to provide certain designated executives of the employer company with investment and tax counsel at no charge to these executives. If the Internal Revenue Service taxes the value of such counsel to an executive as additional compensation, then he is entitled to deduct this amount either as an expense related to investments held for the production of income, or as payments for tax assistance.[303]

If a corporation loses part of a compensation deduction because it is deemed to be unreasonable, the payee (usually an officer or executive) may be called upon, directly or indirectly, to restore to the company the amount of its lost tax deduction. All sorts of pressures may be placed upon him to do so. But if he does repay the amount of disallowed compensation for the prior year, he will not get a tax deduction; business expenses must be ordinary and necessary, and this is neither. It is not ordinary for an executive to pay back money his employer could not justify to the Internal Revenue Service as reasonable. It is not necessary to make the payment in the absence of a legal obligation to do so. But his deduction in case of repayment can be assured in any of these ways:

1. Notation in the directors' minutes. *Actual example:* Salary payments made to an officer of the corporation that shall be disallowed in whole or in part as a deductible expense for Federal income tax purposes shall be reimbursed to the full extent of the disallowance. It shall be the duty of the board of directors to enforce payment of such amount disallowed.[304]

2. Corporate bylaws. *Actual example:* Any payments made to an officer of the corporation, such as salary, commission, bonus, or rent or entertainment expense incurred by him, which shall be disallowed in whole or in part as a deductible expense by the Internal Revenue Service, shall be reimbursable to the full extent of the disallowance. It shall be the duty of the directors, as a board, to enforce payments to each such amount disallowed. In lieu of a payment by the officer, subject to the determination of the directors, proportionate amounts may be withheld from his future compensation until the amount owed to the corporation has been recovered.[305]

3. Provision in an employment contract. *Actual example:* The parties specifically agree that if any payments are disallowed, in whole or in part, as deductible expenses for Federal income tax purposes, the employee shall mandatorily reimburse the company to the full extent of the disallowance.[306]

An executive may guarantee a bank loan to his employer corporation because if the corporation fails, which is quite possible, commitments he has made to customers will not be honored. That could hurt his reputation and employability as an executive. If he has to make good because the corporation fails, he has a fully deductible business bad debt.[307] *See also* **Guarantor, payments by.**

Sometimes an executive arranges to have some of his personal bills paid by the corporation for which he works. If he is a stockholder, the Internal Revenue Service will treat the company's payment of his bills as though they were dividends to him. If the personal bills paid by the corporation were medical expenses, the employee can deduct them on his own tax return although he did not actually pay the physicians himself.[308]

Similarly, if a corporation pays a financial counseling firm a fee to provide personal advice to specified executives, this payment is regarded as taxable compensation to each such executive. But the executive may deduct the equivalent of any part of the fees that represents advice on tax planning and tax-return preparation.[309] *See also* **Bad debt; Conventions; Education; Employment-agency fees; Entertainment; Guarantor, payments to; Legal fees; Ransom; Release from liability; Reputation, maintenance of; Settlement payments; Travel.**

Executive-search-agency fees. *See* **Employment-agency fees.**

Executor's fees. As a general rule, expenses of a casual executor, administrator, or trustee are not deductible. But where an individual undertook the duties of executrix with intent to secure compensation therefor, and she was in fact allowed a substantial fee by the probate court, her services could not be deemed to be so insignificant as to deny them the characterization of business activities.[310]

Similarly, a trustee could deduct legal expenses resulting from a suit by a beneficiary which demanded an accounting, sought restoration by the trustee of losses from improper investments, and attempted to have a new trustee appointed. On a do-it-yourself basis, she also could deduct the cost of law texts for her own use.[311]

A fiduciary may deduct the cost of litigation in order to obtain his fees.[312]

An individual had been named by the decedent, his father, to be one of the three coexecutors. The son had limited business and financial experience. But the administration of the estate required financial and business skill ordinarily associated with the conduct of large enterprises and available only to persons who had years of intimate knowledge of the details of the business. The other two coexecutors had such experience, and the son felt that his own heavy responsibilities should be delegated to them. He arranged to pay them for relieving him of unfamiliar chores in the form of a percentage of the executor's fees he would receive. The fees he thus paid them were deductible by him as nontrade or nonbusiness expenses incurred for the production of income.[313]

Where an executor agreed to turn over his executor's fees to a financial firm for taking over his accounting and appraisal responsibilities in connection with the estate, he could deduct these payments.[314]

Ex-employee, inducement to return after military duty. *See* **Ordinary and necessary business expenses.**

Expenditures for benefits lasting more than one year. Ordinarily, expenditures for business benefits which will be enjoyed over a period of years must be capitalized rather than expensed currently. Following are areas where the full expense could be taken in the year of payment or incurrence:

1. Survey of future financing requirements.[315]
2. Fees paid to an accountant to investigate the advisability of a change in the taxpayer's accounting system.[316]
3. Management survey.[317]
4. Fees of efficiency engineers to increase the taxpayer's production at reduced cost.[318]
5. In many states, employers subject to the state unemployment insurance law are permitted to make voluntary payments in excess of the regular rate. Inasmuch as the state unemployment insurance tax rate in such places is based upon a ratio of employer contributions to claims filed by ex-employees now out of work, a favorable ratio will entitle the employer to a lower tax rate in the future. Such voluntary payments are deductible as ordinary and necessary expenses when made, although the objective is to reduce the rate of *future* tax payments to the state.[319]

That a future benefit has been established by an expenditure does not necessarily mean that the expenditure must be capitalized instead of being deducted at once. In one case, an expenditure was made for the right to use a new credit system that was licensed by a franchisor. Although future benefits from the expenditure were possible, deduction was allowed because the payment was made to promote the taxpayer's existing business and did not create a separate and distinct asset.[320]

The cost of items which ordinarily have a life of more than one year is deductible if it can be shown that in this particular instance, life was less than one year. The cost of tires purchased for a vehicle used for business purposes was deductible where it could be demonstrated that the tires would be used up in less than a year. It does not matter that this life extends into part of the following year.[321]

This rule has also been applied in the case of a purchase of used tires and tubes.[322]

Where a doctoral degree is necessary for a university teacher to obtain a permanent appointment to the staff, the tuition costs for the degree are deductible, even though possession of this degree may be expected to be useful in the teacher's career for many years after the expenses are made. Such educational expenses, in the words of one court, have a "now-or-never status."[323]

Expenses for obtaining a long-term lease (*e.g.,* a broker's commission or lawyer's fee) are amortizable over the life of the lease, regardless of the taxpayer's accounting method.[324] Any renewal period is to be considered in determining the period over which amortization of cost is allowed, but *only* if less than 75 percent of the cost is attributable to the portion of the lease (excluding the renewal period) remaining on the acquisition date. This rule will apply unless it is established at the close of the taxable year that the lease probably will not be renewed.[325]

Where loan commitment fees are for a short period, they are deductible. They must be amortized over the period of a loan or mortgage for a period of more than a year.[326]

Individuals must capitalize the costs of producing motion pictures, records, and similar properties, including the cost of making prints of a film for distribution. These capitalized costs may be deducted over the life of the income stream generated from the production activity. This provision applies to amounts paid or incurred after December 31, 1975, with respect to property the principal production of which began after that date.[327]

The cost of a license or franchise is amortizable over its life.[328] Where a franchise is indefinitely renewable so that there is no reasonably determinable life over which to spread the cost, there is no amortization deduction.[329] But where the holder of an automobile distributorship franchise which was indefinitely renewable could show that General Motors Corporation had the authority to terminate a franchise upon the holder's death, and in fact frequently did so, he could amortize the cost over his own life expectancy.[330]

A business operating permit was renewable by a municipality each year. Although the Internal Revenue Service claimed that for practical purposes the permit was permanent and expenses in connection with it had to be capitalized, it was held that the annual payment was deductible. The renewal of the permit would be in great jeopardy if some governmental law or regulation was violated, and hence the permit could not be regarded as permanent.[331]

A physician paid a onetime hospital-staff-privilege fee. He was permitted to deduct his cost ratably over the number of years in his life expectancy.[332]

But where the hospital was due to be replaced by another one, depreciation could be deducted for the privilege over the remaining life of the first hospital.[333]

The costs of acquiring a license to practice law in California could be amortized over his remaining life expectancy by a lawyer who already was licensed to practice in New York.[334]

An individual paid a fee to become an underwriting member of Lloyd's of London. The membership was for life and nontransferable, and for Federal income tax purposes, he was permitted to amortize and to deduct the amount of this fee ratably over his remaining life expectancy. The court pointed out that if in the future he resigned from Lloyd's, he could deduct any remaining unamortized cost at that time.[335]

Ordinarily, payments to eliminate competition are not deductible. But where the elimination of competition was for a fixed and limited term, the cost could be spread and deducted over that period.[336] Similarly, the cost of a covenant from the former owner of a business not to compete with the new owner is not deductible unless the covenant is for a stipulated number of years, in which event the cost can be amortized.[337] In order to get the deduction, the buyer must show that he would not have purchased the business unless assured that the seller would not go into competition with the buyer for a period long enough so that the seller could not be a threat in getting back former customers. So when the seller agreed not to be a competitor for four years, what the buyer paid for that commitment could be deducted ratably over the four-year period.[338] "The greater the allocation of the purchase price to the covenant not to compete," said one court, "the greater the tax advantages for the buyer since the buyer can deduct payments made for the covenant."[339]

In general, the cost of construction of property with estimated business usefulness of more than one year must be capitalized over the period of contemplated benefits; in the case of a road, where that period may be unmeasurable, no deductions at all may be available. Payment of the cost of construction of a new highway was deductible by a food processor whose property otherwise would have been substantially destroyed by a new state highway running through it. The cost of a new alternative road to be paid for by the food processor was acceptable to the state for its purposes, and the company could deduct this amount because the expenditure did not add to the value of the property but was for the purpose of reducing or minimizing loss or injury to existing property.[340]

A taxpayer was allowed to deduct the cost of moving waste materials from one business premise to an unused piece of land which he also owned. This was not an expenditure which had to be capitalized as part of the cost of the vacant land, for it was not certain at the time of the expenditure whether or not the empty land was being benefited. What was certain was that operation of the existing business property was being benefited by removal of the waste. Observed the court: "The tax does not require that a business be run inefficiently."[341]

Expenses of a trip to Washington in connection with an additional tax assessed on the taxpayer's trade or business are deductible.[342]

Amounts paid to an appraiser to determine the proper amount of a casualty or theft loss may be deducted.[343]

Amounts paid to a title insurance company to determine whether local tax assessments were properly made against property held by the taxpayer are similarly deductible.[344] *See also* **Cattle feed, deductibility of; Construction-period interest and taxes; Depreciation; Election to deduct or capitalize; Farmers; Legal fees; Loan expenses; Maintenance; Medical expenses; Obsolescence; Pollution-control facilities; Reforestation expenditures; Rehabilitation expenses; Removal of impediments to the physically handicapped; Repairs; Start-up expenses; Surveys; Termination of a business.**

Expenses of another person. The general rule is that a taxpayer may not deduct the payment of another person's expenses. One individual formed a corporation to sell a product he had developed. A major customer agreed to sell defective merchandise it had received from the corporation only if the individual agreed to indemnify the customer for any loss resulting from sale of this merchandise. The individual could deduct the amount of a loss reimbursement he paid to the customer. The corporation lacked the resources to make an indemnification promise. If the customer had returned the merchandise and word of defective quality got about, the individual could lose the income he expected to receive from the corporation's profits. His payment was an expense to protect his own income.[345]

A taxpayer was a broker of agricultural products and his name was well known in the trade. He formed three corporations to sell products labeled as his own brands. When the corporations were unable to pay their creditors, he made the payments. They were deductible as payments made to prevent loss of his own earnings had his good will been destroyed by corporations using his trade name.[346]

An investment banker made a payment to a corporation in which he was a stockholder and director in order to avoid possible liability under the Securities Exchange Act of 1934, and to protect his business reputation; this was deductible.[347]

A taxpayer's voluntary payment of a predecessor's business debts, to the extent that they had not been paid off in a bankruptcy settlement, was deductible. Only by making this payment could a first-class credit rating be obtained. So the voluntary payment was a natural and reasonable operating cost.[348]

Some physicians who specialized in accident and industrial injury practice organized a nonprofit organization to operate a private hospital. Purpose: to provide hospital care exclusively for their own patients. The physicians received fees from the hospital for the referral of patients. Although it had been believed that the hospital's current receipts would exceed its current expenses, such was not the case. In order to keep the hospital solvent so that the doctors would continue to receive medical fees from it, the physicians paid the hospital's operating deficits; the payments were deductible because they were made to protect the doctors' own incomes.[349]

A landlord was permitted to deduct the cost of advertisements he had placed in the name of a tenant. The tenant was unwilling to pay for advertising. But if this unenterprising tenant failed financially, the landlord predictably would have difficulty in leasing the aged structure. He could deduct the advertising costs.[350]

A business could deduct the legal fees of its president, who was involved in a tax-evasion matter. The business would not have been able to exist without his presence.[351]

Where Federal income taxes were assessed against a dissolved corporation, which already had distributed all of its assets to its shareholders, a stockholder who felt he could be held responsible for these taxes as transferee liability (up to the value of what he had received in the liquidation) was permitted to deduct fees paid to a lawyer to resist imposition of the corporate taxes. The intention of the stockholder was to protect himself.[352]

Officers of a corporation, under a state's law, were personally responsible for state sales tax deducted from customers' payments but not transmitted to the tax authority. Officers who had this liability could deduct the payments that they made to the state.[353]

See also **Executives; Government employees; Legal fees; Medical expenses; Ordinary and Necessary business expenses; Partnerships; Ransom; Reputation, maintenance of; Taxes.**

Experimental expenses. In the case of research and experimental expenditures, a taxpayer may elect either to deduct them as expenses or to capitalize them for amortization and deduction over a period of not less than sixty months.[354]

Expenses relating to the acquisition of inventory are not currently deductible but are added to the cost of inventory. You must add to the cost of inventory research and experimental costs incurred in the fabrication of your products, the IRS told a manufacturer of office equipment. To the contrary, ruled the court, for research and experimental costs may be deducted, if the taxpayer wants to handle them in that way, even though they relate to inventory or production equipment.[355] Nearly eight years later, the Internal Revenue Service announced that it will be guided by the court's decision.[356] *See also* **Depreciation; Election to deduct or to capitalize; Legal fees; Mortgage loan fees and commissions; Refinancing fee; Repairs; Research and experimental expenses.**

Expropriation losses. *See* **Foreign expropriation losses.**

Extortion payments. *See* **Casualties.**

Eyeglasses. *See* **Medical expenses; Safety equipment.**

E

1. *Ranchers Exploration and Development Corporation v. United States,* DC, N.M., 1978.

2. *Tax Information on Educational Expenses,* IRS Publication 508, 1976 edition, page 1.

3. Regulations Section 1.162-5(b)(2)(i)(2).

4. *Laurano et al. v. Commissioner,* 69 T.C. 723 (1978).

5. *Jouett et al. v. Commissioner,* T.C. Memo. 1982-99, filed February 25, 1982.

6. *Toner v. Commissioner,* 623 F.2d 315 (3d Cir., 1980).

7. *Granger et al. v. Commissioner,* T.C. Memo. 1980-60, filed March 5, 1980.

8. *Kilroy et al. v. Commissioner,* T.C. Memo. 1980-489, filed October 22, 1980.

9. *Sherman v. Commissioner,* T.C. Memo. 1977-301, filed September 7, 1977.

10. *Heffernan v. Commissioner,* T.C. Memo. 1979-363, filed September 10, 1979.

11. *Williams et al. v. United States,* 238 F. Supp. 351 (DC, SD N.Y., 1965).

12. *Smith et al. v. Commissioner,* T.C. Memo. 1981-149, filed March 30, 1981.

13. *Albert C. Ruehmann III,* T.C. Memo. 1971-157, filed June 30, 1971.

14. *Picnally v. Commissioner,* T.C. Memo. 1977-321, filed September 20, 1977.

15. *Peter G. Corbett et al.,* 55 T.C. 884 (1971).

16. *Furner et al. v. Commissioner,* 393 F.2d 292 (7th Cir., 1968).

17. *John C. Ford,* 56 T.C. 1300 (1971).

18. Regulations Section 1.162-5(a)(2).

19. *Toner v. Commissioner,* 623 F.2d 315 (3d Cir., 1980).

20. *William et al. v. United States,* 238 F. Supp. 351 (DC, SD N.Y., 1965).

21. *Marvin Leroy Lund et al.,* 46 T.C. 321 (1966).

22. *Ruth Domigan Truxall,* T.C. Memo. 1962-137, filed June 5, 1962.

23. *Tax Information on Educational Expenses,* IRS Publication 508, 1976 edition, page 1.

24. *William J. Brennan et al.,* T.C. Memo. 1963-243, filed September 10, 1963.

25. *John S. Watson,* 31 T.C. 1014 (1959).

26. *Greenberg et al. v. Commissioner,* 367 F.2d 663 (1st Cir., 1966).

27. Regulations Section 1.162-5(b).

28. Regulations Section 1.162-5(c)(1).

29. *Iglesias v. Commissioner,* 76 T.C. 1060 (1981).

30. Revenue Ruling 74-78, 1974-1 CB 44.

31. *Petersen v. Commissioner,* T.C. Memo. 1980-338, filed August 26, 1980.

32. Regulations Section 1.162-5(c)(1).

33. *Blair et al. v. Commissioner,* T.C. Memo. 1981-634, filed October 27, 1981.

34. *McIlvoy v. Commissioner,* T.C. Memo. 1979-248, filed June 28, 1979.

35. *Coughlin v. Commissioner,* 203 F.2d 307 (2d Cir., 1953).

36. *Cosimo A. Carlucci,* 37 T.C. 695 (1962).

37. Revenue Ruling 69-199, 1969-1 CB 51.

38. *Kosmal et al. v. Commissioner,* T.C. Memo. 1979-490, filed December 6, 1979.

39. *Ben (Bong) H. Kim et al.,* T.C. Memo. 1969-126, filed June 23, 1969.

40. *Ralph A. Fattore,* T.C. Memo. 1963-219, filed August 20, 1963.

41. *Sabinof Ciorciari,* T.C. Memo. 1963-162, filed June 11, 1963.

42. *John D. Glascow et al.,* T.C. Memo. 1972-77, filed March 28, 1972.

43. *Cosimo A. Carlucci,* 37 T.C. 695 (1962).

44. *Beatty et al. v. Commissioner,* T.C. Memo. 1980-196, filed June 4, 1980.

45. *Peggy A. King,* T.C. Memo. 1962-93, filed April 23, 1962.

46. *Donald C. Hester,* T.C. Memo. 1963-107, filed April 15, 1963.

47. *Damm et al. v. Commissioner,* T.C. Memo. 1981-203, filed April 27, 1981.

48. *James E. Lane et al.,* T.C. Memo. 1962-179, filed July 26, 1962.

49. *Ralph A. Fattore,* T.C. Memo. 1963-219, filed August 20, 1963.

50. *Walter C. Lage et al.,* 52 T.C. 130 (1969).

51. *Frieda Hempel,* T.C. Memo. Docket No. 7993, entered June 23, 1947.

52. *Elliott v. United States,* 250 F. Supp. 322 (DC, ED N.Y., 1965).

53. *Cecil Randolph Handley, Jr.,* 48 T.C. 339 (1967).

54. *Beckley et al. v. United States,* 490 F. Supp. 123 (DC, SD Ga., 1980).

55. *Boser et al. v. Commissioner,* 77 T.C. 1124 (1981).

56. *Alan Aaronson,* T.C. Memo. 1970-178, filed June 25, 1970.

57. *Keith W. Shaw et al.,* T.C. Memo. 1969-120, filed June 16, 1969.

58. *Knudtson et al. v. Commissioner,* T.C. Memo. 1980-455, filed October 8, 1980.

59. *Cooper et al. v. Commissioner,* T.C. Memo. 1979-24, filed June 25, 1979.

60. *Colangelo et al. v. Commissioner,* T.C. Memo. 1980-543, filed December 8, 1980.

61. Regulations Section 1.162-5(b)(3).

62. *Marshall L. Helms, Jr., et al.,* T.C. Memo. 1968-207, filed September 19, 1968.

63. *Richard M. Baum et al.,* T.C. Memo. 1964-37, filed February 18, 1964.

64. *Donald P. Frazee et al.* T.C. Memo. 1963-217, filed August 19, 1963.

65. *Campbell et al. v. United States,* 250 Supp. 941 (DC, ED Pa., 1966).

66. *Walter T. Charlton et al.,* T.C. Memo. 1964-59, filed March 10, 1964.

67. *Welsh et al. v. United States,* 210 F. Supp. 597 (DC, ND Ohio, 1962), *aff'd,* 329 F.2d 145 (6th Cir., 1964).

68. Ibid.

69. *Regan v. Commissioner,* T.C. Memo. 1979-340, filed August 28, 1979.

70. Revenue Ruling 69-607, 1969-2 CB 40.

71. *Walter C. Lage et al.,* 52 T.C. 130 (1969).

72. *Voigt et al. v. Commissioner,* 74 T.C. 82 (1980).

73. *Educational Expenses,* IRS Publication 508 (Rev. Nov. 1980), page 2.

74. *Khinda v. Commissioner,* T.C. Memo. 1982-42, filed January 29, 1982.

75. Regulations Section 1.162-5(d).

76. Regulations Section 1.162-5(d).

77. *Duncan v. Bookwalter,* 216 F. Supp. 301 (DC, WD Mo., 1963).

78. *Stanley Marlin et al.,* 54 T.C. 560 (1970).

79. *Gladys M. Smith,* T.C. Memo. 1967-246, filed December 8, 1967.

80. *Tax Information on Educational Expenses,* IRS Publication 508, 1976 edition, page 3.

81. *Gibbons, Jr., et al. v. Commissioner,* T.C. Memo. 1978-75, filed February 27, 1978.

82. Revenue Ruling 64-176, 1964-1 CB (Part 1) 87.

83. *Tax Information on Educational Expenses*, IRS Publication 508, 1976 edition, page 3.

84. *John C. Ford*, 56 T.C. 1300 (1971), *aff'd*, 487 F.2d 1025 (1973).

85. Regulations Section 1.162-5(e).

86. *Reuben B. Hoover*, 35 T.C. 566 (1961).

87. Revenue Ruling 62-213, 1962-2 CB 59.

88. *Gudmundsson et al. v. Commissioner*, T.C. Memo. 1978-299, filed August 1, 1978.

89. Revenue Ruling 70-471, 1970-2 CB 199.

90. Regulations Section 1.266-1(b).

91. Regulations Section 1.612-4.

92. IRC Section 616.

93. IRC Section 617.

94. IRC Section 191.

95. IRC Section 174.

96. Revenue Ruling 71-162, 1971-2 CB 97.

97. IRS Letter Ruling 8211004, November 27, 1981.

98. *Martin Mayrath et al.*, 41 T.C. 582 (1964), *aff'd*, 357 F.2d 209 (5th Cir., 1966).

99. Revenue Ruling 80-245, 1980-2 CB 72.

100. Revenue Ruling 76-324, 1976-2 CB 77.

101. *James v. United States*, 366 U.S. 213 (1961).

102. Ibid.

103. *In the Matter of Thomas L. Woodward et al.*, DC, WD Wash., 1979.

104. Regulations Section 1.274-3(b)(2)(iii).

105. Revenue Ruling 72-305, 1971-2 CB 116.

106. Revenue Ruling 72-328, 1972-2 CB 224.

107. Revenue Ruling 62-180, 1962-2 CB 52.

108. Revenue Ruling 80-331, 1980-2 CB 29.

109. *Ditmars et al. v. Commissioner*, 302 F.2d 481 (2d Cir., 1962).

110. *Howard v. Commissioner*, 202 F.2d 28 (9th Cir., 1953).

111. *Imhoff et al. v. Commissioner*, T.C. Memo. 1980-30, filed January 31, 1980.

112. Revenue Ruling 70-475, 1970-2 CB 35.

113. *Damm et al. v. Commissioner*, T.C. Memo. 1981-203, filed April 27, 1981.

114. Revenue Ruling 73-356, 1973-2 CB 31.

115. Revenue Ruling 82-33, I.R.B. 1982-10, 4.

116. *Nidetch v. Commissioner*, T.C. Memo. 1978-313, filed August 11, 1978.

117. *Wolfson et al. v. Commissioner*, 651 F.2d 1228 (6th Cir., 1981).

118. IRS Letter Ruling 8032084, no date given.

119. Revenue Ruling 71-470, 1971-2 CB 121.

120. *Steadman et al. v. Commissioner*, 424 F.2d 1 (6th Cir., 1970).

121. *Banks et al. v. Commissioner*, T.C. Memo. 1981-450, filed September 9, 1981.

122. *Robert E. Cooper*, 67 T.C. 870 (1977).

123. *Plante et al. v. United States*, 226 F. Supp. 314 (DC, N.H., 1963).

124. *Other Miscellaneous Deductions*, IRS Publication 529, 1976 edition, page 3.

125. *Protecting Older Americans Against Overpayment of Taxes*, Special Committee on Aging, United States Senate, 1976, page 5.

126. *Albert L. Sanderson*, T.C. Memo., Docket No. 56830, entered January 31, 1957.

127. *Arthur Brookfield*, T.C. Memo., Docket No. 51372, entered March 12, 1956.

128. *Irving L. Schein*, T.C. Memo., Docket No. 32717, entered February 29, 1951.

129. *Ronald D. Kroll*, 49 T.C. 557 (1968).

130. *Emil J. Michaels*, 53 T.C. 269 (1969).

131. *Beatrice H. Albert*, 13 T.C. 129 (1949).

132. *Brewin et al. v. Commissioner*, CA, DC, 1980.

133. *Your Federal Income Tax*, 1976 edition, page 70.

134. IT 3728, 1945 CB 78.

135. Form 2106, "Employee Business Expense."

136. *Kenneth Waters*, 12 T.C. 414 (1949).

137. *Darrell Spear Courtney*, 32 T.C. 334 (1959).

138. *Daly et al. v. Commissioner*, F.2d (4th Cir., 1980).

139. *Richard Keith Johnson*, T.C. Memo. 1972-192, filed September 6, 1972.

140. *LeRoy W. Gillis et al.*, T.C. Memo. 1973-96, filed April 24, 1973.

141. *Virginia C. Avery*, T.C. Memo. 1970-269, filed September 23, 1970.

142. *Albert R. McGovern et al.*, 42 T.C. 1148 (1964) *aff'd on another issue*, 6th Cir., 1966.

143. *Oliver W. Bryant*, T.C. Memo., Docket No. 27114, entered May 2, 1952.

144. *Boyle, Flagg & Seaman, Inc.*, 25 T.C. 43 (1955).

145. Revenue Ruling 60-365, 1960-2 CB 49.

146. *Raymond Warren Jackson*, T.C. Memo. 1975-301, filed September 30, 1975.

147. *Drury v. Commissioner*, T.C. Memo. 1977-199, filed June 2, 1977.

148. Revenue Ruling 58-382, 1958-2 CB 59.

149. SM 4078, V-1 CB 226.

150. *Murphy et al. v. Commissioner*, T.C. Memo. 1980-25, filed January 28, 1980.

151. *Other Miscellaneous Deductions*, IRS Publication 529, 1976 edition, page 3.

152. *Dean L. Phillips*, T.C. Memo., Docket Nos. 18410-2, entered June 9, 1950.

153. *Miscellaneous Deductions and Credits*, IRS Publication 529, 1976 edition, page 1.

154. *McCollum et al. v. Commissioner*, T.C. Memo. 1978-435, filed November 1, 1978.

155. IT 3634, 1944 CB 90.

156. Revenue Ruling 72-463, 1972-2 CB 93.

157. *McKinley et al. v. Commissioner*, T.C. Memo. 1978-428, filed October 30, 1978.

158. *Miscellaneous Deductions and Credits*, IRS Publication 529, 1976 edition, page 2.

159. Revenue Ruling 54-190, 1954-1 CB 46.

160. Revenue Ruling 69-214, 1969-1 CB 52.

161. IRS Letter Ruling 7828050, April 13, 1978.

162. Internal Revenue News Release IR-1967, March 10, 1978.

163. IRC Section 62(2)(c).

164. Regulations Section 1.62-1(e).

165. *United States v. Correll,* 389 U.S. 299 (1967).

166. *Floyd DeRieux,* T.C. Memo. 1958-146, filed July 29, 1958.

167. *Robert E. Cooper,* 67 T.C. 870 (1977).

168. *Your Federal Income Tax,* 1976 edition, page 70.

169. *Harold A. Christensen,* 17 T.C. 46 (1952).

170. *Edward A. Walsh et al.,* T.C. Memo. 1961-80, filed March 22, 1961.

171. *Julius (Jay) C. Henricks.* T.C. Memo., Docket No. 16192, entered November 8, 1949.

172. *Norman E. Kennelly et al.,* 56 T.C. 936 (1971).

173. *Howard Veit et al.,* T.C. Memo., Docket Nos. 15552-3, entered October 11, 1949.

174. *Herman E. Bischoff et al.,* T.C. Memo. 1966-102, filed May 19, 1966.

175. *Brandt et al. v. Commissioner,* T.C. Memo. 1982-180, filed April 7, 1982.

176. *Neal et al. v. Commissioner,* T.C. Memo. 1981-172, filed April 9, 1981.

177. *Holland et al. v. United States,* 311 F. Supp. 422 (DC, CD Cal., 1970).

178. *Fallon et al. v. United States,* DC, ND Texas, 1957.

179. *Marshall J. Hammons et al.,* T.C. Memo., Docket No. 31518, entered November 24, 1953.

180. *Thomas M. B. Hicks, Jr., et al.,* T.C. Memo. 1960-48, filed March 24, 1960.

181. Regulations Section 1.162-10(a).

182. IRS Letter Ruling 8113020, November 30, 1980.

183. Revenue Ruling 60-223, 1960-1 CB 57.

184. *David J. Primuth,* 54 T.C. 374 (1970).

185. *Kenneth R. Kenfield,* 54 T.C. 1197 (1970).

186. *Leonard J. Cremona et al.,* T.C. Memo. 1972-66, filed March 14, 1972.

187. *R. E. Blewitt, Jr., et al.,* T.C. Memo. 1972-247, filed December 12, 1972.

188. *Miller et al. v. United States,* 362 F. Supp. 1242 (DC, ED Tenn., 1973).

189. Revenue Ruling 66-41, 1966-1 CB 233.

190. Revenue Ruling 75-120, 1975-1 CB 55.

191. Revenue Ruling 77-16, 1977-1 CB 37.

192. *Leisner et al. v. Commissioner,* T.C. Memo. 1977-205, filed July 5, 1977.

193. *Regan v. Commissioner,* T.C. Memo. 1979-340, filed August 28, 1979.

194. IRC Section 274.

195. Regulations Section 1.274-2.

196. Revenue Ruling 63-144, 1963-2 CB 129.

197. Ibid.

198. Ibid.

199. Revenue Ruling 68-144, 1963-2 CB 129.

200. Ibid.

201. *Howard et al. v. Commissioner,* T.C. Memo. 1981-250, filed May 21, 1981.

202. *Richard A. Sutter,* 21 T.C. 170 (1953).

203. *Hughes v. Commissioner,* 451 F.2d 975 (2d Cir., 1971).

204. *Russo et al. v. Commissioner,* T.C. Memo. 1982-248, filed May 5, 1982.

205. *LaForge et al. v. Commissioner,* 434 F.2d 370 (2d Cir., 1970).

206. *Max Plishner et al.,* T.C. Memo. 1962-208, filed August 30, 1962.

207. *Dowell, Jr. et al. v. United States,* 370 F. Supp. 69 (DC, ND Texas, 1974).

208. Revenue Ruling 63-144, 1963-2 CB 129.

209. Revenue Act of 1978, Section 361.

210. Conference Committee Report on Revenue Bill of 1978.

211. *Nicholls, North, Buse Company et al.,* 56 T.C. 1225 (1971).

212. *Samuel Abrams et al.,* T.C. Memo. 1964-256, filed September 29, 1964.

213. *Wolf v. United States,* DC, WD Mo., 1964.

214. *Victor J. McQuade,* 4 BTA 837 (1926).

215. *Cambridge Hotels, Inc.,* T.C. Memo. 1968-263, filed November 19, 1968.

216. *First National Bank of Omaha v. United States,* 276 F. Supp. 905 (DC, Neb., 1967).

217. *Hernandez et al. v. Commissioner,* T.C. Memo. 1982-327, filed June 10, 1982.

218. *George Durgom et al.,* T.C. Memo. 1974-58, filed March 7, 1974.

219. *Berkley Machine Works & Foundry Company, Inc. v. Commissioner,* T.C. Memo. 1977-177, filed June 13, 1977.

220. *Abe Brenner et al.,* T.C. Memo. 1967-239, filed November 28, 1967.

221. *Dowell, Jr., et al. v. United States,* 370 F. Supp. 69 (DC, ND Texas, 1974).

222. *Lennon et al. v. Commissioner,* T.C. Memo. 1978-176, filed May 11, 1978.

223. *LaForge v. Commissioner,* 434 F.2d 370 (2d Cir., 1970).

224. Regulations Section 1.274-5(a)(3).

225. IRC Section 274.

226. Regulations Section 1.274-5(b)(3).

227. *Custis et al. v. Commissioner,* T.C. Memo. 1982-296, filed May 26, 1982.

228. *Dowell, Jr. et al. v. United States,* 370 F. Supp. 69 (DC, ND Texas, 1974).

229. Regulations Section 1.274-5(c)(2)(ii)(c).

230. *Pimpton et al. v. Commissioner,* T.C. Memo. 1981-3, filed January 5, 1981.

231. *Diller et al. v. Commissioner,* T.C. Memo. 1978-321, filed August 16, 1978.

232. *Sap et al. v. Commissioner,* T.C. Memo. 1981-167, filed April 8, 1981.

233. Revenue Ruling 65-38, 1965-1 CB 151.

234. Regulations Section 1.274-5(b)(3)(v).

235. *Savage et al. v. Commissioner,* T.C. Memo. 1981-278, filed June 2, 1981.

236. *Travel, Entertainment, and Gift Ex-*

penses. IRS Publication 463 (Rev. Nov. 1979), page 15.

237. *George G. Ebner et al.,* T.C. Memo. 1958-108, filed June 9, 1958.

238. *Sullivan et al. v. Commissioner,* T.C. Memo. 1982-150, filed March 24, 1982.

239. *LaForge et al. v. Commissioner,* 434 F.2d 370 (2d Cir., 1970).

240. *Dowell, Jr. et al. v. United States,* 370 F. Supp. 69 (DC, ND Texas, 1974).

241. Regulations Section 1.274-5(c)(2)(i),(iii).

242. *Andrews Distributing Co., Inc.,* T.C. Memo. 1972-146, filed July 3, 1972.

243. Regulations Section 1.274-2(b)(1)(ii).

244. *Russo et al. v. Commissioner,* T.C. Memo. 1982-248, filed May 5, 1982.

245. *Denison et al. v. Commissioner,* T.C. Memo. 1977-430, filed December 22, 1977.

246. *Dukehart-Hughes Tractor & Equipment Company, Inc. v. United States,* 341 F.2d 613 (Ct. Cl., 1965).

247. IRS Letter Ruling 7726018, March 29, 1977.

248. Public Law 96-598, Section 5, enacted December 24, 1980.

249. Regulations Section 1.274-5(c)(5).

250. *Murray v. Commissioner,* T.C. Memo. 1980-500, filed November 6, 1980.

251. IRS Letter Ruling 7811004, November 29, 1977.

252. Revenue Ruling 72-316, 1972-1 CB 44.

253. *Sidney Merians et al.,* 60 T.C. 187 (1973).

254. *Ditmars et al. v. Commissioner,* 302 F.2d 481 (2d Cir., 1962).

255. *Harold A. Christensen,* 17 T.C. 1456 (1952).

256. Revenue Ruling 72-192, 1972-1 CB 48.

257. Revenue Ruling 76-77, 1976-1 CB 107.

258. *David N. Smith et al.,* 66 T.C. 622 (1976).

259. *Ingalls v. Patterson,* 158 F. Supp. 627 (DC, ND Ala., 1958).

260. *Stanley V. Waldheim et al.,* 25 T.C. 839 (1956), *aff'd on other issues,* 244 F.2d 1 (7th Cir., 1957).

261. *E. L. Potter,* 20 BTA 252 (1930).

262. *Nidetch v. Commissioner,* T.C. Memo. 1978-313, filed August 11, 1978.

263. *J. Leroy Nickel, Jr., Estate,* T.C. Memo. 1962-55, filed March 15, 1962.

264. *William L. Butler,* 17 T.C. 675 (1951).

265. *Peoples-Pittsburgh Trust Company et al.,* 21 BTA 588 (1930), *aff'd,* 60 F.2d 187 (3d Cir., 1932).

266. Revenue Ruling 68-662, 1968-2 CB 69.

267. *Ditmars et al. v. Commissioner,* 302 F.2d 481 (2d Cir., 1962).

268. *Hochschild v. Commissioner,* 161 F.2d 817 (2d Cir., 1947).

269. *The First National Bank of Atlanta et al. v. United States,* 202 F. Supp. 702 (DC, ND Ga., 1962).

270. *Graham et al. v. Commissioner,* 326 F.2d 878 (4th Cir., 1964).

271. *DePinto et al. v. United States,* 585 F.2d 405 (9th Cir., 1978).

272. *Frank W. Byrne,* T.C. Memo., Docket No. 4090, entered September 7, 1945.

273. IRS Letter Ruling 7802005, September 29, 1977.

274. IRS Letter Ruling 7728004, April 6, 1977.

275. *Charles E. Adams et al.,* T.C. Memo., Docket No. 112228, entered April 2, 1943.

276. *Dixon Fagerberg,* BTA Memo., Docket No. 103449, entered February 6, 1942.

277. *William L. Butler,* 17 T.C. 675 (1951).

278. Revenue Ruling 61-115, 1961-1 CB 46.

279. *Nathan Cummings et al.,* 60 T.C. 91 (1973).

280. *Mitchell et al. v. United States,* 405 F.2d 435 (Ct. Cl., 1969).

281. *Conley et al. v. Commissioner,* T.C. Memo. 1977-406, filed November 23, 1977.

282. *Murray R. Denemark et al.,* T.C. Memo. 1976-267, filed August 23, 1976.

283. *James O. Gould et al.,* 64 T.C. 132 (1975).

284. *Arrigoni et al. v. Commissioner,* 73 T.C. 792 (1980).

285. *Steadman et al. v. Commissioner,* 424 F.2d 1 (6th Cir., 1970).

286. *Cosimo A. Carlucci,* 37 T.C. 695 (1962).

287. *Dan R. Hanna, Jr., et al.,* T.C. Memo., Docket Nos. 25706 and 25707, entered June 6, 1951.

288. *John S. Thompson,* T.C. Memo., Docket No. 23817, entered August 14, 1950.

289. *Kornhauser v. United States,* 276 U.S. 145 (1928).

290. *Schmidlapp v. Commissioner,* 96 F.2d 680 (2d Cir., 1938).

291. *Dowell, Jr. et al. v. United States,* 370 F. Supp. 69 (DC, ND Texas, 1974).

292. *Albert L. Sanderson et al.,* T.C. Memo. 1957-23, filed January 31, 1957.

293. *Penn et al. v. Robertson,* 29 F. Supp. 386 (DC, MD N.C., 1939), *aff'd on other issues,* 115 F.2d 167 (4th Cir., 1940).

294. *Robert J. Harder et al.,* T.C. Memo. 1958-97, filed May 27, 1958.

295. *Holland et al. v. United States,* 311 F. Supp. 422 (DC, CD Cal., 1970).

296. Revenue Ruling 57-502, 1957-2 CB 118.

297. IRS Letter Ruling 7811004, November 29, 1977.

298. *Herman E. Bischoff et al.,* T.C. Memo. 1966-102, filed May 19, 1966.

299. *John Lockwood et al.,* T.C. Memo. 1970-141, filed June 8, 1970.

300. *Lillian M. Goldsmith,* 7 BTA 151 (1927).

301. Revenue Ruling 70-253, 1970-1 CB 31.

302. Revenue Ruling 71-308, 1971-2 CB 167.

303. Revenue Ruling 73-13, 1973-1 CB 42.

304. Revenue Ruling 69-115, 1969-1 CB 50.

305. *Vincent E. Oswald et al.,* 49 T.C. 645 (1968).

306. *John G. Pahl et al.*, 67 T.C. 286 (1976).

307. *Arnstein et al.*, T.C. Memo. 1970-220, filed July 29, 1970.

308. *Estate of W. Favre Slater*, T.C. Memo. 1962-256, filed October 31, 1962.

309. Revenue Ruling 73-13, 1973-1 CB 42.

310. *Mildred W. Wallace Estate v. Commissioner*, 101 F.2d 604 (4th Cir., 1939).

311. *A. M. Barnhart Estate*, T.C. Memo. 1959-42, filed February 27, 1959.

312. *Buder et al. v. United States*, 235 F. Supp. 479 (DC, ED Mo., 1964), *aff'd on another issue*, 342 F.2d 941 (8th Cir., 1966).

313. Revenue Ruling 55-447, 1955-2 CB 533.

314. *O'Connell et al. v. Commissioner*, T.C. Memo. 1980-432, filed September 25, 1980.

315. *Herbert Shainberg et al.*, 33 T.C. 241 (1959).

316. *Meldrum & Fewsmith, Inc.*, 20 T.C. 780 (1953).

317. *Goodwyn Crockery Company*, 37 T.C. 355 (1961), *aff'd on another issue*, 315 F.2d 110 (6th Cir., 1963).

318. *Evans & Howard Fire Brick Company*, 8 BTA 867 (1927).

319. Revenue Ruling 71-246, 1971-1 CB 54.

320. *Iowa-Des Moines National Bank et al.*, 68 T.C. 872 (1977).

321. Revenue Ruling 69-560, 1969-2 CB 25.

322. Revenue Ruling 73-357, 1973-2 CB 40.

323. *Damm et al. v. Commissioner*, T.C. Memo. 1981-203, filed April 27, 1981.

324. Revenue Ruling 70-408, 1970-2 CB 68.

325. *Tax Information on Business Expenses*, IRS Publication 535, 1966 edition, page 12.

326. *Longview Hilton Hotel Company*, 9 T.C. 180 (1947).

327. Tax Reform Act of 1976, Section 209.

328. *Riis & Company, Inc., et al.*, T.C. Memo. 1964-190, filed July 14, 1964.

329. *Richmond Television Corporation v. United States*, 354 F.2d 410 (4th Cir., 1965).

330. *Hampton Pontiac, Inc. v. United States*, 294 F. Supp. 1073 (DC, SC, 1969).

331. *Marcell v. United States*, DC, Vt., 1961.

332. Revenue Ruling 70-171, 1970-1 CB 56.

333. *Wells-Lee et al. v. Commissioner*, 360 F.2d 665 (8th Cir., 1966).

334. *Sharon v. Commissioner*, 591 F.2d 1273 (9th Cir., 1978).

335. *Snell, Jr., v. Commissioner*, T.C. Memo. 1979-141, filed April 11, 1979.

336. *Farmers Feed Co.*, 17 BTA 507 (1938).

337. *Carboloy Company, Inc.*, T.C. Memo., Docket Nos. 101345 and 101920, entered July 2, 1943.

338. *O'Dell & Company*, 61 T.C. 461 (1974).

339. *Ulllman v. Commissioner*, 264 F.2d 305 (2d Cir., 1959).

340. *Seufert Bros. Co. v. Lucas*, 44 F.2d 526 (9th Cir., 1930).

341. *H. G. Fenton Material Company v. Commissioner*, 74 T.C. 584 (1980).

342. OD 849, CB 123.

343. *Tax Information on Disasters, Casualty Losses, and Thefts*, IRS Publication 547, 1976 edition, page 2.

344. *Byron H. Farwell et al.*, 35 T.C. 454 (1960).

345. *James L. Lohrke et al.*, 48 T.C. 679 (1967).

346. *Lutz et ux. v. Commissioner*, 282 F.2d 614 (5th Cir., 1960).

347. Revenue Ruling 76-203, 1976-1 CB 45.

348. *H. Hamburger Company*, T.C. Memo., Docket No. 19840, entered August 30, 1949.

349. *Charles J. Dinardo et al.*, 22 T.C. 430 (1954).

350. *Hennepin Holding Co.*, 23 BTA 119 (1931).

351. *Jack's Maintenance Contractors, Inc. v. Commissioner*, T.C. Memo. 1981-349, filed July 6, 1981.

352. *National Association of Schools and Publishers, Inc.*, T.C. Memo., Docket No. 16433, entered September 17, 1948.

353. *Arrigoni et al. v. Commissioner*, 73 T.C. 792 (1980).

354. IRC Section 174(b).

355. *All Steel Equipment, Inc.*, 54 T.C. 1749 (1970).

356. 1978-2 CB 1.

F

Face-lifting. The cost of a face-lifting operation for the purpose of improving a taxpayer's personal appearance was allowed as medical expense, even though the operation was not the result of a recommendation by a physician.[1] *See also* **Medical expenses.**

Faithful performance bonds. *See* **Insurance.**

False pretenses, losses arising from. *See* **Reliance upon misrepresentation.**

False teeth. *See* **Actors; Medical expenses.**

Family transactions. In general, tax deductions arising from transactions between members of the same family are allowed in the same manner as any other deductions. The only practical distinction is that the Internal Revenue Service is going to be more suspicious about the legitimacy of the deduction and might feel that the taxpayer is trying to beat them out of some tax dollars. This means that the taxpayer has a great burden of proof in establishing his entitlement to deductions resulting from intra-family transactions.

In one case, a celebrated actress made payments in a contractual arrangement with her stepfather for business assistance. The payments made proved to be far greater than either of them had anticipated due to a "contingency arrangement" in the contract. The IRS claimed that the payment was really a disguised form of support and not a *bona fide* business arrangement. But it was proved that the stepfather performed his role of business adviser under the terms of the contract as well as any unrelated party would have done, and therefore the payments, which were made at the prevailing percentage rate of the theatrical industry, were allowed.[2]

A professional singer could deduct the cost of meals and lodgings paid by her husband while he was acting as her business and road manager.[3]

Payments by a famous theatrical producer to his wife for obtaining for him the rights to produce *A Tree Grows in Brooklyn* were deductible as a finder's fee. She was also a theater personage who had been associated closely with the stage for years, and the amount of his payment to her was reasonable in terms of what he received.[4]

Similarly, a salary paid by an individual to his wife as the manager of his ladies' garment factory was fully deductible and considered reasonable because prior to marrying the boss, the woman had worked as a machine operator in the garment factory, and she was thoroughly familiar with all phases of the operation. Her salary became a business deduction for the husband just as if it had been paid to an unrelated person.[5]

An individual was permitted to deduct the amount he had paid to his wife under a contingent compensation arrangement for serving as his business agent. She had experience which he lacked in this field, and he had had the same financial arrangements with her before they were married.[6]

Compensation paid to a son-in-law was deductible as reasonable where this person was paid in line with other employees and his former compensation from an unrelated employer was not substantially different.[7]

A parent may be entitled to the services of his child by having parental rights and duties in respect of the child. But the father is entitled to deduct *reasonable wages* for personal services *actually rendered* by the child as a *bona fide* employee in the conduct of a trade or business or in the production of income.[8] Note the words italicized.

The operator of a mobile home could deduct compensation paid to his three children, aged seven, eleven, and twelve. They performed janitorial and delivery services that could not have been performed by the existing staff.[9]

The proprietor of an engineer procurement agency was allowed to deduct compensation paid to his three sons, aged from seven to eleven, for maintenance work, running errands, addressing and stamping mail.[10]

An attorney was permitted to deduct a portion of the payments he made to his daughter for doing office work for his law firm at the time she was a student. About 30 percent of the amount claimed was determined by the court to be allowable.[11]

A rookie baseball player entered into a contract with his father, a former semiprofessional player and coach, to share equally any bonus the youngster got for signing a contract that his father would procure for him. The son was entitled to deduct the amount which he paid to his father as an expense related to his business.[12]

Other payments made to a relative, if made in good faith for a legitimate business purpose, are deductible in the same manner as payments made to nonfamily members. One individual was permitted to deduct interest payments which he made to his wife for the use of her securities. He had used the securities to provide capital for his business.[13]

A husband could deduct interest on money his wife had advanced him from her own funds to pay off an existing indebtedness. He gave her a note bearing the same interest rate he had been paying a bank, which had thought him a good enough risk to make the loan in the first place. The court felt that she was entitled to a return on the moneys advanced.[14]

An individual borrowed money from his mother for a business deal. The deal subsequently fell through, and he used the funds for household necessities. The Internal Revenue Service sought to disallow part of his interest deduction on the ground that his payment was made to a relative who was now retired, and in a low income bracket, and that he himself had set the rate. Full deduction was allowed. The son had borrowed from his mother because he lacked the credit to borrow elsewhere. The amount was regarded by his mother as a genuine loan, for any time the interest payment was even one day late, she *demanded* that he pay up.[15]

An individual was trustee of two bank accounts in the names of his children. He borrowed money from those accounts for his own use, with the knowledge of his children. He could deduct the interest payments which he deposited in the trust accounts.[16]

A businessperson could deduct consulting fees paid to an engineering consultant company, whose stock was owned by his son. They held frequent consultations concerning technical problems, for the son was an experienced registered professional engineer.[17]

An individual was engaged in the business of yacht chartering. He could deduct the salary paid to his brother to serve as captain, as the latter possessed the skills necessary for this type of employment.[18]

A father could deduct his share of the losses of a partnership where he and his son were equal partners. The son performed most of the daily farm work, while the father was a paid employee of another business. But the father had supplied all of the capital, and father and son participated in the making of all major management decisions.[19]

Parents may legitimately deduct interest on loans from minor children.[20]

An insurance broker could deduct compensation paid to his widowed mother-in-law for working in his office a few days a week, three or four hours a day. The office manager testified that the mother-in-law assisted the regular staff in filing, preparing mailings, and answering the telephone.[21]

A husband and wife jointly owned some real estate. He used the property in his business, paying his wife as rent one-half of the fair rental value of the property. Inasmuch as each spouse filed an individual Federal income tax return, the husband could deduct the rental payment he made to his wife.[22]

To get a rent deduction on a lease involving one's minor children is difficult but possible. Two physicians owned the building which they leased to their medical partnership. They then transferred the building to a bank as trustee for their minor children, and their medical partnership leased the property back from the trust. The partners could deduct the rent paid to the trust which they had created for the young children. The bank served as an independent intermediary between parents and minor children.[23]

A physician owned a building where he practiced. He transferred the structure to a trust for the benefit of his children and leased it back. An independent trustee represented the children, and he negotiated the lease terms and other business aspects of the transaction on behalf of the children. The physician could deduct the rent payments as business expenses. This was not just a tax dodge. There was a business reason for the arrangement: to avoid loss of the property to creditors in the event of a malpractice suit or other action against the physician.[24]

A physician transferred his medical equipment and furnishings to a trust for the benefit of his children, the trust to last for ten years and a month. The assets then were leased back to the professional corporation which the doctor used to conduct his practice. His attorney was the trustee, and the rent income was distributed annually to the children. Here, the rent payments unquestionably were fair in amount. And the trustee was not the father's stooge who meekly followed his wishes. This trustee on several occasions refused the doctor's request to use trust funds for the purchase of equipment which would be leased to the physician's corporation, on the ground that the items were too expensive. So the rent payments were held to be deductible.[25]

A world-famed concert singer could deduct the travel expenses of his wife when he went on a professional engagement to Europe because she was professionally competent to be his theatrical consultant in studying for his roles, choosing costumes, and other necessary chores related to his engagements.[26] In connection with a business matter, legal fees paid to an attorney who happened to be the payor's brother were deductible.[27]

An individual owned a tenement house containing eight apartments. He paid his teen-age sons for janitor and repair services, which were performed after school or on weekends or school-vacation days. The court was satisfied that the sons indeed had rendered some services, but there was nothing to substantiate the $900 business deduction claimed by the father. Because of the absence of substantiating records, the court allowed a deduction of $500 for the work performed by the young sons.[28]

A druggist could deduct payments made to his son for working in the former's pharmacy part-time during the summer. Even though this summer work afforded Junior the hours necessary for compliance with the apprenticeship requirements of the State Board of Pharmacy, work which was helpful to the father's business had been performed.[29]

An attorney could deduct the amount he paid to his daughter for helping out in his office at lunchtime when his assistant was away. But payments to his two sons, who were attending junior college, were held to be only partially for business services. Although the sons performed chores in the office, they also washed his car and performed nonbusiness jobs. The attorney filed salary information returns on Form W-2 for about half of what he actually paid his sons. These reported amounts were held to be the allowable deductions.[30]

An engineer paid "salaries" to his three sons, aged seven to eleven, for "helping out." The court allowed about 12.5 percent of the amounts claimed as business deductions.[31]

In special cases, a husband can deduct the travel expenses of his wife (or other related person) who accompanies him on a business trip. One man, who was a diabetic, could travel only if accompanied by someone who had been specially trained to deal with the demands of his ailment, which his wife had been. Since the expenses certainly would have been deductible if paid to a similarly trained nonrelative, the family relationship in this case was irrelevant.[32]

A corporation was permitted to deduct the expenses of its president's wife when she accompanied him on business trips. He had a serious heart condition and was permitted by his physician to travel only in the company of a knowledgeable person who knew precisely what to do in a crisis situation. She had been instructed specifically on how to minister to him by her father, a prominent physician. Helpful in rebutting the Internal Revenue Service allegation that the trips amounted to vacations to the wife was evidence that she was not enthusiastic about having to accompany her husband on these trips.[33]

Parents who owned a building for rental purposes could deduct rental expenses and depreciation on a unit rented to their daughter at a figure which was less than their expenses. They had rented the space to her at a figure comparable to what other tenants in this slum area were paying.[34]

Losses on sales or exchanges of stock or other property are *automatically* disallowed if the transactions took place between an individual and certain designated family members. The designated family members are a spouse, brothers, sisters, ancestors, and lineal descendants (sons, daughters, grandchildren, etc.). This applies in any case, no matter if the price or terms are identical to those offered by unrelated persons.[35]

Losses on the exchanges or sales of stock or other property with family members other than those designated above are not automatically disallowed and will be recognized if legitimate. These include losses that occur in transactions between an individual and his mother-in-law. This can be true no matter how emotionally close the two are.[36]

Loss on a sale to one's *former* spouse is deductible where the transaction is at arm's length.[37]

Similarly, losses are allowed in the case of transactions with one's son-in-law.[38]

The credit for household and dependent-care services necessary for gainful employment is not allowed for payments to a person for whom a dependency exemption is allowable, either to the taxpayer or his spouse. But payments to nondependent members of the family, such as grandparents, may qualify for the credit.[39] (*See also* **Child-care and disabled-dependent care.**)

An individual was entitled to deduct a loss on the sale to his nephew of stock in a corporation which he controlled. Although the seller arranged for the financing of the transaction, he did not have a sufficient degree of control over the stock after this sale to cause the deal to be disregarded for tax purposes as a sham.[40]

Losses which occur in transactions with *both* eligible and ineligible relatives can be partially allowed but must be prorated. For example, one individual sold property to his daughter and her husband, receiving their joint promissory note in payment. When they defaulted on the payment, the father claimed a loss on the transaction. In this case, the sale had been to "tenants in common" (the husband and wife shared equally in the possession of the property) and there had been no legally authorized inheritor (for example, the property was not deeded to a blood relative of the father if the two died) nor were there any other legal complications in the ownership of the property. Therefore the half of the loss which was sold to the daughter's husband could be recognized by the father for a tax deduction.[41]

For a real family-style transaction, one that could hardly be more complex, take this example: An individual sold assets to his nieces' husbands at a price previously set as fair by an independent expert. The father of the nieces (the individual's brother) had lent his daughters the money to purchase the assets. The husbands then used the borrowed money (which had been deposited in a joint husband-wife account) for purchasing the assets. The loss occurring in the transaction was allowed as a deduction, even though this circuitous method was used for the purpose of saving taxes in the first place. The motive behind the sale was immaterial as long as the sale was *bona fide* and there was no evidence that the assets were being held for the benefit of the individual's brother, who had, after all, put up the money for the purchase.[42]

If one spouse decamps with property belonging to another (*decamp* literally means to pack up equipment and leave a camping ground, but in this case it would mean a wife packing up her husband's valuable stamp collection and running away with the gasoline serviceman), the victim can deduct this as a theft loss in the same manner as if a stranger had taken the property, *provided the laws of the state where this took place recognize that the theft of property by one spouse from another is a legal theft.* There is a question arising over what the victim can call the loss of his property in states which do not recognize intraspousal theft, but in any case, where it is recognized (in Iowa and states with similar laws), the loss is deductible.[43]

A father could deduct as an embezzlement loss the amount he had to pay to recover securities which his son, without permission, had taken from a safe-deposit box to which they each had access. The son had used the securities as collateral with his own broker.[44]

An individual was permitted to deduct as a bad debt the amount she lent to her son-in-law for personal expenses. Inasmuch as she had already lent him a large amount for his business, she felt she had to lend him the additional amount to protect her investment.[45]

An individual can include in deductible medical expenses not only those for himself but also those for his spouse and for persons defined as dependents in the Internal Revenue Code.[46]

An individual can deduct expenses proper for his wife to take *only* if a joint return is filed. And a joint return can be filed by a man and a woman who are unmarried if they live where common-law marriages (those marriages where a man and woman live together as man and wife but have never gone through an official ceremony) are recognized as lawful (*e.g.*, the District of Columbia).[47]

Not all dispositions of capital assets are taxable (for instance, because the disposition might be more in the nature of an exchange than a sale), but a taxable disposition of capital assets will produce a gain or loss which is not changed by the fact that the parties involved in the transaction are married to each other. Thus, if a husband transfers securities to his wife under a court-approved settlement, and his cost is more than the fair market value at the time of the transfer, that deduction which is proper for a *capital loss* can be taken.

In the case of the husband giving the wife the securities, it is not considered a division of property. It is considered a sale or exchange of the securities for something of value—namely, the husband's freedom.[48]

When a husband gives property to his spouse in a divorce settlement, and this property has appreciated in value since he acquired it, he has disposed of property in a taxable exchange and thus has gain to report. It is not a sale but a taxable exchange, for property was transferred in return for something else. The same rule applies to losses. Where a husband transferred to his wife, in a divorce settlement, certain stock which had gone down in value since he acquired it, he had a loss, deductible to the same extent as other capital losses borne by individuals.[49]

The satisfaction of a legal obligation (the payment of a debt, for example) by the transfer of co-owned property from one co-owner to the other is considered a legal taxable transaction and can be a deduction if a loss is realized by the co-owner transferring the property. For instance, if John Smith by reason of a divorce settlement owes Shirley Smith money which he pays by transferring ownership of a jointly held parcel of land to her, John can claim a loss (and therefore a tax deduction) if the cost of the transfer is costlier to him than if he paid the money in cash to satisfy the debt. The amount of the deduction is the sum of money above the amount of the debt which John Smith had originally owed.[50]

An individual may deduct a net operating loss from the income of his (or her) spouse on a joint income tax return, but *only if* a joint return can be filed at the time the loss is suffered.[51] *See also* **Alimony; Business-related losses; Carry-overs; Casualties; Child-care and disabled-dependent care; Interest; Medical expenses; Travel.**

Farmers. A farmer is entitled to a certain particularized tax treatment in a manner which is different from that applicable to other taxpayers. The most frequently litigated issue of farmer versus nonfarmer involves deduction of farm expenses and losses. Inasmuch as farming so frequently is engaged in for reasons of pleasure or other not-for-profit purposes, the issue is whether this really is a transaction entered upon for profit. Says the Internal Revenue Service:

A taxpayer is engaged in the business of farming if he cultivates, operates, or manages a farm for gain or profit, either as an owner or tenant. . . . [A] taxpayer who receives a rental (either in cash or kind) which is based upon farm production is engaged in the business of farming. However, a taxpayer who receives a fixed rental (without reference to production) is engaged in the business of farming only if he participates to a material extent in the operation or management of the farm. . . . A taxpayer is engaged in "the business of farming" if he is a member of a partnership engaged in the business of farming.[52]

A farm which had shown losses over a continued period was held to be a business operation which could beget deductible expenses and losses. It was stated by the court that a taxpayer is entitled to embark on his own business enterprises no matter how impractical.[53] Another court added:

Certainly a taxpayer is entitled to embark on a business enterprise and if in fact that enterprise is a business enterprise is entitled to deduct his losses. The impracticality of the enterprise and the unlikelihood of making a profit are merely factors to be considered along with all other evidence in determining whether the intent of the taxpayer is to make a profit.[54]

It is not for the Internal Revenue Service to criticize the particulars of the management of a business by the taxpayer. A third court noted:

Such Monday morning quarterbacking [by the IRS] is easy, but it should be acknowledged somewhere along the line that if the success of American business should be made to depend upon the business acumen of the Collector of Internal Revenue rather than the enterprise, imagination, initiative and gambling instinct of the American businessman, little progress would be probable.[55]

In another case, the court stated that "if losses, or even repeated losses, were the only criterion by which farming is to be judged, then a large proportion of the farmers of the country would be outside the pale."[56]

A taxpayer has the burden of proving that the transaction was entered upon with the expectation of making a profit. Expenses were adjudged to be deductible where an individual had a panel of experts to advise him on his farming enterprise and where he had an elaborate accounting system so that he could operate the venture in a business-like way, regardless of what the profit-and-loss statement actually showed.[57]

A farmer is permitted to deduct losses even after the venture has been unsuccessful for several years if he can show that at all times he had the true intention of making a profit. So it was in a case where lack of success could be related to the inability to get the necessary machinery and labor to operate the farm because of shortages precipitated by World War II.[58]

Whether a farming operation represents a transaction entered upon for profit must be determined from all the facts and circumstances in each case. The Internal Revenue Service will not consider that an individual has operated a farm for profit if he raises crops or livestock mainly for the use of his family, although he derives some income from incidental sales.[59]

A person is presumed to be operating his farm for profit by the Internal Revenue Service if in two or more years out of five consecutive taxable years ending with the current taxable year (seven years in the case of an activity which consists in major part of the breeding, training, showing, or racing of horses), his gross income from the activity exceeds the deductions attributable to it. He may elect to suspend the application of this presumption until there are five consecutive taxable years (seven in the case of horses) in existence from the time he first engaged in farming. If a person makes this election, the presumption will apply to each taxable year in the five- or seven-year period.[60]

The choice is made by filing Form 5213, Election to Postpone Determination, with your Internal Revenue Service Center within three years after the due date of the tax return, without regard to extensions, for the first taxable year in which you engage in farming.[61]

The cost of ordinary tools of short life or small cost, such as hand tools including shovels, rakes, etc., may be deducted.[62]

If a farmer does not compute income upon the crop method, the cost of seeds and young plants which are purchased for further development and cultivation prior to sale in later years may be deducted as an expense for the year of purchase, provided the farmer follows a consistent practice of deducting such costs as an expense from year to year.[63]

The purchase of feed and other costs connected with raising livestock may be treated as expense deductions insofar as costs represent actual outlay, but this does not include the value of farm produce grown upon the farm or the labor of the farmer.[64]

The cost of feed, labor, and similar items utilized in raising turkeys could be deducted; these items were valid business expenses and did not have to be considered part of the cost of the turkeys.[65]

A farmer was permitted to deduct as expense a payment for feed to be delivered in the *following* taxable year when a drought situation, which could have caused a feed shortage, indicated that the farmer was not merely seeking a tax deduction by claiming an expense and later changing his mind about making the purchase.[66]

A farmer using the cash basis (that is, income was reported for tax purposes when actually received, and expenses were deducted as paid) could deduct a check for feed which he gave to a dealer on the last day of the taxable year, even though deliveries were not to be made until the following year. This was not a mere deposit for future orders. There was a business purpose for the expenditure prior to the time the feed was needed—namely, to protect the farmer against a price rise in the event the market price went up. Also, because he held a valid contract to acquire feed, he was in a preferred position to get delivery of the items purchased in case of a feed shortage.[67]

Deduction was allowed for the cost of feed purchased in advance where the purchaser believed prices would go up, even though there was no evidence that his fears were correct.[68]

Deduction for feed prepayments was allowed in the case of a "passive farmer" as well as a full-time farmer. In one case, the "gentleman farmer" who was permitted to deduct his prepayment was treasurer of the United States Steel Corporation.[69]

Deduction was allowed for purchase of feed late in the year, for use in the following year, when it could be established that a professional in the field had advised the taxpayer that the price of corn to feed cattle was generally lowest at the end of the year. Statistical tables were used to support this belief.[70]

A cash-basis individual who raised hogs was permitted to deduct the cost of feed which was purchased in advance of the year of its intended use. There had been a justifiable business purpose: fixing his costs in the event of a rise in the price of feed.[71]

Farmers employing the cash method of accounting may deduct in the year of payment the cost of baby chicks and egg-laying hens purchased for raising and resale, or for egg-laying, provided this method is followed consistently and clearly reflects income.[72]

On December 26 of one year, a farmer purchased a one-year supply of feed corn and silage, borrowing money for the purpose. Although the expenditure created an asset which had a useful life extending beyond the close of the taxable year, virtually all of the feed actually was consumed within one year of its purchase. Proration of feed expenses, unlike rental payments, requires the maintenance of consumption records, which the taxpayer kept. They won the case for him.[73]

Other deductible farm expenses may include farm organization dues, farm magazines, stamps and stationery, advertising, livestock fees, account books, litter and bedding, ginning, tying materials and containers, insect sprays and dusts, trucking, farm business travel, and accounting fees.[74] Veterinary medicine is also deductible.[75]

The expenses of maintaining houses and their furnishings for tenants and hired help are deductible farm business expenses. These expenses include repairs, heat, light, insurance, and depreciation.[76]

Transportation costs of obtaining livestock are deductible by a cash-basis farmer in the taxable year he sells the animals.[77]

Where a cash-basis farmer made a twenty-year business lease calling for annual payments to be made on December 1 each year, deduction was allowed in the first year for a full twelve months' rent, even though eleven-twelfths of the period covered by his payment was in the following taxable year. Although a cash-basis taxpayer usually must prorate prepayments to the periods covered, here it was felt by the court that simplicity of the cash-basis method would be sacrificed for an inconsequential change in the timing of deductions.[78]

Management and service fees paid to an agent were deductible.[79]

A cattle breeder could deduct amounts expended for cattle-embryo transplant operations, reduced by the amounts allocable to the cost of the cows receiving the transplants.[80]

Repairs to an earthen dam to prevent further leaks were deductible, even though the original dirt in one area was replaced with clay. Declared the court: "Fixing leaks on a dam on a farm . . . can hardly be considered an extraordinary or unsuspected expense. Nor can such expense be considered other than necessary in the conduct of the business of farming.[81]

Casualty losses are deductible in the case of such happenings as the destruction of trees by chestnut blight.[82]

Removal expenses for dead and blown-down trees were properly deductible.[83]

For taxable years beginning after July 12, 1972, where a farmer is engaged in producing crops, and the process of gathering and disposal of such crops is not completed within the taxable year in which the crops were planted, expenses may, with the consent of the Commissioner of Internal Revenue, be determined under the crop method, and these deductions may be taken in the taxable year in which the gross income from the crop has been realized.[84]

A farmer may elect to treat as deductible expenses those expenditures otherwise chargeable to capital account which are paid or incurred by him during the taxable year for the purchase or acquisition of fertilizer, lime, or other materials to enrich, to neutralize, or to condition land used in farming. And those expenditures which otherwise would be chargeable to capital account but which were paid or incurred for the application of such listed items and materials to the land may likewise be treated as deductible expenses.[85] If a farmer chooses to capitalize these expenditures over a period of years, the portion of the cost deducted each year need not be the same if the benefits are clearly greater in the early years.[86]

Amounts expended in the development of farms, orchards, and ranches prior to the time when the productive state is reached may at the election of the taxpayer be regarded as investments of capital to be recovered over the period of expected useful life.[87]

"Expenses of maintaining agricultural items in the preproductive state are deductible if they are sufficiently similar to the expenses that will be required to maintain them once they are productive."[88]

Cultivation and maintenance expenditures incurred during the preproductive years of farmers' pecan orchards were deductible by them where the outlays were for services which would be required in the regular care and maintenance of the orchards once they became productive. This included spraying, watering, pruning, and irrigating.[89]

Expenses attributable to the planting, cultivation, maintenance, or development of any citrus or almond grove (or part of one) which are incurred before the close of the fourth taxable year beginning with the year in which the trees are planted must be capitalized. But current deduction is allowed where such a grove is replanted after having been lost while in the taxpayer's hands by reason of freeze, disease, drought, pests, or casualty.[90]

A farmer may deduct his soil and water conservation expenditures which do not give rise to a deduction for depreciation and which are otherwise not deductible. The amount of the deduction is limited each year to 25 percent of the taxpayer's gross income from farming. Any excess may be carried forward and deducted in succeeding taxable years. As a general rule, once a farmer has adopted this method of treating soil and water conservation expenditures, he must deduct all these expenditures, subject to the 25 percent limitation, for the current and subsequent taxable years. If a farmer does not adopt this method, such expenditures increase the basis of the property to which they relate.[91]

A taxpayer engaged in the business of farming may elect to deduct certain expenditures paid or incurred by him in any taxable year in the clearing of land to make the "land suitable for use in farming," but only if such expenditures are made in furtherance of his business of farming. The amount deductible for any taxable year is limited to the lesser of $5,000 or 25 percent of the taxable income derived from farming. Expenditures in excess of the amount thus deductible are treated as capital expenditures and constitute an adjustment to the basis of the land.[92]

Clearing of land includes (but is not limited to) (1) the removal of rocks, stones, trees, brush, or other natural impediments to the use of the land in farming, (2) the treatment or moving of earth, including the construction, repair, or removal of nondepreciable earthen structures such as dikes or levees, if the purpose of such treatment or moving of earth is to protect, level, contour, terrace, or condition the land to permit its use as farming land, and (3) the diversion of streams and watercourses, including the construction of nondepreciable drainage facilities, provided that the purpose is to remove or to divert water from the land to make it available for use in farming.[93]

Also included in land-clearing expenses are stump blasting, grass planting, and river protection.[94]

A farmer purchased cotton acreage allotments, which allowed the holder to market his agricultural products without penalty despite existing production limits imposed by law. When the government cancelled these allotments, he was entitled to a deductible loss.[95]

Federal benefits were available to qualifying rice farmers who limited their acreage under the Agricultural Adjustment Act of 1938. When that act was repealed on December 22, 1981, there was deductible loss on property which thus lost its privileged status because of the end of entitlement to Federal benefits.[96]

As a general rule, penalties are not deductible for tax purposes. But if a farmer participates in an acreage-reserve program, and he markets an amount in excess of his quota, the marketing-quota penalty imposed on him is deductible as business expense.[97]

Qualified notices of allocation issued by farming cooperatives to their members are written notices of rights of redemption given by the cooperative separately to each patron. They are taxable, to the extent of their stated dollar value, when received and are redeemable in cash within a period of at least ninety days after issuance unless the taxpayer has consented with the cooperative to include the notices to the extent of their stated dollar value in income when received. A loss incurred on the redemption of a qualified written notice of allocation, received in the ordinary course of one's farming business, is deductible as an ordinary loss. The loss is measured by the difference between the stated dollar amount included in income upon receipt and the amount received upon redemption.[98]

The cost of a commodity futures contract purchased solely for protection against commodity price fluctuation is a form of business insurance and is deductible as an ordinary and necessary business expense.[99] But the cost of a futures contract purchased for speculative purposes is not deductible.[100]

The Federal use tax on highway motor vehicles paid on a truck or truck-trailer used in a farming business is a deductible expense.[101]

To the extent that there was no prospect of recovery by insurance or otherwise, deduction was allowed for flood damage to land planted with cranberries.[102] Deduction was allowed for frost destruction of grass on land purchased for purposes of harvesting.[103] Where a windstorm damaged the topsoil of a farm, a casualty-loss deduction was allowed to the extent of the difference in the fair market value of the farm immediately before and immediately after the happening. The court regarded the precipitating event as sufficiently unexpected and unusual to constitute a casualty, although the Internal Revenue Service had argued that this type of windstorm occurred every year, usually in February or March (this one hit in March).[104] Casualty-loss deduction was allowed in the case of damage from drought and early freeze in the case of plants and shrubs.[105]

Loss of bees that had been exposed to pesticides was deductible.[106]

A farmer was allowed to take a deduction for the partial destruction of his own vineyards and orchards, by his own hand, in order to check the further spread of disease.[107]

A farmer claimed as a casualty loss the cost of three heifers that died as the result of eating corn. The Internal Revenue Service questioned whether this was a casualty loss. Without deciding that question, the court allowed the deduction because the heifers were a part of the farm operation. Hence their cost was deductible as a loss in the operation of a farm as a trade or business.[108]

A cattle farmer suffered a significant loss of feed as the result of a drought. In the same year he applied for and received authorization pursuant to the Emergency Livestock Feed Assistance Program for partial reimbursement of the anticipated cost of replacing the lost feed. Shortly afterward he purchased the authorized replacement feed, but he was not reimbursed for his expenditures until the following year. He could not deduct the portion of the feed expenditures for which he had received prior authorization for partial reimbursement, before these feed costs were reimbursed, but the remaining portion of the expenditures for which reimbursement was not available were deductible.[109]

Appraisal fees for the purpose of establishing a casualty loss by reason of subsoil shrinkage resulting from prolonged drought were deductible.[110]

Property used in the business of farming, or for the production of income from rent and royalties (if subject to an involuntary conversion after having been held for more than one year), is included in the definition of "Section 1231 property." Gain on the *net* of all transactions involving Section 1231 property held for more than one year is treated as long-term capital gain. If the netted result of transactions in Section 1231 property of the taxable year results in a loss, the loss is fully deductible.[111]

The following transactions represent areas where losses involving Section 1231 property are fully deductible:

1. Livestock acquired before 1970 (not including poultry) held for draft, breeding, or dairy purposes and held for twelve months or more.
2. Cattle and horses acquired after 1969 for draft, breeding, dairy, or sporting purposes and held for twenty-four months or more.
3. Livestock (except cattle, horses, and poultry) acquired after 1969 for draft, breeding, dairy, or sporting purposes and held for twelve months or more.

If diseased livestock held for the above purposes are destroyed or disposed of by or on account of the disease, any recognized gain or loss must be included.

Section 1231 property also includes:

1. Depreciable property used in the business, such as farm machinery, trucks, barns, sheds, livestock, etc., except for gain attributable to depreciation.
2. Real estate used in the business, such as a farm or ranch land, except for gain attributable to depreciation or for soil and water conservation and land-clearing expenses.
3. Unharvested crops on land used in farming if the crop and land are sold, exchanged, or involuntarily converted at the same time and to the same person. Growing crops sold with a lease on the land, even though to the same person in a single transaction, are not included. Also not included is a sale, exchange, or involuntary conversion of an unharvested crop with land, where the taxpayer retains any right or option to reacquire the land, directly or indirectly (other than a right customarily incident to a mortgage or other security transaction).
4. Timber, the cutting of which the taxpayer has elected to treat as a sale, and timber disposed of under a contract by which he retains an economic interest in the timber.
5. Coal or iron ore disposed of under a contract by which the taxpayer retains an economic interest in the coal or iron ore.
6. Property held for the production of rents or royalties.
7. The taxpayer's distributive share of partnership gains and losses from the sale, exchange, and involuntary conversion of the above items held for more than one year (or the period specified for livestock under specified circumstances), except for gain attributable to depreciation.
8. Involuntary conversions of business property and capital assets held for more than one year (or the holding periods specified for livestock) resulting from casualties and thefts (whether insured or uninsured) or from condemnations for public use.[112]

A deduction is denied in the case of a contribution to an approved charitable organization (except in transfer in trust) of a partial value of a charitable contribution (not in trust) consisting of an irrevocable remainder interest in a farm which is not the donor's entire interest. For example, if an individual contributes (not in trust) to an approved charitable organization a remainder interest in a farm and retains an estate in the farm for life or for a specified number of years, a deduction is allowed for the value of the remainder interest not transferred in trust.[113]

Legal expenses incurred in defending an action for damages by a tenant injured while at work on the taxpayer's farm were deductible as business expenses.[114] *See also* **Agricultural allotment cancellation; Casualties; Cattle feed, deductibility of; Forest management expenses; Hobby losses; Reforestation expenditures; Repairs; Water erosion, correction of.**

Faulty driving, expenses resulting from. *See* **Casualties.**

Feasibility studies. Feasibility studies were made by a taxpayer in order to determine whether and where new facilities should be opened in order to serve customers better in future years. Deduction of expenses for these studies was allowed to the extent that review of current income-producing activities was involved, because assumptions about the future called for an analysis of present activities. But deduction was not allowed for the cost of studies relating to the planning and expansion that were concerned with the production of income in future years.[115] *See also* **Investors; Ordinary and necessary business expenses; Research and experimental expenses.**

Federal Employees. *See* **Government employees.**

Feed, purchases of. *See* **Farmers.**

Fidelity bond premium. *See* **Insurance.**

Fiduciaries. The business which begets business deductions may be any form of activity entered upon with a reasonable expectation of profit. One who regularly engages in the business of serving *for pay* as a trustee, who is required to pay a sum as a liability growing out of the conduct of fiduciary affairs, such as a lawyer who devoted about half of his time to acting as an attorney and as a trustee, may deduct amounts claimed against him.[116] Such deduction was not allowed in the case of a trustee who was not in the *business* of being a trustee.[117] A casual executor, administrator, or trustee cannot deduct business expenses, not being engaged in a trade or business as fiduciary. But it is possible that a person's activities in handling a single estate may be of sufficient scope and duration to constitute his being engaged in a trade or business as fiduciary.[118] (A fiduciary is one who holds something in trust for another party.)

An individual accepted the trusteeship of a trust containing assets with a definite dollar value. He was not regularly engaged in the business of performing services as a trustee. Pursuant to the laws of the state where the trust was created, he was entitled, without court allowance, to annual commissions of 6 percent of all the income from the trust which was handled by him. In order to protect his personal estate from claims or lawsuits which could arise from his activities as trustee, he purchased a one-year trustees' errors and omissions policy with his own funds. Inasmuch as the premium was reasonable in amount compared to the commissions he expected to receive during the policy term, the premium was deductible as an ordinary and necessary expense paid or incurred for the collection of income.[119]

When an individual engages a fiduciary in connection with the production of *taxable* income or for the management, conservation, or maintenance of property held for the production of taxable income, the fee is deductible. Thus, to the extent that tax-free municipal bonds in a trust produce taxable income or are held for that purpose, the fee of the fiduciary, whether measured by the income or by the value of the municipals in the trust, is deductible. A reasonable basis for determining the extent to which the fiduciary's fee was related to taxable income and thus was deductible is the ratio of taxable income to nontaxable income over the life of the trust.[120] *See also* **Coexecutor's fees; Compensable injuries; Executor's fees; Legal fees; Termination of trust or estate; Unused carry-over of fiduciary.**

Fiduciary responsibility, defense of. A corporate director could deduct attorneys' fees in defending a suit against him for improper conduct.[121]

Finance charges. *See* **Interest,**

Financial counseling fees. Fees paid for the services of investment counsel in connection with securities held for the production or collection of income are deductible.[122]

A corporation engaged a financial counseling firm to provide advice to designated executives in the handling of their personal financial affairs. The fees paid by the corporation were treated by the Internal Revenue Service as additional compensation to each of the executives who benefited by the arrangement. But each executive in turn could deduct the amount taxed in this manner as financial counseling fees incurred for the production or collection of income or for the maintenance of investments.[123]

Finder's fee. Reasonable amounts paid as a commission to a person for obtaining something of business value (not a capital asset), or referring parties to the payor, are deductible as ordinary and necessary business expenses.[124]

Payments made in order to get names of prospective customers were deductible.[125]

Fines and penalties. *See* **Punitive damages; Settlement payments.**

Fire damage. *See* **Casualties.**

Firemen. *See* **Employees; Ordinary and necessary business expenses; Telephone; Uniforms.**

Fishermen. *See* **Work clothes.**

Fixed mileage allowance. *See* **Mileage allowance.**

Flight instruction. *See* **Education.**

Floods. *See* **Casualties.**

Flowers. An attorney could deduct the cost of flowers sent to a deceased client. (Presumably the court meant flowers sent to the late client's funeral.)[126]

Fluoride additions to water. Amounts paid to have a device for adding fluoride to an individual's home water supply and the monthly rental charges for this device were deductible where the installation was undertaken on the advice of a dentist.[127]

Food additives. *See* **Medical expenses.**

Food, as business expense. A psychotherapist could deduct the cost of food provided at his office to patients whom he was counseling.[128]

Foreign countries, conventions in. Deductions for the cost of attending conventions outside of the country are subject to severe limitations.[129] *See* **Conventions.**

Foreign expropriation losses. If an individual has net operating losses as a result of expropriation by a foreign government, they may not be carried back but may be carried forward ten years. In the case of Cuban expropriation losses, the carry-over period is twenty years.[130] To qualify, the individual must have been a citizen or resident of the United States on December 31, 1958. This rule applies also to investment property.[131] *See also* **Casualties; Government seizure.**

Foreign income taxes. *See* **Taxes.**

Foreign organizations, contributions to. *See* **Contributions.**

Foreign study. *See* **Education.**

Forest management expenses. Forest management expenses of the owner of timber land were deductible despite the fact that sales of timber were treated as capital gain, even though a small part of those expenses was attributable to the negotiation and supervision of timber-cutting contracts. Here the court declared that selling expenses related to the disposal of timber are treated in a manner somewhat inconsistent with that accorded selling expenses related to most other kinds of capital assets.[132]

The costs incurred for the shearing and basal pruning of trees grown for the Christmas-tree market are deductible business expenses.[133] *See also* **Reforestation expenses.**

Forfeited interest, premature withdrawal of. *See* **Premature withdrawal of interest.**

Forfeitures. *See* **Cancellation and forfeiture.**

Forgiveness of rent. *See* **Rent, forgiveness of.**

Forwarding fees. *See* **Referral fees.**

Foster parents. Foster parents may deduct as charitable contributions unreimbursed out-of-pocket expenses which they pay to provide gratuitous foster-home care for children placed in their home by a charitable organization.[134]

Founder's fee. *See* **Retirement homes.**

Franchise agreement, payments for release from. Payments involving the sale of a franchise are nondeductible capital expenditures. Payments geared to sales made under a franchise are deductible business expenses. One distributor was licensed to operate a franchise for as long as it paid 6 percent of its gross sales to the franchisor. The franchisor later brought suit to recover such fees as had not been paid. Amounts paid by the distributor to obtain a release from all claims under the franchise agreement were deductible business expenses.[135]

Fraud, loss resulting from. *See* **Casualties; Reliance upon misrepresentation.**

Fringe benefits. *See* **Compensation; Ordinary and necessary business expenses.**

Front-foot benefit charge. To pay for the construction of a water system, a city assessed a "front-foot benefit charge" against properties that would benefit from the new facility. This charge was added to the regular real property taxes, with a breakdown of how much of the charge was (1) for construction, (2) for interest, and (3) for maintenance costs. Items (2) and (3) were deductible as taxes.[136]

Funeral expenses. *See* **Flowers.**

Futures contract in commodities. *See* **Farmers.**

F

1. Revenue Ruling 76-332, 1976-2 CB 81.
2. *Olivia de Havilland Goodrich et al.*, 20 T.C. 323 (1953).
3. *James E. Wood et al.*, T.C. Memo. 1971-125, filed May 27, 1971.
4. *Mary Sinclair et al.*, BTA Memo., Docket No. 91164, entered March 14, 1939.
5. *Blanche Rosenzweig*, T.C. Memo. 1955-57, filed March 22, 1955.
6. *Craig Earl*, T.C. Memo., Docket No. 110850, entered May 25, 1943.
7. *Liberty National Bank & Trust Company as executor of Estate of John D. Stewart et al. v. United States*, DC, WD Ky., 1967.
8. Revenue Ruling 72-23, 1972-2 CB 43.
9. *West Eller Trailer Sales of Modesto, Inc. et al. v. Commissioner*, 77 T.C., No. 66 (1981).
10. *Nathaniel A. Denman et al.*, 48 T.C. 439 (1967).
11. *Terrell et al. v. Commissioner*, T.C. Memo. 1979-222, filed June 5, 1979.
12. *Cecil Randolph Hundley, Jr.*, 48 T.C. 339 (1967).
13. *M. A. Long*, 8 BTA 737 (1927).
14. *Dorzbeck v. Collison*, 195 F.2d 69 (3d Cir., 1952).
15. *Barton et al. v. Commissioner*, T.C. Memo. 1979-234, filed June 13, 1979.
16. *Charles R. Godard*, T.C. Memo. 1962-83, filed April 13, 1962.
17. *John E. Walsh, Jr., et al.*, T.C. Memo. 1961-278, filed October 5, 1961.
18. *Thomas W. Jackson*, 59 T.C. 312 (1972).
19. *Palmer et al. v. Commissioner*, T.C. Memo. 1981-354, filed July 9, 1981.
20. *Cook et ux. v. United States*, DC, WD La., 1977.
21. *Laputka and Sons, Inc.*, T.C. Memo. 1981-730, filed December 28, 1981.
22. Revenue Ruling 74-209, 1974-1 CB 46.
23. *Serbousek et al. v. Commissioner*, T.C. Memo. 1977-105, filed April 11, 1977.
24. *May et al. v. Commissioner*, 76 T.C. (1981).
25 *Lerner et al. v. Commissioner*, 71 T.C. 290 (1978).
John Charles Thomas, BTA Memo., Docket No. 91164, entered March 14, 1939.
27. *George S. Groves*, 38 BTA 727 (1938).
28. *Charles Tschupp et al.*, T.C. Memo. 1963-98, filed April 4, 1963.
29. *Adam C. Croff*, T.C. Memo. 1957-163, filed August 27, 1957.
30. *Roundtree et al. v. Commissioner*, T.C. Memo. 1980-117, filed April 14, 1980.
31. *Nathaniel A. Denman et al.*, 48 T.C. 439 (1967).
32. *Allenberg Cotton Co., Inc., et al. v. United States*, DC, WD Tenn., 1960.
33. *Quinn et al. v. United States*, DC, Md., 1977.

34. *Keenon et al. v. Commissioner*, T.C. Memo. 1982-144, filed March 23, 1982.
35. IRC Section 267.
36. Revenue Ruling 71-50, 1971-CB 106.
37. *William E. Robertson et al.*, 55 T.C. 862 (1971).
38. *Fervel Topek et al.*, 9 T.C. 763 (1947).
39. IRC Section 44A(f)(6).
40. *First Teachers Investment Corporation et al. v. Commissioner*, T.C. Memo. 1980-302, filed August 7, 1980.
41. *Walter Simister, Jr., et al.*, 4 T.C. 470 (1944).
42. *Maurice B. Saul et al.*, T.C. Memo., Docket No. 7679, entered June 26, 1947.
43. *Vesta Peak Maxwell*, BTA Memo., Docket Nos. 86186-7, entered February 7, 1940.
44. *Earle v. Commissioner*, 72 F.2d 366 (2d Cir., 1934).
45. *Sidney Dembner et al.*, T.C. Memo. 1974-180, filed July 8, 1974.
46. IRC Section 213.
47. *James M. Ross*, T.C. Memo. 1972-112, filed May 25, 1972.
48. *Wallace et al. v. United States*, 439 F.2d 757 (8th Cir., 1971).
49. *Worthy W. McKinney*, 64 T.C. 263 (1975).
50. *United States v. Davis*, 370 U.S. 65 (1962).
51. *Zeeman v. United States*, 275 F. Supp. 235 (DC, SD N.Y., 1967), *aff'd on this issue*, 395 F.2d 861 (2d Cir., 1968).
52. Regulations Section 1.182-2.
53. *Wright v. United States*, DC, Nev., 1965.
54. *Leonard F. Barcus et al.*, T.C. Memo. 1973-138, filed June 25, 1973.
55. *Wright et al. v. Commissioner*, 249 F. Supp. 508 (DC, Nev., 1965).
56. *S. Riker, Jr.*, 6 BTA 890 (1927).
57. *Plant v. Walsh*, 280 F.2d 722 (DC, Conn. 1922).
58. *Otis Beall Kent*, T.C. Memo., Docket No. 37332, entered December 31, 1953.
59. *Farmer's Tax Guide*, 1976 edition, page 24.
60. IRC Section 183.
61. *Farmer's Tax Guide*, 1981 edition, page 10.
62. Regulations Section 1.162-12(a).
63. Ibid.
64. Ibid.
65. *McCulley v. Kelm*, 112 F. Supp. 832 (DC, Minn., 1953).
66. *Cravens v. Commissioner*, 272 F.2d 895 (10th Cir., 1959).
67. *Mann et al. v. Commissioner*, 483 F.2d 673 (8th Cir., 1973).
68. *De La Cruz et al. v. Commissioner*, T.C. Memo. 1978-8, filed January 9, 1978.

69. *Frysinger et al. v. United States,* 645 F.2d 523 (5th Cir., 1981).

70. Ibid.

71. *Mann et al. v. Commissioner,* 483 F.2d 673 (8th Cir., 1973).

72. Revenue Ruling 60-191, 1960-1 CB 78.

73. *Commissioner v. Van Raden et al.,* 650 F.2d 1047 (9th Cir., 1981).

74. *Farmer's Tax Guide,* 1976 edition, page 27.

75. Schedule F listing for Form 1040.

76. *Farmer's Tax Guide,* 1981 edition, page 13.

77. Revenue Ruling 80-102, 1980-1 CB 108.

78. *Zaninovich et al. v. Commissioner,* 616 F.2d 429 (9th Cir., 1980).

79. *De La Cruz et al. v. Commissioner,* T.C. Memo. 1978-8, filed January 9, 1978.

80. IRS Letter Ruling 8007002, October 30, 1979.

81. *Evans et al. v. Commissioner,* 557 F.2d 1095 (5th Cir., 1977).

82. *Cinelli et al. v. Commissioner,* 502 F.2d 1695 (6th Cir., 1974).

83. *Thomas O. Campbell et al.,* T.C. Memo. 1973-101, filed April 25, 1973.

84. Regulations Section 1.162-12(a).

85. Regulations Section 1.180-1.

86. *Farmer's Tax Guide,* 1976 edition, page 25.

87. Regulations Section 1.162-12(a).

88. *Maple v. Commissioner,* 440 F.2d 1055 (9th Cir., 1971).

89. *Vinson et al. v. Commissioner,* 621 F.2d 173 (5th Cir., 1980).

90. IRC Section 278(b)(1).

91. IRC Section 175.

92. IRC Section 182.

93. Regulations Section 1.182-3(a).

94. *Arthur William Peterson et al.,* T.C. Memo. 1970-181 filed June 29, 1970.

95. *Greaves et al. v. Commissioner,* T.C. Memo. 1980-535, filed December 4, 1980.

96. Revenue Ruling 82-67, I.R.B. 1982-16.

97. Regulations Section 1.61-4(a)(4) and 1.61-1(b)(4).

98. *Farmer's Tax Guide,* 1976 edition, page 23.

99. *Corn Products Refining Company v. Commissioner,* 350 U.S. 46 (1955).

100. *Henry I. Seroussi,* T.C. Memo. 1963-233, filed August 29, 1963.

101. *Farmer's Tax Guide,* 1976 edition, page 26.

102. *F. H. Wilson,* 12 BTA 403 (1928).

103. *Flona Corporation v. United States,* 218 F. Supp. 354 (DC, SD Fla., 1963).

104. *Barry et al., v. United States,* 175 F. Supp. 308 (DC, WD Okla., 1958).

105. *Alfred M. Cox et al.,* T.C. Memo. 1965-5, filed January 14, 1965, *aff'd on another issue,* 354 F.2d 659 (3d Cir., 1966).

106. Revenue Ruling 75-381, 1975-2 CB 25.

107. *H. B. Hooper,* 8 BTA 397 (1927).

108. *Cooper et al. v. Commissioner,* T.C. Memo. 1981-369, filed July 16, 1981.

109. Revenue Ruling 79-263, 1979-2 CB 82.

110. Revenue Ruling 58-180, 1958-1 CB 153.

111. IRC Section 1231.

112. *Farmer's Tax Guide,* 1976 edition, page 40.

113. Regulations Section 1.170A-7(b)(4).

114. OD 1117, CB No. 5 (1921).

115. *NCNB Corporation v. United States,* 651 F.2d 942 (4th Cir., 1981).

116. *John Abbott,* 38 BTA 1290 (1938).

117. *Commissioner v. Heide,* 165 F.2d 699 (2d Cir., 1948).

118. *A. M. Barnhart Estate,* T.C. Memo. 1959-42, filed February 27, 1959.

119. Revenue Ruling 72-316, 1972-1 CB 44.

120. *Whittemore, Jr., et al. v. United States,* 383 F.2d 824 (8th Cir., 1967).

121. *Hochschild v. Commissioner,* 161 F.2d 817 (2d Cir., 1947).

122. Regulations Section 1.212-1(g).

123. Revenue Ruling 73-13, 1973-1 CB 42.

124. *Mary Sinclair et al.,* T.C. Memo. 1960-113, filed May 31, 1960.

125. *Doris Jones,* T.C. Memo., Docket No. 26195, entered May 29, 1952.

126. *Gilman II et al. v. Commissioner,* 72 T.C. 730 (1979).

127. Revenue Ruling 64-267, 1964-2 CB 69.

128. *Fanning v. Commissioner,* T.C. Memo. 1980-462, filed October 14, 1980.

129. IRC Section 274(h).

130. Tax Reform Act of 1976, Section 2126.

131. IRC Section 165(i).

132. *McMullan et al. v. United States,* Ct. Cl., 1978.

133. Revenue Ruling 71-288, 1971-2 CB 319.

134. Revenue Ruling 77-280, 1977-2 CB 14.

135. Revenue Ruling 79-208, 1979-2 CB 79.

136. Revenue Ruling 79-201, 1979-1 CB 97.

G

Gambling losses. Income from gambling is taxable, but it may be offset or even cancelled completely by gambling losses.[1] The difficulty is that significant gambling "wins" are reported to the Internal Revenue Service by the racetrack or other payor, at least in theory. The taxpayer has to prove the losses himself. When a taxi driver who went to the track several times a week finally won a $21,854 twin double on April 5, this payout was reported by the track. Forewarned, he showed a Revenue Agent $23,680 in losing tickets he allegedly had purchased between April 6 and May 21. The only trouble was that many of the losing tickets unmistakably bore heel marks, such as often appear on tickets that disgusted bettors throw away after their horses have lost. Instead of $23,680 the court allowed him $2,000 as a deduction against gambling gains.[2] Damon Runyon could have written a dandy story on this one, but the bettor did not do too badly, considering the nature of his "evidence."

A factory worker was a racetrack addict. To offset wagering gains one year, he showed "losing" tickets of an amount almost as large. But unlike other taxpayers who had displayed randomly numbered tickets which often bore heel marks or other evidence that they had been picked off the turf by persons whose horses had not come in, his tickets were clean and untorn, most bearing sequential serial numbers which indicated that they had been issued to the same purchaser at the same time. A racetrack companion testified that he had never seen the taxpayer pick up ticket stubs flung to the ground by unsuccessful bettors. The court allowed two-thirds of the amount claimed as offsets against gambling wins.[3]

In one case, a bettor added his unsuccessful tickets each night and attached them to the adding-machine tape. He made a schedule each month of the transactions and turned all of this material over to his accountant at tax time. The court accepted these records as proof of the loss offset.[4]

A part-time gambler had one substantial win on the horses in the taxable year. To offset this, he turned over to the tax examiner a shoe box of unsuccessful gambling tickets which allegedly totaled virtually the same amount as the wagering income. The court allowed the claimed deduction as an offset to the successful bet, although the Revenue Agent had not bothered to add up the losing tickets. The judge felt that this taxpayer would not have exaggerated the amount of his losses, "knowing," added the court, "that the audit agent was likely to count them."[5]

Even in the absence of detailed records which meet all of the requirements of the Internal Revenue Service regulations, deduction of losses may be accepted by a court if orderly records have been maintained regularly by a competent accountant and these records are still available in their original, untranscribed form for examination by a Revenue Agent. The court noted in one such case that gambling operations must be assumed to have losses as well as gains.[6]

A court allowed the deduction of dog-racing losses because of evidence that the taxpayer had repeated domestic quarrels with his wife— by reason of his sustained gambling losses.[7]

In one case, a court allowed the claimed loss offsets because the taxpayer kept a monthly diary in which he recorded his wagers, both wins and losses. The court accepted these figures, because the diary's list of wins pretty well matched what the payor's information returns had reported to the Internal Revenue Service.[8]

One individual's records for 1975 were lost when he changed his residence. But he produced his 1974 records: notations on racing programs of how much he had placed on various horses and the amounts he had received back, with notations each day in a spiral notebook, which was summarized on a schedule attached to his 1974 Federal income tax return. His winnings on the schedule were the same as reported by the racetracks on Information Forms 1099. His 1975 return had a comparable schedule, without the lost back-up substantiation. The court allowed the total losses he had claimed as offsets to winnings for 1975, believing that that year's figures must have been as accurate as his painstaking records for the previous year.[9]

To prove gambling losses, the Internal Revenue Service recommends that an accurate diary or similar record regularly be maintained, supplemented by verifiable documentation. In general, the diary should contain at least the following information:

1. Date and type of specific wager or wagering activity.
2. Name of gambling establishment.
3. Address or location of gambling establishment.
4. Name(s) of other person(s), if any, present with the taxpayer at the gambling establishment.
5. Amount(s) won or lost.

Adds the IRS: "Verifiable documentation for gambling transactions includes but is not limited to Forms W-2G; Forms 5754, Statement by Person Receiving Gambling Winnings; wagering tickets, cancelled checks, credit records, bank withdrawals, and statements of actual winnings or payment slips provided by the taxpayer to the gambling establishment.

"Where possible, the diary and available documentation generated with the placement and settlement of a wager should be further supported by other documentation of the taxpayer's wagering activity or visit to a gambling establishment. Such documentation includes, but is not limited to, hotel bills, airline tickets, gasoline credit cards, cancelled checks, credit records, bank deposits, and bank withdrawals.

"Additional supporting evidence could also include affidavits or testimony from responsible gambling officials regarding wagering activity."[10]

Gambling losses may be offset against gambling gains whether the wager occurred as part of a trade or business or for "sport and recreation."[11]

If an expense arises out of the conduct of a business and is a required outlay meeting the standard definition of "ordinary and necessary," it is allowed, even though the business activity is illegal under the laws of the state where it operates. The United States Supreme Court has said that "the federal income tax is a tax on net income, not a sanction against wrongdoing."[12] Where state law banned bookmaking, payments of wages and rent by the bookmaker were deductible for tax purposes because they were ordinary and necessary expenses in the accepted meaning of those terms and were not devices to avoid the consequences of violations of the law.[13]

Other expenses of an unlawful business, conceivably, could not be deemed deductions. *See also* **Bribes and kickbacks; Illegal business activity.**

Gasoline taxes. For taxable years beginning after December 31, 1978, gasoline taxes no longer are deductible, except when the fuel is used in business or investment activities.[14]

General sales taxes. *See* **Taxes.**

"Gentleman farmer," expenses of. *See* **Farmers; Hobby losses; Transactions entered into for profit.**

Gift and leaseback. If a person owns property that is needed in his trade or business, he can create a tax deduction for himself by transferring the property to another party and leasing it back, the rent being deductible. The transfer can be a sale, but this produces taxable gain when there is a profit. And if there is a loss, this is not recognized for tax purposes where the buyer is the seller's spouse, brother or sister, ancestor, or lineal descendant. Rather than a sale and leaseback, a gift and lease-back may be used. Most commonly, the donee is a minor child (or children) of the donor or is his spouse, so that the property remains in the family. In order for the donor to get a rent deduction when he leases back the property for use in his business, these four conditions must be met:

1. The donor cannot retain substantially the same control over the property that he had before the gift.

2. The leaseback normally should be in writing and must require payment of a fair rent.

3. The leaseback (as distinguished from the gift) must have a substantial business purpose.

4. The donor must not possess a disqualifying equity in the property; that is, a meaningful interest in it or control over it.[15]

The "reasonable rental" element is customarily lacking where the donor appears to control the rate of rent and other aspects of the transaction. In order to avoid even the appearance of unfair rent because of conflict of interest, a trust frequently is set up where the donee is a minor or is financially unsophisticated. Rent is deductible as reasonable where an *independent* trustee (for example, a bank) negotiates rent and other terms with the donor.[16] A pediatrician-allergist could deduct the rent he paid to a trust he had set up to hold property gifted to his children, even though the trustees were his attorney and his accountant. Here the rent had been determined by an independent appraisal firm, and the work of the trustees was purely ministerial, such as collecting rents and paying bills.[17]

There must be a business reason for the donor to lease back what had been his property. Such an arrangement was found where a physician gave his business assets to his children in order to avoid the risk of having this property pass from the family if he should be involved in a malpractice suit in excess of his liability insurance.[18] Or the justification may be that the donor had wanted to make a gift of his building, but he requires it in order to conduct his medical practice there.[19]

As to (4), the deduction is not otherwise lost where the donor retains no right to get the property back again, such as upon the donee's death or his reaching a specified age.[20]

Although the most common form of gift and leaseback involves an individual and his minor child or children, the opportunity is not confined to that situation. Rent deduction was allowed where a physician assigned his building to a bank as trustee for the benefit of his wife and then leased back part of it for use as a medical clinic.[21]

Despite the frequency with which this procedure is used by doctors, it is available to any other persons who presently own property that is needed in their trade or business. Deduction for rent was permitted in the case of two attorneys who owned an office building and transferred it to a bank as trustee for the benefit of their minor children. The lawyers then leased back the premises to use as their professional office, with deductible rent.[22]

The property that is given away and then leased back most frequently is a building. But it likewise may consist of other costly assets, such as where an ophthamologist leased back medical equipment and furnishings he had given away.[23] *See also* **Family transactions.**

Gifts. *See* **Business gifts; Compensation; Contributions; Ordinary and necessary business expenses.**

Goodwill, expenses to create. A businessperson can deduct expenses for the purpose of creating goodwill, such as through the purchase of tickets to benefit performances to raise funds for approved charitable organizations.[24] *See also* **Advertising; Contributions; Ordinary and necessary business expenses.** *For discussion of the treatment of goodwill entertaining expenses, see* **Entertainment.**

Government employees. Dues paid to a chamber of commerce or similar organization represent ordinary and necessary expenses where this membership is used as a means of advancing the business interest of the employee, such as carrying out duties imposed upon him solely because of his governmental employment.[25]

Expenses paid by a foreign-service officer of the United States in excess of those expenses which are either reimbursed or certified as properly reimbursable by the State Department are deductible, if he can establish that they are ordinary and necessary in the performance of his duties.[26]

An employee of the Federal government represented a fellow employee in the presentation of an antidiscrimination complaint. Expenses in gathering data used to justify the allegations contained in the complaint were deductible because they were incurred while he was acting within the scope of his employment in representing the complainant. Civil Service regulations authorized a complainant to be represented by a person of his choice in the presentation of a complaint.[27] *See also* **Education; Expenses of another person; Ordinary and necessary business expenses; Travel.**

Government seizure. Deduction was allowed for the cost of business property which had been seized by a foreign government during wartime. The owner was given no right to demand compensation, a situation which was dependent upon the hazards of war then in progress.[28]

Government service, company employees in. *See* **Compensation.**

Graduated payment mortgages. *See* **Interest.**

Graduate studies. *See* **Advanced degree, study for; Education.**

Gratuities. *See* **Tips.**

Grooming. A saleswoman at a drugstore could deduct the cost of special hair-do's which she considered to be helpful in carrying out her duties.[29] *See* **Personal grooming.**

Ground rent. Ground rent is a payment for the right to make use of another person's property—for example, to build a structure there. Payments made annually or periodically on a *redeemable* ground rent are deductible as interest. Here land is leased for a term of more than fifteen years, and the lessor's interest in the land is primarily a security interest to protect the rental payments to which the lessor is entitled. Payments on a *nonredeemable* ground rent are not interest. But they are deductible as rent if the property is used for business or rental purposes.[30]

Group legal-services plan. Payments made by an employer to a qualified group prepaid legal-services plan that provides legal services for an employee or his spouse or dependent are deductible for taxable years ending before January 1, 1985.[31]

Group-term life-insurance premiums. *See* **Compensation.**

Guarantor, payments by. Where a corporate employee was advised by his supervisor that if he did not act as guarantor of a bank loan made by his company, his present position and future possibilities would be jeopardized, he guaranteed the loan. His sole purpose was to protect his employment. When the loan could not be repaid by the corporation and he was obliged to honor his guarantee, this was a fully deductible business bad-debt deduction.[32]

If an individual suffers a loss resulting from the guarantee of a loan which he has to make good, the nature of the deduction will depend upon the reason for which the loan guarantee was made. The loss is fully deductible only if it arose in connection with the taxpayer's business.[33] Otherwise, it may be regarded as a nonbusiness bad debt, and treated as a short-term capital loss. The proper time to determine the guarantor's motivation is when the agreement was made, not at the time the payments were made under the guarantee.[34]

An individual was permitted to deduct losses arising from her guarantee of a corporation's obligations, where she had entered the guarantee transaction for profit in terms of increasing the value of the stock held by her in this corporation.[35]

An individual guaranteed the obligation of a corporation that had never defaulted in the past. If in the future the corporation defaulted, he would have no possibility of being reimbursed by the company for any amount he had to pay out. Accordingly, payment which he made to be relieved of his potential liability was deductible as a loss on a transaction entered into for profit.[36]

Legal expenses incurred by a guarantor in obtaining a release from his liability are deductible, if the guaranty resulted from a transaction entered into for profit: *e.g.,* where a note was guaranteed with the expectation that the proceeds of the note would be used to buy stock in a corporation in which the guarantor would be elected a director. It was believed also that this corporation would deposit its funds in a bank of which the guarantor was a stockholder.[37] *See also* **Business-related losses; Legal fees.**

Guarantor, payments to. Where businesspersons required surety bonds in order to make bids and surety companies were unwilling to issue such bonds without personal guarantees by financially responsible individuals, compensation paid to persons who signed the guarantees were deductible.[38]

Guardians, expenses of. Reasonable amounts paid for the services of a guardian or committee for a ward or minor, and other expenses of guardians and committees which are ordinary and necessary in connection with the production or collection of income of the ward or minor, or in connection with the management of his property, are deductible.[39]

Guide dogs. *See* **Medical expenses.**

Guile, loss resulting from. *See* **Reliance upon misrepresentation.**

Gun, cost of. An individual performed surveillance work for a United States government agency. Although in general he was reimbursed for his out-of-pocket expenses, such was not the case where from personal preference he supplied his own job-related equipment. The cost of a firearm which he purchased because it was smaller and more concealable than the pistol furnished him was deductible; but as the gun had a useful life of more than one year, the cost had to be deducted proportionately over its estimated life.[40]

Gymnasium. *See* **Actors; Handball court, rental of.**

G

1. IRC Sections 165(d).
2. *William H. Green*, T.C. Memo. 1972-131, filed June 20, 1972.
3. *Salem et al. v. Commissioner*, T.C. Memo. 1978-142, filed April 13, 1978.
4. *Wolkomir et al. v. Commissioner*, T.C. Memo. 1980-344, filed August 27, 1980.
5. *Jones v. Commissioner*, T.C. Memo. 1981-458, filed August 25, 1981.
6. *Gene P. Green et al.*, 66 T.C. 538 (1976).
7. *Sandor Kovacs et al.*, T.C. Memo. 1967-214, filed October 30, 1967.
8. *Faulkner v. Commissioner*, T.C. Memo. 1980-90, filed March 25, 1980.
9. *Rockin v. Commissioner*, T.C. Memo. 1980-418, filed October 7, 1980.
10. Revenue Procedure 77-29, 1977-2 CB 538.

11. *Humphrey v. Commissioner*, 162 F.2d 853 (5th Cir., 1947).
12. *Commissioner v. Tellier*, 383 U.S. 687 (1966).
13. *Commissioner v. Sullivan*, 356 U.S. 27 (1958).
14. Revenue Act of 1978, Section 111.
15. *Hobart Lerner*, 71 T.C. 290 (1978).
16. *Engel v. United States*, DC, WD Pa., 1976.
17. *Rosenfeld et al. v. Commissioner*, T.C. Memo. 1982-263, filed May 12, 1982.
18. *Brooke v. United States*, 468 F.2d 1155 (9th Cir., 1972).
19. *Alden B. Oakes et al.*, 44 T.C. 524 (1965).
20. *May et al. v. Commissioner*, 76 T.C. 7 (1981).

21. *Skemp v. Commissioner,* 168 F.2d 598 (7th Cir., 1948).

22. *Quinlivan et al. v. Commissioner,* 8th Cir., 1979.

23. *Hobart Lerner,* 71 T.C. 290 (1978).

24. *Victor J. McQuade,* 4 BTA 837 (1926).

25. Revenue Ruling 66-261, 1966-2 CB 47.

26. Revenue Ruling 65-125, 1965-1 CB 88.

27. Revenue Ruling 74-514, 1974-2 CB 41.

28. *United States v. S.S. White Dental Manufacturing Company of Pennsylvania,* 274 U.S. 398 (1927).

29. *Key et al. v. Commissioner,* T.C. Memo. 1980-67, filed March 10, 1980.

30. *Tax Information for Homeowners,* IRS Publication 530 (Rev. Nov. 80), page 3.

31. IRC Section 120.

32. Revenue Ruling 71-561, 1971-2 CB 128.

33. *Ways and Means Committee Report on the Tax Reform Bill of 1976,* page 176.

34. *B. B. Rider Corp. et al. v. Commissioner,* T.C. Memo. 1982-98, filed February 23, 1982.

35. *Marjorie Fleming Lloyd-Smith,* 40 BTA 214 (1939), *aff'd on other grounds,* 116 F.2d 642 (1941).

36. *Shea v. Commissioner,* 327 F.2d 1005 (5th Cir., 1964).

37. *Imel et al.,* 61 T.C. 318 (1973).

38. *A. A. and E. B. Jones Company,* T.C. Memo. 1960-284, filed December 30, 1960.

39. Regulations Section 1.212-1(j).

40. IRS Letter Ruling 8125006, February 27, 1981.

G

H

Hair-do's. *See* **Grooming.**

Hairpieces. *See* **Actors; Medical expenses.**

Hair removal. Hair removal through electrolysis involves attachment of a fine needle with a rounded tip to an electrode, which is inserted into the hair follicle. Electric current permanently destroys the hair root. The process affects a structure of the body, the skin and subcutaneous layers. The cost is deductible as an amount paid for medical care, within the guideline limitations for the medical expense deduction.[1]

Hair transplant. The cost of a hair transplant was a deductible medical expense. *Why* the twenty-four-year-old taxpayer had the work done (vanity, embarrassment at his premature baldness, need to appear youthful in his work) was deemed to be irrelevant.[2]

Halfway house. *See* **Medical expenses.**

Handball court, rental of. An actor who was obliged to keep himself in first-class physical condition could deduct rent for handball courts and gymnasium facilities.[3] *See also* **Entertainment.**

Hand controls for car. *See* **Medical expenses.**

Handicapped persons. *See* **Blind persons, expenses of; Child-care and disabled-dependent care; Deaf persons, expenses of; Education; Medical expenses; Removal of impediments to the physically handicapped.**

Hard hat. Where an employee was required to supply his own safety equipment, the cost of a protective hard hat was deductible.[4]

Health and accident insurance premiums. *See* **Medical expenses.**

Health foods. *See* **Medical expenses.**

Health institute fees. Payments for use of the facilities of a health institute are usually only deductible where the treatment was prescribed by a physician as a necessary medical treatment.[5] *See also* **Actors; Medical Expenses.**

Hearing aid. A lawyer could deduct the cost of a hearing aid as a business expense.[6] *See also* **Medical expenses.**

Hearing Ear cat. *See* **Deaf persons, expenses of.**

Hearing Ear dog. *See* **Deaf persons, expenses of.**

Hedging operation. *See* **Insurance.**

Highway patrolman. The cost of uniforms made to the specifications of a state highway patrol was deductible. They were not worn off duty, inasmuch as civilian attire was more comfortable and less expensive.[7]

Hobby, income-producing, expenses of. Expenses of an income-producing hobby are deductible.[8]

Hobby losses. Although expenses of a business are deductible whether or not profits are made, real doubt exists as to whether an activity actually is a business if profits are nonexistent. That is especially the presumption if the alleged business is something that the taxpayer enjoys doing. Rarely does a court admit, as in one case, that a "business will not be turned into a hobby merely because the owner finds it pleasurable; suffering never has been made a prerequisite to deductibility.[9] As the court stated in another case, "A farm is no less a business simply because its operation gives the owner pleasure."[10]

An individual who was engaged in a variety of businesses could deduct his expenses in developing and raising a new strain of dog and wolf for use as guard dogs. Said the court: "Raising vicious wolf dogs who can tear through chain-link fences and devour cattle seems to us . . . a completely different prospect than playing with Rin-Tin-Tin. [This individual's] enjoyment would have been served by raising more congenial, orthodox breeds; to create an entirely new and unpredictable canine species seems to us a step beyond personal pleasure."[11]

An activity may not be classified as a trade or business unless an individual can prove that he has a *bona fide* intention of making a profit therefrom. It is not necessary, however, that the expectation of profit be a reasonable one, as long as it is genuine.[12] Deduction depends not on whether a person *expected* to make a profit but on whether he engaged in the activity with the *objective* of making a profit.[13]

An individual became interested in the writings and teachings of Joanna Southcott, a religious teacher and prophetess who died in 1814. The taxpayer read Southcott's sixty-five works which were in libraries; the teacher's other works were supposed to be sealed in an ark in the custody of the British Parliament, which was to be opened in 1914 or whenever the nation's troubles demanded that it be opened. (The year 1914 seemed to qualify.) The taxpayer arranged for the publication of Southcott's works in the United States. There were some 50,000 disciples in this country, and efforts were made to disseminate the wisdom of the prophetess. With a disciple, the taxpayer traveled widely and distributed pamphlets. Her expenses were allowable deductions. Whether the publication project would ever be financially successful was not the determining factor in whether the transaction was one entered upon for profit; more significant was whether the taxpayer thought it could be financially viable. And she was believed to have entered upon the undertaking in good faith for the purpose of making a profit. Had the ark been opened, the profit potential would have been increased greatly. She showed a willingness to invest time and capital in the future outcome of the enterprise, regardless of what actually happened. She thought it was a proper and commendable enterprise. It was not carried on primarily for recreation or pleasure; she was in dead earnest.[14]

A diplomat who had long been interested in farming got advice on the running of his farm from a consulting firm and showed cognizance of the profit motive by eliminating unsuccessful activities and substituting others with more promise. His expenses were deductible. Perhaps he did not operate the farm in the most efficient manner, but it was not the quality of his judgment which was at stake.[15]

A government employee could deduct his expenses at the business of lapidary (the cutting, polishing, or engraving of precious or semiprecious stones). He displayed his wares at a rock showing and sold many items, he had a sales tax license, and he advertised in a national magazine. The court rejected the Internal Revenue Service claim that this was a hobby, its expenses nondeductible:

A trade or business is something more than a hobby; a trade or business, as the names imply, connotes the hope of profit. Though it also connotes something more than an act or course of activity engaged in for profit. It must refer not merely to acts engaged in for profit but to extensive activity over a substantial period of time during which the taxpayer holds himself out as selling goods or services.[16]

Another government employee, who was an Internal Revenue Agent, was permitted to deduct his expenses in racing stock cars for prize money. He had submitted an outside business request to his employer before starting the racing actively.[17]

A businessman who collected postage stamps was allowed to take a deduction when he ultimately sold his collection for less than his cost. He was active in various enterprises and served as a director of the Philadelphia National Bank. He became impressed with the investment possibilities of stamps and was recommended to a professional philatelist. The philatelist discussed the investment features of stamps and their history of increasing value over a period of time. The businessman purchased stamps regularly, following the consultant's advice in most instances. The professional philatelist did not regard his client as a collector or a hobbyist, and for that reason no recommendations were made as to stamps that seemed to be selling over the market value (or what was generally accepted as the current market value) of the stamps. The stamps were fully insured against loss, and meticulous account books were kept. When the stamps were sold, the motive was to achieve liquidity. The court believed that the businessman's single objective was financial reward. Thus he had the "requisite greed" for a transaction entered upon for profit.[18]

An individual acquired land for the purpose of quarrying and selling rock. But because of time-consuming construction activity in the area, the roads were virtually impassable, and he had difficulty getting his product to market. His sales efforts were not conspicuously successful. The Internal Revenue Service sought to disallow his maintenance and other expenses as hobby-related, not a transaction entered upon for profit. The court disagreed. Although hindsight revealed that there were insurmountable obstacles in the way of making the venture profitable, these were not realized during the taxable year. And this was not the familiar situation of a hobby loss, where a taxpayer does not care that the undertaking will never make a cent so long as he has fun on his farm or other outlet for pleasure. The court concluded, "Try as we might, we cannot conjure up a picture of [the taxpayer] mirthfully driving his fully reconditioned 1948 GMC flatbed truck or 1948 FWD telephone pole truck along the countryside with nothing but pleasure on his mind."[19] (The year in question was 1963.)

A business will not be turned into a hobby merely because the owner finds it pleasurable.[20] In the words of one decision, "Success in business is largely obtained by pleasurable interest therein."[21]

A practicing attorney worked on a book of photographs of the high country in Colorado. He expected to publish and to sell the finished product. He spent about thirty hours a week on the project, in addition to the forty hours devoted to his law practice. He visited several publishers to discuss publication possibilities, and he received encouragement to complete the project although no one made a commitment to publish it. It was held that he was in the trade or business of producing a book.[22]

A psychoanalyst was permitted to deduct her expenses in connection with photographic activities related to a book which she hoped to have published. The court found that she sincerely and in good faith expected to make a profit out of her activity in these years or at least an ultimate profit. It mattered not that this was a secondary occupation to her, for it was carried on in a regular, continuous manner and in a businesslike way. The court's most significant words were, "I do not think she played at this as a dilettante."[23]

An individual was allowed to deduct expenses and a loss incurred in his photographic activities. It was believed that photography was more than a hobby to him. The equipment owned and used by him was of the type employed by professional rather than amateur photographers. And his limited income did not show him to be a rich person who was engaging in a hobby.[24]

A professor's wife had been engaged in artistic endeavors for twenty years. Her income from painting, etc., never equaled her expenses, but she kept steadily at work with the encouragement of some sales, various prizes, exhibits, and good critical reviews. She satisfied the court that she had pursued her activities in the taxable years with the objective of making a profit. Perhaps her expectations of profit were not reasonable, but the court was convinced that she had a *bona fide* intention of making a profit and a belief that she could do so. She kept all the receipts of her art expenses and kept a journal recording what she had sold and to whom, which indicated that, said the court, "she carried on her activities in a businesslike manner for profit." She had a mailing list of persons to whom she sent regular notices of her exhibits and she sought to get galleries to have her work shown.[25]

A chemical engineer who became interested in a career in acting was able to deduct his theatrical school expenses and his costs in getting to class, some fifty miles from his home or place of employment. In addition to the time he took off from his engineering job, he "spent a great deal of time simply driving to and from the classes." Although he derived some pleasure from the classes, the court suggested that these facts showed a serious and studied effort to launch a profitable acting career.[26]

When he was let go after reaching his employer's mandatory retirement age, a person who had been engaged in scientific research decided to continue in his familiar field of expertise on his own, and he solicited engagements. The first couple of years, he received little income from his activity, but he was permitted to deduct his losses. Losses incurred during the start-up phase of a business do not necessarily indicate lack of a profit motive.[27] And even if his efforts in the first few years had not been profitable, it was reasonable to believe that his hard work would be rewarded with substantial income if his research proved to be successful.[28]

A realtor acquired an airplane, which he was licensed to fly. The court accepted his statement that he expected to profit from making commercial charter flights, which actually materialized in only a minor way. Although the realtor was a man of means, observed His Honor, the jet had cost him a very considerable sum, and the taxpayer "could ill afford a hobby of such dimension."[29]

To maximize the possibility of having deductions allowed as business-oriented even though the activity is one which most people pursue as a hobby, an individual should attempt to observe these court findings:

1. Operate the activity under a trade name. This is an indication that it actually is a business rather than a hobby.[30]
2. Where animals are involved, engage professional trainers.[31]
3. Be personally involved in the project. A nonfarmer who maintained a farm impressed the court with the fact that he had consulted with the county agent on agricultural problems, subscribed to Doane's *Agricultural Services,* and obtained various government and university publications on farming.[32]
4. Form a panel of experts to render advice.[33]
5. Keep good accounting records. One taxpayer had one of the eight largest accounting firms in the country audit the books.[34] Complete and accurate records indicate a businesslike conduct of the activity, which evidences a profit objective.[35]
6. Keep funds for the activity separate and distinct from your personal funds.[36]
7. Constantly review operations to weed out unpromising lines.[37] In one case where a transaction was deemed to have been entered upon for profit, it was shown that its complete advertising campaign was totally revised three times.[38] A salaried person convinced the court that he had been operating a boat for its commercial-charter income by changing his method of soliciting business when the original mode proved to be unsuccessful.[39]
8. Where animals or produce are involved, advertise the venture. Compete in shows.[40]
9. Market the product in accordance with the standards of the trade or business.[41]
10. Undertake profit-feasibility studies.[42] One taxpayer evidenced his business goals by having calculated a break-even point before commencing his activities.[43]
11. Do not fail to maintain adequate insurance coverage on the assets allegedly held for business purposes.[44]
12. Where licensing by a state, county, or other governmental unit is required to carry on a particular activity on a commercial basis, be certain that the necessary permits are obtained.[45]

Losses sustained because of unforeseen or fortuitous circumstances beyond the control of a taxpayer do not indicate that the activity was not engaged in for profit.[46]

If profits do not materialize, a taxpayer may be able to show that there was a reasonable expectation of financial success, which had been thwarted by such factors as these:
1. The taxpayer had sustained a nervous breakdown which kept her from spending enough time on the venture.[47]
2. A farmer's house with all its contents had burned to the ground and his wife had left him.[48]

3. Lack of success of a racing-car venture was attributable to the fact that there had been mechanical breakdowns and several cars had crashed.[49]

4. Although the venture had been operated in a businesslike manner, a depression had prevented success.[50]

5. Most of the puppies raised by a dentist's kennel died of a virus infection despite the efforts of several veterinarians to curb the disease.[51]

6. For a number of years, an individual was involved as a party in a series of lawsuits which prevented him from spending as much time attending to farm matters as he otherwise would have.[52]

Persistent losses limit the amount of a person's deductions. A taxpayer is presumed to be engaged in an activity for profit in the current taxable year, unless established to the contrary by the Internal Revenue Service, if in two or more years of the period of five consecutive taxable years ending with the current taxable year (seven years in the case of an activity which consists in major part of the breeding, training, showing, or racing of horses), the activity was carried on at a profit; that is, if the gross income from the activity exceeds the deductions attributable to the activity which would be allowed if it were engaged in for profit. For this purpose, all deductions attributable to the activity other than that allowed for net operating loss carry-overs are taken into account.[53]

An individual may elect to suspend the application of the presumption until there are five consecutive taxable years (or seven in the case of horses) in existence from the time he first engages in the activity and then to apply it to any years in the five- or seven-year period.[54] If the activity is not deemed to be one carried on for profit, hobby losses are deductible only to the extent that there are gains from this activity.[55]

Deduction of a loss from what *could* have been a hobby requires positive proof. A physician inherited a farm. He took a great interest in activities there, maintaining sizable herds of cattle. He sold animals that proved unsatisfactory. He experimented with various strains until he found what appeared to be cattle with good profit potential. He raised horses, an operation he closed out when it proved to be unprofitable. His catfish-pond activities were terminated for the same reason. He sought advice and assistance from expert farmers, cattlemen, and machinery mechanics, constantly attempting to improve his profit picture by altering his methods of operation and by abandoning those operations which proved incapable of profit. But for twelve years, the farm failed to show a profit. The Internal Revenue Service claimed that his business was medicine and the farm was primarily for recreation, so his losses were personal and nondeductible. But the court felt that he had established that his dominant motive or intention had been to derive a profit. There were no recreational facilities at the farm. He engaged in manual farm labor and machinery repair, activities that could scarcely be regarded as recreational. Although his activities evidenced a lack of good business judgment or farming knowledge, he had tried with the aid of competent advisers to operate the farm as a business for profit. Therefore the losses were deductible.[56]

A New York banker established a ski lodge in Vermont. He had researched the profit potentialities carefully; the place was operated in a businesslike manner; there were adequate books of account; advertisements and brokers were used to generate business. But the national gasoline shortage at that time resulted in poor bookings. Losses and expenses could be deducted because, under the circumstances, the losses were not an indication that the activity was not engaged in for profit.[57]

Home care. *See* **Medical expenses.**

Home expenses. Deduction is not allowed for expenses of one's home, unless they qualify in part as business expenses. (*See also* **Office at home.**) But deduction is allowed for expenses specifically permitted under other provisions of the tax law, such as interest, property taxes, and casualty losses.[58] These are discussed under the appropriate headings in this book.

Home for the aged. *See* **Contributions.**

Home leave expenses. *See* **Travel.**

Home mortgage. *See* **Interest.**

Home, office at. *See* **Office at home.**

Home, sale of. *See* **Residence sold at a loss; Transactions entered into for profit.**

Home stereo system. *See* **Medical expenses.**

Home, taxpayer's. *See* **Interest; Taxes.**

Home telephone. *See* **Employees; Executives; Telephone.**

Horses. *See* **Advertising; Farmers; Hobby losses.**

Hospitality room. *See* **Entertainment.**

Hospital services. *See* **Medical expenses.**

Hospital staff fees. Annual staff fees paid in order to continue receiving hospital privileges, which privileges originally were made available by payment of a sum for lifetime privileges, were deductible.[59]

Host's own meals, deductibility of. *See* **Entertainment.**

House calls. A chiropractor could deduct the cost of transportation from his office to the homes of patients when he was making house calls.[60]

Household expenses. *See* **Child-care and disabled-dependent care.**

Household improvements for the handicapped. *See* **Medical expenses; Removal of impediment to the physically handicapped.**

Hunting, expenses of. A businessperson could deduct the cost of leasing deer-hunting rights when it appeared that entertainment of certain persons in a secluded environment could lead to the solving of a business problem—namely, the obtaining of employees for a highly specialized type of work who were difficult to find.[61] *See also* **Entertainment.,**

H

1. Revenue Ruling 82-111, I.R.B. 1982-22, 10.
2. *Mattes, Jr., v. Commissioner*, 77 T.C. 650 (1981).
3. *Charles Hutchison*, 13 BTA 1187 (1928).
4. *Broughton v. Commissioner*, T.C. Memo. 1979-77, filed March 8, 1979.
5. Revenue Ruling 55-261, 1955-1 CB 307.
6. *Paul Blanchard, Jr.*, 23 T.C. 803 (1955).
7. *Commissioner v. Benson et al.*, 146 F.2d 191 (9th Cir., 1944).
8. *Miscellaneous Deductions and Credits*, IRS Publication 529, 1976 edition, page 1.
9. *Thomas W. Jackson*, 59 T.C. 312 (1972).
10. *Fields, Jr. et al. v. Commissioner*, T.C. Memo. 1981-550, filed September 28, 1981.
11. *Sampson et al. v. Commissioner*, T.C. Memo. 1982-276, filed May 18, 1982.
12. *Margit Sigray Bessenyey*, 45 T.C. 261 (1965), *aff'd*, 379 F.2d 252 (2d Cir., 1967).
13. *Dreicer v. Commissioner*, CA, DC, 1981.
14. *Doggett v. Burnet*, 65 F.2d 191 (CA, DC, 1933).
15. *Patterson et al. v. United States*, 459 F.2d 487 (Ct. Cl., 1972).
16. *Estes et al. v. United States*, DC, SD Ala., 1969.
17. *Bryson, Jr., et al. v. Commissioner*, T.C. Memo. 1982-424, filed July 27, 1982.
18. *George F. Tyler*, T.C. Memo., Docket No. 5508, entered March 6, 1947.
19. *Claude L. Crespeau*, T.C. Memo. 1969-236, filed November 5, 1969.
20. *Thomas W. Jackson*, 59 T.C. 312 (1972).
21. *Wilson v. Eisner*, 282 F. 38 (2d Cir., 1922).
22. *Snyder et al. v. United States*, 674 F.2d 1359 (10th Cir., 1982).
23. *Young v. United States*, DC, Md., 1971.
24. *Charles D. Eggert et al.*, T.C. Memo. 1957-221, filed November 29, 1957.
25. *Churchman et al. v. Commissioner*, 68 T.C. 696 (1977).
26. *Regan v. Commissioner*, T.C. Memo. 1979-340, filed August 28, 1979.
27. Regulations Section 1.183-2(b)(6).
28. *Stahnke et al. v. Commissioner*, T.C. Memo. 1980-369, filed September 10, 1980.
29. *Louismet et al. v. Commissioner*, T.C. Memo. 1982-294, filed May 26, 1982.
30. *Rex B. Foster et al.*, T.C. Memo. 1973-14, filed January 23, 1973.
31. *Joan F. (Walton) Farris et al.*, T.C. Memo. 1972-165, filed August 3, 1972.
32. *Patterson et al. v. United States*, 459 F.2d 487 (Ct. Cl., 1972).
33. *Plant v. Walsh*, 280, F. 722 (DC, Conn., 1922).
34. *Patterson et al. v. United States*, 459 F.2d 487 (Ct. Cl., 1972).
35. Regulations Section 1.183-2(b)(1).
36. *Monfore et al. v. United States*, 214 Ct. Cl. 705 (Ct. Cl., 1977).
37. *Patterson et al. v. United States*, 459 F.2d 487 (Ct. Cl., 1972).
38. *Siegel et al. v. Commissioner*, 78 T.C., No. 46 (1982).
39. *Mc Larney et al. v. Commissioner*, T.C. Memo. 1982-461, filed August 9, 1982.
40. *Rex B. Foster et al.*, T.C. Memo. 1973-13, filed January 23, 1973.
41. *Howard et al. v. Commissioner*, T.C. Memo. 1981-250, filed May 21, 1981.
42. *Irving C. Ackerman et al.*, 24 BTA 512 (1931), *aff'd*, 71 F.2d 586 (9th Cir., 1935).
43. *Mc Larney et al. v. Commissioner*, T.C. Memo. 1982-461, filed August 9, 1982.
44. *Eastman et al. v. United States*, Ct. Cl., 1980.
45. *Ladner et al. v. Commissioner*, T.C. Memo. 1982-207, filed April 19, 1982.
46. Regulations Section 1.183-2(b)(6).
47. *Thelma C. Whitman*, T.C. Memo. 1960-88, filed May 6, 1960.
48. *Woodrow L. Wroblewski*, T.C. Memo. 1973-37, filed February 14, 1973.
49. *L. A. Bolt*, 50 T.C. 1007 (1968).
50. *Lucien H. Tyng et al.*, 36 BTA 21 (1937), *aff'd and rev'd on other grounds*, 106 F.2d 55 (2d Cir., 1939), *rev'd*, 308 U.S. 527 (1940).
51. *Amos S. Bumgardner et al.*, T.C. Memo.

Docket Nos. 40912-3, entered February 10, 1954.

52. *Otis Beall Kent,* T.C. Memo., Docket No. 37332, entered December 31, 1953.

53. IRC Section 183(a),(d).

54. IRC Section 183(e).

55. IRC Section 183(b).

56. *Gregory, Jr., et al. v. United States,* DC, WD La., 1976.

57. *Allen et al. v. Commissioner,* 72 T.C. 28 (1979).

58. IRC Section 280A(b).

59. *Wells-Lee et al. v. Commissioner,* 360 F.2d 665 (8th Cir., 1966).

60. *R. O. Watts,* T.C. Memo. 1975-131, filed May 7, 1975.

61. *Sealy et al. v. Commissioner,* T.C. Memo. 1980-7, filed January 14, 1980.

H
─────

I

Icestorms. *See* **Casualties.**

Illegal business activity. Expenses of an illegal business are deductible if not of a type forbidden by law, such as bribes to police officers. Accordingly, wages and rents are deductible by a gambler even though his betting establishment is forbidden by state law.[1]

Advertising expenses of a gambling establishment were deductible despite a state's ban against gambling.[2]

Even where the Internal Revenue Service contends that a person is in the trade or business of swindling, he is entitled to deduct the expenses which he can prove that he incurred in carrying on his trade or business.[3] Although the laws of one state prohibited lotteries, the cost of producing lottery tickets was deductible as a business expense.[4]

A taxpayer could deduct depreciation on business equipment placed in a customer's store, although installation of the equipment was forbidden by state law.[5]

In this highly regulated age, some business activities may be contrary to a local law. One taxpayer illegally manufactured amphetamines and other controlled drugs. Volatile chemicals exploded and the plant was destroyed by fire. To the extent that the structure was uninsured, the loss was deductible. The fact that the taxpayer suffered his loss in connection with an illegal enterprise was no bar to the deduction, for this loss was incurred in the operation of a trade or business for profit.[6]

The operator of a house of prostitution could deduct amounts paid to her "girls."[7]

A dealer in illegal drugs, whose only office was in his home, was entitled to a home-office expense deduction.[8]

For many years, an individual had been in the business of making loans. Under state law, he could not sue to recover amounts that he had loaned at interest rates in excess of what was permitted under the usury laws. But he could deduct the unrecovered amounts as business bad debts. "There is nothing . . . requiring the taxpayer to be engaged in a 'legal' business to qualify for the statutory deduction," held the court.[9] *See also* **Bribes and kickbacks; Gambling losses; Legal fees.**

Illegal discounts. *See* **Bribes and kickbacks.**

Illegal operation. *See* **Abortion; Medical expenses.**

Improvement of employee morale. Where an employer transfers employees to a new location, some of these persons are likely to be resistant to the move or resentful because of the problems of disposition of their old homes. One employer was permitted to deduct payments made to an unrelated company for helping displaced employees to sell their homes. Deduction is allowed, declares this ruling, as "various types of benefits, provided by an employer to its employees, can bear a direct relationship to the business of the employer by bolstering employee morale and thereby increasing employee productivity and efficiency."[10]

Expenses incurred by an employer in encouraging the employees to vote in general elections, in allowing time off with pay to register and vote, and in deducting and forwarding employee political contributions to designated organizations are deductible as expenses to improve employee morale.[11] *See also* **Day-care center, financing of; Training expenses.**

Improvement of skills. *See* Education.

Improvements of a capital nature. In general, all construction costs of a business must be capitalized and written off over the estimated useful life of the facility. But when the purpose of temporary partitions, heating, and the like was to allow existing buildings to operate during major construction operations, the cost was deductible.[12] Deduction was also allowed for the cost of enlarging and improving an office when the work was not in the nature of permanent improvements but was to facilitate the transaction of increasing business.[13]

Expenses related to the installation of capital equipment with a useful life of more than one year customarily must be capitalized. But labor and transportation costs in connection with moving certain of a taxpayer's capitalized assets to another location were deductible, for the relocation did not add to the value nor appreciably prolong the useful life of these assets.[14] *See also* **Election to deduct or to capitalize; Expenditures for benefits lasting more than one year; Removal of impediments to the physically handicapped.**

Inclinator in home. *See* **Medical expenses.**

Income beneficiaries. *See* **Depreciation.**

Income in respect of a decedent. Sometimes a person receives income which would have been paid to the one who earned it, if he had lived. For example, a widow may receive a year-end Christmas bonus which would have been paid to her husband except that he died in early December before payment was ready to be made. Or an insurance salesman may have sold a policy to a client but died before he received his commission, so that the check eventually goes to his son, the wife having died many years earlier. The *right* to receive this money must be shown as property owned by the person who died, and if his estate was large enough to be taxable, that right was part of the total property subject to Federal estate tax. The person who eventually receives income earned by the one who died must show this income on his own tax return. But he gets a deduction for *income in respect of a decedent.* He must determine what the proportion of the value of the right to receive this income in respect of a decedent is to the total property which is subject to tax. That ratio or percentage is multiplied by the estate tax paid, and the resultant figure is deducted by the person who receives the income in respect of a decedent.[15]

Sometimes each of several persons receives income in respect of a decedent in the taxable year. Each of these persons may deduct a prorated portion of the Federal estate tax paid by the estate by reason of the inclusion in the estate of the value of the right to receive the income. This proration is on the basis of the proportion of the income in respect of a decedent received by each of the persons getting the income. The actual computation of the estate tax allocated to each person is very involved. If you are one of several persons who receives income of this type in any one year, you or your accountant should look at the detailed computation released for this purpose by the Internal Revenue Service.[16]

Incurable disease. A person may have a physical or mental condition which medicine cannot alleviate. But expenses for the purpose of offsetting the effect of this condition may be deducted as medical expenses. *Example:* parents could deduct the fees paid to a teacher who had been specially trained in reading and study skills which enabled that teacher to alleviate the condition of a child with incurable brain damage.[17]

Indefinite living-away-from-home expenses. *See* **Travel.**

Indemnitors. *See* **Guarantor, payments by.**

Indemnity bond premiums. *See* **Insurance.**

Individual retirement account. Prior to 1982, an Individual Retirement Account (IRA) was restricted to a person who was not an active participant in a qualified employer-sponsored or government pension plan. The assets of the IRA may be invested in a trustee or custodial account with a bank, savings and loan association, or credit union, or in a qualified retirement bond.[18]

The acquisition by an IRA of any "collectible" after December 31, 1981, is treated as a distribution from the IRA to the participant, taxable to him as a dividend at the collectible's cost. A collectible for this purpose may be a work of art, rug or antique, any metal or gem, stamp or coin, alcoholic beverage, and the like.[19]

For taxable years beginning after 1981, a person can put into an IRA and deduct the lesser of $2,000 or 100 percent of his compensation for that year. If a joint Federal income tax return is filed, a working individual also can contribute to a spousal IRA for a nonworking spouse, for a combined contribution of up to $2,250. But the combined contribution may not exceed 100 percent of the compensation includable in the working spouse's gross income for the year. The deduction for either spouse's contribution may not exceed $2,000.[20]

A divorced spouse is allowed a deduction for contributions to a spousal IRA established by the individual's former spouse at least five years before the divorce if the former spouse contributed to the IRA under the spousal IRA rules for at least three of the five years preceding the divorce. If these requirements are met, the limit on the divorced spouse's IRA contributions for a year is not less than the lesser of (1) $1,125 or (2) the sum of the divorced spouse's compensation and alimony includible in gross income.[21]

If an employee is an active participant in an employer's plan, he is allowed a deduction for contributions to an IRA or for voluntary contributions to the employer's qualified plan providing that the plan permits this. The first $2,000 of the voluntary employee contribution to a plan will be allocated to the employee IRA unless he designates otherwise. He can allocate voluntary contributions to employee IRAs under all qualified plans in which he participates, so long as the total amount allocated does not exceed the deduction limit for that year.[22]

A deductible contribution may be made up to the prescribed date (including extensions) for filing the Federal income tax return. The IRA is considered to have been set up on the date the contribution was made.[23]

No deduction is allowed for any contributions into an IRA made during or after the year when a person reaches age 70½ unless a simplified employee pension is used.[24] (*See* **Simplified employee pension plan, deduction for.**)

An annuity sometimes is used as an IRA. The insurance company or other party which issues it may provide a waiver-of-premium rider in certain circumstances, such as the buyer's disability. Deduction is then allowed for the cost of the waiver to the extent that this cost, plus the cost of the annuity itself, does not exceed the limit for deductions to an IRA; that is, 100 percent of compensation or $2,000, whichever is lower.[25]

Individuals, contributions to. *See* **Contributions.**

Informant, tax, return of fees by. Where a cash-basis individual receives an advance from the Internal Revenue Service for supplying information about violations of the tax law by someone else, with the understanding that he will receive more if his leads justify it, but will have to refund any portion of his receipts if they are higher than the amount of the award as finally established on the basis of tax yields, he is taxable upon the full advance. But he can deduct the amount of anything he is obliged to give back at the time of the repayment.[26]

Inheritance, expense of collecting. *See* **Contested inheritance, expenses of.**

Initial service charge. *See* **Interest.**

Initiation fee. An initiation fee paid to a labor union to obtain employment is deductible.[27] *See also* **Union dues.**

Injuries to employees. *See* **Compensation; Ordinary and necessary business expenses.**

Insider profits. *See* **Executives.**

Installment purchases, carrying charges on. *See* **Interest.**

Institutional care. *See* **Medical expenses; Retirement homes.**

Instruction. *See* **Advanced degree, study for; Education.**

Insulin. The cost of insulin had been deductible in accordance with the deduction permitted for medicine and drugs. (*See* **Medical expenses.**) For taxable years beginning after December 31, 1983, insulin is deductible as a medical expense even though medicines and drugs in general no longer will be deductible.[28]

Insurance. Deductible business-insurance premiums include:
1. Fire, theft, flood, and other casualty insurance on property used in the trade or business.
2. Merchandise and inventory insurance.
3. Credit insurance on policies covering losses resulting from the non-payment of debts owed to the business.
4. Employees' group hospitalization and medical insurance paid or incurred by the employer.
5. Public liability insurance covering liability for bodily injuries sustained by nonemployees and for damage to the property of others.
6. Workmen's compensation insurance.
7. Overhead insurance.
8. Use and occupancy insurance and business-interruption insurance.
9. Employee performance bonds. Fees are deductible in the case of fidelity, indemnity, performance, and other types of bond to ensure faithful performance by employees.
10. Bonds that must be furnished by reason of law or a contract to ensure the company's performance in a business undertaking.
11. Automobile and other vehicle insurance.[29]

Premiums against accident losses are deductible if they are business-related.[30]

Malpractice insurance premiums were deductible by a physician who could become personally liable for negligence.[31]

Insurance premiums paid or incurred by a taxpayer as the mortgagor on a mortgaged loan, which are attributable to the loan during the period of construction of business improvements covered by the loan, are deductible as business expenses.[32]

Amounts paid by policyholders as premiums on business insurance to a mutual insurance company are deductible even though there is a likelihood that a portion of the premium may be returned to them by the company.[33]

A person may deduct the insurance on his car if he uses it exclusively for charitable purposes.[34]

An investor was allowed to deduct premiums he paid on property owned by a corporation in which he had a substantial stock interest, since this was to protect his investment should anything happen to this property.[35]

Premiums paid on an errors and omissions policy are deductible where the risks covered are related to the taxpayer's trade or business.[36]

An employer may deduct indemnification insurance premiums of two types: (1) where the employer would be indemnified against damages sustained as a result of wrongful acts committed by executives in the line of their duties and (2) where executives would be indemnified for their expenses arising from wrongful acts committed or alleged to have been committed in their capacity as executives.[37]

Hull insurance is deductible by a commercial fisherman.[38]

Standard marine insurance policies have a $100,000 deductible provision. A shipowners' protection and indemnity association set up a fund to provide insurance protection left void by that deductible clause. Amounts paid by a shipper into this fund for protection were deductible as ordinary and necessary expenses.[39]

Credit insurance premiums on policies covering losses resulting from the nonpayment of debts owed to the business are deductible.[40]

An installment seller of real estate could deduct the premiums on the lives of purchasers covering their unpaid balances.[41]

Premiums on the life of a business debtor are deductible, the payment being, in the words of one decision, "related to its business, to wit, the preservation and conservation of its funds."[42] Ordinarily, a creditor cannot deduct premiums paid on a policy on the life of a debtor assigned as collateral. But where a creditor paid premiums on life insurance on the debtor which had been given as collateral for a loan, and there was no reasonable expectancy that the debtor would reimburse the creditor for these premium payments, they could be deducted.[43]

Deduction was allowed for premiums paid on insurance on the life of a debtor who had pledged the policy as collateral for a loan but was unable to meet his repayment obligations.[44]

A seller of homesites on the installment plan took out insurance on the life of a purchaser in the amount of the unpaid balance. Upon the death of the insured purchaser, title would be conveyed to her heirs. The seller could deduct the premiums as business expense.[45]

An employer may deduct insurance premiums he pays on the life of an employee, the latter's wife being the beneficiary, where there was a clear intent that the insurance premium be a form of compensation.[46]

Where a taxpayer purchases an insurance policy which, in accordance with its terms, would reimburse him to the extent specified in the policy for certain business overhead expenses incurred by him during prolonged periods of disability due to sickness or injury, any premiums paid are deductible business expenses.[47]

Amounts paid on premiums under Part B of Medicare (Supplemental Medical Insurance for the Aged) are deductible as medical expenses.[48]

The expenses of a hedging operation were deductible by a manufacturer which was interested in protecting itself against fluctuations in the price of its raw materials.[49] Deduction is not permitted where there is merely a transaction in future contracts rather than in commodities.[50]

For group-term life insurance, hospitalization, and medical insurance paid by one's employer, see **Compensation; Medical expenses.** See also **Title insurance company, payments to.**

Intangible drilling and development costs. See **Election to deduct or to capitalize; Prepaid expenses.**

Interest. Interest paid or incurred on indebtedness is tax-deductible.[51] There are few significant exceptions to this rule. One exception is that interest in connection with the purchase of single-premium life insurance is not deductible. Interest to buy or carry tax-exempt bonds generally is not deductible, although exceptions to this provision are given later in this section. And "interest" where the indebtedness is not genuine is nondeductible.

Interest payments are not deductible if they are part of a transaction where no economic gain can be realized except for a tax deduction. But interest is deductible when borrowed to purchase "flower bonds." These are certain issues of United States Treasury bonds which can be presented at face value in payment of Federal estate taxes, although the bonds, because of their low interest rates, are sold well below face value. Money was borrowed in order to get a benefit—namely, the bonds could be used to make payment at par although they were purchased at a substantial discount. But as the purchase was not made to get a *tax* advantage but a *payment* advantage, deduction was proper.[52]

Some insurance companies permit loans against the cash-surrender value of a policy at a rate well below present commercial interest, the policy itself being the only security. By borrowing against such a policy, a purchaser may get the cash to take out additional life insurance. But where a person's chief purpose is to obtain additional insurance protection for his family, interest deductions on the money he borrows against the policy are deductible because they are not merely a part of the cost of buying more insurance than his cash position would permit.[53]

What constitutes compensation for the use or forbearance of money is controlled by the facts, not the language. To avoid state usury laws, one taxpayer agreed to pay a certain interest rate plus a bonus. Though the bonus for the loan could not be enforced in the state courts because of the limit on permissible interest, for Federal income tax purposes it was deductible.[54]

It is not necessary that the lender charge as interest a percentage of the sum loaned. To be deductible, interest need not be computed at a rigid stated rate. All that is required is that a sum definitely ascertainable be paid for the use of borrowed money, pursuant to the agreement of the lender and the borrower.[55]

Under certain circumstances, part of the payments in connection with installment and other deferred payment sales is treated as interest. This amount, referred to as imputed or unstated interest, arises when the sales contract either makes no provision for the payment of interest or provides for a very low interest rate. In addition, the sale price must be more than $3,000 and at least one payment must be due more than one year after the date of sale. The amount of imputed interest is determined by application of a 7 percent discount factor. For details, see *Installment and Deferred-Payments Sales,* IRS Publication 537.[56]

Deduction was allowed for payments for the use of borrowed money, even though both parties had agreed that the size of the payments to be made would be contingent upon the occurrence of certain events.[57]

Insurance policy loans are debts for the purpose of the interest deduction.[58]

Interest is deductible on money borrowed on an employee's annuity contract.[59]

Unlike so many forms of tax deduction, interest need not be related to the taxpayer's trade or business. Thus, interest on notes given to a taxpayer's ex-wife as part of the property settlement was held to be deductible.[60]

Deduction is allowed for interest paid with borrowed funds, unless the lender retains control over the loan proceeds.[61]

Deduction was allowed where money was borrowed from a party to whom interest on a prior loan was still owed, where the purpose of the second loan was not limited to payment of interest on the first loan.[62]

Although an individual cannot deduct amounts he pays in Federal income taxes, he can deduct interest on money borrowed to make these payments.[63]

A corporation permitted certain employees to purchase from it residential real estate. The employer had an option to buy back this property at its then appraised value if the employee left his employment other than through retirement and ceased to use it as his principal residence. The employer supplied financing at 4.5 percent below the commercial rate. Employees covered by the plan could deduct this interest.[64]

Where a lender withholds the interest which was payable to him on a loan in advance, a cash-basis borrower can deduct interest only as principal payments are made by him. The interest charge is deemed to be paid by him ratably over the life of the loan.[65]

Interest or broker's charges on a margin account are deductible at the time the broker receives payment.[66]

Interest is deductible in the case of delinquent payments even where the payments themselves are not deductible, as for example, when a Federal income tax deficiency is imposed, the tax is not deductible but interest on the belated payments is.[67]

A state penalty for tardy payment of income taxes, which was a stated percentage of the tax regardless of how late the payment actually was, was nondeductible as a penalty. But an additional charge based upon the time elapsed between due date and actual payment was deductible as interest.[68] The same treatment applied where the taxes were state real-estate taxes.[69]

Interest incurred to purchase an automobile is deductible even if a person uses the standard mileage rate instead of itemizing expenses of using a car for business purposes.[70]

Payments of carrying charges on installment purchases are deductible as interest.[71]

Where the sole beneficiary of a decedent's estate is obliged to pay an estate tax deficiency because no assets are left in the estate, he can deduct the interest which accrued on the deficiency subsequent to the distribution. Interest which accrued on the deficiency prior to the distribution is not deductible as it was not his primary obligation.[72]

Interest on a Federal gift tax deficiency is deductible.[73]

Unlike many other forms of expenditure, such as compensation or rent, interest need not be reasonable to be deducted.[74] If a taxpayer borrows money at a usurious rate, interest is deductible regardless of what it has been labeled to circumvent a state law on maximum percentages.[75]

Expenditures related to the acquisitions of property with a remaining life of more than one year, such as a building, customarily are not deductible when made but are considered an additional cost of the property, subject to the depreciation deduction where business property is involved. But interest does not represent a cost of acquiring or developing property. It is, rather, the price paid for the use of borrowed money even where the loan is used to improve or to secure an asset with a life of more than a year. So the interest is deductible.[76]

Ordinarily, a taxpayer on the cash basis deducts expenses when paid, regardless of the period covered by his payments. However, prepaid interest in general is not deductible in this manner. A deduction for interest paid in advance on indebtedness for a period not in excess of twelve months of the taxable year immediately following the taxable year in which the payment is made will be considered on a case-by-case basis to determine whether a material distortion of income has resulted. Factors to be considered include the amount of income in the taxable year of payment, the income of previous taxable years, the amount of prepaid interest, and the existence of a varying rate of interest over the period of the loan. If a material distortion of income results from the prepayment, interest will be deductible on a prorated basis over the period covered.[77] The taxpayer has the burden of showing that prepayments on interest did not result in this material distortion.

In the case of prepayments of interest on or after January 1, 1976, the Treasury Department is authorized in certain cases to treat interest payments under a loan with variable interest rates as consisting partly of interest computed under an average level effective rate of interest and consisting partly of an interest prepayment allocable to later years of the loan.[78]

An individual borrowed money from an insurance company against a policy on his life. He was on the cash basis; that is, he reported income on his tax return when he actually received it and took deductions when payments were made. The insurance company deducted interest on his loan in advance, when he borrowed the money in 1970. His tax deduction was in 1972, when he actually paid off the loan.[79]

An individual on the cash basis borrowed money, and a loan fee was deducted by the lender from the loan proceeds at that time. This fee was deductible on a *pro rata* basis at the time the borrower made payments on his indebtedness.[80]

Interest paid to a related party is deductible if for a *bona fide* indebtedness, as in the case where the husband agreed to pay his wife for securities he borrowed from her to provide capital for his business.[81]

Parents may legitimately deduct interest paid on money borrowed from their minor children.[82]

Loan fees withheld by a bank from the amount given to a borrower are deductible as interest.[83]

Amounts charged to customer accounts under a bank's credit-card plan and designated as "finance charges" pursuant to the Truth in Lending

Act are deductible as interest where no part of the charge is a carrying charge, loan fee, or similar charge.[84] Amounts levied by retail stores on customers' revolving charge accounts and designated as "finance charges" pursuant to that same act are deductible as interest; *e.g.,* customers with approved credit may charge their purchases and then either pay for them in full or in installments. If payment is made within thirty days from the date of the statement billing date, no charge is made to their account by the store. If full payment is not made within thirty days, a charge is made to their account on their unpaid balance at the beginning of the month.[85]

An individual who uses a credit card issued by an oil company can purchase gasoline, oil, special products, and services. The credit-card agreement provides for the payment by the purchaser of a "finance charge" that is expressed as an annual percentage of the purchaser's billing statement. The charge is based on the customer's unpaid balance and is computed monthly. This finance charge is deductible as interest.[86]

A bank operated a credit-card plan under which retail customers who were cardholders could obtain cash advances and overdraft advances. At the time an advance was made by the bank, the amount was added to the cardholders' credit-card account balance, the bank charging the cardholders' account with a one-time charge of 2 percent of the amount of each cash advance and 1 percent of the amount of each overdraft advance, these charges being in addition to its regular monthly finance charges on overdue accounts. The charges for advances were held to be deductible as interest.[87]

Treated similarly are amounts paid under a department store's "budget charge account," which were percentage charges based upon balances still unpaid after a specified payment period.[88]

Carrying charges on installment purchases were deductible as interest.[89]

Finance charges paid by customers under a retail installment contract and charges for the privilege of prepaying their accounts are deductible as interest.[90]

If flat fees or service charges on installment purchases are separately stated on a customer's bill, but the interest cannot be ascertained, the deduction is the lesser of (1) an amount equal to 6 percent of the average unpaid balance of the installment contract during the year or (2) the portion of the total fee or service charge allocable to the year.

The average unpaid balance in (1) is determined by totaling the unpaid balances on the first day of each month in the year and dividing this total by twelve. The unpaid balance at the beginning of each month is determined by taking into account the payments in the amount and at the time called for in the contract, even though such payments are not made when due.

The amount in (2) is determined by dividing the fee or service charge by the total number of monthly payments to obtain a prorated monthly finance charge. This amount is then multiplied by the number of months the installment obligation was outstanding during the year.[91]

A late-payment charge of 5 percent of the amount of the bill of customers who paid later than twenty days after the due date was deductible as interest. It was not necessary for the parties to label a payment made for the use of money as interest for it to be treated as such for tax purposes.[92]

Commitment fees incurred by a merchant under an agreement with a bank which guaranteed to have business funds available on a standby basis in case of need were deductible as charges to carry on a business. They were deductible as ordinary and necessary expenses not representing interest.[93]

A building contractor paid a loan commitment fee in order to have funds available for a specified period at a fixed interest rate. Inasmuch as the project for which these funds were desired, a hotel, had not yet been begun, the Internal Revenue Service sought to disallow the standby fee as start-up expenses for a new business in which the contractor was not yet engaged. Deduction was allowed by the court. The taxpayer already was in the business of development, construction, and operation of hotels. So the payment to assure that funds would be available on a standby basis related to the taxpayer's existing business.[94]

Commitment fees or standby charges incurred under a mortgage agreement providing for construction funds to be available in stated amounts over a specified period are similarly deductible as current business expenses. These fees are considered to be carrying charges which the borrower may deduct currently or elect to capitalize as part of construction costs.[95]

Penalty payments made by a taxpayer to his mortgagee for the privilege of prepaying his mortgage indebtedness are deductible as interest.[96]

Prepayment charges in the case of a loan are in reality an additional fee for the use of the lender's money for a shorter period of time than originally agreed upon. The fee represents the generally higher cost of a short-term loan as opposed to a long-term loan.[97]

Under the Graduated Payment Mortgages (GPM) plan of the Department of Housing and Urban Development, the mortgagor pays to the mortgagee the principal amount borrowed, plus interest at a fixed rate per annum on the unpaid mortgage balances. Various plans are available. Some plans provide for annual increases in monthly payments for a fixed period of years with level payments made thereafter. Other plans permit five years of increasing payments with annual increases, and some permit ten years of increasing payments with annual increases at 2 percent and 3 percent respectively. For the early years of the mortgage term, when the amount of monthly payment does not fully cover the interest owed, the entire amount represents interest and is deductible by the mortgagor when paid. That part of the interest owed but not paid is not allowed as a deduction to the mortgagor until paid. For subsequent years of the mortgage term, when the amount of the payments has increased to the extent that it now exceeds the current interest charge owed, the excess is to be applied against the unpaid balance of the loan. This excess will be treated as discharging first that part of the unpaid balance of the loan that represents accumulated interest carried over from prior years and is deductible by the mortgagor as interest at that time.[98]

A loan-processing fee, sometimes referred to as points, paid by a borrower as compensation to the lender solely for the use or forbearance of money is deductible in full in the year of payment.[99]

However, the term *points* is sometimes used to describe the charges paid by a mortgagor-borrower to a lender as loan origination fees, maximum loan charges, or premium charges. Expenses incident to acquiring a mortgage loan are not deductible as interest nor are they deductible in full as business expenses in the year paid. These expenses are capital expenditures, which are deductible on a *pro rata* basis over the life of the mortgage.[100] So the payor has the obligation of showing that the loan fees were an additional cost of the borrowing of money, as opposed to a charge for compensation for services rendered in obtaining the loan.[101]

Where instead of a higher interest rate points are charged by the lender at the time the loan is made, any prepayment of interest which has taken the form of points is deductible with the following limitation: The use of points in the geographical area where the loan is made must be a regular practice, and deduction of the prepayment is limited to the number of points generally charged in that area for a home loan.[102]

A negotiated bonus or premium paid by a borrower to a lender in order to obtain a loan is characterized as interest.[103] Whether the amount of the bonus or premium is withheld by the lender rather than paid back to the lender is immaterial.[104]

Points paid by a cash-method taxpayer on indebtedness incurred in connection with the purchase or improvement of (and secured by) his principal residence may be treated as paid in the taxable year of actual payment. This exception applies only to points on a home mortgage and not to other interest costs on such a mortgage. In addition, in order to qualify for this exception, the charging of points must reflect an established business practice in the geographical area where the loan is made. The deduction allowed under this exception may not exceed the number of points generally charged in that area for a home loan.[105]

A premium charge paid by a buyer to a savings and loan association was deductible where this represented a charge of one-half of 1 percent per year for the privilege of being granted the loan.[106]

Where, in addition to other costs for borrowed money, a borrower had to pay a lender 2 percent "initial service charge" or "financing fee," little if any of the charge or fee was for services of any kind. The fee was deductible as interest.[107]

If a borrower is obligated to sign a note for more money than he receives from the lender because the interest is subtracted from the face amount of the note, the interest is deductible on this note discount when payments are made. Assume that a borrower signs a note for $1,200 on March 27, agreeing to pay it in twelve equal installments beginning on April 30. The interest ($1,200 $\times$ 6 percent = $72) is subtracted from the face value of the note, and the borrower receives $1,128. If he uses the cash method, the interest is considered to be repaid in twelve installments of $6 each. If he makes only eight payments in that year, his deduction is $48. Accrual-method taxpayers, however, prorate the interest over the period in which it accrues. So $54 (nine-twelfths of $72) is deductible in the following taxable year.[108]

If a party owes both principal and interest, any payment he makes to his creditor is credited first to his interest obligation, the balance going toward principal. If debtor and creditor agree in an arm's-length transaction that interest is to be allocated differently from what this general rule requires, the Internal Revenue Service will respect the agreement unless the Service finds that the method of accounting does not clearly reflect income. So debtor and creditor can work out an agreement which provides the debtor with the tax treatment he prefers, usually a larger tax deduction for that year. Where the parties fail to do so, the debtor is bound by the usual rules as to the application of the payment he makes.[109]

Interest that is included in a lump-sum compromise of tax deficiency, penalty, and interest is deductible.[110]

Where additional taxes, penalty, and interest are assessed for one or more taxable years against a person and he makes a partial payment without giving specific instructions as to how his payment is to be applied, the Internal Revenue Service will apply it to tax, penalty, and interest in that order, starting with the earliest period involved. The portion of the payment applied to interest for any period will be deductible for the year in which the partial payment is made.[111]

Payments made annually or periodically on a redeemable ground rent are deductible as interest.[112] Although payments on a nonredeemable ground rent are not interest, they may be deducted as rent to the extent they are business expenses or are attributable to rental properties held for the production of income.[113]

The owner of a condominium can deduct the interest on mortgage indebtedness allocable to his property.[114]

Interest rates sometimes are so high that they exceed state limits as to what can be charged to individuals under usury laws. A standard ploy is for a bank to tell an individual who applies for a loan to form a dummy or sham corporation in order to get around the interest ceilings, which generally apply only to individual loans. One corporation was formed to borrow from a bank, the individual guaranteeing the loan. Then he paid the corporation's interest on its indebtedness, as the corporation had no funds of its own. He could deduct the interest, regardless of whether he was viewed as paying interest to the dummy corporation or directly to the bank as the corporation's agent.[115]

Where two or more persons are jointly and severally liable on an obligation (that is, each person has liability for the full amount of the indebtedness), and only one of these parties makes an interest payment in a taxable year, he is entitled to the full interest deduction.[116]

Where a husband and wife jointly owned a residence and the husband made the mortgage payments, he could deduct the entire amount of the mortgage interest paid.[117] Where a son borrowed money under a student-loan program in order to pay tuition and other expenses, his father had to cosign a promissory note. Actually the father paid each interest installment. He could deduct the full interest as paid.[118]

Husband and wife held their personal property as tenants by the entirety. The property was encumbered with an indebtedness evidenced by a promissory note and secured by a mortgage. The note, signed by each spouse, required each and both of them to pay the mortgage interest in monthly installments. The schedule of payments given to each spouse by the mortgagee showed separately the amount of interest payable. Where the spouses filed separate Federal income tax returns, the amount of interest actually paid by the wife was deductible on her individual tax return for each year.[119]

If a husband and wife jointly own their residence as tenants by the entirety with a right of survivorship, and an agreement made a part of a divorce decree provides that, from amounts the wife receives from the husband as support, she is to make the principal and interest payments on the mortgage on the property (an indebtedness for which they are both liable), then the wife must include in her income, and the husband may deduct, one-half of each principal and interest payment as "alimony." He may also deduct the other half of the interest payments as "interest." If the residence is held by husband and wife as tenants in common, the wife owns one-half of the property. Therefore the husband may deduct, as "alimony," amounts he pays on the wife's half of the property for principal and interest on the mortgage.

Amounts paid by the husband on his half of the property are not deductible as alimony, nor are they taxable to the wife. But he may deduct as "interest" the portion he pays for interest on his half of the property. If his wife is sole owner of the property, and her husband agrees to make the mortgage payments on it, he may deduct these payments as "alimony," where they are taxable to her as periodic payments under a decree or agreement. If she itemizes her deductions she may deduct the portion of each payment which represents interest on the mortgage. If the husband is sole owner of the residence occupied rent-free by the wife, he may not deduct his mortgage payments as "alimony." But he may deduct as "interest" any interest he pays on the property.[120]

To be deductible, interest must be on a person's own indebtedness. But where an individual puts up his property as security for another party's loan and pays interest when the borrower cannot do so, the former is entitled to an interest deduction. Example: A stockholder pledges his own property when a corporation cannot get a bank loan.[121]

Under state law, a corporation executive, if his responsibilities include the transmission of state sales and withholding taxes to the state, may be personally liable for such taxes which the corporation has collected but failed to transmit. That portion of the interest on the delinquent tax payments which accrued after he became primarily liable for the obligation is deductible.[122]

When an individual was obliged to pay another party's indebtedness that he had guaranteed, he could deduct that part of the interest which accrued after he became primarily liable for the obligation subsequent to the time when this other party defaulted.[123]

Where a bank informed individuals who desired a business loan that funds would be lent only to a corporation so as to circumvent state law on the maximum rates chargeable to individuals and partnerships, a corporation was formed to borrow the money. The funds were used to acquire realty, which immediately was conveyed to a partnership. The corporation did nothing except act as a conduit for funds. Interest was deductible by the partnership rather than by the "straw" corporation. That meant that each partner could deduct his proportionate share of the interest.[124]

An individual endorsed the promissory note of a corporation, which became unable to pay it. He was obliged to pay the indebtedness and unpaid interest upon it. He could deduct the interest he paid.[125]

A father could deduct interest he paid on a student loan taken out by his son, where the father had been required by the lending bank to cosign the son's note.[126]

An interest deduction is allowed when a taxpayer is secondarily liable only if the interest was paid in connection with a real-estate mortgage and the taxpayer is the legal or equitable owner of that property.[127]

Interest on indebtedness incurred or continued to purchase or to carry tax-exempt obligations is not deductible.[128] But it does not follow that interest paid to lending banks or other parties must be disallowed simply because the taxpayer happens to own tax-exempt bonds. When an individual borrowed funds to operate various business ventures at a time when he was holding tax-exempt bonds, the Internal Revenue Service claimed that interest on the undeniably business indebtedness must be disallowed because to some extent at least this money *could* have been used to carry the tax-exempts. In rejecting this position, the court pointed out that this rule applies only where a taxpayer borrows and uses the borrowed funds to purchase the tax-exempts. Such was not the case here. There was no relationship between the incurring of various indebtedness by the taxpayer and his holding of tax-exempt bonds except for the general fact that incurring of indebtedness allowed him to retain his tax-exempt holdings.[129] A loan not incurred to purchase tax-exempt obligations but for the purpose of operating a taxpayer's business was not "incurred or continued to purchase or carry" tax-exempt securities, even though such securities were hypothecated (deposited as security) for the loans.[130]

The Internal Revenue Service has stated that interest incurred to buy or to carry tax-exempt bonds will not be disallowed where the investment in tax-exempts is insubstantial. In the case of an individual, investment in such bonds is presumed to be insubstantial only where during the taxable year the average amount of the obligations valued at their adjusted basis (tax cost) does not exceed 2 percent of the average adjusted basis of the taxpayer's investment portfolio.[131] "Investment portfolio" for this purpose includes transactions entered into for profit (including investment in real estate) which are not connected with the active conduct of a trade or business.[132]

Deduction was allowed where the proceeds of a *bona fide* indebtedness were temporarily invested in tax-exempt obligations because the intended utilization of the borrowed money had to be deferred for reasons beyond the borrower's control.[133]

Generally, interest is not disallowed if an individual's indebtedness is of a personal nature as opposed to investment; for example, where he holds municipal bonds and takes out a mortgage to buy a home instead of selling the municipals in order to finance the purchase. Here the purpose of incurring the indebtedness is so directly related to the personal purpose of acquiring a home that there is no inference of a direct relationship between the borrowing and the investment in tax-exempts.[134]

An individual who owned quantities of tax-exempt bonds was one of nine persons who carried on real-estate activities. He and the other persons bought nine parcels of land for business purposes, giving mortgages and cash for their acquisitions. Such mortgages were the customary way of financing purchases of this nature. Interest on the mortgages was deductible.[135]

A person may rebut the presumption that borrowing was for the purpose of continuing to hold previously purchased tax-exempt bonds by showing that he was unable to sell the municipals.[136]

A person who owned a large quantity of tax-exempts could deduct interest for money borrowed to pay income and gift taxes. True, she could have sold some of her securities in order to pay these taxes. But inasmuch as the securities had a low-cost basis, she would have had taxable gain had she done so. Borrowing to pay taxes was an alternative to increasing taxable income. The indebtedness being to pay taxes and not to carry tax-exempt bonds, it was deductible. Although the borrowing to pay taxes enabled her to get the benefit of tax-exempt bonds, that was not enough to require disallowance of her interest expense.[137]

Interest expense on the revolving account of a brokerage house (the account was used to purchase both taxable and tax-exempt securities for resale) was deductible. The tax-exempt securities represented only a small fraction of the bonds purchased, inasmuch as the firm had a policy against investment in tax-exempts. The statute makes no provision for proration of interest.[138]

Another broker carried on a general securities business, including tax-exempts, which amounted to less than 1 percent of the average monthly value of the firm's assets and less than one-fourth of 1 percent of the gross income. Money was borrowed to finance customers' purchases of securities in margin accounts and for general cash requirements for purchasers. It was not possible to determine how much of the loans represented dealings in tax-exempt obligations. Only that portion of the interest deduction not allocable to investments which were not tax-exempt was deductible.[139]

In the case where an individual, as the distributee of an estate's assets, paid an estate tax deficiency and interest thereon by reason of the fact that the estate no longer had assets, he could deduct the interest which had accrued on the deficiency *subsequent* to the distribution. Interest which had accrued on the deficiency prior to the distribution was not deductible.[140]

A somewhat limited deduction is allowed for interest on money borrowed for investment purposes ("investment interest"). Such interest is deductible by an individual up to the aggregate of:

1. $25,000 ($12,500 in the case of separate returns filed by married persons).

2. The amount of net investment income.

3. The excess of net long-term capital gain over net short-term capital loss for the taxable year.

4. One-half the amount by which investment interest exceeds the total of items 1, 2, and 3.

This does not refer to investment interest on indebtedness incurred before December 7, 1969, or incurred after that date pursuant to a written contract which was binding on that date.[141]

For taxable years beginning after December 31, 1975, there is a limitation on the deduction of nonbusiness interest: $10,000 plus the taxpayer's net investment income. No offset of investment income is permitted against capital gain income. An additional deduction of up to $15,000 per year is permitted for interest paid in connection with indebtedness incurred by the taxpayer to acquire the stock in a corporation, or a partnership interest, where the taxpayer, his spouse, and his children have (or acquire) at least 50 percent of the stock or capital interest in the enterprise. Interest deductions which are disallowed under these rules are subject to an unlimited carry-over and may be deducted in future years, subject to the applicable limitation. No limitation is imposed on the deductibility of personal interest.[142]

Interest on Federal income taxes owing is deductible when paid. It is geared semi-annually to the adjusted prime interest rate.[143] This rate was set at 16 percent on January 1, 1983.[144]

See also **Condominiums and cooperative housing corporations; Discount; Family transactions; Investors; Loan discount; Reverse mortgage loan, interest on; Tuition-postponement-plan payments.**

Interest, forfeiture of. Where an individual makes a bank deposit and there is a substantial forfeiture of interest called for if he withdraws his money before a stipulated time, the amount of the forfeiture is deductible as a loss on a transaction entered into for profit.[145]

Interviews. An employer can deduct the costs of interviewing prospective employees.[146] *See also* **Employment, expenses in seeking.**

Inventors. *See* **Research and experimental expenses; Transactions entered into for profit.**

Inventory write-downs. If a taxpayer's business inventory is valued on the basis of the lower of cost or market value, deduction is allowed when written down to the latter figure.[147]

Any goods in an inventory which are unsalable at normal prices and are unusable in the normal way because of damage, imperfections, shop wear, change of style, odd or broken lots, or similar causes, including secondhand goods taken in exchange, are to be included in inventory at *bona fide* selling prices less the direct cost of the disposition.[148] A deduction for this write-down is allowed.

Unsalability for this purpose is not limited to damage, imperfections, etc. Unsalability was found where the only possible purchaser of the inventory, military light cargo trailers, terminated its contract.[149] Write-down was allowed when large quantities of defective merchandise were found in the inventory;[150] when there had been leaks in the inventory;[151] and where there were merchandise shortages.[152]

Inventories of unsalable merchandise are written off in the taxable year when they become unsalable, not when the taxpayer ultimately concludes that they cannot be sold.[153] *See also* **Abandonment loss; Obsolescence.**

Investigatory expenses. *See* **Feasibility studies; Investors; Ordinary and necessary business expenses; Prebusiness expenses; Private investigators; Start-up expenses.**

Investors. Deduction is allowed to an individual for all ordinary and necessary expenses paid or incurred for the production or collection of income and for the management, conservation, or maintenance of property held for the production of income.[154] One of those named characterizations customarily covers what an investor does.

Office rent and similar expenses paid or incurred by an individual in connection with his investments are deductible only if they are ordinary and necessary under all the circumstances having regard to such an investment and to the relationship of the individual to such investment.[155]

If a person maintains an office at which he conducts some other activity of a personal nature, and he also carries on activities as an investor there, an allocation of rent, clerical salaries, and other expenses may be deducted.[156]

A retired octogenarian was permitted to deduct part of the cost of an office maintained for personal use and to handle his investments. Although he personally spent little time in the office, a clerk worked there regularly, collecting and recording the venerable gentleman's income. On the basis of time devoted to the production of income, 50 percent of the office expense was deemed to be deductible.[157] The cost of moving an office was also deductible in a case where the office was used for handling investments.[158]

Postage related to one's investment activities is deductible.[159] To the extent that a secretary's time is devoted to a person's investment activities, an allocation of her (or his) time is deductible.[160]

An individual may properly deduct an investment counsel's fee.[161] That includes investment counsel and advice concerning existing and future or potential investments.[162]

Costs incurred in the acquisition of a capital asset (such as stock customarily is in the hands of an investor) are not deductible but are treated as part of the cost of the investment. Fees were paid to an investment advisory service which specialized in minimizing a client's income taxes while enlarging his estate. These fees were of two kinds: (1) a monthly retainer which was payable regardless of whether any investments were made and (2) an investment fee which was a specified percentage of the cost of a project in which the client actually invested. A client's investment in a recommended project took the form of a limited partnership interest, created by the advisory service primarily for appreciation and tax shelter potential, the intention being for the client to close out his investment when the desired tax benefits were no longer available. Fees paid for (1) were deductible, those made for (2) were not.[163]

An attorney who had often been asked by clients to evaluate prospectuses of real-estate syndications decided to research such ventures on his own. When he found a venture which appeared sound, he put interested clients directly in touch with the syndicators. Clients who invested in such syndications were billed by the lawyer in accordance with his research-time cost. Investors were not able to deduct these fees. But they could deduct any part of the legal fees that could be shown to be incurred for tax advice and tax planning.[164]

The chief stockholder of a closely held corporation engaged a broker to find another company into which to merge, so that he would not have the bulk of his estate in stock of his own company, which produced little income and which was not readily marketable. The broker spent a great deal of time trying to find another company with which to exchange shares, but without success. Eventually the stockholder found and made his own deal. The fees he paid to the broker were not for the acquisition of a capital asset, stock, but were compensation for time and effort which had been fruitless. The expenses were deductible.[165]

The cost of statistical service is deductible if used in the management and conservation of investments.[166] An attorney who bought and sold securities for his own account could deduct his expenses for a statistical service.[167]

An investor properly deducted fees for the collection of income. This includes fees paid to a broker, a bank, or a similar agent to collect bond interest or dividends.[168] But a fee paid to a broker to acquire investment property is not deductible and is added to the cost of the property. A fee paid in connection with the sale of investment property is a selling expense and may be used only to determine gain or loss from the sale.[169]

Rent for a safety-deposit box is deductible if the box is used for the storage of taxable income-producing stocks, bonds, and the like. The rent is not deductible if the box is used to store personal effects or tax-exempt securities.[170] Deduction was permitted for the rent of a safety-deposit box which was used to hold Series EE Treasury bonds, although no income was reportable in the taxable year, election having been made to report appreciation in the year when the bonds matured.[171]

Where a person was unable to rent a safety-deposit box for the purpose of storing his securities and other financial investments, he purchased a safe for the purpose. The cost of the safe was not deductible at the time of purchase but annual depreciation was allowed.[172]

The cost of custodian services is deductible.[173]

Entertainment in connection with investments in taxable securities was deductible where an investor wined and dined knowledgeable persons in an effort to get investment advice from them.[174]

An individual gave purchase orders for stock, and the necessary funds, to a New York Stock Exchange member firm, calling for immediate delivery of his shares. After nine futile months of demanding his stock, he brought suit against the broker for cancellation of his orders; the stock, meanwhile, had declined drastically in value. He also sought the return of his funds. He was awarded judgment for the amount of his cash advances. But inasmuch as the broker faced bankruptcy, the customer accepted cash and stock worth considerably less than the judgment. The loss was fully deductible, for although the broker owed money to his customer, he did not owe it as a debtor and hence it was not a debt. As far as the customer was concerned, this had been a transaction entered upon for profit.[175]

A loss sustained during a taxable year with respect to expenditures incurred in search of a business or investment is deductible only where the activities are more than investigatory and the taxpayer actually had entered into a transaction for profit and the project later is abandoned. The loss is allowable only in the taxable year in which the project is abandoned.[176]

The following case is a good example of the above. After investigating a mine operation owned by another person to determine whether it might be a suitable investment for himself, an individual contributed cash and hired several men for about thirty days to rehabilitate mining equipment and to operate a mine temporarily to ascertain whether future investment was warranted. The results of the temporary operation were unsuccessful, and the project was abandoned. The individual never acquired any interest nor made any other investment in the property. A deductible loss was sustained in the taxable year in which the project was abandoned because his activities in connection with the project were more than investigatory; he had actually entered into a transaction for profit which he later abandoned.[177]

An individual sought to operate a Holiday Inn under a franchise. He obtained a "hold" from that organization, subject to the acquisition of an appropriate site in a designated community. He found land to his liking, arranged for the financing, and was ready to go forward, when for reasons beyond his control and without his fault or neglect the land became unavailable. He was permitted to deduct his expenses for attorney, architect, and feasibility studies because they related to a transaction entered upon for profit, although this venture was not connected with his regular profession (he was a lawyer) and the motel venture never became operative.[178]

A taxpayer sought, with several associates, to incorporate a savings and loan association. Funds were expended to obtain the necessary charter from the state savings and loan commissioner. The taxpayer's activities in investigating the project, in holding discussions with professional advisers, and in studying the economic chances of success indicated that this was a transaction entered upon for profit. Expenses merely representing the cost of an investigation of a possible business opportunity are not deductible, but here the project could be said to have proceeded sufficiently far to establish that this was a transaction entered upon for profit, even though the deal subsequently fell apart because the charter was not issued.[179]

One case lost by a taxpayer revealed what an investor has to show in order to deduct travel expense. He studied financial data relevant to corporations in which he was interested, including annual reports, production data, and newspaper articles. As part of his investment method, he also visited corporate factories and retail outlets to see things for himself. In one year, he made fifteen trips through parts of the United States and Europe. But he could not deduct his travel expenditures as expenses for the production of income, for it appeared that he managed to visit members of his far-flung family on these trips. The value of this decision is that the court specifically stated what a traveling investor can do to get his tax deduction: "If proof had been adduced that such a trip was part of a rationally planned, systematic investigation of the business operations of such a company, if the level of costs involved had been reasonable viewed in relation to the magnitude of the investment and the value of the information reasonably expected to be derived from the trip, if the circumstances had negated a disguised personal motive for the travel, and if there had been some showing of a practical application through investment decisions of the kind of information gained from such trips, we might have been favorably disposed to [the investor's] contentions. We need not, and do not, hold that as a matter of law the legitimate costs of travel by an investor to places of business of firms in which he holds a substantial stake may never be deducted. We hold merely that under the circumstances of this case [the investor] has not persuaded us that the costs he incurred here were ordinary and necessary."[180]

If an individual's attempts to acquire a business are unsuccessful, deduction is not allowed for expenses incurred in the course of a general search for, or preliminary investigation of, a business or investment. This includes expenses related to decisions *whether* to enter a transaction and *which* transaction to enter. Typical are expenses for advertisements, travel to search for a new business, and the cost of audits that were designed to help the investor to decide to attempt an acquisition. But once efforts are made to acquire a specific business or investment, expenses for attorneys to draft purchase agreements and any other costs incurred in an attempt to complete the purchase of the business are deductible.[181]

Expenses incurred in the search for suitable business income are not deductible; they are not business expenses before the taxpayer is engaged in that business. But if a transaction has reached the point where he is justified in thinking he has found such a business, the expenses are deductible on the ground that they are related to a transaction entered upon for profit. An individual sought to make a substantial investment in some business. Through a broker, he made contact with a distributing corporation. After consultations with bankers, accountants, and lawyers as to the status and prospects of the corporation, plus considerable personal investigation, terms were worked out and a draft acquisition agreement was prepared. But before the papers were signed, he discovered that there had been some misrepresentations to him and that the company's financial position was not so rosy as he had believed. He called off the deal. His expenses for legal and accounting fees, and for travel and living expenses in investigating the proposition, were deductible. These expenses had not been incurred by him in preparing to consummate the purchase. So they were not nondeductible prebusiness expenses before he could be said to have entered upon a transaction for profit.[182]

An individual was a corporate employee and never was in the business of buying and selling oil leases or other mining property. But he did purchase interests in leases and royalties solely for the purpose of utilizing his personal funds. It was held that expenses incident to travel to investigate investment possibilities were deductible when the investigations did not result in the acquisition of leases or royalties as investments.[183]

A United States investor could deduct his expenses in looking after his investments in Canada. The properties were held for the production of income, and legal matters in connection with these properties called for the investor's attention.[184]

A shareholder of a corporation could deduct travel expenses, including meals and lodgings, while attending a stockholders' meeting in another city for the purpose of taking action aimed at prevention of dilution of stock through issuance below book value.[185]

A taxpayer was an employee of a bookshop. She also managed her own investments, noted the court, "in a businesslike manner." She subscribed to the *Wall Street Journal* and several investment services; she also collected a variety of information about investments such as corporate financial reports, news releases, and brokers' recommendations. She was permitted to deduct the costs of weekly trips to the manager of her custodial account and monthly trips to meet with her broker.[186]

A substantial investor in a corporation's stock could deduct his travel expenses in attending the annual shareholders' meeting in another city. He attended in order to present a shareholder resolution requesting management to stop diluting stockholder equity by issuing common stock directly through public sale and through the company's dividend reinvestment and stock purchase plans, at prices below book values. The resolution was passed by 97 percent of the shareholders.[187]

Investors in securities or investors in real estate may deduct stock transfer and real-estate transfer taxes, respectively, to the extent that they are expenses incurred in carrying on a trade or business or are an activity for the production of income.[188]

Taxes incurred in the production of rental income, such as real property taxes and personal property taxes, are deductible as rental expenses.[189]

Transfer taxes imposed by state and local governments in a transaction entered upon for profit are deductible.[190]

A shareholder was permitted to deduct premiums he had paid on a corporation's primary asset in order to protect his investment.[191]

If a dealer in securities makes a short sale of stock and is required to pay the lender for dividends distributed while he maintained his short position, he may deduct this amount as a business expense. These payments made by individuals who are investors may be claimed only when deductions are itemized on Schedule A ("Itemized Deductions"), which certainly means a substantial proportion of all investors.[192]

If the payment is in lieu of a liquidating or stock dividend or if the borrower buys additional shares of stock equal to a stock dividend issued during his short position, that amount must be added to the cost of the stock sold short, whether the payment is made by the dealer or an investor.[193]

Loan premiums equal to cash dividends paid by an investor on stock borrowed to cover short sales are similarly deductible.[194]

Where a stockholder surrenders a part of his stock to improve the financial condition of the corporation, he sustains a deductible loss, measured by the cost or other basis of the stock surrendered, less the resulting improvement in the value of the stock retained.[195] Where a stockholder surrenders to the issuing corporation some of his shares disproportionately with respect to other shareholders, for no consideration other than whatever enhancement in the book value results from this surrender, he realizes an ordinary as opposed to a capital loss.[196]

Generally, a payment by a stockholder to his corporation to protect his existing investment and to prevent a loss is regarded as a capital contribution and must be added to the cost or other basis of his stock.

But when a stockholder surrenders a part of his stock to improve the financial condition of the corporation, he has a deductible loss, measured by his basis in the shares surrendered. Such was the case where the two principal stockholder-officers of a corporation with more than 800 shareholders transferred some of their stock back to the corporation. All they received in return was a belief that the corporation would not be plunged into insolvency, a circumstance which might have caused the company's principal creditor to sue these officer-shareholders for mismanagement that had triggered bankruptcy and creditor losses.[197]

Several individuals owned the controlling stock interest in a corporation. In order to prevent a takeover of their interest by another group, they engaged counsel. Legal fees were deductible as an expenditure for the conservation of property held for the production of income. The stock could be regarded as held for the production of income if the individuals' continued gainful employment would be lost as the result of the takeover, or if continuance of dividends on their stock was likely to be jeopardized.[198]

A minority stockholder in a Delaware corporation was dissatisfied with the terms of a merger that the corporation entered into with a larger company. As authorized by Delaware law, inasmuch as she had dissented from the merger, she was entitled to be paid a price based upon an appraisal of the value of her stock. She could deduct her legal fees in forcing the appraisal and the correlative payment to her. She incurred the legal expenses solely in an attempt to increase the amount of income the sale of the stock would produce over the amount she previously had been offered. Although the fees related to a capital asset, they were not necessary to the disposition of a capital asset and hence were not capital expenditures. Her purpose in engaging counsel was to determine the amount of income due her from the sale of her stock.[199]

Pro rata expenses of members of a stockholders' committee were deductible where far-reaching changes in the management of the corporation were sought. These objectives were sought by attempting to elect a new board of directors. The payments by the stockholders were made in anticipation that profit would result, as shown in a document published by the committee entitled *Let's Rebuild Montgomery Ward*. It may have been a long chance that a stockholder was taking, but it was an attempt (actually successful) to increase corporate profits and stockholder dividends.[200]

Payments by an investor to a bondholders' protective committee as a proportionate share of expenses were deductible as money paid for the conservation of property held for the production of income.[201]

Assessments by a bondholders' reorganization committee were deductible.[202]

A director who also held a substantial minority interest in a corporation could deduct his expenses in going to directors' meetings. He believed that the policies of the majority would endanger the value of his investment and that what he was engaged in was damage control: a fight for the life of his investment.[203]

Costs incurred by a stockholder in a proxy fight opposing management are deductible, at least to the extent that they are closely related to his income-producing activities.[204] Deduction similarly is allowed where the existing management is being supported in a proxy fight.[205]

A director and stockholder of a major railroad corporation joined with other individuals in soliciting proxies from the stockholders in an attempt to unseat the incumbent management. The group's efforts were unsuccessful, and the corporation saw fit to reimburse their expenses. Several other stockholders brought suit against this group for improperly claiming this reimbursement, and each of the group members bore his proportionate share of the compromise settlement worked out with those bringing the suit. The amounts paid out in the compromise were deductible. The expenses arose because of an effort by major stockholders to affect the policies of the railroad corporation and were moneys spent to conserve and to maintain income-producing property (stock) which they held.[206]

That situation differs markedly from the following: A person holding a small stock interest in a large corporation takes it upon himself to crusade for a particular point of view on a particular issue. However worthy his motives, he cannot reasonably expect to affect his dividend income in relation to his corporate investments to such an extent as would justify defining his activity as an ordinary and necessary expense.[207]

If holders of stock decide to sell their shares by means of a public offering of their holdings, the cost is not deductible, being deemed to be capital. But if they change their minds and abandon the project, they can deduct the costs which they incurred.[208]

There are two types of fees paid by subscribers to sponsored investment plans:

1.   The creation fee is deducted by the custodian from subscriber deposits and is paid to the sponsor for its services in developing, selling, and administering the plan. It is a fee paid for the privilege of acquiring stock through the plan and is not deductible. This fee is a capital expenditure and must be added to the cost of the shares acquired through the investment plan.[209]

2.   The custody fee is paid for services performed by the custodian in holding the shares acquired through the plan, maintaining individual records, and providing detailed statements of account to subscribers. This is deductible.[210]

A bank established a plan known as the automatic dividend reinvestment service. Under the plan, cash dividends paid by the corporation were reinvested by the bank as agent for participating shareholders in full or fractional shares of the corporation. The bank was authorized by each member to receive all the cash dividends from the payor corporation that were otherwise payable to the shareholders. The bank's service charge and brokerage commissions were apportioned among subscribers to the plan. The service charge was deductible.[211]

Deduction is allowed for service fees charged by a bank in connection with the operation of an automatic investment service in which depositors, with the bank acting as their agent, may elect to invest a portion of their checking accounts in the common stock of specified corporations.[212]

If an individual purchases a fully taxable bond at a premium (above par), he may elect to amortize the premium over the life of the bond. The amortizable bond premium is then subtracted from his basis or adjusted basis for the bond. This treatment is mandatory in the case of tax-exempt bonds.[213]

Premiums paid to purchase a bond of indemnity so that a new stock certificate will be issued to replace a missing one are deductible.[214] So are incidental expenses to secure replacement if securities are mislaid, stolen, or destroyed.[215]

A theft-loss deduction depends upon whether the event meets the definition of "theft" under the law of the state where it takes place. When investments are made with a certain party under fraudulent misrepresentations by him, and under state law the taking of money under false representations or false pretenses is theft, there is a theft-loss deduction for tax purposes.[216] An individual loaned money to a corporation in exchange for an unsecured interest-bearing note of the corporation. His decision to loan the corporation funds was based upon information contained in financial reports issued by the corporation. Subsequently, it was established that the financial statements were fraudulent in that they did not reflect large liabilities which made the corporation insolvent. Inasmuch as the misrepresentation as to the corporation's financial condition had been deliberate, the lender was entitled to a theft-loss deduction.[217]

Loss from failure to exercise a stock option is deductible if the option is not a capital asset in the holder's hands.[218] (Whether or not the option is a capital asset is a technical question, which the taxpayer may have to ask an accountant, lawyer, or IRS employee.)

An expense incurred for the acquisition of capital assets is not deductible and must be added to the cost of the property. But deduction for lawyers' expenses in getting back investment property is deductible, as where a minority stockholder loaned shares to the corporation because it needed collateral for a bank loan and subsequently the corporation became reluctant to give back the stock. Her status as a lender was independent of her position as a shareholder.[219]

If an individual holds income-producing securities, expenses in connection with incompetency proceedings which involve the securities' holder are deductible as expenses for the management and conservation of property. Without the appointment of a committee to handle her affairs, the income-producing property could not be conserved.[220]

If an individual incurs expenses to produce both taxable and tax-exempt income, but he cannot identify specifically the expenses which produce each type of income, then he must prorate them in order to determine the amount deductible.[221] Typical items subject to such proration are investment counsel fees, accounting services, interest on borrowed money. Where an investigator borrowed money to make real-estate investments when he was also holding tax-exempt bonds, the interest was deductible. A reasonable person is not expected to sacrifice liquidity and security by selling tax-exempt bonds in lieu of incurring mortgage indebtedness for business purposes.[222]

Fees paid to a fiduciary for the management, conservation, or maintenance of a trust were deductible to the extent that taxable income was involved. When both taxable and tax-free securities were in the same trust fund, deduction was determined upon the ratio of taxable to nontaxable income.[223]

Other interest paid by an investor is determined in the same manner that applies to individuals in general. Interest on margin accounts is deductible for the taxable year when it is paid.[224]

For taxable years beginning after 1975, the amount of any loss (otherwise allowable for the year) in connection with one of certain activities cannot exceed the aggregate amount with respect to which the taxpayer is at risk in the activity at the close of the taxable year. This "at risk" limitation applies to the following activities: (1) farming (except farming operations involving trees other than fruit or nut trees), (2) exploring for, or exploiting, oil and gas resources, (3) holding, producing, or distributing motion-picture films or video tapes, and (4) equipment leasing. A taxpayer is generally considered "at risk" with respect to an activity to the extent of his cash and the adjusted basis of other property contributed to the activity, any amounts borrowed for use in the activity with respect to which he has personal liability for payment from his personal assets, and his net fair market value of personal assets which secure nonrecourse borrowings. This provision does not apply to net leases under binding contracts for equipment-leasing activities finalized on or before December 31, 1975.[225] For taxable years beginning after 1978, the specific "at risk" rule applies to all activities other than real estate.[226] *See also* **Accounting expenses; Amortization of bond premium; Automatic dividend reinvestment plan; Capital losses; Condominiums and co-**

operative housing corporations; Mineral leases, cost of acquiring; Office at home; Registered mail; Reliance upon misrepresentation; Small-business corporation stock; Small-business investment company; Start-up expenses; Tax-option corporations.

Involuntary conversions. *See* **Property used in the trade or business and involuntary conversions.**

IRA. *See* **Individual retirement account.**

Iron lung, operating expenses of. Expenditures for the operation of an iron lung and associated equipment are deductible medical expenses.[227]

I

1. *Commissioner v. Sullivan et al.*, 356 U.S. 27 (1958).

2. *George G. Ebner et al.*, T.C. Memo. 1958-108, filed June 9, 1958.

3. *Afshar v. Commissioner*, T.C. Memo. 1981-241, filed May 18, 1981.

4. *Louis Cohen*, T.C. Memo., Docket No. 63366, entered April 8, 1958.

5. *Marigold Foods, Inc. v. United States*, DC, Minn., 1965.

6. *Hossbach v. Commissioner*, T.C. Memo. 1981-291, filed June 15, 1981.

7. *Conforte et al. v. Commissioner*, 74 T.C. 1160 (1980).

8. *Edmondson v. Commissioner*, T.C. Memo. 1981-623, filed October 26, 1981.

9. *Herbert E. Tharp et al.*, T.C. Memo. 1972-10, filed January 12, 1972.

10. IRS Letter Ruling 8113020, November 30, 1980.

11. Revenue Ruling 62-156, 1962-2 CB 47.

12. *Robert Buedingen*, 6 BTA 335 (1927).

13. *Connecticut Mutual Life Insurance Company v. Eaton*, 218 F.206 (DC, Conn., 1914).

14. Revenue Ruling 70-392, 1970-2 CB 33.

15. IRC Section 691(c).

16. Revenue Ruling 67-242, 1967-2 CB 227.

17. Revenue Ruling 69-607, 1969-2 CB 40.

18. Pension Reform Act of 1974, Section 2002.

19. IRC Section 408(n).

20. IRC Section 219(b)(1).

21. IRC Section 219(b)(2)(C).

22. IRC Section 219(b)(2)(3).

23. IRC Section 219(f).

24. IRC Section 219(b)(2)(B).

25. IRS Letter Ruling 7851087, September 22, 1978, using figures contained in IRC Section 219(b).

26. Revenue Ruling 76-374, 1976-2 CB 19.

27. IT 3634, 1944 CB 90.

28. Tax Equity and Fiscal Responsibility Act of 1982, Section 202.

29. *Tax Guide for Small Business*, 1975 edition, page 112.

30. Regulations Section 1.162-1(a).

31. Revenue Ruling 60-365, 1960-2 CB 49.

32. Revenue Ruling 56-264, 1956-1 CB 153.

33. Revenue Ruling 60-275, 1960-2 CB 43.

34. *Orr v. United States*, 343 F.2d 553 (5th Cir., 1965).

35. *Harold Mortenson*, 3 BTA 300 (1934).

36. Revenue Ruling 72-616, 1972-1 CB 44.

37. Revenue Ruling 69-491, 1969-2 CB 22.

38. *Tax Guide for Commercial Fishermen*. IRS Publication 595 (Rev. Oct. 1981), page 10.

39. Revenue Ruling 55-189, 1955-1 CB 265.

40. *Tax Guide for Small Business*, 1976 edition, page 112.

41. Revenue Ruling 70-254, 1970-1 CB 31.

42. *General Smelting Company*, 4 T.C. 313 (1944).

43. *The First National Bank and Trust Company of Tulsa v. Jones*, 143 F.2d 652 (10th Cir., 1944).

44. Revenue Ruling 75-46, 1975-1 CB 55.

45. Revenue Ruling 70-254, 1970-1 CB 31.

46. *N. Loring Danforth*, 18 BTA 1221 (1930).

47. Revenue Ruling 55-264, 1955-1 CB 11.

48. *Donovan et al. v. Campbell, Jr.*, DC, ND Texas, 1961.

49. *Corn Products Refining Company v. Commissioner*, 350 U.S. 46 (1955).

50. *Farroll v. Jarecki*, 231 F.2d 281 (7th Cir., 1956).

51. IRC Section 163.

52. *Wachovia Bank & Trust Company et al. v. United States*, 499 F. Supp. 615 (DC, MD N.C., 1980).

53. *Golsen et al. v. United States*, Ct. Cl., 1980.

54. *Wiggin Terminals, Inc. v. United States*, 36 F.2d 893 (1st Cir., 1929).

55. Revenue Ruling 72-2, 1972-1 CB 19.

56. IRC Section 483.

57. *Kena, Inc.*, 44 BTA 217 (1941).

58. *Rufus C. Salley et al.,* 55 T.C. 896 (1971).

59. *Minnis et al. v. Commissioner,* 71 T.C. 1049 (1979).

60. *Thomas v. Dierks,* 132 F.2d 224 (5th Cir., 1942).

61. *Richard S. Heyman et al.,* 70 T.C. 482 (1978), *aff'd,* 633 F.2d 215 (6th Cir., 1980).

62. *Newton A. Burgess,* 8 T.C. 47 (1947).

63. *Canfield v. Commissioner,* T.C. Memo. 1980-533, filed December 3, 1980.

64. IRS Letter Ruling 8104139, October 31, 1980.

65. *Stewart et al. v. Commissioner,* T.C. Memo. 1980-496, filed November 4, 1980.

66. Revenue Ruling 70-221, 1970-1 CB 33.

67. Revenue Ruling 70-284, 1970-1 CB 34.

68. Revenue Ruling 60-127, 1960-1 CB 84.

69. Revenue Ruling 60-128, 1960-1 CB 85.

70. Internal Revenue News Release IR-81-121, October 6, 1981.

71. *Oliver W. Bryant et al.,* T.C. Memo., Docket No. 27114, entered May 2, 1952.

72. Revenue Ruling 72-544, 1972-2 CB 96.

73. *Estate of Jane deP. Webster,* 65 T.C. 968 (1976).

74. *Goldstein et al. v. Commissioner,* 364 F.2d 734 (2d Cir., 1966).

75. *Arthur R. Jones Syndicate v. Commissioner,* 23 F.2d 833 (7th Cir., 1927).

76. *Margaret E. Johnson Malmstedt et al.,* T.C. Memo. 1976-46, filed February 24, 1976.

77. Revenue Ruling 68-643, 1968-2 CB 76.

78. Tax Reform Act of 1976, Section 208.

79. Revenue Ruling 73-482, 1973-2 CB 44.

80. *Burton Foster,* T.C. Memo. 1973-53, filed March 5, 1973.

81. *M. A. Long,* 8 BTA 737 (1927).

82. *Cook et ux. v. United States,* DC, WD La., 1977.

83. *Dustin et al. v. Commissioner,* T.C. Memo. 1977-409, filed November 29, 1977.

84. Revenue Ruling 71-98, 1971-1 CB 57.

85. Revenue Ruling 72-315, 1972-1 CB 60.

86. Revenue Ruling 73-136, 1973-1 CB 68.

87. Revenue Ruling 77-417, 1977-2 CB 60.

88. Revenue Ruling 67-62, 1967-1 CB 44.

89. *Oliver W. Bryant et al.,* T.C. Memo., Docket No. 27114, entered May 2, 1952.

90. Revenue Ruling 73-137, 1973-1 CB 68.

91. Regulations Section 1.163-2.

92. Revenue Ruling 74-187, 1974-1 CB 48.

93. Revenue Ruling 54-43, 1954-1 CB 119.

94. *Duffy et al. v. United States* Ct. Cl., 1981.

95. *Tax Information on Business Expenses,* IRS Publication 535, 1976 edition, page 3.

96. Revenue Ruling 57-198, 1957-1 CB 94.

97. *General American Life Insurance Company,* 25 T.C. 1265 (1956).

98. Internal Revenue News Release IR-1795, April 15, 1977.

99. Revenue Ruling 69-582, 1969-2 CB 29.

100. *Tax Information on Business Expenses,* IRS Publication 535, 1976 edition, page 14.

101. *Herbert Enoch et al.,* 57 T.C. 781 (1972).

102. IRC Section 461(g).

103. Revenue Ruling 74-395, 1974-2 CB 45.

104. *L-R Heat Treating Company,* 28 T.C. 894 (1957).

105. Tax Reform Act of 1976, Section 208.

106. Revenue Ruling 69-290, 1969-1 CB 55.

107. *Wilkerson et al. v. Commissioner,* 70 T.C. 240 (1978).

108. *Your Federal Income Tax,* 1976 edition, page 98.

109. *Mason et al. v. United States,* 453 F. Supp. 845 (DC, ND Cal., 1978).

110. *Max Thomas Davis et al.,* 46 BTA 663 (1942).

111. Revenue Ruling 73-305, 1973-2 CB 43.

112. IRC Section 163(c).

113. *Your Federal Income Tax,* 1976 edition, page 96.

114. Revenue Ruling 64-31, 1964-1 CB (Part 1) 300.

115. *Beran et al. v. Commissioner,* T.C. Memo. 1980-119, filed April 15, 1980.

116. *Kate Baker Sherman,* 18 T.C. 746 (1952).

117. *Castaneda-Benitez v. Commissioner,* T.C. Memo. 1981-157, filed April 2, 1981.

118. Revenue Ruling 71-179, 1971-1 CB 58.

119. Revenue Ruling 71-268, 1971-1 CB 58.

120. *Income Tax Deductions for Alimony Payments,* IRS Publication 504, 1976 edition, page 3.

121. Regulations Section 1.163-1(b).

122. *Arrigoni et al. v. Commissioner,* 73 T.C. 792 (1980).

123. *Tolzman et al. v. Commissioner,* T.C. Memo. 1981-689, filed December 2, 1981.

124. *Schlosberg v. United States,* DC, ED Va., 1981.

125. *Burgher et al. v. Campbell, Jr.,* DC, ND Texas, 1958.

126. Revenue Ruling 71-179, 1971-1 CB 58.

127. *Abdalla et al. v. Commissioner,* 69 T.C. 697 (1978).

128. IRC Section 265(2).

129. *Edmund F. Ball et al.,* 54 T.C. 1200 (1970).

130. *R. B. Machinery Co.,* 26 BTA 594 (1932).

131. Revenue Procedure 72-18, 1972-1 CB 740.

132. Revenue Procedure 74-8, 1974-1 CB 419.

133. Revenue Ruling 55-389, 1955-1 CB 276.

134. Revenue Procedure 72-18, 1972-1 CB 740.

135. *Israelson et al. v. United States,* 367 F. Supp. 1104 (DC, Md., 1973), *aff'd,* 508 F.2d 838 (4th Cir., 1975).

136. *Norfolk Shipbuilding and Drydock Corporation v. United States,* 321 F. Supp. 222 (DC, ED Va., 1971).

137. *Estate of Dellora A. Norris v. Commis-*

sioner, T.C. Memo. 1981-368, filed July 16, 1981.

138. *Wynn, Jr., et al. v. United States*, 288 F. Supp. 797 (DC, ED Pa., 1968).

139. *Leslie et al. v. Commissioner*, 413 F.2d 636 (2d Cir., 1969).

140. Revenue Ruling 72-544, 1972-2 CB 96.

141. IRC Section 163(d).

142. Tax Reform Act of 1976, Section 209.

143. IRC Section 6621(b).

144. Revenue Ruling 82-182, IRB 1982 44.

145. Revenue Ruling 73-511, 1973-2 CB 402.

146. *Charles O. Gunther, Jr., et al.*, T.C. Memo. 1954-181, filed October 21, 1954.

147. *E. W. Bliss Company et al. v. United States*, 351 F.2d 449 (6th Cir., 1965).

148. Regulations Section 1.471-2(c).

149. *Space Controls, Inc. v. Commissioner*, 322 F.2d 144 (5th Cir., 1963).

150. *Celluloid Company*, 9 BTA 989 (1927).

151. *Otto Huber Brewery Company*, 2 BTA 1193 (1925).

152. *Long Broom Co.*, 9 BTA 39 (1927).

153. *C-O- Two Fire Equipment Company v. Commissioner*, 219 F.2d 57 (3d Cir., 1955).

154. IRC Section 212.

155. Regulations Section 1.212-1(g).

156. *Charles Oster*, T.C. Memo. 1964-335, filed December 20, 1964.

157. *Kenneth A. Scott*, T.C. Memo. 1972-109, filed May 10, 1972.

158. *Samuel Abrams et al.*, T.C. Memo. 1964-256, filed September 29, 1964.

159. *E. N. Fry*, 5 T.C. 1058 (1945).

160. *Frederick B. Rentschler*, 1 T.C. 814 (1943).

161. *Raymond Fitzgerald*, T.C. Memo., Docket No. 52539, entered December 27, 1956.

162. *Mallinckrodt v. Commissioner*, 2 T.C. 1128 (1943), *aff'd*, 146 F.2d 1 (8th Cir., 1945).

163. *Honodel et al. v. Commissioner*, 76 T.C. 351 (1981).

164. IRS Letter Ruling 8108008, October 31, 1980.

165. *Picker et al. v. United States*, 371 F.2d 486 (Ct. Cl., 1967).

166. *Edward E. Bishop*, 4 T.C. 862 (1945).

167. *L. T. Alverson*, 35 BTA 482 (1937).

168. *Miscellaneous Expenses*, IRS Publication 529 (Rev. Nov. 1980), page 4.

169. *Tax Information on Investment Income and Expenses*, IRS Publication 550, 1976 edition, page 22.

170. Ibid.

171. *Daniel S. W. Kelly*, 23 T.C. 682 (1955), *aff'd on another issue*, 228 F.2d 512 (7th Cir., 1956).

172. IRS Letter Ruling 8218037, February 2, 1982.

173. *M. A. P. Coolidge et al.*, T.C. Memo., Docket Nos. 103648-103653, entered December 31, 1942.

174. *Samuel Abrams et al.*, T.C. Memo. 1964-256, filed September 29, 1964.

175. *Fred G. Meyer et al.*, T.C. Memo. 1975-349, filed December 8, 1975.

176. Revenue Ruling 57-418, 1957-2 CB 143.

177. *Charles T. Parker*, 1 T.C. 509 (1943).

178. *Finch et al. v. United States*, DC, Minn., 1966.

179. *Farris W. Seed et al.*, 52 T.C. 880 (1969).

180. *William R. Kinney*, 66 T.C. 122 (1976).

181. Revenue Ruling 77-254, 1977-2 CB 63.

182. *Johan Domenie et al.*, T.C. Memo. 1975-94, filed April 7, 1975.

183. *Colman et al. v. United States*, DC, Utah, 1946.

184. *E. M. Godson et al.*, T.C. Memo., Docket Nos. 4913-4, entered July 24, 1946.

185. IRS Letter Ruling 8042071, July 23, 1980.

186. *Martha E. Henderson*, T.C. Memo. 1968-22, filed January 13, 1968.

187. IRS Letter Ruling 8220084, February 19, 1982.

188. Regulations Section 1.164(a).

189. *Income Tax Deduction for Taxes*, IRS Publication 546, 1976 edition, page 5.

190. Revenue Ruling 65-313, 1965-2 CB 47.

191. *Harold Mortenson*, 3 BTA 300 (1934).

192. *Tax Information on Business Expenses*, IRS Publication 535, 1976 edition, page 4.

193. Ibid.

194. Revenue Ruling 72-521, 1972-2 CB 178.

195. *Commissioner v. Burdick*, 59 F.2d 395 (3d Cir., 1932).

196. *Estate of William H. Foster*, 9 T.C. 930 (1947).

197. *David N. Smith et al.*, 66 T.C. 622 (1976).

198. *Powell, Jr., v. United States*, 294 F. Supp. 977 (DC, SD S.D., 1969).

199. *Stemfel v. United States*, DC, MD Tenn., 1969.

200. *Surasky v. United States*, 325 F.2d 191 (5th Cir., 1963).

201. *Truman H. Newberry et al.*, T.C. Memo., Docket Nos. 4122-3, entered June 6, 1945.

202. *Charles Goodman et al.*, T.C. Memo., Docket No. 4976, entered December 18, 1946.

203. *Stranahan, Jr., et al. v. Commissioner*, T.C. Memo. 1982-151, filed March 25, 1982.

204. *Graham v. Commissioner*, 326 F.2d 878 (4th Cir., 1964).

205. *Locke Manufacturing Companies v. United States*, 237 F. Supp. 80 (DC, Conn., 1964).

206. *Graham et al. v. Commissioner*, 326 F.2d 878 (4th Cir., 1964).

207. *J. Raymond Dyer*, 36 T.C. 456 (1961).

208. Revenue Ruling 79-2, 1979-1 CB 98.

209. *Tax Information on Investment Income and Expenses*, IRS Publication 550, 1976 edition, page 23.

210. Revenue Ruling 55-23, 1955-1 CB 275.

211. Revenue Ruling 70-627, 1970-2 CB 159.

212. Revenue Ruling 75-548, 1975-2 CB 331.

213. IRC Section 171.

214. Revenue Ruling 62-21, 1962-1 CB 37.

215. *Tax Information on Investment Income*

I

253

and Expenses, IRS Publication 550, 1976 edition, page 23.

216. *Michele Monteleone et al.*, 34 T.C. 688 (1960).

217. Revenue Ruling 71-381, 1971-2 CB 126.

218. Regulations Section 1.1234-1(b).

219. *Cruttenden et al. v. Commissioner*, 70 T.C. 191 (1978).

220. *Elsie Weil Estate*, T.C. Memo. 1954-96, filed July 12, 1954.

221. *Tax Information on Investment Income and Expenses*, IRS Publication 550, 1976 edition, page 23.

222. *Edmund F. Ball et al.*, 54 T.C. 1200 (1970).

223. *Whittemore, Jr., et al. v. United States*, 383 F.2d 824 (8th Cir., 1967).

224. *Miscellaneous Deductions and Credits*, IRS Publication 529, 1976 edition, page 3.

225. Tax Reform Act of 1976, Section 204.

226. Revenue Act of 1978, Section 201.

227. Revenue Ruling 55-261, 1955-1 CB 307.

I

254

J

Job evaluation. *See* **Career counseling.**

Job hunting. *See* **Employment, expenses in seeking; Employment-agency fees; Résumés.**

Jockeys. A professional jockey who is required to supply his own uniforms, without possibility of reimbursement, is entitled to deduct the cost.[1]

Joint Federal income tax returns. *See* **Carry-overs; Child-care and disabled-dependent care; Contributions; Medical expenses; Taxes; Tax-option corporations.**

Joint ownership of property. *See* **Interest; Taxes.**

Judgment payment. An individual, while driving his car for business purposes, fatally injured another person. Payment of a court judgment on behalf of the victim, in excess of insurance settlements, was deductible.[2]

A businessperson can deduct the amount of a judgment arising from a suit brought by someone injured by an automobile driven by an employee on company business.[3] (*See also* **Pedestrian, cost of hitting.**)

A professional writer could deduct the amount of a libel judgment rendered against him for something which he had published. (*See also* **Business-related losses.**[4])

J

---

1. Revenue Ruling 70-475, 1970-2 CB 35.
2. *Anderson v. Commissioner*, 81 F.2d 957 (10th Cir., 1936).
3. *Mulgrew Blacktop, Inc. v. United States*, 311 F. Supp. 570 (DC, SD Iowa, 1969).
4. *Cornelius Vanderbilt, Jr.*, T.C. Memo. 1957-235, filed December 23, 1957.

K

Kennel, dog. *See* Transactions entered into for profit.

Keogh plans. *See* Self-employment plans.

Kickbacks. *See* Bribes and kickbacks.

Kidnapper, payment to. *See* Casualties.

Kidney transplant, expenses related to. *See* Medical expenses.

Kiting of checks. *See* Check kiting.

L

Laboratory services. *See* **Medical expenses.**

Labor problems, expenses due to. *See* **Ordinary and necessary business expenses.**

Labor union. *See* **Union dues.**

Laetrile. The cost of laetrile is deductible as medical expense if prescribed by a doctor, provided the product was purchased and used where legally permitted.[1]

Land clearing. *See* **Farmers.**

Land surveys. *See* **Surveys.**

Late payment charge. *See* **Interest.**

Laundry expenses. If the cost of a uniform is deductible as a business expense (*see* **Uniforms**), maintenance costs are likewise deductible.[2] Thus, the cost of cleaning work clothes was a deductible expense to a factory worker whose dirty clothing was a hazard because it sagged and was apt to catch in revolving machinery.[3]

Deductible travel expenses while away from home include cleaning and laundry costs.[4] Such was the situation where a university professor, who took an assignment with a government agency in a distant city, could deduct laundry and certain other expenses during his eleven months of duty there.[5] *See also* **Work clothes.**

Law school, study at. *See* **Advanced degree, study for; Education.**

Lawyers, expenses of. Bar association dues are deductible by an attorney.[6] So are subscriptions to professional publications.[7]

A lawyer could deduct annual depreciation on his professional library.[8] *See also* **Answering service; Bad debts; Conventions; Disbarment, expenses to resist; Education; Expenditures for benefits lasting more than one year; Hearing aid; Hobby losses; Legal fees; Professional negligence.**

Learning disabilities, expenses to cope with. *See* **Education; Medical expenses.**

Lease, cancellation payments to obtain. *See* **Cancellation and forfeiture.**

Leasehold improvements as rent. *See* **Rent.**

Leases, expenses for obtaining. *See* **Expenditures for benefits lasting more than one year.**

Legal fees. Legal expenses which are a necessary factor in producing taxable income normally are deductible. Deduction is allowed where legal assistance is related directly to keeping one's employment, whether in performing duties or in litigating to keep one's job.[9] Legal fees incurred in an effort to get a person rehired by a corporation after his dismissal were deductible.[10]

Attorneys' fees in connection with resisting demotion are deductible.[11]

An individual took an examination for assistant building inspector of the New Jersey Civil Service Commission, and he was certified number one on the list. There was then a vacancy, and his appointment to the post was mandatory. But at the request of the municipality where the vacancy existed, his name was removed. He sued and won reinstatement. His attorneys' fees were deductible. Although he had no "job" in the usual sense, there was a position of status to be protected. It related to the production of future income. He was endeavoring to protect an already existing employment advantage.[12]

A judge could deduct legal fees incurred for the purpose of protecting his employment, where charges brought against him, if unrefuted, would have subjected him to removal from office.[13]

A faculty member brought suit against his employer for damages as a result of statements made about his employment status. Attorney fees in negotiating a settlement were deductible.[14]

Attorneys' fees incurred to protect one's employment are deductible despite the apparently indirect nature of the expenditures in some circumstances. In order to keep stockholders from voting her out of office, the president of a corporation needed all of the votes she could muster. Previously she had transferred stock amounting to about 5 percent of the shares outstanding to trusts for the benefit of her children. As the trustees might vote this stock against her retention of her salaried position, she engaged counsel to arrange for the replacement of the trustees with other persons who would vote on her side. The fees were deductible.[15]

Expenses of resisting his attempted discharge were deductible by a corporate officer.[16] Attorneys' fees paid by the president of a corporation were similarly deductible, as action had been brought against the corporation to remove him from control and management.[17]

An officer and director of a corporation which was involved in various litigation properly deducted the fees of a lawyer he had engaged to advise him as to his liabilities, if any, as an officer and director.[18]

An individual was president and a stockholder of a family corporation in which his father was the dominant person. The father was strongly opposed to his son's expressed intention of marrying a certain woman. The father threatened that if the marriage was consummated (presumably in the legal sense) against his wishes, he would starve his son into submission by cutting his income from all sources. When the son got married anyway, the father discharged him. Then, as the son now was "retired," the father sought to have the corporation reacquire the son's shares under a buy-sell agreement which had been adopted. The purchase price offered was totally inadequate.

The son's mother was loyal to her husband and sought to have the son declared mentally incompetent. The son engaged counsel, and there were thirty instances of litigation in the next four years, including derivative suits by minority shareholders. Typically, the son filed suit against the corporation to require it to pay dividends because he continued to hold some stock. After the father died, an accommodation was reached, and the son regained his presidency, with substantial salary increases. His legal fees were deductible, for, said the court, without the assistance he received from his lawyers, he would not have regained his executive position, which provided the compensation on which he paid substantial income tax. And his stockholdings would have been swept away by an inadequate purchase price. Dividends would have been much smaller if not nonexistent. The fees were to protect his position and his income.[19]

A director could deduct legal fees in defending himself against stockholder allegations of improper conduct.[20]

The United States government brought suit against the directors of a corporation which went into bankruptcy, seeking to recover $250,000 from the directors collectively. The matter was settled. A director could deduct legal fees related to her participation in the matter, for they were in line with the performance of her duties.[21]

An individual could deduct legal fees to defend himself against charges of breach of fiduciary duties owed to a corporation as a director and officer.[22]

A retired businessman properly deducted his attorneys' fees in defending himself in a lawsuit directed against his activities while still a corporate director and officer. The suit had resulted from his business as a director and officer, when he was still engaged in the business.[23]

An individual was secretary-treasurer of a corporation with the responsibility of filing the corporation's Federal income tax returns. He diverted substantial corporate funds to his personal use and did not report these amounts as income on either the corporate or his personal income tax return. As a consequence he was indicted for causing the corporation to file a fraudulent tax return and for filing a false individual return. He employed counsel and incurred legal fees. Inasmuch as his duties included the filing of the corporate tax returns, the legal expenses incurred in his defense for evading the corporation's taxes by filing a false return arose in connection with acts committed by him in his trade or business as an employee of the corporation and were deductible as ordinary and necessary expenses on his own return. He could, moreover, deduct attorneys' fees in connection with his own defense of tax evasion.[24]

Fees paid to an attorney for advice on a person's liability as stockholder, director, and officer were deductible.[25]

In general, attorneys' fees are deductible only if related to the taxpayer's trade or business or to the production of income. Such was the case where an individual paid a lawyer for claims resulting from a business in which he was no longer engaged.[26]

A business could deduct legal fees paid to defend an executive who had been indicted for Federal tax evasion in years before the business was organized. He was indispensable and irreplaceable, and the business could not have continued without him.[27]

The president of a corporation was sued by a purchaser of land on the ground that, as chief executive, he had made fraudulent representations. The president could deduct both the legal fees and any settlement payments he ultimately made as ordinary and necessary expenses related to his business.[28]

Legal expenses in defense of professional acts arising from one's trade or business are deductible.[29] An individual may deduct fees in defense of his own activities in connection with an antitrust suit involving his corporation as long as they are incurred in defending activities related to the business of the corporation and not to personal policies.[30] A broker was put to the cost of defending a lawsuit wherein he was charged with "churning" the portfolio of a trust under his supervision simply for the purpose of increasing his commissions. His expenses incurred in resisting the claim were held to be deductible.[31] An attorney could deduct legal fees related to his successful defense against disbarment.[32] Legal expenses incurred by a physician in defending a suit for malpractice were deductible.[33]

But the person paying the fees must establish that they were related to his trade or business. That could not be done by a physician who had to pay substantial costs arising from a stockholder's suit for mismanagement against a board of directors of which he was a member. This director served solely at the request of the chief stockholder and was not paid for so doing.[34]

A purchasing agent for a municipality could deduct legal fees in answering charges that he had accepted illegal kickbacks in return for the placing of municipal contracts.[35]

An author could deduct legal fees in connection with the negotiation of contracts and the resisting of a libel suit.[36] Legal expenses were allowed in a matter involving alleged violation of the Fair Labor Standards Act.[37]

A physician could deduct fees paid to an attorney to settle any possible civil action which might have arisen out of an altercation with a third party resulting from the doctor's attempt to remove a patient from a hotel.[38]

Deductibility of counsel fees is not limited to instances where the defense was successful, however, because deduction was allowed for the defense of a damage suit based on malpractice or fraud or breach of fiduciary duty without regard to the success of the defense.[39]

Legal fees are deductible in the case of an unsuccessful defense of a criminal action arising from the carrying on of a trade or business. In the words of one decision which the United States Supreme Court affirmed:

So long as the expense arises out of the conduct of the business and is a required outlay it ought to be considered ordinary and necessary. . . . There had been no "governmental declaration" of any "sharply defined" national or state policy of discouraging the hiring of counsel and the incurring of other legal expense in defense of a criminal charge. In fact, it is highly doubtful whether such a public policy could exist in the face of the Sixth Amendment's guaranty of the right to counsel.[40]

Attorneys' fees and related legal expenses paid or incurred in the unsuccessful defense of a prosecution for violation of the Sherman Anti-Trust Act or of claims by the government under the Clayton Act or the Federal False Claims Act, if otherwise deductible as ordinary and necessary expenses, no longer will be denied deduction on the ground that allowance of these deductions would frustrate sharply defined public policy.[41] Attorneys' fees in connection with defense before the National Labor Relations Board are also deductible.[42]

The president of a labor union was allowed to deduct the cost of defending an action arising from the performance of his official duties.[43]

In a community-property state, a wife could deduct half of the legal fees paid by her husband in an unsuccessful defense against charges resulting from his participation in a fraudulent income tax refund scheme.[44]

A realtor could deduct legal fees in defending himself against a charge of tax evasion.[45]

A university professor was allowed to deduct attorneys' fees in connection with his indictment for preparing false tax returns for clients.[46]

Attorneys' fees resulting from resistance to foreclosure suits for alleged nonpayment of bills were deductible.[47]

Attorneys' fees in an action to recover the amount of a bill which a customer or client refused to pay are deductible.[48]

And an executor could deduct the legal expenses involved in collecting his fee.[49]

Deduction was allowed for the fees of attorneys hired to collect a business insurance claim. The expenditure was to collect a sum of money, and the dispute did not concern title to a capital asset or an additional expenditure undertaken to improve or to increase the value of any capital asset then owned by the taxpayer.[50]

Deduction was allowed for attorneys' fees in connection with the recovery of stolen property.[51]

Legal fees in connection with the acquiring of capital assets are not deductible. One law firm was asked by many clients to evaluate tax savings prospectuses, some of which involved real-estate syndications. Eventually the law firm began researching such syndications itself; and if one appeared to be sound, clients were put in touch with the syndicators. Clients who entered upon such investments were charged a fee based upon the time spent on research. Such fees are not deductible, being deemed to be part of the cost of the investment. But any part of the fees which could be shown to be for tax advice or tax planning could be deducted.[52]

Legal expenses in an attempt to recover damages for illegal patent infringement were allowed.[53]

Legal fees paid to collect income are deductible, even though the income collected happens to be capital gain.[54]

Legal fees incurred in connection with a suit to recover interest on a loan are deductible, but that portion of the legal expenses attributed to the collection of the principal of the loan is not.[55]

Although consulting fees pertaining to the acquisition of additional business properties with a life of more than one year are not deductible, deduction is allowed for that part of the fees which relates to problems of administration of property already held.[56]

Lawyers' fees in connection with the leasing of land are not currently deductible, for they must be spread over the life of the lease. Deduction is proper, however, where the efforts to acquire leases were unsuccessful.[57]

Legal fees in the compromising of litigation with a one-time business associate were deductible, even though the suit had been brought against other persons in addition to the taxpayer.[58]

An individual could deduct attorneys' fees paid in an effort to salvage something from the dissolution of a corporation in which he was interested.[59]

An individual was actively engaged in the hotel business. He was a stockholder in a hotel corporation while also serving as its president and manager. When the hotel defaulted on a mortgage obligation, the mortgage holder brought suit against the corporation to enforce his lien. The stockholder engaged attorneys to resist the action. He could deduct the legal fees, although he had not been named in the legal proceedings, as his interests would have been vitally affected by a foreclosure (for example, he might have been removed from control of the corporation).[60]

Persons who had guaranteed a corporation's note held by a bank engaged lawyers when the corporation discontinued operations. The legal fees were deductible as expenditures for the sole purpose of reducing the individuals' liabilities under the guaranty. They and not the corporation would bear the cost of the corporation's impending insolvency.[61]

Fees paid to an attorney to obtain the payor's release from an indemnification contract were deductible.[62] It must be shown that the guarantee arose in connection with a transaction entered into for profit.[63]

Costs of legal work in applying for a Federal income tax ruling were held to be deductible.[64]

Fees paid for consultation and advice in tax matters arising from a divorce settlement are deductible.[65] (See the discussion on legal expenses related to divorce proceedings later under this heading.)

Legal fees incurred in defending the legality of a divorce are not deductible. Expenses for getting tax advice, however, are deductible. Where a lawyer handling divorce litigation shows a breakdown on his bill of how much of it represented the tax problems involved, that portion could be deducted, whereas nothing is deductible in the absence of such an analysis of his charges.[66]

Legal fees paid in connection with a compromise of taxes are deductible.[67]

Fees paid to an attorney in connection with the defense of a criminal indictment for tax evasion are deductible.[68]

Fees paid to a law firm to prepare an estate plan for an individual and his wife are deductible to the extent that the services involve Federal income, estate, and gift tax advice. A proration which includes an itemized list of the services performed and the time spent on each element of the estate planning must therefore be made available, preferably on the lawyer's bill. Without such a proration into the deductible and nondeductible portions of the estate-planning work, the entire deduction may be lost; otherwise, an allowable percentage of the bill is deductible.[69]

Deduction was permitted for attorneys' fees in a case where the fees were to pay for a study of the merits and legal aspects of a plan to rearrange and to reinvest an entire estate. The plan had been submitted by a firm of estate planners.[70]

Amounts received (1) in settlement of claims for compensatory damages because of slander or libel are not income. But amounts received (2) as punitive damages from wrongdoers because of their unlawful conduct are considered as income to the recipients. Legal fees are deductible only in the case of (2), inasmuch as expenses related to tax-exempt income are not taxable and hence the deductions are similarly treated. Where a legal fee is paid and payments are received under both (1) and (2), that proportion of the fee arithmetically allocable to (2) is deductible.[71]

Professional fees in connection with obtaining a ruling from the Internal Revenue Service on the tax consequences of corporate reorganization were deductible in part. That part of the fee which was allocated to ascertain the basis of a shareholder's stock under the proposed reorganization was not deductible.[72]

Deductible attorneys' fees are not restricted to litigation or even to essentially legal work. A business could deduct fees paid to lawyers to work on credit problems.[73]

The expenses incurred in hiring an attorney to determine the advisability of a change in organization are deductible.[74]

Payments to a law firm to study the feasibility of undertaking a complete business organization change were deductible.[75]

Fees paid to a lawyer to facilitate the shipment of undelivered purchases could be deducted.[76]

Payments to an attorney for collecting a business debt were properly deducted.[77]

A creditor was able to take a deduction for his payment to a lawyer for locating a debtor's property.[78]

Legal expenses arising from the defense of a suit for an accounting are deductible.[79] Where a former partner sued a copartner for an accounting of the receipts of the dissolved partnership, the copartner could deduct legal expenses arising from his defense of the suit.[80] Also, a legal expenditure made in defending a suit for an accounting and damages resulting from an alleged patent infringement was deductible as a business expense.[81]

Expenses to resist an injunction sought by a competitor because of alleged unfair methods of competition were deductible.[82]

Ordinarily, attorneys' fees incident to a condemnation action, which is an involuntary conversion, are capital expenditures. But in a case in which the owner of a building held as rental property brought suit for negligence against a salvage company (the negligence had resulted in the destruction of her building) she could deduct the legal fees. They were spent in an attempt to require a negligent party to pay for the loss of an income-producing property; that is, they were expenses in connection with the conservation of property held for the production of income.[83]

A retired noncommissioned officer in the United States Army could deduct legal fees related to successful efforts in increasing his retirement pay.[84] And the cost of court-martial counsel was deductible by a member of the Army Reserve.[85] (*See also* **Armed Forces.**)

A stockholder of a dissolved corporation was permitted to deduct fees paid to a lawyer in contesting Federal taxes imposed against the corporation, which taxes could have been assessed against the stockholder as transferee liability up to the value of the property he had received in the liquidation.[86]

Expenses incurred in "defending or perfecting title to property" are nondeductible. The Internal Revenue Service sought to use this principle to disallow legal expenses of an individual who had inherited corporate stock from her father. A shareholder in the corporation in which her father had been an officer instituted a shareholder's derivative suit claiming that her father and other officers had obtained the stock in breach of their fiduciary duty to the corporation and that the corporation should have been the owner of the shares. This suit was unsuccessful. The daughter could deduct her legal expenses in connection with the conservation of the shares, for she was protecting her income; that is, dividends on these shares. The issue of title was not the main and primary purpose of her expenditures.[87]

An individual owned a minority interest in a brokerage corporation. He lent his stock to the corporation so that it could increase its borrowing capacity. But the corporation then was acquired by another company, which refused to return the stock to the lender. His payments to a lawyer to recover the shares were deductible. Payments to defend title to property are not deductible, but he never had relinquished title when he made the loan. His payments were for the conservation and maintenance of property held for the production of income.[88] When the broker to whom an individual had given funds to buy stock became financially unable to do so, the individual went to an attorney to cancel the agreement and to get back his money. A settlement was reached, under which the customer got back most of his advances in the form of cash and stock. Legal fees are not deductible if incurred in connection with the acquisition of a capital asset, as the stock was. The total dollar value of what the broker paid over was split percentagewise into stock and cash ratios. The legal fee was multiplied by the ratio representing the stock, and the result was nondeductible as a capital expenditure. The legal fee then was multiplied by the ratio representing the cash proportion of the total proceeds, and this was a deductible legal expense.[89]

An individual could deduct the amount of his expenses in recovering his own property which a governmental agency had seized from the custody of a third party.[90]

A dentist could deduct fees paid to an attorney for services in evicting a tenant from space needed by the dentist for a laboratory for her clinic.[91]

Even though defense of title (for example, title of stock) ordinarily is a nondeductible capital expenditure, an individual was permitted to deduct legal fees in defending her title to stock in a suit which was completely without merit and was utterly unjustified.[92]

When the holders of a substantial minority interest in a corporation became dissatisfied with the manner in which it was operated, they sought the advice of counsel. He ascertained that enough stock could be purchased to acquire control. Legal fees for his services were deductible, being for the rendition of advice as to a method by which the shareholders could protect their existing interests in the corporation.[93]

Individuals were permitted to deduct legal fees incurred in an effort to prevent a takeover of their controlling interest in a corporation. Inasmuch as the litigation represented an attempt to conserve property held for the production of income, this was not a capital expenditure.[94]

In another stock case, a minority shareholder of a corporation, who had dissented from a merger, could deduct her legal fees in demanding an appraisal of her stock; under state law she was permitted to be paid for her shares on the basis of an appraisal and she was merely enforcing this right.[95]

The successor to a defunct business could deduct attorneys' fees in resisting taxes imposed against the defunct company, whose liabilities the successor had assumed.[96]

Legal fees relating to the payment of alimony were deductible to the extent that they were concerned with the tax deductibility of such payments.[97]

A contractor could deduct legal fees in connection with damage claims against him for inadequate construction work.[98]

The sole stockholder of a corporation was able to deduct legal expenses in resisting claims that charged him and other officers with conspiracy against the corporation after it had been liquidated, for he could look to no one else for reimbursement.[99]

In general, attorneys' fees in connection with a divorce, separation, or decree for support are not deductible by either the husband or the wife. But the expense of legal advice to determine the tax consequences incident to divorce is deductible in each of these situations:

1. Where at the time of his divorce a taxpayer engaged a law firm specializing in taxation to advise him as to a proposed settlement agreement in which he transferred his interest in certain properties to his wife in exchange for the transfer to him of her interest in other properties and the release by her of marital rights in certain other properties owned by him.

2. Where at the time of his divorce the taxpayer engaged tax counsel to advise him of the Federal income, estate, and gift tax consequences

to him of establishing a trust to make periodic payments to his wife during her life in discharge of his obligations under state law to support her, with a remainder interest in the property to pass to their children at her death.

3. Where for an agreed fee the taxpayer engaged a practitioner to represent him in connection with his divorce, the services including tax counsel concerning the right of the taxpayer to claim the children as dependents for Federal income tax purposes in years subsequent to the divorce. The practitioner's statement allocated his fee between the deductible tax advice and other nondeductible nontax matters.[100]

Any part of an attorney's fee paid in connection with a divorce, legal separation, written separation agreement, or a decree of divorce which is properly attributable to the production or collection of money includible in one spouse's gross income is deductible by that spouse.[101]

Where tax advice is given in a divorce settlement and one spouse pays the fees for the attorneys of both spouses, the payor cannot deduct both fees as legal fees.[102] But he can deduct payments made under a divorce decree or settlement not as legal fees but as alimony. (*See also* **Alimony.**)

Attorneys' fees for collecting alimony which is owing are deductible.[103]

Fees in connection with the enforcement of a promissory note given by the taxpayer's former husband were deductible.[104]

A large investor incurred legal expenses in objecting to Securities and Exchange Commission proceedings for the dissolution of a corporation. These costs were deductible. Inasmuch as the SEC objective was dissolution of the corporation, which could have resulted in the loss of an attractive investment, the expenditures were a necessary expense of carrying on the investor's business of conservation of existing investments. The attorneys' fees were not for the primary purpose of realization of a capital gain. That a gain did in fact result from the contest was a consequence of the investor's unsuccessful effort to hold on to an investment and of being forced to sell; that did not change the nature of the expenditures.[105]

Legal fees paid by shareholders in defending an action instituted by the SEC for the purpose of imposing trusts on the shareholders' stock were deductible as ordinary and necessary expenses for the collection of income. None of the issues in this litigation was of a nature which would require disallowance of the deduction to prevent the frustration of public policy.[106]

An individual who had served as trustee of a trust could deduct the fees of an attorney who represented her in actions against her personally and as a fiduciary in regard to alleged maladministration.[107]

An individual was allowed to deduct legal expenses incurred in reestablishing her right to act as coexecutor of an estate after her disqualification by a state court.[108]

A life tenant properly deducted legal expenses arising from a contested will involving the amount of income payable to her.[109]

Legal fees incurred in settling a claim for an inheritance are not deductible insofar as what is received is characterized as inherited property, for such property is excludible from a beneficiary's gross income and hence the legal fees allocated to obtaining the property are not related to the production or collection of income. But legal fees for any part of what is received representing improperly withheld income are deductible. A proportionate amount of the attorneys' fees attributable to the recovery of such income therefore is deductible.[110]

The remainderman of a trust receives whatever principal is left after the termination of the interest of the life tenant, who receives the trust income for as long as he lives. A remainderman could deduct fees paid to an attorney in order to be kept advised as to how the trust property was being handled, for the remainder interest qualified as property held for the production of income.[111]

A life tenant could deduct the fees of attorneys who investigated the question of whether she was receiving sufficient income from the trust.[112]

Attorneys' fees in acquiring a life estate for an individual, while not deductible in the year of payment, may be spread over the acquirer's life expectancy for tax purposes.[113]

An individual who had acquired property by gift contested the Internal Revenue Service valuation of the property. He was required to pay the Federal gift tax because the donor, who should have done so, had not made this payment. Accordingly, the recipient of the gift was permitted to deduct his cost in keeping the valuation, and his tax upon it, low.[114]

An individual whose professional livelihood was dependent upon the goodwill of the public before whom he appeared as an entertainer could deduct legal fees in undertaking suit against a person who allegedly had libeled him publicly. The primary purpose of the litigation was to vindicate the personal reputation and character of the taxpayer in order to protect his business.[115]

Litigation expenses may be incurred both to defend title and to protect the production of income. In such a situation, there may be an allocation of the expenses between these objectives.[116]

Attorneys' fees incurred in resisting condemnation of business property by a state agency were deductible. The court pointed out that an individual undoubtedly could deduct payments to a watchman to remain on this very property to prevent unlawful entry or misuse by trespassers. And if court action was necessary to oust the trespasser from this property, the fee of a lawyer engaged to eject him would be a business expense. Here the state agency proved to be the trespasser, and legal fees were deductible just as the watchman's wages would have been.[117]

Expenditures made in order to produce a benefit lasting more than one year generally must be capitalized, deduction each year being the amount spread ratably over the period of benefit. But legal fees could be deducted in full when incurred to have declared invalid a municipal ordinance which would have prohibited the operation of the taxpayer's business. Here it was deemed to be immaterial that the benefits gained would last indefinitely.[118]

In one case, the total amount paid for legal fees was deductible even though the advice may have extended for periods beyond the one in which given.[119]

A Federal regulatory agency revoked a taxpayer's license to do business. After legal proceedings, the revocation was cancelled. The Internal Revenue Service claimed that the legal fees were not deductible, being capital expenditures; that is, payments to obtain benefits lasting for more than one year. And expenses in connection with defending or perfecting title are specifically called capital expenditures. Here the fees were deductible, however, not as an expenditure to obtain a capital asset but as an effort to survive, for loss of this license would have put the taxpayer out of business.[120]

A professional writer was permitted to deduct legal fees for obtaining advice on his rights when he appeared before a Congressional investigation.[121]

Where property which had been contributed to a tax-exempt organization was in danger of having a public highway constructed through it, the original donor of the land could deduct the legal fees spent in resisting condemnation as a charitable deduction.[122]

When an attorney's fee covers both business and personal matters, an allocation into the deductible and nondeductible portion is allowed. However, the burden of establishing the percentage to which he is entitled rests on the taxpayer. A yacht was used only to the extent of 5 percent for business purposes. In a case in which a lawyer was engaged to handle an action brought by a member of the crew against the taxpayer for false imprisonment, 5 percent of the fee was the allowable deduction.[123]

Legal fees in connection with an individual's bankruptcy were deductible where his insolvency had resulted from the failure of his retail store.[124]

If legal expenses are necessary in order to authorize a method of medical treatment for mental illness of a dependent, they are amounts paid for the diagnosis, cure, mitigation, or treatment of disease and are deductible as medical expenses.[125] *See also* **Adoption expenses; Contested inheritance, expenses of; Employees; Executives; Expenditures for** payments lasting more than one year; Investors; Group legal-services plan; Tax rulings, expenses in obtaining.

Legal separation. *See* **Alimony.**

Letter-carriers. *See* **Uniforms.**

Liability insurance. *See* **Executives; Insurance.**

Libel award, payment of. *See* **Business-related losses; Judgment payment.**

Libel suits. *See* **Legal fees.**

Library, depreciation on. A depreciation deduction is allowable for a library which is used in the taxpayer's trade or business. *See also* **Depreciation.**[126]

License and franchise costs. *See* **Expenditures for benefits lasting more than one year.**

License maintenance. A dentist could deduct the cost of attending seminars approved by the California Dental Association, which were utilized to satisfy the state's continuing professional education requirements.[127]

Licenses and fees. Licenses and regulatory fees paid by a business venture to a state or local government are deductible.[128]

A county coroner was employed on a part-time basis by a funeral home as a mortician. He could deduct the annual cost of an embalming license. Although this license was not specifically required of him as a coroner, it was helpful to him as a mortician.[129]

Life care. *See* **Retirement homes.**

Life insurance. *See* **Alimony; Compensation; Insurance.**

Life tenant. *See* **Depreciation; Legal fees.**

Lifetime privilege. Fees paid by physicians to acquire lifetime hospital privileges could be amortized and deducted over each doctor's remaining life expectancy.[130]

Limited partner. *See* **Carry-overs.**

Lip reading. *See* **Deaf persons, expenses of.**

Liquidated damages. *See* **Settlement payments.**

Liquor. *See* **Medical expenses; Ordinary and necessary business expenses.**

Little League baseball teams. *See* **Contributions.**

Livestock feed. *See* **Farmers.**

Living expenses. *See* **Employees.**

Loan commitment fees. Where loan commitment fees are paid in order to have capital available for acquisition of a long-lived asset, the fees become part of the cost of the property acquired upon exercising of the right to receive the money. If the right is exercised and the loan is taken out, the commitment fee becomes part of the cost of obtaining the loan and is to be deducted ratably over the term of the loan. But if the right is not exercised, the taxpayer is entitled to a loss deduction when the right expires.[131] *See* **Expenditures for benefits lasting more than one year; Interest.**

Loan discount. A loan discount, where the lender delivers to an individual borrower an amount that is smaller than the face amount of the loan and the difference is the agreed charge for the use of borrowed money, is regarded as interest. If the borrower is on the cash basis, the discount is deductible by him when he actually pays it.[132] *See also* **Discount.**

Loan expenses. Expenses incurred in connection with obtaining a loan are not deductible currently but must be spread over the life of the loan. When the loan has been repaid *prior* to maturity, however, the unamortized expenses may be deducted fully in the year of repayment.[133]

Where a new loan is taken out with the same lender, expenses to repay the first loan are deductible, provided the two loans are separate transactions, with different principal sums and freshly negotiated interest rates.[134] *See also* **Interest.**

Loan fee. *See* **Interest.**

Loan origination fee (points). *See* **Interest.**

Loan premiums. *See* **Investors.**

Loan processing fee. A loan processing fee (points) paid by a mortgagor-borrower as compensation to a lender solely for the use or forbearance of money is deductible as interest.[135] In such a situation, the borrower must establish that the fee was not paid for any specific services that the lender had performed, or had agreed to perform, in connection with the loan.[136]

Loan repayment. *See* **Penalty fee for loan prepayment.**

Loans and advances. A bank director and several of his associates personally advanced funds to the bank's creditors in an effort to relieve the institution, which had been paying them compensation, of certain obligations when its financial situation became precarious. When this advance became uncollectible, he could deduct it as related to his trade or business of being a director.[137] *See also* **Bad debts.**

Lobbying. Expenditures in an effort to influence legislation are not deductible, but deduction is permitted for certain types of activity dealing with legislative matters:

1. Appearances before, or communications with, committees or individual members of Federal, state, or local legislative bodies.

2. Communication of information on legislative matters to business or trade organizations.

3. The portion of membership dues in such organizations which are attributable to the activities mentioned in items 1 and 2.[138]

An individual who operated an advertising and public relations firm could deduct payments made to Democratic Party committees that sought to register Democrats to vote, hopefully resulting in some benefits for persons on the ticket. (No one actually knew for whom the new registrants actually would vote, or whether they would vote.) These payments were not deemed to be political contributions.[139]

An individual was permitted to deduct as a business expense his costs in lobbying for employment benefits for all the state employees of a department in which he worked.[140]

A professional lobbyist acting in a representative capacity may deduct secretarial salaries and other general office expenses incurred in his business. Such also is the case with transportation and travel expenses (including meals and lodgings while traveling away from home overnight), if they are incurred as general business expenses not directly related to lobbying.[141]

A taxpayer was permitted to deduct as business expense a payment to an individual to reimburse him for lobbying expenses incurred on behalf of the taxpayer.[142]

Local benefit taxes. *See* **Taxes.**

Local taxes. *See* **Taxes.**

Long-service award. An employer may deduct the cost, but not in excess of $400, of tangible personal property awarded to an employee by reason of length of service.[143] *See also* **Employee awards.**

Looting, losses from. *See* **Casualties.**

Losses. *See* **Abandonment loss; Agricultural allotment cancellation; Bad debts; Business-related losses; Capital losses; Casualties; Demolition; Employee benefit-plan losses; Family transactions; Gambling losses; Government seizure; Hobby losses; Illegal business activity; Inventory write-downs; Purchase of stock to get assets; Small-business corporation stock; Small-business investment company; Tax-option corporations; Termination of a business; Transactions entered into for profit.**

Low-income housing amortization. *See* **Rehabilitation expenses.**

Low-income rental housing. *See* **Depreciation; Rehabilitation expenses.**

1. Revenue Ruling 78-425, 1978-2 CB 113.
2. Revenue Ruling 70-474, 1970-2 CB 34.
3. *Elwood J. Clark et al.*, T.C. Memo., Docket Nos. 9059, 9135, and 9167, entered April 1, 1964, *aff'd*, 158 F.2d 851 (6th Cir., 1947).
4. Revenue Ruling 63-145, 1963-2 CB 86.
5. IRS Letter Ruling 8121050, February 26, 1981.
6. *Henry P. Keith*, T.C. Memo., Docket No. 108883, entered December 9, 1942.
7. *Julius I. Peyser et al.*, T.C. Memo., Docket Nos. 108711-2, entered March 23, 1943.
8. *Edgar W. Waybright, Sr.*, T.C. Memo., Docket No. 27461, entered June 21, 1951.
9. *Miscellaneous Deductions and Credits*, IRS Publication 529, 1965 edition, page 3.
10. *Stanley V. Waldheim et al.*, 25 T.C. 839 (1956), *aff'd on another issue*, 244 F.2d 1 (7th Cir., 1957).
11. IRS Letter Ruling 8032084, no date given.
12. *Caruso et al. v. United States*, 236 F. Supp. 88 (DC, N.J., 1964).
13. Revenue Ruling 74-394, 1974-2 CB 40.
14. *Wolfson et al. v. Commissioner*, 651 F.2d 122.8 (6th Cir., 1981).
15. *Nidetch v. Commissioner*, T.C. Memo. 1978-313, filed August 11, 1978.
16. *Stanley V. Waldheim et al.*, 25 T.C. 839 (1956), *aff'd on other issues*, 244 F.2d 1 (7th Cir., 1957).
17. *E. L. Potter*, 20 BTA 252 (1930).
18. *Durden v. Paterson*, DC, MD Ala., 1956, *rev'd and rem'd'd on another issue*, 5th Cir., 1957.
19. *Ingalls, Jr., et al. v. Patterson*, 158 F. Supp. 627 (DC, ND Ala., 1958).
20. *Lomas & Nettleton Company v. United States*, 79 F. Supp. 886 (DC, Ct., 1948).
21. *Mrs. A. B. Hurt, Jr., et al.*, 30 BTA 653 (1934).
22. *Hochschild v. Commissioner*, 161 F.2d 817 (2d Cir., 1947).
23. *The First National Bank of Atlanta et al. v. United States*, 202 F. Supp. 702 (DC, ND Ga., 1962).
24. Revenue Ruling 68-662, 1968-2 CB 69.
25. *Patterson v. Durden*, 5th Cir., 1957.
26. *Sylvester G. Miller*, T.C. Memo., Docket No. 111238, entered July 21, 1943.
27. *Jack's Maintenance Contractors, Inc. v. Commissioner*, T.C. Memo. 1981-349, filed July 6, 1981.
28. *Russell et al. v. Riddell*, DC, SD Cal., 1966.
29. SM 4078, V-1 CB 226.
30. *Central Coat, Apron & Linen Service, Inc., v. United States*, 298 F. Supp. 1201 (DC, SD N.Y., 1969).
31. *Ditmars v. Commissioner*, 302 F.2d 481 (2d Cir., 1962).
32. *Morgan S. Kaufman*, 12 T.C. 1114 (1949).
33. SM 4078, V-1 CB 226.
34. *DePinto et al. v. United States*, 585 F.2d 405 (9th Cir., 1978).
35. *Murphy et al. v. Commissioner*, T.C. Memo. 1980-25, filed January 28, 1980.
36. *Cornelius Vanderbilt, Jr.*, T.C. Memo. 1957-235, filed December 23, 1957.
37. IT 3762, 1945 CB 95.
38. *Henry M. Rodney et al.*, 53 T.C. 287 (1969).
39. *Commissioner v. Heininger*, 320 U.S. 467 (1943).
40. *Tellier et al. v. Commissioner*, 342 F.2d 690 (2d Cir., 1965), *aff'd*, 383 U.S. 687 (1966).
41. Revenue Ruling 66-330, 1966-2 CB 44.
42. Revenue Ruling 69-547, 1969-2 CB 24.
43. *James B. Carey et al.*, 56 T.C. 476 (1971).
44. *Johnson v. Commissioner*, 72 T.C. 340 (1979).
45. *Paul Caspers et al.*, 44 T.C. 411 (1965).
46. *Terry et al. v. Commissioner*, T.C. Memo. 1979-284, filed July 26, 1979.
47. *Lena G. Hill*, 8 BTA 1159 (1927).
48. *Kornhauser v. United States*, 276 U.S. 145 (1928).
49. *Buder et al. v. United States*, 235 F. Supp. 479 (DC, ED Mo., 1964), *aff'd on another issue*, 354 F.2d 941 (8th Cir., 1966).
50. *Ticket Office Equipment Co., Inc.*, 20 T.C. 272 (1953), *aff'd on another issue*, 213 F.2d 318 (2d Cir., 1954).
51. *Katherine Ander*, 47 T.C. 592 (1967).
52. IRS Letter Ruling 8108008, October 31, 1980.
53. *Urquhart v. Commissioner*, 215 F.2d 17 (3d Cir., 1954).
54. *Commissioner v. Doering, Jr., et al.*, 335 F.2d 738 (2d Cir., 1964).
55. *John Kurkjian et al.*, 65 T.C. 862 (1976).
56. *Harry Bourg et al.*, T.C. Memo. 1961-95, filed March 31, 1961.
57. *Watson P. Davidson*, 27 BTA 158 (1932).
58. *H. M. Howard*, 22 BTA 375 (1931).
59. *Jay A. Mount*, T.C. Memo., Docket No. 8401, entered November 29, 1946.
60. *E. L. Potter*, 20 BTA 252 (1930).
61. *Mozelle Rushing et al.*, 58 T.C. 996 (1972).

62. *Worrell et al. v. United States*, 269 F. Supp. 897 (DC, SD Ga., 1976), *rev'd and rem'd'd on another issue*, 398 F.2d 427 (5th Cir., 1968).

63. *Imel et al.*, 61 T.C. 318 (1973).

64. Revenue Ruling 67-401, 1967-2 CB 123.

65. *Davis et al. v. United States*, 287 F.2d 168 (Ct. Cl., 1961).

66. *Hall et al. v. United States*, Ct. Cl., 1977.

67. *B. E. Levinstein*, 19 BTA 99 (1930).

68. Revenue Ruling 68-662, 1968-2 CB 69.

69. *Sidney Merians et al.*, 60 T.C. 187 (1973).

70. *Nancy Reynolds Bagley*, 8 T.C. 130 (1947).

71. Revenue Ruling 58-418, 1958-2 CB 18.

72. *Kaufman et al. v. United States*, 227 F. Supp. 807 (DC, WD Mo., 1963).

73. *Meldrum & Fewsmith, Inc.*, 20 T.C. 790 (1953).

74. *Francis A. Parker*, 6 T.C. 974 (1946).

75. *Marcell v. United States*, DC, Vt., 1961.

76. *B. F. Crabbe et al.*, T.C. Memo. 1956-52, filed March 5, 1956.

77. *Richard Croker, Jr.*, 13 BTA 408 (1928).

78. *H. R. MacMillan*, 14 BTA 1367 (1929).

79. *Kornhauser v. United States*, 276 U.S. 145 (1928).

80. Revenue Ruling 72-169, 1972-1 CB 178.

81. *F. Meyer & Brother Co.*, 4 BTA 481 (1926).

82. *Graphic Business Systems, Inc. et al. v. Commissioner*, T.C. Memo. 1982-167, filed March 30, 1982.

83. *United States v. Pate et al.*, 254 F.2d 480 (10th Cir., 1958).

84. IT 3325, 1939-2 CB 151.

85. Revenue Ruling 64-277, 1964-2 CB 55.

86. *National Association of Schools and Publishers, Inc.*, T.C. Memo. Docket No. 16433, entered September 17, 1948.

87. *Sergievsky v. McNamara et al.*, 135 F. Supp. 233 (DC, SD N.Y., 1955).

88. *Cruttenden et al. v. Commissioner*, 644 F.2d 1368 (9th Cir., 1981).

89. *Fred G. Meyer et al.*, T.C. Memo. 1975-349, filed December 8, 1975.

90. *Powell, Jr., et al. v. United States*, 294 F. Supp. 977 (DC, SD, 1969).

91. *Cabieles v. Commissioner*, T.C. Memo. 1982-421, filed July 26, 1982.

92. *Samuel Galewitz et al.*, 50 T.C. 104 (1968).

93. *Straub et al. v. Granger*, 143 F. Supp. 250 (DC, WD Pa., 1956).

94. *Powell, Jr., v. United States*, 294 F. Supp. 977 (DC, SD S.D., 1969).

95. *Stemfel v. United States*, DC, MD Tenn., 1969.

96. *W. D. Haden Company v. United States*, 165 F.2d 588 (5th Cir., 1948).

97. *Carpenter et al. v. United States*, 338 F.2d 366 (Ct. Cl., 1964).

98. *Connecticut Valley Realty Co.*, BTA Memo., Docket No. 62678, entered April 8, 1933.

99. *Russell et al. v. Riddell*, DC, SD Cal., 1966.

100. Revenue Ruling 72-545, 1972-2 CB 179.

101. Regulations Section 1.262-1(b)(7).

102. *United States v. Davis et al.*, 370 U.S. 65 (1962).

103. *Ruth K. Wild*, 42 T.C. 706 (1964).

104. *Wildes et al. v. Commissioner*, T.C. Memo. 1980-298, filed August 6, 1980.

105. *Allied Chemical Corporation v. United States*, 305 F.2d 433 (Ct. Cl., 1962).

106. *Guttmann et al. v. United States*, 181 F. Supp. 290 (DC, WD Pa., 1960).

107. *A. M. Barnhart Estate*, T.C. Memo. 1959-42, filed February 27, 1959.

108. *Annie Laurie Crawford*, 5 T.C. 91 (1945).

109. *Stella Elkins Tyler*, 6 T.C. 135 (1946).

110. *Parker et al. v. United States*, 573 F.2d 42 (Ct. Cl., 1978).

111. *Hobart J. Hendrick*, 35 T.C. 1223 (1961).

112. *Ila B. Mann*, T.C. Memo. 1965-161, filed June 17, 1965.

113. *Marianne Crocker Elrick*, 56 T.C. 903 (1971).

114. *United States v. Bonnyman et al.*, 261 F.2d 885 (6th Cir., 1958).

115. *Paul Draper et al.*, 26 T.C. 201 (1956).

116. *Larchfield Corp. v. United States*, 373 F.2d 159 (2d Cir., 1966).

117. *L. B. Reakirt*, 29 BTA 1296 (1934).

118. Revenue Ruling 78-389, 1978-2 CB 125.

119. *Saks & Co.*, 20 BTA 1151 (1930).

120. *BHA Enterprises, Inc. v. Commissioner*, 74 T.C. 593 (1980).

121. *Waldo Salt*, 18 T.C. 182 (1952).

122. *Archbold v. United States*, 449 F.2d 1120 (Ct. Cl., 1971).

123. *Larrabee et al. v. United States*, DC, CD Cal., 1968.

124. *Cox et al. v. Commissioner*, T.C. Memo. 1981-552, filed September 28, 1981.

125. *Gerstacker v. Commissioner*, 414 F.2d 448 (6th Cir., 1969).

126. *Beaudry v. Commissioner*, 150 F.2d 20 (2d Cir., 1945).

127. *Blair et al. v. Commissioner*, T.C. Memo. 1981-634, filed October 27, 1981.

128. *Tax Guide for Commercial Fishermen.* IRS Publication 595, 1979 Edition, page 15.

129. *Burdett et al. v. Commissioner*, T.C. Memo. 1981-739, filed December 31, 1981.

130. Revenue Ruling 70-171, 1970-1 CB 56.

131. Revenue Ruling 81-160, IRB 1981-23, 12.

132. Revenue Ruling 75-12, 1975-1 CB 62.

133. *Andover Realty Corp.*, 33 T.C. 671 (1960).

134. *Buddy Schoellkopf Products, Inc.*, 65 T.C. 640 (1975).

135. Revenue Ruling 75-187, 1974-1 CB 48.

136. Revenue Ruling 69-188, 1969-1 CB 54.

137. *Stephenson v. Commissioner*, 42 F.2d 348 (8th Cir., 1930).

L

138. IRC Section 162(e).

139. *James P. Keene et al.*, T.C. Memo. 1979-121, filed March 29, 1979.

140. *James M. Jordan*, 60 T.C. 770 (1973).

141. Revenue Ruling 68-414, 1968-2 CB 74.

142. *Republic Petroleum Corporation v. United States*, 397 F. Supp. 900 (DC, ED La., 1975), *aff'd and rev'd on other issues*, 613 F.2d 518 (9th Cir., 1980).

143. IRC Section 274(b)(3)(B), as amended by the Economic Recovery Tax Act of 1981, Section 265.

L

M

Magazines. *See* **Subscriptions to periodicals.**

Mailing expense. *See* **Postage.**

Mailpersons. *See* **Uniforms.**

Maintenance. The operator of a drive-in food stand could deduct the cost of cleaning a canopy and coating it with a plastic finish. Although there was a five-year guarantee for the plastic finish, the work was not done to prolong the life of the building but to maintain it in an efficient operating condition.[1] *See also* **Repairs.**

Maintenance of employment, expenses for. Legal expenses paid by an employee to help to keep his job are deductible.[2] *See also* **Employees; Executives; Legal fees.**

Maintenance payments. *See* **Alimony.**

Malpractice insurance. Premiums on malpractice insurance were deductible by a doctor who could become personally liable for negligence.[3]

Similarly, a corporate executive may deduct the cost of liability insurance protecting him against the financial consequences of his acts.[4]

Malpractice judgments. A physician was permitted to deduct malpractice judgments and attendant costs.[5]

Malpractice suits. *See* **Legal fees.**

Management fees. Fees paid for management and financial advice during negotiations for the acquisition of stock were deductible when the negotiations broke down. Expenditures in connection with the acquisition of stock generally are not deductible. But here no stock or anything else was obtained as a result of the expenditure.[6]

Management survey. *See* **Expenditures for benefits lasting more than one year.**

Managerial skills, improvement of. *See* **Education; Executives.**

Margin account, charges on. Brokers' charges or interest on a margin account are deductible when the broker receives payment.[7]

Marketing services publication, cost of. A securities salesman was permitted to deduct the cost of a marketing services publication.[8]

Marriage tax penalty, deduction for. For taxable years beginning after 1981, two-earner families who file joint Federal income tax returns are allowed a deduction from gross income in arriving at adjusted gross income. This deduction may be claimed even if personal deductions are not itemized. Starting in 1983, the deduction will be 10 percent (1) of $30,000 or (2) the qualified earned income of the spouse with the lower qualified earned income. In 1982 the deduction is 10 percent of the smaller figure. Maximum deduction: $1,500 for taxable years beginning in 1982, $3,000 in later years. If the qualified earned income of each spouse is the same, deduction may be made for either. Qualified earned income is determined without the 30 percent limitation on compensation from a trade or business in which both personal services and capital are material income-producing factors. The term does not include untaxed income, retirement-plan distributions, and deferred compensation.[9]

Massage. Payments for manipulative treatment were deductible when they were incurred at the direction of an osteopathic physician.[10]

Materials used to build a new home, sales tax on. *See* **Taxes.**

Mattress, cost of. The cost was deductible where a mattress was specially made in accordance with a physician's instructions for the purpose of alleviating the pain of a patient's arthritis.[11]

Meals. An individual can deduct the cost of his own meals when he is away from home overnight for business purposes.[12] But when he is in his home community, deduction is limited to the costs for persons that he entertains or with whom he has business discussions.[13]

One businessperson considered it necessary to attend dinners of certain organizations at which there were discussions related to his line of work. Even though these dinner meetings were held in the city where he lived, so that he was not away from home overnight, he could deduct the excess of the cost of the meals over the amounts he normally would have spent had he eaten at home or at a place of his own selection.[14] *See also* **Employees; Entertainment; Overtime meals.**

Meals and lodging as medical expense. *See* **Medical expenses.**

Medical bill of employee injured on job. *See* **Ordinary and necessary business expenses.**

Medical-care plan. *See* **Medical expenses.**

Medical expenses. An individual may deduct expenditures which qualify as "medical expenses" for himself, his spouse, and his dependents as defined in the tax law. The allowable deduction is that amount which exceeds 5 percent of his adjusted gross income.[15] (For an explanation of "adjusted gross income," see the box below.)

Adjusted gross income is the total of all your income less the following deductions:

Expenses that are ordinary and necessary to a trade or business, other than as an employee.

Ordinary and necessary expenses and certain other deductions in connection with property held for producing rents and royalties.

Expenses incurred by an employee in connection with the performance of services as an employee. These may include travel, meals, and lodging away from home, local transportation expenses, moving expenses, and other reimbursed expenses if they otherwise qualify.

Certain losses on sales or exchanges of property.

60 percent of the excess of net long-term capital gain over net short-term capital loss.

Payments by self-employed persons to their own retirement plans.

Allowable depreciation and depletion if you are a life tenant or an income beneficiary of property held in trust or are an heir, legatee, or devisee of an estate if the depreciation or depletion is not deductible by the estate or trust.

One of the tests for a dependency exemption in computing Federal income tax is that the dependent not have gross income in excess of $1,000 for taxable years beginning after 1978. But medical expense of a dependent otherwise qualifying for this treatment may be taken even though the dependent's income is in excess of this figure.[16]

The deduction allowed for medical expenses includes expenditures on behalf of a person whom the taxpayer can claim as a dependent under a multiple-support arrangement, except to the extent that the taxpayer is reimbursed by other relatives or friends.

Multiple-support arrangement. In some cases, no one person contributes more than half the support of a dependent. Instead, two or more persons—any one of whom could claim the individual as a dependent if it were not for the support test—together contribute more than half of the dependent's support.

In such a case, any one of those who individually contribute more than 10 percent of the mutual dependent's support, but *only one* of them, may claim the exemption for the dependent. Each of the others must file a written statement that he will not claim the exemption for that year.

The statements must be filed with the income tax returns of the person who claims the exemption. Form 2120 may be obtained for this purpose from your Internal Revenue Service office.

For example, Fred Johnson and his brothers Harry and Jack each contribute equally to the support of their aged mother. Fred, however, claims his mother as a dependent under a multiple-support arrangement. (See the box above for an explanation of "multiple-support arrangement.") Because Fred claims his mother as a dependent, he also pays her medical bills. He may deduct the expenditure even though he does not contribute more than half of her support. If Harry or Jack reimburse Fred for any part of the medical bills, Fred must reduce his medical deduction by the amount of the reimbursement. And neither Harry nor Jack can deduct their share of the medical bills. Therefore, a deduction is lost for this amount.[17]

Medical care, the basis for the deduction, means amounts paid for the diagnosis, cure, mitigation, treatment, or prevention of disease or for the purpose of affecting any structure or function of the body.[18]

Mental disorders constitute "disease" for purposes of the medical expense deduction.[19] Likewise covered are emotional disorders resulting in learning disabilities.[20]

It is irrelevant that the medical expense is incurred in connection with a self-inflicted condition.[21]

Mental defects or illnesses are covered as well as the physical ones.[22]

A mental disorder is a "disease" for this purpose.[23] Expenses to provide care for the mentally ill in order to keep them from harming themselves or others constitute deductible medical care.[24]

Deductible medical expenses include payments primarily for medical care made for the following:

1. Hospital services.
2. Nursing services (including nurses' board when it is paid by the taxpayer).
3. Medical, laboratory, surgical, dental, and other diagnostic and healing services.
4. X rays.
5. Medicine and drugs to the extent that they exceed 1 percent of the taxpayer's adjusted gross income.[25] For taxable years beginning after December 31, 1982, this 1 percent floor under drug expenditures is eliminated; the only deductible drug expenditures are those for drugs that legally require a prescription or for insulin.[26]
6. Artificial teeth and limbs.
7. Ambulance hire.[27]

Also covered are expenditures for the following:

1. Chiropodists (podiatrists).
2. Chiropractors.
3. Christian Science practitioners.
4. Crutches.
5. Dental care; dentists.
6. Doctors.
7. Guide dogs and their maintenance.
8. Hearing aids and their component parts.
9. Meals and lodging furnished by a hospital or similar institution incident to medical care.
10. Optometrists; eyeglasses. This includes contact lenses.[28]
11. Psychiatrists.
12. Special equipment, such as wheelchairs.
13. Therapy.[29]
14. Vaccines.[30]

Elastic stockings qualified as medical expenses in the case of an elderly woman.[31]

One individual's physician prescribed high-top orthopedic shoes. The right leg was shorter than the left, and the right foot was smaller. The shoes had a lift and a Thomas heel on the right foot. Deduction was allowed for the excess of the cost of the orthopedic shoes over normal ones.[32]

Amounts paid to licensed osteopaths for medical care are deductible.[33]

Deduction is allowed even though the practitioners who perform the services are not required by law to be, or are not (even though required by law), licensed, certified, or otherwise qualified to perform such services.[34]

Drugs and medicines are ordinarily deductible even if they have not been prescribed by a physician. But they must have been obtained legally.[35]

The cost of a sacroiliac belt prescribed by a doctor was deductible.[36]

The cost of a back brace is deductible medical expense.[37]

The cost of high blood pressure medication and a blood sugar test was deductible.[38]

Payments for vitamins, iron supplements, and the like may qualify for medical expenses if prescribed or recommended by a physician.[39]

An important condition which a taxpayer must satisfy if his claim for a medical expense deduction is to succeed is that the expenditure would not have been made if there had been no illness or condition to be alleviated.[40]

On the advice of a dentist, an individual paid for a device for adding fluoride into a home water supply and also paid monthly rentals for the equipment. The fluoridating device was installed for the purpose of adding fluoride at a controlled rate into the home water supply. It was represented that fluoride is a chemical which strengthens the dental enamel as the teeth grow, making them more resistant to decay. The primary and only purpose of the installation and use of the device was to prevent tooth decay. The costs were deductible.[41]

Amounts paid for "medical care" may be deductible even if they were for purposes which do not have the sanction of the medical profession or if the payments are made to persons without medical qualifications. Thus, payments to qualified psychologists are deductible medical expenses even though such persons may be devoid of any medical training.[42]

Payments by a Navajo Indian to tribal medicine men for "sings" were deductible in accordance with traditional medical care in connection with healing ceremonies. (The court had to estimate the amount of payments to one medicine man, as he had died at age 106 before the tax hearing.)[43]

Where a taxpayer was receiving manipulative treatment from an osteopathic physician, payments to masseurs were deductible.[44]

Payments for acupuncture treatments qualify as medical expenses, even if the medical association in the state where the treatment was performed did not sanction this procedure.[45] Whether laetrile is an effective drug or a food is a controversial question in the medical profession. But its cost was deductible as medical expense where a taxpayer's physician has prescribed the use of laetrile for treatment of illness and the prescribed quantity was purchased and used in a locality where sale and use of the product were legal.[46]

Amounts which are paid to practitioners such as psychotherapists for services rendered are categorized as medical care for tax purposes even though those who perform the services are not required to be, or are not (even though required by law), licensed, certified, or otherwise qualified to perform such services. In other words, payments to unlicensed practitioners are deductible if the type and quality of their services are not illegal.[47]

An individual paid amounts to a nonprofessional person who helped conduct "patterning" exercises for his mentally retarded child. One system of therapy consists mainly of coordinated physical manipulation of a child's limbs to stimulate crawling and other normal movements. The manipulation exercises, known as "patterning," are conducted in an attempt to trace the pattern of normal physical movements on undamaged portions of a child's brain, thereby causing the undamaged portions to assume the function of controlling the child's basic movements. After his evaluation at a medical institute, physical therapists designed a therapy program for this child and instructed the parent in the techniques of patterning so the therapy could be continued at home. The physical therapists at the institute periodically reevaluated the program and the child's responses to the therapy. The costs were deductible as medical expense, because the program was given for the purpose of alleviating physical and mental defects.[48]

A taxpayer's son had a congenital defect which resulted in severe malocclusion (an improper meeting of the upper and lower teeth). An orthodontist recommended that the child take lessons in playing the clarinet because he believed the continued practice with the clarinet would serve as therapeutic treatment and alleviate the severe malocclusion of the boy's teeth. The cost of the clarinet and the lessons necessary for the child to play the instrument to the degree required to obtain the benefits of the prescribed treatment were deductible.[49]

The purchase of birth-control pills by a woman for her personal use was a deductible medical expense since she obtained the pills under prescription provided by her physician.[50]

Where, in the opinion of a physician, conception of children would be a serious threat to a woman's health, the cost of oral contraceptives was deductible.[51]

Also, the cost of an operation legally performed on a taxpayer at her own request to render her incapable of having children qualified as a medical expense.[52]

A vasectomy performed at a man's own request in a doctor's office, under local anesthetic, for the purpose of preventing conception is a deductible medical expense.[53]

Expenditures to terminate pregnancy are deductible if the operation is not illegal under state law.[54]

A husband and wife underwent treatment for sexual inadequacy and incompatibility at a hospital which utilized procedures developed by foundation researchers. The couple followed its own doctors' recommendations in taking this treatment. In the opinion of the psychiatrists conducting the program, the probability of a successful treatment was greater if their patients resided at a hotel in the vicinity of the hospital during the two-week duration of the treatment. Fees paid to the psychiatrists were deductible as medical expenses, although deduction was not allowed for payments for hotel accommodations, these not being a part of the institutional medical care.[55] Possibly the couple would have won a complete victory if their doctors had testified that hotel occupancy was an indispensable part of the therapy, the home environment being hostile to their treatment because of the presence of certain other parties.

Payments made in lieu of what would have been a deductible medical expense are allowable as a legal medical expense. For example, a businessman was obliged to be in his office during normal working hours. His wife, a semi-invalid after a series of strokes, was unable to take care of herself, nor was she able to get about without the benefit of a walker. In addition, she had to take certain pills for her ailment three times a day. Rather than put his wife in a nursing home, he engaged a woman to attend to his wife's needs while he was away at work. The hired woman's only duties were to give the wife her medication at prescribed times, to wash and dress her, and to cook her meals. She also prepared evening dinner for the couple and did some light housework and laundry. The hired woman had absolutely no training in nursing nor was she qualified to provide medical care. But the businessman's deduction of her salary, which was labeled "nursing care," was allowed by the court to the extent of 75 percent of what the businessman claimed. The unallowable portion presumably was what had been spent (estimated) for purposes other than caring for the semi-invalid. Because the cost of a nursing home would have been included in medical-care expense, the cost of the hired woman was merely an acceptable substitution.[56]

One person's nonagenarian mother was hospitalized. His doctor advised him that the patient would need nursing care for an extended period and she could receive better care at less expense in accommodations away from the hospital. The son rented a small two-room apartment in the building where he lived, equipped it, engaged full-time nursing care, and kept his mother there under the doctor's care and supervision for seven months, when she left to live with a daughter. Full deduction was allowed, for the expenditures were similar to room rent in a hospital during an acute period of convalescence.[57]

An individual had the problem of having someone take care of his seventy-eight-year-old wife, who had a bad case of arthritis and was unable to take care of herself. Her physician advised the husband to engage a person to take care of her, and so the man had his wife brought to the home of their daughter, who took care of the physical and other needs of her mother. The father paid his daughter $72 a month to take over this care, which he deducted as medical expense. The court allowed one-half of that amount on the ground that some of the assistance was personal and did not relate to physical or mental matters. That the payee was a close relative without medical or nursing training was deemed to be irrelevant.[58]

An individual who was paralyzed from the waist down required someone to perform nursing services. She also did some light housework and cooking for him, and in consideration of her services, he paid $400 in rent on her apartment and an unspecified part of her telephone and water bills. He was allowed to deduct the $400 as a medical expense.[59]

When hospital stays failed to alleviate his wife's mental disorders, an individual obtained her release by agreeing to have a woman reside in his home to look after her. Failing to find anyone available in the vicinity of his farm, he prevailed upon his niece to move in with her seven children, the oldest of whom was fourteen, in return for their board and lodging. He was permitted to deduct the value of such board and lodging as medical expense. The cost of maintaining his wife in a hospital would have been deductible. So was this alternative arrangement. "It is the nature of the services and the purpose for which they are rendered," said the court, "rather than the place where they are performed or the title of the person performing them that determine whether they constitute [deductible] medical care. . . ."[60]

An aged lady who lacked muscular and other physical control engaged an untrained woman to help her to stay clean, to take her medicine, and to move about. This person also cooked for her employer, but she performed no household chores, as a maid was paid to do these things. The court held that the unskilled so-called "nurse" was more than just a companion, and allowed 40 percent of her compensation to be deducted as medical expenses.[61]

An octogenarian had arteriosclerosis (hardening of the arteries) in an advanced stage and his physician felt that "constant attendance of an attendant was necessary," as the senior citizen should not be left alone. For this purpose, the patient engaged a woman with no special qualifications for nursing but who rendered the kind of care which he required. She prepared his meals, helped him about, and changed his bed linen when circumstances required prior to the visits of the regular cleaning person. He claimed her salary as a medical expense. The court allowed a deduction of slightly more than 50 percent of this amount, as some strictly domestic services had been rendered.[62]

When his mentally retarded dependent son was released from a mental hospital, the father was advised by a psychiatrist to have the youth spend a transition period in a private home with these specifications: (1) that it be near the hospital, (2) that there be in the home both a husband and a wife who were emotionally stable, (3) that they accept the doctor's recommendations regarding the manner in which they related to the patient, and (4) that there be no other patients ("rivals") in the house. The costs qualified as medical care, although this care was provided by persons with no medical training at a place without hospital facilities.[63]

A Milwaukee businessman, while on a trip to New York, had an attack of appendicitis and underwent immediate surgery. Seventeen days later he was still too weak to return to Milwaukee. His wound was still draining, but the hospital needed his room. On the recommendation of his doctor, the Milwaukee businessman stayed in a New York hotel until he was recovered enough to return home. His wife changed his bandages, assisted him in walking and bathing, and provided him with such nursing services as he required. The hotel room was a substitute for a hospital room, and the cost was similarly deductible.[64]

A ninety-year-old woman had a brain hemorrhage. She wished to stay at the home of her daughter rather than in a hospital. The daughter agreed to take care of her mother if her brother paid the salary of a clerk to take her (the daughter's) place in her husband's store during her absence. The brother could deduct the store clerk's salary as medical expense, for it avoided a larger, more direct expenditure for the required nursing care.[65]

One taxpayer had a seven-year-old child who was blind. Because of this condition the child was unable to attend school unless someone accompanied him throughout the day and guided him about. An individual, not a dependent, was engaged by the taxpayer solely for the purpose of guiding the child's steps throughout the school day. Inasmuch as the expenditure was to alleviate the child's physical condition of blindness, the expenses constituted medical care.[66]

An individual's three-year-old child suffered lead poisoning, which was traced to paint on the outside of his parents' home. A physician recommended, and the local health authorities required, that the existing lead-based paint be removed from any surfaces reachable by the child, up to four feet in this instance. These costs were deductible medical expenses.[67] Costs of removing paint more than four feet from the ground were regarded as nondeductible, as there was no medical justification for the expense, but the parents seemed assured of future medical expense deductions for the cost of removing an additional couple of inches of paint each year as the child grew. A high-protein diet might increase the deductible medical expense deductions.

An individual was susceptible to nasal infections. His physician advised him to replace the moldy shingles on his house, which had permitted dust and mold irritants to enter freely. The cost of replacement of these shingles with wood clapboard was deductible to the extent that this expenditure exceeded the increase in the value of the house as a result of the new siding.[68]

Medical expense includes amounts paid for oxygen equipment and for oxygen used to alleviate difficulty in breathing due to a heart condition.[69]

The cost of a reclining chair purchased on his doctor's advice by a person with a cardiac condition qualified as medical-care deduction but only under the condition that such "equipment" was not used generally as an article of furniture.[70]

A special mattress and a certain thickness of plywood boards had been prescribed for an individual who had arthritis of the spine. The cost of the mattress and the plywood boards was deductible.[71]

An individual was seriously disabled and required crutches or a leg brace. He was able to drive his automatic shift car to and from work, but it was difficult and dangerous for him to get from his house to his car in the wintertime. He had a garage built as an attached extension of his house. He was allowed to deduct this cost, reduced by the estimated increase in the value of his house resulting from the extension, as a medical expense.[72]

The cost of an iron lung and associated equipment constitutes medical expenses.[73] The maintenance costs of such equipment are also treated as medical expenses.[74]

A medical-expense deduction was allowed when a sick or disabled person acquired an "autoette," or wheelchair that was manually operated or self-propelled. This equipment was primarily used for the alleviation of his sickness or disability and was not merely to provide transportation between his residence and his place of employment.[75] Deductible also is the cost of operating and maintaining the equipment.[76]

The medical expense for equipment used primarily for the alleviation of sickness or disability includes depreciation.[77]

An individual paid fees in connection with plastic surgery that improved the taxpayer's personal appearance. The operation, commonly referred to as face-lifting, involved the elimination or removal of chin and neck sag, jowls, bags under the eyes, and excess tissue under the eyelids. Although the operation was not the result of a recommendation by a physician, the cost was deductible as medical care, the purpose being to affect a structure of the human body.[78]

A twenty-four-year-old man who suffered from premature baldness could deduct the cost of a surgical hair transplant, which was performed by a physician.[79]

The cost of a whirlpool for baths for medical purposes was deductible.[80]

The cost of a wig was deductible when purchased on a physician's orders as necessary to avoid mental upset by a patient who had lost her hair.[81]

Capital expenditures generally are not deductible for Federal income tax purposes. That means those expenditures, for example, which add to the value or prolong the life of some property and whose benefits are expected to extend beyond one taxable year. But in the case of medical expenses, an expenditure which otherwise qualified as medical expense will not be disqualified merely because it is a capital expenditure. If the primary purpose of the expenditure is for the medical care of the taxpayer, his spouse, or his dependent, it may qualify as medical expense. However, the "capital nature" of the asset will be a consideration in determining the amount of medical-expense deduction. If such expenditures are for permanent improvements which increase the value of any property, they will be allowed as medical expense only to the extent they exceed the increase in the value of the property.

Let's take a couple of examples. In the first case, an individual with a heart ailment, on his doctor's advice, installs an elevator in his home so that he will not need to climb stairs. The elevator costs $1,000. A competent appraiser says the elevator increases the value of the home by $700. The $300 difference is medical expense. If the elevator had not increased the value of the home, the entire installation cost would have been medical expense.[82]

In the second case, that is what happened. The physician had advised the installation of an elevator to alleviate an acute coronary insufficiency of a taxpayer's wife. The elevator was regarded as a permanent installation, but in the court's judgment it did not have the effect of increasing the value of the property. The full cost was deductible.[83]

Deduction depends upon showing that installation of a long-lived asset in one's home did not increase the value of the home. As the court noted in one case, "A photograph of the elevator clearly reveals that it does not constitute an improvement and that under no circumstances could it be considered a capital improvement.[84]

An individual paid $3,400 for the installation of a health spa in his home. The spa was installed as the result of advice from a physician that it would be beneficial in relieving pain of severe multiple joint arthritis suffered by this individual's wife. Installation required the removal of landscaping which had been acquired at a cost of $1,900. A medical-expense deduction of $1,500 was allowed, as the court believed that the spa added value to the individual's residence beyond the value of the landscaping removed.[85]

One taxpayer had suffered an attack of coronary thrombosis. She had no bedroom or bath on the first floor of her home. At her physician's urging, to avoid further damage to her heart she had installed along a channeled steel rail attached to the wall side of the stairs to the second floor a collapsible chair propelled by an electrically driven cable. The sales representative of the supplier testified that, to his knowledge, he had never installed such an inclinator in the home of a person of robust health. The contraption added nothing to the value of her home, and the full cost was deductible as medical expense.[86]

A man with a similar medical problem had an electrically operated device installed on his property so that he could make use of the two-thirds of his property which was on a lower level of the slope on which he lived. Deduction was allowed for the amount by which the cost of the installation exceeded the value added to the property by this installation.[87]

Deduction was approved for the cost of an inclinator which was detachable from the residence and had been purchased only for the use of a sick person.[88]

A taxpayer who was physically unable to walk and was confined to a wheelchair purchased an automobile that was specially designed for transporting people confined to wheelchairs. The vehicle had ramps for entry and exit, rear doors that opened 180 degrees, floor locks to hold wheelchairs in place, and a raised roof giving the required headroom to accommodate wheelchair patients. The individual paid $6,000 for this specially designed automobile, whereas the cost of a comparable car of standard design was $4,500. Inasmuch as the car was designed for transporting persons confined to wheelchairs, the cost to the purchaser of the special model was a capital expenditure which was related only to the sick person. So the amount paid which was attributable to the special design, $1,500, was deductible as medical expense.[89]

An individual purchased a van on which he had a wheelchair lift installed solely for the purpose of transporting his son, who had muscular dystrophy, for medical treatment. Only the cost of the wheelchair lift and its installation were deductible medical expenses.[90]

A taxpayer's wife had multiple sclerosis. Special features in a residence built for her were allowed to the extent they did not add to the value of the house. This included a stereo system.[91]

A man was handicapped with arthritis and a severe heart condition. As a result, he could not climb stairs or get into or out of a bathtub. On the advice of his physician he had bathroom plumbing fixtures installed on the first floor of a two-story house he rented. The lessor (an unrelated party) did not assume any of the costs of acquiring or installing the special plumbing fixtures nor did he reduce the rent; the entire costs were paid by the tenant. As the primary purpose of the acquisition and installation of the plumbing fixtures was for medical care, the tenant could deduct them as medical expenses.[92]

Improvements to a person's grounds to enable him to move more freely to get from one part of a split-level home to another were deductible by a handicapped person. "There is nothing in the statute, regulations, or the cases," said the court, "which limits deductions to those which are necessary for eating, sleeping, and using the bathroom."[93]

The expense of a pool may or may not be a medical deduction even though it was installed in the first place because of a physician's recommendation. If the person who installed the pool on his property cannot prove that the installation of the pool alleviated in any way his physical condition, then a deduction is not allowed.[94]

On the other hand, if it can be proved that the pool was installed on the advice of a physician and was used for a specific medical purpose—for example, to provide hydrotherapeutic treatment—and did therefore serve a medical purpose, the deduction is allowed.[95]

Evidence that air-conditioning equipment was for the alleviation of a physical condition was established by allergic reaction to dust, cardiac condition, or special respiratory problems.[96]

After being advised by a physician to provide pure, humid air for his child, who was restricted to her home by cystic fibrosis, an individual installed central air-conditioning in his home. The alternative, air-conditioning the child's room and confining her to this area, was thought by the taxpayer to be psychologically dangerous. The cost of the installation was $1,300; the value of the house was increased $800 according to the authoritative estimates. The $500 difference could be deducted as medical expense.[97] (*See also* **Air-conditioning equipment.**)

To the extent that medical expenses for a year exceed 5 percent of adjusted gross income, there may be question as to *how much* a person may deduct. In most areas of taxation, there *is* a limit: an individual may deduct an expense, such as business salaries or entertainment, only to the extent that they are reasonable. One person, on doctor's orders, installed a swimming pool on his estate in an effort to prevent his wife's spinal disorder from resulting in lifelong paralysis. "Permanent" improvements to a home to alleviate one's physical condition are deductible as medical expenses to the extent that they do not increase the value of the property. Addition of this pool increased the value of the estate, but certainly not by the amount which had been lavished on the pool, housed as it was in a building that matched the palatial residence, with similar hand-cut stone, cedar woodwork, and a cathedral ceiling built without thought of cost. Taxpayers are not limited to choosing the cheapest form of medical treatment available to them, held the court which originally heard the case, and a taxpayer of means can deduct the cost of an extremely expensive private room at a hospital instead of entering a ward. True, an appeals court subsequently ruled, but at the hospital the costs incurred were directly related to medical care. That was not the situation here. The use of ceramic tile and fantastically luxurious appointments for this oversized pool were not necessary for medical care. The first court was directed to find out how much of the cost of the pool could be said to provide a functionally adequate facility for therapeutic purposes. But, admitted the higher court, in the market of potential buyers of luxury residences, a facility of mere functional adequacy might add nothing to the property value of the taxpayer's swank estate, in which event the entire cost of the pool would be deductible medical expense.[98]

It was medically necessary for an individual to increase his breathing power after an operation known as total thorasoplasty. He had a pool constructed that took up most of his backyard. Inasmuch as exercise to improve his breathing was the sole purpose of the pool, it was only four feet deep, with no improvements such as copings or diving boards. He could deduct the difference between the cost of the pool and the amount which it added to the value of his home, as determined by an appraiser engaged for mortgage purposes, taking into account such factors as its shallowness and extraordinarily large space utilization.[99]

An individual had severe osteoarthritis, a steadily degenerative disease affecting the use of the legs, that results in a progressive weakening and decreased functional ability in the knees. His physicians advised him to swim several times a day to slow down the effects of this disease, or he might be limited to moving outside his home with the aid of crutches or a wheelchair. There were no adequate facilities convenient to his residence to pursue the prescribed regular daily swimming exercises. He had built an indoor exercise or "lap" pool attached to his home. The pool was eight feet wide and thirty-six feet long, with depth variations from three feet nine to five feet three. It was equipped with specially designed steps, wider and with a smaller rise than normal, with a steam hydrotherapy device. It had no diving board and was not suited for general recreational use. Deduction was allowed for the costs of the exercise pool and housing structure to the extent that they did not exceed the minimum reasonable costs of a functionally adequate facility and to the degree that these costs exceeded any increase in value of the house.[100]

Deduction was allowed for the cost of a pool installed on the advice of attending physicians by a person whose wife suffered an attack of paralytic poliomyelitis. Here the special design incorporated a ramp to facilitate entry into the pool from a wheelchair.[101]

If the capital expenditure relates to the permanent improvement or betterment of property (such as a swimming pool or an elevator in a home), the cost is not deducted but becomes part of the total cost of the property. Otherwise, it is deductible as medical expense, such as in the case of oxygen equipment used to alleviate difficulty in one's breathing due to a heart condition. Medical expenses are deductible only to the extent that in total they exceed 5 percent of the taxpayer's adjusted gross income for the year. So part of the cost of the oxygen equipment may not have been deducted as medical expense up to the time this equipment subsequently is sold. In that case, for the purpose of determining any gain on the sale of the equipment, its cost is deemed to be increased by amounts not deductible as medical expense because of the 5 percent limitation.[102]

Deduction was allowed for the cost of hand rails installed in one taxpayer's home for the accommodation of a blind, elderly dependent.[103]

Generally, the cost of special food or beverages does not qualify as medical expenses. But in special cases, depending upon the circumstances, such costs are deductible medical expenses. If the prescribed food or beverage is taken solely for the alleviation or treatment of an illness, is in no way a part of the nutritional needs of the patient, and a statement as to the particular facts and as to the food or beverage prescribed is submitted by a physician, the cost may be deductible.[104] "You should attach to your return a statement from your doctor showing that you need the special foods."[105]

An individual had hypoglycemia, a condition caused by abnormally low blood sugar in the body. A specialist prescribed frequent feedings of a high-protein diet as the major treatment. The high-protein supplements were not in addition to her normal nutritional needs and, not being replacements for any of her normal consumption of food, qualified as medical expense. By comparing her food bills with those of her friends without this condition, she estimated that 30 percent of her bills represented the cost of the extra protein needed to treat her disease. This additional cost was deductible.[106]

A professional blood donor could deduct the additional cost of high-protein foods and diet supplements for maintaining the quality of the blood plasma she sold.[107]

In a case where a physician had prescribed that a person take two ounces of whiskey twice a day for relief of angina pain resulting from a coronary disease, the cost of the prescribed amount of whiskey was a deductible medical expense.[108]

An individual had been placed on a salt-free diet regimen by his physician. The additional charge made by restaurants for preparing such meals was deductible as medical expense. And for good measure, the court allowed as additional medical expense the cost of getting to and from such accommodating restaurants.[109]

Artificially ripened, stored, sweetened, colored, and preserved foods, or those which have been canned in phenollined tins, cause allergic reactions in some persons which bring about headaches, nausea, or other severe distress in some bodies. Such was the situation of both a husband and wife, whose physicians testified that the only treatment was to restrict their patients' diets to uncontaminated organic foods. Specially grown, transported, packaged, and marketed foods were used exclusively by the spouses at a cost of approximately double that of ordinary foods. So 50 percent of the cost of the specially processed foods was deductible as medical expense. The organic foods were not a substitute for ordinary nondeductible food but represented an additional cost for the relief of medical infirmities.[110] This decision is not likely to give comfort to people who buy "health foods" for philosophical or other personal reasons.

"Where an item purchased in a special form primarily for the alleviation of a physical defect is one that is used ordinarily for personal, living, and family purposes, the excess of the cost of the special form over the normal cost of the item is an expense for medical care."[111]

An individual who had an allergy to household dust purchased an air cleaner for his home. He also purchased a new vacuum cleaner that functioned as an ordinary household cleaning device and, in addition, purportedly functioned as an air cleaner which would alleviate his allergy. No deduction was allowed for the cost of the vacuum cleaner, as the taxpayer presented no evidence, such as a medical prescription, that the vacuum cleaner had been purchased primarily for medical care.[112] The inference is strong, however, that had there been some form of medical directive, deduction would have been allowed.

Where a taxpayer's four-year-old daughter was severely brain-damaged and incontinent, the cost of disposable diapers was deductible. The child was long past the age when diapers would be a normal living expense. But her physician had stated that she required diapers on a constant basis; because of her skin breakdown potential, absorbent paper-product diapers had to be used.[113]

Expenses paid for transportation primarily for, and essential to, the rendition of medical care are allowed as medical-care expenses. This does not include, however, the cost of any meals or lodging while away from home receiving medical treatment.[114] If a trip is undertaken for medical reasons, it should be ordered, directed, or at least suggested by a physician.[115]

To be deductible, said one court, "there must be some existing or imminent illness or existing physical defect which the trip is supposed to alleviate, cure, or prevent." Desire merely to benefit or to improve the general health is not enough.[116]

Where it was necessary for a mother to move for health reasons to a state where climatic conditions were more friendly to her medical problems, upon the advice of her physician, the family costs of moving the parents and two children were not deductible, but only that part of the total purely attributable to the mother's travel was a deductible medical expense.[117]

Transportation to and from a physician's office, such as taxi fare, is deductible.[118]

The cost of going to a pharmacist is deductible.[119]

Food and lodging expense while traveling to the place of medication and incurred prior to receiving medical treatment is deductible.[120]

Amounts paid for bus, train, or plane fares or ambulance hire are similarly deductible.[121]

Expenses paid for transportation primarily for and essential to the rendition of medical care are expenses paid for medical care. But this does not include the cost of meals and lodging while away from home receiving medical treatment, as where a person goes to a warm climate to alleviate a specific chronic ailment. If a doctor prescribes an operation or other medical care and the taxpayer chooses for personal considerations to travel to another locality, such as a resort area, neither the cost of transportation nor of meals (except where paid as part of a hospital bill) is deductible.[122]

Travel expenses were allowed for a trip from Cleveland to Florida where a physician advised the taxpayer (who was in his seventies) to stay out in the sunlight every day during the winter, in order to get the heat of the sun which would dry up the catarrhal inflammation at the back of his nose and throat and decrease mucous secretion and congestion. Then he probably would not get respiratory and ear infections such as he got in Cleveland in the winter.[123]

Travel expenses were deducted properly when a severely depressed woman, at the recommendation of her psychiatrist, took a trip from her home in New York to visit her sister in California. The doctor thought this trip would be of great therapeutic benefit and might be an alternative to institutionalization.[124.]

An individual's son, while on a vacation cruise at sea, manifested signs of mental disorder and threatened to blow up the ship. He was put ashore by the captain at the nearest port. The father, after having been notified by the ship's doctor that the youth could not travel by himself, flew to where his son had been disembarked. The father could deduct as medical expenses his round-trip costs in flying to Europe to fetch his son, as well as the excess cost of the son's return trip by air over the cost of sea travel.[125]

When a patient uses his own automobile for transportation to and from a physician's office or for other medical-care purposes, a flat figure of nine cents per mile may be claimed in lieu of itemizing expenditures. Parking fees and tolls attributable to such transportation may be deducted as separate items. If the patient prefers, he may deduct his actual substantiated expenditures.[126]

Where a person decides to use this alternative method, the write-off is limited to the first 60,000 miles of a vehicle's life, regardless of the age of the car.[127]

Taxi fares for getting to and from work were deductible where a doctor advised the taxpayer to seek remunerative employment as and for occupational therapy.[128]

If on the basis of competent medical advice it is deemed necessary for the parents of a child at a specially equipped psychiatric therapy center to visit their child, the cost of the transportation for these visits qualifies as the cost of transportation primarily for, and essential to, medical care and is therefore deductible.[129]

The deductions for medical expenses also include the money paid for the transportation of a parent who must accompany a child to get medical care as well as for the transportation expenses of a nurse familiar with injections, medications, and other treatment required by a patient who is traveling to get medical care and is unable to travel alone.[130]

If a wife has been trained to handle emergency situations which ordinarily a nurse would take care of, then the deduction would also apply to the taxpayer's wife.[131] Such was the situation in one case where, on occasions when the wife was unable because of responsibilities to the children to accompany her diabetic husband, he would travel with one of his salesmen who had knowledge enough to supply supportive assistance.[132]

A deduction was allowed for the transportation costs of both a taxpayer and his nurse when in accordance with his physician's advice he went to a predetermined location where the temperature was suitable to his condition (the taxpayer had arteriosclerotic heart disease) and where he would receive proper medical care. Any further travel or sightseeing was precluded by his physician's orders. The nurse was necessary to give him medication and injections which he required continually.[133]

Expenses which were incurred annually by an individual who traveled from Los Angeles to New York and back to consult a physician in whom he had confidence were regarded as medical-care expenses. It was determined that such consultation was the primary purpose for the travel and otherwise the patient would not have made the trip.[134]

Unable to find medical relief from a skin disorder known as vitiligo in the United States, an individual went to see a physician in Europe who had experience in this field. She could deduct her doctor's bills and travel costs as medical expenses. But as she was an outpatient, she could deduct nothing for board and lodgings.[135]

An individual who went to Europe on a freighter for a vacation was afflicted with a severe kidney ailment. He could deduct as medical expense the higher fare for an airline trip back to San Francisco for treatment by a urologist there.[136]

A taxpayer could deduct the cost of transporting his wheelchair-confined daughter, the victim of an incurable disease, to a public high school. Although the child could have received competent instruction at home, the taxpayer's primary purpose in sending her to a public high school was for psychotherapeutic reasons, as explained by her physician, to keep her in school with children of her own age.[137]

The cost of operating an automobile as a means of transportation that is not primarily for, and essential to, medical care is not an allowable medical expense. In other words, Mrs. Martha Hennings, who is confined to a wheelchair but who uses her specially equipped automobile to drive around for shopping and pleasure purposes, cannot claim the operating expense of her automobile as a medical-care deduction when the automobile is used for those purposes.[138]

But driving a car was part of a doctor's prescribed treatment for one patient, and therefore the cost of operating the car was deductible as medical expense. The doctor had advised the taxpayer, who had suffered severe facial mutilations after an accident, to mix with other people. Driving a car was part of the doctor's treatment for her mental state.[139]

A war-wounded veteran could deduct that portion of his automobile expenses in going from home to work at a veterans' hospital which the mileage involved bore to the total miles he drove that year. His physician had recommended employment as therapy for his physical condition, and the use of a car also had been advised for improving the patient's physical health. He testified that after he started to work, he felt much better.[140]

An individual who was almost wholly disabled was advised by her physician to seek remunerative employment as occupational therapy. It was understood that in so doing, she would be obliged to spend sums in excess of what a normal person would have to pay for transportation. She had to travel by taxi, with special demands upon drivers for assistance. Her expenses were deductible in the course of occupational therapy as, and for, medical expenses.[141]

To distinguish when it is allowable to deduct the cost of operating an automobile as medical expense, here are two examples. In the first case, an individual could deduct the cost of driving to work because his physician had recommended that he undertake employment and that he use a car for the improvement of his health. His driving was part of a physician's prescribed treatment and therefore deductible.

In the second case, where the cost of operating an automobile was not deductible, the individual had an artificial limb, and she used her car to get to work as she could not use public transportation. But there was no determination that driving a car was in any way an alleviation of her physical or mental condition, and there was no evidence to support her allegation that she had to work "for physical and occupational therapy," because her physician had not prescribed it.[142]

Special equipment such as hand controls and other devices which are especially adapted to permit the operation of an automobile are medical expenses.[143]

How to get a medical-expense deduction for the cost of installation of a telephone in one's car is suggested by how one person lost such a deduction. He was paralyzed from the waist down. Subsequently he suffered a heart attack. When he was able to drive again, he had his automobile equipped with a mobile telephone service, the cost of which he sought to deduct as medical expense. This, he claimed, was so that he could contact a doctor immediately in the case of another heart attack while on the road. But if that was primarily the reason for installing a car telephone, why did he have this phone number listed in the public directory? That careless act cost him a tax deduction, for the directory listing indicated that social or other nondeductible personal purposes might have been the reason for this printed announcement of where he could be contacted by callers.[144]

An individual was under a psychologist's care in connection with a drug-abuse problem. She lived 350 miles from her psychologist, with whom there was a weekly counseling session by telephone. The cost of the calls was deductible as medical expense.[145]

When an individual is in an institution because his physical condition is such that the availability of medical care in the institution is the principal reason for his presence there, the entire cost of medical care, including meals and lodging at the institution, is deductible as medical expense. For example, medical care includes the entire cost of institutional care for a person who is mentally ill and unsafe when left alone.[146] Likewise included are meals and lodgings provided by a center during treatment for alcoholism or drug addiction.[147]

While ordinary education is not medical care, when the individual is attending a special school for a mentally or physically handicapped individual, his medical care includes the cost of attending such a school. However, the following requirement has to be met: His condition has to be such that the resources of the institution for alleviating such mental or physical handicap are a principal reason for his presence there.[148]

Deduction of the entire cost of a special school for mentally retarded children is allowed. The cost of ordinary education provided by a special school is deductible only if it is incidental to medical care.[149]

For example, a taxpayer's daughter, a girl of average to above-average intelligence, suffered from an emotional disturbance which caused her to withdraw from reality and to be incapable of functioning normally at school. Upon the recommendation of a psychiatrist, the taxpayer enrolled her in a private school which specialized in treating children with problems of this nature and in remedying their learning disabilities. The institution was regarded as a "special school," and the tuition paid by the taxpayer as medical care.[150]

Tuition of an individual's deaf son was deductible at a school where individual attention and opportunity for lip reading was available. The special resources of the school were the primary and principal reason for enrollment, and the enrollment was also at the recommendation of an otologist, a physician who specializes in treatment of diseases of the ear.[151]

A university provided medical and hospital care for its students, contracting such care at a stipulated rate per student and paying actual hospital bills for those students hospitalized during the academic year. The amount of the fee for the health plan, which was included in the tuition charge, was not billed separately. It was ruled that if a student pays a lump-sum fee which includes his education, board, medical care, etc., and no breakdown is made of this fee as to the amount apportioned to medical care, no specific part of the tuition fee is deductible medical care. But if this breakdown is provided or is readily obtainable from the university, that portion of the fee which is allocated to medical care will constitute a proper deduction.[152]

Advised that their two children had learning disabilities, particularly in the area of language arts, the parents sent their son and daughter to a private school, which had a program for children with learning disabilities. Remedial education was provided in the Department of Language Development by a staff of educators who were specially trained to work with learning-disabled children. Tuition at the school was not deductible. But the additional charge for enrollment in the Department of Language Development was held to represent medical expense—namely, payment for services which would alleviate or mitigate mental problems which prevented the children from progressing in a normal educational environment.[153]

A court may make its own estimate as to what part of a flat fee represents the medical expense for a physical examination and minor medical care.[154]

In some cases an allocation is made between deductible medical-care cost and nondeductible personal expenses. One individual sent his son, who had hearing and vision difficulties, to a school for boys of normal intelligence who had failed to achieve success at other schools because of mental or emotional problems. This was not a "special school" for a mentally or physically handicapped person. Nevertheless, an allocation of the school's $10,682.81 fee was allowed between deductible medical-care and nondeductible education expense. That portion of the fee which was in excess of what other private schools in the state were charging was characterized as medical expense.[155]

In another case where an allocation was made, an emotionally disturbed child, who was not retarded or physically handicapped, was sent to a school primarily to receive an education. The desire to obtain psychological and psychiatric help was merely *one* of the reasons for selecting this particular school. The court allowed $3,000 of the $6,270 fee as medical-care expense.[156]

Following the recommendation of his psychiatrist, an individual paid the cost of maintaining his mentally retarded dependent son in a specially selected home to aid his adjustment to life in the community after life in a mental hospital; the expenses were deductible.[157]

Parents could deduct the fees paid to a teacher who was specially trained and qualified to teach remedial reading to mitigate the dyslexic condition of their child. The dyslexia was caused by congenital damage to the brain; the only treatment is training and study skills which permit the student to overcome the results of his handicap.[158]

Fees paid to a special school were deductible, where there was a program designed to educate children with severe learning disabilities so that they could return to a regular school within a few years. Here a taxpayer's minor child had congenital impairment in the areas of visual memory and visual matching. Competent medical authorities who examined the child determined that the learning disabilities were caused by a neurological disorder, and the child's physician recommended special schooling.[159]

Similarly, deduction was allowed for expenses of maintaining a dependent at a "halfway" house which aided individuals in adjusting from life in a mental hospital to life in the community after such people had outgrown the protective environment afforded by psychiatric institutions and for whom further hospitalization was not indicated.[160]

A person could deduct his expenses as an inpatient at a therapeutic center for alcoholism. The center was maintained by a private, nonprofit organization, but patients had to pay for their own care, including room, board, and treatment.[161]

Amounts paid by a taxpayer to maintain a dependent in a therapeutic center for drug addicts, including the cost of the dependent's meals and lodging at the center which were furnished as a necessary incident to his treatment, were expenses for medical care.[162]

Ordinarily, fees paid to a health institute where a taxpayer takes exercise, rubdowns, etc., are nondeductible personal expenses. But fees paid to health institutes may be deductible as medical expenses when such treatments are prescribed by physicians and are substantiated by a doctor's statement that the treatments are necessary for the alleviation of a physical or mental defect or illness of the individual receiving the treatment.[163]

The amount of bills paid to a nursing home, including the costs of meals and lodging, were deductible if the principal reason for a person's presence in the home was the availability of medical care for him.[164]

A professional singer, in order to maintain the vocal standards required by his engagements, was frequently treated by a physician who was a throat specialist. The singer's payments were deductible as medical expense.[165]

Social Security taxes on wages of private nurses providing medical care are deductible as medical expense.[166]

An individual entered a hospital as a patient for a kidney transplant. The donor traveled from a distant city and was entered at the same hospital for the purpose of donating a kidney to the patient. The patient paid all surgical, hospital, and transportation costs of the donor and was entitled to deduct such payments as medical expenses.[167] Ordinarily, only medical expenses for the benefit of the taxpayer, his spouse, or a dependent are deductible by him. But surgical, laboratory, and transportation expenses paid by a donor and a prospective donor in connection with a kidney transplant operation were deductible medical expenses.[168]

Attorneys' fees to collect for the cost of medical care following an accident can be deducted under certain circumstances as medical expenses. To be deductible, they must exceed the amount of insurance recovered or other reimbursement for the expenses.[169]

Legal expenses incident to the establishing and conducting of an individual's guardianship were deductible as medical-care payments in this special case: The taxpayer's physicians had advised that the girl for whom he was a potential guardian should be treated for mental and emotional problems and that the treatment would be successful only if she were institutionalized. The girl refused voluntary institutionalization; therefore, the taxpayer became her legal guardian in order to give the girl the necessary medical treatment which she needed. His expenses incident to the establishment and conduct of the guardianship were therefore deductible.[170]

Legal fees paid by a father in connection with the commitment of his son to a state mental institution are deductible as medical care.[171]

Psychoanalysis is usually deductible as medical expense. However, if an individual undertakes psychoanalysis for the purpose of qualifying for admission to a psychiatric or psychological institution or to equip himself for specialization as an analyst, the costs are nondeductible. The reason, of course, for the nondeduction in the above case is that the psychoanalysis was undertaken not for the purpose of affecting the health of the taxpayer but for qualification of that taxpayer for a job or profession.

But where the psychoanalysis is obtained for the purpose of diagnosis, cure, mitigation, treatment, or prevention of disease or for the purpose of affecting any function of the body, the amount spent for the psychoanalysis is therefore medical care, *even though* a further and additional benefit is obtained as qualification for admission to a school of psychoanalytic training. Here the individual's purposes were dual and of equal weight. That is, to help alleviate his own problems and to qualify for admission to the training curriculum of an institute.[172]

The cost of psychoanalysis may be deductible as an ordinary and necessary business expense in certain situations. A clinical social worker was allowed the deduction upon a showing that what she learned about the nature of her own conflicts made her better able to deal with those of her patients.[173]

The cost of psychoanalysis may be deducted as a business expense if it amounts to education which will maintain or sharpen one's skills in one's present trade or business. So it was in the case of a licensed physician who was on the psychiatric staff of a hospital. His psychoanalysis enabled him to understand aspects of his patients' problems, which permitted him to deal more effectively with these problems.[174]

An internist who underwent psychoanalysis could deduct his costs as educational expenses because he used psychiatric methods in the diagnosis and treatment of his patients' psychosomatic illnesses.[175]

Payment of an ex-wife's medical and dental expenses under a divorce decree or agreement qualifies as deductible alimony if the amounts meet the test of periodic payments and if separate tax returns are filed. (Periodic payments are payments of a fixed amount [for example, $100 per month] for either a fixed or indefinite period. The payments need not be made at regular intervals.) The wife includes the payments in her gross income. But she may claim them as medical expenses if she itemizes her deductions.[176]

If a court decree orders the husband to pay his ex-wife's medical expenses and also the premiums on medical insurance for her, these costs are deductible by him as alimony.[177] Where he is ordered to pay her medical expenses, and he chooses to finance these through medical insurance, the premiums are deductible as alimony.[178]

In a *community property state,* such as California, married couples are treated as though each spouse earned one-half of the income and owned one-half of the property of the other spouse. Where a husband and wife reside in a community property state and file separate income tax returns on a community property basis, amounts paid for the medical care of one spouse out of funds they both own are considered as paid one-half by each spouse. Where expenses are paid out of the separate funds of one spouse, only the spouse paying the medical expense is entitled to the deduction.[179]

Medical care includes amounts paid for insurance covering medical care.[180] Amounts paid for hospitalization insurance for membership in an association furnishing cooperative or so-called free-choice medical service, or for group hospitalization and clinical care, are expenses for medical care.[181] Premiums are deductible for policies covering accidental loss of life, limb, sight, and time.[182] Premiums on disability insurance are medical expenses deductible within the limits applied to medical expenses in general.[183]

An otherwise allowable medical expense is deductible even if paid to a party other than the one who or which provided the services. An individual's medical bills were paid by his parents, who brought along a standard form of promissory note for him to sign on their condolence call. The individual paid off the note to his parents a year later. Medical-expense deduction was allowed in the year his parents paid the physician.[184]

If an individual is fitted with contact lenses by an optometrist, the individual may make an agreement with the optometrist, for a non-refundable fixed amount, to replace the lenses if they become lost or damaged within one year. Or the individual may take out insurance on the lenses, covering replacement if they are lost or damaged within that time. In either event, the payments are deductible as medical expenses.[185]

Medicare A is that part of the Social Security program which covers basic Medicare. An individual may deduct premiums which he voluntarily pays for Medicare A coverage if he is sixty-five or older and is not entitled to Social Security benefits. These premiums are not deductible if they are part of one's Social Security tax.[186]

Premiums voluntarily paid by a person who is sixty-five years of age or older, and not otherwise entitled to Social Security benefits, in order that he may obtain basic Medicare coverage may be deducted as medical expense.[187]

Amounts paid as premiums under Part B of Medicare (Supplementary Medical Insurance for the Aged) are deductible as medical expenses.[188]

A middle-aged couple had an eighteen-year-old daughter who was physically and mentally handicapped to the extent that she was confined to a wheelchair and required continued and expensive care. To ensure that the daughter received appropriate care after their death or at such time as they would otherwise be unable to care for her, they entered into a contract with a private institution specializing in the care and custody of such individuals to provide for her care, supervision, and training in the institution during her lifetime. In order for the girl to be accepted in the institution and receive lifetime care, the institution required payments from the couple of a specified amount, 20 percent payable when the contract was signed, 10 percent within twelve months, an additional 10 percent within twenty-four months, and the final 60 percent when the daughter entered the institution. No portion of the payments was refundable. The fee was not medical insurance, being calculated without regard to contracts for care involving other patients. Under the contract, the obligation to pay was incurred at the time the payments were made, and the payments were made to secure medical services for a dependent, even though these services were not to be performed until a future time, if at all. The payments were deductible as expenses for medical care in the year paid.[189]

A couple living together as common-law man and wife in a state recognizing such marriages can file a joint return on which medical-care expenses can be claimed for a woman's dependent parents.[190]

Preadoption medical expenses are deductible if the child adopted qualifies as a dependent *when* these expenses were paid or incurred. If, for example, the taxpayer reimburses an adoption agency or other persons for medical expenses they paid out under an agreement with the taxpayer, the taxpayer is considered to have paid these expenses, and they are deductible if the adoption has been completed at the time of reimbursement.

On the other hand, if the reimbursements of such expenses are incurred and paid *before* the adoption negotiations, then the taxpayer is not allowed the medical expenses as a deduction.[191]

The above two paragraphs refer both to doctor and to hospital bills.[192]

It is immaterial that the taxpayer's adopted child was not born at the time the medical services were rendered.[193]

One can deduct the cost of a periodic physical examination if it is required by an employer.[194] When an employee is required by his employer to take a physical examination to establish his fitness for his job, the cost of a periodic routine examination is deductible as an ordinary and necessary business expense. But any additional expenses that the employee incurs for medical aid or physical correction so that he can retain his job are deductible medical expenses.[195]

Physicians, psychologists, and others frequently notice that the payments they receive for personal services are in the form of company checks. But when a revenue agent seeking substantiation for such a medical-expense deduction sees these checks, he is likely to disallow the deduction with some witticism such as, "If the company is sick, the company gets the medical deduction." One individual subjected to that treatment won his case by showing that the company checks had been left over from the days when he was still in business for himself and that the bank actually charged the medical-expense payments to his personal account.[196]

Payments were made on a subscription basis to a plan that provided for the storage and locating of personal medical information by a computer data bank. The services thus provided by the computer equipment consisted of storing medical information that was furnished by the personal physician of each subscriber regarding his illness, diseases, allergies, medication prescribed on a long-term basis, vital-sign statistics, blood type, and family medical history. This information could be located and furnished rapidly to any physician who was attending the subscriber, subscribers being furnished with a special identification card to facilitate speedy supplying of data. The subscription cost of this service was deductible as medical expense.[197]

A cruise was organized to provide medical services such as seminars relative to patient-passengers' medical conditions and dietary problems. A group of physicians aboard reviewed each patient's medical records, performing certain tests upon a person as directed by his personal physician or as indicated by the patient's condition, and reporting the result of the patient's medical progress to his physician. The one part of the cruise expense which was deductible was the amount charged for reviewing the patient's medical records, performing tests, and reporting them to his physician.[198]

It is not exactly news that corporate executives sometimes arrange to have personal bills paid by their corporations. If the executive is also a stockholder, the amount of the personal bills paid by the company will be taxed to him as a dividend by an alert Internal Revenue Agent. But if the personal charges that the corporation paid were physicians' and hospital bills, he can deduct the corporate payments as his own medical expenses, which the Internal Revenue Service, in effect, had back-charged to him.[199]

One of the major requirements of allowable medical-care deduction is concrete *proof.* But in at least one case the court was willing to estimate what the allowable medical expenses were. The case was that of an elderly taxpayer who had no such proof, but there was credible testimony that the woman was consulting a physician. Evidently the court believed that a person of her advanced years could be presumed to have physical infirmities, and without concrete proof it allowed an estimate of medical expenses to be deducted.[200]

Poorly documented medical expenses were allowed where the husband was seventy-nine and his wife was seventy-eight, the court deeming the total claimed as not too unreasonable in the light of their advanced ages.[201]

In *any* situation where an individual can show that he had some medical expenses but has little specific proof of the amount he actually spent, the court, if it chooses, may arrive at its own figure for the medical-expense deduction, treating the taxpayer rather severely because the insufficient records resulted from his own doing.[202] So it was where an individual supplying services which alleviated a physical condition required food and lodging at substantial cost, although actual figures were not available.[203]

Medical expenses are deductible in the year actually paid only if an individual pays on a cash basis, as virtually every individual does. But if he charges medical expenses to his credit card, they are deducted in the year the charge is made. It does not matter when he pays the amount charged.[204]

One court made its own finding as to what portion of payments made to a person who performed both individual services and household chores for the taxpayer's mentally ill wife could be considered a medical expense.[205]

Expenses for the medical care of an individual who died are treated for tax purposes as *his* medical expenses if they are paid out of his estate by his executor during the one-year period beginning with the day following his death. But this can be done only if the executor agrees not to deduct the same amount on the Federal estate tax return as a debt of the deceased taxpayer.[206]

If a medical expenditure is deducted on the decedent's final Federal income tax return, it is subject to the regular limitation that medical expenses are deductible only to the extent that in aggregate they exceed 5 percent of adjusted gross income. There is no limitation to the amount that the decedent's estate can deduct. Where part of the medical expenditure is taken on the decedent's income tax return and the remaining portion is shown as a claim against the estate on the Federal estate tax return, the 5 percent portion of the medical expenses not allowable on the income tax return is also not deductible from the gross estate on the estate tax return.[207]

Medical expenses are deductible only to the extent that, in aggregate, they exceed 5 percent of an individual's adjusted gross income for the taxable year. Business expenses are fully deductible. When a businessperson has medical expenses so that he can transact business, the question is whether such expenses are characterized as *medical* or *business*. Here is how the Internal Revenue Service draws the line: (1) A businessperson was paralyzed from the waist down. When he had to go to business meetings out of town, his wife, a friend, or an associate went along to help him negotiate the stairs and narrow doors and to handle baggage. He needed no such assistance in his hometown. (2) Another individual, an amputee, required medication several times a day. When he went out of town on business, his wife, a friend, or an associate helped him to get about, as in (1). But his helper also took care of the replacement and removal of his prosthesis (artificial limb) and the daily administration of his medicine, and was prepared to render assistance should an allergic reaction to his medication occur. In both (1) and (2), the taxpayer did not pay for this aid, but he assumed all travel, meal, and lodging expenses. The expenses of the helper in (1) were deductible as *business expenses,* inasmuch as they were intrinsically a part of the expenses for travel paid by an individual in connection with business services. But the outlays in (2) were *medical expenses,* being more in the nature of payments for nursing services, the services being required *regularly* in the conduct of the individual's personal activities as well as incidentally in his business activities.[208]

Allowance of the medical expenses deduction can depend upon willingness to identify names. An individual considered it to be damaging to the patient to write down the name of a dependent who was getting psychiatric treatment. He was also concerned lest identification of the doctors lead to tax investigation of them. (The record did not indicate *whose* idea that was. Result: loss of the medical-expense deduction for lack of substantiation.)[209]

In order to get the full medical expense deduction to which you are entitled, you must claim all medical and drug reimbursement available to you under your own or your employer's insurance program. The medical deduction for Federal income tax purposes does not include amounts which you could have claimed under an insurance policy.[210] *See also* **Alcoholics Anonymous; Blind persons, expenses of; Credit card, charges to; Cooperative health association membership; Deaf persons, expenses of; Incurable disease; Retirement homes; Weight-loss program; Wigs.**

Medical malpractice insurance. Certain physicians formed a trust for the creation of a statewide medical malpractice insurance risk pool to provide coverage to participants for any medical malpractice claim in excess of a specified amount. Each physician was obliged to arrange for coverage up to that specified amount. Compliance was effected with the state insurance department's rules as to reserves, deficit assessments, and the like. Premiums paid by the physicians could not be recovered by them. Premiums paid for medical malpractice insurance paid by the participating doctors were deductible as ordinary and necessary business expenses.[211]

Medicare, premiums under Part A. *See* **Medical expenses.**

Medicare, premiums under Part B. Premiums on Part B of Medicare Supplemental Medical Insurance for the Aged are deductible.[212] *See also* **Medical expenses.**

Meetings. *See* **Conventions.**

Membership fees. Professional society fees paid by a scientist were deductible.[213] Farm organization dues were held to be a deduction.[214]

Likewise, membership in the Sanitarians' Association by a person engaged in the septic-tank business was deductible.[215]

An actor could deduct his membership fee in the Screen Actors Guild.[216]

An officer in a publishing company could deduct dues paid to the Cleveland Ad Club.[217]

An active real-estate saleswoman could deduct the cost of her multiple listing membership.[218] *See also* **Dues, association.**

Membership in cooperative health association. *See* **Cooperative health association membership.**

Mental illness. *See* **Medical expenses.**

Merchandise shortages. *See* **Inventory write-downs.**

Mileage allowance. In the case of expenses for business travel away from home (other than costs of transportation to and from the destination), the requirements of substantiation are deemed to be met where an employer reimburses his employees for subsistence in an amount not exceeding $44 per day or in lieu of subsistence provides his employees with a *per diem* allowance not to exceed $44 a day. But the employer must reasonably limit payment of such travel expenses to those which are ordinary and necessary in the conduct of his trade or business, and the elements of time, place, and business purpose of the travel must be substantiated. For this purpose the employer must maintain adequate internal audit controls, such as verification by a responsible person other than the employee himself. The term *subsistence* includes, but is not limited to, cleaning and pressing of clothes, and fees and tips for services. Alternatively, in the case of travel away from home, a fixed mileage may be used.[219] This standard mileage rate for the first 15,000 miles of business use of an automobile is twenty cents a mile. The rate is ten cents a mile for business travel in excess of 15,000 miles per year. The rate for an automobile used for charitable, medical, and moving expenses is nine cents a mile. Actual expenses may be used if they are higher— and documentable. Parking fees and tolls may be deducted in addition to either mileage rate.[220] Such an arrangement is not acceptable where an employer and an employee are related parties unless the related parties are other than an individual and his spouse, brothers and sisters, ancestors, or lineal descendants. If the employer is a corporation, the employee may not own, directly or indirectly, more than 10 percent of the stock.[221]

This treatment applies to passenger cars, including vans, pick-ups, and panel trucks.[222]

Interest as well as state and local taxes are deductible in addition to amounts computed under the standard mileage rate.[223]

If an employee or self-employed person uses different automobiles on different occasions for business travel, the aforementioned rates are applied to the *total* business mileage of the cars, as if they were one, to arrive at the deduction. Similarly, if he replaces a car during the year, the total business mileage for the year of both vehicles must be computed as though they were one, in applying the standard mileage rate. This optional method cannot be used for computing the deductible costs of two or more cars used simultaneously, such as in fleet operations.[224]

Where husband and wife use a jointly owned car in their individual businesses, only twenty cents a mile for the first 15,000 miles of annual business travel may be used whether joint or separate returns are filed.[225]

One individual was allowed by his employer to use a company car or his own for the conduct of his duties. If he used his own vehicle, he would be reimbursed by the employer at the rate of ten cents a mile. He could deduct the difference between the optional mileage allowance rate and ten cents a mile as business expense.[226]

Where employer reimbursement exceeded the optional mileage allowance, an employee could deduct the total of actual expenditures in excess of reimbursement where there was credible evidence as to the amount of these expenditures.[227]

Even where an individual has not maintained records as to the number of miles he traveled for business purposes, his employer's records may substantiate the amount. In one case, deduction was allowed to an employee for the excess of the standard mileage rate over the amount of employer reimbursement because the court accepted the employer's records as to the number of business miles traveled by the employee.[228]

If an employer's mileage allowance exceeds twenty cents per mile, the presence of unusual circumstances which account for his excess may constitute grounds for considering the higher allowance as equivalent to substantiation and adequate accounting to the employer. But the Internal Revenue Service refused to allow any more per mile to be used even where local gasoline prices were running above the national average or other normal operating costs had been increasing.[229]

An automobile driven by a taxpayer who uses the optional method of computing costs of an automobile for business purposes is considered to have a useful life of a total of 60,000 miles of business use at the maximum standard mileage rate without reference to the age of the vehicle. After 60,000 miles of business use at the maximum standard mileage rate, the car will be considered fully depreciated.[230]

Where a car used for business purposes is fully depreciated for tax purposes—that is, the amount of its cost already has been deducted over a period of years—the standard mileage deduction is ten cents per mile for all miles of business use.[231]

Interest to finance the purchase of a car is also deductible even where a person uses the standard mileage rate.[232]

The maximum automatic allowable rate can be greater than $44 if the maximum *per diem* rate paid by the government is higher in the locality in which the travel is performed, as may be the case where travel is outside the United States.[233]

Where a person uses a car for the rendering of gratuitous services to a charitable organization, for transportation for medical care, or for allowable moving expenses, nine cents per mile may be claimed as a deduction in lieu of itemizing costs individually.[234]

An Internal Revenue Service district office has given these suggestions for utilizing the optional mileage deduction:

"Business expenses are claimed on Form 2106, moving expenses on Form 3903, but medical and charitable expenses can be claimed only as itemized deductions on Schedule A.

"Records must be kept describing the qualifying miles driven. A simple log in a 3″ × 5″ notebook, listing the date, beginning and ending mileage, and purpose of each tax-deductible trip is sufficient. Using separate pages for business, medical, charitable and moving expense mileage will simplify preparation of the tax return."[235]

A salesman was allowed to deduct business mileage for 26,000 miles in one year. He met his burden of proof by the evidence of his odometer, purchases of gasoline, and the statement of his territory as furnished by his superior.[236] *See also* **Medical expenses; Moving expenses.**

Military officers. *See* **Armed Forces.**

Military-style uniforms. Civilian faculty and staff members of a military school were required to wear at work uniforms of a general "military type," with buttons, insignia of rank, and component designations being established by the school. The cost and maintenance of the uniforms were deductible.[237]

Mine cave-in damage to one's property. The amount of such damage qualifies as a deductible casualty loss.[238]

Mineral leases, cost of acquiring. An individual may pay fees to a person who solicits applicants to participate in the bidding on noncompetitive government oil and gas leases on Federal lands which are held monthly by the United States Interior Department's Bureau of Land Management. The fees may cover such services as: expert geological advice on government lands available for noncompetitive leasing, timely and accurate filing of offers to lease approved lands on behalf of the applicant, and payment of the standard filing fee to the Bureau on behalf of the applicant. If no lease is obtained, the fee is fully deductible.[239] The portion of the fee which is deductible is not limited to amounts expended merely to obtain advice on available leases.[240] If a lease is obtained, the cost is a capital expenditure recoverable through annual depletion deductions.[241]

Mink coat. *See* **Uniforms.**

Minor children, interest paid to. Parents legitimately may deduct interest on loans from minor children.[242] *See also* **Family transactions.**

Minority stockholders, expenses of. *See* **Investors; Legal expenses.**

Minors, expenses for. *See* **Guardians, expenses of.**

Misappropriation losses. *See* **Casualties.**

Misappropriation, restitution for. *See* **Restitution payments.**

Mismanagement charges. An executive could deduct the cost of resisting mismanagement charges. These were business expenses incurred in an effort to maintain his existing employment.[243]

Mismanagement suits, cost of. *See* **Executives.**

Misrepresentation. *See* **Reliance upon misrepresentation.**

Missing property, reward for return. A reward for the return of stolen business property was deductible.[244]

Mortgage, payments on. *See* **Interest.**

Mortgage insurance premiums. *See* **Insurance.**

Mortgage loan fees and commissions. Ordinarily, fees and commissions paid in connection with a mortgage loan are not deductible, for the benefit of the expenditures is expected to last over the period of the loan. The deduction of fees must be spread over the life of the loan. But the unamortized portion of the fees and commissions is deductible in the year the mortgaged property is sold.[245] If the loan is called ahead of time by reason of a default, any unamortized portion of the fee is deductible in the year the property is disposed of.[246] *See also* **Expenditures for benefits lasting more than one year.**

Mortgage payments as alimony. *See* **Alimony.**

Mortgage points. *See* **Interest.**

Mortgage prepayment fees. Fees paid for the privilege of prepaying mortgage indebtedness are deductible by the mortgagee.[247]

Motor fuel tax. Except in the case of vehicles used for business and investment purposes, gasoline, diesel fuel, and other motor fuel taxes are not deductible in taxable years beginning after December 31, 1978.[248]

Moving expenses. The rules as to moving expenses apply both to employees and to self-employed persons. Moving expenses are deductible if an individual can meet these guidelines:

1. The distance between his new place of work and his old principal residence is at least thirty-five miles farther than the distance from his old residence to his old place of work. The distance between the two points is measured by the shortest of the most commonly traveled routes between the two places. A part-time residence or a seasonal one, such as a summer beach cottage, does not qualify for this purpose.

2. The individual must work at least thirty-nine weeks during the twelve-month period immediately after his arrival in the general location of his new principal place of work. It is not necessary that he work for a single employer for that thirty-nine weeks, nor must the weeks be consecutive. It is required only that he be employed on a full-time basis within the same general commuting area. Whether a person is deemed to be employed full-time depends upon the customary practice for a particular occupation. For example, a schoolteacher whose employment contract covers a twelve-month period and who teaches on a full-time basis for more than six months is considered a full-time employee during the entire twelve-month period. A person is considered to be working during any week he is, through no fault of his own, temporarily absent from work because of illness, strikes, shutouts, layoffs, natural disasters, and the like. Self-employed persons must perform services on a full-time basis for at least seventy-eight weeks during the twenty-four-month period immediately after their arrival.

The thirty-nine- or seventy-eight-week test is waived only if an individual is unable to satisfy it because of death, disability, involuntary separation from work (other than for willful misconduct), or transfer for the benefit of the employer after obtaining full-time work in which he reasonably could have been expected to satisfy the test. In the case of married persons filing a joint Federal income tax return, if both spouses are employees either one may satisfy the full-time work requirement. But the weeks worked by the two spouses may not be added to satisfy the requirement.[249]

One individual moved to a distant location in order to accept employment which he expected to last for more than thirty-nine weeks. But his employment was terminated after four months because he was too "outspoken" with his superior. Moving expenses were deductible.[250]

The move must be reasonably close in time and in place to a person's commencement of work at his new principal place of work. In general, moving expenses incurred within one year of the date of commencement of work are considered to be reasonably close in time. Moving expenses incurred after the one-year period may be considered reasonably close if it can be shown that circumstances prevented the taxpayer from incurring the moving expenses within the one-year period allowed. An individual was transferred by his employer from Los Angeles to Chicago in December 1974. He and his wife decided that she would remain in Los Angeles until the youngest child was graduated from high school in June 1977. He thereupon rented a furnished one-room apartment in Chicago and lived there until the family home in Los Angeles was sold, at which time his wife and children moved to join him in their newly purchased home in Chicago. The cost of the 1977 move to Chicago was deductible although he already had been working there for two and a half years.[251]

As stated in brief previously, no deduction is allowed for an individual's moving expenses unless his new principal place of work and his old principal residence is at least thirty-five miles farther than the distance from his old principal residence to his old principal place of work. If he had no former principal place of work, the new principal one must be at least thirty-five miles from the former residence. This latter category includes persons who are seeking full-time employment for the first time or those who are reentering the labor force after a substantial period of unemployment or part-time employment. An out-of-work individual found work elsewhere and moved to a new residence. The distance between his former residence and his former principal place of work was twenty-five miles. The distance between his former residence and his new principal place of work was fifty-five miles, thus exceeding by thirty miles the distance from his former residence to his former principal place of work. He could not deduct the moving expenses. Although his new principal place of work was fifty-five miles from his former residence, it was only thirty miles farther than his former residence was from his former principal place of work and thus did not meet the "at least thirty-five miles farther" minimum-distance condition. He was not seeking full-time employment for the first time, nor was he reentering the labor market after a substantial period of unemployment in view of the fact that he had been unemployed for only two months.[252]

The time periods are measured from the date of an employee's arrival in the general location of his new principal place of work. Generally, date of arrival is the date of the termination of the last trip preceding the person's commencement of work on a regular basis and is not the date his family or household goods and effects arrive.

Where a person has more than one place of employment (for example, he works for more than one employer), his principal place of work is determined by his principal employment. The more important factors are: (1) the total time ordinarily spent at each place, (2) the person's activity at each place, and (3) the relative significance of the financial return from each place.

The term *moving expenses* includes only those expenses which are reasonable under the circumstances of the particular move. They cover the following categories:

1.   Travel expenses, including meals and lodging, for the taxpayer and his family while en route from his old principal residence to his new one. Family, for this purpose, includes any member of one's household other than a tenant or employee, unless he happens to be a genuine dependent whose principal place of abode is the taxpayer's residence. It does not include a servant, chauffeur, nurse, or other attendant who is not a member of the household. The deduction for traveling expenses from the taxpayer's former principal residence to his new residence is allowable for only one trip. But it is not necessary that the taxpayer and all members of his household travel together or at one time. If a person used his own automobile for this transportation, he could compute the transportation expense in either of two ways: (1) by actual out-of-pocket expenses, or (2) at a rate of nine cents a mile.[253] Where (2) is used, the mileage deduction applies only where the vehicle has been used for 60,000 or fewer miles.[254]

2.   The cost of moving household goods, personal effects, and automobiles of the taxpayer and of the members of his household as outlined in item 1 above. This covers the cost of transportation from the old principal residence to the new one, the cost of packing and crating, in-transit storage, and insurance. Storage can include charges for a thirty-day period after the day of the move. If the property was not at the taxpayer's old residence at the time of the move, expenses are deductible only if he owned it at the time, and the cost of transportation does not exceed what the tariff would have been from his old residence.

3.   The cost of house-hunting trips prior to the move from the old principal residence to the new principal place of work, including return after

obtaining work. The deduction is not available, however, unless the taxpayer (1) has obtained employment at a new principal place of work before the trip begins and (2) travels from his former residence to the general area of his principal place of work and returns.

4. The cost of temporary quarters (meals and lodgings are covered) at the new location of work during any period of thirty consecutive days after obtaining work.

5. The cost of selling an old, or acquiring a new, residence are deductible. When a person sells his old home he may deduct real-estate commissions, attorneys' fees, title fees, escrow fees, points or loan-placement charges he is obligated to pay, and state-transfer taxes and similar expenses in connection with the sale or exchange of his former residence. When he buys a new residence, he may deduct attorneys' fees, escrow fees, appraisal fees, title costs, points or loan-placement charges not representing payment or prepayment of interest, and similar charges in connection with the purchase of a new residence.

6. The expenses incurred in obtaining a settlement on the lease to a person's former residence and the expenses incident to the acquisition of a lease for a new residence. This includes payments to a lessor for releasing you from the taxpayer's lease.[255]

The total deduction for items 3, 4, 5, and 6 for taxable years beginning after December 31, 1976, is limited to $3,000 (previously it was $2,500), of which no more than $1,500 (previously it was $1,000) can be for items 3 and 4.[256]

If a husband and wife both commence work at a new principal place of employment within the same general location, the same $2,500 limit applies as if there were only one commencement of work. Where a married couple file separate returns, the overall limitation for these additional living expenses is $1,250 for each, and the house-hunting and temporary living expenses are limited to $500 of the $1,250. In those cases where the moving expenses relate to an individual other than the taxpayer, a deduction is allowed only if the individual lives in both the former and the new residence and is a member of the taxpayer's household.

Deductible moving expenses include members of the household provided that their principal place of residence is the same as that of the taxpayer both before and after the move.[257]

Transportation expenses of the move cover any pets owned by the taxpayer.[258] It is not necessary to consider whether a pet is regarded as a member of the household or a personal effect.

The moving-expense deduction is available in the case of a newly elected member of Congress who moves to Washington.[259]

Certain expenses are not deductible if the purpose is to obtain tax-exempt income, such as interest on money borrowed to purchase or to carry state or municipal bonds. (This is discussed under **Interest.**) Similarly, moving expenses to change jobs from one producing taxable income to one producing tax-exempt income are not deductible. A person moved from the United States to a foreign country, where his income was exempt from U.S. tax because his principal residence and his place of work were abroad. No deduction was allowed for moving expenses.[260] (*See also* **Armed Forces; Expenditures for benefits lasting more than one year.**)

In the case of moves to foreign work locations, the period during which the cost of temporary living arrangements is allowed as deductible moving expenses is ninety days rather than thirty, and the ceiling on those temporary living costs is $4,500 rather than $1,500. Moving expenses include the cost of storing goods while abroad.[261] The $3,000 limitation applicable to the deductability of the aggregate qualified residence sale, purchase, or lease expense in the case of a domestic move is $6,000 in the case of a foreign move.[262] The moving expense deduction permits *bona fide* retirees returning to the United States after working abroad and survivors of Americans who die overseas to deduct the cost of moving back to the United States, subject to the regular limitations.[263] Survivors' expenses must be incurred for a move to the United States from a former residence outside the country that was the residence of the decedent and the survivor. The move must begin within six months after the death of the decedent. A move is also considered to begin when the survivor contracts for the moving of his or her household goods and personal effects to a residence in the United States but only if the move is completed within a reasonable time thereafter.[264]

To deduct expenses for a move outside of the United States, you must be a U.S. citizen or resident who moves to the area of a new place of work outside of the United States or its possessions.[265] To establish your entitlement to this treatment, attach to your Federal income tax return Form 3903F, Foreign Moving Expense Adjustment.[266]

A nonresident alien individual (that is, a person who is not a citizen or resident of the United States) could deduct his expenses of moving here in order to obtain further training and experience in his profession during a one-year stay in this country, when he had full-time employment during this period.[267]

When to take the moving expense deduction can be perplexing because it is not known until a year after the move if one really qualifies. Deduction cannot be taken in the later year when one's entitlement to the deduction becomes known. Deduction thus should be claimed in the year of the move, subject to later verification, although at filing time it is not known whether the deduction is proper. Or an amended return may be filed subsequently for that year.[268] *See also* **Medical expenses.**

Moving expenses: business. In the case of business equipment with an estimated remaining life of one year or more, the cost of moving such as freight is added to the cost of the assets and similarly is subject to annual depreciation write-offs. But where equipment is moved from a taxpayer's plant to another of his locations, or from one part of a plant to another, the cost is a deductible business expense.[269]

Such also is the treatment where a taxpayer pays for the moving of equipment to a new plant.[270] This includes the installation cost of machinery which has been moved.[271] A taxpayer could deduct the cost of removing leasehold improvements he had installed in rented premises, after the lease was terminated.[272]

An individual who maintained an office to carry on his investment activities could deduct his expenses in moving his facilities to a new location.[273]

Multiple-support arrangement. *See* **Medical expenses.**

Municipality, contributions to. *See* **Contributions.**

Musicians. A concert harpist could deduct the cost of instruction from a world-renowned musician, depreciation on her harp, repairs to the instrument, and playing costumes.[274] *See also* **Education; Medical expenses; Uniforms.**

Music lessons as medical expense. *See* **Medical expenses.**

M

1. *Giles Frozen Custard, Inc.,* T.C. Memo. 1970-73, filed March 26, 1970.
2. *Miscellaneous Deductions and Credits,* IRS Publication 529, 1979 edition, page 3.
3. Revenue Ruling 60-365, 1960-2 CB 49.
4. Ibid.
5. IRS Letter Ruling 7816021, January 17, 1978.
6. *United States Freight Company et al. v. United States,* 422 F.2d 887 (1970).
7. Revenue Ruling 70-221, 1970-1 CB 33.
8. *Irving L. Shein,* T.C. Memo., Docket No. 32717, entered February 29, 1952.
9. Economic Recovery Tax Act of 1981, Section 103.
10. *Ford et al. v. Commisssioner,* T.C. Memo. 1979-109, filed March 26, 1979.
11. Revenue Ruling 55-261, 1955-1 CB 307.
12. *Commissioner v. Flowers,* 326 U.S. 465 (1946).
13. *Richard A. Sutter,* 21 T.C. 170 (1953).
14. IRS Letter Ruling 8006004, October 26, 1979.
15. IRC Section 213(a)(1), as amended by the Tax Equity and Fiscal Responsibility Act of 1982, Section 202.
16. Regulations Section 1.213-1(a)(3)(i).

17. *Litchfield v. Commissioner,* 330 F.2d 509 (1st Cir., 1964).
18. IRC Section 213(e)(1).
19. *C. Fink Fischer et al.,* 50 T.C. 164 (1968).
20. *Fay et al. v. Commissioner,* 76 T.C. 408 (1981).
21. Revenue Ruling 72-226, 1972-1 CB 96.
22. Regulations Section 1.213-1(e)(ii).
23. *Walter D. Bye et al.,* T.C. Memo. 1972-57, filed February 29, 1972.
24. Regulations Section 1.213-1(e)(1)(v)(a).
25. Regulations Section 1.213-1(e)(ii).
26. Tax Equity and Fiscal Responsibility Act of 1982, Section 202.
27. Regulations Section 1.213-1(e)(ii).
28. Revenue Ruling 74-429, 1974-2 CB 83.
29. Revenue Ruling 55-261, 1955-1 CB 307.
30. *Protecting Older Americans Against Overpayment of Income Taxes,* Special Committee on Aging, United States Senate, 1976, page 2.
31. *Bessie Cohen,* T.C. Memo., Docket No. 22263, entered January 12, 1951.
32. IRS Letter Ruling 8221118, February 26, 1982.
33. IT 3958, 1943 CB 157.
34. Revenue Ruling 63-91, 1963-1 CB 54.

35. *Medical and Dental Expenses,* IRS Publication 502 (Rev. Nov. 1980), page 2.

36. *Protecting Older Americans Against Overpayment of Income Taxes,* Special Committee on Aging, United States Senate, 1976, page 2.

37. *Owens et al. v. Commissioner,* T.C. Memo. 1977-319, filed September 19, 1977.

38. Ibid.

39. *Blackburn et al. v. Commissioner,* T.C. Memo. 1982-529, filed September 15, 1982.

40. *Joel H. Jacobs,* 62 T.C. 813 (1974).

41. Revenue Ruling 64-267, 1964-2 CB 69.

42. Letter from Assistant Commissioner of Internal Revenue to the author, March 19, 1953, on behalf of the Joint Council of New York State Psychologists on Legislation.

43. *Tso et al. v. Commissioner,* T.C. Memo. 1980-399, filed September 18, 1980.

44. *Ford et al. v. Commissioner,* T.C. Memo. 1979-109, filed March 26, 1979.

45. Revenue Ruling 72-593, 1972-2 CB 180.

46. Revenue Ruling 78-325, 1978-2 CB 124.

47. Revenue Ruling 63-91, 1963-1 CB 54.

48. Revenue Ruling 70-170, 1970-1 CB 51.

49. Revenue Ruling 62-210, 1962-2 CB 89.

50. Revenue Ruling 73-200, 1973-1 CB 140.

51. Revenue Ruling 67-339, 1967-2 CB 126.

52. Revenue Ruling 73-603, 1973-2 CB 76.

53. Revenue Ruling 73-201, 1973-1 CB 140.

54. Revenue Ruling 73-201, 1973-1 CB 140.

55. Revenue Ruling 75-187, 1975-1 CB 92.

56. *John Frier et al.,* T.C. Memo. 1971-84, filed April 26, 1971.

57. *Sidney J. Ungar et al.,* T.C. Memo. 1963-159, filed June 10, 1963.

58. *Myrtle P. Dodge Estate,* T.C. Memo. 1961-346, filed December 27, 1961.

59. *George M. Womack,* T.C. Memo. 1975-232, filed July 15, 1975.

60. *Walter D. Bye et al.,* T.C. Memo. 1972-57, filed February 29, 1972.

61. *Marantz v. Commissioner,* T.C. Memo. 1979-463, filed November 26, 1979.

62. *Estate of Jacob Hentz, Jr.,* T.C. Memo., Docket No. 36704, entered April 6, 1953.

63. Revenue Ruling 69-499, 1969-2 CB 39.

64. *Kelly v. Commissioner,* 440 F.2d 307 (7th Cir., 1971).

65. *Sidney J. Ungar et al.,* T.C. Memo. 1963-159, filed June 10, 1963.

66. Revenue Ruling 64-173, 1964-1 CB (Part 1) 121.

67. Revenue Ruling 79-66, 1979-1 CB 114.

68. IRS Letter Ruling 8112069, September 29, 1980.

69. Revenue Ruling 55-261, 1955-1 CB 307.

70. Revenue Ruling 58-155, 1958-1 CB 156.

71. Revenue Ruling 55-261, 1955-1 CB 307.

72. *Karlis A. Pols et al.,* T.C. Memo. 1965-222, filed August 13, 1965.

73. Revenue Ruling 55-261, 1955-1 CB 307.

74. Revenue Ruling 67-76, 1967-1 CB 70.

75. Revenue Ruling 58-8, 1958-1 CB 154.

76. Revenue Ruling 67-76, 1967-1 CB 70.

77. *Sanford H. Weinzimer et al.,* T.C. Memo. 1958-137, filed July 16, 1958.

78. Revenue Ruling 76-332, 1976-2 CB 81.

79. *Mattes, Jr., v. Commissioner,* 77 T.C. 650 (1981).

80. *Protecting Older Americans Against Overpayment of Income Taxes,* Special Committee on Aging, United States Senate, 1976, page 2.

81. Revenue Ruling 62-189, 1962-2 CB 88.

82. Regulations Section 1.213-1(c)(iii).

83. *Berry et al. v. Wiseman,* 174 F. Supp. 748 (DC, Okla., 1958).

84. *Snellings et al. v. United States,* 149 F. Supp. 825 (DC, ED Va., 1956).

85. *Keen v. Commissioner,* T.C. Memo. 1981-313, filed June 22, 1981.

86. *Hollander v. Commissioner,* 219 F.2d 934 (3d Cir., 1955).

87. *Riach et al. v. Frank,* 302 F.2d 374 (9th Cir., 1962).

88. Revenue Ruling 66-80, 1966-1 CB 57.

89. Revenue Ruling 70-605, 1970-2 CB 209.

90. IRS Letter Ruling 8024169, March 24, 1980.

91. *Oliver et al. v. Commissioner,* 364 F.2d 575 (8th Cir., 1966).

92. Revenue Ruling 70-395, 1970-2 CB 34.

93. *Riach et al. v. Frank,* 302 F.2d 374 (9th Cir., 1962).

94. Revenue Ruling 54-57, 1954-1 CB 67.

95. *Mason et al. v. United States,* DC, Hawaii, 1957.

96. *Raymond Gerard et al.,* 37 T.C. 826 (1962).

97. Ibid.

98. *Ferris et al. v. Commissioner,* 582 F.2d 1112 (7th Cir., 1978).

99. *Polacsek et al. v. Commissioner,* T.C. Memo. 1981-569, filed September 30, 1981.

100. IRS Letter Ruling 8208128, November 27, 1981.

101. *Mason et al. v. United States,* DC, Hawaii, 1957.

102. Revenue Ruling 78-221, 1978-1 CB 75.

103. *Beyers et al. v. Commissioner,* T.C. Memo. 1979-353, filed September 5, 1979.

104. Revenue Ruling 55-261, 1955-1 CB 307.

105. *Medical and Dental Expenses,* IRS Publication 502 (Rev. Nov. 1980), page 2.

106. *Von Kalb v. Commissioner,* T.C. Memo. 1978-366, filed September 13, 1978.

107. *Green v. Commissioner,* 74 T.C. 1229 (1980).

108. *Tax Benefits for Older Americans,* IRS Publication 554, 1976 edition, page 25.

109. *Leo R. Cohn et al.,* 30 T.C. 387 (1962).

110. *Thereon G. Randolph et al.,* 67 T.C. 481 (1976).

111. Revenue Ruling 76-80, 1976-1 CB 71.

112. Ibid.

113. IRS Letter Ruling 8137085, June 17, 1981.

114. Regulations Section 1.213-1(e)(iv).

115. *Arthur D. Foyer et al.*, T.C. Memo. 1960-244, filed November 21, 1960.

116. *Samuel Dobkin*, 15 T.C. 886 (1950).

117. *Lawrence Prem et al.*, T.C. Memo. 1962-157, filed June 26, 1962.

118. Revenue Ruling 55-261, 1955-1 CB 307.

119. *Medical and Dental Expenses.* IRS Publication 502 (Rev. Nov. 1981), page 10.

120. *Montgomery et al. v. Commissioner*, 428 F.2d 243 (6th Cir., 1970).

121. *Your Federal Income Tax*, 1976 edition, page 86.

122. Regulations Section 1.213-1(e)(iv).

123. *William B. Watkins et al.*, T.C. Memo., Docket No. 38010, entered March 31, 1954.

124. *Estate of Benjamin F. Pepper*, T.C. Memo. 1956-167, filed July 17, 1956.

125. IRS Letter Ruling 7813004, December 20, 1977.

126. Revenue Procedure 80-32, 1980-2 CB 767.

127. Revenue Procedure 81-54, IRB 1981-44, 21.

128. *Misfeldt v. Kelm*, DC, Minn., 1952.

129. Revenue Ruling 58-533, 1958-2 CB 108.

130. *Your Federal Income Tax*, 1976 edition, page 86.

131. *Allenberg Cotton Company, Inc., et al. v. United States*, DC, WD Tenn., 1960.

132. *Quinn et al. v. United States*, DC, Md., 1976.

133. Revenue Ruling 58-110, 1958-1 CB 155.

134. *Stanley D. Winderman*, 32 T.C. 1147 (1959).

135. IRS Letter Ruling 8126044, March 31, 1981.

136. *William B. Meister et al.*, T.C. Memo. 1959-202, filed October 26, 1959.

137. Revenue Ruling 65-255, 1965-2 CB 76.

138. Revenue Ruling 55-261, 1955-1 CB 307.

139. *Michael R. Bordas et al.*, T.C. Memo. 1970-97, filed April 27, 1970.

140. *Sanford H. Weinzimer et al.*, T.C. Memo. 1958-137, filed July 16, 1958.

141. *Misfeldt v. Kelm*, DC, Minn., 1952.

142. *Ann Coopersmith*, T.C. Memo. 1971-280, filed November 2, 1971.

143. Revenue Ruling 66-80, 1966-1 CB 57.

144. *George M. Womack*, T.C. Memo. 1975-232, filed July 15, 1975.

145. IRS Letter Ruling 8034087, May 29, 1980.

146. Revenue Ruling 58-481, 1958-2 CB 107.

147. *Medical and Dental Expenses*, IRS Publication 502 (Rev. Nov. 1980), page 1.

148. Regulations Section 1.212-1(e)(1)(v)(a).

149. Revenue Ruling 70-285, 1970-1 CB 52.

150. *Lawrence D. Greisdorf et al.*, 54 T.C. 1684 (1970).

151. *Donovan et al. v. Campbell, Jr.*, DC, ND Texas, 1961.

152. Revenue Ruling 54-457, 1954-1 CB 100.

153. *Fay et al. v. Commissioner*, 76 T.C. 408 (1981).

154. *H. Grant Atkinson, Jr., et al.*, 44 T.C. 39 (1965).

155. *C. Fink Fischer et al.*, 50 T.C. 164 (1968).

156. *Hobart J. Hendrick et al.*, 35 T.C. 1223 (1961).

157. Revenue Ruling 69-499, 1969-2 CB 39.

158. Revenue Ruling 69-607, 1969-2 CB 40.

159. Revenue Ruling 78-340, 1978-2 CB 124.

160. IRS Letter Ruling 7714016, January 10, 1977.

161. Revenue Ruling 73-325, 1973-2 CB 75.

162. Revenue Ruling 72-226, 1972-1 CB 96.

163. Revenue Ruling 55-261, 1955-1 CB 307.

164. *W. B. Counts et al.*, 42 T.C. 755 (1964).

165. Revenue Ruling 71-45, 1971-1 CB 51.

166. Revenue Ruling 57-489, 1957-2 CB 207.

167. Revenue Ruling 68-452, 1968-2 CB 111.

168. Revenue Ruling 73-189, 1973-1 CB 139.

169. *Edward J. Cullen*, T.C. Memo. 1973-158, filed July 23, 1973.

170. *Gerstacker et al. v. Commissioner*, 414 F.2d 548 (6th Cir., 1969).

171. Revenue Ruling 71-281, 1971-2 CB 165.

172. *David E. Starrett et al.*, 41 T.C. 877 (1964).

173. *Voigt et al. v. Commissioner*, 74 T.C. 82 (1980).

174. *Iglesias v. Commissioner*, 76 T.C. 1060 (1981).

175. *John S. Watson*, 31 T.C. 1014 (1959).

176. *Income Tax Deductions for Alimony Payments*, IRS Publication 504, 1976 edition, page 1.

177. *Illene Isaacson et al.*, 58 T.C. 659 (1972).

178. *Lebeau et al. v. Commissioner*, T.C. Memo. 1980-201, filed June 12, 1980.

179. Revenue Ruling 55-479, 1955-2 CB 18.

180. IRC Section 213(e)(1).

181. Regulations Section 1.213-1(e)(4).

182. *Richard H. Marriott et al.*, T.C. Memo. 1966-86, filed April 22, 1966.

183. *J. Robert Andrews et al.*, T.C. Memo. 1970-32, filed February 5, 1970.

184. Revenue Ruling 78-173, 1978-1 CB 73.

185. Revenue Ruling 74-429, 1974-2 CB 83.

186. *Medical and Dental Expenses*, IRS Publication 502 (Rev. Nov. 1979), page 2.

187. Revenue Ruling 79-175, 1979-1 CB 117.

188. *Donovan et al. v. Campbell, Jr.*, DC, ND Texas, 1961.

189. Revenue Ruling 75-303, 1975-2 CB 87.

190. *James M. Ross*, T.C. Memo. 1972-122, filed May 25, 1972.

191. *Your Federal Income Tax*, 1976 edition, page 89.

192. Revenue Ruling 60-255, 1960-2 CB 105.

193. *Kilpatrick et al. v. Commissioner*, 68 T.C. 469 (1970).

194. *Protecting Older Americans Against Overpayment of Income Taxes*, Special Committee on Aging, United States Senate, 1976, page 5.

M

316

195. Revenue Ruling 58-382, 1958-2 CB 59.

196. *John B. Dougherty et al.,* T.C. Memo. 1976-135, filed April 20, 1976.

197. Revenue Ruling 71-282, 1971-1 CB 166.

198. Revenue Ruling 76-79, 1976-1 CB 70.

199. *Estate of W. Favre Slater,* T.C. Memo. 1962-256, filed October 31, 1962.

200. *Bessie Cohen,* T.C. Memo., Docket No. 22263, entered January 12, 1951.

201. *Myrtle P. Dodge Estate,* T.C. Memo. 1961-346, filed December 27, 1961.

202. *Teichner et al. v. Commissioner,* 453 F.2d 944 (2d Cir., 1972).

203. *Walter D. Bye et al.,* T.C. Memo. 1972-57, filed February 29, 1972.

204. *Medical and Dental Expenses,* IRS Publication 502 (Rev. Nov. 1979), page 1.

205. *Walter D. Bye et al.,* T.C. Memo. 1972-57, filed February 29, 1972.

206. IRC Section 213(d).

207. Revenue Ruling 77-357, 1977-2 CB 328.

208. Revenue Ruling 75-317, 1975-2 CB 57.

209. *Dodov et al. v. Commissioner,* T.C. Memo. 1977-362, filed October 11, 1977.

210. IRS Letter Ruling 8102010, September 29, 1980.

211. IRS Letter Ruling 7751021, September 21, 1977.

212. *Donovan et al. v. Campbell, Jr.,* DC, MD Texas, 1961.

213. *Mathilda M. Brooks,* 30 T.C. 1087 (1958), *rev'd on other grounds,* 274 F.2d 96 (9th Cir., 1960).

214. *Farmer's Tax Guide,* 1980 edition, page 12.

215. *Marjorie E. Blackburn et al.,* T.C. Memo. 1973-254, filed November 21, 1973.

216. *Regan v. Commissioner,* T.C. Memo. 1979-340, filed August 28, 1979.

217. *Dan R. Hanna, Jr. et al.,* T.C. Memo., Docket Nos. 25706-7, entered June 6, 1951.

218. *Peck et al. v. Commissioner,* T.C. Memo. 1982-506, filed September 8, 1981.

219. Revenue Ruling 71-412, 1971-1 CB 170.

220. Revenue Ruling 75-433, 1974-2 CB 92, as amended by Revenue Procedure 80-32, I.R.B. 1980-29, 27.

221. Revenue Ruling 71-412, 1971-1 CB 170.

222. Revenue Procedure 80-7, 1980-1 CB 590.

223. Revenue Procedure 77-36, 1977-2 CB 568.

224. Revenue Procedure 80-32, 1980-2 CB 767.

225. Revenue Ruling 77-147, 1977-1 CB 41.

226. IRS Letter Ruling 8004052, October 30, 1979.

227. *Chapman et al. v. Commissioner,* T.C. Memo. 1982-307, filed June 3, 1982.

228. *Lewis v. Commissioner,* T.C. Memo. 1982-12. filed January 12, 1982.

229. IRS Letter Ruling 7736018, June 9, 1977.

230. Revenue Procedure 81-54, I.R.B. 1981-44, 21.

231. Revenue Procedure 75-3, 1975-1 CB 643.

232. Internal Revenue News Release IR-81-121, October 6, 1981.

233. Revenue Procedure 72-508, 1972-2 CB 200.

234. Revenue Procedure 80-32, 1980-2 CB 767.

235. *Tax News, Internal Revenue Service,* [*Hartford*] Connecticut, September 1980, page 2.

236. *Raymond M. Martin et al.,* T.C. Memo. 1968-127, filed June 25, 1968.

237. Revenue Ruling 59-219, 1959-1 CB 46.

238. *Tax Guide for Small Businesses,* 1978 edition, IRS Publication 334, page 111.

239. Revenue Ruling 71-191, 1971-1 CB 77.

240. Revenue Ruling 79-346, 1979-2 CB 84.

241. Revenue Ruling 67-141, 1967-1 CB 153.

242. *Cook et ux. v. United States,* DC, WD La., 1977.

243. *J. LeRoy Nickel, Jr.,* T.C. Memo. 1962-55, filed March 15, 1962.

244. Revenue Ruling 67-98, 1967-1 CB 29.

245. *Herbert Enoch et al.,* 57 T.C. 781 (1972).

246. *Malmstedt et al. v. Commissioner,* 578 F.2d 520 (4th Cir., 1978).

247. Revenue Ruling 57-198, 1957-1 CB 94.

248. Revenue Act of 1978, Section 111.

249. This entire section is based upon IRC Section 217 and the correlative Treasury Regulations, as amended by Revenue Procedure 80-32, 1980-2 CB 767.

250. *Lyle et al. v. Commissioner,* 76 T.C. 668 (1981).

251. Revenue Ruling 78-200, 1978-1 CB 77.

252. Revenue Ruling 78-174, 1978-1 CB 77.

253. *Moving Expenses,* IRS Publication 521 (Rev. Nov. 1980), page 3.

254. Revenue Procedure 81-54, I.R.B. 1981-44, 21.

255. *Moving Expenses,* IRS Publication 521 (Rev. Nov. 1980), page 3.

256. Tax Reform Act of 1976, Section 506.

257. Regulations Section 1.217-2(b)(10)(i).

258. Revenue Ruling 66-305, 1966-2 CB 102.

259. Revenue Ruling 73-468, 1973-2 CB 177.

260. *Hartung et al. v. Commissioner,* 484 F.2d 953 (9th Cir., 1973).

261. Foreign Earned Income Act of 1978, Section 204.

262. TD 7810, filed with the *Federal Register* on February 5, 1982.

263. Foreign Earned Income Act of 1978, Section 204.

264. TD 7810, filed with the *Federal Register* on February 5, 1982.

265. *Moving Expenses,* IRS Publication 521 (Rev. Nov. 1980), page 6.

266. Ibid., page 4.

267. Revenue Ruling 68-308, 1968-1 CB 336.

268. *Della M. Meadows,* 66 T.C. 51 (1976).

269. *Addressograph-Multigraph Corpora-*

M

318

tion et al., T.C. Memo., Docket Nos. 108181-108187, 111395, entered February 5, 1945.

270. *The Fowler & Union Horse Nail Co.,* 16 BTA 1071 (1929).

271. *Briar Hill Collieries,* 12 BTA 500 (1928), *aff'd and rev'd on other issues,* 50 F.2d 277 (6th Cir., 1931).

272. *The Uniharbor Corporation v. United States,* DC, SD Cal., 1958.

273. *Samuel Abrams et al.,* T.C. Memo. 1964-256, filed September 29, 1964.

274. *Elliott v. United States,* 250 F. Supp. 322 (DC, WD N.Y., 1965).

N

Narcotics addiction, treatment for. Amounts spent at a therapeutic center for drug abusers are deductible as medical expenses.[1] *See also* **Medical expenses.**

Nationalization by foreign government. *See* **Casualties; Foreign expropriation losses.**

Naval officers. *See* **Armed Forces.**

Negligence. *See* **Casualties; Repairs.**

Net operating loss. *See* **Carry-overs; Family transactions; Foreign expropriation losses; Tax-option corporations; Unused carry-over of fiduciary.**

Newsletter fund, contributions to. *See* **Contributions.**

Nonbusiness casualties. *See* **Casualties.**

Nonbusiness interest. *See* **Interest.**

Noncompetition agreements. *See* **Expenditures for benefits lasting more than one year.**

Nonprofit organizations, contributions to. *See* **Contributions.**

Nonresident alien, deductions of. If a person is not a citizen of the United States and he does not live in this country, deductions are allowed only if and to the extent that they are connected with income from sources within the United States.[2]

A casualty loss of property not connected with a trade or business is deductible only if the loss is of property located in the United States.[3]

Charitable contributions are deductible only if made to corporations chartered in the United States or to community chests, funds, or foundations created here.[4]

A nonresident alien individual came to the United States for a period of one year in order to acquire additional training and experience in his profession. He was employed full-time while in this country. He could deduct his expenses in moving to the United States.[5]

A nonresident alien individual is entitled to deductions he is eligible for only if he files a true and accurate Federal income tax return.[6]

Normal obsolescence. *See* Depreciation.

Notetaker for deaf student. *See* Deaf persons, expenses of.

Nurses. *See* Employees; Uniforms.

Nurses' registry. A nurse was permitted to deduct payments which she made to a nurses' registry.[7]

Nursing home, contributions to. *See* Contributions.

Nursing home, services at. *See* Medical expenses; Retirement homes.

N

1. Revenue Ruling 72-226, 1972-1 CB 96.
2. IRC Section 873.
3. Regulations Section 1.873-1(c)(2)(ii).
4. Regulations Section 1.873-1(c)(2)(iii).
5. Revenue Ruling 68-308, 1968-1 CB 336.
6. IRC Section 874.
7. *Albert R. McGovern et al.,* 42 T.C. 1148 (1964), *aff'd on another issue,* 6th Cir., 1966.

O

Obesity. *See* **Weight-loss program.**

Obsolescence. The depreciation allowance includes "a reasonable allowance for obsolescence."[1] This refers to *normal* obsolescence, the general awareness that sooner or later most depreciable property will be supplanted by something better.

Abnormal obsolescence, which is the subject of this section, is another matter entirely. Here there is not merely a leisurely period during which something becomes out of date; there is a dramatic occurrence, not necessarily all at once, which requires that an asset be replaced before it wears out physically. If this abnormal obsolescence and the steps to replace the asset take place in a single year, there is a deduction at that time.[2] Generally, recognition of the problem and doing something about it take more than one year.[3] Then the unrecovered cost of the asset is amortized over that period.

Where a taxpayer can show that the useful life of business property is being shortened by reason of *abnormal* obsolescence, a change to a new and shorter life computed in accordance with this showing will be permitted.[4] The customary guidelines do not represent a reasonable allowance where abnormal obsolescence is present.[5]

Obsolescence in this sense may arise from changes in state of the art, shifting of business centers, loss of trade, inadequacy, supersession, prohibitory laws, and other things which, apart from physical deterioration, operate to cause business assets to suffer diminution in value.[6] Where an asset is permanently retired from use in the trade or business or in the production of income but is not disposed of by the taxpayer or physically abandoned, loss is recognized upon an abnormal retirement. This is measured by the excess of the adjusted basis of the asset at the time of retirement over the estimated salvage value or the fair market value at that time if it is higher. A retirement may be abnormal if the asset is withdrawn at an earlier time or under different circumstances than had been contemplated, as, for example, where the property has lost its usefulness suddenly as the result of extraordinary obsolescence.[7]

A manufacturer lost a contract to manufacture shells for the government at the war's end. The full value of specialized machinery for such production (less estimated salvage) was deductible as obsolescence upon the termination date of the contract.[8] Additional buildings that had been constructed for a manufacturer under like circumstances were subject to a write-off.[9]

Changes in the character of a neighborhood and in the activities engaged in it by the taxpayer were bound to make the structures economically valueless because the changes had recast the neighborhood from residential to business. An obsolescence deduction was allowed where the conditions were known to exist at the end of the taxable year, although the buildings were not abandoned until the following year.[10]

A dealer in phonograph records could write off the value of his supply of discs when a radically improved new type made sales of the older version impossible. The dealer was not able to return his obsolete records to the manufacturer.[11]

Usually an asset cannot be written off at one time, even though its obsolescent state is recognized, because it takes time to procure a replacement. So the unrecovered cost of the asset is amortized over the length of time that will be required for that.[12] For example, a retail merchant undertook plans to replace his obsolete store with a modern, up-to-date building; he could amortize his unrecovered cost over a period of time until the new facilities would be available.[13]

Occupational taxes. Taxes imposed at a flat rate by a locality, for the privilege of working there, are deductible.[14]

Office at home. An individual is not permitted to deduct any expenses attributable to the use of his home for business purposes except to the extent attributable to the portion of his home that is used exclusively on a regular basis:

1. As his principal place of business: A person can have a principal place of business for each separate trade or business in which he is engaged; and if the regular-and-exclusive-use tests are met, he can deduct the expenses attributable to using his home as the principal place of business for one or more such businesses.[15] A hospital-employed physician was allowed to deduct expenses for a home office which was the principal place of business for his real-estate rental business.[16] Where a person operated a home-repair service from his own house, performing his services in the residences of his customers, his home was his business headquarters, and he could deduct his expenses in going from there to the premises of his customers.[17]

2. As a place of business which is used by patients, clients, or customers in meeting or dealing with the taxpayer in the normal course of his trade or business: An account executive was required by his corporation to discuss matters with customers who wanted to consult with him. Many of these persons could not call him from their places of employment during the daytime, or they were away during regular hours so he could

not call them. He spent about two hours every weekday night on the phone in a room he set aside solely for this purpose. He was not allowed a home-office deduction. But the court indicated it might be allowed if he showed he had sustained major expenses in setting aside this room for phone calls.[18]

3. In the case of a separate structure which is not attached to his dwelling unit (such as an artist's studio in a structure which is not attached to his residence), in connection with his trade or business. An individual operates a small floral shop in town. Behind his house is a greenhouse where he grows the plants that he sells in his home. The greenhouse is used exclusively and regularly in his business. The expenses for this building are eligible for the deduction.[19]

The use of of a portion of a home (such as a den) for both personal purposes and for the purposes of carrying on a trade or business does not meet the exclusive-use test.[20]

An exception to the exclusive-use test is provided where the home is the sole fixed location of a trade or business which consists of selling products at retail or wholesale and the taxpayer regularly uses a separately identifiable portion of the residence for inventory storage.[21]

In the case of an employee, the business use of his home must be for the convenience of his employer. There must be evidence that the employer required an employee to maintain an office in his home.[22]

An individual was employed on a full-time basis by a cosmetics manufacturer as a sales-account manager. She sold merchandise to the manufacturer's customers and developed new accounts in an assigned sales territory. Her employer did not furnish her with an office, so she worked from her home, where she kept her business records and made contacts with customers and with her employer. (1) For part of the year she used areas of her living room as an office, both business and living furniture being located in that room. (2) Later in the year, she moved into a two-bedroom apartment, using one of these rooms exclusively as an office. In the case of (1), she could deduct nothing. In the case of (2), she could deduct that part of her rent and utilities allocated on a space basis as a business expense.[23]

A psychiatrist claimed a deduction for expenses of a home office. The Internal Revenue Service insisted that he produce his appointment books so that some of the patients named there could be contacted for the purpose of verifying the claimed use of a home office. In view of the confidentiality of the physician-patient relationship and the stigma widely attached to persons known to be getting psychiatric aid, the court allowed the deduction without disclosure of the patients' surnames.[24]

Overruling the Internal Revenue Service, a court has stated that one's home office need not be an entire room or some portion or area of a room physically separated in some manner from the dwelling portion of the house or apartment. Even if there is no wall, partition, or other physical demarcation to separate, for example, the office portion of a room from the bedroom portion, the facts may persuade a court that a home office exists for deduction purposes.[25]

Where business use of a home is properly made, the deduction cannot exceed the gross income derived from this use over the permissible deduction, reduced by otherwise allowable expenses, such as taxes, mortgage interest, and casualty losses for the business use.[26]

There is a limitation on the amount that a person may deduct for expenses attributable to the business use of a residence, which in many cases is the rental of a vacation home, if his use of the residence for personal purposes during a taxable year exceeds the greater of fourteen days or 10 percent of the number of days during the taxable year for which the unit is rented at a fair rental. A person is not considered to be using a home for personal purposes if it is rented to anyone (including a relative) at a fair rental for use as his principal residence. A special rule applies in the case of reciprocal ownership and rental arrangements.[27] Nor is the space considered to be used for personal purposes on any day when the taxpayer is engaged in repair and maintenance on a substantially full-time basis, merely because other individuals who are on the premises on that day are not so engaged.[28]

A professional writer could deduct the expenses of maintaining an office in his home where this was his sole place of work. "His only office," said the court, "was that which he kept in his home. Clearly, he could not have engaged in this trade or business without this home office. [His] use of this office was not 'purely a matter of personal convenience, comfort, or economy.' "[29]

Where an office is maintained in one's home, as in the case of a professional writer, she could deduct depreciation and the cost of utilities and insurance on the basis of the amount of space used for business and for personal purposes, such as one-eighth of the total where she used for writing purposes one of the eight equally-sized rooms.[30]

Depreciation is deductible only on that part of the home used for business or rental purposes.[31]

Deduction is allowed for the cost of painting and repairing rooms that are used only for business purposes. An allocated portion of the cost of painting the outside of the home or repairing a roof with comparable materials is allowed.[32]

Where deduction is allowed for home-office expense, there is the problem of proof of (1) what part of the residence was used for business purposes, and (2) the portion of the time when it was so used. One individual lived and conducted some business in her home. She argued that as one-half of the space in her apartment was used as a home office, one-half of the rent was deductible. But inasmuch as she also was employed outside of her home for forty hours a week and was in addition a night student, the court held that one-half of the time that the apartment was actually in use should be allocated to business purposes. Half of the half of the expenses of the home in which she conducted business thus was deductible, or one-fourth of the rent she paid.[33]

The same rule applies in order to determine the proper deduction by an individual who uses a portion of his home in connection with activities for the production of income, such as an investor.[34]

Any space which cannot be pinpointed for business use is mathematically excluded. Requirements of her job obliged one employee to work overtime, which she did in her home rather than at her employer's place of business. The total space in her one-room apartment amounted to 185 square feet. Office appurtenances occupied 120 square feet. Of the remaining 65 square feet, 36 were covered by her bed and dressing table. The unallocated 29 square feet were deemed to have been used for unspecified personal purposes. Annual rent for the apartment was divided by 185. This figure, multiplied by 120, was the home-office deduction.[35]

Where an allocation of home-office expenses is still permitted as a business deduction, water and sewer charges are includable in the amount to be allocated.[36]

Photographs may be a useful mechanism to show what proportion of an apartment or home is used for business purposes.[37]

A prominent entertainer-pianist used a luxurious house as his base of operations, and numerous pictures were taken of him there for publicity and promotion purposes. His pool was piano-shaped, and the elaborate studios were equipped with chandeliers such as those with which the public associated him. Deduction was allowed for 50 percent of the house's depreciation and maintenance because, while he was using the home for business purposes, he was also indulging in the pleasures associated with his possessions.[38]

An otherwise deductible home-office expense was allowed even though the business conducted there was in illegal drugs.[39]

Officers, corporate. *See* **Executives.**

Old-age pension fund assessments. Such assessments, if paid by an individual so that he can remain in the union and hold employment, are deductible.[40]

Olympic games, contributions to sponsoring organization. Deduction is allowed for contributions made after October 4, 1976, to tax-exempt organizations which sponsor athletic competitions.[41] This presupposes that there is no direct benefit from the transfer to the taxpayer or to other persons.[42]

Operating permits. *See* **Expenditures for benefits lasting more than one year.**

Ordinary and necessary business expenses. Deduction is allowed for all ordinary and necessary expenses paid or incurred during the taxable year in carrying on any trade or business.[43] The United States Supreme Court has listed five characteristics essential in establishing a deduction as an allowable ordinary and necessary business expense: "An item must (1) be 'paid or incurred during the taxable year,' (2) be for 'carrying on any trade or business,' (3) be an 'expense,' (4) be a 'necessary expense,' and (5) be an 'ordinary expense.' "[44]

An expenditure that promotes and/or protects a taxpayer's business is deductible as an ordinary and necessary expense, unless the expenditure is for the acquisition of a capital asset; that is, one with an expected benefit lasting for more than one year.[45]

A paid director of a corporation is engaged in carrying on the trade or business of being a director.[46]

The practice of law is regarded as a business for this purpose.[47]

A person who serves the government for an obviously nominal salary, such as $1 a year, can deduct the expenses necessary to carry on the requirements of his employment, even though the trade or business is not carried on for profit.[48]

A professional artist was in the business of being a sculptor.[49]

Likewise subject to the rule was a retired United States Army colonel, who was deemed still to be engaged in the business of being an army officer in view of the fact that he remained subject to recall to active duty.[50]

A person continues to be engaged in a trade or business although temporarily unemployed.[51]

An individual is engaged in the trade or business of being an employee when he is on an employer's payroll.[52]

An expenditure may be regarded as one involved in carrying on a trade or business even before this is a revenue-producing activity. One builder could deduct normal recurring expenses to maintain the business enterprise where these expenses were not in the nature of start-up costs nor had they been intended to provide benefits extending beyond the year of expenditure, even though construction of the building involved could not start before funding was provided by a government agency where there was a temporary moratorium on additional approvals.[53]

Payment of debts for ordinary and necessary business expenses was deductible, even by a cash-basis individual, though made in a year when he no longer was in business. Because of financial problems, he had been unable to pay his debts when incurred, at which time he had made an agreement to pay his creditors when he would be able to obtain funds. The fact that the business had been discontinued prior to the taxable year did not prevent deduction as a *business* expense.[54]

The preceding paragraph applies even to a person who is not engaged in carrying on a trade or business in the customary sense, such as a clergyman.[55]

Automobile expenses in connection with learning the characteristics of the area served by his company were deductible by a city fire-department officer. He knew he would be quizzed by his superiors on his familiarity with the district involved.[56]

Ordinary and necessary business expenses include the cost of education necessary to maintain or to sharpen one's skills in one's present trade or business.[57] (*See* **Education.**) This also includes trips to the offices of one's attorney and one's accountant in order to discuss business problems.[58]

Damages paid to a pedestrian by an individual who had an accident while driving his car for business purposes were deductible.[59]

Ordinary and necessary business expenses for a professional fisherman include galley supplies, bait, ice, and fuel for his boat.[60]

It is difficult to argue that expenditures are *ordinary* if other parties customarily do not make such payments. Disbursements by a brokerage firm to an ordained minister for spiritual help were not deductible in the absence of proof that such help was sought by other concerns in solving business problems.[61] Deduction was allowed for a small part of the payment as compensation because the minister did run some business errands, which the court apparently regarded as an ordinary function for him.

In the case of an individual, deduction is allowed for all ordinary and necessary expenses paid or incurred for all the production or collection of income or for the management, conservation, or maintenance of property held for the production of income.[62]

A builder joined with several other persons in applying to the Federal Home Loan Bank Board for permission to organize a new local Federal savings and loan association. The organizations were required to contribute to the association cash in specified amounts to protect it against losses in its first five years. The builder could deduct his payments as expenses for the production of income. He expected to receive fees from the association as an appraiser and a director; he also expected that his connection with the association would enhance his stature as a community leader and a successful contractor, with the result that he would receive new construction contracts. That, in fact, is what happened.[63]

An executive who is required, such as in corporate bylaws, to reimburse his employer for any of his entertainment expenses which the Internal Revenue Service refuses to permit the corporation to deduct may himself take a tax deduction for the amount of the reimbursement he makes.[64]

Compensation paid by a business to a regular employee who is in the Armed Forces as an inducement to return upon his discharge is deductible as a business expense.[65]

Expenses prior to the time one is engaged in a business are not deductible; prebusiness expenses are not "paid or incurred in carrying on the business," for the business is not a fact as yet. But expenses during a transitional period between businesses are deductible. Thus, gifts and entertainment for buyers of jewelry were deductible by a salesman in that line during a transitional period until he found a new connection.[66] (*See also* **Start-up expenditures.**)

Where a corporation incurs travel and entertainment and other legitimate expenses in territory where it has not yet received state approval to do business, these expenses are not tax-deductible, for they are not related to the corporation's business if it is not authorized to do any there. An individual may get a better deal. A salesman for a prominent national manufacturer had a specific geographical territory, Greater Oklahoma City, where he received commissions on products he sold. He was highly ambitious, so he solicited orders from firms outside his territory. The Internal Revenue Service sought to disallow his expenses in connection with soliciting these outside orders because they did not relate to *his* business, which was restricted by his employer to Oklahoma City. But the court allowed him to take the deduction. Those business trips to cities outside his own territory were made only after approval had been obtained from his sales manager, which legitimized his invasion of districts not his own.[67]

Expenses of trying out a business venture are deductible if the venture is abandoned, provided the activities were more than a matter of investigating or looking into a proposition. The taxpayer must actually have been engaged in a transaction carried on for profit.[68]

Amounts paid to a client by an individual because of his failure to protect the client's interest are deductible.[69]

If a salesman is allowed to draw commissions before they are earned, and he draws against sales not yet paid for by his customers, he may be called upon to repay those commissions he drew out against customer bills that never did get paid. If he paid Federal income tax on commissions when he received them, he is entitled to a business-expense deduction in the year he returns the unearned commissions to his employer.[70]

An employer could deduct fees paid to a tax-exempt organization for advice as to housing for employees of a minority group.[71]

Payments to approved religious and charitable organizations were deductible as business expenses where the purpose of the expenditures was to attract the favorable attention of potential customers who received bulletins from these organizations listing contributors who had assisted in the financing of their good works.[72]

Amounts contributed by an employer to promote the rehabilitation of employees and their families who sustained injuries or damage in a tornado were deductible because the expenses, in the Treasury Department's words, "have a direct bearing on the retention of the employer's good will and the morale of the employees, which in turn are essential to the successful conduct of the business."[73]

Contributions to an irrevocable trust established as the result of union negotiations for the purpose of providing an apprenticeship and training program for employees were ruled to be deductible business expenses.[74]

Sums paid by an employer, pursuant to a union-negotiated agreement, to an irrevocable trust established to develop educational, cultural, and charitable programs for the benefit of individuals working in that industry were deductible business expenses.[75]

An employer, as a matter of policy, may encourage employees to enroll in outside educational courses which will help them more quickly absorb the employer's business background and discharge the duties of their jobs. On behalf of employees who take the courses and maintain satisfactory grades, the employer either pays the tuition costs directly to the educational institution or reimburses the employees for the costs of the courses taken. Assuming that the courses are of a type which will be beneficial to a career in the employer's business and that the employees have the prior approval of the employer, the employer's cost are deductible as business expenses, because the degree to which an employee effectively and successfully performs his duties directly affects the degree to which the employer achieves business objectives. So the employer's costs are deducted as business expenses of a noncompensatory character and are not subject to wage withholding.[76]

Consultation fees for management and financial advice during contract negotiations were held to be deductible. (Such might not have been the case where the transaction involved the sale of capital assets, the cost then appearing to be a capital expenditure.)[77]

Professional or technical journals and books, etc., are deductible if they have short useful lives, such as less than one year; otherwise, the costs would have to be written off as depreciation over the useful lives of the assets.[78]

Gifts to subordinates by a sales supervisor were deductible, because greater cooperation from these persons was likely to increase his own performance.[79]

A businessperson could deduct the cost of liquor purchased in reasonable amounts for people who regularly supplied merchandise.[80]

A business-expense deduction was allowed for payments to a physician for treating someone injured on the premises.[81]

Research expenses incurred by a professor for the purpose of teaching, lecturing, and writing in his own field were deductible as a means of carrying out the duties expected of him as professor without expectation of profit apart from his salary.[82]

Testimonial-dinner costs in the case of important customers were deductible business expenses.[83]

Fines and penalties are not deductible for Federal income tax purposes. But some of the by-products of fines and penalties *are* deductible, such as legal fees and related expenses paid or incurred in the defense of a prosecution or civil action arising from the violation of the law imposing the fine or civil penalty. Court costs assessed against the taxpayer, as well as stenographic and printing charges, are not regarded as part of the fine or penalty, nor are compensatory damages (including damages under Section 4A of the Clayton Anti-Trust Act) paid to a government.[84]

A gambling establishment could deduct the losses of "shills," who were engaged to attract customers to the establishment's card tables.[85]

A partner in a brokerage firm could deduct his contributions to an undertaking which was formed to get evidence against a bucket shop. His payment was to protect his own business interest.[86]

Amounts paid by various employers to a protective service association that was to protect them from unjust labor demands were deductible.[87]

Payments to a nonprofit organization for protection against labor demands were deductible.[88]

Some physicians organized a private hospital to serve their own patients exclusively. To keep the hospital solvent, the doctors paid the operating deficits that resulted at first. Each doctor was permitted to deduct such payments, as the purpose was to continue to earn fees from patients who were hospitalized there. The payments were made to preserve income from loss or reduction.[89]

Lawyers could deduct the operating deficits of a savings and loan association organized as a source of legal business for the attorneys.[90]

As a condition to practicing at a hospital, a physician was required to turn over 5 percent of his income from private practice there to the hospital's research fund. That was deductible as a business expense.[91]

A business was permitted to deduct the legal fees paid when its president and sole stockholder was indicted for personal tax evasion. Without his presence, this personal-service company could not have continued in business.[92]

A taxpayer could deduct payments made to trade creditors of a previously liquidated corporation. Suppliers in this business community generally required that such debts be paid before they would extend credit to the principal of a previously failed enterprise.[93]

A printing concern with labor problems was allowed to deduct the cost of recruiting personnel to break a strike.[94]

Expenses incurred while investigating employees in order to avoid embezzlement losses was a legitimate deduction.[95]

Costs of resisting efforts to put the taxpayer out of business were deductible, as where an entertainer incurred legal fees in a libel action against a person who had called him a Communist and who had published calls to the public "to hit these boys in their box-office."[96]

A director of a corporation could deduct accounting and legal fees incurred in defending himself against stockholders' suits for violation of his fiduciary duties.[97]

A judge was permitted to deduct his expenses in defending himself against charges that he had conducted himself in a manner which called for his removal from office.[98]

Transfers of property to an approved charitable organization which bear a direct relationship to the taxpayer's trade or business and which are made with a reasonable expectation of financial return commensurate with the amount of the transfer may constitute allowable deductions as trade or business expenses rather than as charitable contributions.[99]

The existence of a contractual arrangement between the taxpayer and the "donee" may establish that direct economic benefit is expected. Certain merchants, both owners and tenants, entered into an agreement with the city in which they were located, to pay half of the cost of a parking lot owned by the city. In return, the city restricted the use of this lot for ten years to parking for customers of the adjacent business district in which the merchants were located. The payments made by the merchants were business expenses extending well beyond the taxable year. The business expense could be written off ratably each year of the ten-year agreement.[100]

A commercial firm could deduct payments to the Union of Soviet Socialist Republics that were based upon a percentage of the value of its imports and exports, in order to obtain a license to do business.[101]

Deduction was allowed for the cost of Christmas cards, including the postage thereon, which were sent to customers.[102]

The cost of Christmas parties for employees and customers was deductible.[103]

When an individual engaged in a trade or business makes a payment to an exempt organization with a reasonable expectation of financial return to himself, which is in line with the amount of his gift, it is not subject to the percentage limitations of charitable contributions but is fully deductible as ordinary and necessary business expense. Such was the ruling when money was given to a pollution-control fund established by a municipality where the donor's business had been hurt in the past because of polluted atmosphere.[104]

In order to try to get the goodwill of a potential customer who also happened to be the chairman of a hospital's fund drive, a businessperson made a contribution to the hospital. This could be deducted, not as a contribution subject to percentage limitations, but as a business expense.[105]

A manufacturer can deduct as research and experimental expenditures the cost of developing and designing, at the manufacturer's risk, a specially built automated manufacturing system for a single customer's specific order.[106]

An employer's contribution to an unemployment-benefit fund to pay a "layoff moving allowance," when an employee who is laid off at one plant accepts employment at another plant, is deductible as an ordinary and necessary business expense.[107]

Where income is earned outside the United States by a person under certain conditions, it is not taxed in the U.S. Expenses in connection with that income similarly are not deductible. But expenses not related to income earned outside the country are deductible. Examples of such items include personal and family medical expenses, real-estate taxes on a personal residence, interest on a mortgage on a personal residence, and charitable contributions.[108]

An industry association and a union made an agreement, which provided that companies belonging to the association would make monthly contributions of $X per employee into a trust fund for the benefit of covered employees. The trust was to maintain a health facility for the benefit of the union members and to maintain accident, health, and hospitalization insurance for the employees and their families. If the plan was terminated, any remaining moneys were to be used as the trustees saw fit, which meant that the companies would not get back their contributions under any circumstances. The amounts thus contributed under the plan were deductible as ordinary and necessary business expenses.[109]

Dental bills paid for an employee because of an accident sustained at work are deductible.[110]

A taxpayer could deduct the cost of repairs and replacements in the form of a complete cleaning, overhauling, and replacing of axles, transmissions, and brakes of motor equipment used for business purposes. Although the repairs were extensive and the new materials had some advantages over those replaced, they did not materially increase the value or the life of the equipment but only kept it in usable condition.[111]

The cost of repairs was deductible where business equipment was of no greater utility and was not more efficient after the repair, even if the work done was not a reasonable facsimile of the original item, as in the case of an elevator.[112]

After a fire had partially destroyed a plant, expenditures for temporary electrical installations and other emergency activities to place the plant in running order were deductible.[113] (*See also* **Repairs.**)

Where a vehicle was used for business purposes, the entire cost of air horns was deductible, for they had a very short life span.[114]

The cost of tickets for benefit performances, purchased to maintain goodwill in the community, was deductible as a form of advertising.[115]

A tavern owner was permitted to deduct as advertising the cost of a Christmas party given for the children of the neighborhood to promote goodwill with their parents.[116] A restaurant could deduct the cost of an automobile given to the patron who drew a winning ticket.[117] (*See also* **Advertising.**)

To promote sales and net profits, a business agreed to pay to an approved charitable organization a certain amount for each label from one of its products that the organization mailed to the business enterprise. In return, the charitable organization agreed to permit the use of its name in the business's advertising and to obtain testimonial letters for use in a sales campaign. The amounts turned over to the charity by the business were deductible as ordinary and necessary expenses, without the percentage limitation imposed upon charitable contributions.[118]

A university permitted faculty members of its medical school to engage in private practice provided each doctor turned over to the school the amount of each year's fees (less legitimate professional expenses) to the extent that these net fees exceeded his university salary. The fees were part of each person's gross income. But each could deduct the amounts turned over to the university.[119]

An attorney bought stock in a finance company. When the company became insolvent, his loss on the stock was not a capital loss but a fully deductible ordinary loss. He had purchased the stock, not as an investment, but for the purpose of getting profitable law work for himself. His investment was large enough to enable him to be elected president, and as such, he thought he could turn over some of the finance company's legal work to himself in his capacity as a lawyer. He expected through this connection to be engaged for title searches on property offered as security by borrowers, to obtain collection fees of up to 25 percent when the company had to get *some* lawyer to go after the delinquent parties, and to obtain document recording and notarial fees. The loss was fully deductible, being in connection with a business transaction entered upon for profit.[120] *See also* **Actors; Armed Forces; Bribes and kickbacks; Contributions; Employees; Entertainment; Executives; Reputation, maintenance of; Settlement payments; Teachers, expenses of.**

Organic foods. *See* **Medical expenses.**

Origination fees. *See* **Interest.**

Orthopedic shoes. The cost of shoes worn in order to cope with a physical condition are deductible as medical expenses.[121]

Osteopaths. Payments to osteopaths are deductible.[122] *See also* **Medical expenses.**

Outside salesmen, expenses of. *See* **Employees.**

Overalls. Carpenters are permitted to deduct the cost of protective overalls.[123] *See also* **Work clothes.**

Overhead insurance. Where an individual purchases an insurance policy that would reimburse him, to the extent specified in the policy, for certain business overhead expenses incurred by him during prolonged periods due to sickness or injury, the premiums are deductible business expenses.[124] *See also* **Insurance.**

Over sixty-month period. *See* **Expenditures for benefits lasting more than one year.**

Overtime meals. Ordinarily, the cost of meals purchased because of overtime duties is not deductible. But if a person is required by the nature of his employment to work a considerable distance from his home, on those occasions when duty keeps him at the work site overnight, he may deduct the cost of lodging and extra meals there.[125]

Overweight, mitigation of. *See* **Weight-loss program.**

Oxygen equipment. *See* **Medical expenses.**

O

1. IRC Section 167(a).
2. *Keller Street Development Company v. Commissioner,* 323 F.2d 166 (9th Cir., 1963).
3. *Zwetchkenbaum et al. v. Commissioner,* 326 F.2d 477 (1st Cir. 1964).
4. Regulations Section 1.167(a)-9.
5. *Frito-Lay, Inc. v. United States,* 209 F. Supp. 886 (DC, ND Ga., 1962).
6. *United States Cartridge Company v. United States,* 284 U.S. 511 (1932).
7. Regulations Section 1.167(a)-8.
8. *United States v. Wagner Electric Mfg. Co.,* 61 F.2d 204 (8th Cir., 1932).
9. *United States Cartridge Company v. United States,* 284 U.S. 511 (1932).
10. *Cosmopolitan Corporation et al.,* T.C. Memo. 1959-112, filed June 12, 1959.
11. *Lucker v. United States,* 53 F.2d 418 (Ct. Cl., 1931).
12. *Corsicana Gas & Electric Company,* 6 BTA 565 (1927).
13. *Townsend-Ueberrhein Clothing Company v. Crooks,* 41 F.2d 66 (DC, WD Mo., 1930).
14. *Your Federal Income Tax,* 1978 edition, page 90.
15. IRC Section 280A(c)(1)(A).
16. *Curphey v. Commissioner,* 73 T.C. 766 (1980).
17. *Adams et al. v. Commissioner,* T.C. Memo. 1982-223, filed April 26, 1982.
18. *Green et al. v. Commissioner,* 78 T.C., No. 30 (1982).
19. *Business Use of Your Home,* IRS Publication 587 (Rev. Nov. 1981), page 1.
20. *Your Federal Income Tax,* 1981 edition, page 97.
21. IRC Section 280A(c)(2).
22. *Besch et al. v. Commissioner,* T.C. Memo. 1982-15, filed January 12, 1982.
23. *Gomez et al. v. Commissioner,* T.C. Memo. 1980-565, filed December 18, 1980.
24. *Wisconsin Psychiatric Services, Ltd. et al. v. Commissioner,* 76 T.C. 839 (1981).

25. *Weightman v. Commissioner*, T.C. Memo. 1981-301, filed June 18, 1981.

26. IRC Section 280A(c)(5).

27. IRC Section 280A(d)(1).

28. IRC Section 280A(d)(2).

29. *Gestrich v. Commissioner*, 74 T.C. 525 (1980).

30. *Allen et al. v. Commissioner*, T.C. Memo. 1982-93, filed February 23, 1982.

31. *Tax Information for Homeowners*. IRS Publication 530 (Rev. Nov. 1980), page 5.

32. *Your Federal Income Tax*, 1981 edition, page 98.

33. *Browne v. Commissioner*, 73 T.C. 723 (1980).

34. *Imhoff et al. v. Commissioner*, T.C. Memo. 1980-30, filed January 31, 1980.

35. *Thomas v. Commissioner*, T.C. Memo. 1981-348, filed July 6, 1981.

36. *Locke et al. v. Commissioner*, T.C. Memo. 1979-153, filed April 17, 1979.

37. *Frank A. Thomas et al.*, T.C. Memo. 1969-108, filed May 26, 1969.

38. *International Artists, Ltd. et al.*, 55 T.C. 94 (1970).

39. *Edmondson v. Commissioner*, T.C. Memo. 1981-623, filed October 26, 1981.

40. *Your Federal Income Tax*, 1979 edition, page 98.

41. IRC Section 170(c)(2)(B).

42. Tax Equity and Fiscal Responsibility Act of 1982.

43. Section 162.

44. *Commissioner v. Lincoln Savings and Loan Association*, 403 U.S. 345 (1971).

45. IRS Letter Ruling 8202010, September 28, 1981.

46. *Hochschild v. Commissioner*, 158 F.2d 764 (2d Cir., 1947).

47. *Wm. Armstrong, Jr., et al.*, 51 T.C. 863 (1969).

48. *Frank v. United States*, 577 F.2d 93 (9th Cir., 1978).

49. *Rood v. United States*, 184 F.Supp. 791 (DC, Minn., 1960).

50. *Imhoff et al. v. Commissioner*, T.C. Memo. 1980-30, filed January 31, 1980.

51. *Harold Haft*, 40 T.C. 2 (1963).

52. *David J. Primuth et al.*, 54 T.C. 374 (1970).

53. *Blitzer et al. v. United States*, 684 F.2d 874 (Ct. Cl., 1982).

54. Revenue Ruling 67-12, 1967-1 CB 29.

55. *Onstott et al. v. Commissioner*, T.C. Memo. 1981-50, filed February 10, 1981.

56. *Banks et al. v. Commissioner*, T.C. Memo. 1981-450, filed September 9, 1981.

57 Regulations Section 1.162-5(a)(1).

58. *Boggs, Jr., et al. v. Commissioner*, T.C. Memo. 1981-224, filed May 4, 1981.

59. *Plante et al. v. United States*, 226 F. Supp. 314 (DC, NH, 1963).

60. *Tax Guide for Commercial Fisher-*

men, IRS Publication 595, 1979 edition, page 15.

61. *Trebilcock et al. v. Commissioner*, 557 F.2d 1226 (6th Cir., 1977).

62. IRC Section 212.

63. *D. Holland Wessell et al.*, T.C. Memo. 1963-11, filed January 11, 1963.

64. IRS Letter Ruling 7811004, November 29, 1977.

65. *Berkshire Oil Co.*, 9 T.C. 903 (1947).

66. *Harold Haft et al.*, 40 T.C. 2 (1963).

67. *Raymond Warren Jackson et al.*, T.C. Memo. 1975-301, filed September 30, 1975.

68. *Charles I. Parker*, 1 T.C. 709 (1943).

69. *Henry F. Cochrane*, 23 BTA 202 (1931).

70. Revenue Ruling 72-28, 1972-1 CB 45.

71. Revenue Ruling 68-2, 1968-1 CB 61.

72. *Smith et al. v. Commissioner*, T.C. Memo. 1980-523, filed November 25, 1980.

73. Revenue Ruling 131, 1953-2 CB 112.

74. Revenue Ruling 58-238, 1958-1 CB 90.

75. Revenue Ruling 74-51, 1974-1 CB 45.

76. Revenue Ruling 76-71, 1976-1 CB 308.

77. *United States Freight Company et al. v. United States*, 422 F.2d 887 (Ct. Cl., 1970).

78. *Beaudry v. Commissioner*, 150 F.2d 20 (2d Cir., 1945).

79. *Harold A. Christensen*, 17 T.C. 1456 (1952).

80. *Rodgers Dairy Co.*, 14 T.C. 66 (1950).

81. *Fred W. Staudt*, T.C. Memo., Docket No. 32244, entered December 17, 1953.

82. Revenue Ruling 63-275, 1963-2 CB 85.

83. *First National Bank of Omaha v. United States*, 276 F. Supp. (DC, Neb., 1967).

84. TD 7366, 1975-2 CB 64.

85. *Irving Nitzberg et al.*, T.C. Memo. 1975-228, filed July 14, 1975.

86. *Edward A. Pierce*, 18 BTA 447 (1921).

87. *Mrs. H. A. Allan*, 7 BTA 1256 (1927).

88. *Fritz B. Campen*, 16 BTA 543 (1929).

89. *Charles J. Dinardo*, 22 T.C. 430 (1954).

90. *Cubbedge Snow*, 31 T.C. 585 (1958).

91. IRS Letter Ruling 8110064, December 11, 1980.

92. *Jack's Maintenance Contractors, Inc. v. Commissioner*, T.C. Memo. 1981-349, filed July 6, 1981.

93. *M. L. Eakes Company, Inc. v. Commissioner*, T.C. Memo. 1981-429, filed August 13, 1981.

94. *Queen City Printing Company*, 6 BTA 521 (1927).

95. *Desmonds, Inc.*, 15 BTA 738 (1929).

96. *Paul Draper et al.*, 26 T.C. 201 (1956).

97. *The Lomas & Nettleton Company v. United States*, 79 F. Supp. 886 (DC, Ct., 1948).

98. Revenue Ruling 74-394, 1974-2 CB 40.

99. Regulations Section 1.170A-1(c)(5).

100. *Berglund et al. v. United States*. DC, Minn., 1981.

101. *Allied American Corporation*, 25 BTA 1276 (1932).

102. *Arthur S. McKenzie et al.*, T.C. Memo., Docket No. 30042, entered May 2, 1952.

103. *Robert S. LeSage et al.*, T.C. Memo., Docket Nos. 11239 and 11240, entered December 3, 1947, *aff'd*, 173 F.2d 826 (5th Cir., 1949).

104. Revenue Ruling 73-113, 1973-1 CB 65.

105. *Marcell v. United States*, DC, Vt., 1961.

106. Revenue Ruling 73-275, 1973-1 CB 134.

107. Revenue Ruling 73-245, 1973-1 CB 64.

108. Regulations Section 1.911-1(a)(3).

109. Revenue Ruling 77-406, 1977-2 CB 56.

110. *Bearl Sprott et al.*, T.C. Memo., Docket Nos. 32340-1, entered February 17, 1953.

111. *Mark C. Nottingham*, T.C. Memo., Docket No. 31415, entered May 8, 1953.

112. *Mellie Esperson*, BTA Memo., Docket No. 98737, entered February 5, 1941.

113. *Ticket Office Equipment Co., Inc.*, 20 T.C. 272 (1953) *aff'd*, 213 F.2d 318 (2d Cir., 1954).

114. *Marcell v. United States*, DC, Vt., 1961.

115. *Victor J. McQuade*, 4 BTA 837 (1926).

116. *A.D. Miller et al.*, T.C. Memo., Docket No. 23754, entered January 18, 1951.

117. IT 1667, II-1 CB 83.

118. Revenue Ruling 63-73, 1963-1 CB 35.

119. Revenue Ruling 66-377, 1966-2 CB 21.

120. *Irwin v. United States*, DC, ED La., 1975.

121. IRS Letter Ruling 8221118, February 26, 1982.

122. Revenue Ruling 63-91, 1963-1 CB 54.

123. *Busking et al. v. Commissioner*, T.C. Memo. 1978-415, filed October 16, 1978.

124. Revenue Ruling 55-264, 1955-1 CB 11.

125. *Coombs et al. v. Commissioner*, 608 F.2d 1269 (9th Cir., 1979).

P

Painter. *See* **Artist, expenses of.**

Painting. *See* **Alimony; Repairs.**

Paint removal. The cost of removing a lead-based paint from a fence, contact with which previously had given the taxpayer's child lead poisoning, was deductible as medical expense. Deduction was limited, however, to removal of paint from surfaces which the child could reach.[1]

Parking fees. Where an automobile is used for business purposes, parking charges are one of the legitimate expenses deductible in producing taxable income. Such fees may be deductible even if not used in producing income. Such was the case where an individual was a member of his state's Advisory Committee to the Small Business Administration. He was not compensated for his services in this connection. But he could deduct his parking fees as "out-of-pocket transportation expenses necessarily incurred in performing donated services."[2] (*See also* **Contributions.**)

    The deduction of parking fees presents a difficult problem of substantiation in most instances. One commercial traveler met the burden of proof through notations recorded in his monthly mileage books.[3]

    Parking fees incurred in connection with business are separately deductible even where a person uses the zero bracket amount in lieu of itemizing deductions.[4]

    Amounts deposited in parking meters are deductible if the expenditures are in connection with a taxpayer's trade or business.[5] *See also* **Employees; Medical expenses; Mileage allowance.**

Parking-space permit. The cost of an annual county residential parking permit is not ordinarily deductible. If, however, the space subject to this permit is used in connection with an individual's trade or business, the fee is deductible.[6]

Partnerships. A partner can deduct his appropriate share of losses and deductions.[7]

    In general, a partner's proportionate share of partnership deductions is determined by his respective interest in the partnership. (*See also* discussion of partnership losses under **Carry-overs.**)

A partner can deduct unreimbursed travel and entertainment expenses he incurred for the partnership, where under the partnership agreement he was obliged to assume such expenses.[8]

Two partners in the operation of a tavern agreed to spend as much of their own money as possible to advertise or to promote the business. The partnership was not charged and did not pay these amounts. Each partner could deduct his actual outlays.[9]

A partner, under the terms of a partnership agreement, was required to pay out of his personal funds the compensation of one of the partnership employees who performed some of the duties of this partner. He could deduct this compensation as business expense.[10]

A partner was permitted to deduct his share of a partnership loss that resulted from another partner's embezzlement of cash.[11]

Where a partnership became insolvent because of embezzlements by one of the partners, and the general partners also became insolvent, the limited partners lost their capital investments. Each limited partner could deduct his share of the partnership loss to the extent of his interest.[12]

A sum paid to one's partner to bring about an early dissolution of the partnership is deductible.[13] *See also* **Family transactions; Legal fees.**

Partners, lunches for. *See* **Entertainment.**

Passport. The fee paid for a passport is not deductible as a tax. But if it is procured in connection with a trip for business purposes, it is deductible as a business expense.[14]

Past-due premium on fidelity bond. A belated premium on a fiduciary bond required under a previous employment was held to be deductible.[15]

Patent infringement, losses from. *See* **Compensable injuries.**

Patterning. *See* **Medical expenses.**

Payment of debt of another person. Generally, voluntary payments of the debt of another party are not a deductible business expense. But deduction is allowed where payments are made to protect and to preserve an existing business reputation.[16] *See also* **Reputation, maintenance of.**

Payola. *See* **Bribes and kickbacks.**

Pedestrian, cost of hitting. Where an individual was driving his car for business purposes at the time his vehicle struck a pedestrian, the damage settlement in excess of insurance reimbursement was deductible as a business expense.[17] *See also* **Judgment payment.**

Penalty fee for loan prepayment. A borrower may wish to prepay loan installments to speed up the termination of his loan. Ordinarily, a cash-basis taxpayer is not entitled in a single year to the deduction of interest related to a period of more than twelve months because that would result in a material distortion of his income for that year. One loan agreement allowed the borrower to make prepayments on any future installments. But if prepayments in a twelve-month period equaled or exceeded 20 percent of the principal of the loan, the borrower would be liable to a prepayment penalty equal to 180 days' interest on the original principal of the loan. Prepaid interest in the year of payment was deductible to the extent of the penalty for the prepayment of installments.[18]

Penalty payments, as interest. Penalty payments made by a taxpayer to his mortgagee for the privilege of prepaying his mortgage indebtedness are deductible as interest.[19] *See also* **Interest.**

Pension contributions not completely regained. If an individual contributes his required amount to a plan which is approved by the Internal Revenue Service, he may be entitled to receive from the pension fund when he retires a lump-sum payment of the amount due him. But because of the fund's investment losses, the amount which he receives when he retires may be less than he put into the fund. The difference between what he put into the fund and what he gets out is deductible as an ordinary loss in the year he gets the money.[20]

Pension-fund assessment. An employee may deduct old-age pension-fund assessments which he must pay in order to remain a member of his union, a requirement for holding his job.[21]

Pensions. *See* **Individual retirement account; Self-employment plans.**

Percentage depletion. *See* **Depletion.**

Percentage rental. If business is good, a company can afford to pay higher rent for its premises, and of course the tax deduction goes up. If business is poor, a rent reduction is desirable. Both objectives are facilitated by a percentage lease. The landlord is protected against inflation by the automatic escalation factor, while if the tenant's business deteriorates, the automatically lowered rent is at least better than having the tenant become unable to afford the original rent. Customarily, the percentage lease is geared to receipts or profits, with a minimum rent to provide a reasonable return on the landlord's investment. Even if a tenant's rent is unusually large in a particular year under a percentage lease, no part of the rent will be disallowed as unreasonable. But if tenant and landlord are related parties, the Internal Revenue Service may question the legitimacy of the arrangement. In one case, the Service questioned the tax deduction when a corporation rented its premises from the chief stockholder under a percentage lease, which yielded a rental that exceeded the flat rental rate previously used. But the court permitted the full rent deduction even though the percentage rental had been recommended by the accountant who also handled the company's taxes, because (1) percentage rentals are fair to both landlord and tenant in principle by reason of the factors of inflation and business fluctuations and (2) the arithmetic of this percentage lease was in line with other percentage leases in the area involving unrelated parties.[22] *See also* **Rent.**

Per diem allowance. *See* **Mileage allowance.**

Performance bonds. *See* **Contracts, expenses; Insurance.**

Periodicals. *See* **Subscriptions to periodicals.**

Periodic payments. *See* **Alimony.**

Permits. Ordinarily, payment to a municipality or other governmental authority for a permit to do business is not deductible, if the permission granted is permanent or is renewable automatically. Reason: The expenditure is for benefits lasting for more than one year, usually for a period of unforeseeable duration. But where a permit has to be renewed each year, and may not be, the cost each year is deductible.[23] *See also* **Expenditures for benefits lasting more than one year.**

Personal grooming. Although the cost of personal grooming (such as haircuts) is not deductible as a business expense, an American Airlines pilot could deduct the cost of shoeshines, which the court regarded as part of the upkeep of his uniform. The company had suspended other persons who had failed to present a well-groomed appearance to the public.[24]

An employee was permitted to deduct the cost of the daily cleaning of his work clothes, which, having become saturated with oil, could be worn only one day and then had to be cleaned. Dirty clothing was dangerous in his business, because his garments became saggy and could catch in revolving machinery.[25]

A police officer could deduct the cost of having his uniform cleaned, possibly because he had little choice in the selection of persons with whom he came in contact.[26]

Personal liability insurance. *See* **Executives.**

Personal-property taxes. *See* **Taxes.**

Pesticides, loss resulting from. *See* **Casualties.**

Pets, transportation of. *See* **Moving expenses.**

Photographs. The cost of photographs used to make appraisals and to determine the extent of casualty losses is deductible.[27]

An actor seeking employment could deduct the cost of photographs which he sent to agents and producers.[28]

The author of a profusely illustrated book could deduct the cost of photographs he used.[29]

A newspaper photographer used spot-news aerial pictures he had taken to justify his entitlement to deduct flying lessons as education expense.[30]

A county coroner could deduct the unreimbursable cost of color film that he used in connection with his professional duties in homicide cases.[31]

Physical examination. The cost to an employee of periodic routine physical examinations sufficient to establish his position may be deducted as ordinary and necessary business expenses. But any additional expenses for medical aid or physical correction, which may be required to enable him to maintain the physical fitness necessary to retain his position, are deductible only as medical expenses, within the limits set for that.[32] *See also* **Employees; Medical expenses.**

Physical fitness. *See* **Actors; Handball court, rental of; Weight-loss program.**

Physical training. The physical-training exercise expense of a movie stuntman was allowed as an expenditure related to his trade or business.[33]

Physicians, professional expenses of. *See* **Advertising; Automobile, use of; Commuting; Conventions; Depreciation; Dues, professional societies; Education; Entertainment; Expenditures for benefits lasting more than one year; Hobby losses; Hospital staff fees; Insurance; Legal fees; Malpractice insurance; Office at home; Ordinary and necessary business expenses; Professional instruments and equipment; Professional negligence; Settlement payments; Subscriptions to periodicals; Telephone; Travel; Work clothes.**

Physicians' fees. *See* **Medical expenses.**

Pilots, flight instruction expense. *See* **Education.**

Placement agency fees. *See* **Employment, expenses in seeking; Employment-agency fees.**

Plastic surgery. *See* **Face-lifting; Medical expenses.**

Pleasure farming. *See* **Farmers; Hobby losses.**

Podiatrists. *See* **Medical expenses.**

Points. *See* **Interest; Prepaid interest.**

Policeman. *See* **Personal grooming; Uniforms.**

Political bad debts. *See* **Bad debts.**

Political campaign funds, expenditure of. Campaign funds received by a candidate for public office, in excess of what is necessary to defray his campaign expenditures, may be transferred to an "excess campaign fund" to support his activities as a government officer. These transactions are treated for tax purposes as gross income to him. But he may deduct ordinary and necessary expenses in carrying on his trade or business of being an officeholder.[34]

Political contributions. *See* **Contributions.**

Political expenses. Although a candidate for reelection to public office cannot deduct his campaign expenses, he is permitted to deduct qualifying and committee assessments payable to a state under its law.[35]

Political lobbying. *See* **Lobbying.**

Pollution-control facilities. The cost of certified pollution-control facilities in connection with a plant or other property in operation before January 1, 1969, may, at the taxpayer's election, be amortized over a sixty-month period.[36]

Pool. *See* **Medical expenses.**

Postage. A businessperson could deduct the cost of Christmas cards sent to customers.[37]

Postage was deductible when related to a person's investment activities.[38]

An actor could deduct the cost of mailing résumés and photographs to casting directors, agents, and studios.[39]

The cost of mailing résumés to prospective employers is deductible.[40]

Postage stamps, loss on sale. *See* **Hobby losses.**

Postcards. A physician was allowed to deduct the cost of mailing postcards to his patients back in the United States, for the addressees were persons whose patronage reasonably was expected and who were being reminded of the continuing availability of the sender.[41]

The cost of Christmas cards sent to customers was held to be deductible.[42]

Postmen. *See* **Telephone; Uniforms.**

Practical nurses. *See* **Medical expenses.**

Preadoption medical expenses. *See* **Medical expenses.**

Prebusiness expenses. Ordinarily, expenses of a business before a person is engaged in that business are not deductible. But a builder's normal nonrecurring expenses to keep the enterprise in operation were deductible even though a structure could not be completed so as to generate income, where the necessary approval from a government agency was held up by a temporary moratorium on additional approvals for monetary advances.[43]

An individual acquired a one-half interest in a golf course upon which construction was nearing completion. He could deduct his half-share of the expenses for seeding, fertilizing, watering, and mowing of the playing surfaces, even though the course was not to be open to the public for two months. This care was required in order to maintain playability; that is, business use.[44]

Directly after he left high school, an individual who was actively seeking a professional baseball career engaged his father, a former semi-professional player, to teach him the skills necessary to develop his playing abilities. The Internal Revenue Service sought to disallow the fees the son paid to his father for this guidance because they related to a profession in which the younger man was not yet engaged. But the fees were held to be deductible, because they related to his intended business and could have been deducted only when paid inasmuch as the youth reported on the cash basis.[45]

Where a manufacturer's retail outlets in city stores suffered falling sales, advertising and promotional activities were undertaken in individual suburban stores, in an effort to stimulate products' sales. Such expenses were deductible as an expense of the manufacturer's existing business, not costs related to the development of a new business.[46]

A consultant developed a computer program to keep track of data used in his engagements and to monitor the progress of his activities. By the end of the taxable year, the program had not been perfected to the degree that it could be placed in operation. The Internal Revenue Service sought to disallow his development expenses on the ground that they related to a new business in which he was not yet engaged. Although costs prior to engaging in a business are nondeductible prebusiness expenses, a new method for running an established business is an attempt to apply modern technology to the taxpayer's trade or business and is deductible.[47]

A taxpayer could deduct expenses for wages, utilities, and consumable supplies even before commencement of the business of operating a nursing home. These were expenses in connection with a transaction entered into for profit, even though a state regulatory agency had not yet issued the necessary license. There was no reason to believe that the license would not be issued. The expenses all would produce benefits in the year paid.[48]

Salaries, utility bills, and stationery costs in connection with a transaction entered into for profit are deductible, although the acquisition of income-producing assets has not been completed as yet.[49] *See also* **Feasibility studies; Investors; Ordinary and necessary business expenses; Start-up expenses.**

Pregnancy, termination of. Expenses to terminate a pregnancy are deductible if the operation is not illegal under the law of the state where it takes place.[50]

Premature withdrawal of interest. Some financial institutions offer a higher than standard rate of interest to depositors who agree to leave a designated principal amount on deposit for a period of time which may range from sixty days to ten years. If the depositor withdraws the principal prior to the expiration of the term of the account, he must forfeit an amount equivalent to the interest for a stipulated period. A deduction from principal is made in the event the depositor has made a premature withdrawal and if the interest has already been paid to or withdrawn by him. The financial institution must report to the Internal Revenue Service any interest payments aggregating $10 or more during a taxable year, and the amount thus reported cannot be reduced by any forfeiture incurred. The depositor must report the full interest. But he may deduct the amount of the forfeiture as a loss incurred in a transaction entered upon for profit. Where the deposit arrangement is entered into as part of the depositor's trade or business, the forfeiture is a loss incurred in a trade or business, and in arriving at adjusted gross income, it is deductible in the year of the forfeiture.[51]

The penalty under the Depository Institutions Deregulation Committee Regulations for premature withdrawal of funds from a time savings account that is not connected with a trade or business is an allowable deduction in arriving at adjusted gross income in the taxable year of the withdrawal. The penalty may exceed interest accrued or already paid and require a forfeiture of principal.[52]

Premium charges. *See* **Interest.**

Premiums, insurance. *See* **Executives; Insurance.**

Premiums on medical insurance. *See* **Medical expenses.**

Premiums paid to obtain a loan. A negotiated premium or bonus paid by a borrower to a lender in order to obtain a loan is deductible as interest. Whether the amount of the premium or bonus is withheld by the lender rather than being paid back to him by the borrower is immaterial.[53]

Pre-opening expenses. *See* **Start-up expenditures.**

Prepaid expenses. Although a cash-basis taxpayer ordinarily deducts payments when made, prepayments as a rule must be deducted over the periods covered by these payments. Otherwise it would be easy to take a tax deduction in whatever year would be most beneficial. But a taxpayer engaged in oil and gas exploration could deduct intangible drilling expenses which had been prepaid in accordance with the contract. There had been a business reason for this: namely, to provide a contractor with working capital to conduct the operation and not merely to control the timing of deductions. Prepayment, moreover, was the usual practice in the industry.[54] *See also* **Interest.**

Prepaid feed, deduction for. *See* **Farmers.**

Prepaid interest. Ordinarily, a person who is on the cash basis cannot deduct interest which he pays in advance for future years. But he can deduct points paid for the purchase of his own principal residence. Points of this nature are additional interest charges which may be imposed by the lender instead of a higher interest rate when the loan is made. The amount paid as points is deductible by the borrower if they generally are charged in the geographical area where the loan is made, to the extent of the number of points charged in that area for a home loan.[55] *See* **Interest.**

Prepaid legal expenses. *See* **Group legal-services plan.**

Prepaid rent. Ordinarily, a cash-basis taxpayer can only deduct in any year the portion of a business rent payment which applies to that particular year. Where one such person, under a twenty-year lease, was obliged to make annual payments each December for the succeeding twelve-month period, he could deduct a full year's rent on that first December 1.[56]

Preparation of tax returns, cost of. Deduction is permitted for all ordinary and necessary expenses in connection with the determination, collection, or refund of any tax.[57] Expenses of obtaining guidance on tax matters are deductible.[58] So it is worth preserving the bill or invoice of this book.

Prepayment charges. Charges for the privilege of paying installment charges before they are due are deductible as interest, representing as they do a payment that takes the place of interest.[59]

Prepayment fees. Fees paid by a mortgagee for the privilege of prepaying a mortgage are deductible.[60]

Prepayment of mortgage. A fee charged for the privilege of paying off a mortgage before it is due is deductible as interest.[61]

Prepublication expenses. Research, travel, writing, and arrangement expenses of a professional writer were deductible when paid.[62]

Prescription drugs. Medicines and drugs were deductible to the extent that a person's costs exceeded 1 percent of his gross income, being then includable with deductible medical expenses. (*See* **Medical expenses.**) But for taxable years beginning after December 31, 1983, deduction is allowed only for prescription drugs and insulin.[63]

Preservation of reputation. *See* **Reputation, maintenance of.**

Pressing of clothing. Where traveling expenses are deductible, so are expenditures for pressing, laundering, and cleaning of clothing while away from home on business.[64]

Preventative maintenance. *See* **Repairs.**

Prevention of casualties, cost of. *See* **Casualties.**

Private investigators. The beneficiary of a trust was allowed to deduct fees paid to investigators in order to determine whether she was receiving all that she was entitled to get.[65]

Expenses incurred while investigating employees in order to avoid embezzlement losses are deductible.[66]

Probation, expenses to obtain. *See* **Restitution payments.**

Productivity award. An employer may deduct the cost, but not in excess of $400, of tangible personal property given to an employee for productivity.[67]

Professional expenses. *See* **License maintenance.**

Professional instruments and equipment. The cost of instruments and equipment is deductible by a professional person if the useful life of the equipment is short.[68]

Professional journals. Deduction is allowed for the cost of subscriptions to professional journals.[69]

Professional memberships. An actor was permitted to deduct the cost of membership in the Screen Actors Guild.[70]

Professional negligence. Losses caused by one's professional negligence are deductible as ordinary and necessary business expenses.[71]

Professional seminars. *See* **Conventions.**

Professional-society fees. Fees paid by a scientist for membership in a professional society were deductible.[72]

A physician was permitted to deduct medical-society dues.[73]

Professors, expenses of. A university professor is often expected by his employer to "publish or perish." That is, he will not be able to maintain his employment unless he has the results of his research published. If publication is in a scholarly publication which makes no payment for articles, this is not a transaction entered into for profit. But research expenses, including travel, are deductible if reasonable in terms of maintenance of one's present employment.[74] *See also* **Advanced degree, study for; Books; Depreciation; Doctoral dissertation; Education; Research; Sabbatical leave, expenses of; Taxes; Teachers, expenses of; Travel.**

Promotion expenses. *See* **Advertising.**

Promotion, expenses in obtaining. An employee, dissatisfied with his compensation and prospects at his employer's business, paid a fee to an executive search agency for help in finding him something better. The search agency did locate a better position for him elsewhere, but his old employer matched this with a promotion and higher pay. The fee paid to the agency was disallowed by the Internal Revenue Service on the ground that it was not a payment to obtain another job. The court, however, allowed the deduction.[75] Eight years later, the IRS announced that it will apply this decision in similar situations.[76]

Property used in the trade or business and involuntary conversions. In the case of so-called "Section 1231 assets," long-term capital gain is reported if the assets are sold or otherwise disposed of at a gain after having been held for more than one year. But losses are fully deductible. Section 1231 assets are property used in the taxpayer's trade or business which is either real property or depreciable property. This does not include inventory, copyright, artistic composition, or certain livestock.[77] This treatment also applies under specified circumstances to timber, coal, or domestic iron ore, and to livestock and unharvested crops.[78] This preferential tax treatment applies to the *netted* gain or loss for all transactions in Section 1231 assets within the taxable year.

Capital assets subject to Section 1231 treatment are limited to assets involuntarily converted, as by fire or governmental seizure.[79] *See also* **Farmers.**

Protection. Fees paid to private detectives for protection of business and premises during a period of labor strife were deductible where no police protection was available.[80]

Deduction was allowed for payments to an association created for the purpose of protecting employees from unjust labor demands.[81] *See also* **Bodyguard.**

Protective clothing. *See* **Work clothes.**

Proxy fight. Expenses of an investor in seeking to cause the removal of an incompetent management of a corporation in which he owns stock are deductible.[82]

A corporate president could deduct her costs in a proxy fight where she would have lost her employment if opposition forces gained control of the company.[83] *See also* **Investors.**

Psychiatrists. *See* **Medical expenses.**

Psychoanalysis. The cost of a personal psychoanalysis may be deducted as an ordinary and necessary business expense where it can be shown that the study sharpened an individual's professional skills. A clinical social worker was allowed to deduct her costs where it was shown that she benefited by learning about her own personality conflicts so that she could be more capable of separating them from her patients' problems and thereby was better enabled to diagnose and to treat her patients.[84] *See also* **Education; Medical expenses.**

Psychotherapists. *See* **Medical expenses.**

Public official, defense of position. An individual who had been elected to public office was threatened with loss of his job when voters were asked at a special election to vote whether or not he should be recalled from that office. (A recall is the removal of an official from office by a popular vote.) He waged an active campaign in his own defense and successfully defeated the recall. His costs in defending his existing position were deductible, being expenses in connection with his business of being a public official.[85]

Similarly, a state court judge, when charged with misconduct in office, was required to defend himself before a commission which could have removed him for conduct prejudicial to the administration of justice. He retained legal counsel to represent him before the commission, and after extensive discussions, the charges were dropped. Inasmuch as these charges arose from the conduct of his duties in the business of being a judge, the legal fees were deductible.[86] *See also* **Employees; Government employees.**

Punitive damages. Fines and penalties paid to a government for violation of any law are not deductible. But where a business, as a result of a civil lawsuit by another private party, was ordered by a court to pay punitive damages for breach of contract and fraud in connection with the ordinary conduct of its business affairs, this was fully deductible as a business expense.[87]

Purchase of stock to get assets. In the standard situation, sale of stock at a loss produces capital loss. But the loss was fully deductible as a business expense where the purpose of the stock's acquisition was not investment but a business objective.

A wholesale liquor dealer purchased shares of stock in a distillery during a whiskey shortage in order to exercise rights offered by the distiller to acquire liquor; loss on the sale of the shares after the rights were exercised was fully deductible.[88]

A business enterprise could deduct as a business expense its cost of purchasing stock in a manufacturing company that went bankrupt. The only purpose of the acquisition was to ensure a steady supply of equipment.[89]

Loss similarly was deductible where stock in a retailing organization had been purchased by a manufacturer in order to have a continuing outlet for its products.[90]

Deduction of a loss on the disposition of shares was allowed where the purpose of the acquisition had been to get the technical expertise of the employees of the company taken over.[91]

A manufacturer entered into a contract with the representative of a foreign country for the sale of machinery. The foreign government required that U.S. government bonds be deposited with a New York financial institution as security for the performance of the contract. Such bonds were purchased and were sold at a loss when the contract was completed. The loss was deductible in full, having been incurred in the regular course of the taxpayer's business.[92]

A business paid a certain dollar amount for the stock of a corporation which was dissolved immediately. Inasmuch as the only purpose for acquiring the stock was to be relieved of a burdensome contract, and as there was no intention to buy or to hold the stock as an investment, the payment was deductible as an ordinary and necessary expense of doing business or as a business loss.[93] See also **Ordinary and necessary business expenses.**

P

---

1. Revenue Ruling 79-66, 1979-1 CB 114.
2. *Oliver et al. v. Commissioner,* 553 F.2d 560 (8th Cir., 1977).
3. *Siragusa v. Commissioner,* T.C. Memo. 1980-68, filed March 10, 1980.
4. Revenue Procedure 74-23, 1974-2 CB 476.
5. Revenue Ruling 73-91, 1973-1 CB 71.
6. IRS Letter Ruling 8017001, August 30, 1979.
7. IRC Section 704(b).
8. *Frederick S. Klein,* 25 T.C. 1045 (1956).
9. *Michael L. Dotson et al.,* T.C. Memo., Docket Nos. 40611-2, entered August 6, 1953.
10. Revenue Ruling 70-253, 1970-1 CB 31.
11. *Mann et al. v. Commissioner,* T.C. Memo. 1981-684, filed November 25, 1981.
12. Revenue Ruling 66-93, 1966-1 CB 165.
13. *A. King Aitkin et al.,* 12 BTA 692 (1928).
14. Revenue Ruling 72-608, 1972-2 CB 100.
15. *Raymond Warren Jackson et al.,* T.C. Memo. 1975-301, filed September 30, 1975.
16. *Allen et al. v. Commissioner,* 283 F.2d 785 (7th Cir., 1960).
17. *Dancer et al. v. Commissioner,* 73 T.C. 1103 (1980).
18. *Jackson P. Howard et al.,* T.C. Memo. 1976-5, filed January 7, 1976.
19. Revenue Ruling 57-198, 1957-1 CB 94.
20. Revenue Ruling 73-305, 1973-2 CB 43.
21. *Your Federal Income Tax,* 1980 edition, page 102.
22. *A. H. Phillips Co., Inc., v. Commissioner,* T.C. Memo. 1977-150, filed May 18, 1977.
23. *Marcell v. United States,* DC, Vt., 1961.
24. *Robert C. Fryer et al.,* T.C. Memo. 1974-26, filed January 30, 1974.
25. *Elwood J. Clark et al.,* T.C. Memo., Docket Nos. 9059, 9135, and 9167, entered April 1, 1946.
26. *Commissioner v. Benson,* 146 F.2d 191 (9th Cir., 1944).
27. *Your Federal Income Tax,* 1979 edition, page 90.
28. *Regan v. Commissioner,* T.C. Memo. 1979-340, filed August 28, 1979.
29. *Richard L. Wesenberg et al.,* 69 T.C. 1005 (1978).
30. *Alan Aaronson,* T.C. Memo. 1970-178, filed June 25, 1970.
31. *Burdett et al. v. Commissioner,* T.C. Memo. 1981-736, filed December 31, 1981.
32. Revenue Ruling 58-382, 1958-2 CB 59.
33. *Charles Hutchison,* 13 BTA 1187 (1928).
34. Revenue Ruling 80-331, 1980-2 CB 29.
35. *Maness et al. v. United States,* 237 F. Supp. 918 (DC, MD Fla., 1965), *aff'd on another issue,* 347 F.2d 357 (5th Cir., 1966).
36. IRC Section 169.
37. *Arthur S. McKenzie et al.,* T.C. Memo., Docket No. 30042, entered May 2, 1952.
38. *E. N. Fry,* 5 T.C. 1058 (1945).
39. *Regan v. Commissioner,* T.C. Memo. 1979-340, filed August 28, 1979.
40. Revenue Ruling 77-16, 1977-1 CB 37.

41. *Ralph E. Duncan*, 30 T.C. 386 (1958).

42. *Arthur S. McKenzie et al.*, T.C. Memo., Docket No. 30042, entered May 2, 1952.

43. *Blitzer et al. v. United States*, 684 F.2d 874 (Ct. Cl., 1982).

44. *Berglund et al. v. United States*, DC, Minn., 1981.

45. *Cecil Randolph Hundley, Jr.*, 48 T.C. 339 (1967).

46. *Briarcliff Candy Corporation v. Commissioner*, 475 F.2d 775 (2d Cir., 1973).

47. *Brown v. Commissioner*, T.C. Memo. 1979-434. filed October 24, 1979.

48. *United States v. Manor Care, Inc.*, 490 F. Supp. 355 (DC, Md., 1980).

49. *Blitzer et al. v. United States*, (Ct. Cl., 1981).

50. Revenue Ruling 73-201, 1973-1 CB 140.

51. Revenue Ruling 73-511, 1973-2 CB 402.

52. Revenue Ruling 82-27, IRB 1982-7, 5.

53. *L-R Heat Treating Company*, 28 T.C. 894 (1957).

54. *Dillingham et al. v. United States*, DC, WD Okla., 1981.

55. IRC Section 461(g).

56. *Zaninovich et al. v. Commissioner*, 616 F.2d 429 (9th Cir., 1980).

57. IRC Section 212(3).

58. *Higgins v. Commissioner*, 143 F.2d 654 (1st Cir., 1944).

59. Revenue Ruling 73-137, 1973-1 CB 68.

60. Revenue Ruling 57-198, 1957-1 CB 94.

61. Revenue Ruling 57-198, 1957-1 CB 94.

62. *Stern et al. v. United States*, DC, CD Cal., 1971.

63. Tax Equity and Fiscal Responsibility Act of 1982, Section 202.

64. Revenue Ruling 63-145, 1963-2 CB 86.

65. *Ila B. Mann*, T.C. Memo. 1965-161, filed June 17, 1965.

66. *Desmonds, Inc.*, 15 BTA 738 (1929).

67. Economic Recovery Tax Act of 1981, Section 265.

68. Regulations Section 1.162-6.

69. Ibid.

70. *Regan v. Commissioner*, T.C. Memo. 1979-340, filed August 28, 1979.

71. *Henry F. Cochrane*, 23 BTA 202 (1931).

72. *Matilda M. Brooks*, 30 T.C. 1087 (1958), *rev'd on other grounds*, 274 F.2d 96 (9th Cir., 1960).

73. *Kenneth Blanchard*, T.C. Memo., Docket No. 24010, entered May 21, 1953.

74. Revenue Ruling 63-275, 1963-2 CB 85.

75. *Kenneth R. Kenfield*, 54 T.C. 1197 (1970).

76. Public Law 96-608, Section 3.

77. IRC Section 1231(1),(b)(1).

78. IRC Section 1231(b)(2),(3),(4).

79. Regulations Section 1.1231-1(a).

80. *Carlos W. Munson*, 18 BTA 232 (1929).

81. *Mrs. H. A. Allen*, 7 BTA 1256 (1927).

82. *Central Foundry Company*, 49 T.C. 234 (1967).

83. *Jean Nidetch*, T.C. Memo. 1978-313, filed August 11, 1978.

84. *Voigt et al. v. Commissioner*, 74 T.C. 82 (1980).

85. Revenue Ruling 71-470, 1971-2 CB 121.

86. Revenue Ruling 74-394, 1974-2 CB 40.

87. Revenue Ruling 80-211, 1980-2 CB 57.

88. *Western Wine & Liquor Co.*, 18 T.C. 1090 (1952).

89. *Arlington Bowling Corporation.* T.C. Memo. 1959-201, filed October 26, 1959.

90. *Weather-Seal, Inc.*, T.C. Memo. 1963-102, filed April 8, 1963.

91. *Schlumberger Technology Corporation v. United States*, 443 F.2d 1115 (1971).

92. *Commissioner v. Bagley Sewell Company*, 221 F.2d 944 (2d Cir., 1955).

93. *Pressed Steel Car Company, Inc.*, 20 T.C. 198 (1953).

R

Racial discrimination suit. *See* **Violation of rights, payments to settle.**

Railroad-car inspector, expenses of. A railroad-car inspector was permitted to deduct the cost of shirts emblazoned with an armband bearing his employer's emblem. The armbands were not removable unless the threads were taken out.[1] *See also* **Uniforms.**

Railroad rolling stock. The cost of certain railroad rolling stock may be amortized for Federal income tax purposes over a sixty-month period.[2]

Ransom. An employer may deduct payments made to obtain the release of a valued executive. Although the kidnapper's demands had been sent to the victim's family, the employer's payment was deductible because the payor would have suffered loss if deprived of a valuable asset: an executive.[3]

Razing of property. *See* **Demolition.**

Real estate. *See* **Interest; Taxes.**

Real-estate transfer taxes. *See* **Taxes.**

Real property. *See* **Election to deduct or to capitalize.**

Rebates. Under various circumstances a business is not permitted to sell below stipulated prices. Example: In a regulated industry such as liquor or milk, state law may ban sales below posted prices. In California, state law forbade wholesale liquor dealers from selling below prices on file at a state agency. One dealer billed favored customers at the official prices required by state law but allowed credits which brought down the actual costs to these customers. Then the pet customers asked for wet goods they desired, and these were furnished without cost up to the amount of the credits, cost of sales being charged for the figures represented in the credit memoranda. Gross income of the wholesale liquor dealer for income tax purposes was based upon actual net prices paid by customers and not upon the legal minimum prices which should have been paid. This amounted to a deduction of the amount of the rebates or credits, which served to reduce gross income. The court distinguished between (1) rebates to which customers became entitled at the time of sale, as here, and (2) costs incurred in the form of bribes and kickbacks that were not made pursuant to an agreement that was part of the original sales. Item (2) is not deductible, but item (1) is.[4]

The Internal Revenue Service has changed its position and has announced that price rebates which are illegal payments when made by the seller directly to the purchaser may be subtracted from gross sales in order to determine gross income.[5]

Recapitalization of corporation, contributions opportunity. *See* **Contributions.**

Receptionist. A receptionist could deduct the cost of a nurse's uniform which she was required by her employer to wear at work in a dentist's office.[6]

Reclining chair, as medical expense. *See* **Medical expenses.**

Redecorating. *See* **Repairs.**

Redeemable ground rent. *See* **Interest.**

Redemption penalty. A purchaser of real estate may find later that he is subject to a state- or local-tax lien for delinquent taxes of the previous owner. In order to keep this property, he must pay the back taxes and also a redemption penalty. The taxes are considered part of his cost of the property and are not deductible by him. But he can deduct the redemption penalty, which is regarded as a form of interest for the right to retain the money needed to redeem the property until the redemption period expires.[7]

Reducing, expenses of. *See* **Weight-loss program.**

Referral fees. Payments to persons who are in position to refer business to the payor are deductible.[8] (But *see* **Bribes and kickbacks.**) A salesperson could deduct amounts paid to parties who provided names of potential customers.[9]

An anesthesiologist was allowed to deduct entertainment costs for physicians who referred patients to him.[10]

Refinancing fee. The refinancing fee for a loan customarily is not deductible in the year paid. It provides a benefit intended to last for more than one year and thus has to be deducted ratably over the remaining period of the loan. But if the loan is called prematurely because of a default, any remaining unamortized portion of the fee is deductible in the year the property is sold.[11] *See also* **Expenditures for benefits lasting more than one year.**

Reforestation expenses. Individuals may elect to deduct part of the cost of reforestation expenditures instead of treating the entire expenditure as nondeductible except for annual depreciation write-offs over the life of the property. Up to $10,000 a year is allowed; the figure is $5,000 for a married person filing a separate return. If the election is made, the cost is written off as a deduction ratably over a period of eighty-four months. This refers to direct costs incurred in connection with forestation and reforestation by planting or artificial or natural seeding, and costs for site preparation, seeds or seedlings, labor, tools, and depreciation of equipment used in planting or seeding property held for commercial production of timber.[12]

Refresher course. The cost of a refresher course represents a deduction if it meets the requirements for an education deduction.[13] *See also* **Education; License maintenance.**

Refund of tax, expenditure for. Deduction is allowed for expenses in connection with obtaining a refund of any tax.[14]

Registered mail. An investor was allowed to deduct registered- or certified-mail costs in connection with the sending of securities. *See also* **Postage.**[15]

Rehabilitation expenses. A person may elect to amortize low-income housing rehabilitation expenditures over a sixty-month period. The amount of expenditure eligible for amortization is up to $40,000 if the program meets certain qualifications and is certified by the Secretary of Housing and Urban Development or by a state or local governmental unit.[16]

Reimbursement by trustee. *See* **Fiduciaries.**

Reimbursement of client or customer. *See* **Ordinary and necessary business expenses.**

Related parties. *See* **Family transactions.**

Release from franchise agreement. Amounts paid to a distributor to be released from claims for fees under a franchise agreement were deductible.[17]

Release from liability. The vice-president of a construction corporation was required by a bonding company to sign an indemnity agreement because of the corporation's low capitalization. When the corporation failed, he made a payment to the bonding company to settle his liability. Deduction was allowed for this payment; if he had not made it, he would not have been able to obtain bonding company services for other corporations with which he was affiliated.[18]

Reliance upon misrepresentation. A theft-loss deduction depends upon whether the event meets the definition of "theft" under the law of the state where it takes place. An individual subscribed $25,000 for stock in a corporation, and the persons who solicited the funds kept them. The individual was parted from his money by deceit and trickery amounting to a criminal taking of his property with felonious intent; that is, theft.[19]

A woman received a substantial sum in a divorce settlement, which was publicized in the newspapers. Shortly after this, an individual interested her in a project to acquire a nightclub, and she advanced money for the purpose. She was led to believe that the money would be set aside in a special fund until the club could be purchased. She never saw the money again. Her loss was treated as a deductible theft loss even though the fast talker actually had not been convicted as a criminal.[20]

A theft-loss deduction was allowed where money was given to a person to bet on fixed races, and the trusted recipient disappeared with the funds. The individual who provided the funds had not participated in the fixing of the race.[21]

An investor was told by a business acquaintance that there was an opportunity for each of them to invest $50,000 in the purchase of some patents on recording equipment. The investor gave the latter a $50,000 check, relying on the acquaintance's recommendations, which in an earlier transaction of what seemed to be the same nature had resulted in a small profit. When the investor heard that his acquaintance had been convicted of misapplication of funds, he vainly sought to recover his money. A theft-loss deduction was allowed, because he had been parted from his money by misrepresentation by someone who had even duped the Internal Revenue Service with a rubber check. There was no possibility of recovery, for the perpetrator, who held no assets in his own name, was judgment-proof because legally he owned no property which could be attached.[22]

Where money is parted with under false pretenses of a nonbusiness or personal nature, the first $100 is not deductible.[23]

An individual could deduct the payment he had made to a person who, representing himself to be an attorney, obtained for his client a divorce decree that proved to be a forgery. This was treated as a theft loss, the first $100 of which was nondeductible because it did not result from a business transaction.[24]

If a taxpayer claims a loss because of reliance upon another party's misrepresentation, he must be in a position to prove that he actually had relied upon it. When a certain corporation became insolvent, an investor who had lent money to the company claimed a theft loss on the ground that he would not have advanced the funds had he known that the balance sheet falsely indicated the firm was solvent. But inasmuch as he could not prove that he had ever looked at the balance sheet, he was not able to establish that he had relied upon a misrepresentation.[25]

A bad-debt deduction may be fully allowable as a theft loss, if it can be shown that a loan was made on the basis of a financial statement which was fraudulent by reason of the deliberate omission of large liabilities that made the borrower insolvent.[26]

An individual taxpayer engaged a contractor to build a home. The contractor requested and obtained advance money to buy materials. But he actually ordered the materials on credit and disappeared with the money, as a result of which the taxpayer had to pay the charges to free his property from the lien which suppliers had placed upon it. When the contractor filed a voluntary petition in bankruptcy, the taxpayer objected to releasing the contractor from debts on the ground that the contractor had taken money by fraud. But a state court was not convinced that the contractor had the guilty intent required by law, and he was discharged of his debts. The Internal Revenue Service resisted the theft-loss deduction because the contractor had not been found guilty of fraud. The court allowed deduction, however, because the weight of the evidence was that fraud indeed had been committed although no conviction had been obtained.[27]

The word *theft* covers "any criminal appropriation of another's property to the use of the taker, particularly including theft by swindling, false pretenses, and any other form of guile."[28]

An engineer consulted a business broker about the possibility of buying into a business where his engineering talents would be useful. The broker suggested that his business was a good one in which to invest, as there were acquisitions and merger deals that required the expertise of an engineer. So the engineer, relying upon assurances of important clients, paid $10,000 for a 20 percent interest in the business. The broker and the money disappeared. As the engineer had been parted from his money through trick or deceit after relying upon knowingly false misrepresentations, he had a deductible theft loss.[29] *See also* **Casualties; Investors.**

Relocation. *See* **Moving expenses.**

Relocation of business assets. Expenditures in connection with the acquisition of business assets having a life of more than one year are not deductible but must be added to the cost of these assets and subjected to the annual depreciation deduction. (*See* **Expenditures for benefits lasting more than one year.**) The cost of moving equipment which previously had been purchased, however, could be deducted.[30]

Remainder interest, contribution in form of. *See* **Contributions.**

Remainderman. *See* **Beneficiaries; Legal fees.**

Remedial education. *See* **Education; Medical expenses.**

Remedial reading. A child suffered from a mental handicap known as dyslexia, or cross-dominance, which makes it very difficult to learn to read. Only education, rather than medical procedures, can be used to overcome the results of this condition. Fees paid to a teacher trained to administer such instruction are deductible as medical expenses.[31]

Removal of impediments to the physically handicapped. For taxable years beginning before January 1, 1983, a taxpayer may elect to deduct rather than to capitalize the cost of removing certain impedimenta to physically impaired persons. This refers to the removal of architectural and transportation barriers to the handicapped (including the deaf and blind) and the elderly (age sixty-five or over) in any facility or public-transportation vehicle owned or leased for use in a trade or business. The maximum deduction for a taxpayer for any taxable year is $25,000. In order to qualify for the deduction, the expenses must meet certain government standards.[32] (*See also* **Election to deduct or to capitalize.**)

The election is made by identifying the deduction as a separate item on the taxpayer's Federal income tax return for the taxable year. For the election to be valid, the return must be filed no later than the time (including any extensions) prescribed by law for filing the return.[33]

Renovation. *See* **Repairs.**

Rent. Rent of business premises is deductible.[34] The value of leasehold improvements installed by a tenant on the landlord's property is deductible if the parties intended this to be equivalent to a nonmonetary form of payment for the use of the leased premises.[35]

Taxes paid by a tenant to or for a landlord for business property are considered to be additional rent and are deductible by the tenant.[36]

Where an apartment is used both for business and for personal purposes, an allocation of the rent between these two uses is to be made, and that part of the rent thus allocated to business purposes is deductible.[37] *See also* **Alimony; Apartment used for business purposes; Family transactions; Gift and leaseback; Investors; Office at home; Sale and leaseback.**

Rent, forgiveness of. A taxpayer reported income on the accrual basis. When a business tenant who was in arrears on his rent requested that he be relieved of his back rent although he was not insolvent, the taxpayer forgave the delinquent rent which he had already included in his income. A deduction was allowed for the forgiven rent. The premises benefited from the fine appearance of the tenant's enterprise and attracted a superior type of clientele which the taxpayer felt would improve his own business.[38]

Rental payments by a business tenant to an unrelated landlord are deductible; they may also be deductible when paid to a related party under appropriate circumstances. This simple rule is complicated by a lease with option to purchase. Are the annual payments deductible rent or installments on the purchase price? The test is whether the tenant's annual payments are in excess of the going rental rate, so that actually he is acquiring an equity in the property. If, at the end of the lease, the tenant can buy the property for much less than its worth, usually he is regarded as having in fact paid for the property over the years. But when one tenant at the end of the lease acquired property under the option for $30,000 and immediately sold it for $48,000, his payments in prior years still were deductible. They were just about at the going rate for flat rentals. The low option price, in the court's judgment, had been the result of a fortunate business bargain he had made and had not been an attempt to cast a sales transaction in the form of a lease.[39] *See also* **Ground rent.**

Repairing of damaged property. *See* **Casualties.**

Repairs. The nature of a deductible repair was analyzed by a court decision which has been quoted with approval in hundreds of later decisions:

In determining whether an expenditure is a capital one or is chargeable against operating income, it is necessary to bear in mind the purpose for which the expenditure is made. To repair is to restore to a sound state or to mend, while a replacement connotes a substitution. A repair is an expenditure for the purpose of keeping the property in an ordinary efficient operating condition. It does not add to the value of the property, nor does it appreciably prolong its life. It merely keeps the property in an operating condition over its probable useful life for the uses for which it was acquired. Expenditures for the purpose are distinguishable from those for replacements, alterations, improvements, or additions which prolong the life of the property, increase its value, or make it acceptable to a different use. The one is a maintenance charge, while the others are additions to capital investment which should not be applied against current earnings.[40]

Deductible repairs are confined to business properties, as is indicated by the allowance in the Treasury Regulations under the heading of "business deductions."[41]

Deduction was allowed for the cost of glass window panes which had to be replaced in a business building.[42]

A professional person could deduct the cost of painting his own office building.[43]

Where a building was purchased for business purposes, renovations were made in order to place the property in a condition suitable for rental purposes. Reconstruction expenditures were not deductible as the benefits would last for more than a year. But painting, wallpapering, and redecorating were deductible inasmuch as the work had been performed in contemplation of the rental use of the property.[44]

The general rule is that the cost of a business repair is deductible only if the property is not improved as to length of life or of usefulness.

If the property ends up in some more valuable form, the cost must be deducted over the years of expected useful life.

An individual purchased a farm on which there was an earthen dam. Water subsequently began to seep through the dam. A contractor was hired to drain the reservoir and to excavate soil from one area for replacement with clay. Upon completion of this work, the general appearance of the dam seemed unchanged but the water seepage had stopped. The full cost was deductible. The sole purpose of the expenditure was to prevent leaks and to keep the dam in an ordinary operating condition over its probable useful life for the use for which it was acquired. The work did not create a replacement for the dam but merely restored its original capacity of retaining water. Explained the court: "To some extent, of course, every repair or restoration, no matter how minor or how soon after acquisition it is done, will add some value to the thing repaired or restored." Fixing leaks is hardly extraordinary, and the differences in the condition of the property before and after the work was done were insufficient to require the expense to be treated as a capital expenditure to be spread over the life of the work performed.[45]

About half of one side of the roof of an individual's dairy farm was damaged by a windstorm. The full amount needed to repair the damage was not paid by the insurance company because of the age of the structure. The entire cost of repairing the shingles less what was received from the insurance company was deductible. Replacement of the shingles did not materially add to the property or appreciably prolong its life but maintained it in ordinary efficient operating condition.[46]

A repair is deductible if the purpose of the expenditure is merely a restoration of the *status quo*. Thus, the replacement of pipes containing potential defects was allowed, even though repairs could have been performed on a leak-by-leak basis as they occurred, for the expenditures did not enhance the property's value or adapt the property to a different use. The primary purpose for making these repairs was not to achieve improvements.[47]

Expenditures to place a factory building in good condition after water leakage were deductible. Although the total expenditure was large, amounting to 35 percent of the value of the building, about 80 percent of this expenditure was for labor and about 20 percent for material. No major unit in the structure was wholly replaced.[48]

Deduction was allowed for the cost of replacing rotor bar windings in an electric motor. Parts of the motor wore out because of constant usage. While the restored parts were important and constituted about 20 percent of the entire motor, they did not add materially to the value, life, or efficiency of the motor as originally installed.[49]

Relining the fire box of a boiler was a deductible repair.[50]

A taxpayer's garage was used for business purpose. Salt, carried during winter by automobiles coming into the garage from the street, caused deterioration of the concrete floor and its steel supports. Replacement of large areas of concrete flooring and steel supports represented nondeductible capital expenditures because they added materially to the life of the property. But minor patchwork repairs of concrete were regarded as deductible expenses.[51]

Similarly, deduction was allowed for the cost of replastering, repainting, and mending floors, ceilings, and wiring of a showroom which had been damaged by water leakage.[52]

The cost of repair of a septic sewer system at a taxpayer's farm was fully deductible. It was not a capital improvement to the system, for it did not materially add to the property or appreciably prolong its life, but simply maintained the system in an ordinary and efficient operating condition.[53]

A taxpayer could deduct the cost of repairs and replacements in the form of a complete cleaning, overhauling, and replacing of axles, transmissions, and brakes of motor equipment used for business purposes. Although the repairs were extensive and the new materials had some advantages over those replaced, they did not materially increase the value or the life of the equipment but only kept it in usable condition.[54]

Modifications to a mine hoist made solely for safety reasons, when the anticipated life of the equipment was not extended materially, were deductible repairs even though the asset after this work was not precisely the same as it originally had been.[55]

Where the work is to improve the life, utility, or performance of the asset, the expenditure is not deductible, being considered an investment in a capital asset, recoverable only through annual depreciation deductions. A business experienced many leaks in its underground piping. Rather than replace the pipes, the business installed clamps to cover deteriorated places. Whenever pipes were uncovered in connection with new construction or other activities, clamps would be installed at places which seemed to be weakened. The costs, primarily for excavating to get at the pipes, were deductible as repairs. The clamping of a pipe did not adapt it to a new or different use, nor was the original estimated useful life extended by this work.[56]

Deduction was allowed for the cost of replacement of the entire length of an underground cable. Part of the cable had been damaged by a flood, which at frequent intervals caused the line to "blow up," interrupting the operation of machinery until repairs could be made. The decision to replace the entire patched-up cable with a new one resulted in an allowable deduction in the nature of a repair and not a capital expenditure.[57]

The cost of repairs necessitated by vandalism affecting business property was deductible.[58]

Repairs are deductible even though they are occasioned by the taxpayer's negligence.[59]

An expenditure is more likely to be regarded as a repair for tax purposes if there is no substitution of a different material or structure.[60] Frequently it is stated that a repair, to be deductible, must be made with the same materials as those being replaced, for otherwise the work would be more than a restoration of the *status quo*. That is not necessarily the case. Costs were deductible where a roof was repaired with a different material from the original one, because the new materials did not add to the value or prolong the life of the roof.[61]

The cost of extensive repairs to trucks which had received rough use was deductible, even though, in two instances, the new material had some advantages over that which it replaced.[62]

When a tractor that had been rented to another contractor required overhauling and replacement of many parts to restore it to the condition at the time of rental, the costs were deductible. They did not increase the value or life of the equipment but only kept it in usable condition.[63]

The cost of repairing the leaky roof of business premises was deductible, even though there was some structural change—namely, the insertion of an expansion joint in the roof. But the evidence showed that that was the most economical way to repair the leaks and thus to keep the property in an ordinarily efficient operating condition.[64]

Repairs for the purpose of restoring a business asset to its original operating condition usually are deductible. Where an asset is purchased which is badly in need of repairs, the cost of these repairs is usually treated as part of the cost of the asset; that is, a capital expenditure which is not deductible except in the form of annual depreciation. But deduction of the cost of repairs is permitted where it can be shown that the repairs and improvements had not been anticipated when the asset was acquired.[65]

Deduction was allowed for the cost of replacing the "ammonia parts" of a druggist's refrigerator with "freon parts," as the ammonia parts were difficult to obtain and prohibitive in cost.[66]

The cost of repairs was deductible where the business equipment was of no greater efficiency or utility after the repair, even if the work done was not a reasonable facsimile of the original item, as in the case of an elevator.[67]

Replacement of a malfunctioning unit may give rise to a deduction. Such was the case where the compressor for a business air-conditioning unit became unusable and had to be replaced in the year of acquisition.[68]

When business assets are purchased in poor condition, the cost of repairs is usually not deductible, being deemed a part of the cost of the assets inasmuch as it was known that this work had to be done in order to make the equipment serviceable. But where water leaked through the roof and walls sixteen months after the purchase of a building, repair costs, although amounting to 35 percent of the cost of the structure, were deductible. The work had not been anticipated and merely restored the building to its original condition.[69]

After a fire had partially destroyed a plant, expenditures for temporary electrical installations and other emergency activities to place the plant in running order were deductible.[70]

Deduction was allowed for the cost of lumber used in making temporary doors for a property used for business purposes. As the expenditure was for a temporary repair, it was deductible.[71]

When part of a business building was torn down after it had been condemned as unsafe by municipal inspectors, reconstruction of what had been a plaster interior wall so that it could serve as an exterior wall amounted to a deductible repair. Nothing had been added to the value of the building.[72]

The cost of lowering a concrete culvert on a farm because it had been installed too high in the ground and endangered passing cars was deductible as a repair.[73]

Repair expense was allowed in the case of drilling and grouting (filling with a kind of cement) and some replacements to prevent further cave-ins of a plant.[74]

Subsidence of subsoil under a warehouse caused the posts supporting the roof truss to shift, threatening collapse of the roof. A building inspector warned that if the situation was not corrected, the premises would have to be evacuated. Money spent in order to realign the posts was deductible. The expenditure prolonged the useful life of the building only in the negative sense that if the repairs had not been made, the roof probably would have collapsed and the building would have been ruined.[75]

When business assets are purchased in damaged condition so that it must have been obvious that repairs would need to be made in order to put the property in satisfactory operating condition, usually the cost of repairs is not deductible, being deemed part of the acquisition cost of the assets. But deduction was allowed for the cost of repairing defects which had not been apparent at the time of purchase.[76]

Deduction was allowed for the cost of pushing earth on a farm into ridges which followed the contours of the land in order to prevent further soil erosion from water. Nothing new was added to the farm.[77]

A business owned and operated docks and piers on a river location. Silt accumulated regularly to such an extent that dredging had to be performed at times to maintain the necessary water depth for passage of shipping. The expenses did not improve the taxpayer's property but merely permitted continued operation of its facilities. Deduction was allowed.[78]

Where posts supporting a beach-front residence were damaged by a hurricane, the cost of reposting was deductible, even though not required for another two years.[79]

Where an individual uses his own car for charitable work exclusively, he may deduct the cost of repairs to the vehicle.[80]

A person who is hard of hearing may deduct not only the cost of equipment to alleviate this condition, but the cost of keeping it in a state of good repair.[81]

A farmer could deduct the cost of moving dead and blown-down trees as repair expense.[82] *See also* **Alimony; Casualties; Farmers; Ordinary and necessary business expenses; Watch repairs.**

Repairs as measure of casualty loss. A casualty-loss deduction may be determined by either of two methods: (1) decrease in fair market value as determined by a competent appraiser or (2) the actual cost of repairs.[83]

The amount actually *spent* for repairs, as contrasted to a credible estimate or bid, is what is deductible.[84]

Customarily, the cost of repairing assets damaged by a casualty is not deductible if reimbursement could be obtained from an insurance company. But the repair bill was deductible where a taxpayer's insurance broker had advised against filing the claim lest the taxpayer's large claim history cause the insurance company to cancel further coverage, which was essential to remaining in business.[85]

Repayment of embezzled funds. Repayment of embezzled funds is deductible as a loss in the case of a transaction entered upon for profit.[86]

Repayment of excessive compensation. Where an executive is required by a corporate by-law to reimburse the company for any amount of his compensation disallowed as excessive pay when the Internal Revenue Service audited the corporate tax return, he can deduct the amount he repays to the company.[87]

If he repays an amount disallowed as excessive to his employer, he can deduct only the amounts attributable to the periods after an agreement is signed.[88] *See also* **Executives.**

Repayment of supplemental unemployment compensation benefits. Under defined conditions, a person who has been laid off because of heavy competition from abroad is entitled to "trade readjustment assistance," under the Trade Act of 1974. But a condition is that he repay any supplemental unemployment compensation benefits which he has received as a result of losing his job. Repayment is deductible, effective for taxable years beginning after December 28, 1980.[89]

Replacement of damaged property. A businessperson was allowed to deduct the cost of a bicycle destroyed by one of his trucks.[90]

Representative fees. Employees who do not belong to a union may be required by the union contract to have the equivalent of dues withheld from compensation payments. These withholdings are deductible.[91]

Reprints. A salesperson could deduct the cost of reprints of magazine articles referring to the products he was attempting to sell when the reprints were sent to prospective customers.[92]

Reputation, maintenance of. The regular rule is that a taxpayer cannot deduct the expenses of another party. But deduction is allowed if the expenditures are for the payor's benefit. Such was the case where an individual's name was used by a personal service (public relations) company which he headed. When the company was financially unable to pay its bills, the president paid them. He was allowed the deduction because of his belief, which the court found reasonable, that if he had permitted the corporation which bore his name to go into bankruptcy, his reputation and standing would have been injured in the public relations community where his livelihood was to be gained. So his payments to trade creditors of the corporation were deductible as ordinary and necessary expenditures of his business of being an executive.[93]

Payment by an investment banker to a corporation of which he was a director, to avoid possible liability under the Securities and Exchange Act and to protect his reputation as a banker, was deductible.[94]

An individual was president of a financial institution, which engaged in certain financial irregularities. These could have brought about the institution's insolvency, with resultant probing into his role in these practices. He felt that if the institution failed, an investigation would make it impossible for him ever again to obtain business credit. He was permitted to deduct substantial amounts he contributed to the institution in an effort to keep it solvent. These payments had been made primarily to preserve his business activities and his earnings capacity flowing from them.[95]

A lawyer was engaged in performing legal services primarily for insurance companies. He purchased stock in one such company, which he later sold at a profit. A state attorney-general maintained that under the technical provisions of his state's law, the profit belonged to the corporation. The lawyer doubted this and the matter went to court; but fearful that controversy would damage his status and reputation with the insurance companies, and that his professional career would be endangered, he paid the amount of the profits over to the corporation. He could deduct this amount as an ordinary and necessary expense in connection with his trade or business.[96]

A shoe designer and salesman advanced money to his employer corporations so that they would be in position to deliver to his customers large quantities of footwear he had sold to these customers. He was allowed to deduct as business bad debts the amounts his employers could not repay to him. The loans had been made in order to maintain his reputation and to hold his clients.[97]

Deduction was permitted for worthless bad debts resulting from loans made by a business or professional person in an effort to retain clients and to maintain his reputation.[98] *See also* **Bad debts; Executives; Expenses of another person; Legal fees.**

Research. Research expenses incurred by a professor for the purpose of teaching, lecturing, and writing in his own field were deductible as a means of carrying out the duties expected of him as a professor without expectation of profit apart from his salary.[99]

A university research associate could deduct the cost of printing a scientific article. He was expected by his employer to prepare manuscripts concerning his research pursuits and to secure publication of these in scientific journals in order to meet his present job responsibilities and to obtain promotion. He had not been able to get his research articles published through normal channels of communication because of the controversial position which he took.[100]

A full-time university instructor was permitted to deduct his research expenses in connection with taking courses that would qualify him for a doctoral degree.[101]

A professional writer was permitted to deduct travel and away-from-home lodgings while conducting research for a book he had reasonable expectations of marketing.[102] *See also* **Subscriptions to periodicals.**

Research and experimental expenses. It is not necessary that research and experimental activity relate solely to a person's existing product or services.[103] Such expenses are deductible where efforts are made to develop new products or processes which are unrelated to current product lines or manufacturing processes of the taxpayer's trade or business.[104]

A manufacturer can deduct as research and experimental expenditures the cost of developing and designing, at the manufacturer's risk, a specially built automated manufacturing system for a single customer's specific order.[105]

Expenditures which are expected to produce benefits lasting more than one year must be capitalized and not deducted currently. But the cost of economic analysis of projects which were never undertaken could be written off when the project was abandoned.[106] *See also* **Election to deduct or to capitalize.**

Reserve for bad debts, additions to. *See* **Bad debts.**

Residence sold at a loss. If an individual sells his residence at a loss, deduction depends upon whether this was a transaction entered into for profit or was the sale of his personal home. An individual purchased land and commissioned a builder to construct a home for his family there. But the purchaser and his wife had such violent arguments about the details of their dream house that their marital relationship was threatened. At that point they decided to abandon plans to build a home. The builder was instructed to eliminate all the personalized custom features of the structure and to substitute cheap materials wherever possible so that persons interested primarily in buying a cheap residence would be attracted. But the finished building was sold at a loss. This was deductible because, by abandoning his intention to construct a personal home in which to live, the taxpayer had converted the house's construction and other costs into a transaction entered upon for profit. Actually, he had never lived there.[107]

Rest home, expenses at. *See* **Medical expenses; Retirement homes.**

Restitution payments. Fines and penalties are generally not deductible. Restitution payments are something else. An officer of a contracting company was convicted of misappropriation of funds paid by a client for the construction of a house. As a condition of his probation, the executive was directed by a court to pay $5,000 to the client. This was deductible, not being a fine or similar payment imposed by a state legislature or the local law. It merely represented the payment of an amount due and owing in connection with a business transaction.[108] *See also* **Settlement payments.**

Restitution to customers. *See* **Business-related losses.**

Restoration of damaged property. *See* **Casualties.**

Restrictive easement, contribution in form of. *See* **Contributions.**

Résumés. Expenses of typing, printing, and mailing résumés of one's business or professional qualifications to prospective employers are deductible if one is seeking new employment in one's present trade or business.[109] *See also* **Employment, expenses in seeking.**

Retarded persons. *See* **Education; Medical expenses.**

Retirement homes. If a husband and wife pay a monthly life-care fee to a retirement home and are able to prove that a specific portion of the fee covers the cost of providing medical care for them, that portion of the fee is deductible by the couple as an expense for medical care in the year paid.[110] It should be noted, however, that the extent to which expenses for care in an institution other than a hospital will constitute medical care is primarily a question of fact as to what the payment actually represents.[111]

Ordinarily, personal living expenses, even in a retirement home, are not deductible. And advance payments for medical services to be rendered in subsequent years are not allowed. But where proper records have been kept, a medical-expense deduction is allowed at the time of payment. An individual paid a lump-sum fee to a retirement home under an agreement entitling him to live in the home and to receive lifetime care. The fee was calculated (whether by negotiation or on a what-the-traffic-would-bear basis) without regard to any similar contracts with other patients at the home, and hence no part of it could be called medical insurance. The retirement home demonstrated that a stipulated percentage of the life-care fee covered the home's obligation to provide medical care, medicines, and hospitalization and gave him a separate statement to that effect. It was agreed that on the basis of past experience, the medical-expense allocation of this lump-sum fee conformed to actuality. Because the individual's obligation to pay the lump-sum amount (including the percentage allocable to medical care) was incurred at the time the payment was made in return for the retirement home's promise to provide lifetime care, that part of the charge to secure medical protection was deductible when paid despite the fact that the medical services were not to be performed until a future time—if at all. Accordingly, the portion of the charge allocated to this medical care was deductible as medical expense.[112]

A proper allocation of medical to total life-care fees may be determined by dividing all directly related medical expenses by total expenses. To the extent that they can be substantiated and are allocable medical-care facilities, medically related expenses may include, among other items, real-estate taxes, insurance, and depreciation.[113]

An individual entered into a written agreement with a tax-exempt organization, which provided that he would live at its facility and would receive lifetime care, including his main meal in the dining room and medical attention. The entrance fees charged by this home were determined by a projection of costs of providing services for the average period of residency of each resident. That portion of the entrance fees and monthly service charges were deductible to the extent that they could properly be allocated to medical care.[114]

Entrance fees were paid to a retirement home for providing residence for a dependent of the payor. This home provided no medical care. But in the case of chronic, prolonged, or continuous illness, a resident was entitled to a specified number of days of standard care at a convalescent and rehabilitation center operated by an affiliate of the retirement home. Based on historical costs, 7 percent of the entrance fee paid to the retirement home was estimated to be the cost for providing the cumulative days of prepaid standard care in the convalescent center to residents of the retirement center. Of the fee paid to the retirement center, only this 7 percent was deductible medical expense.[115]

An individual entered into an agreement with a retirement home, under which agreement he became entitled to live there and to receive lifetime care that included specified residential accommodations, meals, and medical care. In consideration for this provision of lifetime care, he paid a "founder's fee" upon commencing residence there plus a specified monthly fee. The fees were negotiated individually with each retiree and were not regarded as a medical insurance. Because the home demonstrated that 15 percent of the monthly fee and 10 percent of the founder's fee would be used to discharge its obligations to provide medical care for its residents, a written statement being provided to the individual to this effect, these percentages of the monthly fees and founder's fee were treated as medical expenses. But an allocation of his payments to the construction of health facilities was not deductible.[116]

A seventy-six-year-old woman with developing cataracts and the prospect of surgery sold the family house and moved with her aging, infirm husband into a retirement center. The center had been built with funds supplied by the corporation which owned it, a charitable foundation, and fees charged to residents did not provide enough money to pay off these construction costs. So "sponsorship gifts" to repay building costs were solicited by the center in its brochures. Two weeks after the couple had been admitted to the center, the woman made a sponsorship gift. She was permitted to deduct this as a charitable contribution, for although 80 percent of the center's population had made such gifts, there was no compulsion to do so, no special benefit was anticipated for making a gift, the center had not prepared the check for her signature, and the couple had been accepted before she made the gift. She had not even known, when she applied for admission and when she was accepted, that a gift was expected.[117]

An individual had a dependent parent who was a resident in a home for the elderly. This home was a member organization of a combined charity fund. The individual was permitted to deduct an unrestricted contribution which he made to the fund, even though managers of the fund made distributions of donations to member organizations, according to a formula, including the home-organization where the contributor's parent was housed.[118]

Retirement of property. *See* **Obsolescence.**

Retirement pay, expenses to establish. *See* **Armed Forces.**

Return of embezzled funds. When an individual returns to his victim any money or property which was embezzled from the latter, a deduction is allowed in the year of this repayment.[119]

Return of tax informant's fees. *See* **Informant, tax, return of fees by.**

Revenue Agents, expenses of. *See* **Books; Education; Subscriptions to periodicals.**

Reverse mortgage loan, interest on. A reverse mortgage loan is based on the value of a person's home and is secured by a mortgage on the home.

The lending institution pays him the loan in installments over a period of months or years. The loan agreement may provide that interest will be added to the outstanding loan balance monthly as it accrues. If he is a cash-basis taxpayer, he deducts the interest on a reverse mortgage loan when he actually pays it, not when it is added to the outstanding loan balance.[120]

Review courses. *See* **Education.**

Revolving-charge-account fees. *See* **Interest.**

Rewards. An individual could deduct the amount of a reward he had contributed to a municipal police department, to be given to the provider of information which would lead to the conviction of the person who had murdered the donor's son. Any money not so awarded was to be used by the police department exclusively for public purposes.[121]

An individual was permitted to deduct the amount of money that he gave to a state enforcement agency to use as rewards to persons who provided evidence to be used against drug pushers.[122] *See also* **Informants, payments to.**

A taxpayer engaged in a trade or business can deduct the amount of a reward given to a person who found and returned stolen property.[123]

Rezoning costs. *See* **Abandonment loss; Zoning change.**

Risk, limitation on investment at. *See* **Investors.**

Robbery losses. *See* **Casualties.**

Rulings on tax matters, expense of obtaining. The cost of legal and accounting work in obtaining a Federal income tax ruling from the Internal Revenue Service is deductible.[124]

R

1. *Lloyd Farrior et al.*, T.C. Memo. 1970-312, filed November 12, 1970.
2. IRC Section 184.
3. IRS Letter Ruling 7946010, no date given.
4. *Max Sobel Wholesale Liquors v. Commissioner*, 69 T.C. 477 (1977).
5. Revenue Ruling 82-149, IRB 1982-33, 5.
6. *George A. Tatum, Jr., et al.*, T.C. Memo., Docket No. 25568, entered June 26, 1951.
7. *Reinhardt et al. v. Commissioner*, 75 T.C. 47 (1980).
8. *Robert Wright et al.*, T.C. Memo. 1967-86, filed April 21, 1967.
9. *Doris Jones*, T.C. Memo., Docket No. 26145, entered May 29, 1952.

10. *Wolf et al. v. United States*, DC, WD Mo., 1964.
11. *Malmstedt et al. v. Commissioner*, 578 F.2d 520 (4th Cir., 1978).
12. IRC Section 194.
13. Regulations Section 1.162-5(c).
14. Regulations Section 1.212-1(1).
15. *Imhoff et al. v. Commissioner*, T.C. Memo. 1980-30, filed January 31, 1980.
16. IRC Section 167(k).
17. Revenue Ruling 79-208, 1979-2 CD 79.
18. *Worrell et al. v. United States*, 269 F. Supp. 897 (1967), *rev'd and rem'd on another issue*, 398 F.2d 427 (5th Cir., 1968).
19. *Paul C. F. Vietske*, 37 T.C. 504 (1961).

20. *Michele Monteleone et al.,* 34 T.C. 688 (1960).

21. *Edwards v. Bromberg et al.,* 232 F.2d 107 (5th Cir., 1956).

22. *Schneider v. Commissioner,* T.C. Memo. 1979-335, filed August 23, 1979.

23. *Charles Edward Shepherd,* T.C. Memo. 1976-48, filed February 26, 1976, *aff'd,* 7th Cir., 1977.

24. IRS Letter Ruling 8146030, August 18, 1981.

25. *Crane et al. v. Commissioner,* T.C. Memo. 1979-276, filed July 14, 1979.

26. Revenue Ruling 71-381, 1971-2 CB 126.

27. *Hartley et al. v. Commissioner,* T.C. Memo. 1977-317, filed September 19, 1977.

28. *Edwards v. Bromberg,* 232 F.2d 107 (5th Cir., 1956).

29. *McComb v. Commissioner,* T.C. Memo. 1977-176, filed June 9, 1977.

30. Revenue Ruling 70-392, 1970-2 CB 33.

31. Revenue Ruling 69-607, 1969-2 CB 40.

32. IRC Section 190.

33. Announcement 80-29, IRB 1980-9, 21.

34. IRC Section 162(a)(3).

35. *Blatt v. United States,* 305 U.S. 267 (1938).

36. Regulations Section 1.162-11(a).

37. *Ray Harroun,* T.C. Memo., Docket No. 5869, entered July 20, 1945.

38. *Lab Estates, Inc.,* 13 T.C. 811 (1949).

39. *Daniel et al. v. Commissioner,* T.C. Memo. 1978-277, filed July 24, 1978.

40. *Illinois Merchants Trust Co.,* 4 BTA 103 (1926).

41. Regulations Section 1.162-4.

42. *Ralph S. Clark et al.,* T.C. Memo. 1966-22, filed January 27, 1966.

43. *R. O. Watts,* T.C. Memo. 1975-131, filed May 7, 1975.

44. *Paul E. Jackson et al.,* T.C. Memo. 1954-235, filed December 27, 1954.

45. *Evans et al. v. Commissioner,* 557 F.2d 1095 (5th Cir., 1977).

46. *Gerald W. Pontel Family Estate v. Commissioner,* T.C. Memo. 1981-303, filed June 18, 1981.

47. *Mountain Fuel Supply Company v. United States,* DC, Utah, 1970.

48. *Buckland v. United States,* 66 F. Supp. 681 (D.C., Ct., 1946).

49. *Apollo Steel Company,* T.C. Memo., Docket No. 3436, entered April 13, 1945.

50. *Wood Preserving Corporation of Baltimore, Inc. v. United States,* DC, Md., 1964, *aff'd on another issue,* 347 F.2d 117 (4th Cir., 1965).

51. *Honigan et al. v. Commissioner,* 466 F.2d 69 (6th Cir., 1972).

52. *Charlie Sturgill Motor Co.,* T.C. Memo. 1973-281, filed December 26, 1973.

53. *Cooper et al. v. Commissioner,* T.C. Memo. 1981-369, filed July 16, 1981.

54. *Mark C. Nottingham,* T.C. Memo., Docket No. 31415, entered May 8, 1953.

55. *Ranchers Exploration and Development Corporation v. United States,* DC, N.M., 1978.

56. *Niagara Mohawk Power Corporation v. United States,* 558 F.2d 1379 (Ct. Cl., 1977).

57. *Apollo Steel Company,* T.C. Memo., Docket No. 3436, entered April 13, 1945.

58. *Shirley S. Imeson,* T.C. Memo. 1969-180, filed September 3, 1969.

59. *Brier Hill Collieries,* 12 BTA 500 (1928), *aff'd and rev'd on other issues,* 50 F.2d 277 (6th Cir., 1931).

60. *Fidelity Storage Corporation v. Burnet,* 58 F.2d 526 (CA, DC, 1932).

61. *Munroe Land Company,* T.C. Memo. 1966-2, filed January 4, 1966.

62. *Mark C. Nottingham et al.,* T.C. Memo., Docket Nos. 31414-5, entered May 8, 1953.

63. *Ibid.*

64. *Oberman Manufacturing Company,* 47 T.C. 471 (1967).

65. *Blake et al. v. Commissioner,* T.C. Memo. 1981-579, filed October 1, 1981.

66. *Adam C. Croff,* T.C. Memo. 1957-163, filed August 27, 1957.

67. *Mellie Esperson,* BTA Memo., Docket No. 98737, entered February 5, 1941.

68. *San Marco Shop, Inc.,* T.C. Memo., Docket No. 39738, entered July 22, 1953.

69. *Buckland v. United States,* 66 F. Supp. 681 (DC, Ct., 1946).

70. *Ticket Office Equipment Co., Inc.,* 20 T.C. 272 (1953), *aff'd,* 213 F.2d 318 (2d Cir., 1954).

71. *Marcell v. United States,* DC, Vt., 1961.

72. *Oscar L. Thomas et al.,* T.C. Memo. 1962-134, filed May 31, 1962.

73. *Thomas O. Campbell et al.,* T.C. Memo. 1973-101, filed April 25, 1973.

74. *American Bemberg Corporation,* 10 T.C. 361 (1948), *aff'd,* 177 F.2d 200 (6th Cir., 1949).

75. *Marion Dodd Gopcevic,* T.C. Memo., Docket No. 2677, entered November 20, 1944.

76. *Parma Company,* 18 BTA 429 (1929).

77. *J. H. Collingwood et al.,* 20 T.C. 937 (1953).

78. *Kingston River Terminal, Inc., v. United States,* DC, SD Ill., 1977.

79. *Willard T. Burkett,* T.C. Memo., Docket No. 27344, entered September 28, 1951.

80. *Orr v. United States,* 343 F.2d 553 (5th Cir., 1965).

81. Revenue Ruling 73-53, 1973-1 CB 139.

82. *Thomas O. Campbell et al.,* T.C. Memo. 1973-101, filed April 25, 1973.

83. Regulations Section 1.165-7(a)(2)(i) and (ii).

84. *Claire Lamphere et al.,* 70 T.C. 391 (1978).

85. *Waxler Towing Company, Inc. v. United States,* 510 F. Supp. 297 (DC, WD Tenn., 1980).

86. *McKinney et al. v. United States,* DC, WD Texas, 1976, *aff'd on another issue,* 574 F.2d 1240 (5th Cir., 1978).

R

370

87. *Vincent E. Oswald,* 49 T.C. 645 (1968).

88. IRS Letter Ruling 7811004, November 29, 1977.

89. Public Law 96-608, Section 3.

90. *Bertha V. Nottingham Estate,* T.C. Memo. 1956-281, filed December 28, 1956.

91. IRS Letter Ruling 7828050, April 13, 1978.

92. *Hobson, Jr., et al. v. Commissioner,* T.C. Memo. 1980-132, filed April 21, 1980.

93. *Conley et al. v. Commissioner,* T.C. Memo. 1977-406, filed November 23, 1977.

94. *Laurence M. Marks,* 27 T.C. 464 (1956).

95. *Elmer W. Conti et al.,* T.C. Memo. 1972-89, filed April 19, 1972.

96. *Joseph P. Pike et al.,* 44 T.C. 787 (1965).

97. *Maurice Arnstein et al.,* T.C. Memo. 1970-220, filed July 29, 1970.

98. *Stuart Bart et al.,* 21 T.C. 880 (1954).

99. Revenue Ruling 63-275, 1963-2 CB 85.

100. *Robert E. Drury,* T.C. Memo. 1977-199, filed June 29, 1977.

101. Revenue Ruling 67-421, 1967-2 CB 84.

102. *Stern et al. v. United States,* DC, CD Cal., 1971.

103. *Best Universal Lock Co., Inc. et al.,* 45 T.C. 1 (1965).

104. Revenue Ruling 71-162, 1971-1 CB 97.

105. Revenue Ruling 73-275, 1973-1 CB 134.

106. *Ranchers Exploration and Develop-ment Corporation v. United States,* DC, N.M., 1978.

107. *Albert W. Bassett et al.,* T.C. Memo. 1976-14, filed January 20, 1976.

108. *Spitz et al. v. United States,* 432 F. Supp. 148 (DC, ED Wis., 1977).

109. *Your Federal Income Tax,* 1979 edition, page 96.

110. Revenue Ruling 67-185, 1967-1 CB 70.

111. Regulations Section 1.213-1(e)(1)(v).

112. Revenue Ruling 75-302, 1975-2 CB 66.

113. IRS Letter Ruling 8213102, December 30, 1981.

114. IRS Letter Ruling 7807093, November 21, 1977.

115. *Estate of Helen W. Smith v. Commissioner,* 79 T.C., No. 19 (1982).

116. Revenue Ruling 76-481, 1976-2 CB 82.

117. *Dowell v. United States,* 553 F.2d 1233 (10th Cir., 1977).

118. Revenue Ruling 80-77, 1980-1 CB 56.

119. *James v. United States,* 366 U.S. 213 (1961).

120. Revenue Ruling 80-248, 1980-2 CB 164.

121. Revenue Ruling 81-307, IRB 1981-52, 8.

122. *Sampson et al. v. Commissioner,* T.C. Memo. 1982-276, filed May 18, 1982.

123. Revenue Ruling 67-98, 1967-1 CB 29.

124. Revenue Ruling 67-401, 1967-2 CB 123.

S

Sabbatical leave, expenses of. The cost of travel by a teacher while on sabbatical leave is deductible as a form of education if the travel is related directly to the teacher's professional studies. *See also* **Education; Travel.**[1]

Safe-deposit box, rental on. *See* **Investors.**

Safety award. An employer may deduct the cost, but not in excess of $400, of tangible personal property given to an employee for safety achievement.[2]

Safety campaign. Payments made to a state to cover the cost of posters and advertising of highway safety were deductible.[3]

Safety equipment. An iron worker was permitted to deduct the cost of safety equipment which he was obliged to furnish for himself, including a hard hat, a safety belt, and steel-toed boots.[4]

A maintenance electrician could deduct the cost of prescription safety glasses.[5] *See also* **Work clothes.**

Safety measures, expenses to achieve. Expenditures to make machinery or other assets safer, or to conform to safety standards, frequently involve costs which provide benefits that will last for more than one year. Such costs, being capital, are not deductible. But modifications to an asset solely for safety reasons, where the life of the asset is not prolonged appreciably nor is the asset improved as to performance, are deductible.[6]

Sale and leaseback. The owner of property may sell it to another party (sometimes called, for the purpose of convenience, the "investor") and then immediately lease it back. Depending upon the relationship of the sale price to the adjusted value at the time, the rent to obtain the use of the property again may be higher than the normal price (if the sale price was more than the property was worth) or lower than the normal rent (if the sale price was less than the property was worth). But even if a higher than normal rent was paid, this is fully deductible.[7] When the parties to such a transaction are related, a rental in excess of normal rates may not be recognized for tax purposes on the ground that the transaction lacks reality.[8]

Deduction of rent under a sale and leaseback arrangement was allowed even where the original owner had sold the building to an unrelated party at a fair price, and then rented it back while still retaining an option to repurchase the property, in which case any rentals already paid would be applied to the purchase price.[9]

Loss on a sale and leaseback may result from the transfer of intangibles, such as a mailing list.[10]

A taxpayer owned and operated a department-store building in a central city area which had deteriorated greatly. In order to finance a suburban store, the building was sold to an insurance company and immediately leased back for thirty years. Deduction of the cost of the store over the sales price was permitted. This was not, as claimed by the Internal Revenue Service, an exchange of business property for property of like kind, gain or loss on which is not recognized for tax purposes. The original owner's money no longer was tied up in like-kind property. The owner had cashed in on his property, preferring to use his limited working capital in his merchandising activities rather than in "bricks and mortar."[11]

Sales and exchanges between related parties. *See* **Family transactions.**

Salesperson. Expenses of keeping abreast of new developments in his field, such as the cost of a marketing service in the case of a securities salesperson, were considered proper.[12] *See also* **Conventions; Employees; Entertainment; Office at home; Travel.**

Sales promotion expense. Deductible advertising includes sales promotion expenses.[13] *See also* **Advertising.**

Sales tax. *See* **Taxes.**

Samples. In some states, distribution of samples by businesses is against the law. That means the cost of the samples is not deductible for Federal income tax purposes because it represents an expense for an illegal purpose. But where the taxpayer can show that the state was not enforcing its own law and in fact had issued an order to enforcement officers to ignore it, the deduction was allowed.[14] *See also* **Bribes and kickbacks.**

Sanitarium, services at. *See* **Medical expenses; Retirement homes.**

Satisfaction of claims, payments in. *See* **Business-related losses.**

Schooling. *See* **Education.**

Schools, specialized, as medical expense. *See* **Medical expenses.**

Season tickets. A business dependent upon the general public for patronage was allowed to deduct its entire expenditure for home-game season tickets for baseball and hockey encounter sessions in Boston. The Internal Revenue Service had allowed deduction of one-half of the cost, but the court considered that the business benefits derived from supporting the local teams and the occasional use of these tickets to entertain customers was justification for full deductibility.[15]

"Section 1231" property deductions. *See* **Farmers; Property used in the trade or business and involuntary conversions.**

Security deposit. Often a landlord requires a tenant to make a security deposit—for example, of the last month's rent under a lease. State law customarily requires the landlord to segregate such deposits and to pay or to credit interest thereon. Often the state law permits the landlord to take as administration expense an amount equivalent to 1 percent per annum of the deposit. When such is the case, a tenant can deduct this 1-percent charge as an expense paid or incurred during the taxable year for the production or collection of income or for the management, conservation, or maintenance of property held for the production of income.[16] Although this deduction would seem to apply to businesses only, it may be taken for residences too.

Seeing Eye dog. *See* **Blind persons, expenses of.**

Seizure. *See* **Confiscation; Foreign expropriation losses; Government seizure.**

Self-employment plans. Self-employed persons may be covered by qualified (that is, Treasury-approved) pension, profit-sharing, annuity, and bond-purchase plans, with some of the favorable tax benefits available to corporate stockholder-employees. These often are referred to as Keogh plans. The owner-employee of a trade or business with earned income from personal services rendered to that trade or business may set up a self-employment plan. A person is an owner-employee if he is a self-employed individual who is a sole proprietor or a partner who owns more than a 10 percent interest in either the capital or profits of the partnership.

If a sole proprietor sets up such a plan for himself, he must cover all full-time employees who have worked for him for three or more years. If he has not been in business for at least three years, he must cover full-time employees who have had as much service as he has had. A full-time employee for this purpose is one who normally works more than twenty hours a week for more than five months a year. A longer waiting period for employees than for the proprietor is not permitted.[17]

For taxable years beginning after December 31, 1981, a sole proprietor's deduction for a self-employed person's pension is the lesser of 15 percent of the earned income from the trade or business, or $15,000.[18] If there are two or more plans, the total deduction may not exceed that amount.[19] This deduction does not cover any amount allocable to the purchase of life, accident, health, or other insurance.[20]

Through 1981, there was a loss of deduction plus a penalty if more was put into the fund than allowed by the IRS limits. Starting in 1982, penalty-free correction of an excess contribution is allowed if the excess is withdrawn before the return filing date due.[21]

Where an individual is covered under a corporate pension or profit-sharing plan and he also derives income from a business he operates during the evening hours, he can set up a plan and make deductible contributions to it out of the self-employment income from his moonlighting operations.[22]

Self-inflicted wounds. Maintenance at a center for drug abusers is deductible as medical expense.[23] *See also* **Medical expenses.**

Seminars. *See* **Conventions.**

Senior citizens. *See* **Blind persons, expenses of; Contributions; Deaf persons, expenses of; Medical expenses; Removal of impediments to the physically handicapped; Retirement homes.**

Separation agreement. *See* **Alimony.**

Services, as contributions. *See* **Contributions.**

Settlement payments. Damages paid for breach of contract entered into in the ordinary course of a taxpayer's business and directly related to it are normally considered to be a business expense, deductible if not a fine or penalty.[24]

Expenses in connection with carrying on one's trade or business are deductible, subject to the general rules that they be reasonable and not of a capital nature. This includes payment of claims arising from driving accidents while carrying on business. As was noted in one decision, "the cost of fuel and routine servicing are not the only costs one can expect in driving a car. As unfortunate as it may be, lapses by drivers seem to be an inseparable incident of driving a car. . . . Costs incurred as a result of such an incident are just as much a part of overall business expenses as the cost of fuel."[25]

When a person, while driving for business purposes, injured a pedestrian, the damage settlement was deductible as business expense.[26] (*See also* **Executives; Violation of rights, payments to settle.**)

A contractor was allowed to deduct a $5,000 restitution payment made on the order of a court to a customer whose money had been misappropriated. Although the contractor had been convicted of misappropriation of this fund, his payment to the customer was not regarded as a fine or penalty inasmuch as it was the payment of a sum due and owing and was not paid to a government.[27]

An officer of an insurance company received an amount from the sale of the company's stock. The state insurance commissioner maintained that the money properly belonged to the company, and the officer turned the proceeds over to his employer. No criminal prosecutions against him were instituted, although the state attorney general claimed a violation of the securities law had occurred. Deduction of the repayment amount was allowed as a payment to protect the officer's reputation.[28]

A corporation's chief executive officer authorized some political contributions to be made by the corporation. Deduction by the corporation was disallowed, and he and the company were fined for violating Federal law. A stockholder brought suit against him for causing the corporate assets to be wasted. The corporation decided to keep him in office on the condition that he reimburse the corporation an amount approximating the cost to the corporation of his actions. Admitting nothing but a desire to avoid further controversy and expense, he made the payment to the corporation. Although the portion of his payment representing payment for the prohibited political contribution was not deductible, the portion representing interest and legal expenses was deductible.[29]

In general, fines and penalties are not deductible. But a carefully worded settlement offer may be used to describe the payment as something which is deductible. The government brought action against a businessperson for violation of the Federal False Claims Act on the ground that shipments to a governmental agency had not lived up to the materials specifications. The business carefully worded a settlement offer, stating that a stipulated amount was being offered for ordinary breach of contract. The government accepted this offer as written, and the payment thus was characterized for tax purposes as a proper business deduction.[30]

One taxpayer was accused of violating the United States Customs laws, and a "Notice of Penalty or Liquidated Damages" was issued with demand for a substantial sum. The taxpayer offered a much smaller amount, as liquidated damages, to settle the government claim if the government agreed to drop its action for penalty. The government agreed. Although fines and penalties are not deductible, this payment was allowed as an ordinary and necessary business expense. The taxpayer had not been convicted of a crime and had not entered a plea of guilty or *nolo contendere* (No Contest). The amount was not a fine or penalty when paid, regardless of what it had been called by the government prior to the taxpayer's offer and its acceptance.[31]

A Department of Energy examination to determine whether a corporation was meeting the rules revealed some violations. The corporation agreed to refund impermissible overcharges to customers who claimed these amounts, any unclaimed portions of the overcharged amounts to go to the United States Treasury. The sums payable to the government were deductible, not being fines but overcharges resulting from alleged pricing violations, proceeds from which the corporation agreed not to keep.[32]

Government claims against a taxpayer for fraud, deceit, malpractice, and the like which involve wrongs of some moral turpitude may be settled by compromise. The amounts paid out in settlement are then deductible as allowable business expenses if there has been no admission of guilt.[33]

A taxpayer purchased the business of a competitor with which it had been engaged in lawsuits involving restraint of trade. The price paid included a negotiated sum to settle lawsuits which had been brought by this competitor. Ordinarily, when a lump sum is paid to acquire the assets of a going business, the amount paid in excess of the value of the operating assets is attributed to intangible capital assets (*e.g.*, good-will) and thus is not currently deductible. But to the extent that the excess amount was attributable to disposition of the lawsuits pending against the buyer, the payment was deductible as ordinary and necessary business expense. Strong support was given to the buyer's claim that no part of the payment was for nondeductible capital assets by reason of the fact that they were not needed or used by the buyer.[34]

A corporate director could deduct settlement costs resulting from lawsuits against him by the stockholders. He was a member of the board of directors of a corporation which had gone through several reorganizations, the results of which the stockholders had felt were not to their best interests. The amount he paid to the stockholders to settle the affair was deductible.[35]

The house physician of a hotel struck another person who was attempting to interfere with the doctor's attempt to remove a patient from the hotel during a party. He could deduct his costs in settling any possible consequences of the incident, which arose from his carrying on his business as a physician.[36]

Severance pay. Payments to terminate the employment of a business employee are deductible.[37] *See also* **Compensation.**

Sex discrimination suit, payments under. *See* **Violation of rights, payments to settle.**

Sexual inadequacy, efforts to overcome. *See* **Medical expenses.**

Shareholders committee, contributions to. *See* **Investors.**

Shingles, replacement of. *See* **Repairs.**

Shoes. *See* **Orthopedic shoes; Uniforms; Work clothes.**

Shoeshines, cost of. *See* **Personal grooming.**

Shooting preserve, expense of. *See* **Entertainment.**

Shop fees. Where a union obtains a contract which requires an employer to check off dues from members, and also an equivalent amount from nonmembers, for transmittal to the union, nonmembers can deduct these shop fees on their income tax returns.[38]

Shortages, repayment of. *See* **Armed Forces; Business-related losses; Cash shortages; Executives; Inventory write-downs.**

Short sales, expenses in connection with. An individual sold stock short, borrowing shares to permit delivery of the certificates sold. She paid to the lender the equivalent of dividends she received on the borrowed stock. This amount was deductible.[39] *See also* **Investors.**

Sick-leave payments. Sometimes an employer has a plan providing that each employee earns one day of sick leave for each twenty working days, or whatever other period is chosen. One such plan stated that the sick leave could be used only in the year following the year in which it was earned; a lump-sum payment for unused sick leave was payable either in January of the year following the one in which the sick leave might have been used or upon termination of employment, whichever occurred earlier. An accrual-basis employer can deduct the amount of sick leave earned by employees that year regardless of when payment actually takes place.[40]

Simplified employee pension plan, deduction for. If a person sets up an Individual Retirement Account (IRA), he may take a deduction for amounts he puts into it up to the lower of 100 percent of his compensation for the year or $2,000. But no deduction is allowed for any contribution made during or after the year when he reached age 70½, unless a Simplified Employee Pension (SEP) is used.[41]

Under this plan, an employer is permitted to contribute into the employee's IRA an amount not in excess of $15,000.[42] That is includable in the employee's gross income for that year. But he may deduct his own contributions up to the deductible amount, in addition to what his employer puts in, even though the employee is over age 70½.[43]

Skills, improvement of. *See* **Education.**

Ski lodge. *See* **Entertainment.**

Small-business corporation stock. An individual may deduct as an ordinary loss, rather than as a capital loss, his loss on the sale, exchange, or worthlessness of certain stock he owns in a small-business corporation. (Gain on this stock, however, is capital gain if the stock is a capital asset in his hands. If in doubt as to the status, he should consult an accountant, attorney, or IRS office.) Small-business stock for this purpose is voting or nonvoting common stock of a domestic corporation, provided:

1. The stock is not convertible into other securities of the corporation.
2. The stock has been offered under a written plan adopted by the

corporation after June 30, 1958. The plan must specify the maximum amount in dollars to be received by the corporation in consideration for the stock to be issued under the plan and the period during which it can be offered. That period must end not later than two years after the date the plan was adopted.

3. At the time the plan in item 2 above was adopted (but not necessarily at the time the stock was issued or the loss occurred), the corporation qualified as a small-business corporation and no portion of any other stock offering was outstanding.

4. The stock was issued under the plan in item 2 above for money or property other than stock or securities.[44]

A corporation qualifies as a small-business corporation if at the time the written plan is adopted the following requirements are met:

1. The amount of the offering, plus money or other property received by the corporation after June 30, 1958, for its stock as a contribution to capital and as paid-in surplus, does not exceed $500,000.

2. The amount offered under the plan plus the equity capital of the corporation (as of the date the plan is adopted) does not exceed $1,000,000.

The amount deductible as ordinary loss on this stock is limited to $50,000 on a separate return and $100,000 on a joint return in the case of stock issued after November 6, 1978.[45] Previously it was one-half of these amounts.

The loss on small-business stock which is treated as ordinary loss is a business loss when determining a net operating loss.[46]

For computing the ordinary loss on small-business stock, the basis of the stock is reduced by the difference between the adjusted basis of the property and its fair market value. The reduction is made for this purpose only and does not affect the basis of the stock for any other purpose.[47]

Small-business investment company. Investors in a small-business investment company are allowed as ordinary loss rather than as capital loss any losses arising from the sale or exchange or worthlessness of stock. Losses of this nature are allowed in determining the net operating loss.[48]

Small-business investment companies, as authorized by the Small Business Investment Act of 1958, are private corporations with paid-in capital and surplus of at least $150,000 which are empowered to provide equity capital and long-term loans as well as management assistance to small business concerns.

Smog damage. *See* **Accident.**

Snow removal. The owner of business property was permitted to deduct the cost of snow removal from the parking areas of his enterprise.[49]

Social-club dues. Dues or fees paid to a social club or organization after December 31, 1978, in taxable years ending after that date, are deductible if the taxpayer establishes that the facility was used primarily for the furtherance of his trade or business and that the expense was directly related to the conduct of his trade or business.[50] *See also* **Entertainment.**

Social Security taxes. Where a businessperson pays the Federal Insurance Contributions Act contributions of his employees, he may deduct these amounts as additional compensation.[51]

Such taxes are deductible if paid by a person who pays wages of private nurses providing medical care. (Here the deduction is characterized as medical expense.)[52]

Soil-conservation expenditures. *See* **Farmers.**

Sole proprietor. *See* **Self-employment plans.**

Sonic-boom damage. A casualty-loss deduction was allowed for damage caused by jet aircraft overflight.[53]

Special assessments, deductibility as taxes. *See* **Taxes.**

Special food. *See* **Medical expenses.**

Special schools. *See* **Medical expenses.**

Speeding charges, expenses to go to court hearing. An individual was permitted to deduct his costs in getting to court to answer charges of unlawful driving, for he was a driver for a trucking company and hence the expenditures related to his trade or business.[54]

Sponsored investment plans. *See* **Investors.**

Sponsorship gift. *See* **Retirement homes.**

Sporting club dues. *See* **Athletic-club dues.**

Spouses. *See* **Alimony; Carry-overs; Child-care and disabled-dependent care; Contributions; Entertainment; Family transactions; Interest; Medical expenses; Taxes; Tax-option corporations; Travel.**

Stamp collection. *See* **Casualties; Hobby losses; Transactions entered into for profit.**

Standby charges. Standby charges or commitment fees incurred by a taxpayer, pursuant to an agreement under which funds will be kept available by a lender for specified times and in stipulated amounts, are deductible.[55] *See also* **Interest.**

Standby expense. A corporation, which operated a shopping center, rented an airplane and pilot. This enabled prospective tenants to visit the center and to return home in a minimum amount of time and to survey the population density of the surrounding areas. In addition, company personnel could make business trips more rapidly. The Internal Revenue Service claimed that the rent deduction of the plane should be limited to the going time rate for leasing, the actual payment made having been much larger because the craft had been rented on a twenty-four-hour-per-day basis so as to have it available at all times on a "standby basis." The court allowed the full deduction. Having the plane available on a standby basis had resulted in some considerable savings to the business. On one of the three occasions when the plane was needed on instant notice, a savings of many times the full rent charge had resulted because an executive was able to obtain a great discount on interest payable on a loan by taking immediate action where a fast decision was necessary.[56]

Start-up expenses. Expenses incurred prior to the establishment of a business normally are not deductible, inasmuch as they are not incurred in carrying on a trade or business or while engaged in a profit-seeking activity. But a person may elect to treat start-up expenditures as deferred expenses, to be written off as deductions ratably over a period of not less than sixty months as selected by the taxpayer beginning with the month in which the business starts.[57] (*See also* **Expenditures for benefits lasting more than one year.**)

For this purpose, the term *start-up expenditures* means costs which are incurred subsequent to a decision to acquire or to establish a particular business and prior to its actual operation. Generally, the term refers to expenses which would be deductible currently if they were incurred after the commencement of the particular business operation to which they relate, if paid in connection with the expansion of an existing trade or business, in the same trade or business.[58] This includes investigatory expenses in connection with business start-up expenses.[59]

Start-up costs may include expenses relating to advertising, employee training, lining up distributors, suppliers, or potential customers, and professional services in setting up books and records. Such costs may be incurred by a party who is not engaged in any existing business, or by a party with an existing business who begins a new one that is unrelated to, or only tangentially related to his or her existing business.[60]

Expenses incurred in developing operating procedures, testing new equipment, and recruiting a work force in connection with the establishment of a new manufacturing facility could be deducted, where no identifiable asset, tangible or intangible, separate and distinct from the existing facility, was secured by the taxpayer as a result of the expansion of its manufacturing capacity.[61]

The expenditures must be of the type that, if paid or incurred in connection with the expansion of an existing trade or business in the same field, would be allowable as a deduction in the taxable year paid or incurred. The amortization period begins with the month in which the business begins or, in the case of an acquired business, the month in which the taxpayer acquires it.[62]

State and local transfer taxes. *See* **Conveyance taxes.**

State disability insurance. Some states have disability insurance laws. One in California, for example, required employers to withhold 1 percent of the first $9,000 of wages for deposit with the California State Disability Fund, which applied unless the employer established a suitable private disability plan meeting all state standards. Employees subjected to this withholding could take a Federal tax deduction of the amount as a state income tax.[63]

Employee contributions to the New Jersey Nonoccupational Disability Fund and to the New York Nonoccupational Disability Benefit Fund are deductible.[64]

State legislators, away-from-home expenses. *See* **Travel.**

State taxes, deductibility of. *See* **Taxes.**

State tax returns, preparation of. Accountants' fees for the preparation of state tax returns are deductible in the same manner as fees for Federal returns.[65]

Statistical services. *See* **Investors.**

Stereo system, as medical expense. *See* **Medical expenses.**

Sterilization. *See* **Medical expenses.**

Stock acquired to get assets. *See* **Purchase of stock to get assets.**

Stockholders. Expenses of a small stockholder crusading for a particular point of view are personal and nondeductible, for he cannot reasonably expect that his efforts will affect his dividend income or stock value in relation to his corporate investment to an extent that would define his activity as an expense in connection with the production of income. But deduction was allowed for the expenses of a large stockholder for the purpose of getting the shareholders to change the management of the company. Here his expenses were related to the production of income or for the preservation of his investment.[66]

A corporate shareholder was permitted to deduct his expenses in attending an out-of-town stockholders' meeting where his purpose was to protect his investment. Up for consideration at this meeting was a proposal which would have lessened the value of his shares by the issuance of additional stock at less than book value.[67]

A shareholder in a corporation was permitted to deduct fees paid to an attorney for advice on the payor's liability as a stockholder.[68]

The treatment of stockholder loans to a corporation that cannot be repaid depends upon whether the advance was for business purposes (fully deductible) or primarily to protect the stockholder's investment in the corporation (additional cost of the stock). Where a stockholder makes the loan primarily so that the corporation will be able to survive and to continue to pay his salary, loss on an unrepayable advance is fully deductible.[69] So it is also where money was furnished to the corporation so that it could create a salaried position for the person (a stockholder) advancing the funds.[70] An unrepaid advance was fully deductible where a shareholder expected to profit from commissions that he would be able to get from the corporation.[71]

Ordinarily, stockholders cannot deduct a corporation's expenses which they pay. Deduction was allowed, however, where the corporation was financially unable to pay its bills and the shareholders would have lost future income from business which they derived from the corporation had it not been able to continue operations.[72]

A commission merchant, who had operated as an individual for many years, formed a corporation to operate in this field in several states. Purpose: to allow employees to benefit from corporate employment. When the corporation was unable to pay its debts, the merchant did so. He could deduct these expenses, for it was necessary for his reputation as a commission merchant to make prompt payment to any person who had relied upon his integrity in settling claims. The Perishable Agricultural Act, under which he operated, required this.[73]

A shareholder paid some of the debts of the corporation when it became unable to do so. He could deduct these payments because the management of another corporation of which he was a director and employee insisted that he do so if he was to remain on the payroll, as suppliers of this second corporation might have been unwilling to extend credit where there was some interrelationship with a company that had defaulted.[74]

A shareholder may deduct the amount of what is necessary to conserve or to enhance his estate, such as the rental of a safe-deposit box, costs of investment counsel or services, and, where appropriate, the salary of a secretary.[75]

A transferee of property is responsible for a transferor's unpaid Federal taxes, up to the value of the property received, if at the time of the transfer the transferor was insolvent or was made insolvent by transferring property without retaining enough to meet liabilities. A stockholder of a liquidated corporation, concerned about his transferee liability for unpaid taxes, which the IRS may assess against a liquidated corporation after audit, could deduct fees paid to a lawyer to challenge the assessment against the corporation.[76]

For treatment of corporate entertainment expenses paid by stockholders, *see* **Employees; Executives.** *See also* **Bad debts; Guarantor, payments by; Investors; Payment of debt of another person; Tax-option corporations.**

Stockholders' committee, expenses of. *See* **Investors.**

Stockholders' suit, defense of. A corporate director was permitted to deduct legal and accounting fees in defending himself against stockholder allegations of violation of fiduciary duties.[77]

Stock transfer taxes. *See* **Investors; Taxes.**

Stolen property, reward for return of. Deduction was allowed for the amount of reward paid to a person who had returned stolen business property.[78]

Stop watch. *See* **Employees; Watch repairs.**

Street closing, payments to obtain. A taxpayer owned all the property on both sides of a street. He gave this property to the city with the understanding that the street would be permanently closed to public use, an action that would benefit the taxpayer's business. Payments to persons who objected to this action, but who actually owned no property rights and were not entitled to anything, were deductible as expenses to expedite the carrying out of the plan, not to acquire property with a benefit lasting for more than a year.[79]

Strikebreakers. An employer was permitted to deduct the cost of recruiting strikebreakers.[80]

Students, expenses of. *See* **Advanced degree, study for; Doctoral dissertation; Education; Tuition-postponement-plan payments.**

Student's maintenance, as charitable deduction. *See* **Contributions.**

Subchapter S corporations. *See* **Tax-option corporations.**

Subscription list. A publisher could deduct the price he paid for another publisher's subscription lists, which were contained on stencils furnished to the purchaser. These lists were not nondeductible intangible assets.[81]

Subscriptions to periodicals. Subscriptions to professional magazines are a deductible expense of being an employee.[82] Likewise, subscriptions to periodicals appropriate to their income-producing activities are deductible by investors,[83] by members of the Armed Forces,[84] by farmers,[85] by teachers,[86] by physicians,[87] by lawyers,[88] by mining engineers,[89] and by securities salesmen.[90]

To be deductible, magazines must be required by the condition or needs or one's employment, which was not the case where a teacher had claimed the periodicals were helpful because they appealed to her grade-school students. The titles included *Architectural Digest, Consumer's Union,* and *House Beautiful.*[91]

A Federal law-enforcement agency issued an official work manual, which was revised frequently. An agency employee, who traveled extensively on business, purchased a year's subscription to the manual at his own expense so that he could have it readily available at all times. This was a deductible business expense.[92]

An Internal Revenue Service field-examination agent could deduct the cost of research materials he used in his work. He spent most of his working hours at the offices of a taxpayer under examination, usually a large corporation, and was away from the library of his IRS office.[93]

A sales manager was allowed to deduct his cost of business journals and magazines.[94]

A salesperson could deduct subscription and single-purchase costs of trade publications which described new products that were competitive to the line she sold, in order to learn what she was up against.[95]

The cost of such subscriptions paid by a professional person likewise is deductible.[96]

An employee at an airplane manufacturing plant could deduct the cost of subscriptions to aviation magazines.[97]

Subsidy, repayment of. A taxpayer received a subsidy payment from the United States government. In a later year, it was determined that he had not been entitled to the payment. Repayment was deductible.[98]

Subsistence expenses. *See* **Conventions; Mileage allowance.**

Substitute, payments to. *See* **Executives; Teachers, expenses of.**

Subterranean disturbances. *See* **Casualties.**

Suggestion awards. Payments to employees for the submission of suggestions to increase the efficiency of a business are considered to be a form of wages.[99] Consequently they are deductible in line with the ground rules for other types of compensation.

Supplemental Medical Insurance for the Aged. Premiums on Part B of Medicare are deductible.[100] *See also* **Medical expenses.**

Supplies. The cost of supplies used in the practice of one's profession is deductible.[101]

A television artist was permitted to deduct the amount he had spent on art supplies.[102]

Support payments. *See* **Alimony.**

Surrender of stock in issuing corporation. *See* **Executives; Investors.**

Surveys. Ordinarily, the cost of a survey is not deductible. Payment for the determination of property lines creates a benefit lasting for more than one year. This is regarded as a capital asset, to be written off, if at all, over the life of the property. But if the survey was conducted primarily to protect income or to avoid expenses resulting from inadvertent use of another party's land, the cost of the survey is deductible. For example, deduction was allowed where a taxpayer's land was near government property and innocent cutting of government trees would have resulted in fines.[103]

Similarly, deduction was allowed for the cost of a survey to re-mark property lines in an attempt to prevent loss of land through adverse possession.[104]

Swimming pool, deductibility of. *See* **Entertainment; Medical expenses.**

Swindling loss. *See* **Casualties; Reliance upon misrepresentation.**

"Swop"-club commissions. *See* **Barter-club commissions.**

Sword. *See* **Armed Forces.**

S

1. Regulations Section 1.162-5(d).
2. Regulations Section 1.274-3(b)(2)(iii) as amended by the Economic Recovery Tax Act of 1981, Section 265.
3. Revenue Ruling 54-532, 1954-2 CB 93.
4. *Broughton v. Commissioner,* T.C. Memo. 1979-77, filed March 8, 1979.
5. *Arnold Bushey,* T.C. Memo. 1971-149, filed June 21, 1971.
6. *Ranchers Exploration and Development Corporation v. United States,* DC, N.M., 1978.
7. *Barran v. Commissioner,* 334 F.2d 58 (5th Cir., 1964).
8. *Shaffer Terminal, Inc. v. Commissioner,* 194 F.2d 539 (9th Cir., 1952).
9. *Belz Investment Co., Inc. v. Commissioner,* 72 T.C. 1209 (1979).
10. *In the Matter of David W. Margulies,* 271 F. Supp. 50 (DC, N.J., 1967).
11. *Crowley, Milner and Company v. Commissioner,* 76 T.C. 1030 (1981).
12. *Irving L. Shein,* T.C. Memo., Docket No. 32717, entered February 29, 1952.
13. Revenue Ruling 56-181, 1956-1 CB 96.
14. *Sterling Distributors, Inc. v. Patterson,* 236 F. Supp. 479 (DC, ND Ala., 1964).
15. *Cambridge Hotels, Inc.,* T.C. Memo. 1968-263, filed November 19, 1968.
16. Revenue Ruling 75-363, 1975-2 CB 463.
17. Regulations Section 1.404(e)-1.
18. IRC Section 404(e)(1).
19. IRC Section 404(e)(2)(A).
20. IRC Section 404(e)(2)(B)(3).
21. IRC Section 219(a).
22. Regulations Section 1.401-10(b)(3)(ii).
23. Revenue Ruling 72-226, 1972-1 CB 96.
24. *Great Island Holding Corporation,* 5 T.C. 150 (1945).
25. *Dancer et al. v. Commissioner,* 73 T.C. 1103 (1980).
26. *Plante et al. v. United States,* 226 F. Supp. 314 (DC, N.H., 1963).
27. *Spitz v. United States,* 432 F. Supp. 148 (DC, ED Wis., 1977).
28. *Joseph P. Pike et al.,* 443 T.C. 787 (1965).
29. IRS Letter 8021015, February 25, 1980.
30. *Grossman & Sons, Inc., et al.,* 48 T.C. 15 (1967).
31. *Middle Atlantic Distributors, Inc. v. Commissioner,* 72 T.C. 1136 (1979).
32. Revenue Ruling 80-334, 1980-2 CB 61.
33. *Milner Enterprises, Inc. v. United States,* DC, SD Miss., 1965.
34. *Entwicklung und Finanzierungs A.G. v. Commissioner,* 68 T.C. 749 (1977).
35. IRS Letter Ruling 7728004.
36. *Henry M. Rodney,* 53 T.C. 287 (1969).
37. *Driskill Hotel Company,* T.C. Memo., Docket No. 31562, entered May 22, 1953.
38. IRS Letter Ruling 7828050, April 13, 1978.
39. *Betty Klinger,* T.C. Memo., Docket No. 18315, entered June 2, 1940.
40. Revenue Ruling 78-116, 1978-1 CB 143.
41. IRC Section 219(b)(2).
42. IRC Section 219(b)(7)(B).
43. *Tax Information on Individual Retirement Arrangements,* IRS Publication 590 (Rev. Nov. 1980), page 8.

44. IRC Section 1244.

45. Revenue Act of 1978, Section 345.

46. *Tax Information on Investment Income and Expenses,* IRS Publication 550, 1976 edition, page 23.

47. Ibid., p. 19.

48. IRC Section 1243.

49. *Ward v. Commissioner,* T.C. Memo. 1978-216, filed June 8, 1978.

50. Technical Corrections Act of 1979, Section 103(a)(10)(A),(B).

51. Revenue Ruling 74-75, 1974-1 CB 19.

52. Revenue Ruling 57-489, 1957-2 CB 207.

53. *Your Federal Income Tax,* IRS Publication 17 (Rev. Nov. 1980), p. 95.

54. *Hamilton et al. v. Commissioner,* T.C. Memo. 1979-186, filed May 10, 1979.

55. Revenue Ruling 56-136, 1956-1 CB 92.

56. *Palo Alto Town & Country Village, Inc. et al. v. Commissioner,* 565 F.2d 1388 (9th Cir., 1977).

57. IRC Section 195(a).

58. IRC Section 195(b).

59. *Summary of Miscellaneous Tax Bills Passed by the Congress in the Post-Election Session.* Report by the Staff of the Joint Committee on Taxation, December 23, 1980, page 19.

60. Senate Finance Committee Report on Public Law 96-605.

61. IRS Letter Ruling 8204061, October 28, 1981.

62. Announcement 81-43, I.R.B. 1981-11, 52.

63. *Anthony Trujillo et al. v. Commissioner,* 68 T.C. 670 (1977).

64. Internal Revenue News Release IR-1967, March 10, 1978.

65. *Myrhl Frost,* T.C. Memo., Docket No. 112333, entered March 31, 1943.

66. *Graham et al. v. Commissioner,* 326 F.2d 878 (4th Cir., 1964).

67. IRS Letter Ruling 8042071, July 23, 1980.

68. *Patterson v. Durden,* 5th Cir., 1957.

69. *Trent v. Commissioner,* 291 F.2d 669 (2d Cir., 1961).

70. *Estate of Kent Avery,* T.C. Memo. 1969-64, filed April 3, 1969.

71. *James E. Gilboy et al.,* T.C. Memo. 1978-114, filed March 22, 1978.

72. *Charles J. Dinardo et al.,* 22 T.C. 430 (1954).

73. *Lutz et al. v. Commissioner,* 282 F.2d 614 (5th Cir., 1960).

74. *James O. Gould et al.,* 64 T.C. 132 (1975).

75. *Jacob M. Kaplan,* 21 T.C. 134 (1953).

76. *National Association of Schools and Publishers, Inc.,* T.C. Memo., Docket No. 16433, entered September 17, 1948.

77. *The Lomas & Nettleton Company v. United States,* 79 F. Supp. 886 (DC, Ct., 1948).

78. Revenue Ruling 67-98, 1967-1 CB 29.

79. *Brown-Forman Distillers Corporation v. United States,* 132 F. Supp. 711 (Ct. Cl., 1955).

80. *Queen City Printing,* 6 BTA 521 (1927).

81. *Zimmerman & Sons, Inc. v. United States,* DC, ED Wis., 1972.

82. *Your Federal Income Tax,* 1976 edition, page 105.

83. *Martha E. Henderson,* T.C. Memo. 1968-22, filed January 31, 1968.

84. *Charles A. Harris et al.,* T.C. Memo., Docket No. 34256, entered January 28, 1953.

85. Schedule F listing for Form 1040.

86. *Beaudry v. Commissioner,* 150 F.2d 20 (2d Cir., 1945).

87. *Wolfson et al. v. Commissioner,* T.C. Memo. 1978-445, filed November 7, 1978.

88. *Julius I. Peyser et al.,* T.C. Memo., Docket Nos. 108711-2, entered March 23, 1943.

89. *J. Bryant Kasey et al.,* 54 T.C. 1642 (1970).

90. *Irving L. Shein,* T.C. Memo., Docket No. 32717, entered February 29, 1952.

91. *Princess E. L. Lingham,* T.C. Memo. 1977-152, filed May 23, 1977.

92. Revenue Ruling 78-265, 1978-2 CB 107.

93. IRS Letter Ruling 8124101, March 19, 1981.

94. *Arthur Brookfield,* T.C. Memo., Docket No. 51372, entered March 12, 1958.

95. *Marilyn Finley,* T.C. Memo. 1977-9, filed January 17, 1977.

96. Regulations Section 1.162-6.

97. *David F. Tautolo et al.,* T.C. Memo. 1975-277, filed September 3, 1975.

98. *Smith v. United States,* DC, Ore., 1958.

99. Revenue Ruling 70-471, 1970-2 CB 199.

100. *Donovan et al. v. Campbell, Jr.,* DC, ND Texas, 1961.

101. Regulations Section 1.162-6.

102. *Herman E. Bischoff et al.,* T.C. Memo. 1966-102, filed May 19, 1966.

103. *The Brier Hill Collieries,* 12 BTA 500 (1928), aff'd on other issues, 50 F.2d 777 (6th Cir., 1931).

104. Ibid.

T

Takeover, expenses to prevent. *See* **Buy-out, expenses to prevent; Executives; Investors; Legal fees.**

Taxes. The following taxes, paid or accrued, are deductible for Federal income tax purposes:

1. State, local, and foreign real property taxes.

2. State and local personal property taxes.

3. State, local, and foreign income, war profits, and excess profits taxes.

4. State and local general sales taxes.

5. State and local taxes on the sale of gasoline, diesel fuel, and other motor fuels, but only if the vehicle is used for business or investment purposes.[1]

An occupational license tax based upon a percentage of compensation and net profits is deductible.[2]

In addition, taxes not described above which are paid or accrued within a taxable year in the process of carrying on a trade or business or an activity relating to expenses for the production of income are allowed as a deduction.[3] This includes state and local transfer taxes.[4]

Ordinarily, taxes cannot be deducted by a party other than the one upon whom that tax is imposed. But if the amount of any general sales tax is stated separately, then to the extent that the consumer pays the tax separately, it will be treated as a tax imposed upon, and paid by, the consumer.[5]

Many states and cities require sellers to collect sales taxes from purchasers. If a corporation collects the taxes but they are not turned over to the governmental agency, some state laws make the company executives *personally* liable for untransmitted taxes. This is rather similar to Federal liability for untransmitted withholding taxes which the responsible corporate executive must pay personally. But where an executive thus has personal liability for untransmitted corporate sales taxes, he is entitled to deduct the amount on his own Federal income tax return.[6]

A *compensating use* tax is treated for deduction purposes as if it were a general sales tax. A compensating use tax means a tax (1) which is imposed on the use, storage, or consumption of such items as would normally have been subjected to a general sales tax under ordinary circumstances and (2) which is complementary to a general sales tax.[7]

As an example of such a tax, consider the following: A municipality has a sales tax upon the purchase of tangible personal property within the jurisdiction of that municipality. To protect local merchants from loss of business in cases where residents go outside the city to make purchases, such as automobiles, a compensating use tax may be imposed upon all residents who have brought in cars without payment of the sales tax. This is deductible.[8]

State income tax withheld from the salary of a cash-basis employee by his employer is deductible on the Federal income tax return of the employee if he itemizes his deductions.[9]

When a joint state income tax is filed and there is joint (and several) liability to pay the tax (that is, each spouse can be held liable not only for his/her portion of the tax but for all of it), if one spouse pays the entire amount, that is what he/she may deduct in computing his/her Federal income tax. It is assumed, of course, that separate Federal income tax forms are filed for the two individuals.

Let's say that George and Mary Travil filed a joint state income tax return in 1976. Although each owed an equal share of the total amount, George paid the entire amount when the form was filed in 1977. George can now deduct the entire amount when computing his Federal income tax, and Mary, who files separately, can deduct none of it.[10]

If husband and wife are each liable for the full amount of the state income tax actually paid, and each paid an equal amount, each may deduct on separately filed Federal income tax returns the amount of state tax actually paid by him or her.[11]

If separate state income tax returns are filed by married taxpayers who at the same time file a joint Federal income tax return, the sum of the state income taxes imposed on and paid by both spouses during the taxable year may be deducted on the joint Federal income tax return.[12] The state income taxes imposed upon a married taxpayer and paid during the taxable year are deductible on a joint Federal income tax return regardless of which spouse actually paid the tax.[13]

An employer can deduct regular contributions under a state unemployment security act, computed on subject payrolls of business employees.[14] In many states, an employer may make voluntary payments, in addition to the required contributions, for the purpose of obtaining a lower regular contribution rate by reason of a very favorable experience factor of former-employee claims to total contributions made. The amount of a voluntary contribution is deductible if it results in a lower rate of regular contribution.[15]

Contributions made by employers and by employees to the Rhode Island temporary disability fund are deductible.[16]

Contributions made by employers and by employees to the New York nonoccupational disability fund under the New York Disability Benefits Law are deductible, but not contributions by employees to private plans for the payment of such benefits.[17]

The same is true in the case of the New Jersey unemployment compensation fund and the nonoccupational disability fund under the New Jersey Temporary Disability Benefits Law.[18]

A similar ruling was issued in the case of the California unemployment compensation fund and the nonoccupational benefit fund.[19]

Foreign income taxes paid to a foreign country or to a U.S. possession may either be taken as a deduction or claimed as a credit against the individual's Federal income tax. Usually such a decision whether a deduction or a credit should be taken on such taxes should be made after figuring out the amounts owed (or to be returned) under each method.[20]

A taxpayer, who was a citizen of the United States residing permanently in the Republic of Ireland, was permitted to deduct the Irish wealth tax, which was levied annually on the net market value each year of every assessable person at 1 percent.[21]

Deduction was allowed for the Zurich, Switzerland, personal fortune tax based upon stocks and bonds owned by a taxpayer and held for the production of income.[22]

Property taxes are deductible even if paid with borrowed money, provided that the taxpayer at that time had sufficient resources of his own to make these payments.[23]

To provide faculty housing for its professors, a university sold to any qualifying professor the ownership of certain land and agreed to pay for the cost of building a home there up to a specified limit. At the time he left the university for any reason except bankruptcy or if he ceased to make this his principal home, his "terminable interest" in the property ended and it passed back to the university for an amount equal to what the institution had made available to build the house. He could deduct the property taxes assessed by the community where his house was located.[24]

A corporation adopted a similar plan, under which designated employees could buy residential property from the employer. Each employee could build any type of house he desired. But when he terminated his employment, conditions similar to those stated in the preceding paragraph allowed the corporation to repurchase the property, including the house, at its then appraised value. Each employee could deduct the taxes he paid on the property while it was his.[25]

Frequently, when a person borrows money from a bank on a mortgage, the bank requires him to put one-twelfth of the estimated real property taxes into an escrow fund each month so that, by the time the tax payment date to the government authority comes around, the bank will have all of the necessary funds in hand, with any shortage to be made up by the borrower on demand. These taxes are deductible by the borrower, not when he pays the bank, but when the bank pays the local taxing authority. And that payment, or a large portion of it, can be in the year after the borrower "paid" his tax installments.[26]

An individual who owed property taxes on his realty could deduct payments made to the governmental authority. The satisfaction of his tax obligation took place regardless of whether the payment had the character of a loan or gift to him or represented some form of income to him.[27]

Real property (or real-estate) taxes are any state, local, or foreign taxes on real property which are levied for the general public welfare. They are deductible.

Local benefit taxes are not deductible in most instances. These taxes are so called because they are for local benefits, such as assessments for local streets, sidewalks, and other like improvements which are imposed because of, and measured by, some benefits applying directly to the property against which the assessment is levied. A "tax" is considered to be assessed against local benefits when the property subject to the tax is limited to the property benefited.

But if these assessments are made for the purpose of maintenance or repair of such local benefits or for the purpose of meeting the interest charges with respect to such benefits, then they are deductible. For example, if your city assesses you a city property tax for the purpose of installing new street lamps on your street, these taxes are not deductible. But if in the future further taxes are assessed for the maintenance of such street lamps, then these future taxes will be deductible.[28]

Thus, when a special assessment was imposed against the owners of property on Main Street and Broadway in Oklahoma City to finance the resurfacing of the pavement when a street railway system was abandoned, this special assessment did not tend to increase the value of the property assessed, for existing curbs, gutters, and surfacing were repaired. None of the streets in the district was widened or lengthened nor was other "new" work done.[29]

Similarly, a sprinkling tax imposed upon the residents of Duluth, Minnesota, for the use of water to sprinkle their lawns, etc., was a deductible tax, for it did not constitute a benefit to the property against which the tax was imposed.[30]

In cases where a front-foot benefit charge was added to a municipality's real-estate bill to pay for the construction of a water system, the bill broke down the benefit charge to show what percentage of the bill was applicable to construction of the system, to interest, and to maintenance costs. The latter two items were deductible as taxes.[31]

If in the case of a local benefit tax assessment the property owner believes at least part of the assessment is going to maintenance, repair, or interest, he may deduct that part of the assessment which he is able to establish is going to such maintenance, repair, or interest.[32]

Water bills, sewerage, and other service charges (*e.g.,* "water taxes") assessed against property used for business purposes are deductible, not as taxes but as business expenses.[33]

Generally, real-estate taxes are an equal responsibility of all the owners of a property, no matter how many there are. Therefore, if one owner, who owns only one-sixth of the property, pays the entire real-estate tax, she may deduct the entire amount.

This is true if the taxpayer in question is a *tenant in common* (defined as having the right to occupy the whole property in common with her cotenants). In order to preserve her individual rights and interest, which she could have lost had she not paid the entire tax (due to a possible foreclosure for nonpayment of taxes), she was entitled to the full deduction.[34]

In the case where the joint owners of property are individually and collectively liable for expenses such as real-estate taxes on the property, whichever owner actually pays the taxes is entitled to the deduction on his or her Federal income tax return.[35]

An individual conveyed his house and lot to the ownership of his church, reserving possession for five years and promising to pay real-estate taxes assessed on the property. He could deduct these taxes because the liability to pay them was his.[36]

A person may deduct taxes on property to which someone else has legal title if the person paying the taxes has a beneficial interest to protect.[37]

Taxes paid by a tenant to or for a landlord for business property are deductible by the tenant as additional rent.[38]

If real estate is sold, the deduction for real-estate taxes must be apportioned between the buyer and the seller according to the number of days in the "real property year" that each held the property (a real property year is the period of time which a real-estate tax covers). The taxes are apportioned to the seller up to, but not including, the date of sale, and to the buyer beginning with the date of sale, regardless of the accrual or lien dates under local laws.

If the seller uses the cash method and cannot deduct the property taxes until they are paid, and the buyer is personally liable for the tax, the seller is considered to have paid the portion of the tax imposed at the time of the sale. This permits him to deduct the portion of the tax to the date of the sale even though he does not actually pay it.[39]

An individual's residence was seized by a municipality for nonpayment of property taxes and was sold to a third party at public sale. Under state law, the original owner could reacquire the property from this third party by paying the latter his expenses of getting the property, including the delinquent property tax. The original owner could deduct the amount of property tax he paid, even though his payment was not made to the municipality.[40]

One person's property was foreclosed for nonpayment of property taxes. He was given the proceeds, less the taxes he owed, when the municipality sold this property to an outside buyer. Inasmuch as the original owner continued to be personally liable for the taxes, the amount thus withheld from the sales proceeds was deductible by him as property taxes paid, even though he had not made any tax payment himself.[41]

Tenant-shareholders in a cooperative housing or apartment corporation who utilize their allotted space as their principal residence may take as their own deductions the amounts they pay to the corporation as their proportionate shares of the real-estate taxes the corporation pays or incurs on the property. But shareholders may not deduct any portion of the real-estate taxes where the corporation does not own the property, even though the corporation pays these taxes under its rental agreement with the actual owner.[42]

The owner of an apartment in a condominium apartment project which he uses as his principal residence may deduct taxes which he pays with respect to the apartment *if* he is liable to the local tax authority for the tax assessment according to his interest in the condominium.[43]

In lieu of itemizing sales taxes, an individual has the choice of using tables prepared by the government for this purpose. These tables are printed in such places as the instruction forms which accompany personal income tax packets. They are also reproduced in various Internal Revenue Service publications such as *Your Federal Income Tax* and *Income Tax Deductions for Taxes*. If he thinks it would give him a higher deduction and if he thinks he can meet the requirements as to substantiation, an individual may elect not to use these optional tables. The tables are geared to an individual's adjusted gross income plus any nontaxable receipts such as Social Security, veterans' and railroad retirement benefits, and workmen's compensation payments.[44]

Should a person use the sales tax tables to determine his tax deduction, he may *add* to the amount shown on the tables the sales tax which he pays on the following five classes of items:
1. Automobiles.
2. Airplanes.
3. Boats.
4. Mobile homes.
5. Material used to build a new home when the individual taxpayer is his own contractor.[45]

If an individual engages a contractor to construct a personal home, the contract can provide for separate listings for supervision, labor, materials, and sales tax on these materials. Sales tax is deductible by the person upon whom it is imposed. In some states the law provides that sales tax on materials which are incorporated into realty are imposed on the purchaser of the realty rather than on the contractor: for example, if the contract identifies the final consumer of the materials as the customer and not the contractor. Where such is the case, the homeowner can deduct sales taxes on materials going into the house.[46]

Where the sales tax is imposed on the seller but is "separately stated" and paid by the consumer, the sales tax is treated as being imposed on the consumer.[47] "Consumer" means for this purpose "the ultimate user or purchaser."[48]

State law determines whether the sales tax liability is upon the buyer or the seller.[49] In a state where the sales tax is imposed directly on the purchaser, such as Connecticut, the tax is deductible by him, even if paid or incurred in connection with the purchase of an asset used in his trade or business.[50]

When an individual engages a private nurse under circumstances which qualify as medical expenses, the Social Security taxes which he pays on the nurse's wages are also deductible as medical expenses.[51]

An employer who absorbs the employee portion of his business employees' Social Security taxes may claim them as a deduction under the heading of compensation, assuming that these absorbed taxes plus regular salary do not constitute unreasonable compensation.[52]

The Federal Insurance Contributions Act (FICA) tax on wages, which are deductible as amounts paid for household and dependent-care expenses, is an essential part of these services and is deductible as employment-related expenses, but only if the expenses are incurred to enable a taxpayer to be gainfully employed.[53]

Dealers or investors in securities can deduct state stock transfer taxes to the extent that they are expenses incurred in carrying on a trade or business or an activity for the production of income. Dealers or investors in real estate may deduct the real-estate transfer taxes in the same manner for the same reasons.[54]

State and local transfer taxes on the conveyance of real estate or securities in a transaction entered upon for profit are deductible.[55]

When the separate taxable existence of a trust was denied the grantor by the Internal Revenue Service on the ground that he had not sufficiently "let go" of control of the trust moneys, the income was taxed to the grantor rather than to the trust.

But by the same token he was allowed to deduct state income taxes originally claimed by the trust.[56]

Taxes paid on real estate which has the complication of being a factor in a divorce case are deductible according to the facts in each particular case. For instance, when a residence is held jointly by the erstwhile husband and wife as tenants by the entirety with a right to survivorship, the husband may deduct any real-estate taxes he pays on the property as "taxes." This refers to real property owned by both spouses, to belong to the survivor after one spouse dies. Neither can sell without the approval of the other.

When the residence is held by the onetime husband and wife as tenants in common, each party owns one-half of the property. So the former husband may deduct, as "alimony," amounts he pays for taxes on the ex-wife's half of the property. The half he pays on his 50 percent of the property he deducts as "taxes."

In the case where the ex-wife is the sole owner of the residence and the former husband agrees to pay the real-estate taxes, he may deduct the payments as "alimony" if they are taxable to her as periodic payments under a divorce decree or agreement. The wife then may deduct the portion of each payment which represents taxes.

If the husband is the sole owner of the residence occupied rent-free by his ex-wife, he may deduct any real-estate taxes he pays on the property.[57]

Mandatory, involuntary extractions by a state are deductible as taxes even if not so labeled. For example, a state's law required candidates in a party's primary to pay qualifying fees and committee assessments to the Secretary of State. These were deductible as taxes.[58] *See also* **Beneficiaries; State disability insurance.**

Taxes, election to deduct or to capitalize. *See* **Election to deduct or to capitalize.**

Tax evasion, expenses relating to. An individual was permitted to deduct attorneys' fees in connection with his defense of the charge of tax evasion.[59]

Such also was the case where an individual engaged an attorney following indictment for preparing false tax returns for clients.[60]

Tax-exempt bonds. If an individual purchases a fully taxable bond as opposed to a tax-free municipal bond at a premium (above par), he may elect to amortize the premium over the life of the bond. The amortizable bond premium is then subtracted from his basis or adjusted basis for the bond. This treatment is mandatory in the case of a tax-exempt bond.[61] *See also* **Interest.**

Tax-free reorganization, use of in obtaining contributions deduction. *See* **Contributions.**

Taxicab fares. The cost of cab fares was deductible where a physician had advised a patient to seek remunerative employment as and for occupational therapy.[62] *See also* **Medical expenses.**

Tax informant. *See* **Informant, tax, return of fees to.**

Tax-option corporations. Under stipulated circumstances, corporate shareholders may elect to have the Federal income tax applied only at the shareholder level. Then there is a pass-through of corporate income and losses (the excess of deductions over income) to the shareholders on a *pro rata* basis. To qualify for the election, the corporation must be chartered by one of the fifty states and not a member of an affiliated group, except that it may own stock in an inactive subsidiary.[63] There can be only one class of stock, which, for taxable years beginning after December 31, 1982, may be held by not more than thirty-five shareholders, who can only be individuals, estates, or certain kinds of trusts.[64] The shareholders cannot be nonresident aliens. Every co-owner is considered a shareholder for determining whether the corporation has more than thirty-five shareholders, and each must file a consent on Form 2553 within specified times.[65] An election can be revoked only by action of shareholders holding more than one-half of the corporation's stock. A person becoming a shareholder, unless he owns more than half of the voting stock, does not have the power to terminate the election; he is bound by the original election.[66]

An individual who is a shareholder of an electing tax-option corporation during the taxable year in which it has a net operating loss is allowed as a deduction from gross income for his taxable year in which or with which the taxable year of the corporation ends, an amount equal to his portion of the corporation's net operating loss. But his share of the corporation's net operating loss for the year cannot exceed the sum of (1) the adjusted basis for his stock and (2) the adjusted basis of any indebtedness of the corporation to him. Both (1) and (2) are determined as of the close of the corporation's taxable year.[67]

For taxable years beginning after December 31, 1982, a corporation with accumulated earnings and profits from years in which it was a regular tax-paying corporation has tax imposed on "passive" income in excess of 25 percent of gross receipts. Passive income for this purpose means income other than from operations, such as rent where the corporation merely provides space or use of facilities.[68] Income was not passive where a corporation's services in leasing out automobiles included full maintenance of the vehicles, supplying of gas and oil, and body repairs.[69] Nor was income passive where a corporation rented dress suits to individuals, with no charge for alterations, and each suit was cleaned and pressed before it was used by a customer.[70]

If a corporation which has accumulated earnings and profits from years before it was a tax-option corporation exceeds this 25 percent limit for three consecutive taxable years, the election is terminated beginning with the following taxable year.[71]

Tax preparation, fees related to. Deduction is allowed for expenses in the determination, collection, or refund of any tax.[72] This includes estate taxes[73] and gift taxes,[74] as well as property taxes. Thus, expenses incurred by an individual for tax counsel or expenses in connection with the preparation of his tax returns or in connection with any proceedings involved in determining the extent of his tax liability or in contesting

it are deductible. Fees paid to a consultant to advise on the tax consequences of a transaction,[75] and fees paid to an appraiser to determine
the amount of a casualty loss for tax purposes,[76] are deductible. Deduction
was allowed for the costs of resisting a tax assessment[77] and for the
defense against a tax-evasion charge.[78] The propriety of a deduction is
not affected by the fact that the taxpayer is unsuccessful.[79]

If a corporation engages a tax consultant to provide specified executives with tax counsel without charge, any executive who utilizes this
service is taxed upon that portion of the employer payment representing
the service rendered to him. But he is entitled to a tax deduction on
his own return.[80]

Deduction is allowed for the cost of preparation of state, as well
as Federal, tax returns.[81]

After a corporation was liquidated, tax was assessed against it; and
as the corporation no longer existed, a stockholder was called upon to
pay this tax up to the value of the property he had received from the
corporation when it was dissolved. In order to avoid this personal tax
liability, he contested the imposition of the tax against the corporation
and was successful in having the assessment cancelled. He could deduct
his legal fees, regardless of the fact that the tax had been imposed against
the corporation and not against him, for as transferee of corporate properties he would have had to pay the tax himself if he had not successfully
resisted the claim against the corporation. His expenses had been to
establish his own tax liability.[82]

Tax rulings, expenses in obtaining. The costs of legal and accounting work
in applying for a Federal tax ruling are deductible.[83]

Tax shelters, out-of-pocket expenses. In an effort to dispose of certain tax-
shelter cases, Internal Revenue Service District Offices have been authorized by the Commissioner to settle these matters by allowing out-of-
pocket expenses in the first year, with the taxpayer signing a closing
agreement that disallows all other credits or deductions claimed. These
expenses represent the taxpayer's cash investments. This offer will not
apply in tax-shelter cases which are designated as matters to be litigated
and to criminal investigation cases. In general, offers are limited to cases
where the initial investment was made in 1980 or earlier.[84]

Teachers, expenses of. Professional or technical journals and books, etc.,
are deductible if they have short useful lives, such as less than one
year; otherwise, the costs have to be written off over the useful lives
of the assets.[85]

Credential renewal fees are deductible.[86]

Depreciation may be taken by a teacher on the price he paid for
books used in his teaching activities.[87]

A teacher of trainable mentally retarded children could deduct the cost of educational materials he purchased for use in his classes or as a student in courses for the handicapped in which he was enrolled.[88]

Grade-school teachers could deduct as business expense the cost of pictures, slides, and children's books and records purchased on a trip abroad in connection with their teaching programs.[89] *See also* **Advanced degree, study for Books; Doctoral dissertation; Education; Educational materials; Employees; Library, depreciation on; Military-style uniforms; Office at home; Research; Sabbatical leave, expenses of; Subscriptions to periodicals; Transportation; Travel; Typing.**

Technical journals and books. *See* **Books; Ordinary and necessary business expenses; Subscriptions to periodicals.**

Telephone. The cost of a telephone is deductible to the extent that the calls are for business as opposed to personal purposes.[90] A businessperson could deduct the expenses of his telephone at a time when he was confined to his home by reason of illness.[91] Telephone expenses are deductible as part of travel expense by a person who is away from home overnight on business.[92]

Telephone costs were held to be deductible expenses of a physician who wrote a 296-page book on infant disorders. Research activities for a business venture were carried on by telephone.[93]

An advertising solicitor could deduct the cost of telephoning his office regularly to check on whether customers had made calls to him.[94]

A physician was permitted to deduct an allocated portion of the cost of her personal home telephone as business expense, for professional appointments also were made on her home telephone.[95]

A business executive was allowed to deduct 15 percent of the cost of having a telephone in his home upon showing that many of the employees with whom he held discussions worked throughout the country in different time zones. By the time they were in their offices, he had returned home at (his) day's end.[96]

A municipal fireman could deduct a portion of the cost of maintaining a telephone in his home, as required by the city.[97] Such also was the situation where firemen were required to provide the authorities with a telephone number where a smoke-eater could be reached in case of emergency. Deduction was allowed where a fireman had a phone installed in his home, although that was not specifically called for by departmental order.[98]

A postal worker who was required by postal regulations to list a telephone number where he could be reached at home by his supervisor could deduct part of the cost of installing a telephone.[99]

An employer required all key personnel to maintain home telephones, so that they could be reached at all times. Although some incoming calls might have been business-related, outgoing calls were not. Fifteen percent of the annual service charge for the home telephone was deductible.[100]

If a person has a telephone in his home which is used both for business and for personal purposes, he may lose a deduction entirely for inability to prove the extent of the business use. But if he makes a credible impression, a court may make its own approximation of deductible business use of the phone: for example, 30 percent in the case of a caterer who made some job arrangements from his home.[101] A probation officer was required to use his personal telephone at night to contact clients otherwise unavailable during the day. The court permitted him to take a business expense deduction of 75 percent of the cost of maintaining a telephone in his residence.[102]

A professional writer could deduct the amount of his telephone bills.[103]

A realtor who conducted business from his home maintained two telephones there, one for personal use and the other for exclusive use in his business. He was permitted to deduct his expenses for the latter.[104]

An individual can deduct the cost of a home telephone if he can show that it was solely for the purpose of receiving calls for the performance of service by him.[105]

An employee was required by his employer to have a telephone in his home. The employee was reimbursed for long-distance calls and for calls made on pay phones, but not for telephone maintenance expenses at home or for local calls. These he could deduct.[106]

A person who telephoned a psychologist some 350 miles away, on a weekly basis, for counseling in a guidance program could deduct the cost of these calls.[107] *See also* **Deaf persons, expenses of; Employees; Executives.**

Telephone answering service. *See* **Answering service.**

Telephone in car. *See* **Medical expenses.**

Temporary employment, expenses of. *See* **Employees.**

Temporary living-away-from-home expenses. *See* **Travel.**

Temporary partitions, cost of. *See* **Repairs.**

Tenants in common, expenses of. *See* **Alimony; Interests; Taxes.**

Tenant-stockholders. *See* **Cooperative housing, deductions of tenant-shareholder in.**

Tennis courts. *See* **Entertainment.**

Tenure, expenses of obtaining. *See* **Advanced degree, study for; Education.**

Termination of a business. A loss incurred in a business, or in a transaction entered upon for profit, which arises from the sudden termination of the usefulness in the business or transaction of any nondepreciable property, is allowed as a deduction at the time the business or transaction is discontinued or the property is permanently discarded from usefulness.[108]

For example, an accountant purchased from another accountant the right to service the account of a particular client. The purchaser properly capitalized the cost for tax purposes; that is, he showed it as a nondeductible expenditure with no annual depreciation write-offs, as the period of useful life of the account could not be measured. Five years later, the client died. At that time the business in connection with the account terminated, and its cost was deductible.[109]

Termination of trust or estate. If an estate or a trust has deductions in excess of gross income and other than personal exemptions and charitable contributions for its last taxable year upon termination of the trust or estate, the excess is allowed as a deduction to the beneficiaries succeeding to the property of the trust or estate. The deduction is allowed only in the taxable year of a beneficiary in which or with which the estate or trust terminates.[110]

Termites, damage caused by. Ordinarily, loss brought about by termite damage is not deductible as a casualty loss because there is not the *sudden* destruction necessary for a casualty deduction; the termites presumably have been at work on a foundation, etc., for a long, long time. But deduction was allowed where it could be shown that the building had been free of termites when examined by an expert less than a year before the loss occurred.[111]

A taxpayer has the opportunity of showing, if he can, that the damage was caused by "fast termites" and hence that there existed the degree of suddenness needed for a casualty deduction.[112]

Testimonial dinners. *See* **Ordinary and necessary business expenses.**

Textbooks. *See* **Books.**

Theft losses. *See* **Casualties; Family transactions.**

Therapy. *See* **Medical expenses.**

Tickets for theater, etc. *See* **Advertising; Benefit performances, tickets for; Business expenses; Contributions.**

Timber. *See* **Farmers; Forest management expenses; Reforestation expenses.**

Time savings account or deposit, premature withdrawal. *See* **Premature withdrawal of interest.**

Tips. Tips for business purposes are deductible. But usually the deduction is lost through lack of proof that the payments were appropriate and necessary or that a specific business purpose had been sought to be gained. In the words of one court decision, "Indeed, a reasonable case can be made that such tips are ordinary and necessary and proximately related to a salesman's duty of entertaining his customers." But here; as usually is the case where there is no contemporary record of who the recipient was and the business purpose, the amount claimed was disallowed for tax purposes.[113]

An actor was allowed to deduct tips which he paid to studio employees in order to get better cooperation from them.[114]

A manufacturing company's field representative could deduct non-reimbursable tips to porters at hotels and service stations.[115]

When an individual's business office was moved, he could deduct cash gratuities given to the mover's helpers, as well as tips given to elevator operators and doormen in both the old and the new buildings.[116]

A businessperson could deduct the amount of tips paid to truck drivers in order to ensure prompt delivery of inventory purchases.[117]

A business executive could deduct payments which he made to employees of the corporation for secretarial and related services in connection with his personal investments. The actual amount of the allowable deduction was set by the court.[118]

Where expenses for gratuities bear a proximate relationship to a taxpayer's business and are for the promotion of that business, they may be deductible even though voluntarily made.[119] *See also* **Bribes and kickbacks; Business gifts.**

Tires, automobile. *See* **Expenditures for benefits lasting more than one year.**

Title, defense of. *See* **Legal fees.**

Title insurance company, payments to. Deduction was allowed for payments made to a title insurance company to ascertain whether local tax assessments made against a person's property were in order.[120]

Tolls. When a car is used for business purposes, highway, bridge, or similar tolls are separately deductible even where the zero bracket amount option is selected.[121]

Tools. Although the cost of business assets with an estimated useful life of more than one year ordinarily must be capitalized and written off only in the form of annual depreciation, the cost of small tools is deductible.[122] But it must be shown that the tools were used in connection with one's trade or business, as opposed to implements utilized for hobby purposes.[123]

A butcher was allowed to deduct the cost of sharpening and maintaining the tools of his trade.[124]

An individual could deduct the cost of tools for use on one particular employment project, where these tools were of no use to him on other assignments.[125]

A sales representative, who had to service equipment bought by his customers, could deduct the cost of tools for which he was not entitled to reimbursement by his employer.[126]

A mechanic could deduct the cost of tools he was required to have in order to meet the conditions of his employment.[127]

Farmers may deduct the cost of ordinary tools having either a short life or small cost, such as shovels, rakes, and other hand tools.[128]

Tools, transportation of. *See* **Commuting.**

Trade or business. Deduction is allowed for all ordinary and necessary expenses paid or incurred during the taxable year in carrying on any trade or business.[129] Where premises are used to carry on a trade or business, depreciation is a proper expense even in the case of assets which ordinarily would be regarded as personal, such as a radio, a cocktail table, a grandfather clock, and a painting in a lawyer's library.[130] *See also* **Ordinary and necessary business expenses; Transactions entered into for profit.**

Traffic accident, outlays resulting from. *See* **Casualties; Pedestrian, cost of hitting; Settlement payments.**

Training expenses. Expenditures in connection with the acquisition of property having a useful life of more than one year ordinarily are not deductible, being considered a part of the cost of the asset. (*See* **Expenditures for benefits lasting more than one year.**) But where a purchaser of business machinery paid employees of the seller to instruct the purchaser's personnel on how to operate the equipment most efficiently, these payments were deductible.[131]

Expenses of training one's own employees were deductible where experience indicated that these persons remained for less than one year and accordingly the expenditure had only short-term value. The benefit of this training did not last for more than a year.[132]

As a result of collective bargaining between an employer and a union, it was agreed that the employer would pay a percentage of its hourly compensation for production labor into an educational fund for the purpose of defraying the cost of daytime schooling of apprentices. This was deductible.[133]

Transactions between related parties. *See* **Family transactions.**

Transactions entered into for profit. Deduction is allowed for losses resulting from "any transaction entered into for profit, though not connected with a trade or business."[134] "[A] taxpayer engages in an activity for profit," said one court, ". . . when profit is actually and honestly his objective though the prospect of achieving it may seem dim."[135]

The term *profit* includes an expectation that the assets used in the activity may appreciate in value.[136] The term *trade or business* includes the arts.[137]

An individual who collected postage stamps was allowed a loss upon ultimate disposition for less than his cost. Evidence disclosed that although he enjoyed his collection, he had been guided in his purchases by the advice of professionals as to which stamps had the greatest potential for enhancement in value because he was interested in making money.[138]

What has been a person's hobby for several years can be converted into a transaction entered upon for profit in a later year when the level of activity and his devotion to it increases. So it was with a county official and a teacher, who collected coins and stamps as a hobby. In a later year, the couple purchased quantities of these "collectibles" and built up inventories of duplicate items for resale. Although the taxpayers continued to work as employees of other parties, they now displayed merchandise for sale at collectors' shows, kept good business records, obtained a municipal business tax registration bearing the classification "Retail Sales," and, to quote the court, showed a "fairly steady march towards establishing a profitable business." Losses from transactions in coins and stamps, which had been held to be nondeductible on tax returns of prior years, were deductible insofar as they related to the year when the activity progressed from a hobby to a profit-oriented business.[139]

An engineer had health problems, which his physician believed would be lessened if he moved to a clean-air environment. He moved to the country and purchased a farm which he operated himself. The fact that he experienced better health from living in the country did not contradict his expressed intention to operate the farm for profit.[140]

An attorney bought stock in a finance company. When the company became insolvent, his loss on the stock was not a capital loss but a fully deductible ordinary loss. He had purchased the stock, not as an investment, but for the purpose of getting profitable law work for himself. His investment was large enough to enable him to be elected president, and as such, he thought he could turn over some of the finance company's legal work to himself in his capacity as a lawyer. He expected through this connection to be engaged for title searches on property offered as security by borrowers, to obtain collection fees of up to 25 percent when the company had to get *some* lawyer to go after delinquent parties, and to obtain document recording and notarial fees. The loss was fully deductible, being in connection with a business transaction entered upon for profit.[141]

Engaging in an activity for profit does not necessarily require a person to earn enough money to support himself.[142] The standard is whether an activity is engaged in for profit.[143]

An enterprise need not demand one's full attention in order for it to qualify as a trade or business.[144] The test is not whether a person's intention and expectation of profit is reasonable but whether the intention and expectation is *bona fide*.[145] But it is important to establish whether a taxpayer's devotion to a project displaced other employment opportunities.[146]

It is irrelevant whether a person intends to make a profit because the profit symbolizes success or because it is the pathway to material achievement.[147]

Telephone, travel, and labor costs are deductible if related to invention activities carried on by an employee on his own time.[148]

Where an employee wishes to establish that a second activity in which he engages is a transaction entered upon for profit, it can be very helpful if he is able to show that he cleared with his employer his undertaking of this second activity.[149]

If a businessperson engages in a second form of activity which he clearly enjoys, such as raising orchids, expenses and losses related to this activity are likely to be disallowed by the Internal Revenue Service. Reason: The expenses and losses do not result from a trade or business entered into for profit but from a personal hobby. If, however, the losses were suffered for reasons beyond the taxpayer's control, they are not an indication that the activity was not engaged in for profit. Such was the case where the vice-president of a major New York bank, who was a long-time ski buff, opened a New England ski lodge. The taxable period was 1973-74, and, because of the gasoline shortage at that time and the long lines at gas stations, people stayed away in droves. His expenses and losses were deductible, because the court believed the taxpayer had had a reasonable expectation of profit.[150]

In the words of one court, "The taxpayer is required to demonstrate that the appearance of a pleasure-seeking motive is misleading and that the motive for the activity was profit making." In this case, the taxpayer was successful in showing that one of the two pleasurable activities in which he was engaged was a trade or business entered upon for profit.[151]

Even if the chances, based upon experience of other persons engaged in this activity, are strong that a person will not find a commercially profitable oil deposit when he drills on land not established geologically to be proven oil-bearing land, on those rare occasions when these efforts do result in discovering a well the operator generally realizes a very large return. Thus, there is a small chance that he will make a large profit from his oil-exploration activity. Under these circumstances, he is engaged in the activity of oil drilling for profit.[152]

But a person must attempt in pragmatic fashion to relate his expenses to his potential income.[153] "Of course," said one court, "the taxpayer may not close his eyes to the facts."[154]

The Internal Revenue Service has announced factors to be taken into account in determining whether an activity is carried on for profit: (1) the manner in which the activity is carried on, (2) the expertise of the taxpayer and his advisers, (3) the time and effort expended by the taxpayer in carrying on the activity, (4) the expectation that assets used in the activity may appreciate in value, (5) the success of the taxpayer in carrying on other similar or dissimilar activities, (6) the taxpayer's history of income or loss with respect to the activity, (7) the amount of occasional profit, if any, which is earned, (8) the financial status of the taxpayer, and (9) whether elements of personal pleasure or recreation are involved.[155] For example, in the case of a farm allegedly operated for profit, it can be helpful to the taxpayer's case if there are no recreational facilities there such as tennis courts or a swimming pool.[156] In one case where a person with a law degree was permitted to deduct losses from the operation of a farm, the court pointed out that "There are no recreational facilities on [the] farms."[157]

Dues of a hunting club were deemed to be for the purpose of business discussions with clients, where an individual testified that there were no entertainment facilities there, that he did not have a gun, and that he did no hunting whatsoever.[158]

But, declared one court, "suffering has never been made a prerequisite to deductability."[159] "[T]he fact that the taxpayer derives personal pleasure from engaging in the activity is not sufficient to cause the activity to be classified as not engaged in for profit if the activity is in fact engaged in for profit, as evidenced by these factors. . . ."[160]

It is helpful if a person can show what was referred to in one decision as "[T]he lack of appeal in the activity other than profit."[161] The size of an undertaking may indicate that it was no mere hobby. In accepting a physician's apple orchard as a transaction entered into for profit, a court declared: "The very magnitude of this operation seems to suggest a business operation for, as [the taxpayer] points out, there is nothing aesthetic or pleasant about thousands of decaying apples on a 10-acre farm."[162]

An individual worked for a farm-implement dealer. His mother gave him a farm, which he enlarged by land purchases. He formed a fifty-fifty partnership with his son, but the father did not participate in the daily farm work, which was performed by the son, a full-time farmer. The father, who had had long experience at farming, pitched in at the farm work when substantial labor was needed and was directly involved with his son in all major managerial decisions. The father could deduct his share of the farm losses as a transaction entered into for profit, for this was a typical partnership where one party supplied the capital and the other, services. He did not have to prove that his expectation of a profit was reasonable, but only that it was genuine.[163]

A practicing dentist had long been interested in bird dogs. Over a period of several years he discussed with recognized authorities on the subject the commercial feasibility of establishing a kennel of championship trial dogs. He engaged a professional handler with vast experience in this area. He spent a great deal of time on the kennels and brought ill puppies to his own home for nursing. He pursued businesslike techniques such as advertising the availability of his leading sire for breeding and keeping an account of his expenses. His losses from his kennel operation were deductible.[164]

An industrialist had been interested in bird hunting for forty years. He decided to start raising bird dogs after discussions with professional trainers. He obtained advice from the head veterinarian at Pennsylvania State University. He regularly visited his kennel to observe the progress of the dogs under experienced handlers. The court noted approvingly that he "maintained records of all the expenses incurred in the kennel operations." He was permitted to deduct his expenses.[165]

For some years, an individual spent most of his time managing his personal investments. Then he became interested in various inventions for mining and manufacturing operations, obtaining several patents. He sought advice from consulting engineers on the marketing potentialities of his inventions, and he wrote to companies that might have been interested in making use of his inventions. He was allowed to deduct his expenses and losses. If he had not been interested in making a profit, there would have been no reason to patent his inventions or to attempt to market them.[166]

A chemical engineer, who had engaged in amateur theatricals, entered upon an acting career professionally. He took lessons at a well-regarded studio, retained a theatrical agent, and sent photographs and résumés to 250 studios, agents, and casting directors. He joined an acting guild. Although it was several years after the taxable year that he left his engineering post and became a full-time actor, the court considered his acting lessons, transportation expenses, guild fees, and the like to be deductible business expenses.[167]

Realizing that his retirement was near at hand, a dentist looked for some business which could supply additional income. He learned from knowledgeable persons that there seemed to be a promising future for breeding and selling American saddlebred horses. He got advice on the general economics of running such an operation, learning that the development time required would be from five to ten years. Actually he had losses for twelve years, the last three of which the Internal Revenue Service disallowed. But a court permitted the deductions, because the dentist had expected that he would make a profit. Complete and accurate books were kept in a manner similar to other comparable *businesses;* business bank accounts were kept separate from personal ones; changes were made in operating methods in an effort to increase profitability; and horses that did not meet breeding expectations were disposed of. Although losses persisted year after year, they were shown to be attributable in part to circumstances beyond the taxpayer's control, such as the medical problems of several of the horses, the failure of a professional trainer to do all that he was expected to do, and a shift in fashion among horse purchasers.[168]

Delayed attainment of financial success in the operation of a herd of registered cattle was attributed successfully to natural calamities, such as an infertile bull.[169]

In the words of one decision, "The fact that [the taxpayer] kept adequate books and records and seeks the assistance of her accountants is also a strong indication of a profit-seeking motive."[170] A person can strengthen his case if he keeps accurate books and records for the alleged business.[171] But although such records are helpful, they are not an absolute requirement in the case of a small operation.[172]

An individual constructed a duplex apartment, occupying the upper unit herself. She was unable to rent the lower portion despite repeated newspaper advertisements and notices in supermarkets. But she could deduct her maintenance expenses for the ground-floor apartment as resulting from a transaction entered upon for profit. Her failure to rent the premises was because the building was in a high-crime, rundown area. She kept the premises in a habitable condition despite frequent vandalism and did not use this space for herself.[173]

Depreciation could be deducted on a house which the owner rented to a tenant at a figure which was less than the depreciation. This was a transaction entered into for profit, for the owner was willing to incur short-term losses on the operation of the house in order to reap the benefits of potentially great long-term appreciation.[174]

A real-estate developer's deduction of operating expenses was disallowed by the Internal Revenue Service on the ground that his business was exclusively in residential properties. Thus, it was claimed, expenses in connection with the development of commercial properties were unrelated to his trade or business. But the court considered the IRS's differentiation to be mere hair-splitting. Enlarging the scope of the developer's activities was only a reasonable and natural expansion of an existing business activity. It was but the cultivation of a business within the normal scope of real-estate development generally.[175] Similarly, a dealer in residential and commercial real estate could deduct professional consultation fees for advice on industrial property development. The court felt that "the line of demarcation between them is obscure."[176]

A licensed real-estate salesperson paid $12,000 to a land promoter for the exclusive right to sell in the Cleveland area certain Florida lots, which the promoter had an option to buy. The promoter never exercised his option to buy the lots, so the salesperson's investment immediately ceased to have any value. This sudden termination of a property right gave rise to a loss deduction.[177]

The basic rule is that a person cannot deduct a loss on the sale of residential property purchased or constructed by him for use as his personal residence and so used by him at the time of the sale. But if this property is, prior to its sale, rented or otherwise converted to income-producing property and is so used up to the time of the sale, a loss sustained on sale is deductible.[178] If he rents out the building to outsiders and subsequently sells the rented property, any loss is deductible.[179]

Loss was allowed on the sale of an inherited house which the taxpayer had never occupied. This at no time had been personal, nonbusiness property but represented a transaction entered into for profit as soon as he acquired his inheritance.[180]

A husband had occupied, for some years, a home owned by his wife, and after her death he inherited it. Four months later he married another woman, at which time he sold the home at a loss. This was deductible, for he had never intended living there after his first wife's death and immediately had set about trying to make a sale. His four-months' occupancy of the house until a buyer was found did not convert the house back to personal as opposed to business property, which it never had been in his hands except for a brief transitional period. He had held it merely with the hope of making a profit.[181]

Expenses of trying out a business venture are deductible if the venture is abandoned, provided the activities were more than a matter of investigating or looking into a proposition. The taxpayer must actually have been engaged in a transaction carried on for profit.[182] *See also* **Hobby losses; Ordinary and necessary business expenses.**

Transcript of court record. The transcript of a court record is deductible if the matter relates to a taxpayer's trade or business and is not of a capital nature; that is, the court proceeding does not involve an expenditure that produces a benefit with a life of more than one year.[183]

Where a person who lost a decision in court purchases a copy of the trial transcript for use in a higher court to which an appeal is being made, the expenditure is deductible.[184]

Transferee liability, payments representing. *See* **Legal fees; Tax preparation, fees related to.**

Translation expense. The cost of translation of documents used in foreign business negotiations was deductible.[185]

Transplant of organs, expenses related to. *See* **Medical expenses.**

Transportation. *See* Conventions; Travel.

Travel. According to the United States Supreme Court, three conditions must be satisfied before a traveling-expense deduction will be allowed:

1. The expense must be a reasonable and necessary traveling expense, as that term is generally understood. This includes such items as transportation fares and food and lodging expenses incurred while traveling.

2. The expense must be incurred "while away from home."

3. The expense must be incurred in pursuit of business. This means that there must be a direct connection between the expenditure and the carrying on of the trade or business of the taxpayer or of his employer. Such an expenditure, moreover, must be necessary or appropriate to the development and pursuit of the trade or business.[186]

Professional football players are engaged in a trade or business and may deduct travel and other expenses related to the business.[187]

Professional baseball players, managers, coaches, and trainers are entitled to deduct their traveling expenses, including meals and lodgings when away from their "club town" in pursuit of their business or employment.[188]

A state legislator could deduct expenses while away from home in order to become better acquainted with his constituents in different parts of the district which he represented.[189] Similarly, a member of a state legislature could deduct unreimbursable expenses incurred in order to ascertain facts which resulted in a proposal and enactment of legislation.[190]

For taxable years after 1981, the home of a United States Congressman is deemed to be in the district from which he was elected.[191]

A state judge was required to be elected from the district where he lived but had to work in the state capital for about two-thirds of the time. He could not deduct his living expenses while in the state capital nor his travel expenses to and from his residence. But he was permitted to deduct his travel and living expenses while at home, the state capital being his principal place of business.[192]

The rule allowing an individual to deduct living expenses while away from home applies when a person who maintains a residence at one location accepts employment away from the vicinity of this residence, the duration of which is *temporary* as distinguished from *indefinite*. A professional news and speech writer was out of employment. He took a job as a construction-site carpenter. The work could have lasted indefinitely, but he intended it to be only temporary because (1) he wanted to get back to his chosen form of work as soon as a position could be found and (2) he was physically unable to perform carpentry for a long period of time because of a muscle condition caused by childhood polio.

Thus he chose not to move to the area of the construction site, and his expenses there were deductible as "away-from-home."[193]

A seventy-one-year-old legal stenographer, after her retirement, found she could not live on her Social Security income. She was unable to find employment in the Florida community where she lived. In the summer months, she moved to New York to work as a replacement for legal stenographers who were on vacation. She could deduct her living expenses in New York and her railroad fares. This was temporary work away from home. The court felt that, because of her age, it was unreasonable to expect that she would move her permanent residence from Florida to New York.[194]

A professional skater was employed by the Ice Follies on a seasonal basis. Employees traveled with the show, and it was understood that they would be in each city visited only temporarily. She never abandoned her permanent home and intended to return to it at the end of her engagement, which she did. She could deduct her "away-from-home" expenses while on the road.[195]

Deduction was allowed where the work away from home was considered to be temporary rather than indefinite because the work was at the construction site for an anti-ballistic missile, and the continuance of construction, in the court's words, "depended on the progress of the Strategic Arms Limitation [SALT] talks."[196]

To qualify for a travel-expense deduction under the temporary employment exception, the employment must be temporary in contemplation at the time of its acceptance and not indeterminate in fact as it develops.[197]

Even if the project on which an individual works is going to continue indefinitely, he can deduct away-from-home expenses where his particular type of work (outdoors in one typical situation) could not be carried on during the severe and lengthy winters which were customary at this place of employment. If he was laid off because of weather-dictated circumstances, his chances of subsequent reemployment were minimal.[198]

A civilian employee of a corporation that performed services for the United States Air Force was assigned as a supervisor to one Air Force base. His work required him to go to other bases as well; and when government transportation was unavailable, he used his own car. He could deduct his travel expenses.[199]

An Air Force major was assigned to temporary duty at an air base in Germany. His responsibilities required him to visit other locations, and transportation was made available by the Air Force. But higher-ranking officers had priority in the assignment of vehicles, and this arrangement was unsatisfactory for the keeping of appointments. Taxis were scarce, and he was not eligible for fare reimbursement because government transportation supposedly was available to him. He could deduct his expenses in using his own car in carrying on his required duties.[200]

Ordinarily, a person cannot deduct travel expenses if he could have obtained reimbursement from his employer or could have made use of a company car. But deduction was allowed where an employee was a "trouble shooter" who had to respond to emergencies instantly, without spending the time required to get authorizations.[201]

Expenses of a university professor while going to technical meetings in cities away from home were allowed as business expenses.[202]

A commercial fisherman's home, for tax purposes, ordinarily will be the home port where he begins and ends his fishing trips. He is considered away from home if the period of absence from his home port is substantially longer than an ordinary work day and his duties require him to sleep away from his home port. If he meets these requirements, and if the time, place, and business purpose of the travel are properly substantiated, he may deduct the reasonable and necessary expenses he incurs for travel, meals, and lodgings.[203]

A university professor who went on sabbatical leave for ten months to pursue postdoctoral research training was deemed to have retained his tax home at the university. His away-from-home travel expenses, including meals and lodgings incurred during that period, were deductible.[204]

Where an individual is engaged in more than one trade or business, and such businesses require a division of his time between two distant cities, he may deduct his travel expenses incurred in discharging his duties at that city which is removed from his principal post of duty. In other words, where a person has more than one place of business or employment his principal place of business or employment constitutes his "home" to serve as a point of origin for determining his deduction for traveling expenses.[205]

In order to determine a "home" for tax purposes, these factors are applied: (1) the length of time that a person spends in each location, (2) the degree of his business activity in each place, and (3) the relative portion of his income derived from each place.[206]

An individual had two offices, one in city X and one in city Y. He worked about fifty hours a week in X and earned about 75 percent of his gross income there. His wife and two of his three children lived in Y. His "tax home" was deemed to be in X, as he earned the majority of his income and spent most of his time there. So he could deduct the cost of his meals and lodgings while his work required him to be in Y. But the deduction was limited to that portion of the family expenses for meals and lodgings which was properly attributable to his presence in Y in the actual performance of his duties.[207]

"Away from home" means overnight if duties require a person to be away from the general area of his tax home for a period substantially longer than an ordinary day's work; and during released time while he is away ("released time" being, naturally, time when he is not actively pursuing business or employment), it is reasonable for him to need and to get sleep or rest to meet the requirements of his employment or business. A person need not be away from his tax home for an entire twenty-four-hour day or from dusk to dawn so long as his relief from duty during his absence is a sufficient period of time in which to get necessary sleep and rest.[208]

The fact that the home from which he was away was the residence of his father did not make it any less the son's home for this purpose, as he paid rent there in the form of contributions to the support of the father's home, had his furnishings there, and made regular trips there while employed on temporary jobs elsewhere.[209]

Where travel by a Minnesota businessman and his wife, who was associated with him in the venture, was to places in the Caribbean where there were potential customers, it was established to the court's satisfaction that these were not pleasure jaunts. He had medical problems that required him to avoid prolonged exposure to the sun, and his wife had comparable problems that ruled out the likelihood that the trip was anything other than business-oriented.[210]

A bank officer was assigned a production quota; his salary increases and bonuses were dependent upon the volume of loans he made. In an effort to develop business, he and his wife went on several tours organized primarily for people involved in the building industry. The officer went on these tours in the belief that they would generate business. Social relationships thus established did result in substantial new business. These trips were strenuous, and the couple, especially the wife, did not enjoy them. He could deduct the travel expenses which were not reimbursed by the bank.[211]

A state legislator may treat his place of residence within his legislative district as his tax home for purposes of computing the deduction for living expenses. If he so elects, he is deemed to have expended for business purposes an amount equal to his legislative days multiplied by the greater of the Federal *per diem* or the state *per diem* (but not over 110 percent of the Federal *per diem*). This amount is deductible, except for legislators living within fifty miles of the capitol building, without regard to the away-from-home rule.[212]

A person who lives in the United States may be required by his employer to work outside of the country. If it is important to his functions abroad that he be fully informed of current trends in American life, he may be *required* by his employer to spend his vacations and other leave time in this country. Then his living and transportation expenses here, if nonreimbursable, are deductible as expenses in connection with his business of being an employee.[213]

Members of the foreign service who are United States citizens are required to take a leave of absence from regular duties upon completion of three years of continuous service abroad, to be spent in the United States. Substantiated "home leave" expenses of the officer are deductible business travel expenses.[214]

A person may deduct his travel expenses if he temporarily leaves his regular place of business to advise or to provide other services to the government while keeping his regular business connection.[215]

Since travel must be business-oriented, a free-lance lecturer and writer could deduct his travel and related expenses in making movies to show at lectures. Although he had a substantial income from a trust fund, his activity was regarded as a trade or business. For many years he had been a journalist, and this activity at one time had supported him and his family. The potential for profit was still good despite some lean years.[216]

An accomplished scientist with a Ph.D. degree and one hundred published papers to her credit went to Europe to do further research in her field. Her objective was to maintain her professional standing in order to be eligible for prospective research appointments and financial gain. Since the death of her husband she needed a source of income; the profit motive was supplied by the good prospects for remuneration by salaries from foundations. Her travel expenses were held to be deductible. The activity engaged in was part of a profit-making scheme. Her activity was not merely a stepping-stone into another type of work; her existing activity was the potentially profitable one.[217]

A physician who ran an alcoholism clinic could deduct expenses of a trip to Europe to study the treatment of alcholism there.[218]

An established professional writer could deduct travel and away-from-home lodging expenses while researching, writing, and arranging material for a book. The manuscript material on which he worked was in a museum 3,000 miles from his home, and he spent most of a year working at the museum. Although he received no compensation for his work on the book that year, it was a transaction into which he had entered with a good-faith expectation of making a profit.[219]

A University of Alabama professor went to Egypt one summer for personal pleasure. While there, he accepted invitations from two universities to lecture upon his field of expertise. As these lectures helped to maintain his professional reputation, although he was not paid for his appearances, he could deduct that proportion of the cost of his trip which represented the number of days devoted to the lectures.[220]

A professor was appointed by the Department of State as a lecturer at a university in France under the Fulbright Act. Travel expense was deductible, including the cost of his meals and lodgings on the round trip to and from the university in France and during his stay there.[221]

Sabbatical-leave travel expenses may be deductible even though the travel is of the "broadening, cultural type, which is generally considered to yield only a personal advantage," if at the same time it "has a direct relationship to the conduct of the individual's trade or business."[222]

An assistant principal of a racially and culturally integrated high school could deduct travel expenses to various countries while on sabbatical leave. Her major responsibilities were the handling of racial and riot problems and attempting to better race relations in a school characterized by racial, cultural, and social diversity. She achieved her objectives by repeatedly visiting foreign schools and talking to teachers, administrators, and students. Upon returning to her school, she instituted a new curriculum concentrating on techniques often used abroad for classrooms of diverse cultural backgrounds.[223]

It is not necessary that the travel be required by one's employer in order to be deductible.[224]

An individual was permitted to deduct his travel expenses to and from Ireland to collect his earnings from the Irish Sweepstakes. There were hazards of loss if the funds were transmitted to him from Europe. He established that no time was spent on unrelated travel or sightseeing.[225]

An individual was permitted to deduct as business expense the cost of traveling to court in connection with speeding charges, for his livelihood depended upon the use of a car.[226]

The holder of a substantial minority interest in a corporation, who was a director, could deduct his expenses in going to directors' meetings, where decisions would be made that might have a substantial effect on the value of his investment.[227]

Deduction is limited to what actually was paid, not to what might have been paid, despite the circumstances. An individual had *bona fide* business to conduct in a foreign country for fourteen days. The charter fare for a twenty-five-day stopover was considerably less, and that was the ticket he purchased. As travel expense, he claimed the right to deduct either (1) the cost of a regular flight, as charter rates did not apply to an eleven-day visit, or (2) expenses for eleven nonbusiness days that the charter flight terms required him to stay abroad. He struck out of both arguments. Deductions are allowed only for actual expenses and not for theoretical calculations based upon expenses which might have been but were not actually incurred on business.[228]

Deduction is allowed for the cost of operating a car for transportation for medical care. In lieu of itemizing medical expense, a standard mileage rate of nine cents a mile may be used.[229]

An individual was permitted to deduct her costs for going to and from Europe to consult a physician who had experience in treating a medical condition which had not responded to treatment she had received from doctors in the United States.[230]

A teacher could deduct his expenses in taking mentally retarded educable students to places where they could be exposed to different aspects of community life.[231]

The cost of vacation travel is personal and not deductible. But an individual who owned a number of rental units could deduct the cost of travel to investigate investment real estate while he was away on vacation. He was able to establish that on this one day, he devoted his full time to investigating real estate and did not mix business and pleasure.[232]

An individual held real estate for investment in a distant city. He received word from county officials where the property was located that under local law he was required to keep unimproved property free from brush, dead trees, and trash or be subjected to a penalty. Inasmuch as he had been unsuccessful in getting anyone else to take care of the property, he was obliged to travel to his land and to perform the work himself. Said the court: "The need to comply with such ordinances makes his travel expenditures . . . both ordinary and necessary."[233]

A businessperson could deduct the expenses of his journey to recruit strikebreakers for his business.[234]

The proprietor of an illegal gambling establishment could deduct the cost of transportation of customers to his place of business.[235]

Unreimbursed travel expenses of a Civil Defense volunteer were deductible when he journeyed to various localities to witness demonstrations and drills.[236]

An employee's expenses while on company business are not deductible if he could have gotten reimbursement from his employer by requesting it. Where one employer banned reimbursement to employees who used their own cars for company business, the executive who had issued that order could deduct his own expenses. Probably he would not have been fired had he ignored the company rule and taken reimbursement. But he had been justified in believing that even he should follow the expressed company policy.[237]

A public official could deduct nonreimbursable travel expenses in connection with receiving an award, which had no cash value, from a nongovernmental organization for the performance of his official duties as an employee of the United States Government. The expenses arose out of the performance of his business duties and advanced the interests of his trade or business.[238]

Deduction of the travel expenses of a businessperson's spouse usually is not allowed because of the strong presumption that the spouse's presence was pleasure- rather than business-oriented. But where an individual is on a valid business trip, the travel expenses of the spouse are deductible if "it can be adequately shown that the wife's presence on the trip had a *bona fide* business purpose.[239] Such was the case where an employee went abroad with the assignment of reporting back on the operation of the foreign branch offices. Specifically, he was to accumulate information on physical facilities, staffing, housing, office space, recreational facilities, school facilities, and other problem areas. His wife, by contacting the families of the foreign employees, was able to relay to her husband information which otherwise he might not have been able to gather.[240]

An individual was a vice-president and director of a tobacco company listed on the New York Stock Exchange. European sales were negotiated primarily by senior executives of the company, who dealt directly with major officials of potential customers. Officers were encouraged and required to have very close friendly relations with foreign customers, and the president told his executives how much his wife had contributed to cementing the type of relationship deemed of greatest value to the company. So the vice-president took his own wife with him on his annual European visits to major customers. She was not a trained salesperson, but a susceptible judge pointed out that she "presents a very personable and attractive appearance." She entertained customers and their wives in her hotel and made it possible and congenial for her husband to be entertained in customers' homes. She was invited to come to Europe by customers. She did no sightseeing on these trips, and the itinerary was constructed solely in accordance with business requirements. The trips were not regarded as for her pleasure or vacation. The only reason she went, concluded the court, was because of her husband's business. Her trip was directly attributable to his business. "It assisted him in his business and assisted in the production of income."[241]

Roy Disney was president and board chairman of Walt Disney Productions, a publicly held corporation engaged in the production of family-type entertainment. He and other executives frequently traveled in connection with business meetings, conferences, meetings with the press, and business-related social engagements. Usually he took his wife with him. On these trips she did nothing of a business nature, such as acting as her husband's secretary, but she attended various events at which women were present. The court found that the trips were part of *his* job. The primary question was whether the dominant purpose of her presence on the trips was to serve her husband's business purpose. And the answer was yes. The company specialized in providing "wholesome entertainment" based largely upon the ideals of Americanism and the home. Inasmuch as executives identified with the company were frequently in the public eye, management believed that the company's special image would be enhanced if its representatives traveled with their wives. True, the chief executive would scarcely be likely to lose his job if he left his wife at home. But he was warranted in believing that even the president should conform to the company's policy.[242]

Expenses of the wife of a businessman who accompanied him to Europe on a *bona fide* commercial trip were deductible. He was a diabetic and could not have made the journey without the constant presence of someone who had been trained to minister to his emergency needs, as his wife had been.[243]

Expenses of an executive's wife on a business trip were deductible. She went on this trip to do secretarial work and to help in entertaining customers. She had been the executive's secretary prior to their marriage and his principal purpose in taking her along was to continue these same duties.[244]

The expenses of a wife in accompanying her husband to an insurance convention were deductible inasmuch as the jury felt that her presence served a *bona fide* purpose related to his business.[245]

A businessman sponsored a contest to advertise his products. The prize winners were to be taken on a fishing trip. It was advertised that if any of the winners were girls, his wife would serve as their chaperone. Two of the winners were girls. He could deduct his wife's travel expenses.[246]

How to get a deduction for travel expenses of a businessman's wife is emphasized by what the Internal Revenue Service says should be avoided: "Although the taxpayer was continually contacting actual or potential customers on these trips, he and his wife generally managed to include stops at resort cities or visits with relatives in their itineraries."[247] The court pointed out that in one case, where a wife accompanied her husband on a business trip to Hawaii, she neither went swimming nor shopping.[248] One must wonder how that was proved.

In a case where a businessman goes on a valid trip and is accompanied by his wife, whose expenses do not qualify for deduction, the couple's cost of transportation and lodging may exceed the cost for single fare and accommodations but is less than twice the single tariff. The amount deductible is the cost at the single rate for similar accommodations.[249]

In addition to the general rules that control tax deductions with reference to being ordinary, necessary, and reasonable, a special section of the Internal Revenue Code disallows travel expenses which do not meet stringent additional requirements as to contemporary recording of the business purpose of each travel expenditure as well as the names and places involved.[250]

These additional requirements, however, apply to travel "away from home."[251] It was held that these requirements do not apply where a person was not away from home overnight, such as where the business use of a car was purely local.[252] Nor do the stringent substantiation requirements have to be applied in the case of the local delivery of goods by a businessperson.[253]

Substantiation is a critical phase of the deduction for travel expense. An interstate truck driver, under Interstate Commerce Commission regulations, carried a driver's log book. He had to show the date of each trip, times of departure and arrival, destinations, and number and place of each stop of any length en route. Entries had to be made within a very short period after completion of each shift. These data were not kept for tax purposes, but they were exactly what the Internal Revenue Service may demand.[254]

One individual undeniably used his car for business purposes and claimed a deduction based upon mileage. In the absence of the required detailed substantiation, the Internal Revenue Service proposed to allow him 70 percent of the amount deducted. But for a month and a half he had kept the proper contemporaneous documentation, and, projecting these figures over the twelve-month period, the court believed the mileage shown in his income tax return was about right despite the lack of full documentation, and it allowed him 85 percent of what he had claimed.[255]

The operation and maintenance charges for a private airplane are regarded as away-from-home travel expenses and are deductible if related to the taxpayer's business.[256]

Payment for transportation necessary for medical care qualifies as a medical expense. This includes transportation expenses of a parent who must go with a child in order to get medical care for the youngster.[257]

Otherwise deductible expenses for business travel and entertainment are allowable only if they can be adequately substantiated as to amount, time and place, person entertained, and *business purpose*. But this purpose can be supported by circumstantial evidence alone. The general manager of an automobile distributorship could deduct his nonreimbursable expenses of going to an automobile show. Despite Internal Revenue Service objections, he was not required to prove that he went to that show for business purposes.[258] See also **Alcoholics Anonymous; Apartment used for business purposes; Armed Forces; Commuting; Conventions; Education; Investors; Medical expenses; Moving expenses; Ordinary and necessary business expenses; Prepublication expenses.**

Trickery, loss because of. *See* **Casualties.**

Trustee. *See* **Fiduciaries.**

Trusts. *See* **Capital losses; Carry-overs; Depreciation.**

Tuition. *See* **Advanced degree, study for; Education.**

Tuition-postponement-plan payments. A university may permit a student to defer the payment of tuition in return for his payment of a certain percentage of his income each year after graduation, until the loan, plus a stated rate of interest, is paid off. Payments made in excess of the amounts allocated to repayment of the deferred amount are deductible as interest.[259]

Turnover, reduction of. A business is permitted to deduct the cost of current expenses which are incurred for the purpose of reducing turnover of employees. Amounts paid to provide child care for the preschool children of employees were permitted where persons on the payroll resigned frequently because of problems connected with not having facilities available to take care of their children during working hours.[260] *See also* **Ordinary and necessary business expenses.**

Tutoring, cost of. Tutoring or tuition fees which you incur on your doctor's advice for a child who has severe learning disabilities caused by a nervous-system disorder are medical expenses.[261] *See also* **Education; Medical expenses.**

Typing. Where a teacher was permitted to deduct the cost of obtaining his Ph.D. degree as a business expense, he could also deduct the cost of having his dissertation typed.[262] *See also* **Résumés.**

T

---

1. Revenue Act of 1978, Section 111.
2. Revenue Ruling 54-598, 1954-2 CB 121.
3. IRC Section 164(a).
4. Revenue Ruling 65-313, 1965-2 CB 47.
5. IRC Section 164(b)(5).
6. *Arrigoni et al. v. Commissioner*, 73 T.C. 792 (1980).
7. IRC Section 164 (b)(1)(D).
8. *Income Tax Deduction for Taxes*, IRS Publication 546, 1976 edition, page 3.
9. Revenue Ruling 56-124, 1956-1 CB 97.
10. GCM 17570, 1937-1 CB 193.
11. Revenue Ruling 72-79, 1972-1 CB 51.
12. Revenue Ruling 74-486, 1974-2 CB 86.
13. Revenue Ruling 75-47, 1975-1 CB 62.
14. Revenue Ruling 71-59, 1971-1 CB 56.
15. Revenue Ruling 71-246, 1971-1 CB 54.
16. Revenue Ruling 81-191, I.R.B. 1981-31, 5.
17. Revenue Ruling 81-192, I.R.B. 1981-31, 6.
18. Revenue Ruling 81-193, I.R.B. 1981-31, 8.
19. Revenue Ruling 81-194, I.R.B. 1981-31, 10.
20. IRC Section 901.
21. Revenue Ruling 78-81, 1978-1 CB 57.
22. Revenue Ruling 70-464, 1970-2 CB 152.
23. *In The Matter of Battelstein*, DC, SD Texas, 1977.
24. Revenue Ruling 73-531, 1973-2 CB 45.
25. IRS Letter Ruling 8104139, October 31, 1980.
26. Revenue Ruling 78-103, 1978-1 CB 58.
27. *Ronald G. Peters et al.*, T.C. Memo. 1970-314, filed November 16, 1970.
28. Regulations Section 1.164-4(b)(1).
29. *Walker v. United States*, DC, WD Okla., 1959.
30. *Oscar Mitchell*, 27 BTA 101 (1932).
31. Revenue Ruling 79-201, 1979-1 CB 97.
32. *Tax Information on Business Expenses*, IRS Publication 535, 1976 edition, page 3.
33. Ibid., page 16.
34. *Lulu Lung Power*, T.C. Memo. 1967-32, filed February 20, 1967.
35. *Gilbert J. Kraus*, T.C. Memo., Docket No. 22594, entered October 31, 1951.
36. Revenue Ruling 67-21, 1967-1 CB 45.
37. *Mary Rumsey Mavius Estate*, 22 T.C. 391 (1954).
38. Regulations Section 1.162-11(a).
39. Regulations Section 1.164-6.
40. *Clarence E. Baldwin*, T.C. Memo. 1955-200, filed July 21, 1955.
41. *Margaret E. Johnson Malmstedt et al.*, T.C. Memo. 1976-46, filed February 24, 1976, *rev'd and rem'd'd on other issues*, 578 F.2d 520 (4th Cir., 1978).
42. IRC Section 216(a)(1).
43. Revenue Ruling 64-31, 1964-1 CB (Part 1) 300.
44. *Income Tax Deduction for Taxes*, IRS Publication 546, 1976 edition, page 6.
45. *William H. Edmister, Jr., et al.*, T.C. Memo. 1977-208, filed July 6, 1877.
46. IRS Letter Ruling 7733068, May 20, 1977.
47. IRC Section 164(b)(5).

48. Regulations Section 1.164-3(e)(2).

49. *William F. Armentrout*, 43 T.C. 16 (1964).

50. Revenue Ruling 70-634, 1970-7 CB 49.

51. Revenue Ruling 57-489, 1957-2 CB 207.

52. *R. J. Nicholl Co.*, 59 T.C. 37 (1972).

53. Revenue Ruling 75-176, 1974-1 CB 68.

54. Regulations Section 1.164-1(a).

55. Revenue Ruling 65-313, 1965-2 CB 47.

56. *United States v. Green, Jr., et al.*, 170 F. Supp. 359 (DC, SD N.Y., 1959).

57. *Income Tax Deductions for Alimony Payments*, IRS Publication 504, 1976 edition, page 3.

58. *Maness et al. v. United States*, 237 F. Supp. 918 (DC, MD Fla., 1965), *aff'd on another issue*, 367 F.2d 357 (5th Cir., 1966).

59. Revenue Ruling 68-662, 1968-2 CB 69.

60. *Terry et al. v. Commissioner*, T.C. Memo. 1979-284, filed July 26, 1979.

61. IRC Section 171.

62. *Misfeldt v. Kelm*, DC, Minn., 1952.

63. IRC Section 1370 *et seq.*

64. IRC Section 1381(b)(1)(A), as amended by the Subchapter S Revision Act of 1982.

65. IRC Section 1371.

66. IRC Section 1362(d)(1).

67. IRC Section 1374(b)(2).

68. IRC Section 1362(d)(3), as amended by the Subchapter S Revision Act of 1982.

69. Revenue Ruling 65-40, 1965-1 CB 429.

70. Revenue Ruling 65-83, 1965-1 CB 430.

71. IRC Section 1375, as amended by the Subchapter S Revision Act of 1982.

72. Regulations Section 1.212-1(1).

73. *Sidney Merians et al.*, 60 T.C. 187 (1973).

74. *United States v. Bonnyman et al.*, 261 F.2d 835 (6th Cir., 1958).

75. *Michael J. Ippolito et al.*, T.C. Memo. 1965-167, filed June 24, 1965.

76. *Ben R. Stein et al.*, T.C. Memo. 1972-140, filed June 29, 1972.

77. *Carlos Marcello et al.*, T.C. Memo. 1964-299, filed November 18, 1964.

78. Revenue Ruling 68-662, 1968-2 CB 69.

79. *W. Brown Morton et al.*, T.C. Memo. 1957-101, filed June 25, 1957.

80. Revenue Ruling 73-13, 1973-1 CB 42.

81. *Myrhl Frost*, T.C. Memo., Docket No. 112333, entered March 31, 1943.

82. *Sharples et al. v. United States*, 533 F.2d 550 (Ct. Cl., 1976).

83. Revenue Ruling 67-401, 1967-2 CB 123.

84. Policy Statement P-4-64, approved by the Commissioner on August 23, 1982.

85. *Beaudry v. Commissioner*, 150 F.2d 20 (2d Cir., 1945).

86. *Collins et al. v. Commissioner*, T.C. Memo. 1979-137, filed April 10, 1979.

87. *Ginkel v. Commissioner*, T.C. Memo. 1980-424, filed September 25, 1980.

88. *Gudmundsson et al. v. Commissioner*, T.C. Memo. 1978-299, filed August 1, 1978.

89. *Hilt et al. v. Commissioner*, T.C. Memo. 1981-612, filed November 23, 1981.

90. *Biggs et al. v. Commissioner*, 440 F.2d 1 (6th Cir., 1971).

91. *Dan R. Hanna, Jr., et al.*, T.C. Memo., Docket Nos. 25706-7, entered June 6, 1951.

92. Regulations Section 1.162-2(a).

93. *Richard L. Wesenberg et al.*, 69 T.C. 1005 (1978).

94. *Julius (Jay) C. Henricks*, T.C. Memo., Docket No. 16192, entered November 8, 1949.

95. *Isabelle M. Cogan*, T.C. Memo. 1971-230, filed September 8, 1971.

96. *Howard et al. v. Commissioner*, T.C. Memo. 1981-250. filed May 21, 1981.

97. *John M. Murphey et al.*, T.C. Memo. 1975-317, filed October 21, 1975.

98. *Banks et al. v. Commissioner*, T.C. Memo. 1981-450, filed September 9, 1981.

99. *Robert H. Lee*, T.C. Memo. 1960-58, filed March 30, 1960.

100. *Drummond et al. v. Commissioner*, T.C. Memo. 1980-416, filed September 22, 1980.

101. *Laurano et al. v. Commissioner*, 69 T.C. 723 (1978).

102. *Charles Edward Shepherd*, T.C. Memo. 1976-48, filed February 26, 1976, *aff'd*, 7th Cir., 1977.

103. *Faura et al. v. Commissioner*, 73 T.C. 849 (1980).

104. *Robbins et al. v. Commissioner*, T.C. Memo. 1981-449, filed August 24, 1981.

105. *Louis M. Roth et al.*, 17 T.C. 1450 (1952).

106. IRS Letter Ruling 8125006, February 27, 1981.

107. IRS Letter Ruling 8034087, May 29, 1980.

108. Regulations Section 1.165-2(a).

109. Revenue Ruling 71-418, 1971-2 CB 125.

110. IRC Section 642(h).

111. *Rosenberg v. Commissioner*, 198 F.2d 46 (8th Cir., 1952).

112. *Rowley et al. v. Commissioner*, T.C. Memo. 1979-338, filed August 27, 1979.

113. *George H. Newi et al.*, T.C. Memo. 1969-131, filed June 26, 1969, *aff'd on another issue*, 432 F.2d 998 (2d Cir., 1970).

114. *William L. Tracy*, 39 BTA 578 (1939).

115. *Marion S. Perkins et al.*, T.C. Memo., Docket No. 31053, entered May 29, 1952.

116. *Samuel Abrams et al.*, T.C. Memo. 1964-256, filed September 29, 1964.

117. *August F. Nielsen Co., Inc. et al.*, T.C. Memo. 1968-11, filed January 18, 1968.

118. *Irving Roy et al.*, T.C. Memo. 1968-99, filed May 27, 1968.

119. *Olivia de Havilland Goodrich*, 20 T.C. 323 (1953).

120. *Byron H. Farwell et al.*, 35 T.C. 454 (1960).

121. Revenue Procedure 74-23, 1974-2 CB 476.

122. *Arnold Roy Bushey*, T.C. Memo. 1971-149, filed June 21, 1971.

123. *Savignano v. Commissioner*, T.C. Memo. 1979-1, filed January 2, 1979.

124. *Charles J. Voigt et al.*, T.C. Memo., Docket No. 15718, entered July 6, 1949.

125. *Kaonis v. Commissioner*, T.C. Memo. 1978-184, filed May 17, 1978, *aff'd*, 9th Cir., 1981.

126. *McCollum et al. v. Commissioner*, T.C. Memo. 1978-435, filed November 1, 1978.

127. *Ion Z. Josan*, T.C. Memo. 1974-144, filed June 6, 1974.

128. Regulations Section 1.162-12(a).

129. IRC Section 162(a).

130. *Beaudry v. Commissioner*, 150 F.2d 20 (2d Cir., 1945).

131. *Knoxville Iron Company*, T.C. Memo. 1959-54, filed March 23, 1959.

132. *United States v. Manor Care, Inc.*, 490 F. Supp. 355 (DC, Md., 1980).

133. Revenue Ruling 58-238, 1958-1 CB 90.

134. IRC Section 165(c)(2).

135. *Dreicer v. Commissioner*, CA, DC, 1981.

136. *Siegel et al. v. Commissioner*, 78 T.C., No. 46 (1982).

137. *Snyder et al. v. United States*, 674 F.2d 1359 (10th Cir., 1982).

138. *George F. Tyler*, T.C. Memo., Docket No. 5508, entered March 6, 1947.

139. *Feistman et al. v. Commissioner*, T.C. Memo. 1982-306, filed June 3, 1982.

140. *Woodrow L. Wroblewski*, T.C. Memo. 1973-37, filed February 14, 1973.

141. *Irwin v. United States*, DC, ED La., 1975.

142. *Casida et al. v. Commissioner*, T.C. Memo. 1979-267, filed July 17, 1979.

143. *Dreicer v. Commissioner*, 78 T.C., No. 44 (1982).

144. *Mercer v. Commissioner*, 376 F.2d 708 (9th Cir., 1967).

145. Regulations Section 1.183-2(a).

146. *Estate of Estelle H. Lanier v. Commissioner*, T.C. Memo. 1981-421, filed August 11, 1981.

147. *C. West Churchman et al.*, 68 T.C. 696 (1977).

148. *Eugene J. Magee*, T.C. Memo. 1973-271, filed December 10, 1973.

149. *Bryson, Jr., et al. v. Commissioner*, T.C. Memo. 1982-424, filed July 27, 1982.

150. *Allen et al. v. Commissioner*, 72 T.C. 28 (1979).

151. *Imbesi et al. v. Commissioner*, 361 F.2d 640 (3d Cir., 1966).

152. Regulations Section 1.183-2(c).

153. *Gloria B. Zimmerman et al.*, T.C. Memo. 1976-1123, filed April 11, 1976.

154. *Proebstle et ux. v. United States*, DC, SD Texas, 1965.

155. Regulations Section 1.183-2(b).

156. *Nickerson et al. v. Commissioner*, T.C. Memo. 1981-321, filed June 23, 1981.

157. *Otis Beall Kent*, T.C. Memo., Docket No. 37332, entered December 31, 1953.

158. *S. Charles Lee et al.*, T.C. Memo., Docket Nos. 5562-3, entered April 5, 1946.

159. *Thomas W. Jackson*, 59 T.C. 312 (1972).

160. Regulations Section 1.183-2(b)(9).

161. *Lawrence D. Boyer et al.*, 69 T.C. 521 (1977).

162. *Robert E. Currie et al.*, T.C. Memo. 1969-4, filed January 7, 1969.

163. *Palmer et al. v. Commissioner*, T.C. Memo. 1981-354, filed July 9, 1981.

164. *Amos S. Bumgardner et al.*, T.C. Memo., Docket Nos. 40912-3, entered February 10, 1954.

165. *Leonard P. Sasso*, T.C. Memo. 1961-216, filed July 31, 1961.

166. *Kilroy et al. v. Commissioner*, T.C. Memo. 1980-489, filed October 28, 1980.

167. *Regan v. Commissioner*, T.C. Memo. 1979-340, filed August 28, 1979.

168. *Engdahl et al. v. Commissioner*, 72 T.C. 659 (1979).

169. *Wright et al. v. United States*, 249 F. Supp. 508 (DC, Nev., 1965).

170. *Joan F. (Walton) Farris et al.*, T.C. Memo. 1972-165, filed August 3, 1972.

171. Regulations Section 1.183-2(b)(1).

172. *Fields, Jr., et al. v. Commissioner*, T.C. Memo. 1981-550, filed September 28, 1981.

173. *Gorod et al. v. Commissioner*, T.C. Memo. 1981-632, filed October 27, 1981.

174. *Langford et al. v. Commissioner*, T.C. Memo. 1981-532, filed September 22, 1981.

175. *Malmstedt et al. v. Commissioner*, 578 F.2d 520 (14th Cir., 1978).

176. *York et al. v. Commissioner*, 261 F.2d 421 (4th Cir., 1958).

177. *Weninger et al. v. Commissioner*, T.C. Memo. 1980-219, filed June 24, 1980.

178. Regulations Section 1.165-9(b).

179. *George H. Frahm et al.*, T.C. Memo. 1974-138, filed May 30, 1974.

180. *George W. Carnick*, 9 T.C. 756 (1927).

181. *H. V. Watkins et al.*, T.C. Memo. 1973-167, filed July 30, 1973.

182. *Charles T. Parker*, 1 T.C. 709 (1943).

183. *Marjorie E. Blackburn et al.*, T.C. Memo. 1973-254, filed November 21, 1973.

184. *Toner v. Commisoner*, 76 T.C. 217 (1981).

185. *Helis et al. v. United States*, DC, ED La., 1973, *aff'd*, 496 F.2d 1319 (5th Cir., 1972).

186. *Commissioner v. Flowers*, 326 U.S. 465 (1946).

187. *John R. Thomas et al.*, T.C. Memo., Docket No. 21780, entered February 16, 1953.

188. Revenue Ruling 54-147, 1954-1 CB 51.

189. *Chappie et al. v. Commissioner*, 73 T.C. 823 (1980).

190. Revenue Ruling 65-224, 1965-2 CB 42.

191. IRC Section 162(a).

192. *Jones et al. v. United States*, 648 F.2d 1081 (6th Cir., 1981).

193. *Waldrop v. Commissioner*, T.C. Memo. 1977-190, filed June 21, 1977.

194. *Virginia C. Avery*, T.C. Memo. 1970-269, filed September 23, 1970.

195. *Judy L. Gooderham*, T.C. Memo. 1964-158, filed June 8, 1964.

196. *Frederick v. United States*, 603 F.2d 1292 (8th Cir., 1979).

197. *Barela et al. v. Commissioner*, T.C. Memo. 1981-405, filed August 6, 1981.

198. *Frederick et al. v. United States* (8th Cir., 1979).

199. *J. B. Stewart et al.*, T.C. Memo. 1976-390, filed December 21, 1976.

200. *Brandt et al. v. Commissioner*, T.C. Memo. 1982-180, filed April 7, 1982.

201. *Howard Voigt et al.*, T.C. Memo., Docket Nos. 15552-3, entered October 11, 1949.

202. *A. Silverman*, 6 BTA 1328 (1927).

203. *Tax Guide for Commercial Fishermen*, IRS Publication 595, 1979 edition, page 15.

204. Revenue Ruling 74-242, 1974-1 CB 69.

205. Revenue Ruling 54-147, 1954-1 CB 51.

206. *Markey v. Commissioner*, 420 F.2d 1249 (6th Cir., 1973).

207. IRS Letter Ruling 8120124, February 23, 1981.

208. *Your Federal Income Tax*, 1976 edition, page 70.

209. *Jim Lee Wilson*, T.C. Memo. 1976-235, filed July 27, 1976.

210. *Louismet et al. v. Commissioner*, T.C. Memo. 1982-294, filed May 26, 1982.

211. *Walliser et al. v. Commissioner*, 72 T.C. 433 (1979).

212. Economic Recovery Tax Act of 1981, Section 127.

213. *Brewin et al. v. Commissioner*, CA, DC, 1981.

214. Revenue Ruling 82-2, I.R.B. 1982-1, 12.

215. *Travel, Entertainment, and Gift Expenses*, IRS Publication 463 (Rev. Nov. 1980), page 4.

216. *Cornelius Vanderbilt, Jr.*, T.C. Memo. 1957-235, filed December 23, 1957.

217. *Brooks v. Commissioner*, 274 F.2d 96 (9th Cir., 1959).

218. *Duncan et al. v. Bookwalter*, 216 F. Supp. 30 (DC, WD Mo., 1963).

219. *Stern et al. v. United States*, DC, CD Cal., 1971.

220. *Ahmed F. Habeeb et al.*, T.C. Memo. 1976-259, filed August 19, 1976.

221. Revenue Ruling 62-2, 1962-1 CB 9.

222. Revenue Ruling 64-176, 1964-1 CB (Part 1) 87.

223. *Haynie v. Commissioner*, T.C. Memo. 1977-330, filed September 26, 1977.

224. Regulations Section 1.162-5(d).

225. *Harry Kanelos et al.*, T.C. Memo., Docket Nos. 112053 and 112090, entered September 21, 1943.

226. *Hamilton et al. v. Commissioner*, T.C. Memo. 1979-186, filed May 10, 1979.

227. *Stranahan, Jr., et al. v. Commissioner*, T.C. Memo. 1982-151, filed March 25, 1982.

228. *Habeeb et al. v. Commissioner*, 559 F.2d 435 (5th Cir., 1977).

229. IR-2165, September 27, 1979, as modified by Revenue Procedure 80-36, 1980-2 CB 769.

230. IRS Letter Ruling 8126044, March 31, 1981.

231. *Gudmundsson et al. v. Commissioner*, T.C. Memo. 1978-299, filed August 1, 1978.

232. *Fairey et al. v. Commissioner*, T.C. Memo. 1982-219, filed April 26, 1982.

233. *Harris v. Commissioner*, T.C. Memo. 1978-332, filed August 23, 1978.

234. *Queen City Printing Co.*, 6 BTA 521 (1927).

235. *George G. Ebner et al.*, T.C. Memo. 1958-108, filed June 9, 1958.

236. Revenue Ruling 56-509, 1956-2 CB 129.

237. *Neal et al. v. Commissioner*, T.C. Memo. 1981-172, filed April 9, 1981.

238. Revenue Ruling 74-208, 1974-1 CB 4.

239. Regulations Section 1.162-2(c).

240. *Wilkins et al. v. United States*, 348 F. Supp. 1282 (DC, Neb., 1972).

241. *Warwick et al. v. United States*, 236 F. Supp. 761 (DC, ED Va., 1964).

242. *United States v. Disney et al.*, 413 F.2d 783 (9th Cir., 1969).

243. *Allenberg Cotton Company, Inc., et al. v. United States*, DC, WD Tenn., 1960.

244. *Walkup Drayage & Warehouse Co. et al.*, T.C. Memo., Docket Nos. 3271-2, entered June 25, 1945.

245. *Kloppenburg et al. v. United States*, DC, SD Ill., 1965.

246. *Albert E. Luetzow et al.*, T.C. Memo. 1973-63, filed March 20, 1973.

247. Revenue Ruling 55-57, 1955-1 CB 315.

248. *Allen J. McDonnell et al.*, T.C. Memo. 1967-18, filed January 31, 1967.

249. Revenue Ruling 56-168, 1956-1 CB 93.

250. IRC Section 274.

251. Regulations Section 1.274-5(a)(1).

252. *Cobb et al. v. Commissioner*, 77 T.C. 1096 (1981).

253. *Allen et al. v. Commissioner*, T.C. Memo. 1982-93, filed February 23, 1982.

254. *B. J. Culwell et al.*, DC, N.M., 1967.

255. *Melville v. Commissioner*, T.C. Memo. 1979-398, filed September 24, 1979.

256. *Gibson Products Company, Inc.*, 8 T.C. 654 (1947).

257. *Medical and Dental Expenses*, IRS Publication 502 (Rev. Nov. 1980), page 3.

258. *Sap et al. v. Commissioner*, T.C. Memo. 1981-167, filed April 8, 1981.

259. Revenue Ruling 72-2, 1972-1 CB 19.

260. Revenue Ruling 73-348, 1973-2 CB 31.

261. *Medical and Dental Expenses*, IRS Publication 502 (Rev. Nov. 1980), page 3.

262. *Donald C. Hester*, T.C. Memo. 1963-107, filed April 15, 1963.

U

Uncollectible accounts. *See* Bad debts.

Undivided interest in property, contribution in form of. *See* Contributions.

Unearned commissions, repayment of. If a salesman is allowed to draw commissions before they are earned, and he draws against sales not yet paid for by his customers, he may be called upon to repay those commissions he drew out against customer bills that never did get paid. If he paid Federal income tax on commissions when he received them, he is then entitled to a business-expense deduction in the year he returns the unearned commissions to his employer.[1]

Unemployment-benefit fund, contributions to. An employer's contribution to an unemployment-benefit fund to pay a "layoff moving allowance" when an employee who is laid off at one plant accepts employment at another plant is deductible as an ordinary and necessary business expense.[2]

Unexercised stock option, loss from. *See* Investors.

Uniforms. The cost of acquisition and maintenance of uniforms is deductible as an ordinary and necessary expense if the uniforms (1) are specially required as a condition of employment and (2) are not of a type adaptable to general or continued usage to the extent that they take the place of regular clothing. The fact that a uniform might be required as a condition of employment is not, of itself, sufficient to allow a deduction, as in the case of military apparel, which replaces regular clothing. Likewise, the deduction is not allowed if the uniform is suitable for ordinary wear.[3]

A person has the opportunity of showing, if he can, that something which he has to wear while on the job cannot be used as everyday attire. Example: A state highway patrolman failed to show that the maroon socks he was required to wear on duty were not usable when he was off duty.[4]

One court set up three criteria for the deduction of the cost of clothing as an ordinary and necessary business expense: (1) the clothing is required, or essential in the taxpayer's employment, (2) the clothing is not *suitable* for general or personal use, and (3) the clothing is not so worn.[5]

The fact that the employer's name could be removed from an employee's jacket did not mean that the garment was adaptable to street use. As long as he still was on the payroll and wore the clothing in connection with his business duties, the cost of the attire was deductible.[6]

A railroad-car inspector could deduct the cost of shirts which had his employer's name displayed on an armband. This armband could not have been removed without taking out the stitches.[7]

A woman employee of an airplane company during World War II was required to wear slacks at work. She was allowed to deduct the cost, for the court believed she would not have worn such apparel other than at work.[8]

An art teacher could deduct the cost of protective-clothing smocks as an ordinary and necessary expense of her business.[9]

The cost of uniforms used by air, rail, and bus employees is deducted if the uniforms are used solely in the course of their employment. But the cost is not deductible if uniforms are equipped with snap buttons that can be removed to convert the uniform to general use.[10]

Deduction is allowed for the cost of uniforms for firemen[11] and for policemen.[12] A California highway patrolman could deduct the cost of his uniform, which he was required to purchase and to wear while on duty. He was not permitted to wear it while employed for compensation outside his official duties. He did not wear the uniform while not working because civilian attire was more comfortable and less expensive.[13] But an examiner in the same state's department of motor vehicles could not deduct the cost of purchasing the prescribed regulation dress for use while on duty in the driver-licensing function. It was a slate-gray suit indistinguishable from regular civilian attire and could have been worn off duty. Perhaps he made a mistake in wearing his uniform to court, for the judge admitted that the most convincing evidence against the taxpayer's argument that the required attire was a uniform was that, in His Honor's words, he "looked too normal and too well in the suit he wore to court."[14] Next time, perhaps, he could do something about *that*.

A commercial airlines navigator was allowed to deduct the cost of his uniforms.[15]

A passenger service agent for American Airlines was obliged to dress in conformity with her employer's "Uniform Regulations" manual. She was required to wear "a dress shoe with a business-like look." She regarded this as "unfeminine" and wore such shoes only at work. In addition, the company manual stated that "no part of the uniform may be worn for off-duty activities." She was permitted to deduct the cost of the shoes as business expense.[16]

A railroad conductor could deduct the cost of his uniforms, where neither the cut nor the method by which they were made was customary for civilian clothing.[17]

A Pullman-car porter was allowed to deduct the cost of his uniforms.[18]

White shirts, black ties, and black shoes represented deductible expenses for a hospital worker who was required to wear this garb at work. These items were not taken home but were kept in a locker at the hospital when he was not on duty. His work brought him into contact with persons who had contagious diseases, so he was careful not to bring this attire home with him.[19]

The cost of a nurse's uniform is deductible.[20] A private-duty nurse properly deducted the cost of her uniform, for it served as a mark of her profession and was necessary in the care of her patient from an aseptic standpoint.[21]

The cost of acquisition and maintenance of uniforms of letter-carriers is deductible if the persons are required to wear distinctive types of uniform while at work and the garb is not suitable for ordinary wear.[22]

The office manager of a dental clinic was allowed to deduct the cost of upkeep of the uniform she wore.[23]

A waitress could deduct the cost of yellow uniforms and aprons, plus appropriate shoes that she wore at work.[24]

Where an employer required his service employees to wear a shirt, jacket, and cap bearing the company name, one of these employees was able to deduct not only the cost of these items but also the cost of trousers made of identical material which were not adaptable to general use.[25]

The cost of clothing specified by an employer for use of service employees was deductible where the garb had been designed for heavy use. This clothing was made of very durable material, with heavy seams, reinforced pockets, and a double seat in the trousers. The price of this attire was about one-third more than the amounts charged for similar articles of regular clothing.[26]

A fashion coordinator was able to deduct the cost of very advanced styles she wore for special meetings.[27] But an advertising executive could not deduct the cost of a mink coat which his wife wore to places where clients were apt to be, because he could not show that a mink coat was an essential uniform for the wife of a successful executive.[28]

A professional musician could deduct the cost of dress clothes which were used exclusively for his business of playing the piano and the Solovox.[29]

A professional baseball player who was required to furnish his own uniform was permitted to deduct its cost even though conceivably this attire could have been worn socially.[30]

A jockey was allowed to deduct the cost of uniforms which he wore professionally, where no reimbursement from anyone was possible.[31]

A plant employee properly deducted as work clothes a plain white coat marked with large letters "Foreman."[32] Presumably his wife would not have let him wear this at home.

The cost and upkeep of uniforms used in charitable activities (for example, as a scoutmaster) are deductible as a charitable contribution.[33]

An individual could deduct the cost and maintenance expenses of distinctive uniforms which he was required to wear when engaged in official Civil Air Patrol activities. He was prohibited from wearing this garb on nonofficial occasions.[34]

An amateur ski enthusiast devoted much of his spare time to serving as a member of the safety patrol of a tax-exempt organization which performed rescues and administered first aid to injured skiers. He was allowed to deduct the cost of a certain type of parka and dark ski trousers which the patrol members were required to wear while on duty.[35]

The cost and maintenance of her Red Cross uniforms were deductible by a volunteer worker.[36]

A civilian employee of an aircraft company could deduct the cost (less salvage value) of an Army officer's uniform without insignia which he was required to wear in combat areas so that if he was captured, he would be treated as a prisoner of war.[37]

A company executive could deduct the cost of blazer and vest sets, which he personally purchased for company representatives at trade shows. Competitors similarly equipped their representatives with such uniforms, and the executive benefited by a profit-sharing arrangement which enabled him to gain from the sales the company made at trade shows and elsewhere.[38]

If the purchase of an item represents an expenditure which is deductible as a business expense, then the upkeep of this item also is deductible.[39]

Where a person required to wear a uniform while on duty also was required to keep the uniform clean and in repair, maintenance expenses were deductible.[40]

An enlisted man in the United States Army could deduct the cleaning costs for his fatigue uniforms.[41] *See also* **Armed Forces; Bus drivers, uniforms of; Cadets, expenses of; Contributions; Highway patrolman; Military-style uniforms; Railroad-car inspector, expenses of; Receptionist; Work clothes.**

Union dues. Monthly dues and assessments paid by members of a labor union are deductible business expenses except for any portion of the assessments used to provide death benefits.[42] An initiation fee is deductible when it is paid to the union in order to obtain employment.[43]

Assessments paid by union members to a pension fund were deductible as business expenses, for assessments had to be paid in order to remain in the union. Membership was essential to keeping one's job. It did not appear here that the personal value of each member's interest in the pension fund ordinarily approximated what he paid into it so as to make his payment a personal expense or consideration for an annuity.[44]

Sometimes a union contract provides that employers must deduct the equivalent of check-off dues from employees who do not belong to the union, which nevertheless receives these amounts. Such employees may deduct the "shop fees."[45]

Fines assessed against a member by his union are deductible, where nonpayment would have meant being dropped from the union.[46] *See also* **Employees.**

United States, expenses related to income earned outside. Where income is earned outside the United States by a person under certain conditions, it is not taxed in the United States. Expenses in connection with that income similarly are not deductible. But expenses not related to income earned outside the country are deductible. Examples of such items include personal and family medical expenses, real-estate taxes on a personal residence, interest on a mortgage on a personal residence, and charitable contributions.[47]

Unlawful business, expenses of. *See* **Gambling losses.**

Unlimited deduction for contributions to a charitable organization. When an individual engaged in a trade or business makes a payment to an exempt organization with a reasonable expectation of financial return to himself, which is in line with the amount of his gift, it is not subject to the percentage limitations of charitable contributions but is fully deductible as ordinary and necessary business expense. Such was the ruling when money was given to a pollution-control fund established by a municipality where the donor's business had been hurt in the past because of polluted atmosphere.[48] *See also* **Contributions; Ordinary and necessary business expenses.**

Unrecovered loss for damages. Damages received under a judgment or settlement of a civil action for U.S. patent infringement, breach of contract or fiduciary duty, and recoveries (except for punitive damages) under the Clayton Act for antitrust violation, are deductible. The deduction is the smaller of (1) the amounts paid in the taxable year concerning the award or (2) the unrecovered loss. The unrecovered loss is the sum of net operating losses attributable to the damages, arising during the period the damages were sustained, to the extent they were not absorbed in carry-overs or carry-backs and also less any deductions for prior recoveries allowed in any prior year.[49]

Unreimbursed expenses. An individual may participate in a Child Care Food Program, under which he agrees to provide day care and nutritional meals to needy children in return for specified Federal payments. As he has a profit motive in participating in this program, should his operating costs be greater than his reimbursement payments, the excess is deductible as a trade or business expense.[50] *See also* **Employees; Executives; Partnerships.**

Unsalable inventory. *See* **Inventory write-downs.**

Unstated interest. Payments made under an installment contract having a sales price of more than $3,000 and containing no interest or an unrealistic stated interest may include an amount of unstated interest.[51] For the mechanics of this rather complex deduction computation, *see Installment and Deferred-Payment Sales,* IRS Publication 537 (Rev. Nov. 1980).

Unsuccessful acquisition costs. *See* **Mineral leases, cost of acquiring.**

Unused capital-loss carry-overs. *See* **Capital losses.**

Unused carry-over of fiduciary. If an estate or trust, when it is terminated, has a net operating-loss carry-over or a capital-loss carry-over, this is allowed as a deduction to the beneficiaries succeeding to the property.[52]

Usurious interest. In order to avoid state-law limitations upon the amount of interest which may be charged, part of the payment for the use of borrowed money may be made under some other label. But any sum "paid as interest, regardless of the name by which it is called, may be deducted by the taxpayer from its income."[53]

U

1. Revenue Ruling 72-28, 1972-1 CB 45.
2. Revenue Ruling 73-245, 1973-1 CB 64.
3. Revenue Ruling 70-474, 1970-2 CB 34.
4. *Christey et al. v. United States,* DC, Minn., 1981.
5. *Betsy L. Yeomans,* 30 T.C. 750 (1958).
6. *Bennie Blatt,* T.C. Memo., Docket No. 10064, entered February 10, 1947.
7. *Lloyd Farrior et al.,* T.C. Memo. 1970-213, filed November 12, 1970.
8. *Morgan et al. v. United States,* 80 F. Supp. 537 (DC, ND Texas, 1948).
9. *Kellner v. Commissioner,* 2d Cir., 1977.
10. *Miscellaneous Deductions and Credits,* IRS Publication 529, 1976 edition.
11. *Jess H. Taylor et al.,* T.C. Memo. Docket No. 28821, entered June 24, 1952.
12. Revenue Ruling 70-474, 1970-2 CB 34.
13. *Commissioner v. Benson et al.,* 146 F.2d 191 (9th Cir., 1944).
14. *Harry J. Sanner,* T.C. Memo. 1969-84, filed April 30, 1969.
15. *Dean L. Philips,* T.C. Memo., Docket

Nos. 18410-12, entered June 9, 1950.
16. *Douglas et al. v. Commissioner,* T.C. Memo. 1979-224, filed June 6, 1979.
17. *Charles and Myrtle Wildman,* T.C. Memo., Docket No. 10061, entered August 14, 1946.
18. *Turner et al. v. Dunlap,* DC, ND Texas, 1950.
19. *Oliver W. Bryant et al.,* T.C. Memo., Docket No. 27114, entered May 2, 1952.
20. Revenue Ruling 70-474, 1970-2 CB 34.
21. *Helen Krusko Harsaghy,* 2 T.C. 484 (1943).
22. Revenue Ruling 70-474, 1970-2 CB 34.
23. *Floyd Gilbert Bickel II et al.,* T.C. Memo. 1966-202, filed September 19, 1966.
24. *Owens et al. v. Commissioner,* T.C. Memo. 1977-319, filed September 19, 1977.
25. *Jerome Mortrud et al.,* 44 T.C. 208 (1965).
26. *Bennie Blatt,* T.C. Memo., Docket No. 10064, entered February 10, 1947.
27. *Betsy L. Yeomans,* 30 T.C. 757 (1958).
28. *Paul E. Jackson et al.,* T.C. Memo. 1954-235, filed December 27, 1954.

29. *Wilson J. Fisher,* 23 T.C. 218 (1954), *aff'd on another issue,* 230 F.2d 230 (7th Cir., 1956).

30. Revenue Ruling 70-474, 1970-2 CB 34.

31. Revenue Ruling 70-475, 1970-2 CB 35.

32. *Morgan et al. v. United States,* 80 F. Supp. 537 (DC, ND Texas, 1948).

33. *Protecting Older Americans Against Overpayment of Income Taxes,* Special Committee on Aging, United States Senate, 1976, page 3.

34. Revenue Ruling 58-279, 1958-1 CB 145.

35. *McCollum et al. v. Commissioner,* T.C. Memo. 1978-435, filed November 1, 1978.

36. Revenue Ruling 56-508, 1956-2 CB 126.

37. *Henry Ralph Leacock,* T.C. Memo., Docket No. 7730, entered December 19, 1947.

38. *Jetty et al. v. Commissioner,* T.C. Memo. 1982-378, filed July 7, 1982.

39. *Robert C. Fryer et al.,* T.C. Memo. 1974-26, filed January 30, 1974.

40. *Commissioner v. Benson et al.,* 146 F.2d 19 (9th Cir., 1944).

41. *Richard Walter Drake,* 52 T.C. 842 (1969).

42. Revenue Ruling 72-463, 1972-2 CB 93.

43. IT 3634, 1944 CB 90.

44. Revenue Ruling 54-190, 1954-1 CB 46.

45. IRS Letter Ruling 7828050, April 13, 1978.

46. Revenue Ruling 69-214, 1969-1 CB 52.

47. Regulations Section 1.911-1(a)(3).

48. Revenue Ruling 73-113, 1973-1 CB 65.

49. IRC Section 186.

50. Revenue Ruling 79-142, 1979-1 CB 58.

51. IRC Section 483.

52. IRC Section 642(h).

53. *Arthur R. Jones Syndicate v. Commissioner,* 23 F.2d 833 (7th Cir., 1927).

V

Vacation expenses. *See* **Travel.**

Vacation home expenses. If a person owns and rents out a vacation home or other dwelling unit which he also uses as a residence for even one day during the taxable year, he must divide his expenses between the rental use and the personal use. He is considered to use the dwelling unit as a residence during the taxable year if he uses it for personal purposes (1) more than fourteen days or (2) more than 10 percent of the number of days during the taxable year it is rented at a fair rental, whichever is greater.[1] Example of deduction computation: He owns a cabin at a ski resort that he rents at a fair rental for 120 days and uses for personal purposes for thirty days. Inasmuch as he used the cabin for personal purposes, he must divide the expenses. Of the total expenses, 80 percent (120 days divided by 150 days) is considered rental expenses and 20 percent is considered personal expenses.[2]

Vaccine. *See* **Medical expenses.**

Vacuum cleaner, cost of. *See* **Medical expenses.**

Vandalism. Deduction was allowed in the case of deliberate destruction of works of art.[3]

A businessperson's cost of repairing glass panes broken by vandals was deductible.[4]

A usual problem in justifying the deduction is proof that the damage was caused by vandalism, and at the specific time claimed. An individual can get a deduction after showing that he had reported promptly to the local police what had happened.[5] *See also* **Casualties; Repairs.**

Vasectomy. *See* **Birth-control measures.**

Vault, safe deposit. *See* **Investors.**

Vestments. *See* **Contributions.**

Veterans. *See* **Armed Forces; Education.**

Veterans' organizations, contributions to. *See* **Contributions.**

Veterinarians. *See* **Depreciation; Farmers.**

Veterinary expenses. A commercial farmer is entitled to deduct costs of this nature.[6]

Violation of rights, payments to settle. Several women brought action against an employer for violations of the Civil Rights Act of 1964. They claimed that they had not been given work because of sex or color or that they had lost their jobs because of pregnancy. To settle the matter, but without admitting violation of the Civil Rights Act, the employer agreed to make settlements to the claimants in lieu of salaries or promotion increases. These were deductible as ordinary and necessary business expenses.[7]

Vitamins. The cost of vitamins is deductible as a medical expense, within the limits for that expense, when prescribed by a physician for health purposes.[8] *See also* **Medical expenses.**

Vocational expenses. The cost of maintenance or improving of skills by means of vocational courses is deductible.[9] *See also* **Education; Ordinary and necessary business expenses.**

Volunteer fire companies, contributions to. Gifts to a volunteer fire company are deductible.[10]

Volunteer firemen. *See* **Individual retirement account.**

V

1. IRC Section 280(a) (d), (e).
2. *Your Federal Income Tax,* 1979 edition, page 43.
3. *Lattimore v. United States,* DC, ND Cal., 1967.
4. *Ralph S. Clark et al.,* T.C. Memo. 1966-22, filed January 27, 1966.
5. *Pickering v. Commissioner,* T.C. Memo. 1978-247, filed October 26, 1978.
6. Per Form 1040, Schedule F.
7. Letter Ruling 7720011, February 7, 1977.
8. *Neil et al. v. Commissioner,* T.C. Memo. 1982-562, filed September 23, 1982.
9. Regulations Section 1.162-5(c).
10. Revenue Ruling 80-77, 1980-1 CB 56.

Wagering losses. *See* **Gambling losses.**

Waiver of premium cost. Where an annuity is purchased for use as an Individual Retirement Account, a charge may be made by the insurance company or other issuer for a waiver of premium rider in certain circumstances, such as the purchaser's disability. The waiver of premium cost is deductible to the extent that it, plus the cost of the annuity itself, does not exceed the limit for the deductions for an IRA; that is, the lower of 100 percent of compensation or $2,000.[1]

Ward, expenses of. *See* **Guardians, expenses of.**

War losses. *See* **Casualties; Confiscation; Foreign expropriation losses; Government seizure.**

War-profits taxes. *See* **Taxes.**

Watch, cost of. If a person's use of a watch is incidental, such as being used only to ensure that he arrives at work or meetings on time, no business deduction is allowed. But if his employer requires him to wear a watch, or the necessities of the job require it, the cost of the timepiece represents a business expenditure. Where the watch also is worn while not on business, there must be an apportionment. Should the watch have a useful life of more than one year, its entire cost is not deductible currently in the year of purchase but must be amortized and deducted ratably over the life of the timepiece.[2]

Watch repairs. Deduction is permitted for the cost of repairs to a personal watch which is required by the nature of the job, as, for example, in the case of a railroad employee.[3] Deduction is not permitted in the absence of evidence that the employer required the employee to carry a watch or that employment was of a character that necessitated such use of a watch.[4] *See also* **Employees.**

Water-conservation expenditures. *See* **Farmers.**

Water erosion, correction of. Terracing of farmland by making ridges or "humps" in the earth in order to channel water in such a way as to prevent further soil erosion was deductible. The farm was not converted for other use, the fertility of the soil was not changed, and farming operations were not made easier.[5]

Water taxes. *See* **Taxes.**

Weevils. Payments by a cotton broker to a fund for the stamping out of boll weevils were deductible.[6]

Weight-loss program. In 1979, the Internal Revenue Service ruled that expenses incurred by participation in a weight-reduction program are not deductible as medical expense if the purpose of the participation is merely for improving an individual's general health and well-being. Later in that same year, however, the IRS decided that deduction was permitted where two physicians had prescribed for an individual a weight-reduction program for the treatment of hypertension. Here the treatment was not for general health but for the alleviation of a physical or mental defect or illness.[7]

Well, abandonment of. *See* **Abandonment loss.**

Wheelchair. *See* **Medical expenses.**

Whirlpool bath. *See* **Medical expenses.**

Whiskey. *See* **Medical expenses.**

Wigs. Where a doctor prescribed the wearing of a wig in order to alleviate mental distress of a patient who had lost her hair, the cost was characterized as deductible medical expense.[8] Where a businessperson finds it necessary to wear a hairpiece in order to achieve the appearance of youth called for by the job, this is treated as a business expense.[9] *See also* **Actors; Medical expenses.**

Will contest, expenses of. *See* **Legal fees.**

Withdrawal of interest, premature. *See* **Premature withdrawal of interest.**

Work clothes. A maintenance electrician and electronics technician could deduct the cost of prescription safety glasses and special work clothes that would tear readily in the event that his clothing should be caught in any of the machinery around which he worked daily.[10]

Amounts expended by surgeons for the purchase and maintenance of distinctive types of uniform which are not adaptable to ordinary wear and which the surgeons are required to wear while on duty are deductible as ordinary and necessary business expenses.[11]

Deduction was allowed for the cost of cleaning work clothes which an employee wore only at the factory where he worked. Dirty clothes were deemed dangerous to wear on the job, because they became baggy and would catch readily in the revolving machinery.[12]

An airline stewardess was allowed to deduct the cost of an inflight smock.[13]

Work shoes that were not suitable or acceptable for general usage were a business expense.[14]

A worker at a chemical plant could deduct the cost of work clothes, safety shoes, and gloves in order to protect himself from the acid fumes of the plant.[15]

The cost of a protective hard hat is deductible.[16]

A car repairman could deduct the cost of high-top shoes, jumpers, and leather-palm gloves.[17]

A welder could deduct the cost of heavy boots and other heavy clothing which was not suitable for street or social use.[18]

A welder could deduct the cost of insulated boots, overalls, a welding jacket, and welding gauntlets used only while at work.[19]

Linemen's boots were an allowable deduction for a telephone worker.[20]

A construction worker was allowed to deduct the cost of safety lenses, shoes, and equipment.[21]

A carpenter was allowed to deduct what he paid for overalls and special work shoes.[22]

A truck driver could deduct the cost of safety gloves and special shoes he wore when driving loads of blacktop because of the high temperature to which he was exposed.[23]

A roughneck for various oil-well drilling companies could deduct what he paid for steel-toe boots and special protective clothing.[24]

A worker at a fish-processing plant was able to deduct the cost of rubber gloves and boots. The court was willing to assume that these particular items could not have been used socially after work.[25] Commercial fishermen were allowed to deduct the cost of oil clothes.[26] *See also* **Actors; Costumes; Uniforms.**

Workmen's compensation insurance. *See* **Insurance.**

Worthless debts. *See* **Bad debts.**

Worthless stock. *See* **Capital losses.**

Write-downs, inventory. *See* **Inventory write-downs.**

Writers, expenses of. An individual can deduct his expenses in the trade or business of being a writer, if he can show that he engaged in this activity in good faith for the purpose of making a profit. This is true even if he has not yet produced a book, for, in the words of one court, any contrary finding "would have an unwarranted and undesirable chilling effect on budding authors who are serious in pursuing a writing career."[27]

A free-lance writer could deduct as ordinary and necessary business expense his automobile, telephone, travel, and kindred expenses in connection with his business of writing magazine and motion-picture stories.[28]

An established author was permitted to deduct prepublication expenses of writing a book: research, travel, writing, and arranging materials.[29]

A writer of radio broadcasting scripts could deduct the costs of script preparation, including musical arrangements and recordings.[30]

One writer was allowed to take a current deduction for story-preparation expenses which consisted of salary he paid to another writer and furnishing meals to agents.[31]

A writer could deduct his expenses in advertising his book.[32] *See also* **Author's expenses; Judgment, payment of; Legal fees; Office at home; Research; Travel.**

Wrongful death claim. *See* **Judgment, payment of.**

W

1. IRS Letter Ruling 7851087, September 22, 1978.

2. IRS Letter Ruling 8125006, February 27, 1981.

3. *O. G. Russell,* T.C. Memo., Docket No. 26963, entered April 2, 1952.

4. *Charles H. Boston et al.,* T.C. Memo., Docket No. 25564, entered June 17, 1952.

5. *J. H. Collingwood et al.,* 20 T.C. 937 (1953).

6. *Alexander Sprunt & Son, Inc.,* 24 BTA 599 (1931).

7. IRS Letter Ruling 8004111, October 31, 1979.

8. Revenue Ruling 62-189, 1962-2 CB 88.

9. *Reginald Denny,* 33 BTA 738 (1935).

10. *Arnold Roy Bushey,* T.C. Memo. 1971-149, filed June 21, 1971.

11. IT 3988, 1950-1 CB 28.

12. *Clark et al. v. Commissioner,* 158 F.2d 851 (6th Cir., 1946).

13. *Stiner et al. v. United States,* 524 F.2d 640 (10th Cir., 1975).

14. *Cavic et al. v. Commissioner,* T.C. Memo. 1977-192, filed June 21, 1977.

15. *Joseph Swiderski et al., T.C. Memo., Docket No. 33281, entered August 27, 1952.*

16. *Your Federal Income Tax,* 1979 edition, page 98.

17. *D. D. Lanier et al.,* T.C. Memo., Docket No. 30294, entered May 2, 1952.

18. *Key et al. v. Commissioner,* T.C. Memo. 1980-67, filed March 10, 1980.

19. *Gallagher v. Commissioner,* T.C. Memo. 1979-412, filed September 12, 1979.

20. *John Young et al.,* T.C. Memo., Docket No. 27611, entered March 19, 1952.

21. *Armes et al. v. Commissioner,* T.C. Memo. 1978-258, filed July 12, 1978.

22. *Busking et al. v. Commissioner,* T.C. Memo. 1978-415, filed October 16, 1978.

23. *Robert S. Henke,* T.C. Memo. 1973-186, filed August 21, 1973.

24. *Davis et al. v. Commissioner,* T.C. Memo. 1982-82, filed February 18, 1982.

25. *Clark v. Commissioner,* T.C. Memo. 1978-276, filed July 24, 1978.

26. Revenue Ruling 55-235, 1955-1 CB 274.

27. *Snyder et al. v. United States,* 10th Cir., 1982.

28. *Eugene Delmar,* BTA Memo., Docket Nos. 83047-8 and 89223-4, entered April 5, 1938.

29. *Stern et al. v. United States,* DC CD Cal., 1971.

30. *Leona Anderson,* T.C. Memo., Docket No. 22222, entered April 18, 1952.

31. *Freda W. Sandrich et al.,* T.C. Memo., Docket Nos. 5372-3, entered April 1, 1946, *supplementary opinion,* June 13, 1946.

32. *Joseph Sheban et al.,* T.C. Memo. 1970-173, filed June 22, 1970.

Y

Yacht. *See* **Entertainment.**

You can deduct the expenses of obtaining guidance on tax matters.[1] That includes the cost of this book.

Y

1. *Higgins v. Commissioner,* 143 F.2d 654 (1st Cir., 1944).

Z

Zoning change. Deduction was allowed for legal fees to prevent rezoning which would adversely affect a going business.[1]

Zoning costs. *See* **Abandonment loss.**

Z

1. Revenue Ruling 78-389, 1978-2 CB 125.

About the Author

ROBERT S. HOLZMAN, Ph.D., is one of the country's leading tax experts. He was Professor of Taxation at the Graduate School of Business Administration of New York University for more than twenty years. He has written numerous articles for national magazines and is the author of forty previous books, including *Dun & Bradstreet's Handbook of Executive Tax Management*.